IMMANUEL KANT

Lectures on Anthropology

The purpose of the Cambridge edition is to offer translations of the best modern German editions of Kant's work in a uniform format suitable for Kant scholars. When complete, the edition will include all of Kant's published works and a generous selection of his unpublished writings, such as the *Opus postumum*, *Handschriftlicher Nachlaß*, lectures, and correspondence.

Kant was one of the inventors of anthropology, and his lectures on anthropology were the most popular and among the most frequently given of his lecture courses. This volume contains the first translation of selections from student transcriptions of the lectures between 1772 and 1789, prior to the published version, *Anthropology from a Pragmatic Point of View* (1798), which Kant edited himself at the end of his teaching career. The two most extensive texts, *Anthropology Friedländer* (1772), and *Anthropology Mrongovius* (1784–5), are presented here in their entirety, along with selections from all the other lecture transcriptions published in the Academy edition, together with sizeable portions of the *Menschenkunde* (1781–2), first published in 1831. These lectures show that Kant had a coherent and well-developed empirical theory of human nature bearing on many other aspects of his philosophy, including cognition, moral psychology, politics, and philosophy of history.

D1590596

THE CAMBRIDGE EDITION OF THE
WORKS OF IMMANUEL KANT IN TRANSLATION

Theoretical Philosophy, 1755–1770
Critique of Pure Reason
Theoretical Philosophy after 1781
Practical Philosophy
Critique of the Power of Judgment
Religion and Rational Theology
Anthropology, History, and Education
Natural Science
Lectures on Logic
Lectures on Metaphysics
Lectures on Ethics
Opus postumum
Notes and Fragments
Correspondence
Lectures on Anthropology

IMMANUEL KANT

Lectures on Anthropology

EDITED BY

ALLEN W. WOOD
Stanford University

ROBERT B. LOUDEN
University of Southern Maine

TRANSLATED BY

ROBERT R. CLEWIS,
ROBERT B. LOUDEN,
G. FELICITAS MUNZEL,
AND ALLEN W. WOOD

CAMBRIDGE
UNIVERSITY PRESS

CAMBRIDGE
UNIVERSITY PRESS

University Printing House, Cambridge CB2 8BS, United Kingdom

Cambridge University Press is part of the University of Cambridge.

It furthers the University's mission by disseminating knowledge in the pursuit of
education, learning and research at the highest international levels of excellence.

www.cambridge.org
Information on this title: www.cambridge.org/9781107583504

© Cambridge University Press 2012

First published 2012
Reprinted 2013

A catalogue record for this publication is available from the British Library

Library of Congress Cataloguing in Publication data
Kant, Immanuel, 1724–1804.
[Lectures. Selections. English]
Lectures on anthropology / Immanuel Kant ; edited by Allen W. Wood, Robert B.
Louden ; translated by Robert R. Clewis, Robert B. Louden, G. Felicitas Munzel,
Allen W. Wood.
pages cm. – (The Cambridge edition of the works of Immanuel Kant in translation)
Includes bibliographical references and index.
ISBN 978-0-521-77161-0
1. Human beings. I. Wood, Allen W., editor, translator. II. Louden, Robert B., 1953–
editor, translator. III. Clewis, Robert R., 1977– translator. IV. Munzel, G. Felicitas,
translator. V. Title.
B2758.C54 2012
128 – dc23 2012036793

ISBN 978-0-521-77161-0 Hardback
ISBN 978-1-107-58350-4 Paperback

Contents

General editors' preface

Within a few years of the publication of his *Critique of Pure Reason* in 1781, Immanuel Kant (1724–1804) was recognized by his contemporaries as one of the seminal philosophers of modern times – indeed as one of the great philosophers of all time. This renown soon spread beyond German-speaking lands, and translations of Kant's work into English were published even before 1800. Since then, interpretations of Kant's views have come and gone and loyalty to his positions has waxed and waned, but his importance has not diminished. Generations of scholars have devoted their efforts to producing reliable translations of Kant into English as well as into other languages.

There are four main reasons for the present edition of Kant's writings:

1. *Completeness*. Although most of the works published in Kant's life-time have been translated before, the most important ones more than once, only fragments of Kant's many important unpublished works have ever been translated. These include the *Opus postumum*, Kant's unfinished *magnum opus* on the transition from philosophy to physics; transcriptions of his classroom lectures; his correspondence; and his marginalia and other notes. One aim of this edition is to make a comprehensive sampling of these materials available in English for the first time.

2. *Availability*. Many English translations of Kant's works, especially those that have not individually played a large role in the subsequent development of philosophy, have long been inaccessible or out of print. Many of them, however, are crucial for the understanding of Kant's philosophical development, and the absence of some from English-language bibliographies may be responsible for erroneous or blinkered traditional interpretations of his doctrines by English-speaking philosophers.

3. *Organization*. Another aim of the present edition is to make all Kant's published work, both major and minor, available in comprehensive volumes organized both chronologically and topically

so as to facilitate the serious study of his philosophy by English-speaking readers.

4. *Consistency of translation.* Although many of Kant's major works have been translated by the most distinguished scholars of their day, some of these translations are now dated, and there is considerable terminological disparity among them. Our aim has been to enlist some of the most accomplished Kant scholars and translators to produce new translations, freeing readers from both the philosophical and literary preconceptions of previous generations and allowing them to approach texts, as far as possible, with the same directness as present-day readers of the German or Latin originals.

In pursuit of these goals, our editors and translators attempt to follow several fundamental principles:

1. As far as seems advisable, the edition employs a single general glossary, especially for Kant's technical terms. Although we have not attempted to restrict the prerogative of editors and translators in choice of terminology, we have maximized consistency by putting a single editor or editorial team in charge of each of the main groupings of Kant's writings, such as his work in practical philosophy, philosophy of religion, or natural science, so that there will be a high degree of terminological consistency, at least in dealing with the same subject matter.

2. Our translators try to avoid sacrificing literalness to readability. We hope to produce translations that approximate the originals in the sense that they leave as much of the interpretive work as possible to the reader.

3. The paragraph, and even more the sentence, is often Kant's unit of argument, and one can easily transform what Kant intends as a continuous argument into a mere series of assertions by breaking up a sentence so as to make it more readable. Therefore, we try to preserve Kant's own divisions of sentences and paragraphs wherever possible.

4. Earlier editions often attempted to improve Kant's texts on the basis of controversial conceptions about their proper interpretation. In our translations, emendation or improvement of the original edition is kept to the minimum necessary to correct obvious typographical errors.

5. Our editors and translators try to minimize interpretation in other ways as well, for example, by rigorously segregating Kant's own footnotes, the editors' purely linguistic notes, and their more explanatory or informational notes; notes in this last category are treated as endnotes rather than footnotes.

We have not attempted to standardize completely the format of individual volumes. Each, however, includes information about the context in which Kant wrote the translated works, a German–English glossary, an index, and other aids to comprehension. The general introduction to each volume includes an explanation of specific principles of translation and, where necessary, principles of selection of works included in that volume. The pagination of the standard German edition of Kant's works, Kant's *Gesammelte Schriften*, edited by the Royal Prussian (later German) Academy of Sciences (Berlin: Georg Reimer, later Walter de Gruyter & Co., 1900–), is indicated throughout by means of marginal numbers.

Our aim is to produce a comprehensive edition of Kant's writings, embodying and displaying the high standards attained by Kant scholarship in the English-speaking world during the second half of the twentieth century, and serving as both an instrument and a stimulus for the further development of Kant studies by English-speaking readers in the century to come. Because of our emphasis on literalness of translation and on information rather than interpretation in editorial practices, we hope our edition will continue to be usable despite the inevitable evolution and occasional revolutions in Kant scholarship.

Paul Guyer
Allen W. Wood

Preface

Kant's lectures on anthropology were first published in the Akademie Ausgabe of Kant's writings in 1997. It was soon decided to add to the Cambridge Edition a volume translating selections from them, as has been done for Kant's lectures on logic, ethics, and metaphysics. As with other volumes in the Cambridge Edition, this one includes a general introduction, brief introductions to particular selections, informational endnotes, and a glossary. The translation of the Mrongovius text was made by Robert R. Clewis, who is grateful to Brian Jacobs, Henry Pickford, and Holly Wilson for allowing him to consult their translations of certain passages.

ALLEN W. WOOD
ROBERT B. LOUDEN

Abbreviations

Ak   *Immanuel Kants Schriften*. Ausgabe der königlich preussischen
      Akademie der Wissenschaften (Berlin: Walter de Gruyter,
      1902–). Unless otherwise noted, writings of Immanuel Kant
      will be cited by volume:page number in this edition.

ApH   *Anthropologie in pragmatischer Hinsicht* (1798), Ak 7
      Anthropology from a Pragmatic Point of View, Ca
      Anthropology, History and Education

Ca   *Cambridge Edition of the Writings of Immanuel Kant* (New
      York: Cambridge University Press, 1992–) This edition
      provides marginal Ak volume:page citations. Specific works
      will be cited using the following system of abbreviations
      (works not abbreviated below will be cited simply as Ak
      volume:page).

G   *Grundlegung zur Metaphysik der Sitten* (1785), Ak 4
      Groundwork of the Metaphysics of Morals, Ca Practical
      Philosophy

KpV   *Kritik der praktischen Vernunft* (1788), Ak 5
      Critique of Practical Reason, Ca Practical Philosophy

KU   *Kritik der Urteilskraft* (1790), Ak 5
      Critique of the Power of Judgment, Ca Critique of the Power of
      Judgment

MS   *Metaphysik der Sitten* (1797–1798), Ak 6
      Metaphysics of Morals, Ca Practical Philosophy

RM   *Die verschiedenen Racen von Menschen* (1775), Ak 2
      The Different Races of Human Beings, Ca Anthropology,
      History and Education

VA   *Vorlesungen über Anthropologie*, VA 25
      Lectures on Anthropology, Ca Lectures on Anthropology

VPG   *Physische Geographie*, Ak 9
      Lectures on Physical Geography, Ca Natural Science

General introduction

Immanuel Kant is best known to us as a systematic metaphysician who defended the *a priori* status of both the principle of morality and the fundamental principles of a science of nature. It may therefore come as a surprise to learn that as a university teacher, Kant's most frequently offered and most popular courses had to do with empirical materials to which he had difficulty giving any systematic form. These were lectures on what Kant called the two kinds of "world-cognitions" (*Welterkenntnisse*): *physical geography* and *anthropology* (VPG 9:157, ApH 7:122n, RM 2:443). Both deal with the environment in which human beings live and act, the former with the outer, natural environment, the latter with both the constitution of the human soul and the social and historical environment in which human beings, both individually and collectively, shape their own nature as rational creatures. Both of these empirical sciences were new in Kant's time, and he could even claim to share in their invention.

Kant began his academic career as a natural scientist, whose special interest in geology and earth sciences is clear from his early treatise *Universal Natural History and Theory of the Heavens* (1755). In this work he proposed the earliest version of the nebular hypothesis of the origins of the solar system (though the hypothesis became well known only after its later and more mathematically sophisticated presentation by La Place). For most of the previous decade, Kant had been writing treatises on physics, astronomy, and geology, discussing such subjects as earthquakes and questions of meteorology. He began lecturing on physical geography in 1756, offering the same course on a more or less regular basis during the summer semester. His interest in anthropology, or at least one side of it, appears to have grown out of this, insofar as Kant sought to "display the inclinations of human beings as they grow out of the particular region in which they live" (Ak 2:9). It was for this reason that Wilhelm Dilthey argued that Kant's interest in anthropology should be fundamentally understood as arising out of his interest in physical anthropology – focusing, however, not on the natural environment as such but on human beings' activities in it.

1

Kant was not appointed to a professorship until 1770; from 1755 until then he was an unsalaried *Privatdozent*. Two years later, in the winter of 1772–1773, he announced a new course on anthropology, which he taught every winter without fail until his retirement from teaching in 1796. His textbook for these lectures was always A. G. Baumgarten's empirical psychology, and already in the early 1760s, Herder lists "anthropology" among the topics Kant taught under the heading of 'metaphysics'.[1] This has led to a fundamentally different interpretation of Kant's interest in anthropology from Dilthey's, arising out of an interpretive tradition affiliated with Benno Erdmann and Erich Adickes, which links Kant's anthropology in its origins to his metaphysics, and more specifically to the portion of metaphysics having to do with psychology and the theory of the human mind.

Kant's anthropology lectures were, year in and year out, the most popular of his lecture courses. They were attended by his professorial colleagues as well as students, registering an average of more than forty paid students every time they were given. In 1798, Kant finally published a textbook based on these courses. In the years after his retirement, Kant also encouraged the publication, in editions prepared by others, of versions of his lectures on logic, physical geography, and pedagogy. But Kant's *Anthropology from a Pragmatic Point of View* is the only textbook on any subject that Kant ever published under his own name drawn from his own lecture courses.

PRAGMATIC ANTHROPOLOGY

The study of human nature was of course not an entirely new subject when Kant took it up in the 1770s. It had already been a focus of attention for some of the greatest minds of the eighteenth century, including Vico, Montesquieu, Wolff, Voltaire, and Hume. Even before Kant, "anthropology" was already being taught in Germany at the Universities of Leipzig (by G. P. Müller and J. Kern) and Halle (by C. D. Voss).[2] But Kant's approach to anthropology was new, and even played a role in the emergence of the field of anthropology in the next century, in part through the influence of his student J. G. Herder.[3] One fashionable approach to the study of human nature at the time was physiological, or even medical. The radical French Enlightenment attempted to understand the human being as a physical mechanism, following Julien Offray la Mettrie's *Man a Machine* (1748). Diderot's dialogue *D'Alembert's Dream* (probably composed in 1769) provides us with a lively record of a range of such materialistic speculations. Le Comte de Buffon, Albrecht von Haller, and Charles Bonnet were among those who took a physiological approach to understanding human beings.

Kant himself should also be accounted among the representatives of the "medical" approach to human nature, as is evident from short works such as *Essay on the Maladies of the Head* (1764), *Review of Moscati's "On the Essential Corporeal Differences Between the Structure of Animals and Human Beings"* (1771), *Note to Physicians* (1782), and the third essay in *Conflict of the Faculties* (1797). But he was also persuaded that the value of this way of studying human nature was sharply limited, and his conception of 'pragmatic' anthropology was deliberately intended to contrast with it. The immediate incitement for him to think critically about the medical or 'physiological' approach was provided by Ernst Platner's *Anthropology for Physicians and Philosophers* (1772), and a review of this book by Kant's student (also a physician) Marcus Herz. In a letter to Herz, Kant projected a new science of anthropology which would avoid Platner's "futile inquiries into the manner in which bodily organs are connected with thought" (Ak 10:146). Later that year, Kant offered his first course on anthropology that same winter, employing the contrasting approach to which he gave the name "pragmatic."

This term, as Kant uses it, combines several different meanings. First, he means to contrast the "pragmatic" approach with the "physiological": Anthropology, he says, "can exist either in a *physiological* or a *pragmatic* point of view. – Physiological knowledge of the human being investigates what *nature* makes of the human being; pragmatic, what *he* as a free acting being makes, or can and should make of himself" (ApH 7:119). Closely related to this is Kant's intention to provide lectures on anthropology that will be "pragmatic" in the sense that they will be *useful* to the audience. Kant hopes his observations about memory, for example, can be used to help people increase the scope and efficiency of their own faculties of recollection (ApH 7:119). He intends a parallel with what was then called "pragmatic" history – history written with the aim of learning from it about how to act successfully in human affairs (Hume's *History of England* was considered the paradigm) (VA 25:472, 1212).

"Pragmatic" anthropology is also contrasted with a "scholastic" approach (ApH 7:120). Here Kant may be seen as taking up, in his lectures on human nature, the task of a "popular" philosopher, in the tradition of Christian Thomasius and of the Berlin Enlightenment philosophers, such as Garve and Mendelssohn. This was a role that he deliberately declined to play in many areas of philosophy, such as metaphysics, pure moral philosophy, and the new discipline of transcendental philosophy through which he hoped to provide a critical grounding to the sciences. But it was one that he apparently thought appropriate for the study of anthropology. Scholastic studies, Kant says, involve knowledge or acquaintance with the world (*die Welt* **kennen**), while a pragmatic anthropology involves "having a world" (*Welt* **haben**): "The first only understands the play [*Spiel*], of which it has been a spectator, but the other has participated [*mitgespielt*] in it" (ApH 7:120, cf. VA 25:9, 854–855, 1209–1210).

Following this intention, Kant also attempts to give lectures on anthropology that will be popular and entertaining (evidently with some success, in view of their popularity). Some topics, according to Kant, such as the critique of reason or the metaphysical foundations of ethics, resist popularization (KpV Axviii, G 4:409, MS 6:206). But pragmatic anthropology is not such a topic. "Our anthropology can be read by everyone, even by women at the dressing table [*Damen bei der Toilette*], because it has much about it that is engaging" (VA 25:856–857). (This remark might conjure up the image of the Marschallin Maria Theresa in the first act of Richard Strauss's *Der Rosenkavalier*, perusing a copy of Kant's *Anthropology* while having her hair done – amusing and edifying herself with Kant's anthropological observations as she haggles with tradespeople, converses with her boorish country cousin Baron Ochs, and listens to the aria of the Italian tenor.)

The term "pragmatic" in Kantian terminology also means "prudential" – both in the sense of reason used in the pursuit of happiness and in the shrewder sense of the rational manipulation of other people (G 4:415–416, MS 6:215–216, ApH 7:312, 322, VA 25:469, 855, 1037, 1210, 1296, 1436). Kant clearly intends his anthropology lectures to be *pragmatic* in this sense too, by providing us with self-knowledge about human follies and foibles, so that we may be in a position to protect ourselves against our own and perhaps also take advantage of the failings of others.

It is a more difficult question how Kant's *pragmatic* anthropology relates to what he sometimes calls "practical anthropology" – the *empirical* part of morals, which Kant claims is required if the *a priori* moral law is to be applied to human actions (G 4:388, 410n, MS 6:217–218). The term "pragmatic" ought to suggest that Kant's lectures *do not* have this aim, but deal at most with empirical information of *prudential* value. But the matter is more complicated than this, as we shall see later.

Kant's text for the anthropology lectures was always the empirical psychology sections of Baumgarten's *Metaphysica*. There is a history of controversy (already mentioned), that began with an exchange between Erich Adickes and Wilhelm Dilthey, over whether Kant's anthropology is rooted in his reception of empirical psychology in the Wolffian tradition, which belonged to his lectures on metaphysics, or represents a different project entirely, one that allies it more closely to his lectures on physical geography.[4] Without attempting to settle the question, it can be noted that there are such weighty arguments on both sides as to render any simple view on either side difficult to maintain. The structure of Kant's lectures, especially at the beginning, is oriented to Baumgarten's text and makes use of the faculties of the human mind as organizing principles. These contents bear a decided affinity with the discussion of empirical psychology that takes place in Kant's lectures on metaphysics. At the same time, it is Kant's clear intention to develop an approach that is "pragmatic" in the multiple senses we have just been describing, and over time his organization of the material came more and more to include a separate division on human character, following the division on human mental faculties, in which the materials from empirical psychology are developed and applied in this new way.

THE LECTURE TRANSCRIPTIONS

The materials on which Kant drew in his anthropology lectures is impressively broad. The official text for the lectures was always the paragraphs from Baumgarten's *Metaphysica* dealing with empirical psychology, but Kant is critical of Baumgarten's approach and always leaves this text far behind almost from the beginning. In the lecture notes from which the selections in this volume were translated, Kant refers to nearly a thousand different sources.[5] Many of them are literary: Horace, Lucretius, and other classical writers, but also modern writers including Molière, La Fontaine, Rabelais, Klopstock, Swift, Fielding, Richardson, Sterne, Goldsmith, Shakespeare, Cervantes. Other sources are historical: Tacitus, Livy, Polybius, Hume, Robertson; or philosophical-literary, Montaigne, Voltaire, Addison, Shaftesbury; or travel narratives written by European explorers: Hearne, Sherlock, Cook, Marion-Dufresne, Bougainville. This erudition no doubt contributed to the popularity of Kant's lectures, but also indicates his aim of writing about human nature based on a wide-ranging consideration of human interactions, observations, and sources of information.

Kant's published *Anthropology from a Pragmatic Point of View* has been translated by Robert B. Louden in the Cambridge Edition volume of *Kant's Writings on Anthropology, History and Education*. The present volume contains excerpts of the lecture notes and transcriptions included in Volume 25 of *Kant's Schriften* in the Prussian Academy Edition (1997), but includes the translation of two complete texts: *Friedländer* (1775–1776) and *Mrongovius* (1784–1785). What we have in these texts is unlikely to be a verbatim report of what Kant said on any single occasion; they seem to be compilations of accounts from different students and other auditors of Kant's lectures. There was an established tradition in German universities of taking notes at oral speeches (sermons, lectures, public addresses), sometimes based on the transcriptions of professional note-takers. After 1770 there seems to have been a lively market for copies of notes from many of Kant's lectures: metaphysics, ethics, logic, rational theology, and anthropology.[6] The texts of Kant's anthropology lectures are probably compilations produced for this purpose. As I have just observed, they cannot be regarded as trustworthy word-for-word transcriptions, but are syntheses of different sets of notes, aiming at the preservation of those contents that would be of most interest and value to the purchasers of such documents. The texts we translate here (like most of the other lecture texts translated in other volumes of the *Cambridge Edition of the Works of Immanuel Kant*) are thus a critically edited version of what students in Königsberg might have purchased, in the form of manuscript copies, either to substitute for their not being able to attend Kant's lectures or to supplement their own recollection of them. Although the texts are identified by a single name, most of them seem to combine notes from different sources. Thus the earliest source from which we excerpt – called *"Collins"* – appears to be a collection of transcriptions by seven different note-takers. *Friedländer* draws from two: Friedländer and Prieger.

The exceptions to this are *Pillau* and *Busolt*, which are apparently the work of a single transcriber, and the *Menschenkunde*, which is based on an edition published in 1831 attributed to the editorship of "Friedrich Christian Starke" – a pseudonym for Johann Adam Bergk (1769–1834) – a nineteenth-century popularizer of Kantian philosophy who used the name "Starke" in other such activities as well. The text of the published *Menschenkunde* was based on a manuscript now in the possession of the Russian National Library in St. Petersburg. This manuscript has also been used in the preparation of the version edited by Werner Stark and Reinhard Brandt, published in the Akademy Edition, on which the present translation is based.

Volume 25 of the Academy Edition (which encompasses two very thick bound volumes, totaling over 1,800 pages) contains seven distinct texts:

Collins (1772–1773, 239 pages)
Parow (1772–1773, 226 pages)
Friedländer (1775–1776, 263 pages)
Pillau (1777–1778, 120 pages)
Menschenkunde (1781–1782, 356 pages)
Mrongovius (1784–1785, 226 pages)
Busolt (1788–1789, 102 pages)

The present volume includes *Friedländer* and *Mrongovius* complete, substantial excerpts from *Menschenkunde*, and smaller excerpts from each of the other texts. *Friedländer* was the most complete of the anthropology manuscripts dating prior to the *Critique of Pure Reason* in 1781. *Menschenkunde* and *Mrongovius* represent the most complete versions during the period of Kant's maturity. In addition (though the matter is uncertain) *Menschenkunde* probably dates from the year following the publication of the *Critique of Pure Reason*, while *Mrongovius* more certainly dates from the year in which Kant wrote *Groundwork for the Metaphysics of Morals*.

It would be a complex task to trace the development of Kant's views through the nearly two decades encompassed by these lectures. This would require a number of distinct narratives, corresponding to the many topics Kant takes up in his anthropology lectures, and their relation to other parts of his philosophy. Paul Guyer, for example, has used these lectures to trace the development of Kant's views on aesthetics from the early 1770s up to the composition of the *Critique of the Power of Judgment* in 1790.[7] What we can usefully do here is only to provide a brief overview of the alterations in structure and organization that Kant's anthropology lectures seem to have undergone from the first version (*Collins*) until the last complete version (*Mrongovius*), the fragmentary *Busolt* version, and the *Anthropology from a Pragmatic Point of View* (1798).

The *Collins* transcriptions (1772–1773) are not organized according to any major divisions, but consist of a series of notes under separate headings. But there is nevertheless even at this early stage a discernible structure to their ordering. It has already been mentioned that throughout their long history, Kant always used Baumgarten's empirical psychology as his text and structured his anthropology lectures (or at least their first division, once he had come to see them as falling into two main divisions), around a theory of the faculties of the human mind. The earliest lectures devote nearly the first half to a discussion of conscious mental processes, before turning to a roughly seventy page long discussion of human mental capacities and incapacities. This is followed by sections dealing with imagination and taste (about thirty pages), fifteen pages on the faculty of desire, and then the final twenty pages on human character and temperament.

The *Parow* text, dated the same years, is similarly without large-scale divisions, but the structure of Kant's lectures emerges a bit more clearly. Kant appears to be organizing his discussion around the three principal faculties of the human mind, as he will later present them in the *Critique of the Power of Judgment* (KU 5:198): First, the faculty of cognition, second, the feeling of pleasure and displeasure, and third, the faculty of desire. The account of mental representation is included, as in the Collins lectures, under the first heading and the account of human character is included under the third.

The *Friedländer* lectures, dated three years later, is (as noted above) the longest and most complete account of anthropology prior to the publication of the *Critique of Pure Reason* (1781). In *Friedländer*, anthropology is for the first time divided into two major parts: the first dealing with human mental capacities, and the second with temperament and character, which is now clearly separated from treatment of the faculty of desire. These are the divisions which, in the published *Anthropology*

7

of 1798, Kant was later to call (respectively) "Anthropological Didactic" and "Anthropological Characteristic." *Pillau*, two years later still, is a fragmentary text, covering only the faculty of cognition, and organized explicitly as commentary to the relevant paragraphs in Baumgarten.

Menschenkunde is the first text dating from after the first Critique. It retains Friedländer's division of anthropology into two main parts: the second now explicitly given the title "characteristic." But it also makes explicit within the first part the three-part division of human faculties into cognition, pleasure and displeasure, and the faculty of desire.

Mrongovius (1784–1785) again divides anthropology into the same two main parts, and also provides a much clearer set of subdivisions beyond this. There is an introductory chapter dealing with self-observation and methodology in anthropology, followed by an explicit three-part division of the human faculties. The cognitive faculty is treated in nine separate chapters. The feeling of pleasure and displeasure is grouped together with the faculty of desire in a second section of the first part, with one chapter devoted to pleasure and displeasure, and three further chapters devoted to the faculty of desire. *Mrongovius* also dates from about the time when Kant was composing the *Groundwork*, in which he divides moral philosophy into a "metaphysics of morals" (or *a priori* part) and an empirical part, called "practical anthropology" (G 4:388). This division is reflected in the structure of the lectures, where the second main part (earlier called "characteristic" is now (temporarily) re-named: "Second or practical part of anthropology," which is divided into two sections: "The character proper of the human being." The first of these sections has four chapters: 1. "On nature [*Naturell*]"; 2. "Temperament"; 3. "Physiognomy"; and 4. "The character proper [*eigentlichen Character*] of the human being." The second section deals with "The actual character [*wirklichen Character*] of the human being," that is, with the character of sexes, nations, and the species as a whole.

Busolt, the latest set of lecture transcriptions, is again fragmentary, dispensing with the organizing divisions found in *Friedländer*, *Menschenkunde*, and *Mrongovius*. But its headings follow the same general order, and the "characteristic" part of anthropology is now introduced as a "doctrine of method" – perhaps in a sense intended to be related to the one Kant used in structuring his published works, such as the three Critiques and the *Metaphysics of Morals*.

When we consider the reference of Kant's term "practical anthropology," we see that over the years, it tended to include three distinct things:

First, in a few earlier reflections, Kant seems to have thought that it was the task of practical anthropology to decide the scope of human moral responsibility, and to show that human beings are capable of doing what morality asks of them: "These two sciences [morality and practical anthropology] are closely connected, and moral philosophy cannot endure without anthropology, for one must first know of the agent, whether he is also in a position to accomplish what is required of him that he should do" (Ak 27:244). "The human being, however, the subject, must be studied to see whether he can even fulfill what is required of him, that he should do" (*Friedländer* 25:471–472).[8] Yet by the time of the second Critique, Kant does not seem to have thought any longer that regarding rational beings, the *general* issue of moral responsibility was even one for empirical inquiry. Instead, he argues that we learn from the command of morality itself that we have the capacity to obey it: "[The human being] judges, therefore, that he can do something because he is aware that he ought to do it and cognizes freedom within him, which without the moral law would have remained unknown to him" (KpV 5:30). (There are still presumably empirical issues regarding whether and to what extent a human being might be regarded as capable of rational action and moral responsibility.)

Second, Kant regards moral anthropology as dealing with "the subjective conditions in human nature that hinder people or help them in the carrying out of the laws of a metaphysics of morals" (MS 6:217). This would appear to include what Kant describes elsewhere as helping moral laws to obtain "access" (*Eingang*) and "emphasis" (*Nachdruck*) (G 4:389, 412, 436), that is, roughly speaking, increasing their psychological appeal to people, human nature being what it is.

Third, practical anthropology is needed in order to apply the *a priori* law of morality to the nature of human beings and the circumstances of human life in the derivation of specific duties. Kant appears to be asserting both the second and third functions of practical anthropology when he says that the *a priori* laws of morality "require a judgment sharpened through experience, partly to distinguish in which cases they have their application and partly to obtain access for them to the will of the human being and emphasis for their fulfillment" (G 4:389).[9]

In the *Metaphysics of Morals*, however, Kant appears to be reassigning this third function, withdrawing it from "practical anthropology" and attaching it to "metaphysics of morals" itself, which, he says, "cannot dispense with principles of application, and we shall often have to take as our object the particular *nature* of human beings, which is cognized only by experience, in order to *show* in it what can be inferred from universal moral principles" (MS 6:217). But it may be cutting things too fine to take this too precisely, as saying that Kant had definitively redefined the scope of "practical anthropology," or excluded from it the task of applying moral laws to human nature and human life. What is clear, however, is that Kant regarded empirical knowledge of human nature, as well as consciousness of the *a priori* moral law, as required both for knowing specifically what morality requires of us and for helping people to fulfill these requirements.

If, finally, we compare with the *Anthropology from a Pragmatic Point of View* the principles of organization that developed through time in these lecture transcriptions, it is easy to see how Kant retained the basic divisions that emerged over time. As already mentioned, Part One is now called "Anthropological Didactic" and Part Two "Anthropological Characteristic"; Part One is divided into three Books, dealing with cognition, pleasure and displeasure, and the faculty of desire. And the "Characteristic" is divided into five sections: A. The Character of the Human Being; B. The Character of the Sexes; C. The Character of Nations; D. The Character of Races; and E. The Character of the Species. It is noteworthy that after *Mrongovius*, Kant did not retain "practical anthropology" as an explicit title for the "characteristic" part, or indeed for any part of his anthropology. This raises the question whether lectures on "pragmatic" anthropology were supposed to include moral (or "practical") anthropology as a part, or were rather meant to exclude this (focusing on the "pragmatic" as the *prudential*, in contrast to *moral* anthropology). Yet the concluding section of the *Anthropology* of 1798, with its discussion of the historical vocation of the human species and its moral destiny, should be enough to justify our dismissing any suggestion that through use of the term "pragmatic" Kant intended to ban moral considerations from his anthropology lectures.

Kant's anthropology has always been an important part of his philosophy, contributing to both his theoretical and practical philosophy, and being the principal site of the development of his views on aesthetics. This importance has long been ignored on account of simplistic views of Kant based on the importance for him of *a priori* cognition, both in the theoretical and practical realms. But to hold that there are *a priori* cognitions and principles, and even that these ground the principal philosophical sciences, is not to deny that empirical cognitions are also indispensable to them. The importance of Kant's anthropology has received increasing attention in recent years, as attested by the works listed in the Bibliography at the end of this volume. It is to be hoped that an English translation of Kant's lectures on anthropology will contribute further to this trend.

Anthropology Collins 1772–1773

Translator's introduction

Kant began lecturing on Anthropology in the winter of 1772–1773. The earliest transcriptions of these lectures that have come down to us are the Collins text and the Parow text. Both are evidently lectures on Baumgarten's empirical psychology; and both texts are fairly extensive: Collins is nearly 240 printed pages. It is a compilation from notes taken by seven transcribers. After a brief "Prolegomena" and introductory "Treatise," it begins by treating the human understanding, or faculty of theoretical cognition, followed by discussions of special talents and diseases of the mind, then passes on to a treatment of the faculty of taste, and ends with a discussion of the faculty of desire, including a treatment of affects and passions, and of human character.

The selections translated here include the opening Prolegomena and Treatise, which discuss the aims and method of anthropology, a selection from Kant's discussion of taste, and a very brief excerpt presenting Kant's conception of character, as it appears in his earliest lectures.

Lecture of the Winter Semester 1772–1773 based on the transcription Collins, Philippi, Hamilton, Brauer, Dohna, Parow, and Euchel

[Excerpts]

PROLEGOMENA

The science of the human being (anthropology) has a similarity to the physiology of outer sense, insofar as in both the grounds of cognition are drawn from observation and experience. Nothing indeed appears to be more interesting for the human being than this science, and yet none is more neglected than precisely this one.[1] The blame[a] for this probably lies in the difficulty of undertaking this species of observation, as also in the odd illusion that one believes himself to know that with which he is accustomed to dealing. For in some sciences important parts have thereby been withdrawn from consideration,[b] because one did not consider them worthy of it. One cause might be that one conjectures he would not find much to rejoice at if he were to undertake the difficult descent into Hell toward the knowledge of himself.[2]

But why has no connected science of human beings been made out of the great stock of observations made by English authors? It appears to come from this: one has considered the science of human beings as a dependent part of metaphysics, and has therefore applied only as much attention to it as the larger parts of metaphysics permitted.[3] This mistake has perhaps arisen out of the error that in metaphysics one must take everything out of himself, so that one has regarded all parts of metaphysics as consequences of the doctrine of the soul. But metaphysics has nothing to do with experiential cognitions. Empirical psychology belongs to metaphysics just as little as empirical physics does. – If we regard the knowledge of human beings as a special science, then many advantages arise from this; since 1) for love of it one need not learn the

[a] *Schuld*
[b] *Betrachtung* (after Philippi); but Collins reads *Beobachtung* (observation).

whole of metaphysics. 2) before a science comes into order and regularity of *disposition*,[a] it must be pursued in academies alone; this is the only means of bringing a science to a certain height; but this cannot take place if the science is not precisely separated. One does not retain anything from books for which one has no pigeonholes,[b] as it were, in one's understanding. The *disposition* is therefore in a science the most excellent thing; if one has this from the natural cognition of human beings, then one would collect inestimable reflections and observations from novels and periodicals, from all writings and from all one's dealings.[c] We will consider the human mind in all its conditions, in health and in sickness, in a confused and uncultivated condition, to establish the first principles[d] of taste and the adjudication of the beautiful, the principles[e] of pathology, sensitivity and inclinations. We will mention the different ages and especially the sexes in their character, and seek to draw them from their sources. From this will follow what is natural to the human being and what is artificial or habitual about him; that will be the most difficult and our chief object, to distinguish the human being insofar as he is natural from the human being as he has been transformed by upbringing and other influences, to consider the mind separated from the body, and to seek, mediated by observations, whether the influence of the body is necessarily required for thinking. If experiences show us the contrary, then a mere corollary from experience will provide us with the most secure proof of the immortality of the soul.

25:9

The knowledge[f] of how to apply the sciences properly is knowledge of the world.[g] This worldly knowledge consists in the knowledge of the human being, how we can give him what he likes, etc. Worldly knowledge also prevents learning from becoming pedantry. The knowledge of natural curiosities is also counted as worldly knowledge. Thus physical geography and anthropology constitute worldly knowledge. The knowledge of the subject is the foundation of all cognitions. It is from lack of it that so many practical sciences have remained unfruitful. For example, moral philosophy; Spalding's writings refer[h] to human nature in such a way that one cannot read them with agreeableness.[4] But the majority of moral philosophers and divines lack this knowledge of human nature. When we possess such skills, which have, as it were, a motivating use[i] [this] is of great value. For although the utility of it each time is very small, it will still be large through multiplication.

[a] This word is lower case, probably indicating it is being treated as a Latin rather than a German noun.
[b] *Fächer*
[c] *aus dem Umgange*
[d] *principien*
[e] *principien*
[f] *Kenntniß*
[g] *Weltkenntniß*
[h] *beziehen sich so auf*
[i] *moventen Gebrauch*

Conversations about human nature appear to be the most agreeable in social intercourse,[a] for the subject matter is societies must be such that everyone can pronounce judgment on it.

The spirit of observation makes one lenient and liberal.[b]

We will estimate a human being not in accordance with his hidden qualities, such as serve only for speculation, but chiefly in accordance with his practical qualities.

The transition from the corporeal motion to the spiritual cannot be further explained, so Bonnet and various others[5] are in great error when they believe they can infer with certainty from the brain to the soul.   25:10

TREATISE

The first thought that strikes us when we observe ourselves expresses the I; it expresses the inspection of oneself. We want to analyze the I. All the proofs that have been presented of the simplicity of the I are nothing more than analyses of the I. In the little word 'I' is not a mere intuition of oneself, but also the simplicity of our Self, for it is the most perfect singular. Moreover, it expresses my substantiality, for I distinguish the I, as an ultimate subject that cannot be further predicated of any thing, and that is itself the subject of all predicates. The little word also expresses a rational substance, for the I expresses that one makes oneself into an object of thoughts with consciousness. In it there also lies personality. Every human being, every creature, that makes itself into an object of its thoughts, must regard itself not as a part of the world, filling up the void of creation, but rather as a member of creation, as its center and its end.

The I is the foundation of the capacity for understanding and reason, and the entire power of cognition, for all these rest on my observing and inspecting myself and what goes on in me. It is difficult to make oneself into an object of thoughts, which is why one so often omits to do so. In the little word 'I' one finds even the concept of freedom, the consciousness of self-activity; for the I is not an external thing. From this analysis of the I we see that what many philosophers pass off as profound inferences are nothing but the immediate intuitions of our self.

Every being that can say I and can make itself into an object of its consideration, has an immediate value, all others have only a mediated one; the attentiveness and intuition of oneself must not be easy, hence children up until their third year do not attain to this concept of their Self at all, but as soon as they do attain to this thought, then that appears to be the point at which their capacities develop.

[a] *im Umgange*   [b] *nachsichtig und milde*

17

25:11   An author allows the reader also a vote in his judgments when he speaks in the plural, hence the word we is modest.

Whoever inquires into the inwardness of incentives, as Montaigne does, can hardly speak in anything but the singular; hence Pascal and Malebranche blame him without good grounds.[6]

Personality is that something can be imputed to me, and personality arises from the thought I. From the combination of several simultaneous ideas into a single one is inferred the existence of our simple, indivisible I.

It is unfortunate that one is made conscious of one's state; hence a creature which cannot say 'I' might well suffer many pains but is not unhappy on that account. Thus only through the I are we capable of

25:12   happiness or unhappiness. The entire proof in philosophy that the soul is a simple substance is grounded on the I, because this is the most perfect singular.

Logical egoism consists in regarding the judgment of all others as superfluous in regard to the decision about what is true and untrue.

"*Étant continuellement affecté des sensations, ou immédiatement, ou par la mémoire, comment puis je savoir si le sentiment du moi es quelque chose hors de ces mêmes sensations, et s'il peut être indépendant d'elles?*" Rousseau. "*L'identité du moi ne se prolonge que par la mémoire.*"[a]

In conversations when one often talks of himself, even if he blames himself, he is annoying to society; for every human being regards himself as a chief part of creation, and does not want to place himself in the standpoint of individual persons, unless perhaps it is an important encounter. Human beings would rather regard the world generally from an indifferent standpoint. Reflections have something very agreeable about them: if one is accustomed to reflect tranquilly, then all affairs in the world are going well for him. Leibniz carefully placed the little worm he was observing back on its leaf,[7] and everyone loves what gives him occasion for contemplation.[b] That is the cause why Montaigne pleases us so much. If one talks in society about one's ends, exertions, and private circumstances, then that is the way to make one's hearers perplexed

---

[a] "Being affected continuously by sensations, whether immediately or by memory, how do I know if the feeling of myself is something outside those same sensations, and if it might be independent of them?" (Rousseau, *Émile, Oeuvres complètes* (Paris: Gallimard, 1969) 4:571. Cf. "*Ce que je sais bien c'est que l'identité du moi ne se prolonge que par la mémoire, et que pour être le même en effet, il faut que je me souvienne d'avior été*" (*ibid.*, 4:590). "What I know well is that the identity of myself prolongs itself only through memory, and that to be the same in fact it is necessary only that I remember having been." The most influential modern proponent of memory as the criterion of personal identity is John Locke, *Essay Concerning Human Understanding* (ed. Peter Nidditch) (Oxford: Clarendon Press, 1972) Book II, Chapter XXVII, Sections 6–26.

[b] *Betrachtungen*

and silent; but if one prattles on*ᵃ* about his own affair, then the company   25:13
gladly hears about it and one does not have to sacrifice his worth in doing
it. So there are no rules about this, each is so intent on his own I that he
does not like to hear about another I. Within ten years the body is made
up of other matter, like a stream flowing with other water, yet the I is
unalterable, and this I is indivisible. If all the members were separated
from my body, and I can speak only the I, then I would be conscious
of no diminution in me. Every human being has in himself a double
personality, as it were, the I as soul and the I as human being.

The real*ᵇ* I is something substantial, simple and persisting; whereas
one on the contrary regards the I as human being as alterable, one says
for example, 'I was tall', 'I was short'. The I would not alter if one were
in another body.

Regarding his body, the human being is little different from the animals, and the Hottentot is so near to the Orangutan that in estimating
the mere shape, if one looks at the speciation he might be dubious about   25:14
it. If one were to remove reason from the human being, then the question
is: What sort of animal would the human being then be? He certainly
might not be the last one, but his animality, since it is moderated by the
human soul, is hard to recognize; for who knows what kind of animality
the Deity mixes with reason in order to make a human being. The Stoics
want to posit animality entirely uncombined with the human soul, for
they regard the body not as a part of the self, but as something belonging
to us, from whose intimacy we must withdraw ourselves; it is like the shell
of the snail, merely our dwelling, and the body itself, along with its alterations, belong to our contingent state.[8] Epicurus, by contrast, asserted
that there are no other beings except the objects encountered by the
senses, so what pertains to the body, only that pertains to our self.[9] I am,
that is an intuition, and not an inference as Cartesius believed.[10] But <u>my
body is</u>, that is a mere appearance. In me, namely, there is nothing but
the representation of my self, I intuit only myself. Insofar as there are
alterations in me corresponding to objects, they are called 'appearances'.
We have no intuition in the whole world except the intuition of our self;
all other things are appearances. The I is the mere soul, the body is the   25:15
husk. There is no human being who would not like to exchange his face
for another's, or his whole physique, or even indeed the qualities of his
soul; but to exchange his entire I, no one resolves to do that: this is in
itself a contradiction, hence it is really nothing at all obscure.

In our soul we find two sides, as it were, one in accordance with which
it is passive, the other in accordance with which it is active. According to
the first I am a play of all the impressions that happen to me from nature,

---

ᵃ *railliert*   *ᵇ* *eigentliche*

according to the other I am a free self-active principle,[a] the human being recognizes himself as so much lower to the extent that he is passive and bound in regard to self-activity.

If a human being in his external demeanor shows no marks of an inner worth, then we despise him, but if the contrary, then we say that he possesses respectability.[b] But he must also provide marks[c] that he does not fail to recognize the worth of others, which one calls 'modesty'.

The question is: Where do we locate the source of ill in the human being? We find it in the human being's animality. In some human beings there are such strong incentives that it is hard for his intelligence to discipline them. And the difference between human beings appears to rest more on their animality than on their spiritual nature.

The human being makes himself as far as possible into an intelligence, and acts as if he wholly neglects his animality.

We have capacities, faculties and powers.

A capacity is the quality of mind to be modified by alien impressions. We can have great faculties and yet only a small power. Thus powers are sources of execution, and the faculty is the sufficiency for certain actions. It is not easy to gain insight into[d] what must be added to a faculty in order that it should become an active power.

The capacity to be modified, or to be passive, one calls the lower power of the soul; the capacity to act self-actively[e] is the higher power. Insofar as the soul is capable of impressions that the body suffers passively,[f] it is called *anima*,[g] but insofar as it is capable of self-active action, it is called *mens*.[h] Insofar as both are united and the former capacity stands under the moderating influence[i] of the other, it is called *animus*[j] – *anima* is called 'soul', *animus* 'mind', *mens* 'spirit'.[11] These are not three substances but three ways we feel ourselves living. In regard to the first way we are passive, in regard to the other, passive but simultaneously reactive, in regard to the third way we are entirely self-active. We can distinguish in the case of agreeable and sad sensations.

1) The feeling of enjoyment, and
2) Cheerfulness about this enjoyment.

Likewise one can distinguish in the case of painful sensations

1) The pain itself or the grief
2) The painful sensations about the grief

25:16

---

[a] *Principium*
[b] *Anstand*
[c] *Marquen*
[d] *einsehen*
[h] mind, though Kant here equates it with spirit (*Geist*).
[i] *moderation*, written lower case, as a Latin word.
[j] soul (m.), though Kant here equates it with mind (*Gemüth*).

[e] *selbstthätig to handeln*
[f] *leidet*
[g] soul (f.)

The Stoics understood by a sage the human being who is never miserable; he feels, indeed, all the pains in his soul, though they never get to his mind, but let him react. A human being can feel the most sensitive pains in his soul and yet be of cheerful and tranquil mind. The mind is also called the 'heart', which borders on the higher powers of the human mind. A good mind or heart[a] is the good relation between sensations or inclinations and the reaction[b] of the understanding. Socrates had an evil heart,[c] but the principles of his understanding overpowered sensibility and made the relation between it and reason correct again.[12] Thus besides pleasure and displeasure in the soul and in the mind, there is also a pleasure and displeasure in the spirit, which is approvals of his good or reproaches[d] of his evil actions. The soul can be swimming entirely in pain, and yet in the spirit there can be great gladness,[e] just as on the contrary, the spirit often looks gloomy when sheer joys in the soul delude the mind. Sicknesses of the mind are the strongest ones – Depression[f] is worse than pain – it is displeasure with my entire state. Dissatisfaction with my own person is spiritual sadness and the worst one of all. It is wonderful that the stronger and more pressing enjoyments are, the more delicate they are and the most sublimely removed from sensibility.

25:17

25:18

What ascends from pleasure or displeasure to the spirit, comes back again into the mind with redoubled strength. Hence the most desperate actions are from self-reproach, just as the most sublime have arisen from self-approval. It is sometimes said that human beings, societies or speeches have spirit, i.e. moving force. We call 'spirit' what contains real moving force, e.g. the spirit[g] of liquors. We always gladly seek out what sets our heart[h] in motion; one sees the spirit in the human being is the same as his life, or the first ground for life in the human being. All depression comes largely from the fact that one makes a great idea of the importance of life. A sage regards everything in the world, even his life, as unimportant. That helps him to outweigh and react[i] against strong sensible feelings.[j] As for what further pertains to the mind or heart,[k] I remark that the heart[l] is usually an object of love. A good heart[m] is still

---

[a] Reading with the Philippi transcription, *Gemüth oder Herz*; in the following passage, *Gemüth* will sometimes be translated 'heart' when that makes for more idiomatic English. But such cases will also be noted.
[b] *reaction*, written lower case, as a Latin word.
[c] *Gemüth*
[d] *reprochen*, written lower case, as a French word, though with a German plural.
[e] *Heiterkeit* [f] *Betrübnis*
[g] *Spiritus*, the Latin word, but capitalized as a German noun.
[h] *Gemüth*
[i] *reaction*, written lower case, as a Latin word.
[j] *Empfindungen* [l] *Gemüth*
[k] *Gemüth* [m] *Gemüth*

loved even when all else is sacrificed to evil excesses. There are *aimables debauchés*, lovable debauchees. One has complete confidence in such good hearts,[a] and sooner in them than in those who act well from principles. In regard to the practical the mind[b] is usually called the 'heart'. As for the spirit, one never says that a human being has an evil spirit, for the spirit is not affected by any inclinations, and since it judges everything merely from reason, not from sense, it judges the good and is the principle[c] of judgment about the good, hence nothing evil can derive from it, from it all good is derived, but evil from the mind. But if one attends to the common opinion of human beings, especially of savages, then the word 'spirit' signifies that which animates the inert matter in the whole of nature. Thus chemists have their *spiritus rectores* in oils, *et cetera*.

25:176

CONDITIONS OF TASTE

Beauty pleases immediately; we can say that something is agreeable mediately (as a means), e.g. an inheritance. One can also say that something is '*mediately* good', but to call it 'mediately beautiful' will not do. Are the sciences mediately or immediately good? – Do they increase the perfection of the human being in themselves, or do they only contribute something to this? – Whether a person is beautiful or ugly one sees through intuition. – The bad features of an ugly face cannot be beautified by any treasure.[d] Beauty has to do with the judgment about intuition, and intuition is something immediate. Beauty is always only something contingent and is easy to do without. But it can be that if beauty is united with utility, the liking for it becomes more well-grounded and enduring. Just the same, pure beauty, which is only for taste and furnishes a certain pure gratification, remains void of all utility. It pleases us whenever we set our collective living powers[e] in activity; but it is a gratification *apart*[f] only if one sets an activity into play. We like to have everything pure, e.g. gratification in mathematics. In the same way, if taste is to be satisfied,[g] then one must see the beautiful alone without regard to utility. If, therefore, one wants to gratify taste purely and for itself, then no utility in the object must be conspicuous. A silver receptacle pleases because it has an inner value, but an enamel[h] is always more beautiful; with an enameled golden receptacle, one seems to pay no attention to the gold. This paying no respect to value is always a chief ingredient in beauty

25:177

---

[a] *Gemüther*
[b] *Gemüth*
[c] *principium*
[d] The text provides no punctuation here, but a new sentence seems to begin at this point.
[e] *Lebhaftigkeiten*
[f] aside (Fr.)
[g] *satisfacirt*
[h] *emaille*

and in the effect of gratification from it. The taste in porcelain service is more refined than that in silverware – the essay by Brabanter Kanten, for whom nothing is beautiful as soon as it sustains a crack: taste is a sensible judgment, but not a judgment of sense and of sensation, but of intuition and comparison, of receiving pleasure and displeasure through intuition. A choice is to be made without reflecting on utility; that we would like to investigate, strain out[a] and refine; indeed, this also contributes much to the perfection of the human being. If I see a farmer who buys a beautiful painting when he could have bought a good cow, then I do not take him to be the best economist, but I think to myself: the guy must have taste. Beauty *and taste is intuition. Utility and insight is reflection. We will later consider what beauty or gratification in intuition contributes to the perfection of the human being.* We must distinguish taste from feeling; it is not the sensation but only the representation of a thing, not insofar as I sense it but insofar as it appears to me, or better, taste is distinguished from sense in this, that it is the *principium* of gratification in the mere representation. Taste provides gratification that arises from the intuitive.[b] We are effective and active in gratification, but in feeling we are passive. Taste does not consist in the gratification that the thing makes for me – I can call a house beautiful and think I would be ready to pay a penny to see it. Through taste we obtain a satisfaction of intuition. If I see an ugly house, then that does not cause me any pain, for I can laugh heartily about it and amuse myself. With intuition I feel nothing, I only compare the things with my feeling without letting it make any impression on my feeling. In short, beauty effects nothing on my faculty of sensation – I am not passive in it – I only receive[c] appearances and representations and compare them with my faculty of sensation. Some senses are more for feeling, others more for appearance. The sight of a beautiful object can make for gratification when one sees it for the first time, but only because one looks forward to being able to tell others about it.

Yet about beauty merely as beauty I do not at all judge in accordance with feeling, but in accordance with appearance compared with feeling. To feeling belongs sense; to taste, the power of judgment. Feeling is therefore very easy to have, for only sense belongs to it. Taste is rare,[d] for to it belongs the power of judgment. In regard to ideal things one can have feeling. E.g. when one represents a thing to oneself in a lively

---

[a] *excolirt*; this is an artificial German verb, apparently derived from *excolo* (Lat.). *Excolo* has two meanings: 'to strain' (first conjugation) (cf. the vulgate of Matthew 23:24) and 'to cultivate' (second conjugation). Either meaning might fit the present context; but only the first conjugation verb would yield the 'r' in '*escoliren*', so we opt for that meaning. See p. 61, note *b*.
[b] *dem intuitiven*   [d] *rar*
[c] *recipire*

manner, when he has a lively imagination. One senses a thing by images of the imagination[a] in just as lively a manner as if one would sense them in their actual existence. But such a person can nevertheless have no correct taste. The one who, e.g., is moved through lively descriptions, has feeling. To feeling belong only susceptibility to stimuli[b] and emotion. Stimulation and emotion arise from feeling; beauty and ugliness, from taste. One can practice feeling, but taste one must learn formally; no one has it by nature. All arts that work much on feeling destroy taste, and persons full of feeling are devoid of taste. Taste is cold and tranquil. Feeling makes me, as it were, into an instrument, and as it were into a keyboard on which everyone to whom it occurs can gratify himself, where one here and there plucks the lyre-strings of feeling, where I am entirely passive and a plaything of impressions. With tasteful writings there arises in me a tranquil gratification; but where we appeal to feeling, there the jurisdiction of the understanding ceases, one commonly acts as if one does not understand a thing. What is supposed to be in accordance with taste must please universally, i.e. the judgment of taste is not made in accordance with the private constitution of my subject to be affected with pleasure by an object, but in accordance with the rules of universal liking. The art of cooking should also have universal rules: tasteful people know well how to encounter what pleases universally or for the most part. But here there is this distinction: In regard to real[c] taste, I must make the judgment about what pleases universally from experience, while in regard to ideal taste one can make it *a priori*. Taste is the *principium* through which human beings can enjoy a socially universal gratification. A human being in the wilderness is not concerned about taste. Everything beautiful one loves and seeks only for society. It is very probable that the man would choose a woman not in regard to her beauty but according to her health and strength. That one now chooses from beauty, one does this from love for society, for one has a particular gratification when one possesses something that pleases others. The satisfaction can be small in relation to gratification, but the universality of the satisfaction elevates it again, and one esteems a human being of taste because his choice has a validity for many. – A garden pleases us if we are in society, but if we were alone then the woods would please us better. The entire beauty of nature would be hidden from the solitary person, he does not reflect on it. Unsociable human beings have no taste. But suppose one would like to object that if what pleases universally has always to be spied out, then taste has no firm rules. It has them, for taste is grounded in humanity, but one can arrive at them only through experience. Fashionable taste is no taste; whoever chooses from fashion because he takes it to be the *principium* of

25:179

25:180

---

[a] *Imagination*
[b] *Reizbarkeit*

[c] *würklichen*

24

the beautiful, he chooses from vanity and not from taste. The man of taste is also guided by fashion, but in accordance with the principle[a] of taste. The woman is just as fashionable, even in judgments, since the man usually judges according to principles. Taste is universal, it indicates a certain agreement. If one disputes,[b] then one wants to prove that our judgment of taste is supposed to be valid for others too. But one does not dispute about taste, because in taste no one demands that anyone should follow the judgment of the other. If there were nothing in taste that pleases universally, then it would be a feeling. About true taste, it must allow of disputing,[c] for otherwise there would be no taste. *De gustu non est disputandum*[d] is a proposition of the ignorant and unsociable. 'Everyone according to his taste' – everyone enjoys only his own gratification; from this follows that everyone should remain by himself. If someone asks good friends over, he certainly does not get information about each one's taste; he is guided rather by the universal. There is much in the *principium* of taste that is empirical, but the grounds of judgment are not merely abstracted from experience, but lie in humanity. – The investigation of taste, where it is accompanied by the judgment of the understanding, is not a private judgment, for human beings have universal rules for the judgment of taste. On account of the validity of private judgments, one notes that if a room is too warm for one and too cold for another, then both of them are right – their two judgments are to be sure opposed, but they do not contradict each other, for there are two sorts of subject, each judges for himself, how he is affected. The air is one and it produces different alterations in different subjects. In the same way, when someone holds this dish to be the best but it tastes differently to another, then both are right, for they are not talking about the object of eating but only about themselves as the subject, about how they are affected. Here one can indeed say *de gustu non est disputandum*, one cannot dispute away the sensations of another, human beings often take their subjective judgments for objective ones. One says of a person that she is ugly, but to another she comes across as pretty, and a third finds some agreeableness in her. They are all judging not of her person but of their sensations, they are judging not objectively but subjectively about the way in which they are affected. Of the agreeable and the disagreeable one must not dispute; that is a dispute about the subject. Good and evil is a matter of the object. If I say: 'The thing is good or evil', then I judge about the object. Judgments about beauty and ugliness are objective but not in accordance with rules of the understanding but of sensibility. Sensibility has its rules as much as understanding. Certain principles of taste must

25:181

---

[a] *Principium*
[b] *disputirt*
[c] *disputiren*
[d] The usual saying is: *De gustibus non disputandum est*: "There is no disputing about taste."

be universal and be universally valid. Thus there are certain rules of aesthetics: with them we must set aside stimuli and emotions.

The representation of the form or figure of things should be made in accordance with the laws of sensibility. – All human beings have certain harmonious laws through which they form objects: those are the laws of representation. What makes sensible intuition easier pleases and is beautiful; that is in accord with the subjective laws of sensibility, and it promotes the inner life, since it sets the power of cognition into activity. This facilitation happens through space and time. Alteration in space is the figure, in time is merely the play. The play of alteration is facilitated through proportion in the parts. Symmetry facilitates comprehensibility and is a relation of sensibility. With a disproportioned house I can represent the whole only with difficulty; by contrast with a well-built house I see the equality of the two sides. Equality of the parts promotes my sensible representation, facilitates the intuition, increases the life of activity and favors it; hence the whole must please me; but for that reason also it must please all, for this rule grounds all of them. Alteration in time is called 'play'. – In music the chief factor^a is the tempo, or 25:182 the determination of the equality of time. Every sound is simultaneous and is distinguished through the equal beat of its resonance. Between the sounds there must be a proportion and symmetry, if it is to please and this is the accord.^{b} This facilitates sensible comprehensibility. – All human beings have conditions under which they can represent a great manifold, hence one also has a theme carried through which must please from the above causes. We call players 'musicians'^{c}; we can term dancers 'players with shapes', just as with pantomimes. In a garden I find beauty through comprehensibility; if there is no order in it, then I can make no image of it; I see too much at once. If I look at a garden, then I am serious at first sight and seek proportion and symmetry, it pleases only because it is usual for me to represent it thus . . .

25:227 Characters are nothing other than that which is peculiar to the higher capacities. Indeed, in each human being there lie the greatest incentives and preparations for every kind of activity, but there also lies *a higher principle in him to make use of all the capacities and incentives*, to sacrifice and to restrain sensations, etc. The constitution of these higher powers makes up the character. Thus one also says nothing, if one says the word 'character' to refer to a human being's capacities. [What matters is] *how he makes use of them*, and what he wills to do.

^{a} *Stück*
^{b} *Accorde*

^{c} *Musici* (It.)

26

Anthropology Parow 1772–1773

Translator's introduction

Kant began lecturing on Anthropology in the winter of 1772–1773. The earliest transcriptions of these lectures that have come down to us are the Collins text and the Parow text. Both are fairly extensive: Parow, at about 225 pages, is just a bit shorter than Collins. Like Collins, it is a compilation from notes taken by seven transcribers (Collins and Parow were contributors to both). Since both Collins and Parow are apparently accounts of the same lecture course, the differences between them may enable us to gauge the extent to which the contents of these transcriptions reflect the transcribers' choices. Like Collins, Parow begins with an introductory and methodological section, but the Parow introduction makes more explicit the focus of attention on empirical psychology (in Baumgarten's sense of the term). It too follows the general account of human faculties – theoretical cognition, taste, and desire (though the Parow account focuses more exclusively on character).

The brief selections translated here are taken from the introduction and from the opening remarks about character near the end of the text.

Lecture of the Winter Semester 1772–1773 based on the transcriptions of Parow, Euchel, Brauer, Hamilton, Philippi, Collins and Dohna

[Excerpts]

TRANSLATED BY ALLEN W. WOOD

LECTURES ON ANTHROPOLOGY

Empirical psychology is a species of natural doctrine. It treats of the appearances of our soul that constitute an object of our inner sense, and indeed just as the empirical natural doctrine, or physics, treats appearances. One also sees[a] how little this doctrine can constitute a part of metaphysics, since the latter has solely *conceptus puri*[b] or concepts which are either given through reason or yet at least whose ground of cognition lies in reason, as its theme.[1] This error derives merely from this, in part because the ancients had collected only a few experiences of the soul, in part because they did not know where they should make room for this doctrine, since they held the whole of metaphysics for an expanded psychology, because the soul is an object of inner sense; but from the soul arise all the concepts of the understanding. But now since we already have obtained a whole collection of this source of human actions or many kinds of appearances of the soul, especially through the English writers, we can expound this doctrine just as we do physics. It is to be wondered at that the ancients did not occupy themselves more with human cognition, even though they declared this endeavor to be the most useful one.[2] But there is nothing more usual than that one believes himself to know that with which one is accustomed to deal, and holds it to be not worthy of his investigation. This opinion, which is implanted in us, has done uncommon harm to the sciences, and deprived us of the cognition of many things. At the same time, it is to be remarked that because the sciences are expounded in academies in a certain order and separate from other sciences, they have grown and expanded greatly. It is precisely so with

[a] *Sieht . . . ein*
[b] pure concepts, but Kant capitalizes the noun as if it were a German noun.

31

25:244 empirical psychology, for as long as it was dependent on metaphysics, and was not expounded especially,[a] it had only a very small range. It even deserves a special set of lectures, in part because it does not at all belong in metaphysics, in part because it can be learned by everyone without requiring any prerequisite sciences. Here one can learn about the source of all human actions and the character of human beings, which one otherwise finds scattered now and again in the sciences, in novels and in some treatises on morality. One can derive from its source every trait of humanity which one notes in some writing, and in this way increase his knowledge of human beings. Montaigne, who over two hundred years ago wrote a book in the old French dialect, is held in respect down to the present day by every reasonable scholar, because from his work one becomes acquainted with human beings in their different circumstances, even though on this account he is otherwise somewhat disagreeable to read, because he is always talking about himself.[3]

In treating this doctrine we want to discuss human beings in different conditions, e.g. in uncultivated and uncivilized[b] conditions, in accordance with their different ages, and to distinguish what is natural and artificial[c] in a human being.

The first thought that arises in a human being when using his inner sense, is the I.

It is noteworthy[d] that we represent so much under the I, for when we analyze it we find that under it we think the following elements:

I.) The simplicity of the soul, since the I expresses only the singular, and if the soul were a composite, and each part might have that thought, then it would have to be called thinking a 'we'.

25:245 II.) The substantiality of the soul, i.e. that the I is not a predicate of any other thing, even though many predicates can be ascribed to it as the subject. For, e.g. when I say "I will this, I think this," then I separate all these predicates off from the I, and consider myself as the subject as of which all this is predicated.

III.) A rational substance, for since I think the I, I feel[e] that I can make myself into the object of my thoughts, but it is the primary expression of reason, or the superior faculty of the soul, that it inspects,[f] as it were, the inferior one, and insofar as I make myself into the object of my thoughts, I reflect upon the faculties that lie in the soul.

IV.) The freedom of the soul. When I think the I, then I separate myself off from everything else, and think myself independently of all external things. Now just this, that when one names the I, one makes oneself as it were into the central point or standpoint of all things, to

---

[a] *besonders vorgetragen*
[b] *roh und ungesittet*
[c] *Natur und Kunst*
[d] or 'strange', *merkwürdig*
[e] or 'sense', *empfinde*
[f] *inspicirt*

which everything has its relation,[a] this makes it the case that one is so reluctantly seen in society, one listens reluctantly to someone who always talks about himself, and even though at the same time one can put oneself in the place of every other who talks about himself, one still does it reluctantly. One would rather have it that no one makes himself into the standpoint on all things, but instead that what gets talked about are universal things which have a relation to all. Hence it is to be regarded as politeness that all princes (the King of Spain in modern times is an exception to this)[4] call themselves not 'I' but rather 'we', because, namely, they formerly did everything only with the consent of the highest estates. The I in a broad sense signifies the human being, in a narrow sense the soul. That the soul is something simple and distinct from the body, one sees from the fact that if one part of the body after another were destroyed, the human being without hands and feet still calls himself the whole I. The Stoics and Plato understood by the I only that immortal being, the soul, and they believed that they had only to carry the body around with them as the snail does its shell.[5] They therefore stood under the delusion that they could not be injured[b] in any way, because no one could gain access to their soul, even if they tortured the body. Every slave among them held himself to be free, for he had a free soul.[6] The Epicureans were of the opposite opinion.[7]

25:246

One must always distinguish in the human being between animality and rationality. In regard to the former, he is little distinguished from other animals. Locke and another Italian physician even wants to assert that human beings were more inclined to walk on 4 than on 2 feet, because the entire constitution of their bodies was so arranged that walking on two feet leads to very many diseases which they would not have known how to remedy in an uncivilized condition.[8]

How little is a Hottentot distinguished from an orangutan, if one took his soul away from him, and it appears actually that if one took the soul away from the human being, he would not be a good, tame animal but even a beast of prey. The human being thus has a double personality, namely as human being and as soul. We are therefore certain that the soul is a simple being, and entirely separate from the body. $\psi\upsilon\chi\eta$ (the soul) properly signifies a butterfly, which, after it has laid aside its chrysalis, has become a bird.[9] The Greeks compared this chrysalis with the body, and the butterfly represented the soul. Already with the Egyptians this butterfly was the sensible image of the soul. When Anaxarchus on the command of a tyrant was being crushed to death by a mortar, he said: *Tunde, non tundis Anaxarchum sed Anaxarchis culeum.*[10] From this we actually see that the human being feels[c] the substantiality of his soul.

25:247

[a] *Beziehung*
[b] *beleidigt*
[c] *empfinde*

From this we actually see and we also feel*a* that our soul is sometimes passive and sometimes active, and hence Lucretius already called the soul in respect of its passive state *anima* and of its activity *animus*.[11]

We observe, however, the soul from three standpoints, namely as *anima* (soul), *animus* (mind) and *mens* (spirit).[12] – Insofar as the soul is thought of in combination with the body and cannot prevent what affects the senses from being communicated to it, it is soul, and there it is merely passive. But insofar as the soul reacts to sensible impressions and proves itself active it is *animus*, and to the extent that it is entirely independent of all sensibility and represents something it is *mens*, e.g. I cannot prevent pain done to my body from passing over into my soul; but I can prevent my soul from reflecting on it, e.g. when I have gout and think what may become of it in the future, how I will be able to earn my bread, and this causes sadness over my state of health, then *animus* is active*b* here. This sickness of the mind is precisely what makes us miserable. Because this reflecting is not attached to animals, they are also never miserable. Finally, however, there arises from this the highest degree of sadness, when my spirit abstracts from all pains, wakens self-blame in me, when it represents to me how I have brought this illness upon myself and have become unhappy through my own guilt. This sadness always works on the body with redoubled forces.

It is very usual that human beings say they would gladly change places with another human being, they wish another's facial appearance or his memory; but if they could exchange everything with another, they would nevertheless not exchange their I, because each regards himself as perfect after his kind. There is something contradictory in this proposition, for they want to exchange, but also not. We often say that a speech has no spirit, the conversation*c* has no spirit, etc. and from this is seen that we understand by 'spirit' the first principle*d* of movement.

In ordinary speech, one calls the mind also the heart. But when one says, that human being has a good mind or a good heart, then we understand by this nothing other than that the human being's bodily constitution is so made*e* that his inclinations could not be otherwise constituted,*f* and hence it probably implies that a human being can be very virtuous but at the same time could have an evil heart. Such is asserted of Socrates, who, although his inclinations did not agree with the principle of reason, he nevertheless knew how to direct himself through reason.[13] Yet we have a greater trust toward someone who has a good heart*g* than

25:248

---

a *fühlen*   *b* *agirt*
c *Gesellschaft*, literally the 'society' or the 'company'.
d *Principium*, but capitalized as a German noun.
e *körperliche Constitution ist so beschaffen*   *g* *Gemüth*
f *beschaffen*

toward someone who is virtuous. Here the cause is this: One is always safer when one entrusts himself to someone whose inclinations already agree with the principles of reason than to someone who always has to struggle with them, for of how often do we not see ourselves surprised by a sensible thought even before we are rightly conscious of it? But it is well to note that one never says, he has an evil spirit – even if he were possessed by the devil – and the cause is that spirit, that is independent of the body and external impulses and always acts in accord with the principles of reason, can never act in a way that is other than good, for it does not choose something beautiful, but what is good. Hence one says that the flesh contradicts the spirit.[14] If now the spirit could act by itself[a] that would be very useful when the flesh contradicts the spirit. The world has a relation as much to our body as to our soul, and according as we have considered the world from the latter or the former point of view, it seems to us one way or the other way. As once an inhabitant of a rocky island, who nothing in the world except these rock and a few islands that lay around it, came upon the grounds of the ruler of the island and saw his palace; he esteemed him happy to be ruler of half the world.[15] If a human being falls into the unhappy situation of being poor and forsaken, then he cannot enjoy all the beauties of nature that surround him; every view is gloomy for him; but if it goes well for him, then everything around him cheers him up . . .

25:249

25:437

OF CHARACTER

The character refers to the complex of the body and consists in what is peculiar of the higher powers of the human mind. The human being has many capacities to assume different forms. He has impulse, desire, passions, he can also have a certain antipathy when he is free from all passions. But he also possesses something distinct from all this apparatus, namely *the faculty to make use of all these powers, faculties, talents*, to let his desires have free play or to hold them back; the character of human beings rests on the constitution of the higher power. Thus the determination of human character depends not on his drives and desires, but rather solely on the manner *in which he modifies these*. We thus ask only about how the human being uses his powers and faculties, to which final end he applies them. In order, therefore, to be able to determine the character of the human being, one must be acquainted with the ends laid in him by nature. The characters of human beings are all moral, for morals is precisely the science of all the ends that are *established through the nature of the will* and that prescribe the objective laws of the will, and according to which we direct and exert our faculties. Character is a certain subjective

25:438

---

[a] *bloß*

rule of the higher faculty of desire. The objective rules of this faculty contain morals, hence constitute what is peculiar to the higher faculty of desire of the human character. *Every will, however, or the higher faculty, is specifically composed* [geartet], *and has its subjective laws, which precisely constitute the character.* Thus one human being considers everything from the standpoint of honor, his entire higher faculty of desire aims only at honor. Another human being has a loving character, whose entire higher faculty of desire leads to beneficence. Very often the character of the human being is uncommonly complicated, because many ends lie in its nature. Then one must separate out the principal ends and determine his character out of them. In youthful years the human character is still not knowable, and a human being of 16–17 years old often cannot himself be acquainted with his character, because no case has yet eventuated where his character may be seen. Then the character forms itself gradually. One says that a human being has made his character worse or has improved it. One can lessen or moderate the propensity one has for something and direct it, only one will not therefore acquire a better character. Whoever has a bad character will never achieve an opposite good one, because the true germ is lacking, which must be laid in our nature to that end.

Anthropology Friedländer 1775–1776

Translator's introduction

The question of the *Bildung* or education of humanity, in particular the Enlightenment goal of human perfectibility, is germane to all the anthropology lectures, but it is especially apropos in the case of the *Friedländer* lectures to situate them historically in relation to the education reform movements of the long eighteenth century. The lectures date from the time of Kant's most active involvement with and support for an institution of education, the Philanthropin (founded in 1774 in Dessau). Its program of education (based on Lockean, Rousseauian, and Enlightenment principles) and the writings of its founder, Johann Bernhard Basedow, inspired the major educational reform movement of his day, Philanthropinismus. In his first set of lectures on pedagogy (also from this period, 1776/77) Kant used Basedow's *Methodenbuch* as the basis for his course. Together with his reading over a decade earlier of Rousseau's *Émile, Or On Education* (with its critique of Locke's educational program laid down in *Some Thoughts Concerning Education*), his interest in the moral weeklies (the English *Spectator*, for example, is referenced in the *Friedlaender* lectures), his correspondence with the education reformers and of course his own experience both as student and teacher, Kant had first-hand knowledge of and engagement in the education reform issues.

Not only do the *Friedländer* lectures for the first time divide the anthropology into two major parts dealing respectively with the human mental capacities and temperament and character, but the final section on education in the second part is unique to these lectures. In fact the last three sections (making up one fifth of the lectures) have an explicitly educational focus. The section on the character of humanity in general, with its references to Rousseau (identified as the most distinguished author on the topic) is replete with allusions to issues of the education debates: for example, how to deal with the natural human desire to dominate others; when and where the cultivation of reason best fits into the education of the child and adolescent (with Locke exhorting that one begin early to reason with the child, while Rousseau insists that one must begin with the body and the passions); the question of reconciling the need for civil constraint – which in turn promotes the development of human talents and skills – with the resulting violence suffered by the natural or animal nature that properly counts as one of the dual determinations (vocations or destinies, *Bestimmungen*) of this being of understanding and sensibility, of intellect (*animus*) and living, organic, ensouled being (*anima*). Awareness of the treatment of such questions in the larger discourse allows one to appreciate the relevance also of discussions in the first part of the anthropology lectures (for example, human self-consciousness as a focal point without therefore conceiving of everything in self-referential terms, the issue of developing skill in transposing the "I" so as to be able to take the point of view of another, the consideration of the body as defining the human being and the relation to it by the operations of the mind, the issue of the obscure basis of the actual reasons for our actions, the uses of the powers of judgment and desire, and so forth). The section on the difference of the two genders entails the question of a distinct education for each sex; this section is found only in a much abbreviated form in four other sets of anthropology lectures (*Collins, Parow, Menschenkunde, Mrongovius*) and it fairly resonates with Rousseau's account in the fifth book on Sophie in his *Émile*.

In the final section entitled "On Education" (or upbringing, *Erziehung*) Kant begins by extolling the "present day Basedow institutes" as "the greatest phenomenon to have appeared in our century for the improvement of humanity toward its perfection" (VA 25, 2.1: 722–723). His personal and public support extended to fund-raising efforts, written communications, and statements printed in the local newspaper in Königsberg (in 1776 and 1777) in which he hailed the school as an "institution of education" whose founders were "dedicated to the well-being and improvement of humanity," whose pedagogy was genuinely "in keeping with nature as well as all civic purposes," and which could thus effect the "development of the natural aptitudes inherent in human nature" (Ak 2: 447–448). He called upon "all humanitarians" (*Menschenfreunde*) to give their support to and inform themselves about this new school and its "true method of education" (Ak 2: 449–450). Besides some initial communiqués with Basedow, Kant maintained correspondence with the school's two main directors, Joachim Heinrich Campe and Christian Heinrich Wolke, offering them his heartfelt encouragement. In a 1778 letter to Christian Wolke, Kant gave an early indication of his conception of education: not the "theoretical learning [*Schulwissenschaft*]" espoused by some of the school's critics, but "the formation [*Bildung*] of human beings, both in regard to their talents and their character" is "the only thing necessary"; he goes on to affirm that both these aims are well served at this institution under Wolke's direction (Ak 10, ¶125, 221).

The educational context gives us another point of view from which to consider the question of the nature of and the need (indeed, urgency) for a science of anthropology, as well as of Kant's effort to distinguish his sense of anthropology from that of his predecessors and contemporaries. Character is not innate, but must be acquired. Good character can overcome an unfortunate temperament and secure the steadfastness which a merely kindly temperament cannot ensure (VA 25, 2.1: 630–654). Since we are responsible for the formation of our character, we are thus also obliged to continue the rearing begun in our youth; such self-education requires self-knowledge, an understanding of human nature. The science of anthropology provides the relevant elements needed for this understanding, and their systematic organization.

The inclusion of all these elements may be best understood under the rubric of the "vocation of humanity" (*Bestimmung des Menschen*) identified in the literature as the programmatic goal of the German reformers of education in the eighteenth century. The concept guided thinking on education toward a human, social, and political order yet to be realized. It was the title of two essays whose appearances in 1748 (by Johann Joachim Spalding) and in 1800 (by Johann Gottlieb Fichte) coincide with the span of Kant's life's work as teacher and philosopher. Initially related in logical and ontological discourse to the Latin *determinatio*, the additional sense of the Latin *vocatio* came into usage in the mid-eighteenth century. In the "Architectonic" of the *Critique of Pure Reason*, Kant introduces it as the concept of the teleological inner order of reason, of the sciences ordered to wisdom: philosophy understood as the idea of legislation or governance inherent in human reason calls upon and orders all other sciences in the service of the *Bestimmung des Menschen* (KpV A838–840/B866–868). Under the aegis of this concept, Kant conceives of human nature as teleologically directed or oriented to the human purpose of the highest good (the unity of complete happiness and perfect virtue), a thematic to which he returns in the second half of the *Critique of Judgment*.

The need for a distinct science of human nature for the sake of the goal of the realization of the vocation of humanity qua human, moral, rational being may be traced also to the nature and status of modern natural science. That modern physics, the science of the nature of things, was wholly inadequate as an account of human nature was a long-standing criticism. A clear statement of the objections is found, for example, in Pope's *Essay on Man* (published in 1733 and praised by Kant in the *Friedländer* lectures). As Pope expresses it, not only do Newton's insights not explain either his own beginning or end, or the workings of his own mind, but in this modern context human nature has paradoxically become an ever greater enigma to itself. Kant repeatedly notes that human nature must be distinguished from the nature of the flora, fauna, and minerals endemic to different lands and climates. In the introduction to the *Friedländer* lectures, he underscores that human nature interests us more than nature itself, for the "human being is the purpose of nature" (*Zweck der Natur*, VA 25, 2.1: 470). Anthropology as the science of the human being as an object of inner sense, he notes, deserves to be accorded a comparable status in academia to that held by physics (the science of objects of outer sense) (VA 25, 2.1: 473). The ensuing discussions in the first part of the lectures of the states of the mind, the issue of its having control over itself, of the clarity or obscurity of its representations, indeed of its capacity to give shape to its world and so to the world in which human beings actually live, are the effort to articulate the elements and divisions of the needed science of anthropology.

This translation was prepared by G. Felicitas Munzel. Reformatting of the textual notes was done by Jeffrey Choi, and some of the informational notes were added by Allen W. Wood.

Lecture of the Winter Semester 1775–1776 based on the transcriptions *Friedländer 3.3* (Ms 400), *Friedländer 2* (Ms 399) and Prieger

TRANSLATED BY G. FELICITAS MUNZEL

Contents

PREAMBLE

In the end, all skill which one possesses requires knowledge of the way in which we are to make use of it. The knowledge basic[a] to application is called knowledge of the world. Knowledge of the world is knowledge of the stage upon which we can apply all skill. It is a twofold kind of knowledge, of theoretical and pragmatic perfection. The theoretical consists in our knowing what is required for certain final purposes and thus concerns the understanding. The pragmatic consists in the power of judgment to avail ourselves of all skill. It is needed to seal all our skill. The basis of pragmatic knowledge is knowledge of the world, where one can make use of all theoretical knowledge. By world we here understand the sum total of all relations into which human beings may enter, where they can exercise their insights and skills. The world as an object of outer sense is nature, the world as an object of inner sense is the human being. Thus human beings can enter into twofold relations, into relations in which they need knowledge of nature, and into relations in which they need knowledge of the human being. The study of nature and of the human being constitutes the study or knowledge of the world. The person who has much theoretical knowledge, who knows a great deal, but has no skill to make use of it, is instructed for school but not for the world. And this skill is pedantry. One can have skill for some relations, for example one does well in school, yet we lack a general skill for all relations that we come across. Since human beings just do not know what relations they may enter into, it is thus necessary to acquire knowledge in all relations indeterminately. Knowledge of all relations is knowledge of the world. In order to have world knowledge, one must study a whole, out of which whole the parts can subsequently be determined, and this is a system, insofar as multiplicity[b] has arisen out of the idea of the whole. The one who knows how to situate multiplicity in the whole of cognition has a system, which differs from an aggregate, in which the whole does not originate out of the idea, but through composition. If I now study the relations of things, and am in a position to assign a place to the multiple parts in the whole, then I have a knowledge of nature. I can however assign things a place in concepts; then this would be a system of nature. Or I can assign things a place in localities, and this is done in physical geography.

The latter belongs to knowledge of the world as its first part, insofar as it is pragmatic. Here many physical observations are omitted; only what is needed in regard to knowledge of the world insofar as it is pragmatic, is taken into account. The second part of knowledge of the world is knowledge of human beings, who are considered inasmuch as their

---

[a] *zum Grunde liegt* [b] *das Mannigfaltige*

knowledge is of interest to us in life. Therefore human beings are not studied in speculative terms, but pragmatic, in the application of their knowledge according to rules of prudence, and this is anthropology. Nothing interests us as much as another human being, not nature but the human being is the object of our affects. We attend to nothing more than we attend to what can accrue to us in other people's regard. Nature can offer us nothing but comfortableness and maintenance, which can only be used among human beings, and only insofar as we cannot have these in common with other people, are we unable to bear all miserable circumstances in regard to comfortableness and maintenance. We do not complain about nature itself in regard to our meager circumstances, but because other people are better off than we are. When my meal is always bread and water, I fret because I know other people are better off. However, when the city is beleaguered, and all in the city must eat the same together, then I am merry and cheerful at heart with my poor fare, because no one is given preferential treatment in this. The human being thus interests us more than nature, for nature exists for the sake of the human, the human being is the purpose of nature.

25:471 It is said: human beings know the world when they have traveled and have seen it. However, that is still no knowledge of the world, but the one who knows human beings knows the world. The knowledge of human beings may however be twofold.

1. The fortuitous behavior or conduct of human beings, or the state of affairs.
2. The nature of humanity.

Anthropology is not however a particular,[a] but a general anthropology. In it one comes to know the nature of humanity, not the state of human beings, for the particular properties of human beings always change, but the nature of humanity does not. Anthropology is thus a pragmatic knowledge of what results from our nature, but it is not a physical or geographical knowledge, for that is bound to time and place, and is not constant. One still cannot say about the person who has traveled and has come to know many people, who has learned the state and fashions of the most famous cities, that he knows human beings, for he has come to know only the state of affairs which is very changeable. However, when I know humanity, then [this conception of humanity] must suit all kinds of human beings. Therefore anthropology is not a description of human beings, but of human nature. Thus we consider the knowledge of human beings in regard to their nature. Knowledge of humanity is at the same time my knowledge. Thus a natural knowledge must lie at the basis, in accordance with which we can judge what is basic

[a] *locale*, also "topical"

48

to every human being. Then we have secure principles in terms of which we can proceed. Hence we must study ourselves, and since we want to apply this to others, we must thus study humanity, not however psychologically or speculatively, but pragmatically. For all pragmatic doctrines are doctrines of prudence, where for all our skills we also have the means to make proper use of everything. For we study human beings in order to become more prudent, which prudence becomes a science. Therefore we should not travel to study human beings, but can examine their nature everywhere. The human being however, the subject, must be studied whether he can even fulfill[a] what we require that he ought to do. Lack of knowledge of human beings is the reason that morality and sermons, which are full of admonitions of which we never tire, have little effect. Morality must be combined with knowledge of humanity.

25:472

Abstention from many vices is not the result of morality and religion, but of refinement. One does not refrain from vices because they are contrary to morality, but because they are so crude. In order that morality and religion obtain their final purpose however, knowledge of the human being must be combined with them. Nature has its phenomena, but human beings also have their phenomena. No one has yet written a world history, which was at once a history of humanity, but only of the state of affairs and of the change in the kingdoms, which as a part is indeed major, but considered in the whole, is a trifle. All histories of wars amount to the same thing, in that they contain nothing more than the descriptions of battles. But whether a battle has been more or less won makes no difference in the whole. More attention should though be given thereby to humanity. In his history of England, Hume provided a proof of this.[1] To observe human beings and their conduct, to bring their phenomena under rules, is the purpose of anthropology. All anthropologies which we still have at this time, have not yet had the idea which we have here before[b] us. Everything that bears no relation to the prudent conduct of human beings, does not belong to anthropology. Only that from which a prudent use in life can immediately be drawn, belongs to anthropology. Everything where ideas arise, belongs to speculation and not in anthropology, in the way Platner delineated it.[2]

---

[a] *praestiren*. Compare the Collins transcriptions of Kant's lectures on ethics: "one must first know of the agent whether he is also in a position to accomplish what it is required from him that he should do" (*Immanuel Kant: Lectures on Ethics*, trans. Peter Heath [Cambridge University Press, 1997], 42). Compare also the Mrongovius transcriptions where Kant is reported to have asserted that the two sciences of practical philosophy and anthropology "cannot subsist as one without the other," for "one must know human beings in order to know whether they are capable of performing all that is demanded of them. The consideration of a rule is useless, if one cannot make people prepared to fulfill it" (Ak 27.2.2, 1398).

[b] Reading *von* as *vor*, per editors' note.

49

25:473

How does anthropology arise? Through the collection of many observations about human beings by those authors who had acute knowledge of human beings. For example, Shakespeare's theatrical works, the English "Spectator";[3] and Montaigne's *Essays* along with his life is also a book for life and not for school.[4] The sphere of human beings is already very spread out, and it thus deserves to be presented together as a whole, and not alongside of other sciences. For physics is knowledge of the object of outer sense, and the knowledge of human beings as the object of inner sense, constitutes just such a sphere. Consequently, it deserves just such effort, and to be treated as such a science in academia, as is physics. Strictly speaking, human beings are sooner worth the effort to be studied, and that they are given their due by such considerations, than the entire physical nature. One believed there to be too little to be said about this in a science; hence one inserted it into metaphysics, and in fact into psychology, which constitutes empirical psychology, where it does not belong at all, in that metaphysics has nothing to do with any empirical sciences.

MORE SPECIFIC TREATISE ON ANTHROPOLOGY

ON THE SELF-CENTEREDNESS[a] OF THE HUMAN BEING

No thought but the thought of the I lies at the basis of other thoughts. This representation of I and the power to grasp the thought, is the essential difference of the human being from all animals. This is the personality to be conscious of oneself. Children belatedly avail themselves of the word I. They cannot yet consider themselves, and do not yet have the power to direct their thoughts to themselves. This concept of the I is one of great fecundity, it is the source from which much is derived.

1. Substantiality. The soul is the real[b] I, it is a subject which is not a predicate of something else.

2. Simplicity. For it is a unity in the strictest sense, and has no plural. It cannot be divided, many cannot constitute an I. Consequently, it is a simple concept.

3. Spontaneity also results from it, for when I say, I act, I am not moved.

25:474

The I itself means the soul, or the inner. The body is an outer object of my senses, but I do not see the I through outer, but through inner sense. I intuit myself. In the soul, we can distinguish intellect and heart.[c]

---

[a] *Selbstheit*: interpreting Kant's sense here from the ensuing discussion and later use of this term.

[b] *eigentliche*

[c] *Geist und Gemüt*: in the context of this discussion, "intellect and heart" seems to capture Kant's sense better than the more common renderings of these terms as "spirit" and

Heart is the way in which the soul is affected by things. It is the power to reflect upon one's state and to relate one's state to oneself and one's personality. Intellect or the soul is the subject which is thinking there, thus it is active, but the heart is passive. Someone who is quick to learn and can be well reared,[a] has a good heart. However the concept of intellect presupposes the concept of activity. A bodily pain concerns our soul, but distress[b] concerns the heart and has its seat there. Many ills exist in our soul, but not in our heart. We not only feel pain in our soul, but besides that we are distressed over this pain in our heart, and we not only feel a joy in our soul, but besides we take delight in the fact that we are joyful, in our heart. It is not a weakness to feel pain in our soul due to a misfortune one suffers, but we find fault with a sober man for distress because of this pain. Likewise it is also not a weakness to feel joy due to good fortune, however it is childish to take extraordinary delight in this joy. Thus when pain passes over into the heart from the soul, it produces distress, and when the joy of the soul passes over into the heart, then a childish enjoyment arises thereby. One thus demands of a wise man that he keep his distance from what belongs to the heart. The heart then is a power of feeling what one feels. Hence, *animus* and *anima*[c] are distinguished. One otherwise calls *animus* also *mens*, only *mens* may also already mean intellect. Thus in the soul, heart is something different, what we otherwise call heart or feeling. Animals are capable of neither distress nor joy, because they cannot reflect about their state. Consequently they are also incapable of happiness and misfortune, for it is through reflection that human beings are only capable of fortune or misfortune; they thus have it in their control. The concept of I, pragmatically considered, is the most interesting thought, to which one applies or reduces everything. In society, human beings are very inclined always to speak about themselves, although prudence limits this somewhat. In his thoughts, every human being is an egoist – but because everyone is like this, one thus limits the other. Montaigne is reproached that he always talks about himself.[5] The German checks this self-centeredness with modesty, by always setting aside the I in letters. The we is really an expression of modesty, as the king thereby includes the advisers, only now it is supposed to mean that

25:475

"mind." The "feeling soul" or "feeling heart" is one sense of *Gemüt* in German, and in this regard *Geist* expresses its opposite, the thinking, cognitive consciousness. The distinction also coincides with the Latin distinction between *animus* and *anima* referred to here by Kant.

[a] *sich gut ziehen läßt*: as becomes evident in the course of these lectures, Kant uses *ziehen* interchangeably with *erziehen*.

[b] *Betrübnis*

[c] *Anima* means soul as the principle of life, while *animus* refers to soul as the principle of intellection and sensation. Its range of meaning includes intellect, understanding, mind, thought, reason, and spirit.

the king represents the entire people. In moral judgments, the power to transpose the I is necessary, and to put oneself in the point of view and place of the other, so that one thinks with him, and has empathy with him. If we want to judge about other people, we must alter our point of view, namely

1. transpose my point of view and then

2. put myself in the other's point of view, and thereupon we can determine the worth of another's actions, when we can alter the two points of view. To take a point of view is a skill which one can acquire by practice. In society, one finds that people are unable to put themselves in the place of another, that they do not have empathy with him, feel with him, and see how this occurs; instead they always look to themselves. All rules of what is permitted there and is in good form are rules whereby I can regard myself from another point of view, and the one who is able to take such a point of view outside of himself knows how to behave properly.

Human beings can thus be considered twofold, as animal and as intelligence. As animal they are capable of sensations, impressions, and representations, as intelligence they are conscious of themselves, which lies at the basis of all higher powers. As intelligence they have control over their state and over their animality, and in this respect this is called intellect. If intelligence is set aside, then the human being is considered as animal. If he considers something as intelligence, then he considers it by means of the understanding. Thus the human being fears much, but as animal, for example when he stands on a high tower; his understanding tells him there is no cause for it. As intelligence he reproves what he desires as animal. In the case of others, we also reprove their temperament and praise their character. Temperament deals with animality. No human being hates himself and wishes himself harm, but he is vexed with himself, especially one who is imprudent and thoughtless. Why is this? There is a twofold subject in the human being. When he reproves himself, then he does so as intelligence, when he is reproved by himself, then he is reproved as animal. Thus the human being considers himself from two points of view, as animal and as intelligence. Intelligence constitutes personality, which is however combined with animality. There is always a natural conflict in this combined personality, since animality is based on the dependence of the soul on the body, and intelligence on the domination of the soul over the body. Thus personality must bring about harmony, which is achieved by compulsion, through self-control in accordance with certain rules and through discipline. The human being distinguishes both sometimes by the senses and sometimes by judgments in accordance with reflection. In accordance with animality he judges what tastes good to him, and on the other hand, as intelligence he judges whether it is good. Likewise in connection with the senses:

25:476

for example, according to animality one judges that everything moves around the earth and that the earth stands still, but not according to intelligence. When the image of the moon is larger as it rises, as animal one judges that the moon is larger, although as intelligence one knows that the moon is continually the same size. And the greatest astronomer cannot prevent this appearance, although he most certainly knows it to be otherwise.

When the human being relates everything to his intelligence, this is self-referential,[a] for all our sensation is either exclusive or participatory.[b] Self-love is fair. Egoism and self-conceit is exclusive. When we read something, a history or a novel, we always put ourselves in the other's place and this is participation. Every human being as person or as intelligence, relates all thoughts to himself by means of the I; there is nothing in the whole world closer to him than himself. Thus in his own regard he is a focal point[c] of the world, but if he relates everything exclusively to himself, then he makes himself the center. Every human being is a focal point of the world, but not the center. Thus every human being likes to speak about himself, and endeavors to make himself the center. Therefore there is always a dispute. However, in order that this does not happen, everyone must observe the limit, and maintain the distance of equality, so that there is an interval between myself and another, and one does not come fully into complete contact, which occurs thereby if one reveals something about oneself to the other. Hence it is also modest on the part of an author if he speaks through the we, for then he shares his judgments with the other. Why is the *ihr*[d] generally used in some languages and in others the *Sie*?[e] The reason seems to lie in respect for the multitude,[f] which we attribute to a person. Hence, our language, which does not have the general *Ihr*, but observes a difference between *Du*,[g] *Er*,[h] and *Sie*, does not have such facility. Instead it has an awkwardness and brings with it a constraint in dispensing these words, which has an influence on genius. It would therefore be good if this would be done away with, which may also make a difference in morals. The Frenchman says *Vous* to the distinguished man and the distinguished man also says *Vous* to the humble man. Consequently there exists no awkwardness, which in our case surely does gradually shackle genius. The body as the subject of animality is so important, that it is through this body that one is precisely the human being one is, and through another body would be

25:477

---

[a] *Selbstsichtigkeit*
[b] *theilnehmend*: taking the term here in its widest sense, since one can take part in something without being necessarily sympathetic.
[c] *Focus*
[d] plural, familiar form of you
[e] formal form of you

[f] *die Menge*
[g] familiar form of you, singular
[h] he

another human being. The body often gives us worth, and intelligence often is not asked for; the officer thus solicits animality in the human being, not intelligence.

ON THE DIFFERENT ACTS OF THE SOUL

Consciousness is twofold, of oneself and of objects. Thus, often a human being who is conscious of objects outside himself, and is very occupied with these in thought, is not conscious of himself. Consciousness of objects is therefore something different from consciousness of oneself. The more we are conscious of objects, all the more are we *outside ourselves, the more we are conscious of ourselves, all the more are we within* ourselves. The observation of things is not as arduous as the observation of oneself, although the observation of oneself is brief. The habit of observing one-self is harmful, provides opportunity for fanaticism, and causes one to be mistaken about the world. Self-observation is difficult and unnatural and may very well take place once for the sake of examination, but should not last long. The main thing must consist in activity. There exists a kind of thoughtlessness and a freeing of oneself in thought, not from other objects, but from oneself, and this is a real recuperation when one has observed oneself. The analytical part of philosophy, where one ana-lyzes one's concepts and also observes oneself, is the most tiring part of philosophy. However, the self-observation of one's sensations and not one's concepts turns one into a fantast.

25:478

Recuperation often consists not in rest, but in other pastimes; thus Schmidt goes bowling in order to recuperate and the philosopher plays cards.

Self-observation in regard to outer appearance, or how one would like to be viewed in another's mind,[a] is affectation. The manners of such a person are forced and embarrassed, or it is affected behavior, which is artificial. Children thereby become habituated to this, when one says to them: how does that seem? how fitting is that? Thereby one fosters in them the behavior of attending to how they would like to be viewed in another's mind. That person makes the best impression[b] who does not even think about what sort of impression he might well like to give others. In the beginning one must indeed make an effort, but in common life one must not observe such a thing. There one must already be proficient in it. Whoever is narrating something, must no longer be attending to himself. If he is, and is artificial in his expressions, then it no longer pleases and is embarrassing, but he must really have acquired proficiency, for example, an author. If someone may not pay attention

---

[a] *dem andern in die Sinne fallen*   [b] *fält am besten in die Augen*

to himself, then he gains naïvety and nature,[a] for art gives rise to the suspicion of semblance and not reality.   25:479

ON THE OBSCURE[b] REPRESENTATIONS OF THE SOUL

The obscure representations contain the hidden vane of what occurs in the open,[c] hence we must examine them. Obscure representations are those of which one is not conscious. How then can one inspect them? Not directly, although I can infer that such representations, of which I am not conscious, are in me. For example, I see the Milky Way as a white strip and through the telescope I see many stars. I have also seen just these stars with my bare eyes, for otherwise I could not have seen the Milky Way, and I was not conscious of this. Therefore I had obscure representations of the stars. In general one notices the following about obscure representations:

1. The human soul acts mostly in obscurity
2. its greatest store of cognitions exist in obscurity.

For example, if an individual[d] reads, then the soul attends to the letters, for if it spells [the words] out, then it reads, [and] then it attends to what it reads. The individual is not conscious of all this. The musician who is improvising must direct his reflection upon every finger he places, on playing, on what he wants to play, and on the new [music] he wants to produce. If he did not do so, then he also could not play, but he is not conscious of this. Here one must admire the quickness of the soul, in that it reflects on all the fingers, on what is being played, and also on what one wants to play in the moment. All this happens in the obscure representations. To observe this is a major occupation of the philosophers.

The soul's greatest store exists in obscurity. A large part of philosophical reflection[e] is already prepared beforehand in obscurity. We must explain and trace judgments which arise from obscure representations. For example, why can we sooner tolerate someone who tries to amass everything together, in order to squander it later, than a frugal, stingy individual, even though the frugal person does no injustice to anyone? And what does it concern us that he lives stingily with regard to himself, as such frugal misers also plead? In what does the cause of this lie? There

---

[a] The sense of "nature" here probably being a "natural demeanor."
[b] *duncklen*. For consistency throughout this section, *dunkel* and *Dunkelheit* (which more commonly mean dark and darkness) will be translated as "obscure" and "obscurity."
[c] *im Lichten*: "in the open" as in a clearing in a forest. At the end of this section Kant also plays on this phrase to mean dawn in contrast to dusk.
[d] *Mensch*   [e] *Gedanken*

25:480 must after all be one, because it is universal: the grounds must after all agree in reason. The cause is: he fixes*a* the use of the goods, this much about him is beyond humanity. One must not regard what is universally judged through sound understanding, to be absurd because it has no basis,*b* but the basis exists in reason, for otherwise human beings could not judge universally. The basis however still exists in obscurity and one must try to establish this basis. For example, a drunken man is more tolerable than a drunken woman. Everyone judges this way. What is the basis? Women*c* are subjected to impugnment. Why does one shake hands with a stranger with one's right hand? The right hand is [our] active one, thus we leave it free for him. Why do we put the most distinguished among three [persons] in the middle? Because he can then converse on both sides. All this lay in reason, only we were not aware of it. Indeed, there exist sciences of the kind, and this is analytical philosophy, in which one sheds light on obscure representations by uncovering them. That is the way it is in morality by the explanation of virtue. One must there make the other person aware of his own ideas, for the concept of virtue already lies in him. Socrates claims to be the midwife of the ideas of his listeners.[6]

If I wanted to become conscious in an instant of all obscure representations all at once, then I would necessarily be very astonished at myself. Thus what lies in my memory is also obscure and I am not conscious of it. What a human being once has in his mind,*d* he does not lose any more, only it is obscure in him and he requires means to draw such out of obscurity. For some, they find it very difficult. Hence if one is supposed to narrate something, one can think of nothing, although if one were to narrate everything one knows, one could write a quarto volume,*e* until a matter is presented. The understanding falls into error through obscure representations and from this scruples arise.

25:481 We take pleasure in letting our mind wander about in obscurity, which the hidden and oblique modes of speech prove. Every obscurity which is suddenly clarified, provides amenity and delights much. The art of an author consists in concealing his ideas in such a way that the reader can immediately resolve them on his own; this takes jests and inspirations. Clarity, however, is soon wearying. Yet, we not only play with such obscure representations, rather we are also ourselves a play of obscure representations. Thus one often prefers to designate natural

a setzen
b Grund: the more natural English term in this context would be "reason," but this would be confusing with the use of "reason" for Vernunft.
c Kant's term here and elsewhere is Frauenzimmer. Regarding this usage, see the comment in the section "On the Difference of the Two Sexes" (beginning on 25:697).
d Gemüt
e A quarto is a book in which there are four leaves to a sheet.

things with an expression from a foreign language, than with a German expression, although the other person understands the expression from the foreign language just as well as his own. Yet the foreign expression must still first be translated in the mind, and only then does the concept come to mind. Thus there is a detour. Through this detour however, the concept is weakened, just like a beam of light through repeated refraction, and therefore we like the foreign expression better; for example, to use *Cour* for "courting." If however, the foreign expression is used altogether too often, and is adopted just the same as one's own, then it loses the veil it initially had. For example, instead of Spanish pox, one said Frenchmen, which has however already been likewise generally adopted. Thus one often conveys the truth covertly to a great and noble [mind], who understands it just the same, as if it were obvious.

Every inspiration which is a riddle in the beginning, but which is immediately followed by elucidation, is also a translation and a detour in the mind, and the mind is pleased to have resolved a difficulty. Thus things happen in the mind in the way they do in an optical box.[7] The art of being obscure in such a way that the other person can see through it, requires much ingenuity,[a] and belongs to modesty and proper behavior, which must be acquired.

In addition, preliminary judgments also belong to the obscure representations. Before an individual passes a judgment which is determinate, he already passes in advance a preliminary judgment in obscurity. This leads him to search for something. For example, who searches for unknown lands, will not simply go to the sea, rather he judges beforehand. Each determinate judgment thus has a preliminary judgment. Hence, the study of the mind with regard to the secret processes of the human soul is very important. On the other hand, we also notice that human beings are themselves a play of obscurity. We are very fond of obscurity, and incline to superstition, fortune-telling, and mystical things, for all this produces greater expectation in the mind, than it has later, when one gains insight into it by light. Just as everything appears larger by dusk, than by light, in this way obscurity also produces greater expectations.

ON DISTINCTNESS

Order precedes all distinctness. Distinctness is a work of the understanding and clarity is a work of the senses, for distinctness is based on reflection. Indistinctness is opposed to distinctness, confusion is opposed to order. Thus order is the condition for distinctness and confusion for

[a] *Witz*

indistinctness. In thinking and acting, order must prevail. However, all order has a rule, and in this human beings are very different. Some human beings already have a spirit of order by nature, they only lack materials which they could order. However, they also produce the little they do know in a certain order, so that the spirit of order is immediately evident, even if it is incidentally completely empty. And since order is only the condition, they thus lack material. For example, in this way someone keeps his books orderly and does not tolerate their being scattered on the table, and for this reason he also does not read them so that he does not bring them out of order. Hence many spend the whole day solely ordering and tidying up. Such order can also take place in thinking, and this is then an awkwardness in the rule which one calls pedantry. The rule must not govern us, we must not do something in order to get a rule out of it, thus to please the rule, for otherwise one is subjugated to the coercion of the rule. One calls such a formal order methodical. Therefore distinctness requires order, and the spirit of order in one's presentation[a] is a great talent. In this way an individual often has a great genius, but no spirit of order for ordering what his mind produces. The spirit of the Germans is methodical and orderly, they produce much for the sake of order. The English lack the spirit of order and of division, by means of which one could have a distinct concept of the whole.

25:483

ON THE VARIOUSNESS[b] OF THE PERFECTION AND IMPERFECTION OF COGNITIONS

The perfection of the cognitions is threefold:

1. The relation of cognitions to the object.
2. The relation of cognitions to the subject.
3. The relation of cognitions among one another.

Truth and certainty appertain to the relation of cognitions to the object, namely in accordance with quality. The means to both is distinctness. In accordance with quantity, cognition in regard to objects is perfect in accordance with size, completeness, and exactness. Facility, liveliness, and novelty appertain to the perfection of cognitions in accordance with the subject. I do not for this reason have better cognition of an object if I find it to be easy, novel, and lively, rather the difference

---

[a] *Vortrag* more narrowly means "lecture," but the context here indicates a wider sense of how people in general express themselves.
[b] *mannigfaltigen*, which is often standardly translated, especially in its nominal form, as 'manifold'.

concerns the human being himself, and not the object. He is fond of the novel because it increases his cognition and is greater than the old [objects of cognition].

Association, order, unity, and then also variousness and contrast, appertain to the perfection of cognitions among one another.

The truth of cognitions is the fundamental perfection, namely in regard to the object; that is not in fact of much interest, but it is the condition of all remaining perfections. Semblance is to be differentiated from truth, it is more convenient and human beings prefer it. In the case of cognition, one must not first regard utility, but rather truth. To the extent that a cognition discovers a law for us, it is thus important, even if 25:484 we do not see any other use for it. For example, the one who first discovered geometrical principles only discovered a rule which had no use at that time, but later could be used in many instances, although he had no immediate insight into them then. *Thus the one who discovered electricity discovered a new law of nature, although he likewise had no insight into its use*. In the hope of utility, one must therefore let oneself be content with truth.

Error and ignorance are the opposite of the perfection of the cognitions. Ignorance is an imperfection of the lazy and error is an imperfection of those who are active. The activity of experimenting is often the mother of errors. A cognition can be small, but secure from errors, but on the other hand, a cognition may be large and extended, but not secure from error. Errors follow from our judgments, especially when we are in the course of making them. They cannot be avoided and also cannot be immediately removed without the means required to help one do so. It is therefore enough if one can secure one's cognition from error, but we should not immediately become impatient due to an error, even if it has been committed by someone else, for one who thinks quickly can commit an error more readily than one who inches along. Paradoxical cognitions are the ones that make error suspect; these cognitions appear strange. Hence, if one judges him, one can learn something new from an author who is paradoxical, because he deviates from the old path and chooses a new one.[8] However, according to reason, such an author is a daredevil, in that he exposes himself both to winning and to losing. If he succeeds, he gains the advantage therefrom, if he fails he still deserves credit for that reason, because he had this much daring to take a risk. Someone else, who is not so daring, holds to common opinion in order not to fail. The French are very fond of daring in thinking, as they take a risk and thereby lay themselves open to praise or blame. That is a narrow-minded person who, in an unfinished book containing errors, 25:485 does not nevertheless see the idea of genius which dared, after all, to say such a thing. One must read such authors who are paradoxical because one finds much that is new in them.

Our cognitions can have clarity in the understanding and intensity[a] in sensation. In the presentation, we can differentiate the emphatic and hypostatic cognitions. This classification is taken from Aristotle, who classified the meteors this way.[9] Thus the rainbow is emphatic, and lightning is hypostatic. What produces an intensity of sensation, would therefore be emphatic and, where there is an independent beauty, it would be hypostatic. The English "Spectator" has independent beauty, the embellishing of speech with images belongs to emphatic beauty.

ON THE DIFFERENCE OF SENSIBILITY AND RELATION TO THE UNDERSTANDING

We hear complaints about sensibility, such as about its being the source of all confusions and errors. Thus it is charged that it is the cause of errors, and one complains that the understanding no longer dominates, but that sensibility does. On the other hand, it has its merits, since it makes intuitable what the understanding coolly reflects upon. And there the understanding is reproached that it is no longer sensible. What are we to make of this? Our perfection consists therein, that we are able to subjugate our faculties and capacities to the free power of choice; but even if this is the case, then it is still necessary that there be in addition a might and a power to carry out such things which the free power of choice devises. It is thus the condition under which the powers can be used. Two elements are therefore necessary for perfection, the power of ruling (*potestas rectoria*) and the power of execution (*executoria*). The power of ruling is blind without the power of execution. Sensibility is a main element of the human being insofar as sensibility has executive force, through which the understanding has an effect, when it is combined with the senses. On the other hand, the senses are not capable of ruling and are often a hindrance. Thus in one respect they are advantageous, and in another respect they are hindering. Our imagination is poorly subjugated to the free power of choice, for the human being cannot have ingenious inspirations when he wants, but must wait. And the matter is also like this for the instincts and inclinations, and that is sensibility's failing. This is a failing of sensibility only insofar as it is not disciplined; if it is to be subjugated to the free power of choice, then it must be disciplined, in order for it to be a tool of the understanding, which the understanding uses to make its ideas intuitable. Therefore it is false that sensibility is the cause of error, for the senses do not judge. Consequently they also cannot err. It is true that a semblance arises with the senses, but it takes place in the understanding; thus the understanding deceives itself. What we can say to the detriment of sensibility is that, according to the proportion, its strength

25:486

[a] *Stärke*

is too great for the strength of the understanding. The understanding cannot carry anything out, rather sensibility must give it the material. It is a great perfection to give much sensibility to the understanding, for sensibility contains the material which the understanding orders. Sensibility makes intuitable what the understanding actually judges. Thus sensibility has the function of making that intuitable upon which the understanding reflects. With regard to the will, the senses are an incentive, but the understanding has no incentive. One does not at all see how the understanding can convey its insight to the senses, and how it can have an effect on the senses, since it has no motive force. We are passive,[a] and sensibility is the passive side of the human being, but the senses are also at the same time passive instruments of the understanding. Hence, sensibility must be cultivated[b] so that it has serviceability, and then it must be disciplined, so that it may be an instrument for the understanding.

25:487

ON FACILITY AND DIFFICULTY

There exists an inner facility and an inner difficulty. An excess of powers for having an effect constitutes inner facility, and the less the excess is, all the more difficult things are. Outer facility is the removal of hindrances; outer difficulty exists where there are hindrances. Wearisome signifies that difficulty which is accidentally accompanied by circumstances. *Ceremonies*, formalities, and compliments are wearisome. There also exist socially wearisome things, for example congratulations and good wishes for one's health. There is nothing more ridiculous than making social intercourse wearisome. Something can be less wearisome, but still more difficult than a religious practice purged of *ceremony*. Where, however, matters depend more on morality, they are less wearisome, but in fact more difficult. Doing something easy is not praiseworthy, but making something easy and doing something difficult, is praiseworthy. Something seems easy for someone and that is what comes easily to him. Something seems difficult for someone and that is what is laborious.

Something requires assiduity without great exertion and that is industriousness, something requires assiduity with great exertion and that is indolence. All who are indolent work themselves to death. They try to get a lot of work done in a short time in order to keep a lot of time left over for leisure. The question thus is, what is better, to carry out

25:488

---

[a] *leidend*, here in the sense of being subject to being acted upon (i.e. passive).

[b] Kant has adapted the Latin *excolere* as the verb *excoliren*. Its meanings include cultivation and refinement, but Kant also uses the terms *cultiviren* and *verfeinern*. Since the basic Latin meaning originates with tending or working the land, the term is here rendered as synonymous with "cultivating" (since Kant also uses both the terms *bearbeiten* and *arbeiten*). See p. 23, note *a*.

one's work in a short time, in order to have the remaining time entirely for leisure, or to carry out the same work very gradually over a long time, without having time left over for leisure? The difference is based on people's temperaments. The choleric person is by nature busy, he chooses to be constantly occupied at all times. The phlegmatic person chooses difficult work in a short time. The sanguine person chooses easy work in a short time, the melancholic one chooses laborious work over a long time. In some cases, the judgment of human beings in the performance of a task[a] is in the first instance easy, and these are thoughtless ones. Someone else finds his initial judgment to be difficult, and these are awkward. The greatest perfection of the powers of the mind is based on our subordinating them to our power of choice, and the more they are subjugated to the free power of choice, all the greater perfection of the powers of the mind do we possess. If we do not have them under the control of the free power of choice, all provisions for such perfection are thus in vain, if we cannot do what we want with the powers of the mind. For this sake, attention and abstraction, as the two formal capacities[b] of our mind, are only then useful for us, if they are under the free power of choice, so that involuntary attentiveness and abstraction produce much harm. We find that people become unhappy, that they attend to, or abstract from something involuntarily. For example, in the case of the affect of love, the individual attends involuntarily to the beauty of a person's figure, and for that reason forgets to attend to all the other things which make his happiness more enduring. Likewise the individual attends in an involuntary way to an offense inflicted upon him in a social gathering, it keeps running through his head, and he cannot rid himself of it. However, the capacity to abstract from it greatly calms

25:489 the mind. If this is not the case, then the mind produces hatred, which is very unpleasant, and the mind is found to be in a condition which is unpleasant for the individual himself, and constantly inconveniences and reproves him. If however I have the powers of the mind under the free power of choice and can attend and abstract when I want, then I dismiss it from my mind. Thus the ill is eradicated, and with it the discomfort and the cause. For if an individual is provoked with someone and the other person notices it, he will offend him still more, but if he dismisses it from his mind, then the offender is all the more willing to apologize.

I must abstract from the ill which can no longer be changed, and from all discomforts; in this way I am sensible of the world's beauty. Just as one overlooks a person's homeliness if good talents of the mind, to which one pays more attention, are evident. A thought which serves to remind me of all ills is one that is not in my control. However, I can remedy it in that I abstract from it and dismiss it from my mind. Many ills thus

[a] *Sache* [b] *Vermögen*

arise in society through the fact that everyone wants to assert himself and another attends to this, but one must try to abstract from it. The only thing an individual can do in regard to all ills and discomforts in life is this, that he seeks to abstract from all of it, and if he has his mind in such control, then he also has his fate in his control and is in a position to enjoy the pleasant things. Hypochondriacs have the failing that they attend to things by involuntary attentiveness and that they would gladly like to dismiss something from their minds, if only they could. Absent-minded people in turn have the failing that they abstract from everything. When hypochondriacs have heard or seen something, it always keeps running through their heads and plagues them constantly, for example if they are present at an execution. One need not fear that they will also commit a wrongdoing, rather it is the failing of their power of choice, which does not have the power to abstract.

One must never give way to a single thought for a long time, the thought may be of whatever kind it will, for the organization of the brain is, so to speak, thereby injured. One may reflect a long time about a subject,[a] but not about a thought, for the trace is not so easily erased from the mind, since all ills are drawn there to where the parts have been weakened, and all thoughts turn there, just as all unhealthy fluids are drawn to an injury one has on one's foot. Therefore one must not give way for long to a thought, whether it be one of joy, or devotion, or sorrow, or speculation. The individual who is practiced in this, can in an instant shift his mind to another attitude; he can become cheerful, when shortly before, he was gloomy. 25:490

We oppose attention with dissipation of the mind or absent-mindedness. This way in society one can take one's mind off things[b] and talk about other things and not of those about which one is thinking. For since one must after all talk, one reflects on what one is talking about, and for this reason forgets the prior thoughts. However, the individual who is only listening adheres to the one thought.

Abstraction seems to be something easy, however it is real work and effort. If one does not have it in one's power to abstract, the imagination runs its course, just like a stream. For example, when I see an individual, I straightaway represent his entire figure, and if there is a peculiar spot on him, then my mind always adheres to the peculiar place. For example, a button is missing on the jacket, or he has lost a tooth; thus one always looks at the missing button and the gap between the teeth. The mind in general has a propensity to complete everything and to produce a certain whole; therefore it is difficult to abstract. If something belongs to the whole of a representation, and something is missing from the whole, then it takes effort to separate such combining representations. The mind has

[a] *Materie*   [b] figurative sense of *dissipiren*

a natural power for attention, and it would be in a position to represent everything for itself all at once, if there were no hindrances. Abstraction must thus prevent this, hence such sciences which require abstraction are also more difficult. Through abstraction, limitations are placed on the mind, and it is kept from the effort of thinking. Thus the power of abstracting requires more cultivation than that of paying attention. People find it difficult to abstract, and especially then, when one makes the greatest effort. For example, if at a given moment one should look respectable and serious, for instance if all get up from the table and want to pray, or in church, and something ridiculous happens, it costs one much effort, and it remains difficult to abstract from it, even though the earnestness is based only on formality.

25:491

ON COMPLEX, PRIMITIVE, AND ADHERING PERCEPTIONS

We must consider every representation in its bare state and separated from everything, or examine it with certain representations that belong and adhere to it, [and give it] a certain accompaniment, and [we must] indeed do so in order to stir up attentiveness and increase the intensity of the impression. For example, thus a gentleman takes many servants with him, even if he does not need them, in order to make an impression, and to stir up others' attention. We also cannot recommend the good to others except by means of the accompaniment and addition of other representations. Rabelais says a sound understanding is like beef and pork for the peasant's supper, but a ragout of folly with the acidity of ingenuity is [meant] for a nobleman's supper.[10] Of what use are images in speech, other than that they are only to embellish the main representation with diamonds and serve as a frame to enhance the picture. In the same way one pays more compliments to that individual who has beautiful clothes than to one who does not, and such representations adhering to it pass on to the main representation and strengthen it.

Where the main representation is not filled in with adhering representations, the representation is dry. This dryness of the representation is often necessary in order to present the main representation all the more clearly and to have insight into it, since the main representation is obscured by the adhering representations. That is what happens in the case of devotion, so that people are more likely to take the adhering representations as devotion, than the main representation itself. Thus when an entire congregation gathers together with a unanimous intent, then this leaves a kind of impression that consists only in the formality, and people call it devotion, while, when they leave the church, they do not know a word from the sermon, that is, from the main representation. Thus the adhering representation is often taken to be the main representation. 25:492

ON THE SENSES

The senses are that through which we directly represent things for ourselves. We can think of two kinds of senses, an inner sense through which we intuit ourselves, and an outer sense, through which we perceive objects outside of ourselves. Inner sense gives the human being the advantage over non-rational animals. His personality is based on this, that he can intuit and consider[a] himself. Through the fact that he is conscious of himself, he is capable of all fortune and misfortune,[b] for pain due to an ill is not misfortune, rather the thought about this pain is. Likewise, joy due to a happiness is also not fortune, rather the thought about this joy is. For example, a young girl going to the ball on another day, feels delight over the joy she will have there. If a man feels delight over a joy he will be relishing, then he is being childish. Therefore distress due to pain and delight due to joy result from the consciousness of inner sense. It is pleasant to occupy oneself with the outer senses, but the attentiveness to inner sense is wearisome and forcible, although it is necessary for re-examination; it only must not be continuous. Hence one who sets great store by his sensations and taste is fantastical. The peasant pays no attention to himself at all, and hardly notices that he is sick, until he is lying in bed. His activities of outer sense keep him from [attending to himself] and that also restores his health.

Whoever does not settle on any object of outer sense is an idealist. There also exist idealists of taste, who indeed say there is no true universal taste, but [there is] custom and received opinion. This principle is a principle of unsociability. If we did not have a universal taste, then we could not eat together from the same dish. We can thus conceive of a rational idealism. It consists in this, that our fortune does not depend on outer things, rather things have the worth we give to them. They must first pass the mind's censorship. For example, if someone is to receive an inheritance, and on account of this represents for himself a paradisiacal fortune, the inheritance is not such a fortune; rather the representation that he has of it is. He takes it to be a great fortune, and thereafter sees that it is a misfortune, since he makes those who also wanted to inherit, 25:493 his enemies, and brings more troubles down upon himself. After that, he attributes the misfortune to things. Therefore fortune does not consist

---

[a] *betrachten*, but the term in the other manuscript (399) is *beurtheilen* ("judge").

[b] *Glück* and *Unglück* may here be intended to be synonymous with *Glückseligkeit* and *Unglücklichkeit*, but since *Glückseligkeit* is also used in the text, the translation is given for the fundamental meaning of the terms (and consistently so throughout this section).

in things, but in the way the mind apprehends it. The mind can do a great deal in this respect, it can reshape the entire world for itself. The emptiness of things and the brevity of life give us an opportunity for it. This is the only thing through which we realize that outer things do not constitute fortune. The mind can thus easily see that true fortune is based on the idea, and this is true idealism which is rational and practical.

The outer senses affect the body. Some affect it externally, others internally. The former are senses of intuition, the others, senses of sensation. Two elements are to be distinguished in all senses, intuition and sensation. The senses of intuition are objective, those of sensation are subjective. The former present objects to us, the others consist in the way in which we are affected by them. For example, when seeing I perceive objects, but when smelling, I have a sensation of an impression. The objective senses are: the feeling of touch (*tactus*) which is different from feeling in general, [and] hearing, and seeing. The subjective senses are smell and taste. If we would include feeling, then there would be six senses, but this is a general sense and is called not touch (*tactus*), but sense (*sensus*). Through objective senses, I am more likely to cognize objects, but through subjective senses I am more likely to perceive enjoyment. Through touch we have cognition of substances; without this sense we could not cognize them, instead we would perceive only appearances.

Hearing is a sense which perceives at a distance. Through hearing we do not obtain any concept of the cognition of objects, rather it is only a play of sensation. Hearing does not present objects in [terms of] their shape; we have no representation and concept of objects other than that an object is merely there. Since hearing does not present any object, but only an impression of it, it has the following uses. It is a sense of sociability, it serves to communicate the signs of thoughts, thus it is a means of speech, it serves as a sign of the object. Figures can thus give us no signs of the objects, rather [they give] the object itself. We divide time through hearing. All tones are equal divisions of time through hearing. Our mind has great keenness to have insight into the division of time in the minutest detail, since it has insight into all the vibrations of the string,[a] which are after all proportioned, although one string produces 6,000 vibrations in a second.

25:494

By means of seeing I cognize objects and determine them. Sight[b] presents the shapes of things in space and divides space. Thus by feeling we cognize substances, by hearing we divide time, and by sight we divide space. Substances, space and time are however the three elements of outer objects.

---

[a] *Seite = Saite* (as confirmed by Werner Stark).
[b] Figurative sense of *Gesicht* as *Sehvermögen*.

The subjective senses are those which change our state. The sense of smell and taste belong to them. The bare state without reference to other things is feeling in general (*generaliter*), and thus is not a special sense, but lies at the basis of all senses. For example, thus a shudder seizes an individual in a tragic performance, [and] in promptings of magnanimity, or thus a person shudders when someone grates a stony stylus on the slate, or if one rasps something pointed or angular. No basis can be given for this in feeling except that, through these piercing tones, the nerves lose their composure. The sense of smell and taste are both senses of sensation, where the effect on the body is chemical, just as in the case of the previous senses, the effect was mechanical. The chemical is an influence through the dissolution of fluids, whereby the body is affected, but the mechanical is when the effect occurs on the surface, as in the case of feeling as a result of pressure, in the case of seeing due to the stimulus of light, and in the case of hearing due to the stimulus of air. But in the case of smelling and tasting, the components of the smell and the salts of the fluids of the body are first dissolved and then absorbed by the organs, and only then do they produce their effect. Therefore no one can taste with a dry mouth. When tasting, saliva is the vehicle; it dissolves the components of the physical thing,[a] it is liquid and is to be distinguished from spittle. In the case of smell, air is the vehicle which dissolves the components which, by means of air, are drawn through the nose into the lungs. Thus, smell and taste are two senses of enjoyment. What we smell blends together with our sense of smell, and tasting blends itself together with the fluids. Thus these are the most powerful senses. Therefore no other sense of loathing exists besides these two, unless, if another sense is combined with them, it can well produce aversion. However, loathing results from contact, hence loathing is difficult to describe. It is an aversion, a particular repugnance, which only occurs in connection with [the sense of] enjoyment. The sense of smell has the least power of discernment,[b] hence too, children and many savages smell nothing. It is the finest, and must be informed. And of all the senses, one can manage without it the most. The external senses are senses of judgment, but smell and taste are those of sensation. We are affected the most by them. Therefore they do not serve as a way of coming to know the object, but only to be sensible of my own state. They thus concern us the most, for if I see, then I attend to an object, but if I smell and taste, then I pay attention to the modification, how my body is affected. Hence they are the senses of the greatest impression. When seeing, the object is more intense than the subject, but in the case of the other senses, the subject is more intense than the object. An ugly object of sight does not

25:495

---

[a] Literally "body" (*Körper*).   [b] *Urteil*

affect me as much as a nasty object of smell, for through the sense of smell, the object is intimately taken in and blended with the body.

The objective senses provide more cognition, and provide occasion for reflection, but the subjective senses have more sensation than reflection. The finer their own matter, the closer the senses come to the processing and representation of the understanding. Thus, in accordance with its matter, feeling is the crudest sense, since we feel physical things only to the extent that they are impenetrable. Taste is already finer, for we taste something by means of the dissolution of the saline material; thus the matter is already finer. The matter of the sense of smell is still finer, for there air dissolves the physical things, a dissolution which is finer than that through saliva. Hearing occurs only by means of pure air, and sight is the finest, since it occurs by means of light. The more human beings can share in them, the nobler are the senses, and the more

25:496 they make objects mutual for us. And these are also the most social. For example, sight is the most mutual sense, for a house can be continually seen at the same time by some 1,000 people. It is also a main significance*a* of taste, since taste has reference to a general communication. Hence people who are social are fond of such objects of general communication, for example, stories. Hearing is the second sense which may be communicated, but the communication does not last as long as for sight. For example, many can listen to a speech, to music. When I hear or see something, I not only judge through my sense, but also by means of the senses of other people. It is also the same in the case of smell, hence everyone will be very concerned that an object might smell good to others as well. Taste is less communicable, for when I am eating, I do not concern myself with how it tastes to others. However, the object of taste may in fact also be distributed, albeit not in the same way as music, for music fills everyone's ears at the same time. Feeling does not participate at all. Thus the advantage of the senses is based on their general communication.

Hearing provides neither the shape nor concept of the object, but it provides sensation. Sight provides no sensation, but it provides the shape. Accordingly, hearing is a play of sensation, and sight a play of shape. Variousness in accordance with time is a play, hence music is a play of sensation. Variousness in accordance with space is shape, hence dancing is a play of shape. It may be called a play to the extent that it occurs gradually, thus in relation to time. Play affects more than shape, because it is sensation. If play buoys up*b* the whole human being, then the individual is animated. The play of shape also has sensation, but

---

a *Hauptsinn*: the context seems to indicate that Kant has here shifted from *Sinn* as "sense," to *Sinn* as "meaning," "significance," or "import."
b *erhält*, literally "maintain, preserve, support," etc.

it pertains more to the object. For this reason we are not as affected. However, it is still sensation through light and through color. These constitute the different kinds of sensation. Therefore we could also have a play of sensation through the eyes. Shape is only the form, but color is a play of sensation. One has already thought of producing consonances and dissonances through colors, in the way it happens through the tones in hearing, and of making a play of sensation through the eyes.[11] However, in the case of tones, a large number of tones occur in a short time, but light is not as intense as the air which affects us. We still hear the sound humming and ringing, thus the impression lasts longer. Since the tone reaches the other person, consequently in the case of hearing there is a continuity, but when the color is past, then the impression is also past. Meanwhile it is still to some degree a play of sensation. This is also the reason why this or that article of clothing becomes one individual better than another. For example, people who are fair must wear light colored clothes. In general, one may notice that when two colors blended together produce a complete color, then it is becoming to the individual, but where this does not occur, then it is not becoming to him. The cause of this is that, at their boundaries, colors are mingled in the eyes, and if a complete color results, then it is becoming. If a complete color does not result, then it does not please. For example, if there is a lot of blue and little yellow, a complete color, namely green, results. Hence a blue jacket and a yellow vest is becoming, but when a lot of yellow and little blue are intermingled, then a dirty color results. Hence too, a yellow jacket and a blue vest is not becoming. Thus too, a blue jacket with a red vest is becoming, but not the reverse. One can judge the taste[a] of human beings accordingly. Hearing is the only sense which can be put into the liveliest play, and it also is pure sensation. The sphere and the range of sight is the greatest, but after that, so too is that of hearing. The sense an old person can dispense with most, would be hearing, but for children it is sight. For hearing is an organ of reason; without hearing there is no speech, and without speech, no signs of the concepts, and without that no use of the understanding can take place. An old person, however, who already has this, can dispense with hearing; but the child without sight devises other sensations for itself for cognizing objects. Hearing is thus the most important sense in the acquisition of cognition, but in regard to use of the world, sight is the most important. All senses have terms peculiar to them; for example, for sight these are red, green, yellow, for taste these are sweet, sour, and so forth. However, the sense of smell can have no terms peculiar to it, rather we take the terms from other senses. For example, it smells sour, or has the smell of roses, or carnations; it smells like musk. These are however all terms

25:497

25:498

[a] *Gout*

from other senses. Consequently we cannot describe the sense of smell. Our sense of smell can be cultivated. It stimulates and delights us not so much through the amenity it provides, as it inconveniences us through its drawbacks. We have a sensation of about ten disagreeable objects of smell, before we have a sensation of one agreeable one. Hence too some persons, such as women, anoint themselves, not in order that they might have a sensation of an agreeable smell, but because they would like to be smelled and sensed by others. Taste, however, delights more than the sense of smell. Thus nothing interested that savage in Paris as much as the diner, and thus all the listeners to Homer's poems ran away when the dinner bell was rung, except for one person who could not hear it. The sense of smell also greatly aggravates the nerves of the person who has refined his sense of smell, so that when the healthy sense of smell is altogether too intense, one can faint. Taste requires the most satisfaction, since everything pertaining to the maintenance of the body occurs through it. It is also connected with people's well-being, for the entire gastronomic tract has a sensitivity through which it expels everything that is offensive to the body and accepts what is agreeable and useful for it. Nature has endowed us with taste so that we should examine through it what is useful for our body, which we do even without being particular about it. And taste also differs in accordance with the difference in the disposition of the body. If the body is sickly, one has a loathing for meat and an appetite for something sour, which is also just what is useful for the body. Therefore the glands, intestines, and everything together must constitute a system, and taste examines what is salutary for it.

ON DIFFERENCES OF THE SENSES, WHETHER THEY ARE KEEN OR FINE, DULL OR DELICATE

Sense is keen for perception and fine for investigation and judgment. A delicate sense is one in which the subject is changed through influence and impression. To be delicate with regard to the senses is not a perfection, but to be keen and fine is a perfection of the senses. A man with a keen sense is not merely changed through an impression, but he is keen in perception and fine in judgment. Women and children have delicate senses. The one who does not feel the state of his body is healthy. We only feel the greater hindrances and the promotion of life. Therefore human beings do not feel their exhalation and blood circulation. But they feel an external drive encouraging movement. One who feels his stomach is sick in his stomach.

We not only include sensation and intuition in the senses, but also judgment and assessment, but we are no longer conscious of this, since we have already been judging since our youth.

The senses must be instructed and cultivated. Thus a blind man can   25:500
cultivate his feeling, so that he can distinguish objects well. Therefore he
can cultivate it. In this way a hunter practices his sight. Likewise those
who drank their anker[a] of wine in the fields had cultivated their taste in
such a way that the one said: the wine tastes like iron, and the other said,
it tastes like leather. Both were right, for a key with a leather band was
in the anker.[12]

Some senses are dull and others fine. Thus one person has a dull
sense, and a fine judgment, and the one who has a fine sense, has a dull
judgment. One acquires judgment for oneself through practice. An old
person judges better than a younger one, since he has had practice. Thus
it must be investigated whether fineness of the senses or judgment is to
be favored. The duller a sense is, all the more would it prefer such objects
which make a strong impression. The Oriental people have dull senses,
for this reason they make use of strong spices. The finer a sense is, the
less it likes such objects which make a strong impression. The Oriental
people have dull senses. People thus reveal a dull sense when they have
objects that make a strong impression, for example, in clothing, or food,
or drink. At first one uses milder things, for example sweet wine, or good
smelling tobacco, but if the senses become duller, then one takes the
strongest things. Recently one has invented a new sense, about which
the ancients knew nothing, namely a taste of the *nose, which is not a
smell, for that deals with evanescent components, but the taste of the nose deals
with saline ones.* The one who demands intense representations in tragic   25:501
performances has a dull sense. Age makes all senses, outer and inner,
dull.

However, the well-being of the older person depends on this dull
feeling. He does not feel the ills of the deterioration[b] of his body.

PROMOTION OF SENSATION AND WEAKNESS
OF THE SENSES

The judgment of the senses about the object becomes easier through
repeated sensation, but the impression of the object becomes all the
keener.[c] Thus a musician knows how to judge music well, but music no
longer makes such an impression on him, it does not excite him in the
way it does another. Other things weaken the sensation of the senses,
such as sleep, drowsiness, opium.

---

[a] A unit of measure used particularly for wine in some European countries. One anker
(also an English term) is equivalent to 10 gallons in the US today.
[b] *Destruction*
[c] The term given is *schärfer*, but this meaning seems to be contradicted by the next sentence. Consistency would seem to call for *schwächer* (weaker).

With regard to the behavior of human beings, distractions thus weaken sensation. In this way, by looking at the torture, a malefactor weakened the sensation of pain. As soon as he was blindfolded, however, he could not stand it. In this way, if one argues with him, a person fond of disputation gets over the pain of gout, just as an illness is often cured[a] through a sudden fright. Thus a servant girl, on whose hand a spark had fallen and who thought about the pain of purgatory, believed that one could become accustomed to it in time. Uniformity weakens the sensation of the senses. Thus, even if he speaks loudly, the preacher's monotony lulls the senses to sleep. As soon as he is quiet, however, everyone wakes up. Novelty intensifies sensation. Thus the day's morning intensifies the sensation of human beings, because it is new; hence morning is highly praised. Variety belongs to this as well. If other representations come in between old[b] ones, then the old ones are renewed. Therefore, one must keep an enjoyment novel by means of the infrequency with which one enjoys such; in this way it will always be agreeable. Contrast also heightens representation. Thus the regions in the East are praised because they are surrounded by deserts. Likewise people from the city find the country air pleasing, because they are confined in the city.

25:502

There exist contrasts which result solely from the unexpected, and which please us merely because we did not anticipate it. In this way an intelligent child pleases us because we do not represent him to ourselves like this. Thus an intelligent woman pleases us for exactly the same reason. It is just the same with soldiers and officers who are gentle, and high ranking people who are gracious.[c] Therefore this makes an impression because we have not anticipated it and we count such as attributable[d] to the objects.

ON SEMBLANCE

A semblance is a basis derived from subjective laws, it is a subjective basis of judgment. Such a basis is always equivocal. Bases must be borrowed from the objects and not from the subjective bases of the mind. True, the subjective is a basis, but it is not adequate. Insofar as semblance is false, it is then either an illusion or a deception. Semblance is not a judgment, but a basis for a preliminary judgment. It would be

---

[a] *verlohren wird*
[b] Given the rest of the sentence, reading *allen* here as *alten*.
[c] *Herablaßend* generally means patronizing or condescending, which does not however fit the context here. The synonym *gnädig* can have the positive sense which has been given in the translation.
[d] *schieben solches auf die Rechnung*

very essential, if in logic there would also be a completely separate chapter on preliminary judgments, which could occasion various sensations. All semblance is first an illusion, if it can harmonize with the cognition of truth. However, all semblance is deception as soon as it does not agree with the cognition of truth. Thus clothes are semblance [in the sense] of illusion. We really have more respect for an individual who has beautiful clothes. They make an impression on us on behalf of the individual, although we otherwise know him very well. Thus the father is better pleased with the son dressed in a new jacket which he himself had in fact had made for him. This way individuals in certain jurisdictions, such as in France, make an impression on people with good-looking clothes, and although the person knows each one of these lords, yet an illusion still takes place with him. In the same way, women's clothes that suggest nicety, give us an illusion, although we know them very well. However, such an illusion in clothes pleases, because the semblance agrees with the cognition of truth. Deception, however, does not please, since it is only makeup, and when it is wiped away, a deathly pallor is revealed. Therefore I know that my judgment here does not agree with the cognition of truth, for this reason it displeases me because I know how I am being deceived; for example, a conjurer. The senses deceive the understanding in just the same way; hence, in retaliation, the understanding must in turn deceive the senses. One cannot oppose the deception of the senses with force, because it is a ruse on the part of the senses. The understanding must however oppose this ruse with another ruse, and the understanding indeed does this and tricks the senses with a ruse. All sensible delights and passions trick the understanding, since they promise more and give greater hope than they afterwards actually yield, and one straightaway trusts the promises of the senses. Thus someone expects to see many new things in his travels and hopes to find in foreign countries what does not exist in his country. Afterwards he discovers that all countries are the same. That's the way it is with all novelties, and everything the senses promise us greatly deceives the understanding. Yet on the other hand, the understanding in turn tricks the senses and this feat lies in human nature. For example, something lies at the basis of the sex drive which exists in all animals, yet here the understanding deceives the senses which aim at animality. Highly enthusiastically, it describes the person's beauty to them, it forms an ideal for them through which they trick themselves. Yet they thereby check themselves and forget the other. That is why relations with women deceive the senses, through the relations they are distracted from what they want to aim for. Just as one tries to distract a child from something else by play, this way the senses are also tricked by the understanding. Hope for a future better state compensates us in our present misfortune. It is a prospect in the future, just as in an optical box, and no reality. We enjoy

25:503

it as long as we see it. Thus death is very near for the 70 year old man, but yet he knows how to flatter himself by means of hope; he has no fear of death although he knows that he must die, and experience also instructs him in this daily. However, he engineers schemes to make his

25:504 life agreeable every day; death appears to him to be still very distant, he does not reckon the time, and thus deceives himself in this.

In general, people in the civilized state*a* play a role, and human society in the civilized state is a theatrical society, and in a society the individual is always in a state of constraint. Thus everyone in society has respect for the other person, he chooses at all times what also pleases others, he is meticulous about his clothes, he assumes such a posture in which he pleases, he conducts himself modestly, and always plays the role of constraint, which is very artificial. We also demand often enough, that persons in a society should adopt another appearance*b* or an assumed role. For example, we want to have the preacher present himself in society in a way that is not as natural as other people, that he instead appear somewhat earnest. Everyone always plays the role of constraint in society. Thus women conduct themselves demurely in society, although we know how their nature is otherwise, and it still gives us an illusion. And if a parliamentary councilor is so earnest, as if he has the most important things on his mind, it gives us an illusion, although we know that at home he pursues frivolous*c* activities. In general, human life and its activities are a game.*d* Such illusions are good-natured and make life pleasant, they please everyone, and who would want to extirpate them would not do humanity*e* any favor. Since they force people to have respect for one another, with time they become accustomed to it. This way the man and wife forced themselves to receive their guests, whom they could not offer much for the noon meal, very courteously, so that they afterwards really became accustomed to it and, with the greatest enjoyment, the guests took their leave from them. Thus in society one is filled with benevolence and good dispositions*f* toward one another, although in such friendship

a *Zustand* (i.e. the state in the sense of condition, and not the political state).
b *Schein*
c *spaßhafte*; frivolous seems to capture the sense better here than "comical."
d *Spiel* (previously translated as "play").   *e* *dem Menschen*
f *Gesinnungen*: disposition(s) is the widely used translation for *Gesinnung(en)* which is problematic for several reasons, including its use also for translating other terms such as *Anlage*, and Kant's own explicit rejection of the Latin cognate *dispositio* because of its too close connection with the sense of habit (something mechanically produced through repeated actions) which he also rejects. In terms of his mature sense of moral character, Kant's use of *Gesinnung* is intrinsically connected with its ordinary-language sense of *sittliche Haltung* (moral comportment [or bearing, or attitude]), that is, with such moral comportment of the mind and *Gesinnungen* in this connection are tantamount to maxims. The use of *Gesinnung* contrasts with Kant's explicit use of *Disposition*, for example in the section "On the Use of Reason in Regard to the Practical" (25:553ff.).

and such a sexual inclination, where one expresses good dispositions of this kind to one another, one still retains much self-love and selfishness in oneself. Thus such a mild illusion surely pleases one and one wants to relieve oneself from the cloak of selfishness. The human being expresses a great benevolence for the other person and he and others are distressed when it happens that another person gets into trouble and an embarrassing position. Thus one retreats. Hence Aristotle rightly said, my friends, there are no friends.[13] However, such a declaration of friendship still pleases us and we are happy to have such a friend, about whom we still know that he would not, as he professes, stand by us in our need. Accordingly, when in need one must never address a friend about something which costs him money, for otherwise one loses him. In reality, in society all expressions are taken to be semblance, and it really is so. Hence in such a society where one does not play the role of constraint, where no one takes offense, everything goes on in a completely dissolute way. Therefore such an illusion is very necessary in human society. 25:505

However deception is irritating, because I know I am being deceived. Hence no individual who has a propensity for truth, takes pleasure in the tricks of conjury, but the optical semblance pleases.

ON REPRESENTATIONS, HOW THEY CONSTITUTE A DIFFERENCE FROM ONE ANOTHER THROUGH DISSIMILARITY, AND HOW THE ONE THEREBY ILLUMINATES[a] THE OTHER; THUS ON CONTRAST, VARIETY AND CONTRADICTION

We can contrast things in order to distinguish them, and to make each of them evident. It is thus necessary to bring an individual, who has been living the good life, into the company of miserable and working people, so that he gains insight into [life's] decline.[b] In the same way, there is a contrast[c] if one all at once takes an individual out of a clamorous company, and places him in complete quiet. If one thus compares conflicting things with one another, a contrast results; for example, the appeal of virtue compared with the odiousness of vice.

Representations are also put into a different light by means of contradiction. This occurs when we unite and connect conflicting things with one another. In the case of contrast, we only compare conflicting things, but when they are united, a contradiction results. Where the contrast is odd ... thus Virgil's Koran is a [mock-] heroic poem.[14] This way it is an odd contrast, for example, splendid clothing and soiled 25:506

---

[a] *ins Licht setzt*   [b] *Abfall*, literally also "waste," or "trash."
[c] *Contrast oder Abstechung*: Kant's inclusion of the synonym indicates the sense in which he means *Abstechung*, translated here as "contrast."

undergarments, good appearance and poor manners, poverty and haughtiness, vulgar behavior and the arrogation of a good, refined education. Such writings which contrast oddly are the most humorous[a] writings and please greatly. Our own view, which we give to things on the basis of the disposition of mind from which we look at it, is [a matter of] mood;[b] more about this below. This way vice can be represented as odious and as absurd. The question is, what is better, to declare vice with the mark of disgust and anger, or, in a mood, to make it absurd, silly and ridiculous. The latter is to be preferred. An individual is improved more through derision than through irate rebuke. The state and situation of the mind is better if one heaps ridicule on vice, than if one regards it with anger and disgust. Fielding writes so humorously, he portrays the miser in the most ridiculous form, whereby he becomes more despicable than if I wanted to describe him from the wicked side. This kind of contrasting is the best way, which sharpens the mind and at the same time makes the vicious person ridiculous. In this way one can search out and present such contradictions, the jests in the speeches of people which are full of contradictions. The English are very attentive to this and then call it a "bull,"[c] since they then say, that one or the other person has uttered a "bull." It helps for the inspirations of ingenuity.

25:507   Novelty, which is opposed to uniformity, is required to put the mind in [a state of] clarity by means of variety. Through the relationship in which they stand, rarity [and] variousness serve to produce representations for the mind. Our mind falls asleep when it is occupied with one and the same thing. Rarity requires a mind limited [in scope], for example, to have high regard for such a book which is only in a few, or only one person's, hands. It is not simply a matter of the relation and of the way in which certain impressions are given to the mind, but also according to the degree. Monotony lulls it to sleep. Hence, springing up and lowering must be alternated. Even pure intervals in representation already produce clarity, just like strokes [of insight] in certain thoughts, where one recollects, grasps the thought and follows it. This way the intervals also increase the impression between one enjoyment and another, which would be insipid if it were to go on continually. A quick leap, which is opposed to continual transition, increases the mind's impression. Continuity makes change in the mind unnoticeable. Thus one can gradually accustom someone, who is used to eating much and eating well, to poor fare and moderation. All

---

[a] *launigsten*: for the range of meanings of *Laune* and its various grammatical forms, see the notes to the section devoted to this notion, 25:563–578.

[b] *launigt*: or "temper" in the sense of "frame of mind" (see 25:563ff.).

[c] The term "bull" here evidently refers to its middle English sense of "absurd and illogical mistake in a statement."

leaps in shapes really hurt the eyes. Thus a leap in the speech arouses the attentiveness of the audience.

The unexpected is a part of novelty and increases the impression. If something is to make a strong impression, then one must not anticipate it beforehand, for otherwise the impression is lost. An individual about whom one has built up great expectations for oneself, does not stir up such an impression on us when we see him, because we have produced a greater representation for ourselves than the subject itself consists in. Hence if an object is to make an impression on us, one must not have any great expectation, so that the object exceeds the expectation. On the other hand, one can in turn say the reverse; that the preparation for a subject produces a stronger impression in us. If we have prepared ourselves for something beforehand, then we are more attentive, and can immediately grasp the subject. This way one finds much understanding in a speech because one has anticipated it, for what one has anticipated, one also finds. Thus one can anticipate of someone, if one puts something into his head, that he will assume it, which afterwards also turns out to be the case. In this way one can convince someone, but only in familiar company, that the other [person] is annoyed[a] and the former will assume such of him, and will also approach him in [this] way, as someone who is annoyed. True, it is very good to prepare someone for whatever, for example for a comedy. However, one must not preoccupy a person, and pronounce a determinate and decisive judgment about an object, for then the object will contain nothing more than a confirmation of what he already knows. 25:508

Through the length of its continuation, the representation loses its clarity. Thus in the beginning, all travelers please, since they present at one time the stories they have gathered, but after three weeks they lose face, and they can no longer maintain themselves in this way, because they have already become completely empty. Their supply of enticements has run out and they cannot present the same joke twice, otherwise it will be spoiled. For the joke is very delicate and is only fitting for the nobleman's supper, as Rabelais says. Therefore, long continuation eradicates and diminishes the impression of the representation. However, that person is very fortunate for whom the object, in the continuation, retains the impression for a long time. Thus, too great a love at the beginning of matrimony soon dies out, and often even turns into loathing. If, however, the love is moderate and accompanied by reason, it is more enduring.

---

[a] *gestört*: the basic meaning of the term is "disturbed," but this again has many other nuances such as being "worried, annoyed, irritated, bothered," etc. The context does not indicate the nuance Kant had in mind.

The state of mind in which one is beside oneself and, with regard to the passions, no longer has control over oneself, greatly transforms the clarity of our representations into obscurity. Thus through great joy or pain, the individual comes to be beside himself, and this is ecstasy, which signifies that state of mind in which the individual is beside himself and is incapable of realizing his actual state, since he has been carried away by the intensity of the inner representations, [and] where the intensity of the inner representation brings him to the point that it dispels the intensity of the outer representation. The taste for the world of spirits is a part of this, where someone claims to have been sensible of the community of spirits. Such fanaticisms provide occasion for ecstasy. Whoever wanders about in his thoughts, without being conscious of the actual world, is dreaming, which is natural. However, whoever is beside himself, is a

25:509   dreamer while awake, which is as harmful as sleepwalking. Our representations are animated through the sensation of a new impression, for example, of a drink. Here we are dealing with the favorable side of the drink, whereby the mind is set into an artificial motion, for the feeling of a greater animation is joy. The ancients did not have such unfavorable concepts of drinking. Sociable and unsociable drinking must be distinguished; the latter is improper and base. Drinking must be sociable, and if it escalates to a certain degree of liveliness, then it promotes the arousal of the mind and makes it sociable. Moreover, in this way it also removes the propensity for dissimulation, and makes one openhearted. For constraint^a exists in all societies, to which one has already accustomed oneself through frequent practice. However, as soon as cheerfulness has been aroused in society through a moderate drink, but where the understanding still need not be befuddled, but only a degree of talkativeness is reached, one sets constraint aside and becomes openhearted. If the cheerfulness becomes widespread, then everyone talks about what comes to mind, and no one weighs the other's words. For this reason, a company of such people does not like to tolerate someone who is completely sober among them, since such a person pays attention to them, and is on the alert with his understanding. If all are however the same, then no one is offended by the other. Who does not, however, want to drink in such a company, because he foresees the consequences of his openheartedness, cannot be much trusted, for he guards himself against being openhearted and must have a great deal to keep reserved. He does not trust himself and hence does not want to relieve the sentinel of his understanding. Therefore, whoever is particular about what is proper, must have a great deal to protect, because he does not want to give himself away. When we are under no constraint, however, then we also need not guard ourselves. However, women must be on their guard, because

^{a} Reading *Zwang* for *Zwanck*.

they are observed and impugned. The ancient Germans reached their decisions while drinking, so they might be courageous, and deliberated about them while sober, in order to give them moderation through the understanding. Drinking brandy is not, however, a means of sociability, but makes one insensible; hence all brandy drinkers are very cautious, and drink in secret. The Italians are open to this, but where a nation is in itself communicative, it then takes drinking to an improper mode of freedom, in which all circumspection is lost. Therefore in such countries 25:510 as France, one finds no drinkers, but in the northern countries it goes on more heavily, and in unrefined nations it goes on the most. Because they are unable to stimulate themselves through anything ideal, they must do so through drinking. All who have reason to be cautious, keep themselves sober, for example, women. Different temperaments also produce different effects of drinking; thus in a hot climate, drinking produces rage. Not only opium does this, but also wine. Hence Mohammed did very well, since he prescribed such as a religious observance, which is more likely to be observed, than if it is included under morality. Drink also produces different effects according to the difference in the substance of which it consists. Thus beer does not seem to be such a means of sociability as is wine; it makes one more absorbed. Through drinks [also] other than wine, one is stirred to joking, merrymaking, and products of wit.

It is a matter for a psychologist to investigate, how opium and also other [forms of] befuddlement, which must however be distinguished from nature,[a] produce such beautiful pictures in the imagination. Not only befuddlement, but also stupefaction, which is the cessation of our entire consciousness, result in our being beside ourselves. In this way, rapture also results in our being beside ourselves. Being enraptured is however used by fantastical rapture. Transport into raptures is, however, to be carried away into the world of spirits, which is not in itself possible, but takes place in the imagination. Thus one can lose one's composure through many things, also in this way, when one is to speak and one prepares oneself conscientiously for it. Hence it is better to reflect about it in general. In fact, it is a principal prerequisite of the mind to be in control of itself. Through the fantastical transport into raptures, the individual forgets his body and accustoms himself to be beside himself. In general, the state of rapture and transport into raptures is the state of displacement. All caprices can only be attained through imagination[b] and not through reality. The transcendent giving of wings to our imagination must be held in limits. 25:511

---

[a] *Beschaffenheit*: presumably Kant's meaning here is that the artificially induced state must be distinguished from the natural state of a given individual.

[b] *Phantasie*

The cessation of all sensation is unconsciousness. If one cannot get out of this state of sensation, then this is death. Sleep is the cessation of all sensation in a healthy state. It is an insensibility to and unconsciousness of outer objects. Drowsiness can become habitual; it is necessary to make a rule for oneself in this respect. Many talents have become blunt through this. Sleep deprives us of the functionality[a] and fineness of the fluids. The fluids are refined and diluted by getting little sleep. Thus recent observations indicate that blood is far colder during sleep, than when one is awake; hence one is cold when one gets sleepy.

ON THE IMAGINATION[b]

Besides the faculty of sensation, we have in addition a faculty to form images of objects, and through special power in the mind to describe and to form what strikes the senses. This is the faculty for forming the impressions of sense.[c] For one who has a vivid imagination and has seen something, the image of it remains indelibly in his mind. This is the faculty of direct image formation.[d] Reproductive image formation[e] is an image of the prior state of the object. It is a faculty of bringing the object forward at one point, thus every memory is a reproductive image formation. Imaginative formation[f] is a poetically invented image, a faculty of invention.[g] It is an image of an object which is neither present, nor future, nor past, but it is a fiction, it is a symbol.[h] Thus figures[i] are images of objects which are not there. The faculty of forming an anticipatory image[j] in advance is the prophetic faculty.[k] Before one even sees it, our mind produces for itself an image in advance of everything about which one hears. Thus everyone produces an image for himself of a king, if he is to see him. If he has heard about him that he is a great hero, then he produces for himself a fairly massive and corpulent image of him, as if it would consist in this. If he later sees him, then he becomes confused if the king looks different from the image which he made for himself of him. The faculty of forming has a propensity to complete the formation[l] of everything in our mind. Hence when we become aware of something, then we form an idea[m] of it for ourselves. If the object does not agree with our idea, then the mind persistently endeavors to complete its formation, for example, an incomplete part in

25:512

---

[a] *Behändigkeit*
[b] *Phantasie*
[c] *facultas informandi impressiones sensuum*
[d] *Abbildung*
[e] *Nachbildung*
[f] *Einbildung*
[g] *facultas fingendi*
[h] *Symbolum*
[i] *Typi*: taking this to be the Latin *typus*, meaning figure or image on the wall.
[j] *vorbilden*
[k] *facultas praesagiendi*
[l] *ausbilden*
[m] *machen uns ein Begriff*: idiomatic phrase (lit. "produce a concept").

the comedy, a gallant knight[a] and an inferior horse. Hence one is less satisfied with something like this, than if it was not there at all, or, if someone has cheated long enough to win 900 florin, then he will keep cheating until he has the full 1000 florin. Thus if one receives 11 ducats someone has sent, then one believes that the servant has the 12th one, because one presumes that the master would have sent a full dozen. In this way 11 pairs of cups are held to be less worthwhile than the first pair constituting what is missing, although one can use them just as well, than if the dozen were complete, and than if there were 13 pair. The one pair is then only casually counted in order that it brings the dozen to its full number one day, if one [pair] were broken. Hence, if something is incomplete, through poetic invention we replace what is lacking to fill it up. This is natural and very good for us; in this way, one seeks out his slight shortcomings in the life of Socrates and fills these in through poetic invention in order to form a complete wise man.[15] This is the faculty of completing the formation, *facultas perficiendi*. We must still especially review the faculty of reproductive image formation. The faculty of reproductive image formation has its law, it follows the law of association, or the association of representations. This is a considerable part of the human mind, and a great deal depends on associating one's representations.

Association is based on three elements, on accompaniment,[b] contiguity,[c] and on relation.[d] Accompaniment consists in representations in accordance with time in this respect, as either following in succession or existing at the same time. Thus if a representation occurs, another is immediately summoned. For example, if we see smoke, then the representation of fire immediately appears. If the clock strikes at whichever time one is accustomed to eat, and one hears it striking, then the representation of food immediately appears. If there were no accompaniment to representations, we could not have any causes and effects. Accompaniment is the first and greatest degree of association. The second basis of association is contiguity. Just as the unity of time constitutes accompaniment, so the unity of place constitutes contiguity. In this way, one's school years come to mind when one goes by the school. If one thinks about the place where one enjoyed oneself, the people who were present there come to mind. If one travels to the place where many events occurred, one remembers these and the mind is stirred up by [the memory of] such events. This way the place where something is to be undertaken makes a big impression. Thus the rogue is more intensely frightened, when he gets to the place where he is to be examined. The third basis of association is relation, insofar as the representations are

25:513

[a] Reading *Ritter* for *Reuter*.
[b] *Begleitung*
[c] *Nachbarschaft*
[d] *Verwandschaft*

related according to their constitution. They are however related due to similarity and derivation. The relation of derivation exists insofar as [the representations] come from one basis, thus the relation of cause and effect constitutes the relation of the effects. For example, if it rains and the sun shines, one immediately looks around [to see] if there is not a rainbow. The relation of similarity exists however if we, for example, assign everything to certain classes, so that if we think of one thing, the other comes to mind.

Because they refer to time and space, the two associations of accompaniment and contiguity are associations of sensibility. The association of relation, however, is an association of the understanding. Therefore if our imagination functions in accordance with sensible association, accompaniment, and contiguity, this is nonsense to the understanding. Thus if someone speaks of English horses, they can think of England itself, of its government and the war in America.[16] There must however be variousness and unity in such social conversations, connection must

25:514 prevail in the understanding, for otherwise it displeases everyone if no connection exists. Often one can guess the means of the transition from one discourse to another. For example, one talks about swindlers and all at once someone talks about a man. Thus everyone thinks he talks about the man for this reason, because he must be a swindler. Carefulness not to disclose the connection of what one has thought, is a shrewdness[a] which one must observe. Hence one must allow the interpolation of an intermediate thought.

THE INTENSITY[b] OF THE IMAGINATION

The imagination is more intense there where other senses are weaker. For example, the imagination of a blind person is by far more intense than someone else's, since it is not disturbed by external objects. Thus in Paris there are blind guides.

The imagination has a more intense effect, if it is combined with inclination, whereby it is animated. The imagination is greater when the object is absent, than when it is present. If the object is present, then the sensible impression is present, and the imagination is obscured by the sensible impression. If however the object is absent, then the imagination is more intense. Hence the sensible impression is weakened by the removal of the object, but the imagination is increased. For example, in the case of one in love, since all shortcomings of the object, which one however surely perceives when it is present, cease to exist in its absence.

There are degrees and qualities of the imagination. A weak imagination is incapable of any impression. It depends on the intensity of the

---

[a] *Feinheit*   [b] *Stärke*

imagination to represent the image for itself in accordance with certain degrees. The description of it does not constitute the intensity. If however the imagination is intense, then the intensity can also be excessive, so that the imagination often outweighs the sensible impression. Hence nothing but the presence of the thing can prevent madness. Passions produce an errant[a] imagination. Thus, *simply due to passion, one can portray something which one has seen as being ugly*. For example, a beautiful, shady forest seems dreadful to me because I was unhappy there.

In the case of hypochondriacs, the imagination is undisciplined,[b] since they represent and imagine many things which they themselves are not fond of and which they do not like to have happen. It consists in the involuntariness of understanding. The imagination must be subjugated to the power of choice, and this is the main thing in extinguishing it; when it is misleading, it is then often the path of many vices.

There exists an erratic[c] imagination, thus not subject to the rule of the understanding, and it is to be differentiated from the undisciplined one. Lack of rules is the effect of a violent temper.

The imagination which plays around has its natural course, so that it is not subject to our power of choice. The power of choice can only do something insofar as it gives direction to the imagination and then it straightaway runs according to its new direction, like water in the stream. For example, if one just hears something being talked about in society, then the imagination at once runs its course so long until one hears something new being talked about, and then the imagination in turn runs according to this new direction. One says of the person who frees his imagination up to take a natural course: he is dreaming. Power of choice does not produce new images, but a new direction.

But one who does not know how to give a new direction to his imagination, is a dreamer. Such people do not think much and do not themselves know what they have been thinking. Excesses of imagination occur when the slightest little thing provides the imagination an occasion to take off. For this reason one often does not know how someone got to something, if one does not know the sequence of the course of his imagination.

ON INGENUITY[d] AND THE POWER OF JUDGMENT

However, we also have a voluntary faculty for comparing images and representations. This faculty is active. Comparison consists in holding

---

[a] *verkehrte*

[b] *Zügellos*: literally "without reins," metaphorical term for "undisciplined."

[c] *regellose*, literally "without rules."

[d] *Witz*. In his *Anthropology from a Pragmatic Point of View*, Kant provides the Latin *ingenium* (7: 201, 220).

representations together. The power of judgment is the faculty of holding representations together according to their dissimilarity. This part
25:516　of judgment is the judgment of discernment.[a] Everyone who can find a
uniformity and similarity in representations does not yet have ingenuity,
but the one who can do so in an eminent way has it. One designates
both ingenuity as well as the power of judgment as fine. A fine ingenuity
is one that can notice the smallest similarity, and a fine power of judgment is one that can notice the slightest dissimilarity. Inasmuch as it is
fine, the power of judgment is called acuity, and inasmuch as it is fine,
ingenuity is called perspicacious.[b] Ingenuity is of service for preliminary
judgments. For example, if grudgingness is being discussed, ingenuity
must summon up everything which pertains to grudgingness; for example, spite, where one begrudges another something, even if one does not
need it oneself. Thus grudgingness occurs with regard to honor, society,
and enjoyment. In this way grudgingness occurs among children, and so
forth. In short, ingenuity summons up all the cases, and looks for a supply
of preliminary judgments. A preliminary judgment is a basis for judging
about things, but which is not sufficient. However, to pass a determinate
judgment is proper to the power of judgment. Ingenuity roams about,
wherever it finds something, and thus is of service for invention. For
that reason ingenuity also leads to errors, for if it takes the insufficient
bases for judging as determinate, it thus leads to error, which happens
then, when one does not feel like reflecting about ingenuity and its preliminary judgments, and combining them with the power of judgment.
The power of judgment however is of service for determinate judgment
and for this reason it also prevents errors. The reason that ingenuity
leads to error is also this: because ingenuity entertains and the power of
judgment satisfies, but people set greater store by entertainment than
by satisfaction, hence ingenuity is better liked and pleases more, and
although one knows it is wrong, it still pleases because it entertains.
Ingenuity is an easy occupation of the mind and is suited to the natural
drive to know. It is easier to search for similarity than dissimilarity, for I
have an immeasurable sphere for finding all similarities. In this way, the
French draw a similarity between the Frenchman and the cooking pot.
25:517　It is more entertaining for the one who is listening, than for the one who
is supposed to rack his ingenuity. If I am to search for the dissimilarity
between two things, then I cannot draw upon a third thing, as in the case
of ingenuity where I can draw upon everything that is similar. [When
searching for dissimilarity], I cannot roam about like this. Thus ingenuity is freer and the power of judgment is bound. Through [my] wants,

[a] *Iudicium discretivum*
[b] *Sinnreich*: translation draws on the Latin cognate *perspicax* which Kant gives in his *Anthropology from a Pragmatic Point of View* (Ak 7: 221; see also 139).

namely in order not to fall into error, I am compelled to [turn to] the power of judgment. Thus, when eating, one should be more particular about health than about amenity, but we still prefer to be more particular about taste, because it is more agreeable. The further reason that ingenuity entertains is because all similarity furnishes a rule, which one afterwards makes into a general rule. All rules, however, enlarge the use of the power of cognition. Every use of ingenuity is, however, to generate a rule in all cases, and it then pleases, where one has been able to generate a rule. For example, someone travels and finds poor conditions at the first two inns; thus he immediately makes himself a rule and says, here poor inns are indeed everywhere. Thus someone also said: in England all the people are rude and the innkeepers are polite, but in France the people are polite and the innkeepers are rude. It is this way with all witticisms. Thus the acts of ingenuity entertain. Ingenuity has inspirations and the power of judgment turns them into insight. Ingenuity produces more, and the power of judgment examines it. In this way, the Frenchman has inspirations and the Englishman strives for insights. Hence the greatest extent of the work of the power of judgment is pondering, and the greatest work of ingenuity is play. If ingenuity is to please, then it must also be easy, but it does not please if it is difficult. Hence it is said: the ingenuity of the English is excessively heavy;[a] for example, Young's satires.[17] Great ingenuity is found therein, yet it does not entertain in the way the ingenuity of the French does, but it satisfies more. The acts of ingenuity can be practical affairs and play. Ingenuity is to serve the understanding, but is not to be substituted for it, for the understanding consists in judging. Consequently ingenuity cannot be put in its place, but ingenuity must administer to the understanding and provide it with inspirations, concerning which the understanding can judge. For otherwise the understanding cannot judge, if it has no material available. Thus philosophy requires much ingenuity. Ingenuity is of service to the understanding for invention and it is also of service to it for clarification of what has already been thought, since it invents examples, analogies, and similarities. Thereby it makes that sensible, what is thought by the understanding in a general way. However, ingenuity is often substituted for the power of judgment. This happens in the case of such persons who have not acquired cognitions scientifically, who have taken to the literary arts,[b] and after that apply ingenuity in the hard sciences[c] in the same way as in the literary arts. However, it is still often necessary that ingenuity be substituted in the place of the power of judgment,

25:518

---

[a] *Centner schwer*

[b] *schönen Wissenschaften.* According to Grimm, in the eighteenth century this phrase was a translation for *belles lettres* and so the counterpart to the *beaux arts.*

[c] *gründlichen Wissenschaften*

especially in society. If in society one presents subjects[a] about which one is arguing, thoroughly and as settled, it is necessary that one then comes up with an inspiration, and thereby puts an end to the entire contentious and exhaustive investigation. Then all start to laugh about it, the grave look ceases, and thereby one promotes the purpose of society, which is not at all that of settling important subjects, but to amuse oneself.[b] I then create a diversion through the inspiration, which all welcome together, since ingenuity pleases everyone without distinction. Consequently it is agreeable and entertaining both for those who are arguing, as well as for those who must listen to it. In this case, ingenuity can be substituted for the power of judgment. Ingenuity is a play, but as a play it can also support the understanding. Thus it must be perspicacious and support the understanding; from this the understanding can produce something. However, babbling ingenuity is empty, and such ingenuity is also called false ingenuity. Thus someone who had soup spilled on him, while having a meal with strangers, said: "greatest sense of justice, greatest injustice."[c] Humorous ingenuity is where one assumes a look, but not in accord with what one wants to say, but its opposite, and therefore it contrasts. *Hudibras*[18] belongs to such ingenious writings. Its ingenuity is humorous, laughter about it is spirited, one's head is filled with ideas.[d] Ingenuity aims more for the novel, hence it is variable, it aims to invent new similarities, but the power of judgment aims more for the old.

25:519

Whoever makes many wisecracks[e] is a joker; such a person may not be worth hating, but he deserves to be mocked, because he is surely seeking to please by his ingenuity. However, when he fails, he still cannot be hated on account of the intention which he had. Whoever makes many overly subtle arguments,[f] is a sophistical reasoner and this person is surely hated and envied even more. The reason is: every individual is more likely to sacrifice something from his memory, but each has the highest regard for[g] his understanding, for he judges his understanding with his understanding, and it is only natural that every understanding judges the best about itself. And I do not judge the other's understanding to

---

[a] *Materien*

[b] Reading *sie* as *sich*, in accordance with the other manuscript. *Sie* would refer to the important matters and then the phrase would be "to lighten them up." But since the purpose of society is geared primarily to its members and not subjects of disputation, *sich* seems to fit better.

[c] *Summum Ius summa iniuria*: the pun here lies in the other meaning of the Latin *ius*, as juice, broth, gravy, soup. Literally translated using this meaning, the phrase reads, "best soup, greatest injury." It is not clear which version Kant intends as an illustration of babbling.

[d] *Gedanken*

[e] *Wercks vom Witz*, literally "works of ingenuity."

[f] *Wercks von der Urtheils Kraft*, literally "works" (or "efforts") of judgment.

[g] *denckt von seinem Verstande das Beste*, literally "thinks the best of his understanding."

be better, and do not see more in his than in mine, for I judge the other's understanding by means of my understanding. Now, I cannot find more in the other's understanding than in mine, for by what means should I find it. Consequently a sophistical reasoner who shows off his understanding angers others, because each one wants to show off his understanding, since each one has the best opinion of his understanding. Hence where there is mutual skill,[a] the other does not easily tolerate it if one makes a big deal of it, but where there is no accord, each one can dredge up his own [reasonings]. For example, if a man of letters, merchant,[b] and soldier are in a social gathering, then each one can talk quite a lot about his own reasonings. The joker is banal if he pursues inspirations. In general, ingenuity must not appear to be laborious, but come to mind without having to search for it. Ingenuity is insipid if no power of judgment is added to it. One calls such a one tasteless, yet in order to be tasteless, ingenuity is required. Hence no one can be so very stupid as can an ingenious person, since because he dares more, he is thus also more likely to fall into confusion. He whose head is completely empty however, is secured by ignorance against error and confusion. Ingenuity becomes disagreeable when it is insipid. Lack of ingenuity is called obtuseness, although that is contrasted with acuity. One also calls lack of ingenuity dryness. Who is dry, and conveys a keen, biting inge-   25:520
nuity behind the dryness, is sly. Consequently one calls such a person crafty. Voltaire has this gift; *The Vicar of Wakefield* and Swift's satires [manifest it].[19] The initial appearance[c] suggests innocence, and when it afterwards becomes clear that something was hidden behind it, then this is crafty. Such a sly individual gets along with everyone. Such people have composure and candidness, and a frank, cool head. One calls the pondering of the power of judgment whims. A "cricket" is a "grasshopper."[d] Who catches such "grasshoppers" is a "cricket-catcher."[e] Thus, whoever pursues empty thoughts which have no use, is a ponderer and a melancholy individual (*Grillenfänger*). The one lacking power of judgment is stupid. Stupidity is not a lack of ingenuity. One who is slow and obtuse seems to be stupid, *yet that is false*. For if he does not immediately have

---

[a] Translation for the second option in the footnotes; i.e. for *Geschicklichkeit gemeinschaftlich*, instead of for *Gemeinschaft der Geschicklichkeit* (community of skill).

[b] Reading *gelehrter Kaufmann* (which would literally translate as a "learned merchant") as *Gelehrter, Kaufmann*.

[c] *Anschein*

[d] As Grimm's etymological analysis shows, this identification of *Grille* (cricket) and *Heuschrecke* was common in the eighteenth century. The play on words here is on *Grille* which is metaphorically a "whim," said here to be the product of judgment's pondering.

[e] *Grillenfänger*: Kant's word play is difficult to render in English. The term is not used in its literal sense in German. It is used in the sense given in the next sentence; i.e. as meaning a melancholy or morose person, especially one having odd, fantastical ideas.

inspirations, then he still can have insight. Hence one must distinguish someone who is stupid from someone who is obtuse. Thus one wanted to turn someone who lacked ingenuity over to the blacksmith; however, in the presence of mathematical books, his insight became apparent. Therefore the one who lacks ingenuity is still not stupid. Ingenuity is hurried, just as the power of judgment is ponderous. Thus cognitions of the ingenious person are transient, they may make an impression, but they do not adhere and do not penetrate. Therefore if one admonishes a person who is in a hurry, these admonitions may make an impression, but they do not adhere and do not penetrate. Thus if one admonishes someone in a hurry, then it is a futile effort. The human mind is indeed something.[a] Whoever has power of judgment, also has constancy, but whoever is ingenious, is also hurried, retains nothing, and is not constant

25:521 in any thing.

ON MEMORY

Memory is the power of producing the recurrence of representations. Our imagination has its natural ebb and flow. Now our power of choice, however, has the power of recalling at will images of the imagination, and not in the way they flowed in the imagination, but at random.[b] Memory is thus a faculty of the power of choice above the imagination. The faculty of remembering belongs to memory. Remembering means however to *recall* the image of the representations. *If I make the effort* to summon *the image of the representations*, then this is recollecting. Recollecting is therefore a means of remembering and of reproduction; it takes no small effort to check the flow of the imagination. The mind strains itself a great deal, when one recollects and checks the stream of the imagination in order to search for what was lost. A threefold distinction is to be made concerning memory: ease in grasping, long retention, and ease in remembering. This rests on certain tricks. Nothing once already in it can in fact be lost from our memory, and it cannot be erased. True, it can be obscured, and then only a good means is required to produce such again and to make it clear. Grasping requires mechanical memorization; this is a frequent repetition of the same kind of things. For example, children thus learn the multiplication tables by repeating them time and again. Mechanical memorization is based on a certain order. If one wants to recollect, then one must follow the order. Hence if one asks children for the multiplication tables out of order, then they recite them from the

---

[a] *Stück*: Kant here seems to be using the term in the same way in which "piece" can be used in English to refer to an individual, or as translated here, the way one says about someone that he or she is quite something.
[b] *willkürlich*: its ordinary language sense seems most appropriate here.

beginning until they reach the number in question. They thus follow the order in which they have learned them. If the order is interrupted, then one cannot think of the link in the chain, but must begin once again from the beginning. Hence if one interrupts an individual who is memorizing, then he knows nothing of what has gone before and must memorize from the beginning. Mechanical memorization has great utility. It is the foundation of the assessment of cognitions. If this were not the case, we would have no cognitions for the understanding. Judicious memorization arises by means of judgments, when one makes a comparison with something. This often happens in the case of the understanding with 25:522 insipid ingenuity. Thus, for example, someone made the following comparison for the title "concerning his legitimate heirs."[a] He conceived a box, which was to signify the inheritance, after that a pig, which was to signify the *suis*, and after that Moses with two law tablets which was to mean legitimate. Such a thing is harmful for the understanding. One can surely preferably compare circumstances, the time, the place; for example, who Julius Caesar was.

Long retention seems to be based on the intensity of the association. I grasp something intensely, if I can associate it with many things. Then if it does not come to my mind with one [association], it will happen with another.

Ease of remembering seems to be based on whether the object is interesting. Hence one easily retains what pleases one. It is said that old people have a weak memory. However, with regard to what they already know, it is just as strong as in the youth, and now that they are old, memory no longer grasps anything new. Consequently old people still know the old precisely, however they cannot grasp the new. Impressions are weaker in their case, thus also the memories. With the youth, however, it is the reverse. They grasp the new quickly, but do not retain anything for long. The reason that the elderly know precisely the old so well is because they have imprinted it so well. Clever people grasp quickly, ingenious people also grasp quickly, however also forget quickly, since they confuse it with other things, for their ingenuity produces many similarities for them. Books have weakened memory, because one does not make the effort to retain what one can find in a book. In the same way one can also say that writing has weakened memory. Thus writing [notes] in lectures has no use at all, if one only does it in order that it serve to retain [the ideas]. However, if it is a form of memory, if one seeks to produce a system out of the science for oneself, then of course it has its use. Whoever has gotten into the habit of immediately writing down what he wants to retain, has weakened his memory a great deal, so that if he has one time forgotten his notepad, he has to strain himself,

---

[a] *de haeredibus suis legitimis*

25:523 in order to retain [the ideas]. Thus through art one can get to the point that one does not have much need for memory. The quality of easily rec-ollecting is superb, and depends on this, that it does not lapse due to the habit of neglect. Forgetfulness is a great misfortune. Those who speak contemptuously about memory, do not bear in mind that it is a great help for cognitions. We know what we retain in our memory.[a] Whoever has an obtuse memory is completely devoid of cognitions. Therefore it is necessary to preserve one's memory. At age 40, memory becomes weak. One cannot learn anything new then; no doubt, however, one can expand what one has learned. A vivid memory lasts only until age 30. In these years, the materials must be procured, in order thereafter to have subject matter for thinking. Hence philosophy should be set aside[b] in school, and only things for memory should be undertaken, because this is the best time for memory. Novels ruin memory, since the mind is there unbridled, adds much to what is there, and produces figments of the mind. Since those reading novels know that they are novels, hence they read these as something which they need not retain. The harm lies not in the fact that one does not retain the novels, which would indeed be fortunate if one could clear one's head of all of them, but because one never reads a novel in order to retain it. Thus one acquires the habit of reading books without retaining what one is reading. Hence people who read novels first and then other books, do not retain anything of what they have read. The unfaithfulness of memory occurs for this reason: when one does not regard something as important to be attended to, and is not concerned about substituting one circumstance for another in a narrative, because one regards it as making no difference. Conse-quently such common people are not to be greatly trusted, especially in a narration, in spite of the fact that these are not lies which they inten-tionally tell, but such reports about which they themselves do not know that they are false. All ghost stories arise from this. Conscientiousness in the observation and recounting of what one has seen and heard is very necessary to keep memory true. However, if people are conscientiously particular about something, then false reports result from good opinion.

25:524 There exist examples of prodigious memory. For example, a gardener's boy took pleasure in a printed book without being able to read it. He was taught to read; after this he could recite from memory everything that he read, so that at one point in time, he dictated word for word a manuscript he had read and which one had taken as lost [on him]. He was an oracle of the men of letters, but indifferent toward the whole world.

[a] *Tantum scimus, quantum memoria, tenemus*
[b] *von der Philosophie abstrahiret werden sollte*

ON THE FACULTY OF COMPOSING[a]

To compose means to create new cognitions and representations. This is either voluntary or involuntary. In the foregoing it has already been said that our imagination runs on with its stream [of images]. That power, however, to produce new representations is an active, voluntary power; it lies at the basis of all initiatives. Before carrying something out, we surely indicate a plan and a means, which all of us compose for ourselves. Composing serves to maintain[b] [this activity] and the more people enlarge their powers of mind, the more dissatisfied they are with the present and produce other new representations for themselves; thus this belongs to nature.

To discover means to first find what is not yet in fact known; it is different from inventing.

To invent means to produce something, which was not at all there, from oneself; however, to discover means only to observe that which was not at all known. In this way magnetic power was not invented, but discovered, in the same way also foreign lands, but one can invent an experiment. *We invent* what depends upon ourselves.

To think up means to find something which has its source solely in thoughts and in the mind:[c] in this way a scoundrel can think something up in his defense. To excogitate is to think of something voluntarily. Thus what composing especially refers to is to produce in general cognitions which did not at all exist in the previous state. However, to poetically invent is to compose something false.

Composing is done in relation to many cases: one poetically invents something for oneself to the advantage of reason in order to invent something. In this way one poetically invents circles in the heavens for oneself. Furthermore one poetically invents something for oneself not for the sake of inventing, but for elucidating, and this serves to the advantage of the understanding, for example, allegories, moral fables. Every fable is thus supposed to be a poetic invention for the elucidation of the understanding, and in the moral world is suited best in order to make morality itself comprehensible. Thus what is expressed in morality by means of universal concepts is made sensible in the fable, which elucidates the understanding. They make a big impression on persons who judge concretely, for example the fable of the stomach.[20] Fables are not for children, since they do not pay attention to the morality, [but] only stay with the external, for example, the fox, raven, cheese, and so forth.

25:525

---

[a] *Dichten*: Kant's usage of this term in this section is wider than its poetic sense.
[b] *zur Unterhaltung*: given the context here, its sense as "support" or "maintenance" seems more fitting than its sense as "entertainment."
[c] *Kopf*

The merit of the fable is to make the understanding sensible and the morality intuitable. Finally, then in addition there exist poetic inventions which oppose the sound understanding, and these are fairy tales which are the opposite of fables. The latter serve for the satisfaction of the understanding, but the former serve to its disadvantage. When we look through the poetic inventions of the nations, for example, the mythology, we can thereby assess the people's genius, for example, of the Greeks, the Romans, and Indians. The Greek and Roman theogony will be preserved as long as the history will remain.

CONCEPT OF THE POET AND OF THE ART OF POETRY

The harmonious play of thoughts and sensations is the poem. The play of thoughts and sensations is the agreement of subjective laws; if the thoughts agree with my subject, then this is a play of the same. Two different things should be noticed about thoughts, that they stand in relation to the object, and there the thoughts must be true, and that the course of thoughts agrees with the nature of the powers of mind, thus 25:526 with the subject, and therefore the succession of thoughts [agrees] with the powers of mind. This harmonious play of thoughts and sensations is the poem. Poetry and eloquence are in this differentiated. The poem is a harmonious play in which the thoughts conform to the play of sensations, eloquence is also a harmonious play, but here sensation must conform to the thoughts. The sensations must promote and enliven the thoughts. To enliven means to give the thoughts intensity, clarity, intuition. The poet carries on the play of thoughts, to the extent they conform to the sensations. The poet has a meter or a rhyme. Such nations which have prosody, have no rhyme, but those who have rhyme, have no prosody. Thus there is always a steady play, which is a matter of expression, and that is the main thing in poetry. If it is omitted, a large part of sensation is omitted. Hence prosody bears a great similarity to music, where there is precisely a higher and lower tone, which is partitioned by the meter into certain intervals. In the art of poetry, the poet has great freedom in thoughts and words, but with regard to the harmony of the play, he has no freedom. Hence a mistake in rhyme is an unpardonable mistake. The art of poetry existed earlier than eloquence, one had poems earlier than orations.[21] The reason is: sensations existed before thoughts; hence one conformed thoughts to the sensations, until the understanding increased, and then one reversed it. In the case of eloquence, the play of thoughts is promoted and enlivened. With regard to sensations, the orator is limited; they must be chosen in such a way that they advance the thoughts of the understanding. If he chooses images, then he becomes a poet. To be 25:527 orator and poet accords greatly. Eloquence makes poetry thoughtful, poetry makes eloquence full of feeling. If the art of poetry is empty, then eloquence must replace the emptiness of thoughts, and if there is little sensation in eloquence, then it is replaced by poetry.

Many poems are mere plays of sensation, for example, love poems. A talented poet must not bother with this, because it is very easy to arouse such sensations, since everyone already has such sensations on their own. However, to bring virtue and its sensations into a harmonious play is meritorious, for it is something intellectual, and to make this intuitable is truly meritorious, for example Pope's *Essay on Man*.[22]

This book sought to *refine* the art of poetry through reason and to animate *reason through the art of poetry*. As to what poetic invention is concerned with, it can thus be written only for entertainment,[a] and then it is called a novel. It is a story poetically invented by analogy with events of the world, but in this way surpasses the events of the world. One places people in novels in quite a lot of situations, so that they ultimately manifest several characters, but the characters from actual history please more. It would be good to describe human beings from the characters of history. Thus Richardson says: people who have a good heart by nature and commit vices, they go further in this than those who are evil by nature. He gave an example from history. Sulla was by nature evil, but after much bloodshed, lived in peace. Nero had a good heart by nature, but through recklessness he degenerated into lewdness and cruelty. Such reflections about human beings which are determined from history, are better than novels. Poetic inventions which are passed off as truths are lies. This attribute is a power of composition with many people, who are only prone to it without the intention of their capacity to compose.

25:528

ON THE STATE OF HUMAN BEINGS IN SLEEP
OR IN DREAMING

Dreams are self-created images of the human mind which one remembers upon waking. With human beings, many dreams make sense,[b] for example, if one is suspended in the air, which is a sign of health, resulting from the fluency of the blood. In this way, dreams can also come *from the disposition of the mind, for example, the dream about* dogs indicates quarreling, especially with people who heed it. The cause is, since already in their sleep, their head was not in the right place,[c] and when they get up, then their mind is also so ill disposed, that they become irritated about everything and start quarreling. Such dreams can always signify something, for it is natural. One also believes one has produced masterpieces

---

[a] *Unterhaltung*: as noted previously, this term also means "maintenance" or "support" and its sense must be interpreted based on context.
[b] *übereinkommen*, literally "agree"   [c] *der Kopf nicht recht gestanden hat*

of ingenuity during sleep, for example, a beautiful poem, but that is an illusion. Presaging dreams are well possible, to the extent that they flow out of the condition of the body. For example, someone dreams about an *illness*, thus the illness already in the body *produces* such a dream. Many dreams arise from the constriction of the blood forced from the heart chamber, especially also from drawing one's breath, which is voluntary[a] while awake, but during sleep is very weak. One has seen dreams as the augury of future things, hence one has wanted to interpret them. All savage peoples have taken dreams to be something divine. A fantast is one who takes his images in the imagination to be actual objects, he is to be distinguished from the enthusiast. The fantast fancies he sees objects of this world, but the enthusiast believes he sees objects of the spirit world. Who watches out for his sensations and is very attentive to them, falls into fantasizing, but who is beside himself, is secure from that.

Enthusiasm is a fantasizing in regard to objects of the understanding, for example enthusiasm of the virtue of patriotism, when an ideal is taken for something real. Madness or delirium is habitual fantasizing, thus taking the images for actual external objects. Who takes his chimera for actual objects of his previous state, for example, he was to have been a prince, is mad. However, who believes he sees external objects, is insane; both are delirium. Mad children do not exist, rather madness arises with reason. Madness due to illness is fantasizing or babbling.

25:529

The one who does not perceive his state in the world is idiotic; for example the cretins in Wallis,[23] also the albinos. If the powers in regard to employment are weak, then these are idiots. However, if the powers in regard to the employment of sensibility are deranged, then these are people who are mad. The idiot is more inept, because he cannot apply his capacities at all, he cannot apply his memory to reproduce what he has seen. Fantasizing is the genus in which one takes images and poetic inventions as actual objects. This fantasizing is twofold, of concepts and of sensations. The fantasizing of concepts arises from a sensation of approval, from a feeling of the good, touching, and charming. This feeling of the concept has the effect that one realizes the ideal, and that it would give us great satisfaction if it were actual. Experience really shows this, that one believes one sees in the object, what one is thinking about it. In this way, when narrating a story, one adds much to it, which one believes it had still been lacking. This fantasizing from ideas, although it is only an effect of the power of composition, but still occurs according to rules of the understanding, is called enthusiasm. He is a fantast of the ideal. These enthusiasts are not all capable, it is a noble fantasizing; where it exists, it presupposes a talent. Many who thus

---

[a] *willkürlich*: Kant's sense here may be that while awake, one has the choice as to how deeply one takes one's breaths, while during sleep it may be very shallow.

dwell on enthusiasm are not free of it through their understanding, but through their stupidity. Enthusiasm presupposes that one makes oneself an ideal of something. There exist cognitions which are archetypes of the thing, so that the things, in accordance with the cognition which is their archetype, are possible. This perfect concept of a thing is the idea, but if one fabricates an image in keeping with this idea, then this is an ideal. Because this idea is the model of perfection, it thus pleases us so, that we are misled to believe that such can actually take place in the world. In this way, everyone has an idea of friendship in its complete purity in his head, although it is not to be found in the whole world. One can assess all friendship in accordance with this idea. However, who realizes this idea, who expects that it should actually take place in the world, and even   25:530
to the degree of it which he produces in his head, he falls into the enthusiasm of friendship. In this way there exists an enthusiasm of patriotism, where one takes an ideal of the perfect connection of civil society, as a general well-being of the entire civil society. Who gives way to this ideal with affect, [to an ideal] that surely cannot be attained, is enthusiastic. Such enthusiasm produces great excesses, so that one who is enthused by this idea sacrifices both friendship as well as natural connection, and everything. Now, if such an ideal is not attained, then such an enthusiasm produces misanthropic individuals. Such a person shuns people not due to malicious intent, because he cannot tolerate them, but because he can nowhere find such people the way he would like them, no such people so grateful, so benevolent toward the whole human race. He is thus a virtuous fantast, he pursues the ideal with affect. True, such an ideal can serve as a rule and for assessment, but it cannot be actually attained. Such enthusiasts are not malicious people, but they are touched with principles of benevolence toward the entire human race, and since they cannot find such, they become misanthropes, for example, Rousseau, and are taken to be absurd, as they have principles like this according to which they are judged by others. One is wont to speak highly of enthusiasm, that it does many great things, and that all the great changes in the world are to have originated from enthusiasm, not from cold judgment, but from intuition.[24] One may call the fantasts of sensation dreamers. Alchemists, chemists, and so forth are of this kind. They still always fancy themselves to attain the stone of the wise man. Such revery takes place due to lack of experience. One calls madness in regard to inner sensation fanaticism.   25:531
All dreamers due to a spiritual sense are fanatics; the one who takes it to be theoretically possible, already has a propensity for it. As noble as is the enthusiast, so base is the fanatic. The enthusiast has after all a true archetype as his object, but the fanatic follows absurdities and figments of the mind. The more one withdraws from the external world, the more harmful it is. But the fanatic is just such a person who withdraws entirely from this world; therefore he is completely unfit for the present world.

All fanatics have no correct philosophy, but the enthusiasts indeed do, only they follow their correct concepts with complete affect.

ON FORESEEING

Foreseeing is the condition under which all our actions occur. We enjoy the present, we make preparation for the future. The more active an individual is, the more he is enticed to direct his attention to the future, but one who in this way has few wants, plans little for the future. Foreseeing increases with age. Young people do not look to the future in the way older ones do, since young people do not have such rooted affairs of life, they have not yet accustomed themselves to many things, they can still change their way of life and make up their minds about everything. However, the older person is more likely to be cautious in regard to the future, because he needs more preparations than the young person, since the young one is livelier. This is the reason that old people are miserly, because they look to the future, although the young ones would have more likely cause to save, since they have longer to live. However, the reason with old people is this, in their old age they find themselves unable to care for their further accommodation; hence they seek to acquire man-made riches for themselves, and hence they save, but the young person thinks, time will bring an answer. Although the representation of something future is just as strong as of something present, yet it interests us more; for example, an enjoyment which one is to relish, seems to be by far more agreeable to one, than one afterwards actually finds it. This is how all marriages are, in which one envisages heavenly delights to be enjoyed, but which afterwards hardly constitute a moderate happiness.

25:532 The thing never accords with the ideal one has made of it for oneself, while it was still in the future. The reason is because we can enhance and refashion the future as we want, but we cannot represent the present as better than it is; hence chimeras refer to the future.

In the same way we greatly delight in future agreeable enjoyment or good fortune, by contrast we find future misfortune to be so much more dreadful than it actually is. Hence one wishes that it would soon be over. In general people divide time up especially with regard to the agreeable and disagreeable. If everyone would have to endure 20 or 30 [years] of nothing but ills, slavery and disagreeableness, and thereafter the remaining time were nothing but good fortune and enjoyment, then everyone would sooner prefer to endure the years of misfortune, just so that toward the end he has nothing but amenities to enjoy. If he undergoes*a* misfortune first, then during it he delights in the prospect of a future agreeable life. But if he would have the agreeable years to enjoy

a genießt

first, then the future misfortune would always torment him. All novels are arranged in this way, they first give the youth all the inconveniences and disagreeableness of life to endure, and they postpone all enjoyment and good living until the end of his life. It is also the same with eating. The best always remains for last. Thus one gives the best wine last to drink.[25] If the best would come first, then the poor things would afterwards not taste [good]. Thus also people, who have had to eschew courtly life, pine away, although their way of life thereafter is not the worst. Thus it depends on the order of sensation, and we all organize our foreseeing this way.

There exist people who nurture themselves with hopes. Some imagine that they are more likely to meet with ill, which threatens them, than that the good fortune will come to pass, for which they could give themselves hope. The one who is moderate in his wishes is more likely to be concerned that he will become unhappier, because he is satisfied with his present state. But who is dissatisfied with his present state, has great hope for future good fortune. One says that one also hopes to attain what one wishes for, yet one often has something else to hope for than one wishes. If one hopes for something and it fails, then the individual becomes despairing, if it has not yet taken place, then hope sustains him, since one still hopes to achieve it in the future; for example a game.

25:533

Youth is full of hope and indeed rightfully so, for it has talents to go to work on such, the old person hopes less and tries only to maintain himself in the possession of what he has.

People are very anxious to know something about the distant future and to effect something in it. To know the distant future has its natural propensity, namely to increase one's knowledge. It is thus not a matter of indifference for us to know what would happen over [the course] of 1,000 years, for example, the astronomical calculations of future changes interest us greatly. The past time with respect to ours, however, is as if it had never been.

The least degree of foreseeing into the future is anticipation, expectation. A greater degree of foreseeing is assuming, and the greatest degree is knowing.

Anticipation is also appropriate to animals. There is a certain order in the sequence of results, which we perceive in regard to the past, according to which everything happened. According to just this order, we also look into the future. The anticipation of similar cases is thus the least degree of our foreseeing. The longer someone lives, and the more he has paid attention to the cases of experience, according to what rules they happened, all the more he is in a position to foresee[a] into the future, since experience makes many rules available to him, according to which

[a] *prospiciren*: Latin, *prospicere* means to foresee, to look into the distance.

he can, in accordance with the rule of similar cases, foresee something. This prudence, which arises from such age, does not proceed from the understanding, but from experience, and is based on similar cases.

To foresee something uncertainly is to assume, *Praevision,*[a] and to foresee something with certainty is to know. Assumption presupposes inference, thus not only experience, but also reason. Knowing, however, presupposes complete reason, in this way an astronomer can know something. One cannot know people's free actions, but can well assume them, and that is prudence. Nevertheless these three faculties are in agreement with the rules of the understanding, and even if anticipation corresponds with the imagination, then it is still in keeping with the understanding. There are however a few *previsions*[b] which have no association at all with the understanding, *indeed that even go against the understanding*, and these are divinations.[c] Divination is supposed to be an immediate intuition of the future, but we can only just intuit the present. Divinations are thus supposed to be not assumptions, but intuitions of the future. In the case of an erroneous and limited understanding, this divination constitutes the greatest part of knowledge. What they assume and know is little. When such persons, especially old women, divine something, it does not occur according to the rules of order and reason, but it is supposed to happen by means of a certain magic power; they feel such anyway in themselves. The question is whether divinations are then without any basis. In a rational sense there can well be a basis for divination in our mind, which we only cannot uncover. For example someone divines that he will be sick, thus the basis lies already in him; or in the game, he [divines] he would lose. Often the divination is the cause of what [occurs], thus someone can divine that he will be happy, which can happen with a cheerful mind, or that he will be unhappy, which can also easily happen with an ill disposed mind, and then the divinations are natural. However, when someone divines something, without connection of the rule with the present, without all laws, by means of a leap, there the divinations belong to figments of the mind. And in this way the inclinations and desires, which step outside their bounds, make the individual superstitious; there he believes he sees and experiences what he creates for himself.

To prognosticate means to predict something. To this extent a man experienced and well-read in affairs of state and justice can often

---

[a] Latin, *praevidere, -vidi, -visum*, is the verb, to foresee. In previous instances in the text, the term has been translated as "foresee."

[b] *Praevisionen*: prevision or anticipatory or prophetic vision.

[c] Reading *Ahnung* for *Ahndung*; latter means punishment or retribution; *Ahnungsvermögen* means intuitive perception or divination, which fits Kant's description in the next sentence. On p. 535, Kant uses the term *Divinationes*.

prognosticate much in accordance with laws of the understanding. *There are however prognoses* which are only addressed to a single person, and one calls these fortune-telling,[a] or those which concern the whole world, and one calls these prophecies.[b] Both can be called divinations. Often one can indicate, for example from his face, what will become of an individual, and thus [one can] prognosticate. This is rational fortune-telling. However, much fortune-telling about individual persons occurs due to lines in the hand, which can be no basis at all for prognosticating. What astronomers are able to say beforehand, are not prophecies. With prophecy, nothing must arise from reason, but it must be a revelation. Fortune-telling may be possible by means of the prospect of distance in space and in time. Yet with regard to the future, no prospects exist. Many philosophers believed this. For example, Leibniz said: if one were completely conscious of the present, then the germ of the future would be inherent in it, just as in astronomy with regard to the constellation of the heavens.[26] Since however in the case of the free actions of human beings, we cannot possibly cognize the determinate causes, in order to predict the future, thus it is not possible. The prophetic gift must concern the free actions of human beings, and such is not possible. It is possible to predict the events of nature, and the more we study nature and can have insight into the causes, all the more likely will it be on target, but even if we come to know human beings ever so well, it still will not be on target. With the ancients, prophet means not the fortune-teller, but the interpreter. The Oriental people take the sayings and the muddled ways of speech of a raving, disturbed individual, who talks about everything all at once, as holy, and say that the soul of such an individual is already with God. Thus someone who stammered and made wry faces, was taken by the inhabitants of that place to be a saint, so that from that hour on they conscientiously helped him get through all the lands.

25:535

25:536

ON THE FACULTY OF CHARACTERIZATION[c]

Characters and symbols are to be distinguished. Symbol is a sensible image,[d] character is merely a designation. A sensible image is an image which bears a similarity to the thing itself. Character means nothing in itself, but is only a means of designating something; for example, ciphers [and] letters are like this. They serve to bring forth other representations,

---

[a] *Wahrsagungen*
[b] *Weißagungen*
[c] Facultate characteristica
[d] *Sinnbild*: the term ordinarily means symbol, emblem, or allegory. In the context of Kant's discussion here, the literal rendering seems to work best.

as [it were] by means of an index.[a] This way the name of an individual is an index of that individual, whom I remember when I have seen him, upon the mention of this name, which according to the analogy immediately signifies something; for example, Henry the Lion. For our cognitions as signs of the understanding, nothing is as fitting as words, because in themselves they do not signify anything else; thus the understanding can connect the relevant concept with it. But when they are pictures, thus signifying something else, then the understanding becomes confused; instead that it should have one, it then has two images. Symbols can only be used there where the representations are not difficult; all symbols are thus means of greater representation. Who speaks by means of symbols indicates that he lacks understanding. In the case of such nations having a symbolic language, the correct concepts of the understanding are very difficult. If they could represent something for themselves by means of concepts, then they would not need any images. All Oriental peoples are like this; they represent all their concepts by means of images. The story of King Nadir belongs to this.[27] Those who imitate this manner of writing in our times, greatly wrong the understanding. It is almost completely impossible for Oriental people to speak by means of concepts. We have the Greeks to thank for it, that they first freed themselves from the jumble of images.

25:537   An anticipatory image[b] of the future is supposed to signify a sign of the future, not as a divination, but as an interpretation and explanation of the future. One has regarded monstrous omens[c] or also dreams, even also the characters of human beings in the hand, as signs of the future. A portent is that which cannot be understood by known laws of nature. In the case of such a portent, the common man immediately asks, what is it supposed to mean? He is thus concerned about the future, which interests him greatly. The philosopher however asks: to what might that be due? Because he is speculative, he is concerned about the causes. The interpretation of dreams is an object which has caused a great deal of sensation among all nations, and pre-eminently so with the savages. Thus one takes something away from the other, because he had a dream, but the other knows how to avenge himself through just such a dream.

---

[a] *Custos*: Kant may here be foreshadowing something like what has been coined in contemporary analytical philosophy as an "indexical sign." To avoid imputing current meanings back into Kant, "index" is used to render the term here. In music, the term "custos" refers to the sign placed on the staff at the end of one line of music to indicate the pitch of the next line. The equivalent in literary texts (in a usage still found in the eighteenth century) is the "catchword," the first word of the following page printed at the lower right hand corner of each page.
[b] *Vorbild*   [c] *Prodigia portenta*

ON THE UPPER[a] FACULTY OF COGNITION

The upper cognitive faculty is the faculty of reflecting on representations given to us. In general this upper cognitive faculty is called the understanding, and this is distinguished from sensibility, or the lower cognitive faculty, through which the representations are generated. The understanding is the power of making use of all representations. Understanding and sensibility are opposed to one another. The understanding is nothing without sensibility, and only a mere faculty, just the same as the government without subjects and the economy without something one can manage. The understanding taken generally, insofar as it encompasses the entire cognitive faculty, is the faculty of reflecting and thinking. Not every memorizing is thinking. Thinking definitely presupposes reflection, that is, bringing representations under the universal rules of cognition. Thinking is not representing things for oneself, which occurs by means of sensibility, but the processing of the materials which sensibility presents. The upper cognitive faculty encompasses three things: understanding, especially insofar as it is opposed to reason, power of judgment, and reason. Understanding is the faculty of concepts. The power of judgment is the faculty of applying concepts in a given case; and reason is the faculty of concepts *a priori* in abstraction. The understanding is the faculty of rules, the power of judgment the faculty of applying rules, and reason the application of rules *a priori*.   25:538

If I cognize something according to a universal rule, then my cognition is not a cognition of the understanding. All cognitions of the understanding are universal cognitions, and all universal cognitions are rules.

[The faculty of] understanding is necessary in order to understand[b] something. To understand is, however, to be distinguished from insights. Insight occurs through reason, understanding through [the faculty of] understanding; hence not all knowing is understanding, but only through [the faculty of] understanding.

The [faculty of] understanding is distinguished into the adroit and the correct. The adroit is one which understands something swiftly, which is easily able to produce a concept for itself, and is especially to be found in ingenious persons. An adroit concept is not always a correct concept, an adroit concept is also a swiftly produced concept, but a correct one originates more slowly. This way ingenious persons are able in a short time to produce universal concepts for themselves, but they

---

[a] *Obererkenntnis* and *Untererkenntnis Vermögen* are here translated as "upper" and "lower" cognitive faculties, indicating simply their relative rank. "Superior" and "inferior" could connote more than what Kant intends here, as could "higher."

[b] *verstehen*: more widely, means to comprehend, grasp.

are lacking in the differentiation and correctness of their concepts. One further distinguishes the understanding into the common and speculative understanding. The common understanding is the faculty of judging concretely, but the speculative is the one of judging abstractly. The common and sound understanding is not therefore called common because it is found in common people, but because it is required everywhere and by all. Such individuals of common understanding judge concretely. Hence if one presents them with something universal and abstract, they instantly demand an example; their understanding is not practiced in judging abstractly, but when it judges concretely, it judges correctly. The speculative understanding must always be a sound one; that necessarily follows, but a sound one is not speculative. The sound one is at the same time the practical understanding, because it can judge only in given cases; however, in order to make plans, a speculative understanding is required.

25:539   The most outstanding main thing to be expected of every understanding, and which is required by everyone, is the power of judgment. One must know how to make use of all the rules into which one has had insight abstractly, and how to apply them. The entire understanding with its cognition is fruitless without the power of judgment. The lack of cognition and concepts produces obtuseness, the lack of power of judgment *produces stupidity. The lack of power of judgment* lapses into the ridiculous, but not the lack of cognitions of the understanding. The one who has much knowledge and insights, but no power of judgment to apply his knowledge in given cases, is a pedant. Such a one is not lacking in the faculty of the power of judgment, but the faculty is just not practiced in applying all cognitions in the world. This arises from a lack of knowledge of the world. The lack of the power of judgment is irreplaceable, because it cannot be replaced by instruction. For the power of judgment does not permit being informed, but the understanding surely does [so permit]. The power of judgment can neither be communicated through schools nor by other forms of instruction, but it is already given by nature; however, one can practice it. One must practice applying what the understanding judges, and then one practices the power of judgment. Thus Queen Christina spoke prudently and acted foolishly.[28]

    The author here remarks incidentally about distraction.[29] One can voluntarily take one's mind off things,[a] but one is involuntarily distracted, especially by the plurality of objects and representations which we perceived in a short time, and which distract us from paying attention. What transposes the mind into an involuntary attitude[b] is a basis

---

[a] *dissipiren*: Kant here adapts the Latin *dissipare*, to scatter, disperse, dissipate. The equivalent German, *zerstreuen*, has the idiomatic meaning of "taking one's mind off things."
[b] *Stellung*

of distraction.[a] Thus every propensity for involuntary imagining, if it becomes habitual, is a great degree of distraction. Persons who reflect abstractly are often distracted; thus, for example, Newton did not know whether or not his supper had been eaten by another person.[30] Such distraction arises from the involuntary reflection where persons reflect in society and in the streets. Thus one such person, without knowing it, went into the street without his wig and in slippers.[31] Because he is absorbed in his thoughts, he does not know where he is. Such thinking has no use; they do not know what they are thinking, they put themselves in the position of being completely beside themselves, and that is not a sign of a thoughtful individual. A thoughtful individual tries to take his mind off things again [when] in society and to be free of his thoughts. Thoughtlessness is either a lively or lifeless one. The lively one is present in an individual through enjoyment and lively conversation; the lifeless one is where the individual is transposed into inaction, and it makes his condition, for the new use of his powers of mind, inanimate. One maintains oneself through lively thoughtlessness; although the conversation is not interesting, yet it cheers one up. It is not only easy to collect one's thoughts[b] from it, but one can also reflect better and more actively.

25:540

25:541

ON THE USE OF THE UNDERSTANDING

The understanding can either be used under the guidance of another, or also without the guidance of another. The first is immature, the other is mature. Thus in mathematics, the Chinese are immature, although with regard to judgment and cognition, they take [their] community to be mature.[c] Thus a professor, when his servant brought him the news that there was a fire in his house, said that such matters belonged to his wife.[32] In this way the clerics take the common people to be immature with regard to religious cognitions, and call them lay people, but call themselves shepherds, which is a very proud name, since all remaining people are then to be seen as beasts.[d] Likewise the rulers call themselves the fathers of the people, since they then take the subjects to be immature children. Thus philosophers also pose as guardians and take all the rest

---

[a] *Zerstreuung*: in the *Anthropology from a Pragmatic Point of View*, Kant gives the Latin *distractio* (VII. 206).

[b] idiomatic meaning of *sich sammeln*

[c] Per also the editors' suggestion, reading *unmündig* as *mündig*. The translation in this section for *Unmündig, mündig* is not the literal translation of minor and major, but the translation usually given for Kant's use of these terms in "What Is Enlightenment?" and for the same reason. The discussion refers to our use of understanding and reason, and our ability or lack thereof to think for ourselves. This choice of translation also distinguishes the terms from Kant's own use of *Majorennitaet* later in the section.

[d] *Vieh*, literally "cattle," a term Aristotle also uses to refer to the popular masses.

25:542 to be idiots, which is the same as the lay people in regard to the clergy. The clergyman has still more right to take the people to be immature with regard to religious cognitions, since he has a divine privilege and authority, but the philosopher does not. There is a certain age where the immaturity of the understanding ceases, but there also exist people who are lifelong immature. Thus someone said of the Russians that they will never be masters and teachers of the sciences, but are only good apprentices; they would, however, always have to get the teachers from foreign countries. True, they could become masters in mathematics, because there [things] proceed according to precepts, but not in other sciences. And since, as it is, one is always accustomed to learning nothing more from the sciences than one provisionally needs for an operation, then in the end there will be no books at all, since a teacher must know not the product of science, but its spirit. The Greeks are the Frenchmen of antiquity, they tolerated no despots in the sciences, but after that everything was subjugated as immature to Aristotle's philosophy, a yoke which has now been shaken off.

It seems that if some people would like to be treated as immature, they would make better progress with regard to their circumstances, but on the whole it is not good, since constraint extirpates genius; and [so], let [us] even [leave] some to be a fool in their own business, if they just have the freedom to be a fool. Universal freedom cultivates genius, and all speeches on the behalf of constraint, for example, by the nobility, who say that the subjects cannot lead their own lives because of their stupidity, are very baseless [in their assertion], since stupidity results from constraint. And they believe that such stupidity will always exist, yet these ills are only consequences of constraint. Constraint makes one mean and stupid. Who is accustomed to it, in the end gives up his understanding. In just this way, someone who has once accustomed himself to it, cannot do without his brandy. Then of course such people cannot rule themselves, but if they would have complete freedom, then they would gradually again get into the habit of ruling themselves, since this stupidity is the consequence of slavery. True, we can of course justify all ills and prejudices, yet these ills can surely come to an end at some point, and a beginning must also be made toward this.

25:543 Women are taken to be immature by the men, which however already lies partly in their nature. If mature were the same as using one's mouth,[a] then they would surely be the most mature, since they have a great talkativeness, an incomparable gift which nature has given them, so that they would have something attractive. However, in what concerns the management of affairs, women are such that they cannot free themselves from a guide, since, in just the same way they cannot even go on the street

[a] The play on words in the German is here on *mündig* and *Mund*.

104

without a guide, they also need the same in all their affairs. True, the feminine understanding is fine in assessing, in pointing out means, they are in fact very shrewd, but when it is a question of what the purpose of something is, then women are immature, and the masculine understanding consists in this [to know the purpose]. [It is] not as if all men actually have [this understanding], but they certainly should have it.

Insofar as it depends on age, maturity is the civilian majority, when people are in the position to provide not only for their own civic affairs, but also for those of the common good. In regard to age, for the understanding which they can attain according to their nature, women can more likely become mature and [do so] earlier. Therefore one will find that women of 16 to 18 years of age are already in the position to preside over the entire household, while men of such age are not in the position to preside over any matter. The majority which is required, to attend to one's state [of affairs] and one's circumstances, can show up in the twentieth year of age, but in regard to money it must be conferred later.

Experience teaches that people of such age are still not at all able to manage money. The reason is because at that age they still do not earn anything, thus also do not know what effort it costs. Thus a prince requires more years for majority, since he has more to administer than a farmer, who can maintain his household earlier. Thus majority must be conferred according to the circumstances of the enterprises, and not in fact according to age.

25:544

ON THE SICKNESS OF THE UNDERSTANDING

The sickness of the understanding consists either in lack of understanding, and this is stupidity, or in its being upside down, and this is insanity, or lunacy. The lack of natural understanding is called stupidity, the lack of practiced understanding is called simplemindedness. Stupidity is not a slowness of understanding. A slow understanding is one that notices few fine differences; then it is obtuse, but still not stupid. It is indeed slow, not adroit, but nevertheless correct. Thus, for example, one must present a matter very slowly and at great length to a judge with a slow understanding, before he grasps it, but then he also judges correctly about it. One must not take guilelessness for stupidity. If someone takes shrewd schemes and duplicities as true, that is not a result of stupidity, but it reveals a good heart. They do not believe the other person has it in him that he would dupe them like this, they always believe the best about everyone, and interpret everything in the best light. This results solely from lack of experience.

One says that the deceiver is always more clever than the one deceived. That is completely false. The one deceived can just be completely inexperienced in the matter, but then he is not otherwise more stupid. And the one who allows himself to be deceived, thereby reveals that he has good dispositions, since he does not suspect such of the other, that he should be a rogue. It is better to be deceived than to harbor such dispositions against another. The other can deceive me, I must guard myself. Who thinks this way about others, already has deceitful dispositions, therefore he also guards himself from others, since he expects to find the same also in them. In just the same way it is also false when one says: the honest person is stupid. Of course a stupid person cannot deceive, because he does not have the cunning, yet uprightness does not at all exist together with stupidity, since one is then honest due to principles.

25:545 Presumptuousness is connected with stupidity. It takes understanding in order to know that one has no understanding. Since a stupid person has no understanding, he thus also does not see that he has a lack of it, for with what will he see it? Accordingly, in regard to himself, the stupid person is not a faultfinder, he is quite well satisfied with himself; and then he also wants that others should likewise take him to be such as he takes himself, and this is impertinence. Self-esteem due to understanding is noble, namely that one takes oneself to be worth just as much as another. However this self-esteem is also at the same time connected with modesty. But with stupidity, there is not such a moderation of one's self-esteem. Experience teaches that impertinence achieves its purpose. Such people get the furthest in the world. Thus many scholars who are held in such high regard, rose to the top not so much through their merit, as through the fact that they first made a hue and cry about themselves, and made a name for themselves. For as stubborn as people are, in the end they still would gladly let themselves be commanded by someone who sets himself up to do so. One will often see in social gatherings, that one conforms and that one afterwards also allows such a worth to the one who is obstinate and values himself, and that is an impertinent individual.

If simplemindedness judges in the case of an understanding that is otherwise correct, but not yet based on experience, then [simplemindedness] is agreeable and noticeable.

ON THE USE OF REASON WITH REGARD TO THE PRACTICAL

Understanding is required for experience and for the assessment of appearances. Experience provides rules and laws which the understanding observes. In order however to judge *a priori* before experience, where no experience any longer guides us, requires reason. Thus in order to carry out the king's orders, a minister only needs understanding, but for making plans on his own he needs reason. Reason is just as creative in the upper powers as the faculty of invention[a] is in the lower powers. Through understanding we only judge, but through *reason* we cognize something due to universal bases[b] and principles. If we could do nothing more than merely judge about experience, and not excerpt something from universal bases, then our judgments would only go as far as our experience goes. As it is, however, we have the faculty of excerpting something from universal bases.

25:546

Ratiocinating means to elevate one's reason beyond the limits of practical use. I can use reason practically and speculatively. Who goes beyond experience, and uses reason speculatively, ratiocinates. Thus subjects are supposed to obey the soldiers, but not ratiocinate. Hence one attempts to deprive people of the use of reason, in order to be able to rule them better. This occurs when one makes them superstitious and shackles them to prejudices. Just as children can be compelled by ghosts, in the same way people can also be compelled by false representations which are repugnant to reason. Thus princes often prohibit the printing press, for its freedom is a means of animating reason, of cultivating knowledge, and therefore of producing ratiocinating human beings. Its prohibition produces just the opposite. For reason makes [them] rebellious against illegitimate compulsion; it wants grounds. Such a government which seeks to prevent this, is very weak as a result; with regard to those who rule, it is indeed very easy, yet the more ignorant and stupid the people are, all the more obstinate they also are. The use of reason beyond the practical is often ridiculous and repugnant, for example when a woman ratiocinates in regard to religion or about the state. Their practical use extends only to the household; there they can ratiocinate, for which they also have a good talent, better than the man. It is just the same when children ratiocinate; in that case one then calls them super clever. In general, where one ratiocinates, and the rules are still derived *a priori*, then it is nonsensical for one who has used his reason for speculation.

Carelessness in the use of reason seems to be a lack of reason. Yet it is often more difficult to use reason than the understanding, since people also like to make use of reason in complicated cases; there [one finds] not a lack of the talent of reason, but carelessness. Hence instruction in universities is properly this, to cultivate the capacity of reason, and to get [students] into the habit of the method of ratiocinating, and to establish the appropriate maxims of reason. Thereby one does not become a scholar, since one does not learn, but only practices using reason. If the

25:547

---

[a] *Facultas fingendi*

[b] *Gründen*: "reason(s)" would probably better translate Kant's use of *Grund/Gründen* in this section, but both the redundancy in English ("reason" for *Vernunft*) and even possible confusion, plus considerations of consistency in translation, serve as grounds to keep "basis/bases."

individual is first accustomed to reason and to reflect about everything, what bases this or that has, then he can adequately use his reason in the world, and later one will yet acquire insights for oneself; one must first remedy[a] carelessness.

The compulsion of emulation is the ruin of reason. Imitation is only a molding, but not something proper to oneself. All learnedness arises from propositions[b] and by means of much memorizing; I have then indeed enlarged cognitions, but have not gotten the capacity of reason into the habit of judging about all universal principles.

If the use of reason is difficult, and one does not concern oneself with ratiocinating, then people greatly welcome it if they are able to thrust the causes and bases of an event onto a universally accepted opinion, and thereby give up the use of reason. The two primary sources to which one is wont to appeal, if one does not want to use reason, are fate and blind chance.[c] Blind necessity is fate and blind chance is fortune. For example, someone is killed on the field; thus one says, who simply must stay, will not escape, that just must be so. Or in a game, there one attributes much to blind fortune. Here the use of reason is somewhat burdensome; hence one gladly withdraws from such principles, in order only not to ratiocinate. There are still many other kinds of methods of considering oneself above the use of reason. Wonders belong to this, for example, birthmarks, the effect of the imagination of pregnant women.[33] Political causes may lie in this, in order to silence the man thereby. Rickmann writes against birthmarks.[34]

Further [examples are] meanings of dreams, which is a great superstition. We are not offended and also do not take them to be inferior for this reason, if women are somewhat superstitious, since they are then more feminine, and those who are not this way, are more masculine, which is just as much to be reproached in them, as the effeminate in men. The reason that such is more respectable for women is because they need the guidance of the man. But if they are free from superstition, then this is a conviction that they need no guidance, [and] thus a signal of domestic turmoil. Moreover, [there is] the superstition of sympathy, the superstition of the divining rod, which is supposed to turn to where the minerals are. With some it is deception, with others delusion. Further, [there are] the influences of the moon. These are not rightly refuted, although also not rightly proven. In general, one attributes much to the heavens. The direction of fates, likewise also the thriving of plants, are attributed to

25:548

---

[a] Reading *haben* as *beheben*, since it makes more sense here to say one must first remedy carelessness, before one concerns oneself with gaining insights, than to say that one "must first *have* carelessness" (which at most would be a statement about the temporal sequence of the state of reason and its subsequent instruction).

[b] *Sentenzen*   [c] *Ohngefehr*

the influence of the moon, which is still not rightly explained, and the peasant especially pays attention to this. But because we cannot particularly explain the laws, we thus must also not yield to believing such. Finally one can also cite in addition the influence of magnetic force on the human body, which in more recent times began to inhibit the use of reason.

Sound reason is the one whose correct use can be confirmed by experience. It does not concern the magnitude of reason, since a modest[a] reason can also be sound. Sound reason is nevertheless already a limitation, since it signifies the adequacy of reason in its narrow limits, which refer only to experience. Everyone wants to have a sound reason. By what, however, does one recognize a sound reason? By the maxims, when its maxims are so constituted, that its greatest use is possible by their means. We reproach an individual who does not have sound reason, just as if it were his fault; we expect[b] of everyone the average in the perfection of human reason, in the same way we expect of everyone the average in the size of the body. It is not possible to determine what degree is required for the average of the sound understanding and sound reason, and of all the powers of mind, also for the size of the body, although all people are in agreement about it, in the way a woman wittily remarked about a homely man: he abuses men's license to be homely. 25:549 Sound reason is more difficult to determine than its artificial use. Sound reason has certain maxims. The maxim of sound reason is as follows: not to accept as valid any other rule in its use than this, [the one] whereby the most universal use of reason is possible, and whereby its use is facilitated. Every nature maintains itself; hence reason also maintains itself, if it does not admit any other rule than such whereby its use is possible. Therefore all wonders and stories about the appearances of spirits and ghosts nullify the use of reason. However, since as it is, reason preserves itself, it thus does not permit that whereby its use is nullified. If it thus were to be assumed that spirits, as beings whose nature we do not at all know, carry on their play in this world and had an influence on us, then the use of reason would cease. In order that this does not therefore happen, sound reason thus rejects such. This is not a theoretical proposition, but a maxim of reason. It would be a theoretical proposition, if reason wanted to settle that there are no such wonders, but as it is, it is a maxim never to appeal to such wonders, [whether] these may exist or not, because otherwise every old woman could put an end to the use of reason by means of such stories of wonders and sorceries. For example, old women thus say of hydrocephalus that it has been foisted on children by spirits, although there are natural causes, since in the case of a few children one finds water which has gathered together under the brain;

---

[a] *kleine*   [b] *fordern*

thus also of the werewolf. *Wehr*[a] is virtually the same as war. In war it has often happened that wolves devoured people on the battlefield. Since they have now become accustomed to human meat, they have also often attacked people and pulled them down, from which the delusion has now originated, that there exists a kind of human being who devours other human beings, and which one then calls werewolves. If one now grants such, that things of this kind exist, then no use of reason is possible whatsoever. Epicurus said: one should not appeal either to gods, or spirits, or anything whatever. Thereby he did not mean to say that he denied such, as if these sorts of things do not exist, but that when one assumes such, one then takes a step beyond the limits of the use of reason.

25:550

Sound reason thus has maxims and speculative reason has rules. Through its maxims, sound reason directs our judgments. Therefore if people tell ghost stories, [and they are people] to whom one cannot prove that no ghosts could exist, then they tell stories which are more nonsensical still, and harm one thereby, since they are telling yet more, which is still more preposterous. Hence in this connection, one must conduct oneself this way, that one does not accept the stories whatsoever on account of the use of reason. Only under such a condition, can reason thus preserve itself, since if such wonders were presupposed, then this is a destruction of reason.

Many things are so constituted, that one can cognize them only exclusively through reason, thus not by means of the understanding. True, there are many things which one cognizes by means of reason, but also by means of the understanding from experience, where then the cognition through reason is more distinct; yet there are many things which can only be cognized solely through reason. These are such [things] where reason provides the idea as the basis, for example, virtue. True, I cognize it through common and sound reason, yet it is still through reason. Experience indeed gives us examples of virtue, yet I must still have the concept to judge such. For all cases of cognition, where it is a question not of how something is, but how it ought to be, there reason is always necessary, since reason indicates how things must be, but experience only how they are. Therefore if I speak about government or education, how it is, then only experience is needed for that, but if I say how it

25:551

ought to be, then reason is necessary for this. The cognition of things which is the model, according to which something is to be arranged, it is this cognition which is the idea. Accordingly there are many cognitions for which ideas lie at their basis. The idea is therefore different from experience; it is found in reason and not in experience. Hence it is false to say, a virtuous man, but [one should say] one who pursues the idea of

---

[a] Arms, also (as verb), to defend or resist. The play on words here refers to the German spelling of *Wehrwolf*.

virtue in a way so as to be equal to it. Plato says that the most important work of the philosopher is to develop the idea.[35] This faculty of
devising something according to an idea is reason. Reason can produce
ideas for itself of its vocation,[a] of its limits of its use. This cognition of
its sphere is the architectonic use of reason. The technical use of reason
thus consists only in the execution, but not in the design of plans. All
of the difference between the *artificer of reason and the one making the
law* of human reason *known*[b] is based on this. Here the difference is just
like the one between a surgeon and a doctor. The latter has the idea
which the surgeon carries out. Thus the mathematician and physicist is
an artificer of reason. The one making the law of human reason known is
a philosopher in the true sense.[c] The latter must draw up the first bases
and have insight into the highest rules and principles of the vocation
of reason and its limits, and that is the philosopher. This name is thus
also only an idea, which one must endeavor to equal. We can indeed
well have insight into laws and rules, but to have insight into the spirit
of the rule and the domain of the use of reason is something entirely
different. Therefore the more he reflects upon the vocation of human
reason, the more the individual approximates the philosopher. Reason   25:552
is further a faculty of cognition from concepts. Different people have a
use of reason on the occasion of intuition, but not from pure concepts,
which is the pure use of reason. Those having insight into something
according to analogy by means of images, have a use of reason, but not
from concepts. It seems that for a large part of the human race, nature
has failed them with regard to the faculty of judging from concepts. All
Oriental peoples belong to this part. From this it follows that with them
the whole of morality cannot be pure, because it must be cognized from
concepts. The pure moral concept is lacking in their morality, hence in
their case nothing can arise from the principle of morality. The desire
for honor of the Oriental people is completely different from the desire
for honor of the people of the Occident. With the latter, the concept
of honor is a true concept, but the Oriental people sought their honor,
for example, in authority, thus from sensibility and not from concepts.
Even in architecture, a concept must lie at the basis, if it is to have taste
and the complete approval of our soul. Thus buildings in the Orient are
indeed rich in gold and precious stones, but they do not originate from
any idea, any plan of the whole. The Orient is the land of sensation,
but the Occident of sound and pure reason. The merit of the Occident
is to judge determinately through concepts; therefore this advantage of
Occidental talent must not be ruined by analogies and images, for it
would otherwise be the degeneration of Occidental taste. There is a big

[a] *Bestimmung*   [c] *Verstande*
[b] *Vernunftkünstlers, Gesetzkundigen*

difference between the kind-heartedness of the Oriental people and the uprightness of the Occidental people. Kind-heartedness also takes place without concepts. It arises solely from sympathy, yet such a kind-hearted person also often becomes exhausted. Therefore this kind-heartedness lacks a concept, that indeed in all cases which one encounters, one nevertheless be kind-hearted, and this is uprightness. The Oriental people lack this and are also not capable of it. Therefore all people who are incapable of the concepts, but who play with intuitive images of spirits which are metaphorical, degenerate into fanaticism.

25:553   One avails oneself of irrationality in the practical [sphere]. Thus irrationality is a procedure in accordance with practical rules. Foolish is contrary to reason in speech and expression. With people one often finds a misology, or hatred for reason. Lack of reason is indeed nothing unusual, but not misology. It arises out of reason's futile effort. It is an attribute of thoughtful persons, who conduct investigations into their future vocation and chief purposes, which finally end in this, that the individual gains insight into his ignorance.[36] If reason just cannot fulfill knowledge, if it cannot satisfy the individual in this, if it deserts him in this, so that the individual cannot foresee the goal and end of all things, then the individual resorts to simplemindedness, and renounces reason altogether, just as someone becomes a misanthrope due to the sensation of virtue, not because he despises people, but because he does not find them to be how he wants them to be. As for the rest, he wishes them all well. Thus one also does not become a misologist out of hatred for reason, indeed one values it, but because it does one a disservice, one thus renounces it. If, however, someone has already gotten into the habit of making use of reason, then it is futile to free oneself from it; who already has a propensity thereto, reflects all his life. Misogyny, or hatred of women, occurs in the same way. It also arises from an ill humor, not because one despises them, but because one does not find in them what one believes, thus from an entirely too great a demand for their perfections. A suitor deceived by a coquette becomes a misogynist. A hatred of reason is also found in the case of those who have no capacity of reason, and these are fanatics. There exist fanatics of religion and of taste. Just because they are incapable of the use of reason, they thus despise those who have this capacity.

As for what concerns the sickness of reason, one notices that both in regard to the understanding and also reason, and all the powers of mind, there exists a sickness, first an indisposition, then sickness, and finally infirmity. The mind becomes well disposed through many circumstances. Thus sleep produces a revolution in the disposition[a] of the

---

[a] *Disposition*; see the footnote (25:504) regarding the difference with the term *Gesinnung* (also translated, in accordance with convention, as "disposition").

human mind, and the palingenesis or regeneration[a] of the human mind occurs in us every night. We regard night as an interval between morning and the immediately following day. Hence we can be differently disposed on the following day, than on the previous one. Thus the mind is more disposed in the morning than in the evening, because it is then not yet so fatigued. The disposition of the mind is in fact very variable from one day to another, indeed from one hour to another. The disposition of the mind takes its bearings especially in accordance with the occasion and the circumstances. Thus one is perhaps ill disposed for deep reflection when one comes from a comedy. One becomes disposed when one recovers self-control from a great distraction and devastation of the mind, or goes from difficult work to agreeable company. The sicknesses of the mind can be twofold. They consist in the weakness and the disturbance of the powers of mind. Thus one often cannot use one's memory because it has been weakened by much grief. The powers of mind can, however, be disturbed, for example by a high fever. But because these are sicknesses which one has contracted, they can thus just as well be remedied, as sicknesses of this kind in the body.

25:554

Infirmity of the mind is just such a crippled state of mind, as infirmity of the body is a crippled state for the body. Infirmities are not hindrances of the powers of mind, but a lack, but the latter exists when the condition for the regular use of the powers of mind is lacking. Idiocy and madness concern the defects of the understanding, about which we already dealt previously. However, lunacy is also an upside down state with regard to the use of reason, and is based on the wrongness of false inferences. Insanity is also an upside down state of the use of reason, and exists when one maintains false principles in the common use of reason, for example, one believes oneself to have invented something.

THE PECULIAR CHARACTERISTIC[b] OF EVERY HEAD

The head is the sum of all powers of cognition, just as the heart is the sum of all powers of desire. The peculiar characteristic of the head depends on the proportion of the powers of mind. If someone is to be beautiful, it is not based on the size of the individual, but on the proportion of his limbs. Every face has something peculiar, whereby it can be distinguished from all others, and its beauty rests on the proportion of its parts. The matter stands exactly the same also with the mind. The peculiar characteristic of the head is based on the proportion of its powers. One often hears complaining about the ingenuity many lack, yet if the individual is to acquire more ingenuity, then he would also have to have more understanding, since one power certainly cannot be increased, and the other

25:555

---

[a] *Wiedergeburt*, literally "rebirth."   [b] *Das eigentümliche*

not, for then there would be no proportion, in just the same way as if one part in the face were to be enlarged and the other not. Therefore it is a great defect if one has more ingenuity than understanding. The understanding is then too weak to keep ingenuity within limits. Thus one also often wishes to have a lot of memory, but then one would also have to possess more power of judgment, since a lot of memory and little power of judgment produces a complete fool. Either all powers would have to be enlarged, or everything must remain as it is, since otherwise the proportion is taken away. However, if all powers of the mind were to be altered, then one would not be the same human being. Therefore everyone must be satisfied with his powers. True, one is dissatisfied with an individual, for example with students with few powers, but not with his powers; but one must be satisfied with the latter. Accordingly a large nose is never too big for the face in which it is found. If the individ-ual would have a small nose, then there would be no proportion, which one has often perceived, when persons who lost their large nose, had a small one made and attached. Therefore in education, one must not be particular about the magnitude of the powers, but about the suitable*ᵃ* proportion of the cast of mind; hence it must not be the case that memory alone is cultivated and the power of judgment is neglected, just as little as one must cultivate ingenuity alone and not the understanding. Yet this is still a problem. One can indeed see how it should happen, namely memory should be cultivated first, so that the power of judgment and

25:556 understanding would have subject matter, but then one would have to cultivate the understanding more than reason, because it is more needed, and ingenuity [is] only [needed] to a slight degree. Yet the rule is lack-ing in order to determine the proportion of cultivation. In the human mind, natural aptitude, talent and genius are to be distinguished. The difference between natural aptitude and talent is this. Natural aptitude is a capacity of mind, but talent is a gift of mind. Natural aptitude is the aptness to grasp something, but talent to produce something. The facility to be cultivated is natural aptitude, but talent [is the facility] in order to invent something; for example, memory is part of natural apti-tude. The difference between talent and genius is: talent is the degree of the powers of mind, whereby something can be produced, when instruc-tion precedes. However, genius is a talent which cannot be a product of instruction. Genius dispenses with all instruction and replaces all art. What belongs to genius is all innate, and thus is contrary to art. A work of instruction is art. However, genius is a creative talent, that is, to pro-duce something without any guidance, without any rule. Therefore it is freedom from the guidance of the rule. Genius is free of rules because it needs none; hence people who are no geniuses, and yet want to be taken

---

ᵃ geschickte: literally, "skillful"

as such, abandon the rules, in order to try to give themselves the reputation of genius. However, the rules retain their value. Whoever is not a genius must not dare to abandon them. Genius cannot be produced. We find cognitions which cannot be produced through any instruction, for example, composing, good penmanship. It is true one can arouse genius, but one cannot produce genius out of talent, since it is not a product of instruction. Thus one cannot teach anyone philosophy, but can arouse his genius for philosophizing; there it becomes apparent whether he has genius or not. Philosophy is a science of genius. Mathematics, however, can be learned through instruction. In it, one's talent can be so perfected by instruction, that in accordance with the guidance of the rules of mathematics, one can invent many things in it. However, one cannot learn to invent a new method through any instruction. Therefore one must invent method from within oneself, for there is no method in order to invent in turn a method. Spirit[a] and genius are also to be distinguished. One has genius without spirit, and spirit without genius. Spirit is a particular attribute of talent. It is based on this, that the mind is animated   25:557 by it, since spirit is the basis of animation. In chemistry, water is the phlegm and alcohol[b] the spirit. Who has the talent to animate, has spirit, for example, [to animate] a social gathering by conversation. A book has spirit, when the reading of it animates. A book can indeed instruct, but not animate. Animating is in all products, for example, in paintings; it has no life, but it has an animation. To animate the products of the understanding is therefore spirit. One often perceives spirit in conversation. Such a person is not a genius, but he has the particular attribute [of being able] to animate, to provide all at once a new impulse. Ingenuity is not always spirit. Spirit is the indescribable in all products. Genius must have spirit; often, however, persons have spirit and no genius. We can differentiate talent as the talent of imitation and as creative talent, and the latter is genius. It takes genius for the invention of sciences, natural aptitude for learning them, and talent for teaching such also to others. All the literary arts[c] are sciences of the genius, poet, sculptor, painter. For copying, however, it only takes talent, since all these items cannot be attained through instruction. Geniuses are rare; that is, something is not invented every day. If something were invented every day, then discovery would not be rare, but something usual. Average genius is a contradiction, this is then only a talent. Genius must always be something extraordinary. Genius is not subject to the compulsion of the rule, but a model for the rule, for we can learn rules, but genius cannot be learned. However, because everything which is produced must after all be

[a] *Geist*
[b] *Spiritus*
[c] *schöne Wissenschaften*

orderly,^a thus genius must be in keeping with the rule; if it is not in keeping with the rule, then one must be able to make a rule out of it itself, and then it becomes a model. Thus, for example, the geniuses of antiquity, Homer, Cicero, are models, and their products are models from which rules can be abstracted. The state of imitation is contrary to genius, just as the awkward observance of rules is also contrary to genius; hence too, mechanism, or proficiency in producing something according to rules, is contrary to genius. Therefore if a certain mechanism is introduced into instruction, then genius is thereby suppressed. This is the failing of all

25:558 our schools, and the reason why few geniuses come out of them. The introduction of mechanism first makes genius dispensable, and finally even causes it to be forfeited. It is true that a certain mechanism is at first necessary in all our cognitions, for example, in history and geography. However, one must procure a free exercise for talent; then genius manifests itself. Mechanism arises out of habit, habit first produces facility, and afterwards necessity. There also exist faulty habits, for example, in writing, in playing, which are very difficult to break. Involuntary habit is a habituated way.^b Someone has a head [for something] to the extent he is inclined to one or another cognition. Thus one finds a talent for mathematics, physics, and so forth. This is the subject's skill in one or another science. Thus one has an empirical, another a speculative head. Would propensity and talent for something be together in one mind? It would be good if it were, but unfortunately it is not. Propensity aims for something else than talent [does]. Thus the individual likes to occupy himself with what is in keeping with his propensity, but not with his talent. He only occupies himself with talent when he must. If both are united, then there is still the question as to whether genius then exists. Genius is admittedly not always needed. It takes a lot to examine what is required for a mathematical, philosophical, physical,^c [or] musical head, but it would be of a great deal of use. For the same thing just does not belong to one talent, as belongs to another. Thus the mathematical talent is very different from the philosophical one, since the one cognition is intuitive, the other discursive. However, for a complete talent it does not so much take the degree of cognition, as the proportion of its powers and their schooling.

With this we have concluded the first part of the psychological considerations, namely of the faculty of cognition. Now follows the second faculty of the soul, namely the feeling of pleasure and displeasure, whereupon the third faculty will then follow, namely the faculty of desire.

---

^a *regelmäßig*
^b *Unwillkührliche Gewohnheit ist Angewohnheit.* The two terms are essentially synonyms (both meaning "habit"), but someone's "ways" may also be referred to as *Angewohnheiten.*
^c *physischen*, undoubtedly in context referring to the physicist's head.

The second source of the phenomena of the soul is the feeling of pleasure and displeasure, of approval and disapproval, of being pleased and displeased. This faculty must be carefully distinguished from the faculty of cognition.

To cognize something and to be pleased with something are two different things. I can have a representation of something, but the effect which things have on the whole of the mind, is the faculty of pleasure and displeasure. The feeling of the hindrance of life is pain or displeasure. 25:559

The feeling of the promotion of life is enjoyment or pleasure. Life is the consciousness of a free and regular play of all the powers and faculties of the human being. The feeling of the promotion of life is what pleasure is, and the feeling of the hindrance of life is displeasure. There can be an enjoyment which diminishes life, but increases the feeling. The feeling of animation is enjoyment. When the blood and animal spirits are set into powerful motion, and when the sensation is more intense on one spot, then this feeling is an enjoyment, although life is itself thereby impeded. In this way the hindrance of life can also be slight and the pain great, and the hindrance of life can be great, and the pain slight; for example, a fine cut is no great hindrance of life, but the pain is great, and damage to the lung is a slight pain, but a great hindrance of life. The cause of this is that where the nerves are not sensitive, there the pain is also not great, but in the hand the nerves have the most intense sensation; hence, the pain in it is also very great. Pain is not related to the proportion of ill, but the proportion of the feeling of ill. Often something which nature has adapted for this end, has produced a feeling of great enjoyment and pain, although the former is no promotion and the latter no hindrance of life. There is [such a thing as] delight merely in the enjoyment of life, without being sensible of the cause which promotes life. Pain is the feeling of hindrance at one place of life. If one feels the whole sum of life, and removes the pain from it, then there is more feeling of enjoyment than hindrance of life. According to this people would rather endure pain than give up their whole life. However if the pain exceeds the whole sum of life, and makes us unable[a] to feel the enjoyment of life, then one would rather give up one's whole life in order to get rid of the pain. Enjoyment is sensual, ideal and intellectual. Sensual enjoyments are enjoyments of the senses, which are easy to gain insight into, but the ideal enjoyments 25:560 require more clarification. They are based on the feeling of the free play of the powers of mind. The senses are the receptivity of impressions, which promote our sensible enjoyment. However, we can produce agitation in our powers of mind by means of objects, not insofar as they make an impression on us, but insofar as we think them, and these are the ideal enjoyments. They are indeed sensible, but not enjoyments of

[a] Reading *unfähig* for *unthätig*, per editors' notes.

the senses. A poem, a novel, a comedy are capable of furnishing ideal delights[a] in us; they arise from the way that the mind produces cognitions for itself out of a lot of representations of the senses. Now if the mind has a sensation of a free play of powers, then what produces this free play is an ideal enjoyment. There exists a pain which serves enjoyment, for example, in tragedy. How does this happen? We must refer to the result. All such impressions are the basis of the promotion of life. The mind which is present at such tragedies thereby becomes agitated, all the organs are thoroughly worked up; there is thus an inner motion, in accordance with which one feels well. Montaigne says: the mind contributes more to health and the promotion of life than all of medicine. If the individual is to be animated, then his mind must thus be agitated. Because this now produces a feeling, it thus delights. The play of the powers of mind must be extremely lively and free, if it is to animate. Intellectual pleasure consists in the consciousness of the use of freedom in accordance with rules. Freedom is the greatest life of the human being, thereby he exercises his activity without hindrance. Life is limited by some hindrances of freedom, because freedom is not subject to the compulsion of the rule. If this were the case, then it would not be free. Since this however brings a disorderliness[b] along with it, if the understanding does not direct this, and yet the disorderliness hinders itself, thus no freedom can please us, except for freedom subject to the rule of the understanding. This is intellectual pleasure, which is concerned with morality.

Although our enjoyments are not uniform in accordance with the objects, they can still be added together later, since they then constitute the whole of well-being, just as if they were uniform. Although these enjoyments are very different, and one is an ideal one, the other a sensual one, we still thus put them together on an equal footing and take them in one sum. The reason is: all delights relate to life. But life is a unity, and to the extent they are all directed at this, they are all uniform. The sources from which they arise may be what they will.

The delights in regard to objects can be different, namely in regard to objects of appearance and of understanding. In regard to the objects, the mind at first behaves indifferently. This indifference can arise from apathy, or from insensitivity, or from equilibrium. Insensitivity is an indifference in regard to the impression, and the indifference of equilibrium is an indifference in regard to choice. Indifference is to be distinguished from equanimity. Indifference due to insensitivity is stupidity, but equanimity is an effect of strength and not of weakness; it consists in the possession

25:561

[a] *Vergnügungen*, which Kant may be using purely synonymously with *Vergnügen*. In this section the terms are translated as "delights" and "enjoyments" respectively.
[b] *Regellosigkeit*, literally "lack of rules."

of well-being irrespective of the condition of the external object, and in the consciousness of the greatness of well-being which outweighs all external circumstances. Equanimity befits philosophers. Sensitivity is the capacity of receptivity of ideal enjoyments; it is contrary to indifference, but not to equanimity.

Touchiness is a weakness, according to which the entire state of a human being is altered; for example, one gets touchy about rudeness, or if a piece of one's china gets broken.

Just as indifference is contrary to sensitivity, so equanimity is contrary to touchiness. Equanimity is actually a self-awareness[a] of a healthy soul, just as the self-awareness of a healthy body is complete health. One feels the source of life within oneself. The health of soul and of body is, of course, the greatest fortune; it is the greatest sum of pleasure and of enjoyment, a greatest sum of pleasure which one still always feels, even if there is pain. The basis for this lies in the human being himself. Who has such strength of mind, that he feels the whole sum of pleasure and of enjoyment, his enjoyment will not be increased either by new additions of enjoyment, nor distressed by some pain; such a person is not glad about the enjoyment, and is not distressed about the pain. One can have a sensation of pain and enjoyment, without being very distressed about the one, and without being very delighted about the other. People who take pleasure in every little thing are also distressed by every little thing. Well-being must thus be a certain sum, which I feel in myself, and which cannot be enormously increased by any small additions of enjoyment, nor be diminished by disagreeable matters. As has already been said, pain is not the hindrance of life, but rather the feeling of the hindrance of life. If we no longer feel our life, then this is not because no hindrance exists, but because we no longer have any feeling. Thus we also finally no longer feel a severe illness, and then death itself will not be painful because we no longer have any feeling. That death is however painful where feeling still remains. Thus it depends on how we feel the hindrance of life. But how can we keep our soul healthy? *Not through the enjoyment of all impetuous joy, not through indifference toward all ill, only through equanimity.* But whoever wants to be quite happy, must remain indifferent toward pain and pleasure; such a person feels a constant enjoyment within himself. It also depends on the body. But how is such equanimity maintained? A deliberation in the particular case cannot do it, but it must be attained by practice; hence one must begin early to express a certain equanimity. Temperament may well contribute the most to this. Since such is life that we are not master over the outcome of things, we must thus really give our mind a steady composure. In any case, human life is composed of nothing but trivialities. We indulge more in our inclination than in

25:562

[a] *Selbst Gefühl*

our true happiness. Not great ills, but the slight offenses of his hobby-horse, depress the individual. Now if one realizes that they are all only trivialities, and if one gets into the habit already early on, not to indulge

25:563 in such trivialities, then one acquires such equanimity for oneself. The most refined is indeed to maintain one's life without reproaches. If one can achieve certain honorary posts in it, so much the better. If this does not come about, that is all right too. Nothing in the world is able to offend me; for example, whether someone makes a straight or wry face toward me, whether he gives me a big or small compliment, and goes out of his way or not. However, whoever is irritated by such trivialities, always loses thereby; afterwards he is vexed with himself about the fact that he became irritated, he realizes it, yet he cannot again soon recover his former composure. In general, such trivialities and irritations harm a great deal; they rob such a person of the taste for life. Once I appreciate^a this, then with great equanimity, I can let very many things pass. If one adds to this the brevity of life, and ponders this, then every rational person will seek to enjoy the brief span of life. In this connection, since we are speaking about equanimity, we come to contemplation.

ON TEMPER^b

Temper is the state in which the individual judges things in the world in accordance with his disposition. We can carry out observations in accordance with objects, and that is a speculative observation, but we can also carry out a tempered^c one, not in accordance with objects, but so that things take on such a shape as accords with our frame of mind.^{d} According to the understanding of the French language, temper means an ill temper, where the individual is ill disposed, and also sees all people this way. There exists a sullen state of the human being, in which he takes everything to be wrong, where everything he sees displeases him, and he also believes himself to be in the right. With such a temper, the individual regards the world [as full of] fools and scoundrels. According to the understanding of the English language, temper means a humor, or a certain self disposition of the mind to judge jestingly about all things and objects and to regard everything as a game. If someone is of this

25:564 temper, then he makes a joke out of everything and that is a good temper. This temper often manifests itself with persons until the end of their life; for example Thomas More let his beard grow, because he was in

---

^{a} *vorsetzen*, literally "put this in front of me."

^{b} *Laune*, which could also be translated 'mood': derived from medieval astrology and the term for phases of the moon and their purported influence on the attunement of mind. "Temper" in the sense of "frame of mind" seems to capture Kant's meaning better than "mood" in this section as a whole.

^{c} *launigte* ^{d} *wie uns der Kopf steht*

litigation with the king about it. If we adapt the German word to the French understanding, then tempered means the false and sullen. Thus the farmer says, that is a temperamental wretch,[a] namely when he is such that, in the bat of an eye, one can soon fall into quarreling with him, which one could not anticipate by his appearance. But if we adapt the German word to the English understanding, then it is a jesting temper. In this understanding [of it], temper must be voluntary. Likewise ill temper must also be voluntary; if ill temper is involuntary, then it is really a melancholy state.[b] Therefore the good, jesting temper is to be distinguished from the melancholy[c] one. The good, voluntary temper is cheerful; such a temper also pleases us in an author. However, the voluntary[d] temper can also be cheerless, namely when authors take it upon themselves to mock something in a jocular[e] [manner]. If we want to make vice sensible, then we can regard it from a melancholic,[f] angry, loathsome, and jocular cast of mind.[g] Through the melancholic cast of mind we become indignant with vice, through the angry one we find it punishable, through the loathsome one [we find it] disgusting, and through the jocular one [we find it] absurd.[h] Among these four situations of mind are two which fit best with the human frame of mind, namely the angry and jocular ones. The melancholic and loathsome situation is such a one in which the individual does not like himself. Loathing is in itself disagreeable; accordingly the rebuke of vice from the standpoint of loathing is to be eliminated. There are vices whose disapproval at all times produces loathing, and these are vices against nature; hence they are also unspeakable. Among all the sensations, loathing has no substitute,[i] because it inhibits the source of life. Sadness does not inhibit the source of life, but is a hindrance over which one must predominate. Thus bitter dishes are more likely to be edible than loathsome ones.

25:565

---

[a] *lünischer Hund*, a phrase pointing to the etymological basis of *Laune*.

[b] *Grille*   [c] *grillenhaften*

[d] Reading *unwillkürlich* as *willkürlich*, in accordance with the editors' footnote and as making most sense in the context.

[e] *launigt*: here Kant seems clearly to draw on the usual meaning of the term in the German language, i.e. prior to adaptation to French or English connotations. The German term for "peevish" or "ill-tempered" is normally *launisch* or *launenhaft*. For the remainder of this section *Laune* will be translated as "temper," but *launigt* as "jocular" (which also seems to capture the element of ridicule better than "humorous").

[f] *melancholischer*   [g] *Gemüths Art*

[h] The editors' note suggests *ungeräumt* ("cheerless") in place of *ungereimmt*; either could fit in the context, but on the following page Kant makes a similar point continuing to use "absurdity."

[i] *ist ohne Ersatz*: *Ersatz* has a range of meaning from "substitute," to "replacement," to "restitution" and it is not clear how strong a sense Kant intends here.

121

All other frames of mind, for example, anger, are agitations, thus also animations, but loathing is a suppression of agitation, and therefore no animation.

Authors reproach vice in a twofold manner, first bitter, with fault-finding, anger, and indignation toward vice, but second, jocular, where they show the absurdity of vice. Such a portrayal of vice must be observed in society. For example, one tells about a mean prank; this must thus not take place with disgust, as the same actually merits, but it must be jocularly ridiculed. One can laugh about it, and still be disgusted by it, and such a portrayal is by far better able to arouse disgust in us against vice than the bitter one. One can read Fielding's *Tom Jones* for this.[37] Everything which disturbs the mind's disposition is disagreeable in society. Hence one must prevent such, and for this reason be jocular and even-tempered about all misfortune and pain. What could cause disagreeable sensations in society, must be jocularly told, for the sensation remains after all in any case, without one arousing it. Jocular authors are peerless also in morality, for even the greatest crime has its farcical side, and it is also possible to portray the greatest crime jocularly; in the end it will no doubt appear sad. One can exhort temper and put oneself in the frame of mind[a] to look at everything as a joke and to make a joke out of everything.

Even in laughter and in temper, the English authors retain the most proper sentiments. It would be desirable for the Germans to imitate the English in this. They are skilled for this; although they do not have such a touching wit, nevertheless despite all temper they do have a rational judgment. In general, everything can be presented in a temper, morality and so forth, except, for the sake of propriety in the pulpit, it would not be fitting for the preacher. For, basically considered, all human actions are a game and full of folly. Someone may wrap himself in ever so earnest a robe, nevertheless when he comes home and into a social setting, he is again the comical man; if he is earnest, then he is certainly playing a false role. Therefore it is also best to get at him on this side.

To the meaning of the expression "temper" which is customary, also appertains still another state of human beings, in which nothing can give them enjoyment, where it is true that no pain due to particular causes affects them, but where they are still incapable of any taste, neither of joy nor of pain. This is a state of [having a] loathing for boredom, it is a state of the melancholic[b] temper. The individual is annoyed that he is bored, that nothing can entertain him, that he finds no taste for anything, whatever various things he might take up; thus everything

---

[a] The editors' footnote suggests *Verfassung* in place of *Gesellschaft* and, in context, *Verfassung* fits better.
[b] *grillenhaften*

becomes a matter of loathing for him. But how does this loathing of boredom arise? The soul here has a horror of the vacuous. The mind is empty, it has no taste for anything, nothing plagues it except empty space, the soul despises this state. Nature is disgusted by such an empty state and the dissatisfaction arises from this. This dissatisfaction extends so far that people also hate their life. Life itself becomes a burden for them. Thus an Englishman hangs himself in order to pass the time. Thus Lord Mordaunt shot and killed himself, in order to see how it looks after all in the other world, since there was nothing more to be done here than to dine and to go courting, and that day in and day out.[38] This is not natural for a human being. If only nothing plagues him, the human being can naturally always be cheerful,[a] even if he is devoid of thoughts and sensations, in the way savages are who can sit all day with a fishing rod by the water. But who has already once aroused[b] his powers of mind, always wants entertainment. But how does this empty and insipid state arise? In the civilized frame of mind, where the mind has already once been aroused, this state arises for two reasons, either that 25:567 sensation is weakened through intense impressions, or that the diversity[c] is exhausted due to far too great a rumination about enjoyments. Just as, in regard to the enjoyment of food and drink, one always helps oneself first to the mild ones, but after that always takes stronger drinks, until finally even these are too weak for us, for example, first poor brandy, or sweet wine, or sweet-smelling tobacco. The more the intensity of the sensation increases however, the stronger the tonics[d] to which one helps oneself, until finally the spirituous brandies make no impression on one's sensitivity. It thus happens likewise with the human being's enjoyment,[e] when the individual at last savors the most intense enjoyments, this way he exhausts all enjoyment and no enjoyment makes an impression on his sensitivity. This is due to our nervous system. When the nerves are overstrained, then in the end they become very weak; this way a far too great a joy is capable of killing an individual, and indeed even more likely than intense distress, for with joy, the individual gives himself entirely over to it, and he bears[f] the entire impression on his nerves. In the case of distress however, he somewhat takes a position. In England, one deduced[g] from an obituary that more people died due to joy than distress. Therefore if one has savored the delights of life to the point of their most spirituous degree, then the nerves at last become dull and nothing stirs them any longer. On the other hand there exist excogitated and studied enjoyments according to all [manner of] diversity. If someone

---

[a] *vergnügt*
[b] *in Bewegung gesetzt*
[c] *Mannigfaltigkeit*
[d] *Mittel*
[e] Reading *Vergnügen* in place of *Vermögen*, per editors' note.
[f] *empfängt*, literally "receives."
[g] *aus ... gesehen*

now even devotes himself to the study of enjoyments, and can no longer produce any new diversity, and contrive nothing more, then he sinks into an empty space of enjoyments. Then he lives and has no taste for life. It has already been said earlier, and will again be reminded, that enjoyment and pain can be in the senses and in the mind. They should be in sense, but not in the mind. We ask a man who has a sensation of pain in his senses not to allow such to pass into the mind. If the individual gives himself over to such impressions, then the pain or enjoyment passes into the mind. For this reason the human being is capable of fortune and misfortune,[a] of which animals are not capable. Fortune must not, then, be diminished by a single impression. For example, one imagines a wealthy man, whose servant due to carelessness has broken a goblet, who immediately flares up over it and is furious, as if the greatest misfortune had happened to him; there really are people who get sick because of it and have to take drugs.[b] This man might want to bear in mind that on the whole it makes no difference whether he has one goblet more or less, and how many people there are who have none such at all and still live happily; then he would not diminish his fortune through such an impression. People who become impatient in the face of adversity[c] are spoiled. People who complain about misfortune, do so only because they have always been fortunate. If they had been unfortunate more often, they would also have learned to endure such. That being so, it is very wise if God sends some adversities to human beings; they then learn to endure such and will not become immediately impatient with every little incident. The main thing is always to keep the impressions away from the mind, except not in [the case of] the moral; there one must consciously bear all one's offenses in mind.[d] How would it be, if an individual were of so staunch a soul, that he would take nothing to heart, in the way other tenderhearted souls [do] when they have played a roguish prank on someone.

Delights are entertaining and animating. To the first belongs, for example, reading books, for which university instruction makes [us] skilled. The sciences are thus greatly entertaining. Sensible occupations, too, for example, drawing, painting, music, optical arts, garden arts, are

25:568

---

[a] *Glück, Unglück*: here (as elsewhere) Kant seems to use these terms as synonyms for "happiness/unhappiness"; to keep them distinct, they are translated as "fortune/misfortune."

[b] *Pulwer*

[c] *Wiederwärtigkeit*, literally "offensiveness," but here and below "adversity" seems to fit the context better.

[d] *zu Gemüthe ziehen*; Kant later draws an explicit distinction between *zu Hertzen nehmen* (take to heart) and *zu Gemüte ziehen*, rendered here as "consciously bear in mind," but in the next sentence as "take to heart."

25:596

a source of a lot of diversions[a] for the mind. However, there also exist delights which are animating. The mind cannot be at rest long, but it must receive a new impetus. Social gatherings which constitute essential enjoyment are a part of this, and are a veritable medicine for the mind; further [examples are] comedies and music, dance, cards and gambling:[b] with every game, the mind is there in a new situation, since each one[c]   25:569 brings some interest with it, either the advantage in winnings, or honor, and so forth. Thus one first has hope, then one makes a call,[d] then one doubts, and then one hopes again. When the play becomes clear,[e] then one is glad. In such a way, the mind is intensely agitated.[f] Finally, when the game has ended, the mind is of a completely different composure and everyone is cheerful after the game, both the winner as well as the loser. But to the extent this is not the case, it has not then been an entertaining or animating enjoyment.

One also calls the entertaining enjoyments calm, and the animating ones heady. In company which is animated, everyone wants to talk, and the more such occurs, the more animated and heady is the social gathering. The next day, the individual is completely animated. Whoever has crude sensitivity, is fond of noisy delights, for example, dinner music, which always already betrays an individual with crude sensations, for with dinner music all entertaining and animating delights cease. Delights tire [one] out, and in the end the powers are wanting; therefore they also need recuperation. The fountains of life must draw a new supply; hence the one who has been for two days in society, gladly stays home on the third day in order to recuperate. Some enjoyments are intermittent, and others are uninterrupted and continual enjoyments. The continual ones are, for example, a meal in a social gathering, both according to taste and the conversation. This enjoyment can last a long time and be repeated every day without exhaustion or loathing. [A] further [example is] social intercourse. Reading is also a continual enjoyment. Intermittent enjoyments are, for example, music, the hunt; there time is needed until the old impression disappears. Thus amusements,[g] which effect a greater agitation and motion of the mind than manual work, are intermittent enjoyments. One sees, for example, a cheerless person on a horse. By riding he will not be as cheered up as through a game. There exist

---

[a] *Unterhaltungen*: elsewhere, *unterhalten/Unterhaltung* has been translated as "entertain/entertainment" in this section.

[b] *Spiel*: the use of the term seems more specific in this context, given Kant's further description, than simply "play(ing)." It is translated as "gambling," "game" and "play" (meaning one move in a game) in this paragraph.

[c] *daßelbe*, literally "the same."

[d] *macht einen Anschlag*

[e] *sich aufklärt*

[f] *starck in Bewegung gesetzt*

[g] *Spiele*

enjoyments in foretaste and aftertaste.[a] For example, the palate finds agreeableness in foretaste, but not in aftertaste. We soon grow tired of such enjoyments which are agreeable in foretaste, but not in aftertaste, but such ones which are bitter in foretaste and agreeable in aftertaste, are

25:570 retained. Thus one drinks first wine with sugar, but afterwards the sour one.[b] Likewise one has enjoyment in aftertaste due to a comedy which ends well; one gets an idea and in the end realizes that it was well thought through, and then it delights. This way a comedy can please in its action, but in the end one does not get what one was looking to get hold of. There are social gatherings which please more in aftertaste than in fore-taste, and in such ones prevailed a spirit, which we do not immediately perceive in it, but are sensible of later. This way a witty idea[c] delights in aftertaste, when one afterwards realizes what it contains. Thus there are persons who please better in aftertaste, others however in foretaste. Travelers all please better in foretaste. The enjoyment of the sex drive also often pleases this way; for example, with a groom more in foretaste, he imagines the enjoyment to be greater than he later finds it. Enjoyment in pleasure discloses the measure of sensation. Enjoyment in aftertaste arises from reflection about the sensation of what preceded. For exam-ple, when the comedy lets out, then everyone does a recapitulation; if it pleases in aftertaste, then this is the true measure of the enjoyment. Likewise enjoyment of society in aftertaste is also true enjoyment. Thus the Russian says: one receives the stranger according to his dress, but when he leaves, one judges him according to his conduct. The conclu-sion of each thing decides about the entire judgment which is aroused in us. The conclusion of a social gathering, of a comedy, or of a speech, must however be certain, because it is that in accordance with which we assess the whole, and through which aftertaste is aroused. Thus the writer of rhyme[d] produces the last rhyme first in thought, with which he afterwards rhymes the first [one]. Such verses are very noticeable, since the word in the second verse fits so precisely, as if it were a [piece] of great luck, that it rhymes so precisely with the first one; yet it after all consisted in the poet's art, who already had the last verse first in his thoughts. It is this way also in society. It would ill please us, if we would be first well received in it, and in the end the host would be sullen. It is

25:571 also likewise in fate, one prefers first to endure the adversities and at last the best, since such produces an aftertaste. Thus it is also more painful[e] if

---

[a] Reading *Vorschmack* as *Vorgeschmack* and *Nachschmack* as *Nachgeschmack*.

[b] Unless Kant intends for the latter to mean a dry wine (which would normally be expressed as *trocken* and not *sauer*) and one more agreeable than a sweet wine, this would of course exemplify the order of enjoyment which he has designated as tiring.

[c] *Einfall*   [e] *empfindlicher*

[d] *Reim Dichter*

a merchant goes bankrupt at an advanced age. Therefore it matters that the entertaining [part] comes at the end. Hence it is good if one is prepared for enjoyment through [the fact] that the arduous things precede; all novels are written this way. In tragedy however, the pain is indeed last. The outcome[a] in tragedy also does not please us. All delights in the end converge in well-being; therefore we need all impressions, tragic, comic, melancholic. Now it makes a difference whether the human being needs such treatment, such anguish of the heart, such agitation of mind. If all this is salutary for him, then the piece pleases him. Tragedy displeases one whose body does not however require such agitations; therefore young people like to see tragic pieces and old people like to see comic pieces, where they have much to laugh about, which is very strange, that age likes to laugh and youth likes to see something tragic.

One could make it a subject of reflection, how things are with adolescent life, that such is in keeping with it. Youth must exercise all its organs and indeed in a good number of ways, in order that the organs can manifest[b] themselves in a good number of ways. Hence young people also like to be mischievous, which is a natural impulse. Since with past representations the agitation of the mind is too weak, but youth must have intense agitations of the mind, hence the tragic pleases them. However, with young persons these impressions also do not stick for long in their minds; true [they stick] in memory, but not in sensation.

There exist delights with which, upon their prolongation, one gets fed up; for example, magic, [or] witty ideas. On the other hand there exist enjoyments with which one does not get fed up upon their prolongation, and through whose repetition one does not get weary. Intellectual enjoyments belong to these, for example [taking pleasure] in the sciences.

Not only sense, but also reason appertains to the estimation of the result of the influence and effect which pain and enjoyment have on the whole of well-being. Thus it badly becomes a sober man to enjoy himself over, or to be distressed about, trifles which have no influence on his entire fortune or misfortune. One can in the end abandon reason, and estimate the worth of a thing not according to the proportion of the entire well-being or prosperity, but in and for itself. This way a wealthy man, just as well as another one, will have misgivings about buying something which serves enjoyment and amenity and, for example,

25:572

---

[a] *Begebenheit*, literally "occurrence"

[b] *sich auswickeln*: literally, unwrap (or uncover) themselves. Kant's terminology here resonates with his account of *Anlagen* and *Keime* elsewhere (e.g. his essays on Enlightenment and on the human race). In the face of varying stimuli, these aptitudes and germs are described as being unwrapped, their outer covering peeled back to reveal and make possible the development of powers lying within.

costs already more than 10 thalers. Although in proportion to the wealth of the rich man, the 10 thalers amount to a negligible trifle, yet the rich man thus estimates this extravagance not in relation to his entire wealth, but in and for itself according to the needs, namely that for this money he could have something more essential. Thus the correct estimation of the thing in comparison with the whole of well-being is very rare. All the absurdities which human beings commit are due to this, when they allow the sum and not reason to estimate; for example, if rich people have lost 1,000 thalers, then they fret a great deal, which they surely would not do, *if they had not had the thalers, if* they had not been so rich. They thus value the 1,000 thalers in themselves and not according to the proportion of their entire wealth.

If the possession of well-being is great, then its decrease to a slight degree is more disagreeable*[a]* than a slight degree of well-being, if one is already accustomed to it, and the increase of my well-being produces a greater degree of enjoyment, than if one had already long savored a greater degree of well-being. What the individual reckons with for the means of his well-being, he no longer has much sensation of; he only counts the increase and decrease of his well-being. For example, if someone received an inheritance of 10,000 thalers, and he loses 1,000 thalers of it, then the pain is greater than if he had only inherited half of this money, namely only 5,000 thalers. And a servant does not count his regular income as his means to increase his wealth, but only the increase, the augment through chance and gifts. Accordingly everyone must make such arrangement in his life, that he can always advance in his life, and not accustom himself to such enjoyment and things with which it is painful to part. It is good to deny oneself much during youth, since one can then always advance, and well-being can increase, for a certain
25:573 curtailment is more painful than the still slighter degree of well-being to which one is accustomed. Hence favorites are ungrateful toward their benefactors, since they already add it to the means of their well-being, and are not sensible of the good granted to them, because they regard this as something constant; they only count the augmentation of this well-being. Since, as it is, no increase is possible in such a circumstance, but on top of that decrease occurs, they thus complain about fate, and feel the slight decrease.

Moreover, one can provide a diversion for someone in the sensation of his pain. For example, if a merchant has lost his only son, which affects him very painfully, one can thus tell him that this pain were not as great, than if his ship had sunk in the sea with his entire fortune.*[b]* If he now

---

[a] Reading *unangenehmer* for *unangenehm*

[b] *Vermögen*, otherwise translated as "wealth" in this section (to keep the distinction with *Glück*).

realizes this, and the news comes that his ship arrived safely, then with the joy of the second case, he overcomes the first pain. Thus one grief[a] can be dispelled by another one, and if the second one is over, then the first one also disappears. The mind can thus be interrupted in the attention which it gives to something, through another object by which it is made more attentive.

Slight vexations and annoyances make one more impatient than great ills, and one is more likely to be resigned in a great misfortune than in a slight annoyance. The reason is: against the slight adversities, the mind does not muster its entire might to resist these; it does not arm[b] itself with all its powers against the slight adversities, because it has little regard for them and does not take them to be worth its while to oppose them. If we are however confronted with a great ill, then one consoles oneself in the face of it with all one's might and all one's powers, and therefore it is more likely to be bearable. Thus it depends on the mind's armament. Where it is thus the case that bearing the ill brings us no   25:574 honor, there we also do not arm ourselves against it; yet it is all the more likely to upset us. But to bear a great ill confers more honor on us, [and] it is indeed worth[while] to oppose it; consequently it also does not upset us so much.

If people become unhappy, then we do not deplore them according to nature's meagerness, in accordance with which they would not be unhappy, but according to the degree to which they were accustomed to be sensible of fortune. For example, if someone is exiled from court and is on his country estate, then he considers himself to be very unhappy because he was accustomed to living at the court, although someone else might consider himself to be very happy, if he would have what has escaped him [altogether, namely such an estate]. If we see such an individual, then we deplore him, yet he himself must not complain about it. Enjoyments acquired by one's own efforts are more agreeable than those obtained by chance, and on the other hand, misfortune is twice as disagreeable, when we have incurred it ourselves, than when it happened by chance. For example, the cards were so good in a card game, that I had to win it; here the enjoyment is not as great than if they had been poorer and I had won the game through my skill, and on the other hand, it is more disagreeable[c] if I had lost the game due to my fault, than if I would have had to lose it according to the cards. The reason is, as soon as the result is due to my skill, then I see in myself a source of more good consequences. It is likewise also in reverse. If the misfortune came

---

[a] *Chagrin* (French)
[b] Reading *sich entrüstet* as *sich rüsten*; *Rüstung* is used five lines later and *rüsten* appears on the next page.
[c] Reading *unangenehm* as *unangenehmer*

about through my clumsiness[a] and incautiousness, then I have a source of more such ills in myself. Thus ills where one is guiltless also do not hurt as much as those where one is guilty. One hears people in misfortune complain and exclaim: I am certainly not to blame for it. But if we are to blame for it, then it pains us all the more, for then self-reproach is added to it, but if one is not to blame, then this is omitted. If one is oneself to blame, then one has a sensation of grief, but if one is not to blame, then one has no grief, but an aversion for and indignation at other persons who are supposedly to blame for it. Enjoyments or pain are sometimes assumed and even absurd. The assumed ones are [those], insofar as we 25:575 fabricate other persons for ourselves, and through fiction pass into the person of the other [individual]; this is the right of a theatrical genius to put himself in the place of other persons, but whom he is not capable of being, and who also do not adhere to him. He can just as well put himself in the place of a patriot as the worst rogue. Thus such persons must be devoid of their own [sensations] and full of sensations belonging to others. Voltaire is a master in this, he can borrow every possible sensation, but in his own person he has no sensations. This way Young[39] also was thoughtless and had a bad character. True, he built a school, but his own students had contempt for him when they buried him. But how could he teach so well? Because he himself had no sensations. The individual who has no sensations of his own, and possesses the spirit to assume others, can do such the best. If he has his own sensation, then he has no expressions and words in his control. In general poets are devoid of their own sensations. Therefore the expressed [opinion] of a porter of a director of a theatrical company, against a scholar who advised him that he might certainly want to admit such persons who had their own sensation as his actors, was quite right when he said: no actor should have his own sensations. Such borrowed sensations only produce a motion with such an individual; yet to have sensation in the place of another and 25:576 under his name, is different from immediately having a sensation with him. The latter is sympathy, it is not due to us, but is involuntary and also proper to animals. For example, when a pig is butchered, then the others scream, but with the human being it exists to a still higher degree. Thus a human being trembles when he sees someone else go under in the water, or fall through on the ice. That is not a play of sensation as [in the case of] the borrowed ones, but it is a true sensation, which is indeed ideal, since we step into his place and have a sensation with him. An object can be disagreeable, but the pain in regard to it can still please; then one calls it a sweet pain. For example, someone who has lost his beloved, gladly gives himself over to this sorrow, he finds sweetness in the midst of this pain and loves it. True, it is a contradiction to take

[a] *Ungeschicklichkeit*

pleasure in pain, for it is a pain of approval; it is noble, but it is also not advisable. If the individual gives himself over to this pain without restraint, then it is also not good.

But on the other hand, the object can in turn be agreeable and the enjoyment in it blameworthy and bitter; for example, a rich inheritance from parents or friends. The inheritance is always an agreeable object, but the enjoyment in it is blameworthy. This is bitter pleasure; also appertaining to this is when the assistant awaits the death of his superior. We also however have a pure enjoyment, where we have nothing for which to reproach ourselves.

There exists a pain due to objects, where the pain itself displeases, for example a lost inheritance; there one denies the pain because it can not be approved. Pain which turns into mournfulness always displeases. The first is natural, but not the second. It is natural to be distressed about the death, but not about the lost inheritance, because we approve of the pain.

One calls some enjoyments rational, not because of the use of reason, but they can also be enjoyments of the senses. There, not the object, but the enjoyment in the object, pleases reason; for example, travels around the world. However, the senses are only pleased by what is agreeable, the disagreeable displeases them.

The third faculty of the soul is the faculty of desire. Satisfaction with   25:577
the actuality of the object is desire. One cannot explain the desires exactly, yet to the extent it appertains to anthropology, it is then that [aspect] in the thinking being, which is the motive force in the physical world. It is the active power of the self-determination of the actions of thinking beings. This is something subtle.

We can take pleasure in objects, although the actuality of the object is [a matter of] indifference to us; for example, when we travel, and we see a house along the country road, then this can please us, although it is all the same to us that it is there [or not]. But since it is once already there, it thus pleases us. The object pleases us, but its existence can be a matter of indifference for us. Accordingly, the assessment of the object is different from the actuality of the object of existence. All desires are directed to activity, for living beings do something according to the faculty of desire, and lifeless beings do something then when they are impelled by an outside force. The involvement[a] of the desires is to determine activity.

The desires can be twofold: idle and inciting desires. The idle ones are those which have no relation to our activity, which have no involvement to determine our activity, but which are only directed to an idea. Inciting desires are the basis of determination, to make the object actual for activity, and to procure.

---

[a] *Beziehung*, literally "reference" or "relation" (also *Verhältnis*, used in the next sentence).

If idle desires exist in their most extreme degree, then they are passions. A great degree of idle desires is longing, a medium degree of the same is wish. Inciting desires carry out a determination in us, in the way applied force does with lifeless things, but nothing results from the idle ones. A desire is not idle if it is preliminary, if it is a basis which determines us to activity. But there are some which are not at all serviceable for this, but only agitate the mind, from which nothing at all results.

25:578   The more sources of activity an individual is sensible of in himself, the more his desires are inciting ones; for example, choleric individuals feel a source of activity in themselves, hence their desires are inciting ones. By contrast, with phlegmatic persons there is a great propensity for idle desires. Novels arouse idle desires in us and make us good at nursing idle desires in ourselves. They empty us and empty effort exhausts the individual, and deprives him of his intrepid spirit;[a] they make him limp and dull. But such desires which do not consist in empty wishes, but have a relation to our activity, produce an intrepid mode of thought in the case of a man, and [produce] an energetic woman, who however languishes due to novels; for example, a person has formed an ideal of a lover from the novel and thus she seeks to achieve the ideal and does not care about how she, as an energetic woman, could preside over her household.

Note: Whether being satisfied is of use then, when someone desires nothing? Such a state is a state of weariness.[b] Someone who desires infinitely much, can still be satisfied; if I am but aware that I desire nothing as a need, then I am satisfied. We do not relate everything we desire to need. For example, one desires to hear music, but if it doesn't come to pass, then one forgets about it. The enjoyment of the mind, in accordance with which need is a minimum, in accordance with which one can sustain needs through the slightest possible condition, that is the most fortunate state of contentedness, upon which satisfaction is based. Satisfaction can be twofold. One is either satisfied if one possesses what one desires, or if one does not do without that which one counts as a need. The first is the natural one and is called contentedness, the other is acquired satisfaction.

ON THE VARIABILITY[c] OF THE DESIRES

The desires are in conflict when one works against the other one. If the conflict on both sides is equal, then there is an equilibrium, however if the equilibrium is lifted on one side, then there is an imbalance. The active state, where the conflict of the desires is at an equilibrium, is indecision.

[a] *Wackerheit*
[b] *Überdrußes*: also "surfeit," but *überdrüßig* has been translated as "weary" in this section.
[c] *Veränderlichkeit*

The desires can be divided into sensible desires and desires of the 25:579 understanding. The sensible desires are desires of sensation and of impression. The desires of the understanding are desires of the effects of deliberation, and these are desires which aim at desires in general. They aim to produce in us an agreement of the desires on the whole, they aim at nothing except the state of deliberation, at the harmony of all our desires in general. Rational desires can be a wish in accordance with desires, therefore they do not come from the impression of objects, but are a wish in accordance with such desires. For example, there is no human being, who if he is a scoundrel, should not wish to become good all at once,^{a} if it just cost him no effort. This wish is a rational desire, he wishes such inclinations for himself, such desires, as others have. Here there is no object which tempts him, indeed the object of the sensible desires^b is more agreeable to him. A good-natured human being seeks to suppress the desires of impressions in himself, he directs his desires to what can put the whole faculty of desire in general into agreement with itself. For example, he likes sleep, but he forces himself and suppresses the sensible desires, and those are rational desires and refer especially to the moral. These rational desires, for example, of a scoundrel to become a good-natured human being, seem to depend on each person's will. Therefore one is wont to say to each one who wishes it, you need indeed only will it, but it is hard to have such a will.[40]

If we use the understanding for nothing except discovering [what will bring about] the satisfaction of sensible desires, then that is not yet a rational desire, but if reason establishes the purpose of the desire, then it is a rational desire. The name is therefore not derived from the means, but from the purpose. In general, rational desire is that one which we ought to desire, and not what we do desire. The sensible desires are threefold. Human [desires] which have as their object something which stirs the senses, but where the understanding prevails, for example, music. The others where the understanding does not prevail, are called brutish, 25:580 for example, hunger, and some are called bestial, where the animality in the human being conflicts with reason, where humanity is violated, for example, voraciousness,^{c} insatiability in all desires, which in a moderate degree would be animalistic, but in an insatiable [degree] are bestial. They conflict with animality^d and are called brutality.

---

^{a} Reading *auch einmahl* as *auf einmahl* per editors' note and as more likely to be Kant's meaning here.

^{b} *sinnlichen Begierden*: it would seem that *vernünftige Begierden* would be more consistent with Kant's point here.

^{c} Reading *Gefräßigkeit* for *Fräßigkeit* (also per editors' note).

^{d} The Prieger lectures have *humanität* here instead.

Propensity and inclination are to be distinguished. Propensity is the inner basis of all possible desires. For example, all savage peoples have a propensity to drink, but no inclination, because they have never yet tasted it, but if one just gives them some, then they have an inclination for it. Future desires are already prepared by a natural propensity of the human being, for example, the propensity in children for sexual love.

Predisposition[a] is the predetermination of the talent of the human being, just as the predetermination of future desires is called propensity. With children such can be discerned very artificially. The propensity may be for evil, yet from which no evil inclination need emerge, namely if the propensity is stifled. We all have a propensity for evil, but no inclination. Many misjudge[b] the propensity. With inclination one must know the object, but not with propensity. Propensity is innate, inclination is acquired through knowledge. However one can also acquire a propensity for oneself, for example for the hunt, which becomes a necessity through the habit. For example, all human beings have a propensity for laziness, only with many it is suppressed by their needs. The savage is lazy because he has no needs. Repose[c] is the frame of reference[d] of all human beings. Everyone thinks in terms of first learning something, afterwards holding an office, then taking a wife, and quietly dying, and this laziness to enjoy repose makes him hardworking. The foretaste of future repose, which is combined with amusements, is what all human beings seek. Thus all human beings have a propensity for laziness, which is only suppressed by other circumstances. Likewise age has a propensity for stinginess. Thus many states have a propensity for barbarity, if they just were not so close to one another, for proximity promotes culture.[41]

We can increase an inclination. Increase happens either through enlargement, or through multiplication. Multiplication is the refinement of the inclination. The state of the refined inclination is luxury,

25:581

---

[a] *Anlage*: "predisposition" has been the customary translation for this term, but Kant uses *Prädisposition* (e.g. Ak 6: 28n) as a description of what a *Hang* is. The term first appears in Kant's biological writings and has an active sense of a 'structuring ability' in many contexts (as Phillip R. Sloan has argued). The translation "disposition" is unsatisfactory both in light of its passive connotation which fails to convey Kant's active sense of the term and the meaning that Kant associates with "disposition"; namely, that dispositions have for their basis circumstantial causes – cultural, empirical origins – not the natural aptitudes (*Anlagen*) found in the nature of every human being (Ak 7: 286) which are themselves the very basis for the organism's response to circumstances. Further, disposition too closely connotes the sense of habit (*Gewohnheit*) which Kant also explicitly rejects – i.e. something mechanically produced through repeated actions.

[b] *verkennen*: the term can also mean to "underrate," but it is not clear whether Kant means here that we underestimate the propensity, or simply fail to know it correctly.

[c] *Ruhe*: repose seems best to capture the wide range of nuances of the German, from rest, calm, tranquility, peace, leisure, retirement, etc.

[d] *Gesichtspunkt*

134

the state of the enlarged inclination is luxuries,[a] if namely the inclination aims for the extent of [one's] abundance,[b] not for the quality, but
for the [enlarged] inclination. [The state of] luxuries is more bestial, but
luxury is already closer to refined taste. [The state of] luxuries is not the
opulence, but the amount. The avaricious person does not have enough
in amount, and for the other it is not good enough. [The state of] luxuries is therefore closer to brutality, but luxury makes the human being
soft. An author thus says: everything which makes the human being soft,
appertains to luxury, for example, riding in coaches; however, riding does
not appertain to luxury.[42]

ON THE OBJECT OF INCLINATION

We can think of two objects[c] of inclination which are completely general,
where the inclinations have no object,[d] but aim for means to satisfy the
inclinations. These are freedom and resources.[e] Freedom is a negative
resource. If I am free, then I obtain nothing thereby. One can always
be free, and still be needy. However, freedom is a negative condition
of all satisfaction of our inclination. Who is not free cannot live how he
wants,[f] but if he is free, then he can live according to his designs,[g] namely
if he presupposes different resources. Freedom is therefore esteemed,
because it is the sole condition for being able to satisfy his inclination.
For example, someone takes the responsibility for another's happiness[h]
upon himself, but in such a way that he entirely loses his freedom,[i] and
it is merely to be based on his will.[j] Everyone would be troubled by this
and could not get the thought out of his mind, to be as of tomorrow   25:582
completely subordinate to the will of another in the provision of one's
happiness, for he[k] cannot then make me happy in accordance with my
inclination. Freedom is therefore a general object to satisfy the entirety
of inclination. This is the first good which human beings wish for themselves, and yet they cannot avail themselves of it; instead [freedom] must
be limited. Still, about the misuse of freedom: for example, one must
not always infer that a former slave would misuse it, and for this reason
give him no freedom at all. He will surely learn to avail himself well

---

[a] *luxuries*   [c] *Gegenstände*
[b] *Grad des Maaßes*   [d] *Object*
[e] *Vermögen*: as Kant explains his usage of the term in this section (25:582), he means wealth
  or fortune, but not simply construed as money, but including health, honor, and riches,
  i.e. in general, "resources" or "means" (but *Mittel* is being translated as "means").
[f] *will*, assuming here the ordinary language sense of the term.
[g] Reading *Sinn* as synonymous with *Absicht* in this context.
[h] *Glück*   [i] i.e. the person being provided for
[j] i.e. the will of the person assuming responsibility
[k] i.e. the person assuming responsibility

of it, and even if in the beginning he is somewhat unhappy through its misuse, then this unhappiness due to his own fault is not too great for him. Everything good is also possible through freedom, for nothing can very well be imputed to one who is not free. Lack of freedom is not felt[a] in the way its loss is, for who has lost it, has already tasted it. However, someone who has never had it is not sensible of its lack, because it is not something positive. The loss is the inhibition of all powers. The more active a subject is, all the more is he sensible of the loss of freedom, but the more indolent one is, all the less one is sensible of it. For the active subject, freedom is therefore the main condition. In the civilized state, one [lives under] social and civil constraint. Children must be accustomed to this in their upbringing; i.e. one must discipline them. One must not, however, accustom them to renounce all freedom, for then they will not become aware of the loss, they must be determined by others, and then are not only open to external constraint, but even have need of it. Therefore a child must enjoy freedom, but in such a way that it recognizes a law, in conformity with which it acts, and yet thinks [of himself as] acting from freedom.

The second general object for satisfying all inclination taken altogether, is resources, whereby we here do not understand merely money, but a positive basis for procuring the actuality of the object for ourselves. We can best express the 3 kinds of resources by strength, means, and reputation, with which health, riches, and honor are placed parallel. Strength of the body, of the understanding, of the spirit of resolve, appertain to strength. Thus health, honor, and riches are the three kinds

25:583 of resources. Health is the possession of all the powers of life, also of the strength and might which accompanies the complete life; that is the complete health and a species of resources whereby it[b] becomes agreeable. One calls riches a resource chiefly because it gets its use from the acquisition of what can satisfy our inclination. For[c] money, one can have everything which human industry produces. Many prefer riches to health, because they believe they can also gain health through money, namely if they retain skilled doctors. However, I maintain that a complete health of body and soul is the greatest fortune, since one can then acquire everything for oneself, and one then also does not need much, for to desire something is already an illness of the soul.

The Englishman places freedom first, then honor, health, and riches, thus honor before health. The Hollander places riches in advance, because he is a merchant.

---

[a] *empfunden*
[b] Per editors' note, if *sie* should be read as *es*, then "it" refers to life.
[c] Reading *für* for *vor*

Reputation and means, or honor and riches, are resources which are determined in the society of other people, in order to satisfy an inclination. Therefore these two resources entail greater inclinations, than the resource of strength and of health, because honor and riches are determined in society, strength however is only meant for us. Society however produces a great inclination to rouse all our impulses.

Reputation or honor is either the honor of esteem, or the honor of might. By [having] the reputation of esteem, we can accomplish much which satisfies our inclination, but through the reputation of might we can compel others to satisfy our will. Human beings prefer to have a reputation [for being] commanding rather than engaging. One can claim and usurp a reputation and an advantage for oneself, so that others do not even know how one got to it. This way one can take on a pretentiousness in society and simply insist on it, thus one also achieves it. One need only adopt an authoritative tone, this way one soon acquires an advantage for oneself, and once one has already achieved it, then it is hard to take such away from him, for if many give him the advantage without knowing why, then no one dares to take it away from him, because he has so many followers; for example, Gellert.[43]

First we distinguished inclination from propensity by means of possibility and actuality. Now we want to distinguish inclination from instinct.   25:584
Both are actual desires. For instinct is a desire in accordance with an object which one does not know, inclination however is a determinate principle *to desire an object*, insofar as it is already known to me. Instincts are therefore principles of desires, which are directed to an indeterminate object; they make us acquainted with the object. We can assume two basic instincts of human nature, which are the most powerful, the instinct for nutrition and for the preservation of one's own person, and the instinct for propagation or for the preservation of one's kind. One knows that children, who are hardly born, show an instinct for nutrition, without knowing what they need, and immediately carry out the art of the physical law to suckle the breast; if they did not have the instinct, but one first had to accustom them to this, then many would perish. However, we have exactly such an instinct for the preservation of [our] kind; that is the sexual instinct. This instinct is thus directed to persons and not to things, and is the principle of the preservation of human nature, just as the first instinct is a principle of the preservation of each human being. We can see that the sexual instinct is a natural instinct by the fact that, even if they were in the monastery, when [the time of] puberty comes, persons are still disturbed by the instinct, and feel the need for an object which they do not yet know. We can call these the original instincts, which are also the strongest.

Love of life and of happiness is no special inclination, but the general condition of the satisfaction of all inclinations.

However, there exist drives[a] which are derived from these original basic instincts,[b] for example, the drive for one's safety, that is derived from the instinct for self-preservation, which is also proper to animals. Thus, for example, a bird always looks round about itself when it feeds. Furthermore, the love of parents for the preservation of the children is a drive which is derived from the instinct to preserve one's kind. With animals this drive manifests itself to a still greater degree, since they entrust their young to no one, but seek to defend them to the utmost extent, 25:585 and protect them with the greatest danger to themselves. Therefore it is barbaric to rob animals of their young, [when animals] have a great attachment to them. But with human beings the natural drives can be suppressed, and in their place others can be invented by reason; for example a Parisian woman would gladly be relieved of bearing a child, and let another woman bear the child for her for money, if it would work, just as also in Paris upwards of 8,000 children are handed over for their upbringing abroad.[c] Savages who are too animalistic, and others who are again too tender, give up such drives. Thus a savage woman offered her child to the traveler. And people who have become absorbed in chimerical inclinations, lose the natural [inclinations].

If we speak of the natural inclination which is based in our nature, then we see that this inclination can be a private inclination and a social inclination. Private inclination is inclination insofar as it can be satisfied solely in us, but the social inclination is inclination insofar as it can only be satisfied in society. The general [aspects] of private inclination are comfortableness and affluence. Comfortableness is the sufficiency of possessions. Some persons dispense with affluence, if they just have comfortableness; the former is an inclination of the lazy. Other inclinations are only those which can be satisfied solely in society. These social inclinations are either sympathizing [inclinations effecting] improvement,[d] associating[e] [inclinations], or self-directed,[f] self-loving inclinations. Associating inclinations are directed to society. Human beings have an inclination to be in society, hence they form families, and like to have social relations,[g] from which larger societies later arise, and upon which we can base the inclination to form nations.[h] But then there exist

---

[a] *Triebe*, essentially synonymous with "*Instinct*," the term used in the previous paragraph, and again in the next sentence; the change in translation serves only to signal the different terms appearing in the original.

[b] *Grundtrieben*

[c] *außer der Stadt*, literally "outside the city" and so "abroad" should be taken in the sense of also including the French countryside.

[d] *theilnehmende beßernde*

[e] *verknüpfende*, i.e. in the sense of forging associations.

[f] *selbstische*, of the self, focused on the self.

[g] *im Umgange stehen*   [h] *Volks Neigung*

social inclinations which aim at ourselves. The desire for dominance, the desire for honor, and all vanities are of this kind. These are inclinations which aim at us, but can be satisfied in society. For the desire for power and honor does not serve to connect society, but to keep others at a certain distance in regard to oneself. Thus not all social inclinations are also sociable inclinations. The unsociable inclinations in society are: 25:586

1. Self-defense and
2. Self-aggrandizement[a]

The first inclination is only negative, the other positive. Just as we before had a drive to preserve ourselves, we have many drives to defend ourselves and to set up resistance against others. This drive is very unsociable and is combined with fear and distrust of others. However, the aggrandizement of one's person or one's influence in society is also unsociable. Everyone seeks to enlarge the circle around himself, everyone would like to have more admirers, he wants to be the most highly respected, and to show off in society, to have sway over others' understanding. We see such arrogances daily in society, but which are obviously unsociable and are also only possible in society. The basis of the unsociable inclination in society lies in distrust and jealousy. The first refers to the inclination to preserve and to defend oneself, where one presupposes that everyone else wants to aggrandize himself, hence we are distrustful of them, since we could thereby come up short. In the case of jealousy we are concerned that we might be infringed upon through the aggrandizement of others. In the first case we are concerned about defending what we already have, but in the latter case we are concerned about attaining what we do not yet have. Thus there is a principle of society and of sociability in the human being, but on the other hand also a principle of unsociability and separation of society. Here both principles collide with one another, which is however wisely arranged by the Creator. First of all human beings have a drive to enter into society, however so that society does not always remain clustered together in one place, human beings have on the other hand another principle of unsociability which separates them; this is the reason that the entire world is populated. Thus if in one place the society is large, then the people separate and go to another place, for example to America. When it multiplies there too, then they will again separate and inhabit new lands. In the end, the entire earth must be inhabited. When many states are together, then they unite, and one engulfs the other. But as soon as the one has become very large, it splits up, and the members try to separate. This is the Creator's special combination and separation, from which the multiplicity arises, and from which the complete perfection of the 25:587

---

[a] *Erweiterung seiner selbst*

human race must afterwards be derived. Then a method of government will arise, which will also remain constant.

On the other hand, with the human being there exists a sympathetic participation in fate and welfare, where human beings are not egotistical. One calls these drives humaneness, humanity.[a] It belongs with[b] the principle of sociability in the social order. We distinguish the inclinations by words of our language which signify either the extended or inner magnitude of the inclination. In the first case we express it by "obsession,"[c] for example, obsessive ambition,[d] obsession with money,[e] in the second case by "stinginess,"[f] for example, ambition,[g] tight-fisted with money.[h] Thus obsession and stinginess refer to the magnitude. One who is obsessively ambitious and obsessed with money can never have enough. One who is mean in his ambition[i] and is tight with money, is one who does not want to do without the least little bit of what he has. Thus one who is mean in his ambition is offended insofar as the slightest little thing [affecting] his honor[j] is denied to him. One who is obsessively ambitious however overlooks the little things, and is not to be satisfied with them, since he is greedy for a great deal.

With regard to the relation of inclination to purpose, [there] are the inclinations of pleasure[k] and of delusion. The inclinations of pleasure are immediately directed to the object insofar as it is an object of sense, however inclinations which are immediately[l] directed to pleasure, are inclinations of delusion. Honor only has value as a means, but whoever seeks to attain it without purpose, seeks the means as the purpose itself, and then it is an inclination of delusion. Obsessive ambition and greed[m] are inclinations of delusion. Delusion is false representation, when one takes what has value only as a means, to be the thing itself. Thus there also exists a religious delusion, namely if one takes the ceremonies to be the worship itself. Thus stinginess is also an inclination of delusion. Money has value as a means, but the stingy person values the money immediately, not as a means by which to acquire an enjoyment for himself, but he has an enjoyment in the empty money. True the stingy

---

[a] *Menschlichkeit, Humanitaet*
[b] Reading *mit*, instead of *nicht*, per editors' note, and as being more consistent with the meaning of the passage.
[c] *Sucht*, mania
[d] *Ehrsucht*
[e] *Geldsucht*
[f] *Geiz*
[g] *Ehrgeiz*
[h] *Geldgeiz*
[i] *Ehrgeiziger*
[j] *Ehre*
[k] *Genußes*; it is in order to reserve "pleasure" for this term that *Vergnügen/Vergnügungen* have been translated as "enjoyment(s)/delight(s)."
[l] Reading *unmittelbar* instead of *mittelbar*, as indicated in second option in editors' footnote and as what would be consistent with the further discussion in the paragraph.
[m] *Habsucht*

person begins by valuing it as a means, which he wants to accumulate for himself; hence he spares the use of this means, in the hope of once using it. But because he finally habituates himself to dispense with that for which he is amassing the money, he thus later sees the money as the immediate purpose. The human being therefore has a folly in himself which no animal has, for animals only have an enjoyment of pleasure. Through this delusion, providence however accomplishes something of which human beings would not have thought. This way the obsessively ambitious person often seeks to promote others' happiness, solely to have the honor, and the stingy person accumulates the money for his descendants, without doing such for that reason, but he accumulates for himself; however just through this, contrary to his will, he also accumulates for his descendants.

ON THE AGITATIONS OF THE MIND

The mind is either calm or agitated.[a] Both occur in regard to the feeling of sensation and in regard to the desires. We can have a sensation and we can desire when the mind is calm, but its agitation is more than having a sensation and merely desiring. Sensations can be found in the mind in a way that the mind is calm, for example being sensible of a beautiful, clear morning. One can also find desires in the mind, in a way that the mind is still calm, for example, being occupied with a plan, or if one is occupied with his office. For it is only an exercise of the mind to direct its occupation[b] to a certain purpose, and also to attain it.

Note: It costs a great deal of effort and practice to maintain the mind's calmness. Thus, for example, unfavorable remarks[c] greatly disturb the mind. However, one must conduct oneself here in such a way, that one resolves to act according to principles, and then one must not bother about the unfavorable remarks; one must behave in such a way that even when people speak badly of us, we do not believe them. One should beware of offending others, because one then suspects the other to have a hatred for us, which arouses in us a still greater hatred against him. One should beware of letting on that one knows that the other person has offended us. The difference in the state of the mind [when] calm and [when] agitated is this: the human being is calm, when he keeps his composure. To keep one's composure means when the state of the mind is subject to our power of choice. Agitation of the mind, however,

25:589

---

[a] *in Bewegung*: "in motion" would literally render this phrase, but in this section, as in his earlier discussions in these lectures, it quickly becomes clear that to be "in motion" is for the mind (*Gemüth*) to be "*beunruhigt*," i.e. disturbed or disquieted. Moreover, the mind "in motion," i.e. occupied with plans, reflection, and the like, is seen as the mind at rest.

[b] *daßelbe*

[c] *nachteiligen Reden*: the sense here could be as strong as "damaging rumors."

is a state where the mind does not have its sensations and desires in its control. What takes away the mind's composure, is the basis of the mind's agitation. We can admit sensations and desires to the mind, only in a way that we do not thereby lose our composure. There exist motions of the mind [which] are spontaneous and also make impressions on the mind.[a] One could also call the voluntary and affected[b] agitation of the mind, the jocular one; for example, if someone wants to act the lover, only in order later to laugh at home about the silly woman who takes him to be ardently in love. Such a person makes better progress in his role, than the one who is really in love, for the latter is thoroughly clumsy, because he is emotional.[c] He cannot talk, but only quivers and quakes.

The agitations of the mind are twofold, affects and passions. One has taken these to be one and the same, however Hutcheson first made here an entirely correct distinction.[44] Affect is a feeling through which we lose our composure,[d] but passion is a desire which takes away our composure.[e] The desire is not a perception of what is actual, but merely of what is possible and future. Feeling however aims at the present. Actual affects therefore appertain to feeling and passions to the desires. Thus fright is a state of feeling, since we do not desire anything there; therefore it appertains to affect. Longing however is a passion. Sadness is an affect. Obsessive ambition is a passion. Both affects as well as passions are an agitation of the mind and not a continual state. Hence one cannot say: the human being has a passion for stinginess, because a passion is not a continual state, but one already calls the propensity for a passion, the passion itself. Passion is to be distinguished from inclination. With human beings, inclination is a continual principle of desires, but passion is not. Inclination is a property of the mind, but passion and affects appertain to the state of the mind. When the mind loses its composure, then it is taken with affect or passion, but if it does not lose its composure, then one could call this temperate sensations and desires. The determination

25:590 of that, through which affect is distinguished from the usual feeling, and passion is distinguished from the usual desires, must be exactly struck. If one posits the difference [as consisting] in a certain degree, then this is a vague concept, which is not at all determinate; in the way, for example, Baumgarten takes stinginess to be a greater propensity and inclination for abstaining from expenditures and for being thrifty.[45] But thriftiness is a virtue and stinginess is a vice. Then however virtue and vice would be distinguished according to the degree, and through reduction of the degree, virtue could become vice, and from this, through the increase of the degree, a virtue could result. That is however not only false, but also

---

[a] *Motus animi spontaneos auch impressos*
[b] *gekünstelte*
[c] *empfindungsvoll*

[d] *aus der Faßung kommen*
[e] *aus der Faßung bringt*

harmful. If therefore every feeling by increasing is supposed to converge on affect, and every desire is supposed to converge on passion, then one would not know how to determine the extent, at which degree feeling becomes affect and desire becomes passion. Therefore it is a specific difference and not [one] according to magnitude. However much virtue may be reduced, it does not become a vice, and the reduction of enjoyment does not become pain. If in the case of feeling and of the desires, the mind's composure is kept, then no matter how intense sensation and desire may be, sensation does not then become affect, and desire does not become passion. We possess great diversity to be affected by sensations of objects. That degree of sensation that makes us unable to estimate and compare the object with the sum total of all our sensation, is affect. For example, joy is an affect; if one is pleased with an object which has no noticeable influence on the whole of our well-being, or if one becomes angry about a dish having been broken in two, which has no noticeable influence on the whole of our well-being, this is affect.

Passion is that degree and state of the desires which makes us unable to estimate the object with the sum total of all inclination. For example, if an individual wants to marry a [woman] and desires her not according to one inclination, but in accordance with all inclinations; if he is particular about her qualities, virtue, station, and skill, then his love arises from deliberate choice, thus not from passion. However, if someone is out to marry a person whom he does not love, but with whom he is in love, which makes a big difference, then it comes about from passion, for with love his mind can be calm. But if he is in love, then his mind is agitated, he values the object not according to all but only in accordance with one inclination, namely according to that one which arises from the sex drive. He is swept away by this inclination, and does not choose according to the proportion of all inclinations; he relegates all advantages which could satisfy his remaining inclinations to the rear, if he can just satisfy this, his one inclination. He imagines everything else to be only minor. If one says, the person is poor, then he is of the opinion he [can] make up for such by his industry, or if one says she is a poor housekeeper, then he is of the opinion: she will yet learn how to keep house. Such a person marries due to passion.

With affect and the passions, there is a certain incongruity, since the one part is greater than the whole, for a sensation and a desire are also a part of our entire sensation, and if this one sensation has a stronger effect and incites more strongly, then as a part it is greater than the whole of sensation and the desires. Accordingly, the affects and passions are something contrary to reason, since reason wants to determine the particular from the universal. If an affect or passion is directed to something good, then they are not yet thereby excused, for they then must also be constituted this way according to the form. The good must be

25:591

143

cognized only through the understanding; therefore the passions must also be in keeping with reason, but then they would no longer be passions, for a passion is indeed just that, which is not subject to our power of choice and reason. The noblest agitations of the mind are therefore the most harmful, for if the object is not an object of the senses and experience, then one needs the guidance of reason; for example, in religion, there no experience can guide him. If this now becomes a passion, then reason also abandons him, since that is precisely passion, and then nothing guides him. Accordingly, to the extent they turn into affect and passion, the noblest agitations of the mind are the most harmful. Affects and passions have still another degree, where they receive special names; namely, affect is called an unrestrained, wild affect, and passion is called a blind passion. That affect which itself nullifies[a] its own natural effect, is a wild affect. For example, one sees a child fall into the water, which one could, however, save through a little assistance, only one is so alarmed, that one cannot do anything in the moment. Fright stuns one so, that one is thereby unable to do anything at all. This way one can also be wholly stunned by joy over an unexpected good fortune, and indeed also in this way, that one is completely limp;[b] whereas joy should surely, on the contrary, have good consequences, however since the affect is wild, it itself nullifies its effect. It is just the same way with the affect of anger. Anger should, after all, have the effect of taking someone to task and reproaching him, yet often the angry person is so stunned that he is irritated, quivers and trembles, and cannot say a word; that is an unrestrained affect. It is just the same way with passion. That degree of passion which itself nullifies its own intention, is a blind passion. True, all passions are blind, and have this feature, that they nullify the individual's rational purpose which agrees with the sum total of all inclinations. These passions can, however, yet be such that they at least can achieve their object. For example, one in love can still, for all his passion, bring it about that he can achieve his object, although to be prudent and in love is contradictory. Nevertheless, that passion whereby the human being gets caught up, and is wholly unable to procure the object for himself because of passion, whereby he completely loses his composure, that is really utterly blind passion. One could also call it brute passion,[c] to distinguish it from others which are also blind. Thus this degree of passion not only does away with the individual's happiness, but because of its own intensity, it also even nullifies his own object and his intention.

---

[a] *umbringen*, literally "kills" or "does away with"
[b] *ganz todt bleibt*   [c] *passionem brutam*

In order that one may consider the affects in different objects, as they are directed to feeling, we thus note some remarks without [any] systematic order. Sensations therefore in themselves have intensity, which is due to the fact that they are unforeseen, and then one calls them surging. This sensation is not penetrating, but it has its intensity from the fact that it is surprising and unforeseen, for example, happy news. But if it is at the same time penetrating, then one calls it an onslaught or excitement, which arises from good and bad causes. [As to] what concerns onslaught in regard to the sensation of the body, one thus calls the shiver[a] a sensation of the body, which lasts only for an instant, and which must be distinguished from the shudder which signifies a lasting fear. One calls this a tremor,[b] which comes on so violently, that one cannot escape[c] it. This tremor[d] overcomes our body, for example, if we hear that someone has fallen asleep on the edge of a guardrail on a high tower, also in the case of a magnanimous, sublime feature in a comedy, for the sublime has something in common with the frightful, and if it is a [case of] sympathizing, then a tremor like this overcomes me. Thus too, prickling is an onslaught which is not penetrating. Fright is connected with horror, but prickling is the beginning of this.

25:593

The object of feeling can be agreeable, but the sensation of it disagreeable, and conversely, the object can be disagreeable, but the sensation can be agreeable. This way, for example, in the case of happy news, in the consideration of reflection, the object can be agreeable, but the sensation disagreeable; i.e. surging[e] and penetrating. But if the object is disagreeable, then the sensation can be agreeable, but only indirectly, if it just serves as a change. Thus, for example, all dissonances are disagreeable, but as a change of tones in music, they are agreeable; therefore, only as a means are they indirectly agreeable. However, the sensation of a disagreeable object is also on the other hand nevertheless agreeable, namely if we are sensible of our cast of mind whereby something pains us; for example, the pain due to the death of a friend. Likewise there is also a wicked joy, for example, due to the death of an enemy, where the object is agreeable, but the joy is blameworthy.

---

[a] *Schauer* [b] *Schauerregen*
[c] Reading *dafür* as *davon*; alternatively, one could read *verbergen* (literally "hide from it") as *vorbereiten* and then the clause would read, "that one cannot prepare oneself for it." If the verb were not in the reflexive form, the sense of *verbergen* could also be that one cannot disguise this sudden, violent onslaught of affect. In the context of the discussion, all three would hold true.
[d] *Schauer*; i.e. the *Schauerregen*.
[e] Reading *aufwallend* for *auffallend*, as indicated in the editors' footnote, and as consistent both with the reference on the previous page and the context in this passage.

25:594   We often confuse sentient*a* pain with reflective [pain], and the sensation of pleasure with reflective pleasure; hence not every pain distresses, but only the reflective*b* one [does].

    The onslaught of an agreeable sensation, which can transpose the individual into another state, is apparent, for example, in the case of a pardon, and on the other hand in intuition, and then one says: the individual stops short due to that which is unexpected. The continuation of this is surprise, a greater degree is amazement, and this being amazed can become stupefaction. Admiration is the agreeable [state], since it is only a feeling, but amazement is an affect, which is a mixture of the agreeable because it animates, and of the disagreeable, due to the embarrassment which the individual suffers, because he cannot make sense of it, and does not know how to reconcile himself to it. Those people who are immediately amazed by everything, show that they are weak, partly because they are immediately sensible of it this way, but particularly because much is unknown to them; hence they are filled with amazement by what is unknown to them. Onslaught of ill due to the representation of ill is a fright. The mind which is disposed to fright is different from the fearful mind, for in the case of the alarmed mind, the mind again plucks up courage when the fright is past, but not with the fearful mind. Fright is the impression which is generated by the reflection on the presented ill. There exists a fright and a fear in regard to certain objects of the imagination, for example falling off the roof. Fear due to imagination is timorousness, timidity;*c* for example, one believes one [will] be struck dumb*d* in a speech, where one gets a fright because of the large audience,*e* although not because of a single person in the audience. This timorousness is different from discouragement, which has actual objects. Courage is contrary to fear, and heartiness to fright. Courage is more mental,*f* and heartiness more physical.*g* Courage is based on reflection, heartiness on sensitivity. The one who does not frighten like this is hearty, but the one who does not fear like this, has courage. Presumptuousness, which is contrary to timorousness, and consists in the lack of imagined fear, must be distinguished from heartiness. The one who takes others' judgments to be nothing with regard to his own is presumptuous; for example, a fop,

---

a *empfindenden*
b Substituting *reflektierende* for *empfindende*, in accordance with the editors' footnote and Kant's earlier discussions, for example, 25:574.
c *Blödigkeit, Schüchternheit*: the first is the now obsolete term for the second one.
d *stecken zu bleiben*, which can simply mean to "get stuck," is used idiomatically in connection with fright to express being rendered speechless, in short getting stage fright.
e *Menge*
f *geistig*; *Geist* is most commonly rendered as "spirit" in English, but in the context here, Kant is clearly juxtaposing mind and body.
g *körperlich*: or, "bodily," or "corporeal"

who in society is a petty ruler,[a] who always shows off, pays no attention   25:595
to any fashion, but produces one himself, when what he does becomes
fashionable. He has to be able to talk about everything, and if he does
not understand it, break off [the discussion], even immediately begin to
talk about something else. He has to be able to do everything indiscriminately, whistle, sing, speak, and so forth. When presumptuousness does
not shrink before the judgment of others with regard to true honor, then
this is impudence; for example, to ask for everything, to freeload.

One cannot get into the habit of presumptuousness through practice,
and it is a great talent.

Daring is courage without reflection. If the human being would
reflect, then no daring would take place. Young people are daring because
of their young blood, but especially due to thoughtlessness, because they
do not reflect. Age however has more courage, because it is more careful, and therefore reflects. If courage remains after reflection, then it is
a sober courage. Bravery aims at human beings, but daring at objects of
nature; for example, a seaman must be daring. All this is different from
steadfastness; it occurs in the case of a continual ill. Someone who does
not lose his courage with continual ill, is steadfast. As it is, someone
can be steadfast in a lasting ill, although at the beginning of the ill, he
had a sensation of fright. There are people who at the beginning of the
ill, for example with combat, had a sensation of fright, but are steadfast in continual ill, for example, with death. Persons who yield to the
sensation of the senses, also yield to fright, but they are steadfast in a
lasting ill. This way persons become frightened in a duel, because the
impression of the senses came as a surge[b] upon them, but in turn they
can die with resolute courage. Thus one who lacks heartiness can, on the
other hand, have much courage. This is based simply on practice and
habit. Thus the butcher does not frighten as easily as the tailor. Likewise
the roofer and the hunter of antelopes in Switzerland know nothing of
dizziness. Dizziness is a queasiness which consists more in the imagination than in the fact. Someone who gets taken by fancied fear, becomes
dizzy. With a timid person[c] fear arises from reflection, but with an easily
frightened one, from the senses. Patience, which is a feminine virtue, is   25:596
different from all of this; on the other hand, steadfastness is a masculine
virtue. Patience does not require any intellect,[d] but [requires] the habit of
resigning oneself to ill. Steadfastness however requires intellect. Hearty
and courageous persons are impatient, not due to lack of courage, but

---

[a] *kleiner Gesetzgeber*, literally "little lawgiver"
[b] Again reading *auffallend* as *aufwallend*, consistent with previous instances.
[c] *zaghaften*; earlier Kant defined "timidity" as fear resulting from imagination.
[d] *Geist*; as in Kant's earlier discussion, "intellect" more adequately renders his meaning   25:474
     than the usual "spirit."

because they have courage, which they cannot however apply here, for in the ills of life where no courage helps, there one must be patient in order to bear it; however one must [muster] courage in ills in accordance with their magnitude, but not of long duration. Sadness is a reflective distress. If one judges that there is nothing at all to be hoped for, then one succumbs to despair, which can be twofold: the headstrong, wild [one, bent on] putting an end to all misery, and timid or crestfallen despair. In the latter, the mind is not in such agitation as in the former. Despair is an effect of impatient heartiness, which one mistakenly confuses with timidity. If it is timidity, then the individual really has a bewildered mind,[a] which sees only the abyss of the ills, and because he cannot rid himself of these, he thus tries to get rid of the sensation of the ills. This can occur if one gets rid of the reflective sensation of the ills; for example, if one does not think about an ill. Thus a merchant who does not want to think about his account books, tries to get rid of the sensation through distractions, or if one gets rid of this sensation by means of opium, [or] drinking, but it will then later surely return even more intensely. Therefore whoever tries to get rid of his sensible sensations, acts contrary to the humanity [in himself]. Some expressions in regard to ills are: to take something to heart and consciously to bear something in mind.[46] The latter appertains to reflective ill. Something can cause me pain, but if I take this pain to heart, then it grieves me, but if I want to bear it consciously in mind, then it distresses me, but if neither of the two is the case, then it merely annoys me. We can take the suffering of our friends to heart, but we cannot consciously bear them in mind. I can take the other's welfare and ills to heart, I can feel the pain, but if I consciously bear it in mind, then I feel unhappy. But I surely have no need to feel unhappy, if others are unhappy.

25:597

We can only take all physical ills merely to heart, but we cannot consciously bear them in mind; however in the moral [sphere] we must bear everything consciously in mind. Thus we deem ourselves unhappy, but we should only then deem ourselves unhappy, if we no longer merit being alive. However, no external ill can make us so unhappy, that we no longer merit being alive, as solely the actions contrary to morality [can do]. Accordingly we should also display courage in the greatest ills, and then we at least still deserve respect. But who bears such ills consciously in mind, degrades humanity, and one loses all respect toward such a person.[47]

Although all feeling is subjective, to which fright, fear, and pain particularly appertain, surely one could thus also assume an objective feeling. True, objective feeling is of course subjective, and here I use the subjective not to assess my state, but to assess the object. The feeling of

[a] *Kopf*

disgust is of this kind. Disgust aims at the quality, not at my state, but at the object. Disgust is either a disgust of loathing, or of hatred, or of contempt. It is not one and the same thing to consider the object as an object of hatred, or of loathing, or of contempt. Among all sensations, loathing has the special [feature], that it entails no compensation,[a] and does not become agreeable through any contrast, because it inhibits the source of life.[48] It is a suppression of agitation, thus no animation. Other sensations, such as fear, [or] sadness, entail a full measure of enjoyment in contrast [with] and among other sensations. However, loathing cannot produce an enjoyment in the least degree, because it is disgust due to the quality of the object; it is in and for itself absolutely a disgust. Agitations of the mind due to loathing suppress all enjoyment; it is the feeling of lifelessness, for the individual is also incapable of [having] other sensations. Thus an individual can displease by his remarks,[b] he can draw hatred upon himself, which is only due to circumstances, but then he is thus less hated by others. However, if he becomes loathsome, then he sinks to the lowest [level]. The physical agitation of hatred is fainting. Thus those vices which entail loathing are unspeakable, because a loathing is already inherent in the naming, and is produced by it. A drunk individual, who is already throwing up, is thus an object of loathing, yet the vice is still speakable. Disgust and hatred are already more objective than [agitation] due to loathing. An object, which is [an object of] disgust due to hatred, is not as untoward as that of loathing, for I can only be hated by enemies, but an object of loathing is the cause of loathing for everyone. 25:598

The object of the disgust of contempt is entirely different from the object of hatred and of loathing. One can always be fond of an object of contempt, not hate it at all, but still have contempt for it; for example, an individual who squanders everything, who makes everything around him cheerful, is in merry and good spirits, why should I hate him? I am fond of him, I deplore him, but I have contempt for him, and cannot think highly of him. Contempt aims at the object of unworthiness and worthlessness. The one who transgresses the duties toward himself, is an object of contempt. He has thereby not insulted anyone, therefore one can also not hate him, but one has contempt for him; for example, a liar is an object of contempt, for who robs himself of his own worth, also cannot demand that others give him a worth. Therefore contempt aims at the inner worth, and for this reason it says far more if I have contempt for someone, than if I hate him. For if I hate someone, then it still does not follow that all hate him, but the object of contempt is held in contempt in the eyes of every human being; therefore [it is] an

---

[a] *Ersatz*: also "substitution" or "replacement"
[b] *in seinen Reden*

25:599 universal object. Accordingly, it is better to be an object of hatred, than of contempt. Utter contempt later becomes loathing, and thus is more likely to border on loathing, than on hatred.

ON THE AGITATIONS OF THE BODY INSOFAR AS THEY HARMONIZE[a] WITH THE AGITATIONS OF THE MIND, THUS ARISING THROUGH AFFECT

Therefore without any systematic order, we just note the following. Some affects produce an agitation of the blood, as [for example], shame about something drives the blood into the face. Some affects produce an agitation of quivering. Quivering is a fluctuation of the nerves. The agitation of anger strains the fibres and muscles of the body: the nerves and fibres are the two sources and principles of life, the nerves for sensitivity, and the fibres for irritability. He who becomes red on the spot due to anger is not to be immediately feared, but he will later at some time avenge himself. He puts his revenge off, since he is ashamed to avenge himself right away. However, he who on the spot becomes pale and white due to anger is to be feared on the spot. If the anger is very violent, then the fibres and muscles are overstrained, so that the person becomes unable to carry out voluntary motions. The agitations of the body are in keeping with the purposes of the affects, but also often opposed, in the way that the most appropriate purpose of fear is flight before the object, yet the individual is often so frightened, that instead of fleeing, he falls down and cannot get away at all. The angry individual's purpose is to heap the greatest reproaches on the other person, yet he stutters. Nature, however, does not produce such agitations which oppose the purposes, but with fear our imagination increases sensitivity, and with anger, the individual is ashamed and has many misgivings.

For what purpose, however, are such agitations of the body placed in us by nature? For example, that upon shame, redness appears in the face? The purpose of shame which nature has placed in us is: to force human beings into truthfulness. In upbringing, inopportune shame can be prevented. Accordingly, one must not say to a child at every occasion, phew, shame on you; that makes children silly and shy. One must either tell them that their action is good or bad. But if the child props itself up, or picks its teeth, then one must not say, that is not seemly, for the 25:600 child does not understand that this should be bad in itself. It must refrain

---

[a] *in Harmonie stehen*, literally "stand in harmony" (or "are in harmony")

from such things due to obedience, because one does not want to permit them. It must obey, yet one must not shame it on account of this. When its character has been formed, then it will thereafter understand by itself that this is not fitting. However, if it lies, then one should say: shame on you; then one must regard it with the greatest contempt, as if one did not regard it even worth looking at. If this is now constantly repeated, then every time the child is about to lie, it will become red, and it will stutter, and the lies will stick in his throat, and thereby he must betray himself, that he has lied. This is therefore the purpose of shame, since the becoming red is a betrayal of what we want to hide. Now since this is a noble purpose, parents should prevent making children [turn] red and shaming them when it is not necessary.

In addition, the affect of sadness produces the physical agitation of sighing, and the affect of fright produces a scream. Thus women immediately scream when they are frightened. Nature has made this sex timid, because it is the sex which is supposed to preserve the species, and what befalls them can easily harm the preservation of the species. Although this sex is very presumptuous, yet with regard to injury it is thus very timid. Therefore women hold their hands in front of their face when they are being beaten. It is healthy for them, if they utter a scream after the fright, since they thereby disperse the blood thrust into their chest by the fright; hence by it one recognizes women behind the masks, for they cannot refrain from this. The man, however, does not take flight in the case of a fright, but stands up to it; hence he remains more mute. Sighing is the expansion of the lungs, in order to facilitate the release of blood. In general, especially with sick persons, the grumbling and clamor is an alleviation of pain. Hence too, children cry after being born, which is very salutary for them, since they thereby disperse the blood from the lungs. Therefore what nature does is good and has its purpose. Laughter and crying are agitations of the body which are produced by affects which are in keeping with them. Laughter is not an agitation of the blood, but a convulsion of the entire system of fibers, and by means of these, also of the nerves. It is not an expansion and tension of the fibers as in the case of anger, but a trembling and back and forth fluctuation of the fibers. The diaphragm is convulsed and the lungs also vibrate. Thereby everything is refreshed and everything receives a greater agitation. Laughter is aroused in the mind by thoughts, by the livening up of life, or also mechanically. Laughter comes from the mind and convulses the body. How does this happen? In order to understand this, we must first explain mechanical laughter. This is aroused, for example, by tickling. Tickling however is a pinching and tugging, as if one wanted to take and let go of something. Thus also here. If I touch a part of the body and let it go again, I thus tug on the muscles. This produces the vibration of the diaphragm

25:601

and the convulsion of the lungs,[a] and this is laughter. It happens just the same with laughter in the mind and in thoughts. For all laughing matter is always a switch. First my nerves are led to a certain prospect; the mind now tries to follow a rational course.[b] If now a switch from the prospect once ensues, and before it realizes what is happening, the mind is on the other side, then it bursts into laughter. Repercussion therefore produces laughter. Completely absurd things do not produce laughter, but it must first have a semblance of truth, and then one must be thrown back from that. For example, someone goes on the street in a respectable and dignified [way], and something has been hung on his back, or he falls; thus here is always the opposite of the dignified. The surprise, the oddity, the unexpectedness, what comes thereafter, constitutes the laughter, but not the affair[c] itself.

Enjoyment arises also from the repercussion of the mind. The joy is not a joy over the affair, but over the animation; it is organic and not ideal, since physical agitation results from the idea, and the agitation produces animation. Crying is an effect of distress, which is not disagreeable. True, the distress is disagreeable, but not the crying about it. After the crying, the heart is pleased, just as sunshine comes after a downpour. Therefore there is something mild in the tears, it is a relief from the constriction which arises from the sadness. Women cry, but men feel the pain. Tears are also taken to be a weakness, but which is in keeping with [the nature of] children and women. In general, one bursts into tears when the heart is affected by something. Every act of magnanimity affects the heart and produces tears; for example, if someone has offended another person, but he is sorry about that, and apologizes to him, [and] the other also forgives him, indeed even overwhelms him with charitable acts. A great charitable act in extreme need also produces tears. How does it happen that acts of magnanimity compel tears?[d] Magnanimity brings us to [the point of] nostalgia, for the human being is filled with longing.[e] Longing, however, is a desire with the consciousness of powerlessness, hence [longing] also produces embitterment [and] tears; for example, with women, because they are powerless to procure gratification for themselves. Much is related to crying. In other respects crying soothes the mind. It is a release from pain. Therefore if one cries over the loss of a beloved, then the distress is far[f] removed from the heart; hence with a

25:602

---

[a] The reversal of which organ vibrates and which is convulsed is in the original text.
[b] Sache
[c] Geschichte
[d] auspressen, literally "squeeze out"
[e] durch Sehnsucht ausgedehnt: one might express this in English as "one's heart swells with longing."
[f] mehrenteils

deep pain which penetrates the soul, one cannot cry so easily. Men, who feel pain better, do not cry.

Such agitations of the mind make a bigger impression on us than others. Hence I will not think about a splendid meal as long as about laughter which was arbitrary[a] and was unexpectedly aroused by sensation. One also laughs otherwise, if one just puts a smile on one's face and pretends to laugh, especially if one wants to do the other a favor, who believes he has told something funny, but which was indeed not the case that [his story] would have evoked laughter due to sensation. If one would not act there as if it were funny, then it might be a reproach for the other person. However, arbitrary laughter, which arises from sensation, produces an innermost agitation of the mind; hence one is also fond of such a comical individual, who can thus arrange all objects in a humorous way, that one bursts into laughter, and one gladly gets on with him in society, because he thereby produces agreeable sensations. Old people gladly like to laugh, but young people like to pass on to all sensations, since they want to try out all their powers in order to get practice. Hence children like to break everything in two, pinch birds in order to hear how they scream, cut up wooden trumpets in order to see what it looks like in them, and so forth. And [hence] young people do much out of thoughtlessness, but in which there probably lies no malice, in order only to experience[b] many changes, and to exercise their powers in this respect, in order to know how far they get with them, and for which they have more propensity since they can still adapt to everything.

25:603

For, just as the same position of the body and its limbs is very disagreeable, indeed one can also torture someone thereby that one leaves him lying in an unvarying position of the body, and just as the changing position of the body is very agreeable, in just this way the changing agitation of the mind is also very agreeable. [Because the changing position of the body is very agreeable,] therefore human beings stretch, and extend their limbs first to this and then to that side, indeed also have their limbs massaged, whereupon they slip into a peaceful lassitude, and are wrapped in a woollen coat. [Since the changing agitation of the mind is likewise agreeable,] young people thus let themselves be worked over[c] by a tragedy and let their sensations be worked up,[d] if only the

[a] *willkürlich*: although it seems that the ordinary language sense of "at random," or "arbitrary" fits here, both Kant's earlier discussion distinguishing laughter arising in the mind from mechanical laughter and his later discussion in this paragraph, indicates that he may intend the usual sense of the term in his philosophy, namely "voluntary."
[b] *kommen*, literally "come to," or "get"
[c] *durchkneten*, literally "kneaded" or "massaged"
[d] *zerarbeiten*

agitation of the sensations is proportioned, for otherwise an organ could very well hurt one. If, therefore, something from the agitations of the sensations stays behind in the mind, then it is disagreeable, but this does not happen with young people the way it does with old ones, since the impressions are not as penetrating with them. However, with the person [where] they penetrate and leave something behind, there they achieve something disagreeable.

One can assess the human being by the way that he laughs, since the idea and his judgment, which produced the laughter, lie at the basis of the laughter. True, one cannot [assess him] by habitual laughter, where one gets hold of everything and summons up everything in order only to laugh, where thus the pleasure of laughing already precedes. Otherwise the high spirits[a] to make all objects [a matter] of laughter is also a good talent, whereby one makes things, which are in themselves disagreeable, ridiculous in a comical way, and thereby makes a social gathering cheerful and sweetens the disagreeable. However, there also exists a malicious laughter, even if it also seems to prove very little; for example, if someone goes down the street, and all at once falls in the mud,[b] then for many [people] laughter arises over this. True, one objects that one would not laugh, if one should see that harm resulted thereby, which one also concedes; nevertheless, ringing laughter about a difficulty another person has suffered, even if not about an ill, for example, if someone has finished writing a page and instead of the blotter, the inkwell falls on it, [such laughter] displeases and annoys the other, although he does not indeed display that he is offended by it, since he will then be made fun of even more; yet it still annoys him. But where the other is annoyed, there is no laughing matter. Such a cast of mind, which laughs about such thwarting of someone's efforts, already has a certain base for malice, and even if he later collects himself and corrects himself, one still sees that the cause of and propensity for such laughter was in his mind.

Note: We can deal with our body in a threefold way, namely through mechanical motive force, for example, by riding, cycling, and so forth, [and] by chemical motive force, where the fluids are dissolved, for example, by medicaments, by salts, and by mineral[c] parts. The third motive force is not through physical things, but through the mind. This is the innermost motive force. We cannot obtain the enlivening, the renewal of the mind, through anything physical or mechanical, much less through medicine. Those are only means of maintaining fading life. With the

25:604

---

[a] *gute Laune*, literally also "good mood"
[b] *Kot*, literally "feces," but also figuratively, the mud or dirt on the street.
[c] Reading *mineralische*, instead of *metallische*, per editors' note.

mind, however, only the hindrance should be alleviated,[a] for there are sicknesses which injure the human machine [and] others which hinder it. The first source of life, however, lies in the mind. We cannot, however, enliven this through physical agitations, but [rather] through agitations of the mind. What is it, for example, that urges the human being to play cards? Not the object, not the interest, since it here really depends on luck, hence one cannot here believe one will gain anything thereby, but the agitation of the mind, the enlivening of the powers of the mind. The human being does not think about it, but he still pursues it, for hardly a social [hour] is spent without a card game. A card game is entertaining for this reason because it is an animation of the mind, for since it here depends on chance, the human being thus lets his imagination dominate, especially if company[b] is added to this. The card game is also to some extent a discipline for the human being, for although the individual is vexed if someone has played a stratagem on him, then he surely must not let it on, since it after all depends on luck; he must control and restrain himself. With time one becomes accustomed to such [self-]control. However, if through habit it becomes an inclination, then it does not have the effect. The intent of the game is the sensitivity of the human being, for since the game always includes a change which depends on chance, we thus also have a play of sensation and this is what enlivens one. In all of life, there is nothing which can transpose the mind in 5 minutes into so much agitation of sensation, as a single game of cards, and in every game the mind is in a new situation. A ponderous company with pipes of tobacco in hand, surrounded by a venerable haze, which entertains itself with reports about the community, does not leave such an animation of the mind behind as does the game. As long as medicine only has mechanical and chemical means of bringing life into motion, and does not try to bring the mind into motion by pneumatic means, its prospects are thus still very poor, since most sicknesses are based only in hindrances lying in the nervous system; hence one must try to enliven the first lifespring of the mind. Therefore, with a sick person, a good, bright friend will accomplish more than all prescriptions, for these touch only the surface of the body, but the enlivening of the mind penetrates to the principle of life. Hence a doctor must seek to inquire of the patient what his enjoyments and enlivening [activities] were, and if he manages to provide such entertainment for him, then such will sooner help him than all medicine. Yet this appertains more to a medical doctor than to a psychologist.

25:605

---

[a] *gehoben*, literally "lifted"
[b] In the other manuscript (per the editors' note) *Geschicklichkeit* (skill) is substituted for *Gesellschaft* (company); either can make sense in the context.

25:606   Finally in addition we can consider sympathetic feeling. [The term] sympathy[a] must not be rendered by "compassion,"[b] but by "sympathizing."[c] Compassion is more concerned with misfortune. However, we have sympathy also in good fortune. We have compassion for those who are weak, but we have sympathy also with those who are strong. Sympathy is thus the genus and compassion the species.

Sympathizing feeling can produce a great effect. Thus we sympathize,[d] for example, if someone gets stuck in a sermon. We sympathize with another's annoyance and offense. This sympathizing is noble. If someone has become unhappy, then I may well feel sorry for him, but if someone is offended, if his right has been violated, then I sympathize with anger toward the other. Those who do not have such sympathy, do not highly value the right of other human beings. Sympathizing with a misfortune, where many thousands have become unfortunate, is not necessarily the same as if one single person had suffered injustice. We are sensible of this sympathizing feeling in our entire soul. For if people, for example [those] subordinate to the aristocracy, are constantly under oppression, then they lose the idea of the right of humanity, for since they have no examples where justice prevails, then they think it must be so. There we must sympathize with the other's right, but not with the physical ill. We sympathize with another individual's joy, we sympathize with the other's pain, with his desires, with his love, with his burden, with his work, for example if someone lifts something very heavy, with his purpose. We sympathize also, for example, if someone falls, or [is] in a dangerous place, where he can fall, as on a boat when it is listing to one side, then we lean over the other side with our body. Likewise when one is bowling, and the bowling ball goes crooked on the one side, one also leans over to the other side with the foot.

Note: The humble individual has sympathy with the sensations of the higher-ranking[e] one, but the distinguished individual has no sympathy with the sensations of the humble one. The humble one puts himself into the disposition of the higher one and has compassion for him, although he is rather[f] more fortunate after his misfortune, than the humble one. If the ills are natural, for example, famine, then the distinguished person sympathizes with the humble one just as well as the latter with him, but
25:607   in the case of the ills of the factitious state, or of the ideal ills, the distinguished one does not sympathize with the humble one, but the latter does in fact sympathize with the former. The feminine sex sympathizes

---

[a] *Sympathie*   [b] *Mitleid*, also "pity"
[c] *Teilnehmung*: fundamental meaning is "participation," while "sympathizing" denotes the particular form of participation that is the subject of the discussion here.
[d] *Anteil nehmen*   [e] *größeren*
[f] Substituting *recht* for *nicht*, per editors' note regarding the term in the other manuscript.

a lot with natural ills, but not with ideal ones, especially toward their sex and persons who are beneath them. Thus one has compassion for an unfortunate king. The reason is because a humble person can easily put himself in the position of the higher one and assume greater dispositions. However, the distinguished one cannot assume the state of the humble one, hence he also does not sympathize with his misfortune. He thinks that the one who is thus not accustomed to the refined life is indeed just a humble man, hence he always gets on [in life], if he can just live. They do not become as aware, for example, of the distance between a citizen and a laborer,[a] as of only the distance of their social standing from the civic one in general. This is also the unfortunate thing with kings. They cannot thus imagine the misfortune of their subjects, and also have no inclination to do so. That is a narrow mind[b] which cannot get beyond the sphere of its upbringing, and transpose itself in another one. The animalistic [aspect] of sympathy is when we are only sensible of what produces physical pain. Sympathy in accordance with ideas is superior,[c] the physical only serves to substitute for the ideal [in the case of] one who is incapable of the latter. It is based not on deliberation, but on animality, if we do not sympathize as much with what we do not see, as when we see it, or if we sooner sympathize with something that has happened to a woman, than with what has happened to someone else. Pity for animals comes from physical sympathy. We need to preserve such sympathies in our nature, because they are means of strengthening the principles of sympathizing. The reason for our duties toward animals not to wrong them, is not their immediate injury, but in order to look after our sympathy and not injure humanity, and to preserve this incentive in its sensitiveness.

On the other hand we can also mention antipathetic feeling here, when one suffers pain because the other rejoices and when one has a sensation of joy because the other has pain. This feeling is nasty and peculiar to the stingy person. One calls sympathetic feeling human,[d] one calls the one who does not have it, inhuman. However, one calls the one who has the opposite, namely the antipathetic feeling, diabolical. One calls the first [case] human, because the human being has a disposition for it, although few have it.

25:608

Yet a basis for such antipathy lies in humanity. Human beings do not in fact take any immediate satisfaction and enjoyment in evil, but only

---

[a] *Handlanger*, literally someone who does the dirty work.
[b] *enger Kopf*
[c] Reading *fürtrefflich* as *vortrefflich*; the editors' note indicates that the term in the other manuscript is *fürchterlich* (terrible), which does not seem to fit the meaning here as well.
[d] *menschlich*: "humane" would also fit the context, but the ensuing discussion focuses on the connection with the species.

insofar as it is a means of satisfying their inclination and of promoting their advantage. This way one is pleased about the death of one's friend, because one thereby inherits. One does not take immediate joy in his death, instead one would like it if he would have remained alive, and one could, without his death, just get such an inheritance. However, if we entertain[a] an immediate enjoyment and satisfaction over the other's harm, then this is diabolical. One calls it diabolical because one cannot comprehend it from humanity, how the human being could take joy in what affords him no use, but brings harm to the other. In general one calls what is below humanity in regard to the moral evil, diabolical. This is therefore an ideal, or a maximum of the moral evil, just as on the contrary we call what goes beyond humanity in the moral, angelic, which is an ideal or maximum of the moral good. Among created beings, angels are the ideal of the good, and the devils the ideal of the evil. The human being who does not lean[b] to either is in the middle. As it is, that evil which cannot be comprehended from humanity, one calls diabolical. To such attributes belong ingratitude toward one's benefactor and gloating. Ingratitude toward one's benefactor exists when one takes an immediate satisfaction in the benefactor's harm. A propensity for envy or for grudgingness lies in the human being. This grudgingness is different between the two sexes. Among men it is not the same as among women. To insert an aside: a stranger said, "The man is jealous

25:609 when he is in love, and the woman is jealous before she is in love." Even if she wants no share of an object, yet she is thus vexed that another member of her sex has it. However, a certain propensity for grudgingness already lies at the basis in humanity, from which gloating afterwards arises. Human beings like to tell about others' mishaps and are eager to know such, which surely betrays a satisfaction in it. If one sees that someone is vigorously[c] rising in reputation and honor, and we learn that he has fallen therein, then we certainly do not have a sensation of indifference, but we express a satisfaction over it. What is the reason for this? Human nature has legitimate pretension[d] to equality. If a certain inequality has already been introduced into the ranks of the civil order, then it is really regarded as an order of nature; therefore we do not take this into account, but with persons of equal rank, everyone strives to preserve equality. The other does not have a sensation of satisfaction with respect to inequality either in honor or talent, or in wealth, but is concerned about being slighted and oppressed. Hence the rich person is contemptuous of the poor one, the distinguished one of the inferior

[a] *concipiren*, from the Latin for "conceive, think, imagine, entertain," etc.
[b] *extendirt*, literally "extend" (as the term is adapted from the Latin)
[c] *mit starken Schritten*, literally "with strong steps"
[d] *Praetension*, in sense of "claim to"

one; indeed it goes still farther, the adult has contempt for the child,[a] the healthy one for the sick, the strong for the weak, the learned [man] for the fool, for the other believes that the fault even lies in him, if he is not the same as he is. The healthy person always thinks about the sick person, he got sick through his fault; hence people also do not like to divulge their state. For this reason all human beings are therefore violent, if they are not limited by the governing authority, which occurs in the states, where the noble [man] seeks to overpower the humble one. The good consequence of antipathy is: human beings are thereby spread out over the entire earth. If they only had a sympathetic and no antipathetic feeling, they would be [clustered together] on one plot of ground. One counts envy and grudgingness to antipathy, insofar as it is universal and natural. However, there also exists an antipathy which is not natural. Thus between 2 greedy persons, between 2 obsessively ambitious ones, there is always an antipathy, for there the one is always against the other, but the grudgingness which lies in humanity is a natural basis of antipathy. In general, we have antipathy for the affects and passions of others, which can be seen by the following general remarks.

25:610

True, we sympathize with another's fortune and misfortune, but not with the other's intense agitations of the mind. We indeed sympathize with another's fortune, which he obtained through an inheritance, however if he is thereby deeply moved, and begins to shout with joy, then we see to it that we take our leave from him. If one person has won the lottery, and the other one says, I am happier than if I had won it myself, then the question is, in what sense[b] is this true? We have two kinds of joy: a rational and a sensible satisfaction. Rational satisfaction arises from reason's sympathy, and the sensible from the judgment of the senses. If I see a human being in misery, who is suffering misfortune [and] watches his family going to ruin, then if I were in a position to do so, I would sooner bestow good fortune on him than on me. If now by chance he does become fortunate, then I am happier than if I had myself been so fortunate, for if I think it over rationally, then I find it agreeable that the purpose was here so fitting, since this miserable man needs it sooner than I do. Joy from private life is a sensible joy. We are pleased with ourselves in such joy, which we take in another's good fortune, but we are not pleased with ourselves over the joy which we take in our own good fortune.

---

[a] *Große ... Kleinen*: as becomes evident later in the lectures, Kant uses these terms to refer to the adult in contrast with the child, and since rich and poor, noble and humble, have already been explicitly named, one can assume that this may be his meaning here. As the discussion continues, the next usage is clearly again in the sense of noble and humble.
[b] *Verstande*, literally "understanding"

However, we do not sympathize with others' agitations of the mind, even if we sympathize with their fate. For example, we sympathize with another's sadness and pain, but if he begins to lament and bursts out weeping, then we distance ourselves from him.

We do not sympathize with another's passions and violent agitations of mind. What is more, our sympathy is then diminished. We sympathize the least with another's anger, indeed we even become angry with the one who tells us something in anger, even if it is of no concern to us, for the agitations of mind deprive us of the state of power over ourselves. As it is, we do not like to be subjugated to our agitations of mind by others, hence we do not tolerate it when the other weeps and moans. With anger, we have antipathy for the other, true we sympathize

25:611 with his indignation, but not with his anger. For example, if someone tells us about another's roguish trick on him, but in a completely unperturbed way, then I harbor a resentment over it and am indignant that he is in addition so unperturbed about it. But if someone tells it in anger, then I have antipathy for him, since anger is dangerous for everyone, for if one is once angry, then one is also capable of becoming angry with the one telling it. If sympathy becomes an affect, then it is a great weakness. Our sympathy is a game, but it becomes serious as soon as it becomes an affect. As soon we have sympathy in our control, as soon as we can let it stop as we like, as long as [this is the case], it is a play, but as soon as I am not the master of it, but am placed in it against my will, then it is an affect. Hence we do not like to sympathize with the affects. We can therefore love a person who is tender like this in sympathy, which is a weakness with him, because we love a human being insofar as we perceive a weakness in him. For this way we have esteem for him, we therefore love him for the reason that he is in union with the other's inclinations, purposes, and intentions. If we were beings who had a greater degree of reason, then we would not need any sympathy, for we could have insight into the other's well-being or misfortune from the principles. Sympathy is therefore only a means of supplementing the lack in principles; to this extent it is also permitted, but if it becomes an affect, then it conflicts with the principles. For example, if a judge is to punish an injustice on [the part of some] persons, and he becomes so touched by compassion, that his sympathy becomes an affect, then the affect takes away his composure of reason. Sympathy makes the heart limp. The Stoic says: I wish a friend for myself, not who helps me in need and sympathizes with my misfortune, but such a one whom I help, and for whom I can employ my powers.[49] On the other hand he says, if you see a friend in misery and ruined, and you cannot help him, then

25:612 look away and say, of what concern is it to me? This really means, if you see a human being in misfortune, sympathize with his ill to the extent that you can help him. However, if you cannot help him at all, if this does not at all lie in your powers, then go away unperturbed. Weeping, mourning, lamenting, surely do not help. The wise man should not sympathize, but act from principles, for if I sympathize with someone, then I make my heart limp by the lamenting, and thereby make the other's misfortune more acute and unbearable for him. The passions are either plucky, for example, jealousy, or languishing, for example, idealistic love. One must guard against languishing passions, for example, novels; one wishes for them and cannot pursue them. Some passions are brooding, for example, stinginess, some are animating, others diminishing; for example, longing impedes activity. Some passions are transitory, others persisting. For example, anger is transitory; hatred is in contrast with it, it persists. Sadness is transitory, grief persists. Anger aims at a single act, and seeks to avenge itself on the spot. However, hatred at once makes a rule for itself, seeks to show itself at an opportune moment, and is vindictive.

The transitory passions, if they are evil, are sooner pardonable, than the [ones that] persist and have taken root, for these commit bad actions in accordance with rules. If the transitory passions are good, then they are all the less reproachable. This way some [people] are wholly taken with benevolence toward another, and it does not take long [before] they have again thus forgotten him. They please everyone, and as soon as they arrive in a strange place, they then have just as many good friends, that they then soon forget the old ones. The transitory passions are turbulent, but the abiding ones are sluggish. The turbulent ones bring ills about in a short time, but the ones which have taken root produce more harm, because they make a rule for themselves. 25:613

GENERAL OBSERVATIONS ABOUT THE PASSIONS AND AFFECTS

There exist some passions, which for that reason, because they are passions, are good-natured, and thus have a greater degree of worth as passions, than if they were only inclinations. [They] arise from reflection or from principles, and the action which arises from the passion thereby receives a worth. Thus, for example, a woman does not like to see it when she is loved by her husband only from duty, from mature deliberation. True, it is agreeable for her that he cares for her as her husband, and gives evidence of genuine benevolence toward her; however, she still considers herself less fortunate if her husband loves her due to reflection and not due to passion, so that he cannot live without her. The reason is this: passion is a means of ruling the other. Who has passion can be ruled by means of it by the one toward whom it is directed, and therefore, if the man loves her due to passion, the woman has power over him. But if the man loves solely due to inclination, so that he is not in love, then he is that much less [subject] to being ruled by his wife, for thereby, that he becomes weak, his wife becomes strong.

Another passion, however, becomes respectable due to the fact that it is a passion, for example, if parents love their children due to passion, so that they risk everything for them. By nature we actually have three drives[a] in us. The one instinct aims for the preservation of ourselves, the other for the preservation of one's kind, the third for the preservation of society. The last drive is only contingent, but the first two are essential drives. The inclination toward the children, or parental love, arises as a consequence from the instinct to preserve one's kind, or from the sex drive. This instinct lies in the nature of the animality of the human being, and naturally only lasts as long as the children need their parents; after that it stops, which we see in all animals, that they desert their young after a time and consider them as strangers, except if this instinct is cultivated in the human being by art. However, even with human beings, the more time separates them, the more indifferent[b] this instinct becomes, and their parents really do love the great grandchildren more than their children [love them].[c] In general, children especially draw love to themselves, because they need care.[d] Therefore, the passion of parental love is authorized by nature. However, one could also ask if the children's love for the parents also lies in nature. Although morality tells us that the children owe love and obedience to the parents, and very much dictates the children's obligation to their parents, yet nature has not thus laid an instinct in their heart. The instinct of the parents toward their children is far stronger, than of the children toward their parents, for the instinct descends and does not ascend. For the instinct which is laid in us by nature is the instinct for propagating the species. Now if with children there would be an instinct to love their parents, then these children could not again have an instinct to love their children. However, this is nature's purpose. The love of children for their parents in old age is also more a love of deliberation, of duty, of gratitude, than a natural

25:614

---

[a] *Triebe*

[b] *je länger, je kälter* (literally "the longer, the colder")

[c] Reading "*die Großenkel haben schon ihre Eltern lieber als ihre Kinder*," as equivalent to "*ihre Eltern haben schon die Großenkel lieber als ihre Kinder*." Given also Kant's continuing discussion about children lacking an instinct to love their parents, the sense that could be consistent with Kant's point would be that the great grandchildren would be in more need of care than the children and, to the extent parental love is tied to the child's need, the great grandchildren would thus evoke more love. Alternatively, if one left the "great grandchildren" (more precisely, the "great grandsons") as the subject, i.e. that the "great grandchildren really love their parents more than their children," then the suggestion might be that these parents are themselves in need of care in their old age, but as Kant goes on in the passage, this is a love based on deliberate reflection, and not a natural instinct.

[d] Reading *Fürsorge*, instead of *Vorsorge*

instinct. The greatest harmony of its purposes prevails in nature, and the philosophy about natural purposes is very agreeable. Thus one will find, that the daughter does not have such love for the mother as the son, and that the mother will also love the son more than the daughter, because she sees her future support in him. The reason, however, that the daughter cannot love the mother as much is this: the daughter is not the maker of her fortune, but her husband is. Therefore her instinct aims more toward taking care of her kind, than providing for others out of magnanimity. Hence one can always take the wife's mother into [one's] home, but not the husband's mother, for if she already has a husband, the daughter does not obey her mother at all, but the man still very much likes to obey his mother. For since the daughter cannot acquire anything for herself, but operates with what her husband has acquired, she thus aims more toward the maintenance of the house, and the house from which she came does not now concern her at all. In general, women are always more frugal, they always gladly accept something indiscriminately, and give no more away, than what they no longer can have any use for; for example, old dresses. The reason is, because they are not the agent of fortune, but only [have it] through the man; since she thus acquires nothing for herself, she has already made her fortune well enough, if she just has married an honest man. Inheriting is fortuitous; thus she can also not be as liberal as the man, and she must also be far more economical, because she is, so to speak, keeping another's accounts. If she would give away what her husband has acquired, then she might have nothing, because she cannot 25:615 acquire anything for herself. Often women acquire more than the man, but this is no longer natural.

This [discussion] served to elucidate that parental love, which is a consequence of the sex drive, is respectable as a passion. The love of life as a passion is not as respectable as the love for children due to passion. We prefer to see that the human being has a deliberate love of life. The reason why sexual love and love for children are sooner respectable as passion, than the love of life, is this: because it is more important to nature to preserve nature than one single individual in himself, for he can always die, if only he has preserved his kind. Therefore the life of a single individual in regard to his entire species is in and of itself fortuitous. However, the passion in sexual love agrees with nature's purposes. Hence the love of life as passion is often only condoned; as sexual love it proves to be its own credit, but the passion of parental love is an elevation. The immediate love of life does not even agree with reason, for one must also live in order to be quite miserable. Therefore life is a condition of fortune and misfortune, thus without determination it still has no amenity. Therefore the love of life as passion is to be approved only in a conditional way. However the instinct of life must come from deliberation, since often someone lives [in a way that brings] disgrace upon himself. If by a higher hand, the choice should be left to an individual, whether he would prefer to live here for all eternity, but in such a way that he would then also have to live and also be subjugated to all fate, and would have to expect fortune and misfortune, or whether he wants to die the way it happens now, then everyone would be appalled at living in the face of an unforeseeable end. This was [the elucidation] insofar as some passions are respectable and honorable.

On the other hand, the human being manifests greater strength in [a state of] affect, and is of more significance and power in this state, than if he is cool-headed. For example, the individual always carries more weight when angry, and is also in some respects seemly. Such affects have something agreeable about them if one is on their edge, so that 25:616 one is emotional*a* with one foot[hold], but not with the other; [this is so] even in sadness, for the borderline has this aspect, that I can let the alternating*b* sensation play, and if I see that it is disadvantageous for me on one side, then I can immediately withdraw the foot[hold]; for example, in tragedy. But he who harbors a resentment, is on the edge of affect, however, he who is furious is already emotional. He who cannot harbor a resentment can affect only little. Therefore anger in the valiant mind has something sublime about it; for example, in Cato. It seems to be this way also in other affects, that in this moment, that is, in their beginning, they can harmonize with principles, and without deliberation give weight to reason. In friendship one must not let it get to the point of affect, for otherwise one will thereby be ruled by the other against whom one is harboring it, and will finally be dragged along by him in all his misfortune. However, the moment of friendship is good; only one must always be on the edge, so that one is always able to withdraw. Therefore it is an intermediate state between affects and cool-headedness. The state of cool-headedness is the state of deliberation and examination of the object by reason. Then, however, this cool deliberation lacks an incentive, which gives it weight. This incentive is affect and passion, but it must be subject to the direction of reason, so that it will be kept in the moment, for if it is once released, then one can no longer check it. When one is only on the edge of affect, one calls this pathetical. For example, if there is only a moment of affect in a speech, the speech of this person is pathetical. However, he who is in an affect cannot talk at all. If he is again cool-headed, then he lacks the emphasis, but in the moment of affect, it is pathetical.

Question: Whether the affects and passions are good, therefore whether one must promote or subdue them? One must here distinguish two elements from one another: whether the passions belong to the great order of nature, or whether they belong to reason's order of rules. The

---

a im Affekt   *b* wechselseitige

first question is affirmed, the other one answered in the negative. For according to the order of nature, the human being is first an animal. Animality is the basis. He lives, preserves himself and his kind, as animal; however he is also an intelligence, or a human being, and there he avails himself of reason to attain his purpose in accordance with deliberate means. The affects and passions necessarily belong to animality. According to the order of nature, the human being must therefore be equipped with affects and passions. However, the affects and passions are contrary to reason, for the affects and passions take the place of reason before the human being comes to reason. However, when he has come to reason, then they should be brought under control by reason. Thus, for example, stinginess is in keeping with the order of nature, for nature wants that the animal does not care for itself alone, but that when it dies, it also leaves something for the descendants, so that it will be easier for them. Therefore in nature there is a propensity to be frugal in old age. However, reason demands this inclination be opposed, and to save only in accordance with intent. Therefore something is good according to the order of nature insofar as we are ruled as animals, but it is not good, insofar as we allow ourselves to be ruled as human beings by reason. This is thus the case with all affects and passions. Affects and passions are means of exerting our powers in animality, and take the place of deliberation. This way, for example, anger is a power of defense; however if reason is already there, then it makes other means available. Therefore to the extent something had to exist provisionally in nature, for the case if reason were not enlightened, and the human being would have had to live as an animal, to this extent it is good and agrees with the order of nature. However, as soon as reason dominates, then we are not justified in using what was an incentive with animality also as an incentive with reason. As human beings we live according to reason, accordingly we should seek to limit the incentive of animality through the maxims of reason, and not allow any inclination to get out of hand. The passions are based on the cast of mind*a* of human beings, and choose an object for themselves according to the constitution of the mind. Passions exist before their objects [do]; the human being has a propensity for honor sooner than he has an object of honor. Then the human being chooses an object for himself to [match] his passions, in accordance with the constitution of his mind. Thus irate persons are very ambitious. They

25:617

---

a As noted near the beginning of these lectures, the actual sense of *Gemüt* in German is "feeling soul" or "feeling heart" (i.e. the opposite of the cognitive consciousness expressed by *Geist*, and consonant with the Latin *anima/animus* distinction which Kant also invokes). In this light, *Gemütsart* is effectively synonymous with temperament, as Kant also elsewhere uses it. So seen, the sense of this sentence is that the passions are based on our temperament and choose their objects in accordance with the constitution of our feeling soul.

25:618 choose ambition on account of the fact that their cast of mind is rash and operative. Honor*[a]* is an object in the idea. It stimulates without sensation; he who has honor enjoys nothing thereby. Hence one also calls honor a delusion, a dupery.*[b]* He who is, however, agitated by an idea, by a dupery, for whatever [end], must be more excitable than the one who is agitated by something sensible. Choleric persons therefore have more propensity for honor. However, the phlegmatic person, who is sluggish, who does not have such excitability, must have something else as an object of his passion, for example, stinginess, lust, voraciousness.*[c]* Therefore the human being chooses as his object of passion what suits him best. Narrow and limited minds are stingy, because their mind*[d]* is not capable of great plans.*[e]* However, those who are capable of this, aim more for honor. Self-seeking persons are envious, for the self-consciousness of their weakness produces the fear of being predominated by others; hence envy arises from the fear of being surpassed by others. Envy and gloating are called malice. Persons who themselves have no joy, take malicious delight in others' misfortunes.*[f]* He who finds a source of joy in himself, likes to see joy in everyone, but he who enjoys none himself is irritated when another has joy. If the other suffers harm in his joy, then this one is pleased, just as a hypochondriac, who looks gloomy all day long, prefers that the weather outside be just as gloomy and overcast. However, if it is a beautiful clear day, then he is irritated, because he cannot enjoy it. It is just the same as if someone should stand before him and laugh when he is afflicted. Thus one says: the unhappy person is malevolent, for since he has no part in another's good fortune, it thus serves to mock him and [give] him a greater sensation of his misfortune; hence he is envious and takes malicious delight in others' misfortunes. Consequently he is to be feared. One is wont to name some passions not from the purpose, but from the means. Among these, stinginess is the only passion which has no purpose at all, no object at all, but only aims for a means. Hence

25:619 stinginess is also nonsensical, because it contradicts itself. He who saves money in order to use it later, in order to distinguish himself, or for the sake of other purposes, is not stingy, but he who saves without any purpose [is stingy]. Here one can conduct philosophical investigations [in regard to the question] how stinginess is possible. Never has a moralist or a preacher improved a stingy person. One may well extort something from him, but then the stinginess is also immediately back. Here reason

---

[a] *Ehre*; the term rendered as "ambition" in English (in this passage and previously), is *Ehrbegierde*, literally "desire for honor."

[b] *Dunst*: literally "to be bamboozled"

[c] As on 25:580, reading *Gefräßigkeit* for *Fräßigkeit*

[d] *Kopf*, literally "head"   *[e]* *Entwürfe*

[f] *besitzen Schadenfreude*; i.e. rendering the term here (otherwise translated as "gloating") in its full sense.

is no help, because he contradicts himself. However, the worth of the human being is very slight, if he only serves as a means. The human being is not a means but an end. One cannot say to a human being: why does the human being exist? For it is good in and for itself, that a human being exists. Therefore it is a great degradation that a human being exists as a means for other people, although this is the end of providence, that the stingy person saves for his descendants. Hence stinginess is the most ignoble vice. Therefore the passions must be named not in accordance with the means, but in accordance with the ends.

The natural disposition and propensity for the passions must be distinguished from the causes by which the passions are aroused. There exist some natural [and] some artificial or unnatural causes which arouse the passions. Thus in the case of affronts to my honor, the presence of another naturally arouses the passion of anger with me. I would not have taken it this way, if no one had been present. Drink, for example, belongs to the unnatural causes. It rouses passion and raises inclination to passion. Thus many are defiant, bold, and presumptuous, [when they are] in a drunken state. Thus the Turks take opium in war, so that they become courageous and daring. This way the passions of love also can be roused by an [artificial means].[a] There can thus be medicaments which rouse some passions, and can also moderate them. Thus Brinckmann[50] 25:620 says, who has stomach acid is a poltroon. Therefore who knows where the cause might often lie. Likewise if news of a battle reaches him [when he is] in his dressing gown, a general will not feel as spirited about it, as [he would] in his full uniform. Hypochondriacs are thus surprised at themselves, when the hypochondria is over, that they had such fantasies. Therefore there exist many causes of arousing the passions.

A distinction in the passions can also thus be made in regard to age and sex. Middle age, or the age of the man, is the age of prudence, where one can rightly estimate the worth of things. One can suppose this age [to be] from the 30th to the 40th year. One can certainly believe that a correct judgment hardly takes place before the 40th year. Judgment about the true worth of things, about what is seemly, and so forth, is found neither at an advanced nor young age. Yet young people do not like to let themselves be bound in marriage by old people. The parents have already forgotten the state of being in love, hence they cannot grasp at all how an individual forgoes wealth for the sake of a beautiful face, and the young person in turn cannot grasp how he is supposed to prefer money to charm. Thus a middle age must take place where both are united, to which youthful sensation still belongs, but which is not as completely spent as in advanced age, but also not as raging as in

---

[a] Latin, *filtrum*, which denotes a strainer or filter. The other manuscripts have *Filtrium* and *siltriam*. The original editors note that the term could not be identified.

youth, and to which the power of judgment belongs, which first shows up with the years, for which thus no great degree of reason is required, for a young person can also have this, but [which consists in] a mature experience and power of judgment which one does not yet have in youth. Therefore there exists a middle age in which one knows how to estimate the worth of things rightly. For there exist follies of youth, just as there exist the eccentricities[a] of old age.

25:621   The difference in regard to sex is: the affects are far more violent with the feminine sex, but they do not penetrate as deeply. Therefore a woman, even if she is so angry that she has turned the whole house upside down, still will not become sick due to anger. Likewise sadness is very violent with them, but soon blows over with them. Anger is really much deadlier in the case of a man, and even if he is not sad, he thus feels the pain more in the soul. Nature has outfitted the woman's machine[b] [to be] very elastic; with them everything happens only on the surface. For the violence of the passions requires strength, hence strong persons are more violently sensible of the attacks[c] in an illness than are weak ones. For where the vital energy is weak, there irregular agitation will also not occur with such strength. The ancients already said: women are easily taken by something, and they also soon tire of it.[51] Something quickly gets hold of them. If they find a difficulty in attaining the object, then they become more curious and vehement, but if they have no difficulty in attaining it, then they soon tire of it. That nothing great can ever be carried out in the world without great passions, that they are therefore the incentives of great actions, is a universal opinion which these persons cite who defend the passions this way, and therefore want that they may not be suppressed at all. It is true great passions play great roles in the world. They produce revolutions and a break with long-standing delusion and the state [of things in which all is] awry. However, although they are of use for revolution, nevertheless they do not thus serve to establish order. Therefore they must have someone who is cool-headed above them to rule them, or to redress [matters after] them.[d] Otherwise they can produce a still greater misfortune. Therefore we can give a worth to passions in and for themselves, however if he has passions, the human being has no honor from this, for they lie in animality. Therefore it is the rule of wisdom and prudence not to tolerate passions in the mind, but courageously to preserve the mind, because they make [the mind] unable to carry out deliberations, and to achieve purpose in accordance with

---

[a] *Narrheiten*, literally "foolishness" or (stronger) "madness"
[b] *Maschiene*; literal translation retained, since the mechanistic terminology here is probably not metaphorical.
[c] Reading *Anfälle* in place of *Zufälle*
[d] *ihnen nachbeßert*, literally "improve upon," "repair"

the prescription of reason. However, we can thereby promote reason's efficaciousness and combine the passions with reason, but not let them dominate.

The sensations of human beings require cultivation and the inclinations require discipline. The sensations should be refined and the inclinations brought under control. He whose sensations have not received cultivation, is unrefined, and he whose sensations do not admit of cultivation, is crude. Hence people who are unrefined are not yet for that reason crude. They are unrefined because their sensations have not yet received cultivation. To this belongs a fine sensation, for example, to feel the duty of gratitude, or to be sensible of the indecency of harboring resentment against one's friend, and still to esteem the former friendship which is finally broken. 25:622

Gallantry and point of honor, *point d'honneur*, arise from the too great refinement of the sensations. Gallantry is thoroughly studied politeness, according to which one notes everything that can in the least flatter one and what the most delicate sense can feel. In regard to this subtlety, the woman is susceptible,[a] but the man should be sensitive.[b] Sensitive here [means] the fine power of judgment in regard to the most subtle objects, to be sensible of what is agreeable with women, and to spare [them] all that is disagreeable, and to be very delicate in the smallest impressions. However, the susceptibility[c] of women [consists in this]: to notice all this delicacy, and to notice the least neglect in the solicitude of this delicacy. Sensitivity or gallantry agrees well with a man's magnanimity, just as the woman's susceptibility accords well with her sex. In the game of gallantry, [there] is great art, for which much time is required. The point of honor is the excessive refinement in regard to paying to another the honor we owe him. Now, the point of honor is connected more with selfishness than with the desire for honor.[d] In ancient times, the desire for honor was very powerful, however the subtlety was wholly unknown, that is, what we call the point of honor. This sophistication which consists in subtle observations of honor, and is called point of honor, is not true honor. For example, if someone does not let me walk in the middle of the street,[e] or on his right, or offends my honor by a small expression: all this is no reason for taking offense. This delicacy in regard to the condition of honor is chimerical, and the satisfaction of its offense is just as chimerical. Often, a clumsy person who otherwise holds

---

[a] *empfindlich*

[b] *empfindsam*

[c] *empfindlichkeit*

[d] *Ehrbegierde*, elsewhere rendered as "ambition," but the reference to the ancients indicates that Kant has the more literal sense in mind.

[e] *Mittelstein*: the main streets in Königsberg had paved strips in the middle which were called (literally) middle stone or stone bridge (Fritz Gause, *Königsberg in Preußen. Die Geschichte einer europäischen Stadt* (Leer: Gerhard Rautenberg, 1987)).

25:623   to no inner, true honor, but seeks his glory in renowned deeds is very delicate in regard to an affront to the point of honor, and immediately tries to obtain satisfaction. Nevertheless, there still is something in this which has a basis. Two elements, gallantry and point of honor are thus connected and are the two incentives; namely, gallantry [is the incentive] of our sensation in regard to women, and point of honor [is the incentive] in regard to refining our [sensation] among one another. They serve as means of preserving a certain fineness and, in social intercourse, of penalizing every rudeness*a* on the spot.

    Just as cultivation aims at sensation, so discipline aims at the inclinations. He whose inclinations have not received any discipline is ill-mannered, however he whose inclinations do not admit of any discipline is wild. In regard to the inclinations, the human being must be brought under control, just as in regard to the sensations, he must be refined. The propriety which one observes in society does not come of itself and by chance, but much time must be spent on it, so that our natural unruliness can be brought under control, until we attain propriety.

    We can mention laziness and negligence with regard to the actions of human beings, with regard to the inclination and disinclination to act and get things done.*b* Laziness is contrary to liveliness, and negligence to industriousness. A lively person can also be negligent, but not lazy.

    In regard to certain actions, we call some people careless. This carelessness is either thoughtlessness*c* or precipitousness.*d* Thoughtlessness is when carelessness manifests itself in regard to the decision and deliberation of the understanding. Precipitousness, however, is when one does not even use one's wits*e* in regard to one's actions; for example, if one walks somewhere and does not at all look out that one can fall. Flightiness is a carelessness in regard to sensation. One brings flighty persons to the point of shedding tears, but it does not take long before they have forgotten it.

    Contrary to all of it is steadfastness, which consists in this: that one does not deviate from one's resolve and [one] firmly insists on one's decision. It is necessary to have firmness in one's decisions, and to persist in one's resolve, and prefer to tolerate disadvantage, than to let resolve go.

25:624   Then the human being knows for sure that he is undertaking something. However, he who is not steadfast in this often lays hold of a resolve, for which he knows for sure that nothing will come of it, because he knows that he has already often broken resolutions. Then the human being is in his [own] eyes a blusterer.*f* He no longer has any confidence in himself;

---

a   *Grobheit*: could mean "crudeness," but "rudeness" is more general.
b   *zu handeln und zu thun*
c   *Unbedachtsamkeit*
d   *Unbesonnenheit*

e   *Sinnen*
f   *Windbeutel*, literally "wind bag"

from this arises hopelessness. That is a disconsolate state, when one always puts off one's hope. This is how it is with late conversions. This is how it is with other things for which one wants to break one's habit of doing them, for example, sleeping in; then it is always said, just this one time more, but then no more, and thus one again philosophizes oneself free of one's plan. In such a state, one never has hope of improving oneself; this is an important point in morality. Hence one must seek to keep one's word to oneself just as conscientiously as to others. From this arises a firm confidence in ourselves. He who knows how to manage himself so that he can be content with himself, is steadfast.

* *
*

PART II. ANTHROPOLOGY

After we have, in the general part, come to know the human being according to his powers of soul and his faculties, we must now, in the particular part, thus seek to apply the knowledge of the human being, and to make use of it. Therefore we here consider the human determinations in connection [with one another], and examine the concept which one makes for oneself of the human being, or the distinctive [mark] of the human being in regard to others. Here we can consider him in regard to his body and in regard to his mind. In regard to the body, we can look to the figure and build[a] of the body, but which we here set aside. With the body, we can here however especially examine the constitution, complexion, and the temperament. As regards the constitution, this is thus the nature[b] of the solid[c] parts, the edifice, the constitution of the body. Complexion, however, concerns the mixture of the fluid parts. Temperament concerns the principle of life, to the extent it is a combination both of the constitution and of the complexion, both in regard to the fluid and the solid parts, to the extent they constitute mechanical powers. The principle of life in regard to the body [consists in] the nerves, muscles, and fibers. As regards the constitution, the human being is thus either of a strong or weak constitution. The constitution is not based on the size, but on the firmness of the nerves and fibers. Complexion signifies more the mixture of the fluid parts in the body. Therefore if I ask about the principle of life, I thus find it in the solid and fluid parts. The possibility of being a living[d] being is the first condition, the motive

25:625

[a] *Gestalt*   [b] *Beschaffenheit*
[c] *festen*: in regard to resolve, etc., rendered as "firm," but here the juxtaposition is of the two kinds of physical parts, solid and fluid, making up the body.
[d] *belebt*, literally an "animated being"

171

spring^a must be sought in the solid parts. No inner motion^b of the solid parts is possible without separation, but with the fluid parts, a motion without separation is possible. Therefore, although they change their position, the fluid parts are in connection [with one another]. However, the vehicle, the first motive force of the solid parts, or rather the instrument of the motion of life, can only be the fluid [part]. The doctors still do not know whether illnesses are to be placed or sought in the fluid or solid parts. Temperament is the unified principle of life from the constitution and the complexion. Here temperament is taken in the physical sense,^{c} and not in the psychological, where the mind does not come into consideration^d at all. Temperament differs in regard to the solid parts, and also differs in regard to the fluid parts. For example, if the muscles are soft and elastic, and the nerves have an ease of motion, then such an individual could be called sanguine. Therefore one could infer something about temperament merely from the motion and from the structure of the parts, which one can already perceive by feeling. This way doctors draw conclusions from the fluid [parts], for example, about temperament from the blood.

25:626 With the human being, we divide everything into nature and freedom. We count natural aptitude, talent, and temperament as nature, but mind, heart, and character as freedom. Something can displease me about a human being due to nature, but I cannot impute guilt to him [for it]. If all is well in regard to nature, then we call it fortunate. Guilt is imputed to the human being for what displeases in regard to freedom. If all is well in regard to freedom, then one calls it good-naturedness. Although the mind^e and heart are not as based on freedom, as is the character of the human being, but we also do not know how much in regard to their goodness^f is to be imputed to the nature of the human being, and how much to freedom, we thus regard everything as if it were to be imputed to freedom and approve or disapprove of it. What appertains to freedom, appertains immediately to the inner goodness of the human being and is good or evil in itself. However, what belongs to nature does not please directly, but as an instrument, which can still be applied to whatever [end].

^{a} *Triebfeder*, elsewhere rendered as "incentive," but here its fundamental mechanical sense is more fitting.
^{b} *Bewegung*, previously rendered as "agitation" in relation to the mind, passions, and inclinations.
^{c} *Verstande* ^{d} *Reflexion*
^{e} *Gemüt*: here, as previously (25:617), the more literal rendering as "feeling soul" would seem to fit the context better. See also the beginning of the next paragraph, where Kant identifies the parts of the *Gemüt* under discussion here as "natural aptitude, talent, and temperament."
^{f} *Bonitaet*

In regard to the mind, we can divide the principles of activity into natural aptitude, talent, and temperament. Natural aptitude is the capacity of receptivity to receive certain objects. Therefore natural aptitude belongs to capacity. Talent is a faculty of producing products; therefore it belongs to power. Temperament is the union of both. In regard to natural aptitude, one calls a human being tractable, quick to learn, mild; in regard to natural aptitude, he is passive. Natural aptitude is required in the case of the apprentice, but talent is required in the case of the teacher. A youth must have natural aptitude [in order] to accept products, but a man must have talent, give shape [to things] himself, in order to produce products. Thus one has a natural aptitude for music, for things [pertaining to] memory, for things [pertaining to] ingenuity. This natural aptitude can take place without talent; thus there exist nations which are only capable students, without producing anything themselves. As regards talent, there thus exists, for example, a talent of cognition for observation, for exact and fine perception, in addition a talent of courage, of [keeping] the spirit alive,[a] a talent of decision, of the quick grasp[b] [of things]. Thus many have a great understanding, but no quick grasp [of things]. There thus also exists a talent of quick resolution; such persons are resolved. This talent is a talent of presumptuousness, in accordance with which one does not at all shy away from the judgments of others, but is very sensitive with regard to them, which every one loving honor must be, but not touchy,[c] for [such a person] is timid in regard to the judgments of others. Therefore there exist all kinds of talents, which are also the condition of our active powers. This way in the case of an orator there exist many talents, for example, naïvety, where one can be thoughtful, affective, also tasteful, in accordance with the simplicity of nature without art. If nature appears as art, then we are taken aback every time, and take enjoyment in it, but if it is the reverse, that art appears as nature, then it pleases still more. Hence such ideas[d] and speeches, which are surely art, but appear in such a way as if they had flowed naturally of themselves, delight greatly. This talent is indeed natural, no one can give it to himself, but it must also be very cultivated. Herein Voltaire is a master, which is also his only merit. His derisive wit comes rolling out so artlessly, as if he had not thought about it at all.

25:627

Temperament is based on the union of natural aptitude and talent, on the practical faculty and on the mind's incentive in regard to natural aptitude and talent. Temperament is of course only the sensible use of the faculties and capacities of the mind. Temperament can be very different in regard to the mind and to talent. For example, he who is sensitive[e]

---

[a] *des gegenwärtigen Geistes*
[b] *behenden Begrifs*
[c] *empfindlich*

[d] *Gedancken*
[e] *empfindlich*

according to his natural aptitude, but possesses strength and fearlessness according to his talent, is choleric. However, he who according to his natural aptitude is sensitive in regard to the ills of life, he who gets intense impressions from the ills of life and has a despondent natural aptitude, but has no hope according to his talent, [and] does not pluck up [his] courage, is melancholic. He is hurt by the ills of life, while the choleric person is furious. However, in regard to the ills [of life], the choleric person is wily and can appease*a* himself with paradisiacal hopes. He has the talent to make up highly arbitrary fantasies according to his pleasure;*b* thus an illusion takes place with him, he deceives himself. Therefore natural aptitude and talent constitute the temperature.[52] The disposition*c* of the mind must be distinguished from temperament. Temperament always remains, [but] one can accustom oneself to the disposition through a habit of mind*d* in regard to feelings and inclinations. The individual who has often had to endure adversities, in the end takes on a misanthropic disposition. The heart of one who forces himself to be genial, afterwards brightens up, and later becomes in fact cheerful. Temper*e* is the peculiarity of the disposition, where one assesses everything in accordance with one's frame of mind.*f* According to ill temper, the vicious person is a fool, and the unfortunate ones are on par with children who cry over their toy which has been taken away.

25:628   By having spoken of natural aptitude, talent, and temperament, we have thus examined the source of the feelings and inclinations of human beings and the principle of life. Now we want to examine the principle of activity, to make use of these feelings and inclinations, thus the practical with human beings. In this respect, we distinguish heart, mind, and character. Not much is required for a genial mind.*g* The genial mind is only

a *abspeisen*, literally "to put someone off" by giving them some token good.

b *Vergnügen*   *c* *Disposition des Gemüths*

d *habitum*; i.e. synonymous with *Disposition*, just as *angewöhnen* (here rendered as "accustom oneself") is literally, "get into the habit of."

e *Laune*: basic meaning of this term is "mood," while Kant's sense of it has been rendered previously as "temper" (25:563ff). The next sentence indicates that Kant's particular sense in this context is the equivalent of *launisch*, or being "ill-tempered" (and hence *Laune* is rendered there accordingly). The editors further note that the Prieger lectures have "the actual dispositions are temper," rather than "the peculiarity of disposition is temper."

f *Kopf*; i.e. literally, according to where one's own head is.

g *zum guten Gemüth*: literally "good mind" but this connotes intelligence in English, while the context here indicates that Kant intends something like "geniality." The problematic nature of rendering *Gemüt* as "mind" (noted on previous occasions) also again arises in the ensuing discussion here. A more literal rendering of Kant's sense here would be to speak of the "good-natured soul," but as becomes clear, he wants to make a further distinction between such in a passive sense (under discussion here) and an active sense (kind-heartedness).

a flexibility, which does not give any resistance to the other [person], which is passive toward others, and gives them no obstacles. The genial mind has no worth in itself, but is only a docility with regard to others. Neither talent, nor a good disposition*a* is required for a genial mind, but only a quickness in acquiescing to every form. One can do this whether one has good or evil dispositions.*b* It is the least [that can be said], if I say of a human being, he has a genial mind. The mind is only something negative, nothing is yet done through a genial mind, but I am merely not in the other's way. All stupid [people] have a genial mind, they are the instruments of others. Therefore a genial mind is only worth being tolerated.

More is already required for a good heart.*c*53 In the practical [sphere], the heart is that which is a principle of activity in accordance with good impulses.*d* Here one is no longer merely passive, but one must be active. One is kind-hearted*e* if one does something good by instinct.*f* Kind-heartedness is thus a good-naturedness*g* from instincts. The good-naturedness of the will from principles is character. Where then there are evil principles, there is an evil character. In the case of one who is kind-hearted, one can also form a good character. In the case of one who is not kind-hearted, it does not yet follow that he has an evil heart. All compassion, all sympathetic enjoyment, all benevolence from instinct appertains to kind-heartedness. Kind-hearted people are seldom strict observers of their owed duties. They will borrow money, and give it as a gift to another person who can plaintively stir their heart. They become infatuated by the sweetness of good actions and forget the owed duties. A great illusion takes place with them. They estimate the actions which they carry out from kind-heartedness as a merit, but if they are, how-ever, supposed to carry out obligatory actions,*h* then they cannot place any merit in it. Hence [this is how] it happens that with the surges of kind-heartedness, people forget the owed duties, and confer the merit [noted] previously. With such people, one is not secure in regard to owed duties; they hate owed duty, and prefer to do everything on their

25:629

---

a *Gesinnung*: see footnote at 25:504.
b *Gesinnungen*; see previous footnote regarding this term (25:504).
c *guten Herzens*; i.e. literally rendered.
d *Trieben*, rendered as "instincts" in other sections, but also meaning "drives" (e.g. the sex drive, or natural drives), or "impulses" (chosen here because it connects slightly with the connotation of "choice" which is also implied in the notion of "principles of activity").
e *gutherzig*, literally "good-hearted," but most generally rendered as "kind-hearted."
f *Instincte*   *h* *Handlungen der Schuldigkeit*
g *Gutartigkeit*

own*ᵃ* out of kind-heartedness and benevolence. He who has to ask for a debt in the case of such a kind-hearted person, is entirely within his rights to ask for it. This is not, however, for the kind-hearted person.*ᵇ* If he [i.e. the debtee] wants to get it [what is owed to him], then he must plaintively ask for it, and touch [the other's] heart, which he indeed does not have to do, yet then he gets it, for then the kind-hearted person thinks he has done him a favor, even if he just pays a debt; this way he has obliged me. For every favor and good deed obliges the other. Kind-hearted persons are often moved to good deeds by the miserable figure of the beggar, but in another case, where the poverty is greater than with the beggar, where it is just not so evident, there kind-heartedness is not likewise moved. Our kind-heartedness is especially manifest toward beautiful young women, indeed [it is so] that the person, who does not let himself be moved by them, is even called a barbarian. Why does kind-heartedness not manifest itself just as well toward an old woman? Because it is a direction of the will from instinct, and not from principles. Kind-heartedness is lovable. The kind-hearted person is a play of impressions, which arouse benevolence in him. Therefore with him it depends on how his heart is moved. In the case of an individual where there is nothing more positive than a good heart, he is good or evil according to the way circumstances affect him. He will also commit evil out of kind-heartedness; he will deny a stingy person, who has a claim against another one, his right. If the other can better move him, and although this one is a miser, then his claim is just after all. Kind-heartedness is without [a] rule. Kind-heartedness can be solely exercised on their part, when one tries to move the mind by impressions. However, it is not good that the human being is solely ruled by the heart. This kind-heartedness must be subject to a rule, so that character is formed [together] with it, for otherwise kind-heartedness predominates over character, and then the human being follows his instinct and his sensible impulses,*ᶜ* but not

25:630 his principles. Gellert's morality teaches [one] to do everything out of kind-heartedness and not out of principles.[54]

Character is the employment of our power of choice to act according to rules and principles. Character is estimable and honorable. One does not exactly love a man of good character, one does not seek out his company, but one values him. If with human beings there is no uniformity of actions according to rules, then there may always be kind-heartedness; but there is no character. People among whom each has a character, cannot harmonize among themselves in one character and unite [as] one universal character. This way each Englishman has [his] own singular

---

ᵃ *von selbst*: i.e. out of their own kindness, and not because it is a prescribed duty.
ᵇ i.e. this is not how such a person sees the matter.
ᶜ *Antrieben*

character; for this reason the whole nation has no character, and the French nation has a universal character, because no Frenchman has his own [character].[55]

Character constitutes the worth of a human being in and for itself, and is the origin[a] of free actions from principles. There exist human beings who have a good, an evil, also no character at all. There do not exist any human beings who could not have a good or evil heart, but there are people who have no character at all. Therefore with a human being, even before a good or evil character is formed, a character must in fact be formed, so that he first has a character in general; i.e. he must first be accustomed to act according to principles. Those who have no charac-   25:631 ter at all, take on a semblance of character. They pretend to have rules and principles, and imitate something character-like,[b] because they do not have any character in themselves. Such people make general rules for themselves, for example, not to lend anything to anyone, or not to believe anyone who promises them something. Such people do not have a bad character, they just have no principles, because they are often deceived by their good heart, and cannot rely on it at all. And because they also lack understanding and power of judgment even to have insight into the rule without being able to apply it in each special case, they thus make a general rule for themselves. A character in fact, it may be good or evil, is one[c] character. One must in the first place have a single[d] character, it may be good or evil; that is, one must act according to principles. Is it better to have an evil character than to have none at all? The individual without any character is not hateful, but he deserves contempt; hence it is better to have an evil character than to have none at all. For who has a single character, it may be good or evil, surely already displays a strength of soul, that one is capable of acting according to principles, and even if the character is evil, then it can still be improved through principles. However, who has no character at all, is not at all in accord with himself; today he gives something to everyone, he is very liberal, but tomorrow he becomes very frugal and stingy, because he sees that he comes up too short, if he does it this way every day. Hence he quickly catches hold of another rule, and thus with him nothing is dependable. Such people are like soft[e] wax; every instant they catch hold of another rule. They are very readily steered to evil, but not to the good, since for this principles

---

[a] *Principium*, Latin (in this case) for ultimate source, origin, cause of something.

[b] *was Charackteristisches*

[c] *ein*: Kant's point here often escapes the English translation because *ein* (as in this sentence) gets rendered as two different words in English, "a" and "one." That character must be "one," i.e. a one, unified character, is fundamental to Kant's mature sense of moral character.

[d] *einen*

[e] Reading *weiches* in place of *zähes*, per editors' note and making more sense in the context.

are already required. With the feminine sex, one sees that it is already not exactly in keeping with their nature to have a character at all. The masculine [sex] is however called^a more to principles; although many likewise have no character, yet character is more in keeping with their nature. Yet principles also do prevail with women, and indeed principles of honor. They are kind-hearted in regard to liberal actions, but they cannot do

25:632 anything from principles, because they acquire nothing, but the man [is the one who acquires things]; hence in this they must be tractable. However, with them the character of the love of honor takes the place of the virtues; hence in upbringing, in virtue, everything must be built on this principle. When I say: the woman has honor or is honor-loving, that is thus already a great deal. Therefore character constitutes the good-naturedness of the subject, and character is also to be peculiarly allotted to the human being; this wholly concerns my freedom. Although mind and heart also appertain to freedom, yet the basis in regard to them also already thus lies partly in nature; however character is to be peculiarly ascribed to the human being. Mind and heart are innate, but character is not innate, but must be acquired. For, because the good-naturedness of the heart is the good-naturedness of the instincts^b and inclinations, but the good-naturedness of character is based on the good-naturedness of the dispositions,^{c} but the inclinations and instincts are innate, but not the maxims, principles, and dispositions,^{d} it thus follows that character must be acquired, but the mind and heart are innate. With character, the understanding comes to the aid; however, it is still based on the good mind and heart. One takes honesty to be peculiar^e to the good mind,^{f} but one must attribute beneficence to the good heart; uprightness however befits character. One is wont to say: he who is honest is also stupid, a good man would be the one who is artless. Honesty can indeed agree with simplicity; with stupidity, however, honesty can always be found, yet it still does not follow that the one who is stupid is also every time honest, and vice versa. Honesty agrees with stupidity for this reason, because honesty takes the straight path, but to take the straight path is very easy and convenient. Roguishness requires more shrewdness and

25:633 speculation to take the crooked path. For if I am asked about something, and I am such a good, honest fellow, I openly say the simple^g truth just as it is, and make no effort to think any more about it, but tell the matter as it was, and thereby I also get by the best and need not [take] any responsibility. However, he who really wants to lie, must deliberate well

---

^{a} *berufen*, or stronger, "destined for"
^{b} *Triebe*
^{c} *Gesinnungen*: see footnote at 25:504.
^{d} *Gesinnungen*
^{e} *zueignen*, archaic for *zugehören*, "to be peculiar to," "inherent in"; in the reflexive form, *sich eignen*, the sense would be that "one finds the good mind to be suited for honesty."
^{f} *guten Gemüth*
^{g} *reine*, literally "pure"

and exert himself to lie in such a way that his lies agree with all the circumstances, so that he does not embarrass himself; consequently it takes more shrewdness than is required for honesty. Accordingly it is not good to pair honesty and stupidity, for otherwise, in order not to be stupid, someone will act the rogue. Uprightness cannot, however, take place at all with stupidity; it really requires reason. For the upright individual acts according to principles, but principles can only be grasped insofar as one is capable of having insight into principles, and insofar as one is capable of having respect for the right of other human beings; however, reason is required for this. A man of upright character does not merely have the faculty of acting according to principles, for the faculty lies in the understanding, but also the good will and good disposition[a] to exercise such principles. However, to have insight into this requires much understanding, therefore understanding appertains to the upright man, which indeed is not speculative, but [it] still must be correct. Accordingly character is not innate, but must be acquired. However, it costs a great deal of effort and takes a long time, before one has accustomed oneself to acting in accordance with principles. That only comes with age, with mature reason. We all believe we are reared[b] in youth, but we are actually not reared, we still must subsequently rear ourselves, and form our character ourselves, which does not consist in this, that one acquaints oneself with certain rules, but that one must think the principles through for oneself. The principles must be learned,[c] and must be understood.[d] One must not afterwards deviate from these principles, for they constitute the law. A law, however, does not admit of any exception, which one is wont to say about a rule. He who is, for example, truthful due to a principle, will never deviate from it. However, this seldom exists, and it takes very long before one is truthful from principles. Human beings are then indeed quite truthful, but they still often deviate from it, because this truthfulness does not arise from principles, but rather from refinement.[e] Can a good character occur there where a maliciousness of mind and heart exists? It is said about Socrates, that he had a malicious mind and heart by nature, but formed his character through his understanding in accordance with correct principles. Therefore it indeed turns out to be so, but for this it takes understanding, to which one can grant the power to act according to principles. However, if the mind and heart are already malicious, then such really proceeds with much difficulty. Such an individual who, despite the maliciousness of his heart and mind, has made the effort to assume a good character, yet cannot thus be quite trusted,

25:634

---

[a] *Gesinnung*: see footnote at 25:504.   [b] *erzogen*
[c] Reading *gelernt* in place of *gelehrt*, per editors' note and as making better sense in the context.
[d] *eingesehen*   [e] *Politur*

for one still does not know whether this good character has already taken root to the extent that it can predominate the maliciousness of heart and mind; one still cannot know whether the maliciousness of his heart and mind wins out over the character.

We can in addition divide character into an assumed and a natural [character]. The assumed one arises from principles which have no basis in nature, but are only assumed due to deliberation. The natural one, however, agrees with the nature of the human being. Human beings have an assumed character, if for example, they are kind-hearted, by which they are often deceived; then they are ashamed, that they come up too short on all sides, and make rules for themselves upon which they firmly want to insist. Or if, in the management of their affairs,[a] they see that small expenditures do finally add up to a quantity, they thus, even if they are otherwise not[b] so frugal, plan from now on to pay attention to all little details. Then they make rules for themselves, for example, not to give anything to any beggar. It seems as if such persons have a character, since they act according to principles; however they have only assumed these rules on an occasion and have suited it to themselves. However, rules are the leading strings of the immature. Who makes a rule for himself and doggedly insists upon it, for example, no longer to lend anything to anyone, indeed in fact falls short the least in the sum of all cases, although he very often falls short, and although there were very often cases where he most certainly could have deviated from the rule; however because he does not know which [ones] are such cases, where he can deviate from the rule, he thus always remains with the rule, the cases may be what they will. Therefore such persons lack the power of judgment to determine such cases, where the rule is to be applied. For this reason many become frugal due to the assumed character, where they have made a rule for themselves never to give or lend anything to anyone. Now it can very often happen, that one cannot refuse persons of position and character something like this; however, because one has often made up one's mind about the latter, since one cannot assess whether this is the case or not where the rule is to be applied, one thus loses one's honor and reputation over it. Mature insight and power of judgment to determine the case, whether it belongs this time under the rule or not, therefore appertains to principles, for otherwise such principles make [one] pedantic. If one has a talent for poetry, and one seeks to cultivate one's talent, then it hinders character. Therefore poets, who have a natural talent for poetry and not only a propensity – for one can also have a propensity for something without [having a] talent for it – also usually have no character. For a poet must be accustomed to put himself into all

25:635

---

[a] *Wirtschaft*: can denote the full range of activity from the economy to the household.
[b] Reading *nicht* in place of *noch*, per editors' note, and as best fitting the context.

situations, and to assume all characters. Then however he has no character peculiar [to him], just as the actor [has no such character].[a] Imitation also greatly hinders character. Therefore in upbringing one must never refer one's children to the neighbor's children and tell them a lot about "phew, that is not seemly," but [one must] form their character directly, [one must] instill principles of good and evil, of the righteous and noble [in them].[56]

Since however natural aptitude, talent, and temperament, are to be distinguished into a fortunate and unfortunate one, character is here likewise distinguished into a good and evil one. One can always have a fortunate temperament, and still an evil character, and in turn, an unfortunate temperament, and still a good character. Who takes immediate satisfaction in the good, has a good character, and vice versa. Evil character can be divided into the deceptive and malevolent [one]. The deceptive [one] is a mean and contemptible character, but the malevolent one is hateful. Malevolent character manifests itself, for example, in the suppression of the right of others, in the assertion of one's will and willfulness, in [taking] enjoyment in the destruction of others' good fortune, in [taking] enjoyment in playing a nasty trick on another. Malevolent character especially manifests itself where an object of nature is not an object of satisfaction, indeed where it is even [an object of] dissatisfaction, and one still has a sensation of enjoyment over it, for example, over another's misfortune. We must be careful about regarding people [as being] of unfortunate temperament, as well as regarding people [as being] of evil character, for that is the worst which one can say: the individual has an evil character, for then [if one had such a character] one does evil from principles.

25:636

ON TEMPERAMENT IN THE SPECIES

Temperament is the proportion of sensible feelings and desires. With the human being, everything depends on the relation and not on the degree of the one or other capacity. The adroit proportion of the powers of cognition, of the sensations and desires constitutes what characterizes the human being in [his] sensibility, with regard to his temperament. With temperament we do not act in accordance with principles and dispositions[b] as with character, but according to inclinations. Two elements are required for temperament: feeling and desires. The proportion of both constitutes temperament.

All temperaments are divided up with regard to feeling and activity. The temperaments with regard to feeling effect the arrangement according to which the human being is capable of well-being or affliction. Two

---

[a] Cf. 25:574–575.   [b] *Gesinnungen*

are included in this: the sanguine and melancholic temperament. If the human being is greatly drawn[a] to enjoyment, then he is sanguine, but if he is more drawn to discontentment,[b] then he is melancholic. Feeling is thus the basis of the human being's condition.[c] With regard to conduct or the activity of human beings, the temperaments are also divided into two: either one feels the source of activity or the powers of life within oneself, or one feels an inactivity and a lack of the powers of life within oneself. The first is the choleric, but the second [is] the phlegmatic temperament. The choleric [temperament] is active, but the phlegmatic [is] inactive.

25:637

All temperaments must not be divided up from one point of view, and one cannot say, there are four temperaments; rather, they must be divided up from different points of view. The sanguine and melancholic do not concern activity, but sensation, and the choleric and phlegmatic concern in turn the source of activity. The sanguine and melancholic in turn concern the capability of living, but the choleric and phlegmatic [concern] the powers of life. If we then want to put the temperaments together, we thus cannot say: someone is sanguine and melancholic, for these are opposites with regard to feeling, or someone is choleric and phlegmatic, for these are opposites with regard to activity.

The temperaments cannot be divided up according to their objects, for example, the sanguine person has lust as his object, the choleric [has] honor, and so forth, for the human being cannot have the objects prior to the temperaments. We bring the temperaments into the world, but not the objects. The human being later chooses the objects according to the proportion of his feelings and inclinations.

As to what then concerns the temperaments in particular, each [taken] by itself, the sanguine person is not then the one who wants all enjoyment and the good life, for everyone wants that, but the one who is thus capable of enjoying it. The sanguine person feels his life everywhere. However, we saw with the faculty of pleasure and displeasure, that life is the feeling of the free and regular play of the powers of the human being, but the feeling of the hindrance of life is pain, and enjoyment is the [feeling] of its promotion.[57] Now the sanguine person regards all objects not as hindrances, but as promotions of his life. He always feels[d] well. Because he is light-hearted,[e] he finds himself affected by the source of life. This disposition[f] is inclined to mirth and cheerfulness; however on the other

---

[a] *hat große Reizbarkeit*, lit. "has a great sensitivity for" or "is easily stimulated by."
[b] *Misvergnügen*   [c] *Befinden*, lit. "state of health"
[d] *sich befinden*: synonymous with *sich fühlen*, where the sense of the latter connotes one's state of health.
[e] Idiomatic: *blut leicht ist*
[f] *Disposition*; i.e. this is how Kant uses the term "disposition," as interchangeable with temperament (as contrasted with *Gesinnung* which is related to character).

hand, it is flighty and thoughtless, for the variations are all enlivening, and always give life a fresh boost.[a] Therefore sanguine persons aim for variableness and are of a changeable cast of mind, and because they take everything in from the aspect[b] how it can be a basis of their well-being, they imagine no danger; they are very sensitive and tender, for the easy motion of the organs of life effects their being thus enlivened. On the other hand, however, this indicates a weakness, they are not toughened up, they are soft. Melancholic persons have a propensity for discontentment, they feel a hindrance of life in themselves. This does not indeed shorten life, but it is a feeling of hindrance, and that is already enough to arouse ill humor in us. Accordingly the melancholic person will not take all the things in the world as promotions of his life, as does the sanguine one, but will regard them from the aspect of danger, for since he does not feel himself to be in good spirits, he thus sees gloom even [when it is] clear. The sanguine person's condition cheers the feeling of life, but the melancholic person does not have such sensations of enjoyment; he is not as thoughtless, because he does not become as animated [and] does not have such elastic organs. The choleric person is active. All choleric individuals must have something to do and they also make themselves busy; hence a choleric cleric likes to meddle in the affairs of the state. They like to conduct legal proceedings, that is very much up their alley; hence they also desire honor, for the one who can be moved to activity by such a small motive of honor, must already be active. Nature has already made such objects, which are in keeping with it, inherent to this temperament. Accordingly, choleric persons are polypragmatics. The phlegmatic person finds no power of activity in himself; he is lax in carrying [things] out.

    Although one cannot put the sanguine temperament together with the melancholic one, yet the one can moderate the other; for they cannot take place together, because they are contrary to one another. Nevertheless, just as the propensity for play must be somewhat moderated by seriousness so that the play does not get out of hand, seriousness however is already a cessation of amusement and a moment of sadness. For if all of a sudden one [goes] from a cheerful countenance [to] assume a serious one, then that is already tantamount to wanting to become sad. Likewise the sanguine temperament must be moderated by the melancholic one, insofar as we count on a degree of seriousness with the melancholic one, which [these persons] attribute to the worth of things. Then we say that the sanguine temperament is moderated by the serious [one]. Now this is not, however, a mixture of both temperaments, but only a moderation of the sanguine one. If one now moderates both, then they can come

25:638

25:639

---

[a] *neuen Stoß und Trieb*, literally "new thrust and drive"
[b] *Seite*, literally "side"

to approximate one another, and in the melancholic one are [found] the positive causes of discontentment, in the sanguine one are [found] the positive causes of enjoyment. Thus one also says of the choleric person: it would be good if a bit of phlegm were present. True, this just cannot happen, that they can be somewhat mixed; yet, to the extent the choleric vehemence is to be moderated by a bit of deliberation it can so happen. The phlegmatic temperament has the worst reputation; the sanguine is the most lovable, because it is inclined to enjoyments and social gatherings. The melancholic [temperament] is not indeed hateful, but pitiable. The choleric person is active; on the other hand, however, he also has something detrimental. Yet all attributes become useless through the phlegmatic [temperament] and therefore also the whole individual, and for this reason it is [held] in great contempt. Phlegm is not an actual passion, but only a great degree of inactivity, which is almost always to be found in the human being. However active he may always be, yet he thus strives for repose. However, if the propensity for repose outweighs everything, then it is contemptible.

If we want to combine the temperaments with one another, then we can only combine them in a fourfold way: the sanguine is the contrary of the melancholic and the choleric is the contrary of the phlegmatic; therefore they cannot be combined in this way. First we can, however, combine the sanguine with the choleric, for the sanguine one takes interest in life;[a] therefore this agrees very well. After this we can combine the melancholic with the phlegmatic, for the melancholic one has an aversion[b] to life, and the phlegmatic one an aversion to acting; therefore this also harmonizes. The sanguine with the choleric is the happiest,[c] but the melancholic with the phlegmatic the unhappiest. Now we can still combine them in a twofold way, namely crosswise, the sanguine with the phlegmatic and the choleric with the melancholic. If the sanguine

25:640 consists in the feeling of life, then it can harmonize well with the phlegmatic, for there are people who pursue enjoyment this way, but who are still very inactive thereby, who do nothing, but still would like to savor all enjoyments. True, they are active, but only to the extent they can procure an enjoyment for themselves. Sanguine phlegmatic persons are satisfied with a little, and are merry thereby, for a lot might cost them effort. With regard to themselves, such people feel very well, but with regard to others they are very useless. The choleric harmonizes very well with the melancholic, for the melancholic provides the choleric with abatement and more deliberation; however, on the other hand, it is very harmful with regard to others, although it is good with regard to itself. For who has a source for all discontentment in himself, is also an

---

[a] *hat Lust zu leben*   [b] *Unlust*
[c] *glücklichste*, here in context, in the sense of *gutgetroffen*

enemy of other's enjoyments; he is all the more intensely sensible of his discontentment. However, the sanguine phlegmatic person has a source of enjoyment in himself, thus he is sympathetic with the enjoyment of others. With regard to itself, the sanguine phlegmatic [temperament] is happy, but with regard to others, the most useless. With regard to itself, the choleric melancholic [temperament] is good, but with regard to others, it is the most harmful. The sanguine choleric [temperament] is the happiest, but the melancholic phlegmatic is the unhappiest.

As to what concerns the difference of the temperaments with regard to outward behavior, we thus first want to compare the sanguine with the melancholic. The sanguine individual is lively, changeable, the melancholic more constant, sober, and uniform. With regard to social intercourse, the sanguine individual is easy to get on with, ingratiating, and with regard to offenses, conciliatory; he avoids his offender, but the melancholic one does not avoid him, but plots revenge and harbors hatred and resentment against his offender. With the sanguine individual, all sensations are intense, but do not penetrate deeply. *With the melancholic individual, however, they are not so intense, but they penetrate more deeply.* The sanguine individual sympathizes with the misfortune of his friend, but he does not take it to heart, and remains fundamentally indifferent. The melancholic one is here again the opposite, he takes everything to heart and in this he again feels badly.[a] It is not good to take everything to heart. In this the teaching of the Stoics is good, although it was taken too far for the strength of human beings. The sanguine individual is inclined to social intercourse and sociability; therefore he is a social friend, but not a supportive friend. In society he is jovial, and sympathizes with other's enjoyment, but if his friend becomes ill, then he takes his leave. The melancholic person is sensible of pain at the misfortune of his friend, and is very inclined to have a sensation of enjoyment in magnanimous pain. He nurtures his pain. No pain, however, except the one over our vices, must be nurtured. With regard to its ills, pain is unfavorable, but not with regard to *others*. Sympathetic pain with regard to the ills of others is lovable, and the moral pain over one's vices is worthy of respect. The melancholic person is affected in friendship; with him it is a matter of the heart, but not with the sanguine individual. However, if the melancholic one is offended in friendship, then he does not become reconciled so easily, and even if he becomes reconciled, yet he still thinks about the past. The wound does not completely heal with him, it still always leaves a scar. However, the sanguine individual, even if he is offended, is immediately again all right, also forgets it and does not even think about it any more. It is just the same in

25:641

---

[a] *fehlen*: its idiomatic sense here constitutes the opposite of indifference.

reflection[a] as in sensation. The sanguine individual is witty, the melancholic one more profound. Wit is based on the liveliness of the spirit, but insight requires more investigation and seriousness. The melancholic person is inclined to seriousness; indeed he gives serious thought to more things which do not even merit it. The sanguine individual is soft-hearted, the melancholic one is soft-spirited[b] and tender, for he not only has sensations, but he is also suited for this. The sanguine individual is open-hearted and keeps no confidentialities; he hides nothing at all, because he is kind-hearted, and also because he has no intentions.[c] He who has more intentions and purposes, however, must be more on guard, and that is the melancholic person. Because the sanguine individual is social and also open-hearted, his garrulousness thus arises from this; therefore he keeps neither his nor his friend's confidentialities. The melancholic person is, however, a better keeper of secrets; he is reserved in talkativeness and the reason is: the melancholic person imagines all people to be worse than they are. By contrast the sanguine individual takes all people to be good. The melancholic one believes himself surrounded by enemies who are poised to ensnare him, and he sees their endearments only as bedazzlements and goads. Therefore he must be secretive in his enterprises and remarks.[d] The sanguine individual, however, has the inclination to be a blabbermouth about everything since, because he is social, he is thus always trying to converse [with others] in [society]; often he also wants to conceal something, but before he realizes it, he has thus blabbed about something, and then it vexes him and he is sorry about it. The melancholic person however is quiet, because he is lost in his thoughts, and although he could be talkative without blabbing about secrets, because he places importance in all things this thus keeps him reserved. He always wants to put something profound forward. Yet the sanguine individual is better in common life, for the whole of life is surely only a game.[e] Society must be maintained not through profundity, but through dalliance. In regard to trust, the sanguine individual is not malicious, but thoughtless; he promises all manner of things, and afterwards does nothing, for he does not know what it takes. After that he believes the other person will be so kind-hearted and excuse him from his promise. The melancholic person does not so easily promise something, he is thoughtful and solicitous, but if he once promises something, then one can rely on him. Because the melancholic person's sensation penetrates more

25:642

[a] *Nachsinnen*, to muse about, or ponder something
[b] *weichmütig*, normally synonymous with *weichherzig*
[c] *Absichten*, here probably bearing the nuance of "schemes," but the term is immediately repeated in the next sentence and there seems to be simply "intentions."
[d] *Gesprächen*   [e] *Spiel*

deeply, he [will] also sooner and with greater earnestness champion the cause of the oppressed. If he is a patriot, then he is impassioned in [his] zeal, but then he is also unbridled with regard to religion. However, the sanguine individual is indifferent, it is all one and the same to him, he conforms in accordance with fashion, he lets himself be persuaded of anything, and lets others do as they please with him. The sanguine individual is easily talked out of his resolve, which others often find agreeable; however the melancholic person is firm, persistent, and obstinate. Hence the sanguine individual is popular, but not dependable. The melancholic person is not, however, so easily steered in an intention which is presented to him, but if he has once really made a resolution, then he is unwavering in it. However, if he here becomes angry,[a] then it is bad, then he gives way to his resolve. The sanguine individual's practice is without any maxims and principles, but the melancholic individual's [practice] is capable of various principles. The sanguine individual acts according to instinct, but the melancholic individual [acts] according to principles. However, the sanguine individual can exercise kind-heartedness and also maliciousness from instincts, and the melancholic individual   25:643 can have kind-heartedness and also maliciousness in his principles.

If we compare the choleric temperament with the phlegmatic one, we will thus find that there is a consciousness of the incentive of activity in the choleric temperament, and a burden[b] of inactivity or lifelessness in the phlegmatic [temperament], that the choleric one is vehement, lighter, and resolute, but the phlegmatic one [is] irresolute. The choleric person is impatient, the phlegmatic, patient, for since the choleric person is active, he thus has a courageous spirit and becomes impatient if he cannot carry anything out, and because the phlegmatic person is inactive, he thus has such apathy [so as] to bear everything. The choleric one rushes [things], the phlegmatic one procrastinates; he finishes nothing because he is sluggish. True, the sanguine individual also does not finish anything, but not because he is sluggish, rather because he is variable in his actions and goes back and forth.[c] The choleric individual, however, overdoes it, he is too vehement, because he applies a greater degree of powers in a short time, but the phlegmatic one uses less power in a longer [period] of time; hence the choleric one is energetic, and he often overdoes [the application] of power, [so] that it cannot last long. In regard to offenses, the choleric person is sensitive; that is, he is easily sensible of something. True, the melancholic person is also sensitive, but he is deeply sensible of [something]. One says of some persons, they are hotheaded but are thereupon also immediately again sweet tempered[d]

---

[a] *böse*; i.e. used here in one of its ordinary language senses
[b] *Gewicht*, literally "weight"   [d] *sanftmüthig*
[c] *wechselt*, lit. changes, alternates

and also quite conciliatory, since they even indeed apologize; yet this is an unmannerliness and a lack of the discipline of one's unruliness, for the human being is, without discipline, by nature unruly like an animal, and without culture [he is] crude. As it is, however, our freedom is limited by other people; hence our natural unruliness must be disciplined. Parents primarily must see to this in bringing up their children, that they discipline their unruliness and do not allow them their will, for to the extent [children] become accustomed to maintaining everything in keeping with their will, they thus become accustomed to dominating, in which one often indulges them out of tenderness, and afterwards they will not tolerate that one contradicts them, but if they are themselves dominated, then they fly off the handle and become hotheaded. Therefore it is nothing more with them than an unmannerliness; their youthful boisterousness has not been cast off,[a] they have not been polished, they do not know that all human beings are equal to one another. This must

25:644   also be seen to in the upbringing of princes, and it does not hurt, if they strike one of their subjects, that they in turn get a blow on the spot. It is said of the Creoles in America that they do not allow themselves to be governed at all, because they are accustomed since youth to domination over the slaves, since a little boy there commands whole armies of slaves, which must altogether strictly obey him. It is very strange and silly for older people of mature reason to complain about the fact that their parents let them have their way,[b] and did not better tame their willfulness.[c] Of course that is a fault of the parents, however, if a person already has a mature reason, and realizes such for himself, then he can also discipline himself and give up his unruliness, and if he does not do so, then others above him will come and make up for the thrashings which he failed to get. One can indeed complain about the parents that they did not break one of the habit of some postures,[d] yet not about unmannerliness, for one has the understanding, after all, to rear oneself. One must greatly beware of such persons who fly into a rage, since one is never quite safe with them. It is said, but such persons have a good heart, yet it is bad to try to gain with the heart, if one has on the other hand, however, sacrificed something. This way many often have contempt for their memory, and regard it as poor, so that one should think them that much more capable of reason.

Although on the one hand the choleric person is productive[e] of many good consequences, since when he is subject to discipline, he is always

---

[a] *nicht abgestoßen*: entire phrase expresses the figurative sense of the term.
[b] *Willen*
[c] *den Sinn nicht beßer gebrochen haben*: reading *Sinn* as *Eigensinn*, thus lit. "did not better break them of their willfulness (or headstrongness)."
[d] *Stellungen des Cörpers*, lit. "positions of the body"
[e] *fruchtbar*, lit. fruitful, prolific

effective, on the other hand he is also likewise in turn productive of vile consequences; he is overbearing, craves dominance, is disparaging, dogmatic in asserting his willfulness, given to conducting legal proceedings, shows off in society, monopolizes the conversation, and in no way wants to bear contradiction. And hard as it is to believe, people are yet fundamentally so submissive and society is so weak, that one will find that such a one in society, who only always insists on doing all the talking, wins out. One yields out of peace-loving intentions, so that one only need not quarrel with him, and then he comes to hold the position of spokesman, and stays in it, and then he is not so easily dislodged. If now the choleric person monopolizes the conversation, then he is very dogmatic and solemn in his presentation, and knows how to present the words with such emphasis, that his speech thereby obtains importance, and through this manner he acquires [his] reputation. Everyone believes him capable of profundity; therefore an illusion takes place. However, as soon as he writes down his speech, this comes to an end, since one cannot there read the pomp and the manner together with [the words]. The choleric person aims for formalities, observances,[a] and the exact keeping[b] of precept, for there he can then demonstrate his domination. He is not open-hearted, but political, hence he does not let himself go, he purports to know a great deal, but he does not say it; he is reserved not out of distrust, as is the melancholic person, but out of the desire for honor, for the one who is reserved discloses that he thinks a great deal. He behaves very affectedly, even in his walk which one can well distinguish, since he takes every step with care and feels every limb when he moves it, just as he hears every word which he speaks. Hence in writing, he is also very precise, quite artificial, stiff, and weighs every word carefully. The choleric person seems to be cleverer than he is, therefore he sets very great store by compliments, but not by flattery, for in the first case one is held in high repute, but in the other case, one is degraded; in general, he is very narcissistic. In religion he is very orthodox, and a strict defender of observances, for since he is on the side of authority, he can thus dominate. However, he does not aim so much for [what is] inner to religion, as he does for form, discipline, and the keeping of precepts. There are not such features of diversity in the phlegmatic temperament, because it is a limitation of activity. The phlegmatic person is apathetic and insensitive and lacks the incentive to act. In regard to inclination, he is more given to wish, than that he should exert his powers to attain such. He feeds himself with hope. In public affairs, he is very tolerant and forbearing; if he is a faculty[c] member, then he is a yes man. At home he is an

25:645

[a] i.e. in the sense of customs, rules, rituals
[b] *Beobachtungen*, lit. observations of
[c] *Collegio*: could also be the council, or the board

25:646 easy-going husband, he does not quarrel over being the master,[a] indeed it suits him fine, if he has nothing to do with it; he is peaceable because he makes no effort to pose difficulties, he does not avenge any offense, because it causes him trouble, he is peaceable out of laziness. True, the sanguine individual is also peaceable, but out of carelessness, which is different from sluggishness. One is careless if one does not accomplish one's work, if one does not employ much industry on it; however one is sluggish if one does not undertake anything at all. The phlegmatic person is not bored; one who keeps busy would rather do evil before he is to do nothing at all. [The phlegmatic person] is friendly in society, he always smilingly approves, and more often than not he takes to his drink. Therefore there is in him an analogue of good-naturedness, not out of positive, but out of negative grounds; he will not do anything evil, he will not undertake anything, because it costs him effort, and that is not his thing. Therefore his phlegmatic temperament also protects him from some vices, for some vices carry a price,[b] since they bespeak great undertakings and activity. One can also find something lofty in great crimes, but other vices disclose meanness. With the phlegmatic person, we indeed approve that he does not practice such vices, yet we have contempt for him, since he is not even capable of such a courageous spirit. His good-naturedness therefore does not come from the goodness of the dispositions,[c] but from inactivity. The phlegmatic person is only useful there where one can give him time, and where one does not need to press him. Where one imposes a lot of work on him, where he must spend a long time without rest, then he might work himself to death, in order to be idle later. The phlegmatic individual is the most placid citizen. He is neutral in civil war and awaits the outcome. He is patient, but not out of a noble cast of mind, rather out of apathy. He is satisfied with a little, if more things cost him effort. True, the sanguine individual is also satisfied with a little, however he produces no sum total of his well-being; the frenzy of enjoyments distracts him from his reflection.

If we compare all the temperaments with one another, and add the talents, we thus find that the sanguine individual is witty, the choleric individual is keen-witted, and the melancholic person is profound;[d] the phlegmatic person, however, has the talent of imitation. The liveliness of 25:647 the sanguine individual makes him witty, and he also needs wit because of the variability. Wit also belongs to sociability; however, the sanguine individual is sociable, but the choleric person is only social. The one who is social likes to go into society, even if they show him the door; the one

---

[a] *um die Herrschaft*
[b] *haben Valeur in sich*
[c] *Gesinnungen*
[d] *tiefsinnig*: also synonymous with melancholic (therefore also with *Schwermütig*).

who is sociable is popular*a* in society. The choleric person is keen-witted, because he wants to have an advantage in everything, and because he is active. His actions must be connected, and be exact in everything. The reason for the melancholic profundity is that he places an importance in everything, thus he is also accustomed to regard all things in terms of an important point, and therefore to inquire into them as being important. Because the phlegmatic person does not put in the effort to produce something himself, he thus imitates; for this reason he also has a good memory.

[As to] what concerns the difference of the nations in regard to temperaments, the French are sanguine, the Italians choleric, the English melancholic, and the Germans phlegmatic. The German likes to imitate, he likes to have models and methods, and prefers to be subject to discipline, than to govern himself. He has no daring to risk anything on his own, which after all belongs to genius.

The faults of the temperaments are: the sanguine individual is thoughtless, disorderly, and a free spirit. The faults of the choleric person are defiance, affectation, dogmatism. [The faults] of the melancholic individual are distrust, secretiveness, obstinacy, [and] resentment; of the phlegmatic individual, [they are] indifference, sluggishness, [and] procrastination. In regard to actions, with the sanguine individual [one finds] candor, with the choleric one, presumptuousness, with the melancholic one, self-possession and resoluteness, with the phlegmatic one, cool-headedness. In regard to society, the sanguine individual is gallant, the choleric individual is pompous, the melancholic one is dreamy, [and] the phlegmatic person does not belong to society at all. In regard to the sex[es], the sanguine individual is a good lover, but a poor husband, the choleric individual is a good master of the house, but a poor marriage partner, the melancholic one is constant and tender in marriage, the phlegmatic one puts up with everything. In regard to objects, with the sanguine individual [one finds] opulence, all amusements and enjoyments; the object[s] of the choleric one are domination, reputation, authority, [and] dogmatism. The object of the melancholic person with regard to maliciousness is envy, with regard to good-naturedness [it is] grudgingness, but in the dispositions*b* [it is] stability; he does not so much aim for external looks, as does the choleric one, but for reality. His qualities relate to solidity and profundity. The sanguine individual is open-hearted, the choleric one presumptuous, the melancholic one distrustful, and the phlegmatic one contemptible. Not even what is negative in the vices can be designated good; nevertheless, who does nothing, is also worth*c* nothing. The one who feels no worth in himself, who does

25:648

---

a Reading *beliebt* for *geliebt* ("beloved").   *b* *Gesinnungen*
c Reading *gilt* (from the other manuscript) in place of *giebt*

not set much store by his worth, but squanders it, is mean; accordingly meanness is also found in one who is worthless. [When] in need, the choleric person will finally sell the sword, the watch, and everything that maintains his honor, for he does not like to lower himself, which is also good, since he then does not trouble the other [person]. Because he [lives] opulently, the sanguine individual will only sell his cufflinks, and so forth, at the end, since he still needs them in order to appear in society. However the phlegmatic individual will sell everything, if he can just afterwards lie on straw, and after that [he] will act in a mean [fashion] and beg, or will send around letters begging for charity, and live off other's charity. The choleric person is greedy, the melancholic one is stingy because he is distrustful. However, miserly frugality, which consists in this that one lets oneself suffer need, dominates with the phlegmatic person. For, since he is lazy and sluggish, he tries to replace power and activity by money.

ON CHARACTER IN THE SPECIES

With human beings, character is the main thing; there is a confluence in their case of everything toward this. Hence it is necessary that we seek out the source of character. The good character would be the good will. Good will is different from good instincts and impulses. We have inclinations and abhor them, we can do evil due to inclination and abhor [such] due to principles; then one has a good will which desires something due to principles. We have a will by virtue of which we desire something due to principles and concepts, so that one can also wish to have good inclinations, since, due to concepts, one realizes that [one's inclinations] are evil. A human being can therefore have an unfortunate temperament, but yet [have] a good will, which is a basis for good character. One also calls character way of thinking,[a] whereby [one] does not however indicate the constitution of the understanding, for, just as will has a general understanding, but by this only disposition[b] is here understood, in the same way the concept of understanding also has a general meaning, but by this only the faculty of making good use of one's understanding is here understood. We esteem something to the extent it is a tool of good use; nothing is unconditionally good, but it depends on the will to make good use of it. The good will is good in itself and unconditioned. To the extent an individual has a good will, he is worth much, through the good will he is good in himself; otherwise, however, the human being can only be good as a means for a purpose. Hence morality is the highest science among all [of them], because through it the human being is good

25:649

[a] *Denkungsart*
[b] *Gesinnung* (comportment of mind, mental attitude)

in himself. The source of good purposes is the *good will, the source of evil purposes is the* evil will. One also calls this way of thinking. Many people do not at all act because they think, but because they have sensation; they perform good actions, but not in accordance with way of thinking, but in accordance with sensation. Conduct of thought, however, is already an origin*a* of acting in accordance with principles.*b* Now on what, however, is this way of thinking of acting in accordance with concepts based, this faculty of maxims and principles in accordance with which the human being has the power of dominating his inclination? The faculty of acting in accordance with principles and maxims is based on this, that the human being can act in accordance with concepts, but the concepts must become an incentive for him. True, the concepts are not in themselves incentives, for what is an object of understanding, can indeed not be an object of feeling; but an incentive is an object of feeling, in order that it can motivate*c* us. Although, as it is, the concepts of good and evil are not objects of feeling, yet they can still serve to rouse feeling to act in accordance with these concepts; then one acts in accordance with principles and maxims. True, one cannot have insight into how the concept, for example of an injustice which has been done to someone, should rouse feeling, and [how] it can motivate [one] to stand by this individual, but still it happens. For providence*d* has only given us instinct for [when] concepts and principles are lacking. Thus concepts are to become incentives in us, they are to rouse feeling, and to motivate us to act in accordance with such concepts, and thus according to principles. Human beings who do not have such a feeling which can be roused through concepts have no moral feeling. This is the sensitiveness, sensitivity, or the feeling through all concepts of the understanding. However, one still finds few people who could be roused through the concept of good and evil; true, they do many good actions, they help the needy, however not from concepts, but from instincts. If one takes away the object through the sight of which feeling is roused, then it will prove difficult to carry out just such actions which one did before, when one was looking at the object itself. Thus one will also hardly refrain from a vile action, if one is supposed to be roused through the odiousness of the concepts. If the action is in keeping with our advantage and our inclination, then one will not be roused by the odiousness of the concept to refrain from such; for example, one is to offer someone a favorable marriage, and one keeps it for oneself. Here one must not say (although it would be hard not to do it) that in that case, where it is in keeping both with advantage and with inclination, such is allowed; true, it is difficult, but the principle

25:650

---

a *principium*: Latin for "commencement, beginning, origin"
b *Grundsätze*   *d* Reading *Vorsehung* in place of *Vorsicht.*
c *bewegen*

still must remain, the law must not be violated. One does not know what the reason is that people do not have moral feeling; one cannot have insight into, also not explain, whether the reason is the amplification or the refinement of feeling. The incentive to act in accordance with good principles could well be the idea that, if all would act this way, then this earth would be a paradise. This urges me to contribute something to this, and if it does not happen, then at least I am not at fault. From my point of view, I am then still a member of this paradise. Now it only depends on this, that everyone would be this way. Therefore the concept of the good can here be an incentive, and then it is the good character.

With the human being, the bad, the good, and the evil character are to be distinguished. Human beings have a bad character, if no faculty of acting in accordance with principles is to be found in them. However, this is not yet an evil character; they can, by the way, have a good heart.[a]

25:651 Bad character betrays a small soul, which fetters itself with rules as if it were on a walking cart. Character is bad if it has nothing noble in it; it consists in the inability to act in accordance with principles. The poor[b] and bad character is an ill which cannot be compensated for; it is almost so, as if one lacked power of judgment. In such circumstances, one can be instructed however much one likes, and attend all schools and academies, this only thus gives one more material for one's foolishness, for one cannot apply it, but through it becomes a complete fool. Therefore a bad character can also not be improved, and even if one had presented him with the whole of morality, he thus approves of everything, and adopts nothing. Where there is no germ, none can be implanted.[c] Where there is an evil character, there is surely still a germ for character; much good can still be generated from it.

We want to search out still ever more and more the sources of good character. The individual who has received no cultivation is unrefined, the one incapable of any cultivation is crude. The individual who has received no discipline is wild, the one who does not admit of any is evil. Now, can one see whether the individual has received no cultivation, or has admitted none? Many people are merely unrefined, but still not crude. On the other hand, can one see whether the individual has received no discipline, or has admitted none? In the first case, he is merely wild, for the human being is wild by nature; he has inclinations which simply take their course, if they are not tamed or curbed through art. Discipline is the constraint of inclination in accordance with rules. Those whose inclinations have received no discipline, do not follow any rule, but are wild. However, there also exist people whose natural aptitude does not admit of any discipline at all, and these are evil people. This is the basis of evil

[a] *Gemüth*
[b] *gering*
[c] *herein gebracht*, lit. "brought in"

character. The greatest scoundrels are often people of the greatest talents and strength of soul, but who have not admitted of any discipline, but wildly follow their propensity; hence scoundrels also manifest untamed strength and obstinacy. The one who admits of discipline and is capable of it, is already good. True, bad character is a lack of the capacity to act according to principles, however evil character is a hatred for and resistance to everything which occurs in accordance with good principles; it is a resolve to resist the principles, thus [to resist] taming the passions and inclinations, and to bring them under the rule whereby human beings are guided to act in accordance with principles. Evil character refers to the constitution of the evil will. One says about the individual who is not compassionate, that he has an evil heart and mind, but the character of the one who has an evil will, is evil. Evil character is either deceitful or malevolent. In accordance with evil character, one is either a deceiver, or a misanthropist.[a] These two elements constitute evil character. Evil character concerns the rights of human beings. For character directs its efforts to morality, to the extent [character] is determined by good or evil. However, in morality two elements are distinguished, the kind and the just will. The kind will relates to the well-being of other people, but the just will relates to the right of other people. In the first case one is kind, in the other upright. The evil character opposes uprightness, just as good character consists in uprightness. One finds people of deceitful character, and others of malevolent character. Those of deceitful character are not malevolent, they take no enjoyment in the suppression of others, they do not have the malice of the misanthropist, but they try to get the better of the other through mean lies. This character is mean and without honor, but the malevolent one is violent[b] and hence hateful. If I now say about an individual: he is a person without conscience and without honor, that is thus all that I can say about him, for to be without conscience, means to be malevolent; the right of human beings offends such a one. But nothing can do away with our honor except lies, duplicity, deception: that makes the individual the object of the greatest contempt, for since deception and the lie are insidious and not apparent, since one does not so easily discern it, thus one cannot oppose such a one with force. Hence one must have contempt for him. However, one can oppose with force [the person] who has malevolence and misanthropy; accordingly this is hateful. The individual can be restored by force from [a state of] malevolence, but nothing except honor can deter the individual from meanness. If an individual thus has no conscience, then a spark of honor can still be in him, which can check him. But if he is without honor, then all is lost with him, then there is nothing more on which

25:652

[a] *Menschenfeind*, lit. enemy or hater of humankind
[b] *gewaltig*

25:653 one can base the good. The human being can be honorable[a] due to his cast of mind,[b] but upright only due to character, for character presupposes understanding. Only the man with a correct understanding can have a good character, but he who does not have this, is indeed capable of a good mind and heart, but not of a good character. Who has an evil character, still proves thereby that he has understanding, since he has contempt for and hates principles.

Can a character also be acquired? Even who does not straightaway have any character, can still have a natural aptitude in him which is capable of a character, and then character can be modeled[c] and established. Through instruction one acquires concepts with which one must become acquainted in order to act in accordance with them. It would be very good if in children's upbringing one would take care that morality would be established on concepts; then one could also establish a character, the will would then also not relate to instincts, but to principles. The principles can now be erected by concepts. All our teachings and speeches, also sermons, are only abstract concepts of instincts, which only move the heart but not the will. Question: whether a good character can still take place in the case of a cast of mind that is not at all the best? In the case of Socrates, a physiognomist discerned that he betrayed an evil mind and heart, and when his students became angered by this, because they knew him from a different side, Socrates then confirmed such, because he really discerned an evil mind and heart in himself, but he suppressed such by good principles. Character cannot be created, but a basis must be there for it; after that, however, one can uncover it through discipline. Therefore in Socrates's case, despite all malevolence, there must also have been a strength of soul and power of understanding, to motivate[d] his will in accordance with concepts, into which he had insight through the understanding. The understanding can be impotent; that is, however, still not incapable; it can have insight into everything, and it does not have the power to motivate the will. True, one cannot gain insight into how the understanding has power to motivate the will; however if an individual has an evil character, then the understanding

25:654 there directs the will in accordance with evil principles. Now in Socrates' case, there could have been such strength and power of understanding to suppress the malevolence of his heart and mind. Therefore it can be the case that with a vile mind and heart, an individual can still have a good character. However, can a good character be assumed in the case of one who has the marks of an evil character? Here one must first investigate

---

[a] *ehrlich*: in high German, came to mean *aufrichtig* (honest, upright), but in this context, the original sense of *ehrenwert* applies better.
[b] *Gemütsart*, which is different from *Denkungsart*
[c] *nachgebildet*   [d] *bewegen*

the marks. The marks of an evil character can already be recognized in the youth, for youth is still incapable of principles; however they do already manifest themselves. If a child is inclined to theft in its youth, then this is already a mark of an evil character, for if there were any reason at all to realize the meanness, then surely the child would indeed refrain from it. Such a character is really hard to set right. However, with grown-ups, character manifests itself through several marks; for example, if someone is pleased about a blow[a] which another person has suffered. The lie is also already a stain in the character which cannot be improved. An established evil character may well never become good, for there the principles themselves are corrupted. Character is set very late, approximately by age forty, for one can there best separate the concepts from the instincts; there the instincts and inclinations have already lost their force, and the concepts are beginning to take up position, and then one makes principles for oneself which constitute character.

ON THE DETERMINATION OF THE CHARACTERS OF THE NATIONS

It is indeed to dare a lot to want to determine the characters of entire nations; however, it is surely possible that nevertheless something characteristic could be determined in the whole of a nation, which through the long duration, through climate and other causes, has in the end received an unique ingrained[b] constitution. The determination of the character must not be taken from contingent matters, for example, from religion; otherwise it is based on chance; rather the hereditary peculiarity, the uniform in the determination, which has yet remained an essential component among all the variations of the nation, must be picked out. That which is characteristic refers here to what is distinctive in regard to the mind of the entire nation. Here character is to have the general meaning of noting the actual difference in regard to talents and mind; hence what has held true for all time must here be drawn out. If we compare the character of the Oriental nations with the character of the Europeans, we here thus find an essential difference, which among all the governments and variations has nevertheless remained in the case of the Oriental nations. A capacity to act in accordance with concepts and principles is required for character. All Oriental nations are completely incapable of judgment in accordance with concepts. It is a big difference to judge a matter according to shape, appearance, and intuition, and to judge [it] according to concepts. All Oriental nations are not in the position to explain a single property of morality or of justice through concepts;

25:655

---

[a] *Streich*: could also mean a "trick" or "prank" which has been played on someone.
[b] *einmahl eingeartete*

rather all their morals are based on appearance. In the beginning this difference seems to be very small; however it comes to the fore[a] in the application. He who is only capable of representing something for himself according to shape and intuition, is completely incapable of what a concept requires; hence they are capable neither of a philosophy nor of mathematics, nor of being able to have insight into something through concepts. Hence all their paintings will indeed have sensible beauties, but neither the idea of the whole nor taste will be found in them. All arts in which the Chinese particularly excel, are sooner cultivated manual exercises than products which are supposed to have flowed from the concept. With the Oriental nations, the beauty of music is completely missing; they do not at all grasp that there is a beauty in it, if many instruments play together harmoniously in different tones. They regard it as confusion, since they are not capable of having insight into the concept of theme which dominates in and is performed in music. There is neither sublimity, order, proportion, delicacy, fineness, nor taste, all of which is based on the concept, in their buildings. True beauty consists in the agreement of sensibility with the concept, and this they lack. Since they are not capable of any concept, thus they also cannot be capable of true honor; indeed

25:656   they know nothing at all about this, for it is something else to have love of honor and desire for honor, than to parade with haughtiness. Love of honor is based on a concept which has another purpose. The lover of honor will therefore seek his honor in this, that he is an upright, magnanimous, kind man; this honor is based on the concept. Their honor, however, will be based on shape and intuition. Accordingly they seek their honor in power, authority, distinguished social position, in vanities which end up in odd things. Therefore they do not aim for taste, but for ostentation, abundance, and wealth. If a great deal is expended for something and a lot of gold is paraded, that is with them an object of beauty and honor, but no one will endeavor to be esteemed. Hence too no love for the fatherland takes place with them. Although they are otherwise kind-hearted people, yet they thus betray their own fatherland, for they do not at all realize why they should not do this, why they owe it to love their fatherland. Hence no minister cares for the welfare of the entire country, but if he does it, then he does it out of obedience, to which he is compelled by the king, who in turn however has his interest. Hence no loyalty exists with them, and no one seeks to be valued for this reason, because he is loyal. They are not capable of any concept of divinity in their books, nothing but ornateness[b] is [found] in their writings; their style is rambling, picturesque, and flowery. Hence we must not at all try to improve the European style through the picturesque, which some want to do, as they then ruin everything, and extirpate the true cognitions

---

[a] *leuchtet hervor*, lit. "shines out"   [b] *Blumenwerck*, lit. flowery works

through concepts, which is the preeminence of the Europeans, and put images in the place [of such cognitions]. True, concepts become more complete if they are made intuitable, but not if images are put in their place. The Greek nation is the first in the entire world which schooled the talents of the understanding and developed the cognitions through concepts. All mathematics with demonstration, we have from the Greeks; hence Hippocrates and Euclid remain models, [and] thus cannot be imitated. Likewise they also surpass all nations in works of taste; they are models in philosophy, oratory, painting, the art of sculpture, and so forth, of whom we are not only students, but will also remain eternal imitators, so that we also will never be able to produce anything better. Here the Asiatic talent for intuition is in moderate proportion consistent with the European talent for concepts. The northern nations of Europe have a greater talent for concepts, but a weak talent for sensible intuition. 25:657

However, if we want to characterize the European nations in themselves, then it will here be more a play of concepts than an assertion. One must here not select any character through which the nation is praised, for otherwise another nation which likewise demands praise will be offended by it; even less should one cite characters of reproach. Therefore the entire characteristic difference of the nations will amount to trifles, about which one can laugh, but which all the same are distinctive marks. In past ages, the Phoenicians, as they traveled to Europe, named the lands according to their products; for example, Spain, the land of horses, England, the land of tin. Therefore we could also imitate a similar way and say: France is the land of fashion, Germany the land of titles, Spain the land of ancestry, England the land of temper, and so forth. We are justified in calling France the land of fashion, for it is a nation of taste. Novelty belongs to taste, variableness to beauty, wherein they surpass all nations. They are lively, merry, carefree, joyful at heart, talkative, inclined to sing, play, dance. No government in the world, be it ever so harsh, can suppress this in them. They turn their whole life into play, they make a trifle out of matters of importance, and importance out of trifles; this is also the course which the human being must take in life, that he treats it as a game[a] and does not cling to things. They surpass all nations in ease, friendliness, independence. One takes only gallantry, not in regard to the sexes, but in all behavior and conversation, which is a politeness without friendship; in it they are thus complaisant, polite to everyone, but without affection, it aims for the fashionable and for external looks. Social intercourse with the French woman schools [one] highly, because they are talkative and sociable, and show off a lot with their talents. If one is to judge impartially, then we would all be bears in our social intercourse, if we would not be refined by the French. In no 25:658

---

[a] *Spiel*; previously translated as "play"

country is conduct as universal as in France, in which every peasant girl can very soon attain the conduct of a princess.

We can call Germany the land of titles, since the German pays great heed to titles. Wives take the title of their husbands. Titles bear a great influence with the Germans, they also occasion much honor. Even the German language discloses such, for it is full of forms of address and observance of the difference in rank; the *du, er, ihr* and *sie*[a] are nothing but observances of the difference in rank. For this reason one is very often embarrassed, since one does not know whether one should say *Er* or *Sie* to one's shoemaker, the first in order not to offend, the latter in order not to overstep the appropriate form of address.[b] The German is therefore very punctilious in the differentiation of rank. The result is this, that [the one of] inferior station is at all times reminded of his inferiority, and gets into [a state of] embarrassment when he speaks with a distinguished person, from which a general awkwardness and constraint arise. It is also likewise in letters, which will always retain the stiffness, and even if one wanted to write with a free hand to a distinguished person, one must always attend to [the fact that] he will take it as disrespect. In France, however, everyone is addressed by *Vous*, whatever the difference may be; hence all conversations are candid, not constrained, not awkward. The complete lack of titles is found in England, from which arises a kind of equality and self-satisfaction. The Germans are methodical, regular, orderly, and precise; hence in all written observances[c] of social standing, they observe order and rule, which has now risen to great heights, and can hardly rise any higher. As it is, the more the mechanism grows, all the more will genius be extirpated; hence they order the products of other's genius, and their books contain much order and [many] parts, but nothing special is dealt with in them. They put much stress on what is useful, hence they will not initiate anything peculiar [to them], and new fashions can also not arise with them, because they believe themselves justified in making fun of the one who starts something new. Those fash-
25:659 ions come into vogue with them, which were already in use in France, and in turn are put to use by [the Germans]. They are therefore very bound to rules, and one can see by looking at them that they subject themselves to constraint. Much is already due to upbringing, since children are already habituated to act according to certain rules at the table, must also observe such in their dress, and are very often referred to what is

---

[a] "you" (familiar form of address), "he" (familiar form), "you" (formal form of address), albeit especially as formal forms of address, these are properly capitalized.

[b] *sich nichts zu vergeben*: *Er* and *Sie* are given in this order in the text, but the reverse order would be the fitting parallel with Kant's further explication.

[c] *Formularitaeten Beobachtungen*: *Formularitaeten* are literally official forms such as one might fill out when applying for something.

seemly or unseemly. It happens likewise also in the schools; there everything is learned according to rules of grammar, the linguistic exercises are arranged according to a certain method, and the letters composed according to all rules of antecedents and consequents; all exercises are copied, from which such a general punctiliousness arises, which is never shed, not even in society. The German is enduring in work, which agrees with his order and punctiliousness according to rules. Hence the German is the pedant in the world, because he is punctilious in the observation of rule, and is lacking in the wisdom and judgment to apply the rule. The German is not as talkative as the Frenchman, but more hospitable; they have a propensity for sociability, which is not content only with words, but also takes care of the stomach. It is a good-naturedness of heart.

Italy is a land of the clever; hence the Italians are very reserved, circumspect, and cautious. In Italy there is nothing but politics. Nowhere does one find it like this as [it is] there; with them everything ends up in craftiness, and by this they make a better living for themselves than if they work out something useful. They manifest a clever and inventive spirit to read the other's taste, and to hit the mark. Hence they greatly emphasize optical things, music, painting. Everything serves to cleverly fleece the rich man. The artists, and the people in general know how to contrive such vanities, to wheedle money from the distinguished persons who had taken it away from them in another way. It is nothing but deception of the senses, for example, the lottery. The fine arts are with them an artificial manner. Their cleverness is also manifest in war and in enmities; hence they make good bandits.

Spain is the land of ancestry. They lay great stress on the longevity of their lineage, on the bloodline, ancestral codes and ancestral customs in religion. Accordingly they greatly esteem, for example, the Gothic blood since it is not mingled with any Moorish blood. With haughtiness and an air of entitlement,[a] they are contemptuous of all other nations. They are very given to superstition, which is then also attended by ignorance.

25:660

England is a land of temper, which is a disposition of the mind[b] to assess all objects according to a particular light. The land of temper is also the land of characters; everyone has his disposition and his peculiar character. Accordingly, no imitators are found among them. The Germans on the other hand, are the greatest imitators. Nothing but original characters are [found] in England. If one has seen ten Frenchmen, then one is acquainted with the entire nation, but in England the difference is very great; hence too the entire nation of the English has no character, because everyone has his own. However, because no Frenchman has a peculiar character, the entire nation thus has one. People who have their

[a] *Vorzugsgeist*, lit. spirit of [making claim] to preferential [treatment]
[b] *Kopfs*

own countries, do not like to conform to a foreign character. Hence popular rule*a* greatly dominates in England. In France one takes pride that the king can do everything, but the subjects cannot get very far at all. The power of the king results from [the fact] that the subjects have nothing, which advantage one also gladly grants to [the kings]. One effect of their temper (of the English) is also suicide. Nowhere do such rich, distinguished, and high-ranking persons commit suicide due to temper, as in England. Eccentricity*b* is the effect of this. Accordingly profundity and melancholy are to be found with them, but not the good taste of the French; although great exactness, durability, [and] proprietorship are found in their products, yet the taste of the French is lacking. True, the product of the French does not endure as long, it is new, [but] all at once also already old; then they again introduce something new, and by this they maintain themselves.

25:661   In the remaining countries and nations of Europe, character is difficult to find out, although a third character results from the union of the characters of two nations. For example, this way the Poles have something from the French and the Spanish character in them, although these characters seem to be opposed to one another. A certain solemnness prevails with the Poles, but later on a Mazurian⁵⁸ indifference results from it. With them everything begins with pomp and splendor, and in the end amounts to something common and base. The Russians must still let themselves be seen more on the stage of the world, in order that one could know and designate their character. Hence it is not advisable to characterize the nations from some minor things, because it could prove to be wrong. The Poles and Russians have a greater Oriental character mixture than all other nations in Europe. Thus in the eloquence of the Poles there is more pomp of declamation than concepts.

ON PHYSIOGNOMY OR THE DETERMINATION OF CHARACTER IN THE HUMAN BEING

Everything which can disclose the character of the human being externally belongs to physiognomy. The curiosity*c* of human beings is directed the most toward this. For since it is partly an art of fortune-telling that nature has given us to discover the projecting character, so the discovery of such a secret greatly flatters the human being, for the more something is hidden from one, all the more one strives to

---

a *Volkrecht*   *b* *Originalitaet*
c Reading *Neugierde* in place of *Neubegierde* (which would literally mean "new desire," but is not a term in the language).

know it. However, this does not serve solely to satisfy human vanity and acuity, but because we are dealing with human beings, and therefore must also come to know them, it is thus also useful. In nature nothing besides another human being is an object of affect and our passion. Other things are only objects of our appetites and desires, but not of our affects and our passions. Therefore this interests the human being the most, to come to know him, and to know his character. Physiognomy teaches us the extent to which we can determine character from the external, and how far our acuity reaches. Physiognomy is the facial form[a] of the human being, from which one can deduce what lies within. However, it should be the science of bringing such under the rule, so that one can   25:662 draw an inference from the outer to the inner.

The human form seems to be the most appropriate for the rational being. We can think of no figure, no poet can boost his fictive prowess so far that he could devise a different figure for the human being than [what] this form of the human being is, which is the most proper and fitting [form] for the rational being. The reason is because no form of our familiar expressions is known to us besides what we have. As little as we can think up another organization of the senses for use in the world,[b] than that which we have, we thus also can not invent any other organization of form than what we have. Just as it is a good moral idea [that] the human being is made in the image of God,[59] one could also on the other hand thus say: the human being makes God in his image, since he cannot make any new form of God. True he can enlarge and augment the human form for God, but he cannot make a new one; he cannot liberate himself from the human form. Likewise one is also wont to affix to angels, to whom one also gives a human figure, wings in addition, which are however very unsuitable, since such an individual who had wings on his shoulders could not fly at all, because the balance is lacking. Therefore we cannot add anything to the human being.

In this form we can consider the figure of the body and the gesture or posture. The pattern[c] of the human being, the proportion of all his limbs, is noticeable in the figure of the body. The proportion of limbs which one could assume to be an universal one is not yet quite determined. For it could also be that one would have accustomed oneself to a certain proportion, and taken this to be the best, and then it would only be taken from experience.

[a] *Bildung*, used in this section in its archaic sense, synonymous with *Gestalt*. One could render it as "features" (i.e. as synonymous with *Züge*) when it is a matter of *Gesichtsbildung*, but Kant in this section also uses *Bildung* in discussing other aspects of the body, indeed for the human form in general.

[b] Reading text according to editors' suggested correction: "So wenig wie wir uns eine andere Organisation von Sinnen zum . . ."

[c] *Schnitt*: pattern in the sense of a dress pattern

25:663   Thus the Chinese seek the beauty of their form in a fat belly, yet one usually seeks and desires beauty in something in which one is wanting. Since, as it is, the Chinese are all very thin, they thus set great store by when they are fully filled out,*a* and place the beauty of proportion in a fat belly. Yet one could surely figure out the true proportion and form from nature, without taking it according to taste. If one wants to figure out the true proportion, one would have to measure the height of 100 individuals, after that the height of the face, then the height of the nose, the forehead, and so forth, of all the limbs. Then one would have to add each height in particular, and then this would be an individual who would be 100 times larger than all 100, and this form would be the proportion of the form of this great giant, and the face would be the proportioned face of this great giant. This would now be a human being of the most proportioned form. If I now divide this proportion by 100, then I get the proportion for every individual of the 100, and this would be the true proportion of the facial form. If, for example, we take the facial form of the Greeks, who would have a straight line in their profile from the forehead to the nose without an indentation, [a] form which indicates something sublime, but is more fitting for Minerva than for Venus, if after that we take the form of the Negro, which in turn has a nose which is altogether too pressed down and flared out, if we now take this together, and after that divide it by the same amount, the median proportion results; neither the profile of the Greek nor the profile of the Negro, and that would be the true beauty of the face. And this way one could also get the true proportion in the form of other limbs. Thighs are said to be larger in India than here.[60] The proportion of the parts also produces in us the judgment of the well-formed figure of the body of the human being; however, from this it does not yet follow that he must be beautiful in the face. For here our judgment is not so much concerned with the proportion, although it is also concerned with it, than it is with the charm which faces have. Therefore Winckelmann also says that we

25:664   corrupt our concepts of the beauty of the form of the face, since we mix up the concepts of the form of the face in itself and its beauty, with the concepts of the beauty of the facial form of women, for there we are not so much concerned with the beauty of the proportion as with the charm, and thereupon try to apply this concept of this beauty to all; for the proportion in the case of the man is after all entirely different, since theirs is different from ours, both in the chest as well as other parts.[61] The Greeks are said to have had the best form of the body, since through their games they thus kept their body naked, trained [it], and did not check the growth of their nature by any constraint. In our case, nature is checked by the constraint of clothes, and thereby the natural proportion of the

a *völlig werden*

body is hindered. Thus the Poles have a thicker neck because it is free, and the English more agile thighs, because the upbringing of children there is not based on the rule of what is fitting and permissible, but the most genteel children run around on the street just as well as the peasant children, which Rousseau also wants to have [be the case], since children are thereby well[a] reared.[62] The German nation is however very bound to rule and custom, hence the upbringing of children is also coercive. The children are always ordered about, they should sit this way and not another way, for that is not fitting, or is not seemly.

What relates to gesture and posture, insofar as it runs through all the limbs, thus depends on the figure and on the form of the body. The less human beings are under constraint with regard to their body, all the more are the gestures in keeping with nature, and all the less does something artificial exist; rather the candor and vivaciousness of nature beams forth at all times, but which in our upbringing is very suppressed by humiliation, and even if a fitting posture and gesture is acquired by coercion, thereby constraint thus certainly takes hold, so that one always maintains the same gesture,[b] and is lifelong unable to transpose oneself into the freedom of nature.

25:665

It is said of the human being: he is handsome [when] well formed. This refers partly to the form of the entire figure of the body, partly to the form of the face. Thus one also says: the human being is ugly. However "ugly" is derived from "to hate."[c][63] But if it is derived from there, one can not thus say, that such a face or figure of the body, which deviates from the true proportion, is ugly; it may not at all be hated because of this. In order to be ugly, something contradicting morality must lie in the face: guile, malice, spite, recalcitrance, crudeness, only that is ugly in the case of the human being. The unproportionate form of the body and the face may not however be ugly because of it. In regard to the two sexes, the judgments are very different, just as the judgments of beauty were, for we assess the beauty of a man and of a woman from different points of view. We consider the man's beauty and ugliness from the standpoint of masculine strength and industriousness, but we compare the beauty and ugliness of the woman with our inclination; hence an old woman always looks uglier than an old man, for we judge the woman according to the charm, but the man according to his manliness. Thus someone does state about Heidegger[64] that he had such a bad facial proportion, that one could not look at him without laughing; likewise he also made jokes about it himself, since he once said he was the ugliest [person]

[a] *wacker*, ordinarily means "brave" or "plucky," but in its archaic sense also means "good" or "honest."
[b] *in allen Geberden den selben blicken läßt*, literally "lets the same be seen in all gestures"
[c] The German terms here are *häßlich* and *hassen*.

205

in the social gathering. When a bet was then made, the other person who had made the bet with him, led an old woman in. All now began to laugh still more about her, as a result of which he lost his bet; however he said: it was still not yet settled with this, because the judgment was here passed from two points of view, [and] one should put the wig on the woman and the cap on him. As soon as this was done, one realized that he was right, and saw on what it is here based. Men must reveal manliness, strength, and industriousness, but the women more meekness

25:666 in their facial form. For just as the feminine face ruins the man, likewise the masculine face ruins the woman; some put the latter forward as a commendation, namely if a woman looks mannish, yet neither the one nor the other*a* can hold good. If there is a disproportion in the face of an individual, then this disproportion cannot even be reversed by the change of one feature, but all features*b* must be changed. For example, if someone's nose is regarded as too big for his face, so that one believes that a disproportion results thereby, the question is whether a smaller nose would become this individual. We can say that no other nose fits so well for his face, as that which he has. By chance it happened that an individual who had a large nose, lost it, and when he had a small one made for himself, it did not at all become him; for this reason he again had as large a nose made as was the one which he had lost. Therefore even in the disproportionate face, there exists such a proportion that one cannot eliminate the disproportion through the change of one feature; rather the entire face would then have to be changed. However, in order to get more to the point about physiognomy, the question thus is, whether a physiognomy is even possible, and if the external could even be regarded as a discovery of the inner of nature, and whether physiognomy permits itself to be brought under certain rules, so that physiognomy would be a science. The extent to which something permits itself to be brought under rules, and the extent to which physiognomy is a science or not, will yet be evident with various things in the following. Strictly speaking, physiognomy cannot be a science, because no rules and principles exist, but it is still a knowledge to deduce the inner from the outer, there is still a basis to surmise that the inner [permits] of being discovered through the outer, and that we can perceive the soul through the body. The

26:667 grounds upon which light may be shed on this are [as follows]: because the mind, if it is agitated, discloses itself through the face, as for example, in the case of anger.

---

a *das eine von einem, noch das andere vom anderen*, literally "the one of the one, nor the other of the other," i.e. neither the feminine of the man, nor the masculine of the woman.

b *Gliedmaaßes, Glieder*: otherwise translated as "limbs" (i.e. of the body) in this section. *Züge* is normally the term for "features" and Kant uses it on 25:667ff.

Before we state whereby the mind reveals itself in the face, we must thus first say in what the face consists. The face, however, consists of the facial form, the facial features, and the facial miens. The facial form is based on the proportion of the face; the face can there be proportioned or disproportionate, about which something has already been said in the figure of the body. The facial feature signifies something characteristic with regard to the mind. Hence one says the face conveys nothing, if it has no noticeable feature which could determine something. The facial features are therefore predispositions[a] for miens. Miens are facial features which have been put into play. Every change and agitation of mind produces miens which harmonize with the change of mind, and no other mien can be found for this agitation of mind; hence the mien of the individual in the case of one listening is different from the one who is surprised, or in the case of the one ridiculing, or of the one who is defiant, or of the one who is convinced about something. Miens are therefore very different, and each is suited for the agitation of the mind. Because, as it is, there does not at all exist any agitation of the mind with which no mien is supposed to harmonize, and because the agitation of the mind is one and the same with all peoples and there thus must also exist one and the same miens, something is here thus planted in nature, where the spirit harmonizes with the body. Accordingly, miens are universally valid and natural signs of the agitations of the mind. Otherwise we have nothing as universal as the miens, for words are not so universal; hence a pantomime comedy which could be valid for all peoples could be staged. Since then, the facial features are predispositions for the miens, but the miens are expressions of the agitations of mind, the agitations of mind, however, arise from the human cast of mind, thus the facial features are also predispositions for the agitations of mind; consequently the cast of mind manifests itself in the facial features. Accordingly the facial feature of the human being will express the constitution and disposition[b] of the mind when he sleeps or is doing anything whatsoever. The miens express the agitations of mind in such a way, that if one assumes certain miens, one is transposed into such agitations of mind. He who wants to give a 25:668 lively portrayal of an angry individual need only pull faces, and assume grim and angry miens; thus he will also be likewise affected. Even some postures produce a state of mind. For example, he who wants to flare up and let [someone] have it, and has to sit down, cannot let [the other] have it. Every time he wants to rail at someone, he gets up from the chair. This way too the straight, stiff[c] posture of the body produces pride; likewise, on the other hand, the state of mind also produces many miens and gestures. However, it is hard to have insight into how human beings bring

---

[a] *Anlagen*   [b] *Disposition*
[c] Reading *geschrobene* for *geschobene*; *geschraubt* is a stiff, stilted bearing.

miens, expressing state of mind, already with them into the world. The body comes into play with the mind, and the mind with the body. If then the body is formed, the soul is thus harmoniously formed with the body, because both constitute a unity; therefore the development[a] of the one must determine the character of the other. Therefore this harmony can already be sought in the initial organization. Travelers who have been to the prisons[b] of Amsterdam note that violent scoundrels have strong facial features.[65] A physiognomist could greatly develop his knowledge there, and build a real school. In order to give some classification to this obscure material, one notes this as the best. Talent is determined by the facial form, the mind by the facial features, and character by the miens or by the look. The profile comprises the facial form, the face[c] comprises the facial features, and the look lies in the action. Thus Lavater[66] in his physiognomy also judges from the facial form to the talent of the human being. With regard to the profile of the human being, one also finds

25:669 many similarities with the profile of some animals, as Buffon, together with several others, says.[67] Thus for example, the skeleton of the human head has much similarity with the skeleton of the sheep's head, only the proportion is changed, [and] thus the profile of some human beings and the profile of some animals deviates somewhat.[68] Hence from the similarity of the profile of a human being with the profile of an animal, one could infer something about the similarity of talent. Caricature is the *exaggeration* of character, which serves to know rightly [what is] characteristic. If one then compares the caricature of the human being with the caricature of animals, it seems as if only the animals have a greater exaggeration[d] of character, and therefore from this an inference can also be drawn about temperament. As to what concerns the facial features, which are reproduced not by the profile, but by the face, one can thus assess the mind from these, which we also usually do in ordinary life. For when we see an individual for the first time in ordinary life, we immediately assess him by the face. It is not a matter of indifference to us what facial features he has; nature has already placed such in us. However, to determine character from the looks is the most difficult. Of course it is important to us to know what sort of mind and heart the human being has, yet it is even more important to us what sort of character the human being has, and what sort of principles he has for making use of his talents. The character of the human being lies in the look. Some individuals have

[a] *Ausbildung*, literally "training"
[b] *Raspelhäusern*: convicts in these prisons had to work with large, heavy rasps to break wood down into small chips, and hence the name of these penal institutions.
[c] *face* per editors; archaic term for *Vorderansicht*, or frontal view.
[d] Reading *Übertreibung*, in place of *Übertretung*, as suggested by the editors and as consistent with the previous sentence.

a look which we cannot bear at all, but others have such a look, on which our eyes can well rest, just as on the blue of the sky, where they find real refreshment. We see the calm soul in them.

Because character is twofold, the deceptive and the malevolent one, we also thus find two sorts of marks, of guileful deception, and of extreme malice. However, because we cannot describe and bring any facial feature, much less a look, under rules, although the profile can be brought under rules, physiognomy thus cannot actually be a science. The other reason is also this, because we cannot have insight through any understanding into what [sort of] a connection there can be between the state of the mind and the motion of the face. The rules of reason are universal and do not permit of any exception, but if we only have empirical rules, then these permit many exceptions. Therefore physiognomy will be more useful for the exercise of our power of judgment, than for the instruction of the understanding, from which the practice [of our understanding] could result. Providence seems here indeed to have made a judgment available to us, and also to have provided a disclosure*a* in the face, so that the human being cannot completely hide, but can make himself known through the face. However, Providence has at the same time also not wanted to manifest this determination too clearly, but has left it only at [the level] of assumption, since this would be very harmful for human circumstances. For suppose someone were to understand the art of precisely determining the character of the human being, this would thus not only be a presumption to judge about everyone, but everyone would also be on guard against it, which would divide human society. Yet because it does however lie in nature, and nature itself furnishes us with the opportunity for it, which Lavater seeks to demonstrate, it does indeed deserve to be cultivated, whereby the art of painting and sculpting would afterwards gain very much. Although human beings differ greatly in their judgments, yet in this they are thus mostly in accord. In his physiognomy, Lavater drew Judas, and everyone judges of him that he would not choose such an individual for his friend.[69] Judgment often hangs by a thread; if one now changes one's face by a little bit, then the judgment immediately turns out differently. Women are more fortunate in hitting it, because they are really shrewder by nature, which must supplement their weakness. Lavater also states this about his wife, that she often hit it better than he.[70] Hogarth, who sought to depict the actions and morals of human beings, knew well how to express character, so that the appearance was immediately convincing about the character, without one first needing to read the explanation about it.[71] In social gatherings he sought to copy the actions which he wanted to depict, [and] the faces of those who carried them out, and when he later wanted

---

a *Ankündigung*, literally "announcement"

to depict one such action, he thus selected that face which was best suited for it, and reproduced it by invention. If however the germ for character already lies in nature, how does Providence agree with this? This is concealed. True, the human being can contend with his character, but not change it, as little as he can change his face. One should note that when individuals have made such persons who are similar to them, the object of their love and inclination, if they live a long life the one person adopts the manner of the other, so that finally a similarity in miens and facial features is to be found. Because some faces bear a resemblance to one another, one can also thus infer the similarity of the character. Hence, if the daughter resembles the mother, then one can infer the character of the daughter from the character of the mother. Question: whom do children resemble more, the father or the mother? Linné says: one resembles the mother in accordance with the shell, but the father in accordance with the kernel; then however temperament and wit would

25:672 have to bear a resemblance to the mother, but talent and character to the father.[72] However, there is nothing certain here. Miens characterize the human being. Thus an unsteady look indicates a dishonest individual. People who lie have something unsteady in their look. Just as their thoughts go left and right, their miens thus also conform with this. People who do not squint, but who look down their nose, surely lie, for just as they are thinking in their head, they likewise also roll the eyes. Thus an unsure look indicates a furtive individual, which one finds with people from the thief's trade. Thus the character of the human being already lies in the look. Here one can note the words[a] of an owner of a theatrical company who, from the facial features of an individual who was presented to him as an actor, concluded and said: if the fellow is no rogue, then the Creator does not write with a legible hand. Only the one who could read such a hand, however, could say this. Thus Pernety also states about Brinvilliers, who was the most malevolent woman known, that when her picture hung among various others in a sitting room, and was viewed by

25:673 some spectators, one of them threw a glance at this picture in particular, and said to the owner: if the painter really hit the character with this idea, then the woman must have been possessed by the devil, which the owner then also confirmed.[73] Therefore although her facial form was very beautiful, yet the features manifested the malice of the character, which lies in the looks. One says of some individuals, they have a distinguished face, of others, they have a common face. Since this refers to social position, one could thus think that it were an assumed mien; yet one does find persons, who are not at all distinguished, and yet have a

---

[a] *Ausdruck*, literally "expression"

distinguished appearance, and in turn, distinguished persons with a common appearance. A common face has the attribute of a base taste and crudeness, which one finds in the case of many distinguished persons. Thus one also finds a distinguished appearance in the case of humble persons, although the expression through the look is lacking, because they are not accustomed to it. Much is based on habit and the adopted manner. Thus aristocratic and bourgeois women have completely different manners; the aristocratic ones manifest presumptuousness in their look, but the bourgeois manifest fearfulness. Therefore with persons who are really distinguished, something distinguished manifests itself in their manner, although their facial form is common. However, it could also be the case, when persons are descended from a pure aristocratic lineage, which nature raised to the peerage on account of its merits, that something sublime lies in their facial features, which is still attributable to a former, nobler mode of thought. Such a lineage of well thinking persons could always be maintained completely pure, if the aberrant shoots would be weeded out; then something noble would always remain in their features. Miens can also be adopted which express a feature that is afterwards permanent.

As to what concerns the facial features which relate to the different social positions and occupations of human beings, one thus finds that [these facial features] greatly conform to them. In just the same way there is thus a difference in the facial features of city dwellers and country people. City people disclose something refined, but country people something stiff, in their facial features. For in the city one must adopt a certain flexibility and urbanity, since one deals with many people; by contrast the peasant does not have so many objects before him, which require him to refine himself. In all things, in clothes, in social intercourse, he is constrained, which also remains characteristic of him for his entire life. Hence one sends young people to the city, so that they become refined.

As to what concerns the occupations, these have a great influence on the facial form, so that one can almost tell by looking at someone, whether he is a tailor or a butcher; for since everyone's way of life is different, the features also conform to it. Thus the butcher's way of life is the vigorous, plucky, dogged way of life which then also remains characteristic of him. If two brothers who resemble one another quite a lot, take up a different way of life, and the one becomes a soldier, the other a cleric, then they will afterwards look completely different, since the expressions of their features have conformed to each one's way of life. Scholars have a gentle expression in their features, because the sciences greatly refine human beings. Men are by far more particular about what is characteristic of women, but women are not at all particular about it,

25:674

for they are only made for preserving the species. If then the man has all possible conditions of social position, of earnings for stability, they do not so much bother with what is characteristic, and they also cannot be so delicate about this, because they are the ones who are chosen, and who cannot choose. And then the man's wicked character is also not as harmful for the wife as for others; his malice does not interest the wife, for if he deceives others, he thus carts it home. However, with regard to this, the man is really more questioning. As to what concerns the physiognomy of entire peoples, it is indeed very difficult thus to say something for certain about it. The Turks have a candid face, which characterizes the defiance, but also the spirit. They admit of no refinement, no discipline. True, the Germans have no genius, but they permit themselves to be refined and disciplined. Many nations do indeed permit themselves to be disciplined, but by force, and not from respect for the universal law. Freedom which arises from respect for the law agrees[a] with every freedom, but license does not agree with every freedom. That already indicates a sublime talent, if human beings are capable of being disciplined by law and not by force. That is the noble [aspect] of the civil order, that when a law is there, all respect it, but woe to the one who undertakes something in opposition to it. The English, for example, are this way. The Poles, however, do not respect any law and want to live in [a state of] license. Every nation does indeed have something special and distinctive in its features, for one can, for example, recognize a Frenchman by his face, without looking at his traditional costume, and thus also the Italians, and other nations.

ON THE CHARACTER OF HUMANITY IN GENERAL

This is an important item about which many authors have already ventured to write, among whom Rousseau is the most distinguished. What should one in fact judge about humanity? Among the animals, and among all beings, what [kind of] a character does it have? How much good and how much evil is in it? Does he contain a source for evil, or for good, in himself? In the first place, the human being must be characterized as an animal. Linné says that, upon all reflection, he finds nothing special about the human being as an animal; hence he must also put him in one class with the ape. If one also wanted to infer the character from this, then it would be very bad, for the apes are very malevolent and deceitful animals. Here, however, we are comparing the human being with all animals in general, and so first of all we ask: if the human being were in a savage state, and had no use of reason, what [sort of] animal would he in fact be there? Would he be a beautiful or ugly, dexterous

---

[a] Reading *übereinstimmen* for *stimmen*

or inept[a] animal? He would not belong to the beautiful animals, but he would be a very dexterous animal, for he has dexterous organs, and for this reason he would not be a weak animal. Examples confirm that human beings in this state, if they were only hearty enough, even subdued wolves, although no one now dares to take part in such a duel. On account of his dexterity and strength, he would therefore be very safe in the forest. However, he would not be a beautiful animal. Imagine,[b] if the human being in the savage state would be naked, and would have kept the beard, but which could also disappear in the naked state, since then the fluids which are now repressed by the clothes, and cause the beard, might evaporate more, and [the human being] would then naturally also be otherwise altogether crude, this then would be a very ugly animal. Thus there can still be much to dispute about beauty. Dampier also notes that savage women look very ugly, since they let their long breasts hang, or throw them over their shoulders.[74] Nowadays the human being makes himself beautiful through the understanding. The seat of beauty consists in the face, where the muscles come into action, and the miens begin to play, but which would not be found in the savage state. However, his dexterity cannot be denied. Further, the question is: how would his figure be constituted? Would he go on two or four feet? This is an important question, once it has been raised. This has still not been rightly investigated, the question must be somewhat ascertained. Because the human being was to have reason, he was thus destined to go on two feet, since [reason] is thereby best cultivated, and because speech is cultivated by reason, the human being must thus indeed be so constituted, that he could produce [such speech] for himself, for even if the first language were revealed, the human being could still thus get into such circumstances where he would forget it. However, if we think of the human being without reason and without speech, how then would the human being in fact be able to live best? Would it be better for him to go on two or four feet? Concerning this one must look up the treatise by von Moscati from Pavia, which is the best and nicest of this kind, and was written with great anatomical skill.[75] Nature's purpose with the human being was to preserve his species; therefore he is built by nature in such a way that he could live in every circumstance. If he were built solely for the civilized state, then he would have to perish if he would fall into savagery. If he were built only for savagery, then he could not cultivate his reason. In order that he could maintain himself as an animal, he thus would have to be built in such a way that it could also stand him in good

25:676

25:677

---

[a] *geschicktes oder ungeschicktes*, otherwise translated as skilled or unskilled, but in the context here, "dexterous" better conveys the sense of bodily skill (rather than that of talents, etc.) which is the subject of the discussion.

[b] *Man stelle sich vor*

stead if he would cultivate his reason, which would still always be fortuitous. If he had reason, then he could afterwards force himself to go on
two feet, for reason can always maintain itself. However, nature has also
provided for him in such a way that he could also exist if he had no reason. However, our build is in fact arranged [so as to go on] two feet. Apes
also have such a build and yet go on four feet, although they can also go
on two, but which is not necessary. True, our arms are too short for our
feet, and those of the apes are very long, so that they almost go upright,
when they go on their forefeet. However, on the island of Madagascar,
there are people who go on four feet, and also have such long hands, for
that can change greatly through the course of time*a* and through long
use. Accordingly one cannot rightly determine the first form.

As an animal, the human being is a very pugnacious animal. In the wild,
he fears nothing as much as another human being. Thus Robinson [Cru-
soe] on the island was alarmed when he discovered human footprints.[76]
The human being can greatly beware of all animals, if he already once
knows their kind and nature, but not of his own kind, for since this is a
cunning creature, he thus cannot detect its snares; he can pretend to be
friendly, and yet act malevolently, he knows how to dissemble, and disguise himself, and always conceive of new means of becoming dangerous

25:678

for the other [person]. Everyone already feels in himself, if he were alone
for a long time on the island, and thus already believed himself to be safe,
that he would become greatly frightened if he would discover a human
being, for now he would no longer be quite safe, now he would have
an enemy who is more dangerous for him than all wild animals, since
he could in fact beware of them, and outwit them, but not the human
being, for this one can set traps for him, watch*b* all his actions, and hinder
him and be dangerous for him in every aspect. Unless, if they have the
same needs, and are in the same predicament, they discover one another,
become acquainted with one another, and live sociably; however even
then the one cannot quite trust the other, he does not in fact know, if
the other is not again plotting against him. Among the animal species,
he is probably not to be ranked as a beast of prey, since it does not seem
that he would have an immediate appetite for others' animal blood, for
mauling everything and tearing it to pieces; moreover his physical build
is not like that of a beast of prey. It thus seems that he would more likely
stick with vegetables. Yet with respect to his own species, with respect to
other human beings, he is indeed to be regarded as a beast of prey, since
he is mistrustful, violent, and hostile toward his own kind, which is no
longer as manifest in the civil state, since the human being is there held
under constraint, but which still does very much sprout up, and a great
deal from the animal state still adheres to us. One has only to attend to

---

a *Länge der Jahre*   *b* *Acht haben*, literally "pay attention to" one society, [to see] whether in it everyone does not take the other to be his enemy, and is very mistrustful of everyone whom he still does not know, and hence is very withdrawn. Suppose that all the constraint of the civil order would suddenly cease, then no one would be safe in his house, everyone would be afraid that someone would break into his house at night, and perpetrate violence. One may not say that only the rabble would do this; by nature all human beings are rabble, and those who are not so now, are refined through the civil order and discipline. But if it would cease, then the refinement would also cease, and all human beings would be such rabble. This maliciousness lies in the nature of all human beings. Since, as it is, this is a universal arrangement of nature, although it immediately aims at something evil, it thus must still indirectly have a purpose. This is a universal rule which one must observe, and which is very philosophical, that one always search for the purpose and intent of something which exists universally in nature, even if it immediately aims for something evil, for nature will not produce such a universal order for nothing. Human beings' desires, jealousy, mistrust, violence, propensity for enmity against those outside the family: all these attributes have a reason, and a relation to a purpose. Providence's purpose is: God wants that human beings should populate the entire world. All animals have their certain climate, but human beings are to be found everywhere. Human beings are not to stay in a small region, but to spread out across the entire earth. The best means of promoting this is pugnacity, jealousy, and disagreement with regard to property. This has separated people from one another, and spread them across the entire earth, for if one family is together, and greatly multiplies and increases in number, then new families develop from this; these fall out with one another and separate, then they must break up after all, and by such a way spread out across the entire earth. Hence one finds human beings everywhere on the most desolate and infertile islands. What prompts them to go there? Not the lack of places to live; there are still many uninhabited lands in Africa and America. But what prompts human beings to go to Greenland, Tahiti, and other lands? Nothing else but pugnacity. If human beings would be peaceable, they would all live clustered together in one place, and no one would separate from society. Therefore this is the one great use which arises from maliciousness. Furthermore, when human beings live beside one another, and begin to cultivate themselves, when they advance from the simple needs of nature to the artificial ones, property is thus instituted, and then human beings always get into war. Human beings all seek to have their property, but this cannot occur without protection and security; accordingly they try to be secure in their property. By nature, however, no one is secure [with regard to] his property, for when one individual fences in an area, and obtains garden produce, then the other one who has spent no effort on it, but has a liking for

25:679

25:680

215

this produce of his, comes and snatches it away from [the owner], if [the newcomer] is stronger than the other one. With effort, one person gets himself some animals, for example, chickens; but the other who does not have them, takes a fancy to them[a] and takes them away. What will he do to him? Therefore if one wants to have property, then one must have protection and security, and this occurs through the coercion of the authorities.

Accordingly a law[b] must be established, which is combined with force. Through what, then, did the most civilized constitution[c] among human beings arise? Through the maliciousness of human nature. Hence this is the other great purpose which arises from it. Through this civil order, a certain whole of human beings comes into existence; regularity, order, reciprocal regulation[d] of one member [in relation] to the other and to the whole of humanity, arise from it. From this arises the development of talents, the concepts of justice and morality, and the development of the greatest perfection of which people are capable. Since everyone in the civil constitution stands in relation to the other, every human being thus becomes [a matter] of great importance to the other one. The judgment of others has a great influence on him, and from this arises the concept of honor; he becomes inspired to undertake a great deal, not only with regard to his needs, but with regard to the common good[e] of life. Arts emerge from this; true, needs grow, yet working these out proves to be a credit to human beings. The human being refines himself with regard to taste, prosperity, and propriety. All these perfections emerged from the maliciousness of the human mind, which first produced civil constraint. The question is, if this maliciousness of the mind did not exist, whether all this would have materialized. Many believe that the human condition would be better, if there were no maliciousness. Yet then human beings would have lived with one another, no one would have concerned himself about the other, everyone would have lived quietly for himself, for the human being is sluggish by nature; if another drive did not pull him up short, then he would also remain sluggish. Accordingly there had to be something which necessitated the human being to [spur himself]. If human beings were meek and good-natured by nature, no civil

25:681

---

[a] *bekommt Appetit dazu*   [b] *Recht*

[c] *Verfaßung*: Kant's usage of this term in the subsequent passages of this section often seems to be more in the general sense of "condition," but since the civil condition is one under a civil constitution, and "constitution" itself connotes the nature, condition, or state of something, the term is rendered by "constitution" throughout.

[d] *Bestimmung*

[e] *allgemeinen Bestens*, literally the "universal best"; that Kant has the notion of the "common good" in mind may also be seen on 25:682, where private needs are again contrasted with the *gemeinen Besten* (i.e. in this second reference, it is unambiguously "common" and not "universal").

constitution would have emerged. This latter is the source of the development of talents, of the concepts of justice and all moral perfection, which is the most distinguished [aspect] of the civil order. If the human being were good-natured by nature, then there would not need to be any authorities, human beings would not stand in any relation to one another, then no one would do his utmost to undertake something which has an influence on the whole, then everything would slack off and one would forget everything, and the complete perfection of human beings which is, after all, the purpose, would come to an end. Just this maliciousness has not only resulted in this civil constitution being established, but it also has the effect of maintaining it, since, because maliciousness consists therein that one individual harbors suspicion of the other, that no one trusts the other, and even if it happens, then it is already a result of the civil order and the refinement of morality, thus the civil order is maintained through this suspicion. For example, 99 out of 100 in an army are so disposed that they prefer to end the war without bloodshed, and would like to go home. How does it happen that they do not do such, that they let themselves be dominated by someone who can do with them what he wants, that often a petty officer keeps them all in fear? Does it perhaps happen because they are all together resolved to comply with such, that they take it to be a duty to promote the well-being of the land or to defend it under the hegemony of one individual? No! The greater part is not so disposed; instead each one would like to be liberated from this hegemony. But if most are so disposed, why do they not do it? Because one is suspicious of the other, and one does not trust the other. Each is concerned about the other, even if they might claim to be in agreement. Thus this mistrust keeps the entire army in order, so that it can be ruled with little effort. This does not only hold good for the military, but also for the civil status. Certainly there are many among the rabble who are disposed to take away from the other what is his, only they cannot come to an agreement, because the one does not trust the other. Accordingly, the civil order is very easily maintained through this maliciousness. Ill is therefore here the source of the good. And if one asks so much, where does evil come from? one should thus rather ask, where does everything good come from? For the human being is not good-natured by nature. The evil in the animal nature is in keeping with animality, and is the source of the development of good in humanity.

25:682

The human being has two determinations,[a] one with regard to humanity, and one with regard to animality. These two determinations

[a] *Bestimmungen*: some usages (such as the one here) would seem also appropriately rendered by "destiny," but since "determination" includes the sense of being directed to an end, and Kant's usages in this section are wider than "destiny," the standard translation of "determination" is here used (without implying its later full critical sense).

conflict with one another. We do not achieve the perfection of humanity in the determination of animality, and if we want to achieve the
perfection of humanity, then we must do violence to the determination
of animality. The age of human beings, and their determination [with
respect to] animality and humanity, can serve as evidence. A child is [a
being] which cannot maintain itself, a youth is one who can maintain
himself, but still cannot reproduce his own kind, or maintain his species.
The man is thus the most complete creature. Therefore, according to
nature, the human being will propagate his species, and at the same time
that he can do this, he will also be able to maintain himself. According to
nature, the human being is then in the position to maintain his species,
when he is in the position to propagate it. According to nature, manhood is combined with maturity; if this were not [the case], then human
beings could not maintain themselves. If the human being, when he can
propagate his species, were not yet able to maintain it, then his species
would have to perish. In the natural state,^{a} the human being is a child
until the sixth year, for until then he cannot maintain himself; in the
tenth year, he is already a youth, [and] then he can maintain himself. In
this age, he can already fish, hunt, gather roots, and if he can do this,
then he can also maintain himself; for this he is already skilled enough in
the tenth year. In the sixteenth year, he can already reproduce his own
kind and propagate his species, and is also in the position to maintain
his species, and then he is also already a man. In this age, he has enough
strength to maintain and to defend himself, his wife, and his own kind.
Here everything is in keeping with nature. However, if we take the civil
state, we thus find that the needs increase, and that the human being must
make himself skilled not only for the fulfillment^b of his private needs,
25:683   but also for the common good.^{c} Hence the inequality between nature
and the civil constitution is very great. For the latter, it takes more skill,
experience, luck, and time to wait such out, until one gets into the position to maintain such. Hence the age of the youth in the civil state is far
more delayed than in the unrefined state of nature. In the civil constitution, the human being is still a child in the tenth year; indeed, until
the fifteenth year, he is then still unable to maintain himself. From this
it follows that the age of manhood is incomparably far more delayed,
than in the natural state, because his, his wife's, and his children's needs
are greatly multiplied, and in order to be able to meet this multitude of
needs, over the course of many years he will have to have acquired the
capacity to be able to provide for them all. Accordingly in the civil state,
the time for being able to get married is set very far beyond the time

^{a} *rohen Zustande*
^{b} *Erwerbung*, literally "acquisition," i.e. by working for/earning one's living.
^{c} *gemeinen Besten*

where nature has given us the capacity to reproduce our own kind. For in the sixteenth year, one is in the position to reproduce one's own kind, but not to maintain it. According to nature, however, at this time one would already be a man. Therefore the determination of nature conflicts with the civil constitution. From this it follows that the interval between the natural and civil determination of manhood should be taken up with the infringement upon and violence to nature which one rightly ought to carry out, but which is presently filled with the vices of opulence; for in the sixteenth year, according to nature one is sexually mature, but nature has not given us the capacity for this, that we should do violence to and infringe upon [nature], or play with [nature], or extirpate [nature], but that we should comply with it. If this were not nature's intention, then nature would have been pulling our leg; nature would have given us a capacity of which we can not at all avail ourselves. As it is, in the civil constitution, we cannot avail ourselves of it until approximately the thir-tieth year of age. Since however the sex drive[a] is operative, and wants to retain its rights, a conflict arises from this, and the civil state is in conflict with the natural one. This can not at all be changed, for surely no one can so easily take a wife in the sixteenth year, but for nearly again the same length of time he must suffer with his sex drive, and do violence to it. Therefore on this side, nature has determined us for animality, but on the other side in turn, for the civil order, namely with regard to the perfection of humanity. Then, through the civil order, we must do vio-lence to the natural state. The luxury and refinement of humanity is the debilitation of animality. The human being is coddled by the amenity of life, and by sparing himself the discomforts against which nature had toughened him, the human being is softened. Many illnesses arise in the civil state which do not exist in nature. A wife of a savage has more strength, and is not as subject to illnesses as here. Therefore the civil constitution does violence to animality.

25:684

Now let us compare the natural human being with the well-bred one, and see how both stand in relation to the highest perfection, and which of them is most in keeping with the true purposive determina-tion. This is the important question of Rousseau, who there investigates whether the state of nature, or of the civil constitution, is the true state of human beings. The concepts must first be rightly determined. The human being of nature is not refashioned and reshaped by any art; art has not suppressed the natural aptitude in his case. However, the civil state is where the human being is disciplined, and through the discipline, violence is done to nature, where the human being is already refashioned and reshaped. One believed that Rousseau favored the human being of nature over the human being of art, and his opinion really does seem to

---

[a] *Triebe*

attach to the side of the natural human being. However, on the other hand, this serves to rouse the attention of the philosophers to investigate how the perfections of the civil state ought to be formed, such that the perfections of nature are not destroyed and no violence would be done to nature, and how the vices and misfortune, which arise through the civil order, can be suppressed thereby that the civil constitution could be united with nature, since the civil perfection greatly conflicts with the natural one. If we now mention the state of nature, then we do indeed 25:685 of course find that the human being of nature is in the first place in fact happier, and then also lives more innocently. However, he is happy and innocent only in a negative understanding [of the matter]; his state does not entail fortune, but also not misfortune. With him, the good is [that there is] no vice, also no virtue. The positive [aspect] of happiness, and the positive [aspect] of virtue is greatly lacking in the natural state. In this state, the human being is a child, where he can do neither good nor evil. The negative perfection of the state of nature consists in the lack of misery and of vice. If we now first take misery [into consideration], then the question is: is the natural or the civil human being miserable? In the first place, in the state of nature there exists a community of goods; there is no property, as long as one has something [to sustain] life, they all have it. Accordingly all conflict, which arises in the civil state due to property, is omitted; the mistrust, the deception, the enmity, the violence are omitted. Everyone is satisfied with the need which he secures daily. But if we take a wealthy citizen in the civil state, who later, however, reverts [to the position] that he must carry out a laborer's work, then this misery is in fact nothing but the opinion of delusion. In this state, he will still always acquire so much, that he need not go hungry. He is not grieved however because he will lack bread, but because he is not in his former circumstances, because his honor suffers due to this and his social standing falls into ruin. Human beings are not grieved because they will lack bread, but because they cannot live like others of their social position; therefore the misery which here oppresses us [consists] in what people will say. Misery here stands in relation to the opinion of human beings, not to the need of nature. The most miserable fare in this state, an oatmeal porridge, is a delicacy for the savages. If we could make do with such a simple fare, then we would spare ourselves much misery and grief. The savage has no concept at all of what [it is to be] well or poorly dressed, about what tastes good or bad, about what is distinguished or base; therefore he need not fear that a distinguished [person] would order him about, since there are no distinguished and no inferior [persons] among them. Thus he cannot comprehend how one human being should be more distinguished than another, or how one human being should limit another, how one could order another 25:686 about. Accordingly, his state exists in complete freedom; his facial features already express something free and unrestrained. Hence an Indian spoke in just the same way with the king of France as with other savages, and was not as embarrassed as a Frenchman often is, who has already been with the court a long time. He paid no attention to all the pomp of the court; for him that was all a trifle. When he girds himself with his golden loincloth,[a] he believes himself to be better and more splendidly dressed up, than anyone else; hence he does not even entertain any desire for the pomp of the Europeans. The civil state, however, makes us greatly dependent on social position, our freedom is fettered in a lot of ways, through the force of the authorities, through our manner, through others' inclinations, through our delusion about social position. Our behavior is constrained and fettered, and not free like that of the savages. The savage is carefree, he relishes the enjoyments of his life without having the discomforts. The natural ills like sicknesses, also do not strike the savage in the way they do the citizen. In this aspect, the savages are like the animals, who are not subject to any sicknesses, and have no presentiment of ill, but live as long as their powers are adequate, and when they cease, then they are also dead. The savage is also just like this. With regard to sicknesses, he is very insusceptible, he does not torment himself with the fear of death, he does not even think about it, but lives as long as his powers are adequate; when they tire, then he is dead. That ill which could still oppress the savage the most is that he is not safeguarded against public violence, as in the civil state. However, although in the civil state we are safeguarded against public violence, and do not run any risk with respect to [our] lives, yet on the other hand, we are also very troubled. Who can say that with regard to his peace, he is very secured, that he is free from all offense, that he is safe from all slander? And then, the wars of the savages are also only a temporary storm; by contrast ours are far more terrible and ruthless, and even peace 25:687 is a constant armament for war, so that the preservation and protection of life costs more effort and work than life is worth. When savages are lured into the civil state, and have already been servants, and had tasted everything which can possibly be enjoyed in the civil state, then one could still not keep them in the civil state, but they left everything and returned to their previous state of nature and freedom. Freedom is thus the bright atmosphere which sweetens everything. With regard to needs, everyone provides so much for himself that he has no want and there is, by the way, no misery which can threaten him, for the natural ills are soon weathered. Ills which oppress us arise mostly from worry about the future. Therefore if we consider happiness negatively, then the human being in the natural state, with regard to physical life, is far happier than is the human being in the civil state. The human being in the natural

---

[a] *Schürze ausputzt*, literally "dressed up in his apron"

state is not only happier, but also more innocent; he is negatively good, i.e. innocent. Innocence is negative moral goodness, but if the human being is innocent, then he is still not virtuous. The unrefined human being is thus negatively good. He has no duties, since he has no concepts of such; he knows no law, hence he also cannot inexcusably violate it, and consequently he cannot be vicious. In the natural state, the incentives for vices are not roused; these are first roused in the civil state by the increase in needs and desires which arise from it. The natural human being thus keeps his word. Among one another they also do not steal, as they only [do] in the case of the neighbor; among themselves they see it as a contract, but because strangers do not concern them, they also do not at all know why they should not take everything away from them. They do not at all comprehend that this is something evil, since they do not even know what good and evil is. Among themselves no theft takes place, for

25:688   nothing tempts them. What one has, every other person can also have. With them there is no incentive of honor, which should induce them to it. In the civil state, however, many vices arise here, such as disloyalty, deception, theft, and so forth. With regard to the sex drive, many vices arise in the civilized state, because in accordance with the civil constitution, it is not possible to make use of the sexual powers when they are given by nature.[a] The cause really lies in the civil constitution, but in the savage state, it[b] is in complete agreement. In the interim period in the civil state, when one reaches sexual maturity,[c] until the time when one is in the position to make proper use of it, nothing but vices occur; the entire interim period is filled with vices, which are all omitted in the savage state. In the civil state, the woman acquires many capacities for attracting the masculine sex to her, from which the vices arise which are directed to different objects. That is not at all [the case] in the savage state. There the drive[d] is not stirred up by allurements, but use is made of it as an animal instinct. The savage woman does not at all entice; on the contrary, the man adorns himself more than the woman. Therefore the savage does not at all comprehend why he should satisfy his instinct with another man's wife, which he can do just as well with his own. Thus all the vices of adultery are omitted, since it already lies in the nature of the state of affairs itself, that such vices are not even possible. All vices which arise from the concept of honor are omitted, because the savage is incapable of such a concept. The powers of the human being are not

---

[a] Reading text in accordance with editors' suggested correction: *Es ist nicht möglich, sich dann des Geschlechtsvermögens zu bedienen.*

[b] i.e. the time of being physically and actually able to use one's sexual powers.

[c] *Geschlechts Vermögen von der Natur bekommt,* literally "receives the sexual power(s) from nature."

[d] *Neigung,* but clearly it is the sex drive which is being referred to.

as weakened as in the civil state. Accordingly, the human being in the natural state lives more innocently, than in the civil one. He lives happily and innocently as a child. However, this is no positive fortune, but also no positive misfortune, just as it is no positive good, but also no positive vice, but negative. In the civil state, the human being sacrifices many of the natural advantages, he sacrifices his freedom in many ways, his carefreeness with regard to his comfortableness, the contentment which arises from the lack of knowledge of greater needs, a great degree of his health through exertion of his powers, and through the wasting away of his life, and through grief, worries, and effort. He becomes subject to the temptation of vices, he gets inclinations from the knowledge of needs, which seduce him into many passions, he comes to know the moral law, and feels the incentive to transgress duties, and since his activity has been aroused,[a] thus evil will grow in just the same way as will the good. Therefore he will feel the incentive to evil just as well as to the good; indeed since we do not have such an incentive for the good as for evil, and the good consists more in the suppression of the incentive to evil, and we do not have any new incentive with which to oppose evil, besides only suppressing it, thus vice will grow in greater proportion than the good. Therefore the human being here gets into the dilemma of virtue and vice. Accordingly, in the civil state, the human being is not as virtuous and happy as in the natural one.

25:689

If we now deal with this on the whole, we thus repeat the question: is the natural state or the civil one more in keeping with the purpose of human beings? In order to approximate more nearly the purpose of humanity, should we all head for the woods, or stay in the civil state? No nation has gone from the civilized state to the wilderness; hence this is not an advance to the perfection of humanity, but on the contrary, the advance is from savagery to the civil constitution, and [entails] that the perfection of the state of human beings is therefore to be placed in the perfection of the civil constitution. For since in the [state of] savagery one lives as innocently as a child, but, as little as it is to be approved that the human being always remain a child, even if he could always be provided for, just as little is it to be approved, that the human being always remain in [a state of] savagery. Rousseau also did not want to say that the determination of human beings is [the state of] savagery, but that the human being should not seek his perfection of his state in such a way that he sacrifices all advantages of nature, by chasing after the civil advantages. This [state] serves only for the plan of education[b] and

[a] *Thätigkeit in Bewegung gesetzt*, literally "activity has been put into motion"; it is also clear from the context that, for Kant, *Tätigkeit* is a very specific term, referring to the activity of the morally conscious being as such a being.
[b] *Erziehung*

25:690 government, through which such a perfect state can be achieved. The human being is determined as an animal for the woods, but as a human being for society, and there he is not to provide for the needs solely for his [own] happiness,[a] but as a part of a whole, to try to promote the happiness of this whole. Since the civil constitution is a constraint, its effect is thus industry and diligence, not only to provide for his needs, but also for the whole. The human being is however lazy by nature; he does nothing other than that to which nature and necessity drives him. However, in the civil state, there exists not only the constraint of the authorities, but also an artificial constraint of the parents, of the circumstances of making a living, of propriety, of honor, and through this arises such diverse activity whereby the human being produces much positive good, which would not at all have existed in the savage state. The human being develops his talents solely in the civil state. With the incentives to evil, his incentives for the good also increase. The civil state has the advantage that it can make the human being positively happy and positively virtuous, while in the savage state, he was only negatively happy and good. Although the human being in the civil state sacrifices many advantages of nature, yet many means are thus furnished to replace such [advantages]. Therefore nature's purpose was the civil society, and the human being is determined to make himself perfectly happy and good as a member of the entire society. Now however, the human being is not yet in the perfection of the civil state. In this constitution of the civil state, the human being has still lost more of the natural [state], than he is supposed to have replaced through the civil one, but he is surely already advancing to the highest happiness of which he is capable in the civil state. When, however, will such perfection be attained? And at what moment in time [will] the perfect civil state [be realized]? This is the establishment of society with all practical conditions, [the establishment] of the society of equal beings. Before this society is established and attained, before [this occurs] we can not believe that the human being will attain the highest degree of civil perfection. As a single individual, the human being cannot yet thus make himself perfect, until the whole of society will be perfect. When such a [political] state[b] will be attained, in which everything will be instituted in accordance with complete rules of

25:691 justice and of morality, this will then be a condition under which everyone will be able to make himself more perfect. True, such a [political] state still does not in fact exist, yet by means of many revolutions which still must take place, it is to be hoped for. What then serves to be able to

[a] *Glück*

[b] *Staat*, usually simply translated as "state," but confusing here because of the translation throughout this section of *Zustand* as state.

produce such [a state]? Here one is still uncertain whether one should start from the bottom, or from the top. Should such a [political] state first be established, so that every single individual could be made perfect, or should every single individual first thus be made perfect through education, in order that finally later, when it has passed through many members, such a state could be established? Does the perfection of every single human being depend on the perfection of the state, or does the perfection of the state depend on the perfection of every single human being? Is the first the condition of the second, or is the second the condition of the first? It seems as if the education of every single human being should constitute the beginning, for the education of one human being educates^a many other human beings, who in turn educate others. In the first place, one must see to it that those, who are afterwards to educate others, are [themselves] well educated. If teachers and priests were educated, if the concepts of pure morality would prevail among them, then they would also soon come to occupy the highest position,^{b} enter the schools of rulers, and through these, the whole could afterwards be educated.

In order that we can survey the entire plan of the advance of the perfection of the human condition, from the [state of] savagery up to the highest perfection of the civil constitution, for the sake of coherence^c we must thus still repeat the following and then continue.

It pleased providence to draw good out of the root of evil,^{d} for, as already stated above, the entire world was populated due to the malevolence of human beings, and since no one could coerce the other, they thus all subjected themselves to common constraint, whereby the civil constitution and civil constraint were achieved. All the talents of the human being were developed in this constitution; there his needs increased, from which all the arts and sciences originated. However, since the constraint of the authorities does not extend to anything beyond the external civil order and the right of others, and [it does] not [extend] to propriety and the moral life, thus another constraint is lacking here which could compel one in the case where civil constraint would be badly misplaced. Since as it is however, human beings became ever more refined through civil constraint, and cultivated themselves more and more, thus the constraint of propriety emerged among them, where human beings

25:692

---

^{a} *bildet*
^{b} *zum Throne hinaufschwingen*, literally "soar up to the throne"
^{c} *Zusammenhanges*, literally "connection," but the sense here seems to be that of how the account being given hangs together.
^{d} *Übel*: *Wurzel des Übels* is how "root of evil" is normally expressed; otherwise, *Übel* has been translated as "ill" (to distinguish it from *Böse*).

compel themselves among one another with regard to taste, modesty, refinement, courtesy, and decorum. For everything [which is a matter of] decency in the good life*a* is not produced by any civil constraint; the authorities do not concern themselves with this at all, with how one treats one's dress, whether one attends to cleanliness, and has chosen tastefully, whether one behaves modestly or crudely in society. If one just does not overtly offend someone, then the authorities are not at all concerned with the rest. However, because of propriety, human beings compel themselves among one another with regard to the rest; they refrain from much because it does not agree with the opinion of others. We are already this far in our civil constitution. We still do not have any other constraint. If, however, our perfection in civil constitution should not rise any further, then we have nevertheless lost more than we have gained. Yet the human race is still progressing ever further in perfection. What kind of additional constraint could still be conceived of here? This is the moral constraint, which consists in every human being fearing the moral judgment of the other, and thereby being necessitated to perform actions of uprightness and of the pure moral life. Human beings have established the constraint of propriety among one another, to which all are subject, and where everyone pays attention to the other's opinion with regard to propriety. Yet human beings have just such a right also to pass judgment about the moral conduct of the human being. First, the concepts of morality must be purified, and respect for the moral law must be instituted; the heart would then already change.

25:693 Then everyone would consider it to be an honor that he is regarded as an upright man by everyone, and not that he could ride in a carriage. The result of this would be that no individual would associate with such [a person] who did not live morally, one would have contempt for that person who has already once lied, and would shun his company, just as everyone shuns associating with that person who has once committed theft, and has thereby infringed upon the civil order and the rights of others. But why should it not also get to the point that one did not desire to associate with such a person who acted contrary to his morality and the duty toward himself. If we take it further, then it follows that when someone would seek office, one would not, as [we do] now, set great store by the outer conduct or skill, but by the moral character. And if such honor would prevail with him, everyone would constrain himself. This moral constraint would make up for the shortcomings of civil constraint and of [the constraint of] propriety. However, because it was based on the opinion of others, it would thus after all be only an external constraint. Accordingly still another constraint remains, and that is the constraint of one's conscience, and indeed of one's own, where every

a im Wohlstande, literally "prosperity"

individual, in accordance with the moral law, passes judgment about his moral conduct through his conscience, and also acts likewise. This is the kingdom of God on earth. Conscience would be our supreme judge, but our conscience is not yet well cultivated, since many still drug[a] their conscience. But if it were cultivated, then this constraint, since it is an inner one, would be the strongest, and then indeed none other would be necessary. We actually have a predisposition[b] for this in us [given to us] by providence, since everyone sentences himself, and also morally sentences the other with reference to himself. Therefore providence has really made us judges, only we do not express our moral judgment, because no moral establishment has as yet been instituted. Should it not, however, be possible that the human race should attain this degree of perfection in the civil constitution, for it seems that every created being would have to achieve the perfection for which it was made; therefore the human race must also actually attain this degree of perfection, which is the purpose of its vocation,[c] and even if it still takes centuries. How- 25:694 ever, if it materializes, then it will also take an unforeseeable [number of] years in an advancement [in perfection]. For it is a philosophy of the lazy, if one believes that [things] will always remain as they are now. For as little as things 1,000 years ago were as they are now, just as little will they be so after [another] 1,000 years; therefore great changes are to be hoped for. One is always accustomed to asking, where does evil come from? But one ought rather to ask, where does the good come from? The beginning is made with evil out of freedom,[77] for evil belongs to the animal perfection of the human being; yet in nature everything is designed to achieve its greatest possible perfection. Just as a man must develop from an embryo, this way everything must indeed rise up to its perfection. Innate[d] to human nature are germs which develop and can achieve the perfection for which they are determined. How many germs have not already developed, about which one could before just as little have believed that they would develop, as we now believe about those which are still not developed. Who has seen a savage Indian or Greenlander, should he indeed believe that there is a germ innate to this same [being], to become just such a man in accordance with Parisian fashion, as another [would become]? He has, however, the same germs as a civilized human being, only they are not yet developed. We equally have reason to believe that there are germs for greater perfection innate to human nature, which could well be developed, and [that] humanity must achieve the degree of perfection for which it is determined, and for which it has the germs within itself, and [that] it will be transposed into

[a] *viele Opium ... nehmen*, literally "take many opiates"
[b] *Anlage*   [c] *Bestimmung*
[d] *liegen*: literally "germs lie in human nature"

the condition which is the greatest possible. This can happen according to just the same degree, as it has already happened, for just as well as civil constraint arose from the maliciousness of the human being, from which in turn very many good consequences emerged; likewise as well after that, through the refinement of human beings from this civil constraint, as from the basis, the constraint of propriety arose, where the opinions of others have a great importance for us, [so] that people also often commit suicide because they do not want that others should think such about them, and from which more refinement and lived morality arises than from religion, and without which human beings, irrespective of the civil order and constraint, would in fact still be very crude; moral constraint can also just as well arise through a greater refinement of humanity. [It is] completely certain [that] the germs for this are innate to human nature, since human beings are very inclined to judge someone according to the morality of his character. Should it not be possible that all could be likewise disposed? Why are the moral germs not developed through education?[a] Great men[b] still do not realize the importance of education and exert no effort on it. One follows religion as a statute; one does not show the odiousness of an action from the action itself, but because it is forbidden. One does not combine inner morality with religion. Therefore immediate aversion for immoral action can also not arise. Yet, just as well as children are taught an immediate aversion for the spider, merely thereby that the nurse shudders when she sees it, children could also just as well be taught an immediate aversion for lies, thereby that one at all times would display the greatest contempt for [lying]. The child may well[c] not even know what lying is, but [the child] learns it thereby that one often tells him [lies]. Therefore if [the child] would be properly reared, then it would have to have just such an aversion for the lie as [it has] for the spider. If human beings would already have come so far, why should the final constraint, namely the constraint of conscience, where everyone would judge in accordance with his conscience about his actions, not arise just as well. This [constraint] cannot, however, be achieved without religion, but religion cannot have any effect without morality; hence religion aims at the highest perfection of human beings. This would be the domination of conscience, and since

25:695

---

[a] *Erziehung*: that "upbringing" is certainly included in a broader concept of "education" is incontrovertible, especially given how this passage continues. Whether Kant has in mind a more restricted sense of the term (i.e. as "upbringing"), or the more comprehensive notion of "education" is a matter of interpretation.

[b] *Große Herren*, probably referring to the present-day authorities.

[c] *dürfte*: alternatively, "should not even be permitted to know." The sense of the verb has to be taken from the context, but the interpretation is not completely clear here. However, it would seem that, if the child is to learn an aversion for lying, then it would indeed have to know what lying is.

conscience is the Deity's vicar, this would thus be the kingdom of God on earth, indeed the heavenly kingdom, for it does not depend on this, where heaven or hell exist. Human beings can make heaven or hell there where they are. Is this state of the perfection of humanity possible, and when is it to be hoped for? Since the germs for this are actually innate in humanity, it is thus possible that they will be developed through cultivation and can achieve perfection. But when is it to be hoped for, and how should it happen, and what can one do in connection with this in order to bring such about? Should one begin from the education of children, or from the education of the entire [political] state? Since the rulers must be educated, they cannot thus be better than the dispositions[a] which are disseminated in the public. The rulers are already educated by corrupted persons. Therefore if they rule poorly, then we have our forebears, who thus have educated them, to thank for such. The rule can therefore not be better than it has been cultivated[b] from the means and constitution of the country. We see that wars arise, and one [political] state overthrows the other one. In time, the princes will have to be sensible of the disadvantage, since with the preparation [for war in times of] peace, they themselves are compelled to employ just such powers as in war. In order, however, that all wars would not be necessary, a league of nations would thus have to arise, where all nations constituted a universal senate of nations through their delegates, [a league] which would have to decide all disputes of the nations, and this judgment would have to be executed through the power of the nations; then the nations would also be subject to one forum[c] and one civil constraint. This senate of nations would be the most enlightened[d] that the world has ever seen. It seems the beginning is to be sought in this, for before the wars do not come to an end, such cannot be achieved, for war makes every [political] state insecure, [and] hence more care is given to the preparation for war than to the internal condition[e] of the [political] state. If, however [the wars] come to an end, then the improvement of the internal government will result, through which human beings are schooled for such perfection. But how can we contribute something to this and accelerate such? The philosopher must make his concepts of this known, and present them for closer examination. The teachers must form character, so that the rulers would have insight into such and bring it about. In such a way, such a state of affairs[f] would exist, for which we have no hope of [living to]

25:696

---

[a] *Gesinnungen*
[b] *gezogen*
[c] *foro*, Latin, also meaning "jurisdiction"
[d] Reading *erleuchteste* for *erlauchteste* (most illustrious), as indicated in the Berlin manuscript (per editors' footnote).
[e] *Beschaffenheit*, previously translated as "constitution," but this could be confusing with the frequent use of the term *Verfaßung* in these passages.
[f] *Zustand*

experience it. This state of affairs cannot be destroyed, but [would] last as long as it pleases God to preserve our earth. This contemplation is very agreeable, since it is an idea which is possible, but for which thousands of years will still be required. Nature will always be sufficient until such a paradise emerges on earth. Just as nature has always developed[a] itself and still develops, and draws nearer to the purpose of destiny,[b] which one can see by the equator and by the ecliptic, which is drawing nearer to fall on the equator, and thereby an equality of day and night arises on the entire earth, but for which 140,000 years are still required. In just the same way, the human race is also forming,[c] and just as many years could go by, before it will attain the greatest degree of perfection.

25:697

ON THE DIFFERENCE OF THE TWO SEXES

The root of the good lies in evil,[d] since evil is the cause of the development of talents, through which everything good afterwards arose. We now come to an instance where very many apparent imperfections, which have their basis in nature, appear to us, and where philosophy must be employed in order to see that these imperfections are purposive and have to do with nature, and that is the investigation of the difference of the two sexes. In this connection we can present tests of the way that the human being should be studied. This is the greatest instance where the study of the human being interests [us], and where the most purposiveness is also discovered in the predisposition[e] of nature. Accordingly we thus say: in all tools, where just as much is accomplished through little power as through great [power], there a more artful[f] mechanism must be provided, than in the tool where there is greater power, for otherwise just the same effect could not be produced. Therefore the less power and might exist in a tool, all the more art there must be. Since, as it is, the feminine sex does not have as much power as the masculine, and it is to produce just as many effects as the masculine, for otherwise it would come up too short, and nature would have done it an injustice, if it were not equal with the masculine sex, thus nature will have given more art to the feminine sex.

25:698 Accordingly the feminine sex and feminine nature merits being studied more, because it has more art, and with them nature achieves by art what she does by might with the masculine sex. Because the man is made for nature, he thus must have the strength and might suited to withstanding

[a] *ausgebildet*
[b] *Bestimmung*
[c] *bildet sich*
[d] *Übel*
[e] *Anlage*
[f] *Kunstmäßig: Kunst* could also be translated as "skill" (especially in the context of this and following passages), but since Kant is not using *Geschicklichkeit* (as he does elsewhere), the further nuances of "trick," "artifice," or "guile" which *Kunst* expresses may also very well be implied.

nature's difficulties,[a] but no art. Since the woman, however, is made for the man, and through the man for nature, thus the woman must have art, in order to withstand nature and its difficulties through the man, and to employ them to her benefit. Because the Germans like to pay compliments, the term "woman"[b] may offend in common life. Woman is the contrary of man, but lady of the gentleman.[c][78] However, just as well as I can say of the king without any offense, that is a brave man, I can say just as well of a princess, that is a beautiful woman. I have said more there than if I said, it is a beautiful lady[d] or princess, for as a beautiful woman[e] she is the most beautiful of the entire sex, but if she is a beautiful princess, then there can still be more beautiful women among the other social stations.

The other principle which we must first mention is this: everything inherent to nature[f] is good. Nature is the condition and reference point of the good, and in nature the good must be unified. Evil[g] is inherent to freedom and the misuse of nature. Now, attention must be given as to whether something is good or evil by nature. It is difficult to find out whether something is inherent to nature or not. If we find that evil is inherent to nature, then it is good for this reason that it is inherent to nature, and it must have a purpose and a good aim, if it is just not misused through freedom. Therefore if we find that a subject is afflicted with ills, and that misuses are taking place, and these misuses are universal, then they are surely inherent to nature, for the cause through which these ills are misused must surely be inherent to nature, because they are universally misused. The cause of the agreement of the misuse of the ills cannot, after all, be sought in freedom, for only fortuitous actions occur through freedom; but it must lodge in the necessity of the action. Therefore this misuse must be regarded as being inherent to nature. However, what is inherent to nature is good, for nature acts until it achieves equality and is in agreement with itself, and this agreement is perfection.

25:699

Therefore in the character of the feminine sex, we will find something which is a particular[h] law of nature, and for this reason, because

---

[a] *Ungemächlichkeiten*

[b] *Weib*: in common German usage, indeed a contemptuous way of referring to "woman," but one of the two contemptuous terms Kant has used throughout (the other being *Frauenzimmer*).

[c] *Mann/Weib, Herrn/Frau*: normally the term for 'lady' is, *Dame* in German, while *Frau* is in fact the term for 'woman' (when 'woman' is used in the neutral sense of being the contrary of 'man').

[d] *Frau*   [e] *Weib*

[f] *in der Natur liegt*, literally "lying in nature"

[g] *Böse*: when Kant uses *Böse* and *Übel* as synonyms, or not, must be assessed from the given context.

[h] *bestimmtes*

it is inherent to nature, it must be good, although it is very hidden and strikes us as imperfect. Accordingly we must seek to discover the purpose, and when we will have discovered the purpose [and] for what it is good, then we can say that it is good. But where should we search for the nature of the feminine sex, and in which state*a* should we study it? With nature, this difference is still to be noted beforehand. Nature can be considered in its simplicity, in the greatest degree of its development, or in its complete development. Since, as it is, there is art in the feminine nature, and strength in the masculine [nature], nature thus coincides with the simplicity of nature, but art with the development of nature. Accordingly the feminine nature must not be studied in its simplicity but in its development, in the state where the predisposition*b* of art could be most developed; the feminine nature cannot be studied in another state. If one takes unrefined nations, then the woman is not at all to be distinguished from the man; she does not have the charms which she has in the developed state, she must work by [employing] strength in just the same way as the man, in the unrefined state she has no opportunity to develop her art. Hence we cannot study the nature of the feminine sex in this state, but only the nature of humanity in general. All the woman's art to get the man, her charms, her amenities, have no effect at all in the unrefined state, because there [the two sexes] only have the senses of needs, they cling to one another in a bond through animal instinct. Therefore, there is no difference in the character of the man and of the woman in this state; the art of the feminine sex is only visible in [the state of] refinement. Thus before we get to this state, they are completely powerless to make
25:700 use of the art of ruling the man; hence among all savages the woman is to be regarded as a domesticated animal, indeed because they have no other domesticated animals, the woman is thus the only domesticated animal. When the man thus goes to the battlefield in war, then the woman carries his weapons behind him, since because she cannot there employ her art on the man, her art also makes no impression on him, because the man is incapable of accepting the woman's art; thus she cannot take over him by any means [and] therefore she must submit. Therefore the feminine sex must be studied in the refined state where the predisposition of the germs*c* of its nature has been able to develop, but the nature of humanity must be studied in the unrefined state. The feminine nature is therefore manifest in the refined state; indeed we can say [that] the nature of the feminine sex makes the state refined. This feminine nature means weakness in the physical and mechanical sense, and it also really is [so], but as the incentive of the man, this weakness is a great incentive whereby the man's strength is constrained and moderated. Therefore with regard to

---

a *Zustand*   *c* *Anlage der Keime*
b *Anlage*

the masculine sex, this feminine weakness is a means whereby it can rule the man and have power over him. Women are also never displeased or indignant about the fun one pokes at their weakness; indeed they not only are not offended by it, but they even seek to behave quite affectedly in this weakness, for example, in fearfulness, fondness, delicacy, whereby they are incapable of more serious work,[a] because they well know that they can get and constrain the man through this weakness. The one who demands masculine strength from women, and has a low regard for them because they do not have it, acts very foolishly, for that is just as absurd as if a man ought to have femininity. With regard to nature and its needs, this sex would be pitiable because of its weakness; yet because it has strength over the man, it thus makes use of nature through the man, whom it rules through its weakness. The purpose of nature with regard 25:701 to the two sexes is perfect unity, which is to be achieved in the human sex. Nature has two aims, the propagation and preservation of the species, and nature has determined the animalistic difference of the two sexes for this purpose, and this is the aim with regard to animality. Nature's second aim with regard to the two sexes is that there should be a social state of affairs. This social intercourse is the aim with regard to humanity, and we are thereby distinguished from the animals. In order to attain nature's first aim, nature has endowed us with instincts which are quite clear, and about which we need not philosophize further; if we only follow this instinct, we thus fulfill nature's purpose, without having the same purpose in view. In order, however, that nature's second aim, that there should be a social constitution and intercourse, could be accomplished, nature must thus have endowed us with sources through which this social intercourse could be accomplished. True, this social intercourse is already partly accomplished through the civil order, but that is through constraint. The greatest social union and the most perfect state of society must occur without constraint. However, this does not happen other than through inclination, therefore by means of women. Women are well equipped for this social state, which is a cause of infinitely [many] consequences, [namely] through the upbringing of children, through talkativeness, which is quite proper to them and wherein a sister who was always at home often outdoes the brother who is far older and was at school, through courtesy, modesty, decency, decorum, refinement, improvement of taste in social intercourse; we have the women to thank for all of this, through which social intercourse is promoted. True, by means of constraint, the civil order produces a civil society; yet a perfect

---

[a] *größeren Arbeiten*: as the passage on 25:704 indicates, Kant has in mind such activities as the sciences which constitute part of the masculine perfection in his account (or see also 25:706, where Kant repeats his statement that women are too delicate for the rigors of mental work).

inner unity is to be established, and women contribute everything to this inner union which occurs without constraint, for nature wanted to achieve a social intercourse without constraint. In order to attain these purposes of social union, a unity had to be established between the masculine and feminine sex, which could bear the fruit of such consequences, in order to achieve a union like this. But through what means is the greatest unity and social union possible? Not through uniformity, but through difference. True union is based on the lack [of something] by one party, and possession of it by the other party. If that is now combined, then a whole of the complete, friendly union arises. In just the same way, the union of the [political] state is based on the mutual need of the members among one another, and not on unanimity. Therefore, if the masculine sex needs the feminine, and the feminine the masculine, then the unity and social union become necessary not only with regard to need, but also with regard to the amenity of social intercourse. Therefore, in order for there to be a difference between the two sexes, and in order that a unity would arise from the difference, the man must have strength there where the woman has weakness, and weakness there where the woman has strength. But the man is strong with regard to nature, the woman is weak in this respect; by contrast, the woman has strength with regard to the man, and the man [has] weakness with regard to the woman, and from this arises the unity, since the lack by the one and the possession by the other sex is the necessary condition under which such a perfect unity and social union can take place. The masculine sex is perfected through the compensation by the feminine, and the feminine through the masculine sex. Accordingly, in his household management the husband will not be so active, energetic, but [instead] lenient, but in this the wife is very active and energetic, puts everything to work, and if it does not happen, then it is very fitting for her that she berates the servants, [and] causes quarreling and strife in the house, and thereby she keeps herself active, and it suits her very well. It is very seldom the case that a wife will become ill due to vexation over the servants, but the husband indeed [will]. By contrast, those women become ill who do not have such an active management of the house, where they can bicker and be vexed. But the man who has his occupation outside the house, and is in turn as active, energetic, and insistent in this, likes to have quiet and peace in his own house, because it is the only place where he can rest; therefore he is very lenient in it. If the wife now wants to carry something out in the household, but which she cannot do without the husband, then she can rule him thereby. Because as it is, the husband is lenient in this, thus he gives in to her, which a modest husband will always gladly do for his wife, since he is much too generous to refuse her such. However, of that man who does not do this, but quarrels with his wife, or beats her, one could say of him, that he is himself really a woman, for that

25:702

25:703

is absolutely not at all seemly for the character of the man. The man is gullible, but the woman is very keen-sighted about that which could be to her disadvantage. The man easily betrays himself, but the woman has such skill to prove her innocence, that one can not at all have the least suspicion; she has such [an] innocent expression and eyes, and can be so indignant, that one becomes completely puzzled by it, and one does not know that such is [a] contrived method which is in keeping with her talent; the man does not have this at all. Her flattery more easily affects the man; thereby, if she has made the man angry, then she also soon again reconciles him. Accordingly the man can sooner forgive the wife, than the wife [can forgive] him. If a woman takes something to be an affront in one matter, then she is not so easily reconciled. This matter is, if one says to them that they are old or ugly. They cannot so easily forgive these judgments, with regard to ugliness not so [much] as with regard to being old, for the judgments with regard to ugliness differ. What seems ugly to one, can please the other, but being old nullifies all the conditions of pleasing.

The feminine sex acquires work for itself in the domestic state, but the man in the civil [state]. As citizen, the man must be a master with regard to his household, he must earn [a living], but with regard to the use of what the man has earned, the wife must have sovereignty. With regard to the affairs of the [political] state, the man participates, and even if he does not have anything directly to do with it, then he still likes to judge. But it makes no difference to the wife who rules there; she does not at all concern herself with it. Women are more inclined to introduce despotism than freedom; if they just have sovereignty in society, then in the [political] state whoever wants may rule there. Poland and Latvia[a] is the only land where the women speak the most on the affairs of state, for there freedom does indeed greatly interest them, for where the aristocracy has the upper hand, there the ladies occupy a high rank, but which ceases [to be the case] if the court rules. Women's two main vocations[b] are: sovereignty in the household, and sovereignty in a voluntary society. The man finds enjoyment in this domination, he wants to be dominated, if it just occurs according to the way that it pleases the man; through his flattery he invites women to [assume] such domination. As soon as the man no longer allows himself to be dominated therein by the woman, he is thus also no longer linked [with her]. The man loves a lack of courage and self-confidence in the woman, for if the woman had this, then he would not serve her with his courage. If the woman would herself have the strength and courage to defend herself, then she would not need to have a man; hence the man loves such shortcomings in his

[a] *Curland*, i.e. the region around the city of Liepāja, in Latvia
[b] *Bestimmungen*

wife, and promotes them. The more nobly a man thinks, all the more does he subjugate himself to a well-thinking person, for he is not coerced to this by force, but it is a voluntary subjugation whereby he is won over, and the more he subjugates himself and expresses his compliance toward his wife, all the more does he gain, and all the more generous does he appear. If we note the determination[a] of this sex, we thus find how a young girl can be in the company of the greatest men, of the greatest insights, without embarrassment, where a youth, if he is far superior to her in insights, becomes greatly embarrassed, and such also pleases the masculine sex, since because women do not have the man's perfection in the sciences, they will thus not esteem the masculine sex more for this reason, for they take the perfections of the man to be serious[b] work for which the man has talent; therefore they are also not embarrassed for this reason. They hold the enjoyment of social intercourse in high regard, and in this they are also completely the master. The education of women may have a greater influence on morals than one believes, for how are women now educated? In reality not at all; if they possess perfections, then they have such by nature. We do not at all count music, dance, and other skills as education, but [what we mean is that] the concepts are

25:705 not at all developed with them, and yet in their younger years, women are far more moral than the masculine sex. They do not acquire this skill by reading books, since thereby more art arises; thus this art also in fact corrupts their natural abilities. A young natural person with natural abilities has something completely different in her understanding which we do not have at all. If, for example, a sister writes a letter, then there will be more naïvety, natural wit, gaiety, jesting, and liveliness in it, than if the brother who has already been to school writes one; he will struggle to get his letter out with all possible formularizations, antecedents, and consequences, that is to say, with much effort. Therefore women need no education beyond a negative [one], whereby they are kept from crudeness and bad manners; they only need social intercourse [and] will thus really school themselves. Yet they are also capable of a more precise instruction, whereby their character is formed. True, the principle of honor is with them the most important; with them everything can be built on this principle. Yet they are also capable of true inner worth, of the moral life, magnanimity, and other masculine endeavors, only they see these endeavors from a completely different point of view, not insofar as they possess such, but their husband or lover [possesses them]. Yet in their education, one should still be careful about true inner moral concepts, for if persons like this would know how to judge the worth of the man by moral concepts, then they would not at all pursue many a flattering dandy

---

[a] *Bestimmung*
[b] *grobe*: in its figurative sense, means "serious" or "grave"; compare 25:700.

of no moral worth. The masculine sex has respect for the feminine [one], about love it goes without saying in any case. However the feminine sex does not have such respect for the masculine [one], no matter how much merit he might have, they always consider themselves important and substantial enough to be respected by the man. The women are judges of taste in social intercourse. Without them, social intercourse is unrefined, turbulent, and unsociable. In a society of nothing but men, one degenerates into conflict, [a] know-it-all attitude, and quarreling, but that is not the case in the society of women. The favor [shown by] the men permits the women to show off, yet if the women always show off, then the conversation will not be interesting; however such social intercourse should also not be interesting, but serve as relaxation. 25:706 Hence women have the good manners to put an end to the serious conversation of the men and to transform the most important matters into fun, which is very nice in society. Indeed, only a woman is enough for well-thinking men to keep them in limits in their serious discussions. Where women are excluded from society, as in the Orient, there the society of men is unrefined. Therefore we have the women to thank for the refinement of society. Accordingly, the education of women is not to be entrusted to the man, for the men would school them in accordance with their [own] character. Therefore we must leave the education in the hands in which it is. The sciences serve them only to the extent that they are an entertainment and play for them; they only have to be reared through social intercourse. They are also much too delicate, than that they should occupy themselves with mental work; hence too, pedantry is more intolerable in a woman than in a man. They are more disposed for play than for important occupations, and that is also in keeping with nature. However, the masculine sex should teach them some soberness, which is very useful in the household. One must be somewhat more particular about principles, sentiments, and domestic duty in their education, for they do not want to know anything about duties in any case; but with them everything is supposed to turn on mere obligingness and kindness. With regard to duty, there is thus still much to improve in their education. In their education, one should also seek to instill in them more importance, regard, and dignity [with respect to] their affairs. With regard to the three items, kitchen, children, and sick room, women are of great importance and an object of high esteem.

These were the sources through which nature maintained its second aim through the feminine sex, namely the social constitution and social intercourse among human beings. However, so that nature could attain its first aim, the preservation of the species, it has thus shown great tenderness in this. Because this aim is entrusted to the woman's womb, nature has thus made the feminine sex fearful. This fearfulness with regard to bodily injury is universal with the feminine sex, and although

25:707 the women among the savages are not as tender as those in the civilized state, they are nevertheless fearful with regard to bodily injury. Hence they do not like to venture out on the water, and in a place where there is cause to be concerned about danger, indeed if a couple of women are having a fight, then each one watches out that the other does not strike her in the face; they hold their hands in front of them and greatly guard against bodily injury. In other cases, where there is no cause for concern about any bodily injury, they are not as fearful; indeed there they even outdo the masculine sex. Hence if it is a matter of the defense of right, or obtaining something, then they are far bolder, more eloquent, and less fearful in this, than the man. Therefore one will find that the workman always prefers to send his wife to city hall and to the city councillor than go himself, since she is more eloquent and also meets with more indulgence from the authorities than the man [does]. This arrangement of nature is unique, for if the wife would venture into all danger in just the same way as the man, then she would also put her offspring in danger, and thereby the species could not be preserved as it now takes place, through a wise arrangement like this which also extends to the animals.

The observation of the difference of the two sexes is an important matter, and it is surely worthy of philosophy that one observe the human species from a certain point of view and search for the purposes of each sex. Since we have already stated the main purposes of nature with regard to the sexes, it is thus still necessary to consider general observations from experience. With regard to the conflict between the two sexes of the human species, which serves more for agreeable entertainment than for stubborn contention, one can pose this question: With regard to inclination and feelings[a] of love, which sex is more tender, the man or the woman? The question does not concern the tenderness of the judgment, but the tenderness of the feeling of the sex drive. Here one must say that the man is more tender than the woman. The man has a fine taste, but the woman a coarser[b] one. For if the woman would have a fine taste with regard to the sex drive, then the man would have to be of a more tender and finer breeding,[c] and if the man had a coarser taste and

25:708 coarser feeling, then the woman would have to be of coarser breeding. As it is, however, it is the reverse, the woman is of a more tender and finer breeding, because the man [has the] finer and more delicate feeling to be sensible of fine breeding like this. The man is however of coarser breeding, because the woman has a coarser taste, and does not at all look for such tenderness in the breeding of the man which she, however, possesses for him. From this one can explain how it often happens that

---

[a] *Empfindungen*   [c] *Bildung*
[b] *gröberen*

beautiful, tender, fine women have coarse, scruffy men, and are very satisfied with them, since they are not at all particular about the fineness and tender breeding of the men, since they are not at all as delicate in their choice, but are more concerned with the industriousness and masculine strength of the man. This serves as evidence for the answer to this question.

Now let us search for nature's purpose and state its cause. It was an essential condition of nature, that the woman must be sought. The man must seek the woman, and not the woman the man. The man therefore had to be [the one doing the] courting, but the woman be [the one] refusing. The man can choose since he can select a woman for himself. However, the woman can only choose thereby that she turns down [the suitors] until [there is] one she cares to accept. The one who is being sought, however, and [who] must wait until someone comes, cannot be so delicate in the choice and pick much out, but must make do with what heaven provides; but the other party who has the choice can be delicate in his feeling, for since he can choose, he can thus choose in keeping with his delicate feelings. Nature has here hit upon a good arrangement, for if the woman were more tender in feeling than the man, then she would come up a great deal too short, since she would not find an object of tenderness like this in the man. But since they are now not so tender in feeling, what has thus already been stated, namely that the finest and most beautiful women often have the ugliest men, can be very well explained. Delicate taste in inclination is a kind of need, which is very hard to please. For the one who has such a delicate taste, things proceed more poorly than for the one who has a crude taste and is not so particular about the delicateness, just as the state of affairs is better for the one who can make do with any fare, than for the one who is so delicate in 25:709 his taste in dishes that he can only satiate it with ortolans[a] and pâtés, and if he does not get these, then he is in poor shape. Hence nature has also taken care of this, and has not given women such delicate taste in feeling, because they are not the ones who can choose according to their taste, but are [the ones] being sought. Some believe that one can dispute this in the way one disputes something from the speaker's lectern [and show it is not inherent to] nature,[b] and [they] believe it to be a matter of fashion; however what is universal and constant, cannot be an object of fashion, but must be inherent to nature. If we want to cast our nets widely to draw this out, we thus find that with animals, where there are many males and one female, that the male sex must be somnolent, but the female must employ enticements in order to attract one or the other

[a] A bird belonging to the finch family
[b] *der Natur abdisputiren*: i.e. rationally demonstrate by argument that this is not a matter of nature, in the manner of the medieval disputation or the disputation of the schools.

of the male sex to her; for example, with bees. If the males were there just as heated, then the female would have to submit to that many. On the other hand, however, where one male has many females, there the female sex must be somnolent, and the male must employ enticements, in order to attract one or the other of the female sex to himself, for if the females would be just as intense in their feeling, then the male would have to submit. But where there is one female and one male, there one sees that the female is the refusing, but the male the courting party; for example, with cats, [or] with dogs, there they even fight over the female. Nature wanted that there should be the greatest liveliness in copulation, so that the greatest fecundity might arise from it. The greatest liveliness is, however, attained through inclination, from which the most fruitful results thereafter arise, when the refusing party yields. Nature's main reason is however this: because receiving is easier than giving, thus the choice to whom he wants to give must there be left to that party who gives. The party receiving, however, is not free to choose what it wants to receive, but is only [free] to refuse to receive what one wants to give it. Since, as it is, the masculine sex is the conferring, but the feminine [sex] is the receiving party, thus the giving party or the masculine sex must 25:710 have the choice to court, while the feminine sex is the refusing party. Accordingly we will find that the woman is the refusing party, and that every woman makes a bid to be demure and decent in society, and to appear completely cold toward the other sex. This is very necessary, and the greater the extent to which she knows how to pursue such, all the more does she attract the other sex to herself. Although it really is such [an] intense love of inclination, through [an] enchanting art they can express their love for the masculine sex more as a favor to the man, than that it should be just such [an] inclination. Although this is obvious, that the feminine sex has a sex drive and instinct just like the masculine, yet it thus possesses such art to conceal this inclination, that one should have doubts about the former. This art of concealment and refusal is however very necessary, for if the feminine sex would express its inclination and instinct toward the masculine, then it would lose much in the eyes of the masculine sex, and then the man may not court them, but because they would have an instinct just like this, they would have to submit to the man; then they would be forced by their inclination to surrender to the man. The one who has needs must submit to the other, but who does not seek and does not have needs, can dominate. Since, as it is, women know how to control their inclinations so artfully[a] that it seems as if they need nothing, but the man expresses his inclination and his needs, thus the man must court, and through her coldness which is an affect,

---

[a] *künstlich*: in this context, could also be translated as "deliberately" (elsewhere rendered as "artificial").

the woman can dominate the man. The man even demands this refusal and coldness of the woman. The man has a great inclination to flatter the woman, and the more a woman assumes a pride and self-sufficiency in this, all the better the man likes it. Thereby the man promotes this sex to such a repute, that the feminine sex is thereby compensated for everything which it misses with respect to nature. For since the man is that party who rules over nature, who engages in business, through whom all arts and sciences are carried out, the feminine sex would thus here lose a very great deal, if the masculine sex had not, on the other hand, compensated it for such. If the man would not give the woman such regard, then there would be no equality between the two sexes, but nature wanted that there should be an equality. 25:711

We notice further that the woman is susceptible, but the man is sensitive. The man's tenderness is sensitive, but the woman's is susceptible. The feminine sex demands tenderness from the man, and is very unforgiving toward every disparagement which it discerns in every detail. Women often accuse the masculine sex of not being tender, yet that is not meant by them as if [to say] the man has no tenderness, but that he does not show enough tenderness toward them. By nature the man is therefore more tender in love than the woman, but the woman does not love as tenderly. The evidence is this: that party who is inclined to take all the troubles and discomforts of the other party upon himself is surely more tender than the party who can demand this, that the other party should do such. Now one finds that the masculine sex is inclined to prove itself to be pleasing to the feminine sex, and to relieve them of all troubles and discomforts, and take them upon itself, and the more the feminine sex needs such, and the masculine sex can render it, all the more does the man like it. Accordingly the man will bother with many a thing through which he can become pleasing to the woman, he will deprive himself of many a thing, only in order to give it to the woman. Accordingly the masculine heart is sensitive, and disposed to a more tender love than the feminine one. But the feminine one is tender in the susceptibility to accept the man's sensitive tenderness. Hence one will find that a woman is very susceptible with regard to the man's tenderness, she will soon take offense at something, every harsh response from the man makes her angry, so that she does not want to speak with him; then the man must flatter her, and do everything to make amends with her again. Thereby however, the man is cultivated in his sensitivity. In the good marriages where fate turned out well, the man is indifferent toward the inclination of other women, and is satisfied with it if he only has the inclination and favor of his wife. He does not concern himself with the favor and kindness of other women, but the woman is never indifferent toward the favor of other men, even though she already has a man, she never resigns [herself] to be completely indifferent toward all

25:712 inclination of the men; she still always exerts her charms on the masculine sex. However, one must not believe that this exertion in marriages is coquetry, rather it is very innocent and has its basis in nature. By nature women have more faithfulness; because they are the object which is to be sought by the other, they must thus generally try to please, until they meet someone whom they suit. This endeavor generally to please also remains later in marriage. Another reason is this: because the woman is always concerned that if the man dies, she is again provided for. With regard to her support, she is always in a predicament. If the man's wife dies, then the man can still always support himself, but if the wife's husband dies, then she must seek to be again provided for; hence the woman must not completely dispense with all favor with the men, since she must again seek to please if her husband has died. Nature has arranged that the woman in marriage is still not completely indifferent how she can please other men, but in marriage still casts her glances about in order to please.

Women adorn themselves for other women and not for the man. For the man they are also well-dressed in their dressing gown; they know that even without the finery of their dress, through the amenity of their person, they have sufficient charms with regard to the men, but they adorn themselves for other women. They do not ask about what the men will say, for they please them in any case by the charms of their person, but with other women, it is difficult, since the charms do not have an effect on other women, but only on the man. Accordingly with them they must try to be conspicuous by means of finery, since a lady scrutinizes the other from head to toe, and completely undresses her in her mind's eye, and inspects every item of the finery; she is fine enough to observe the other's flaws, and to imitate [what] is special [about her]. Now if there is one in society who outdoes the others in this, she thus regards herself as the most distinguished among them, and haughtily ignores the others. In this regard they are very hostile toward one another, and one tries to get the better of the other in this. The man however does not adorn himself for other men, but for the women. In the company of men he prefers to make himself as comfortable as possible, but in the company of women, he tries to be gallant. If the question were asked, by whom women prefer to let themselves be judged, by their [own] sex,

25:713 or by the masculine sex, and before which tribunal they would rather appear, [the one] where the masculine or feminine sex passes judgment, then it is certain that every woman would prefer to appear before the tribunal of the masculine sex, for that would be indulgent toward them, but the feminine sex would know how to judge every hair. Hence it happens that women prefer to seek protection with the masculine sex, and [prefer to] make friends with it, [rather] than among themselves. Their jealousy toward one another with regard to a certain matter is very great. One woman cannot let the other one realize that she would be in the position to captivate the [other's] husband through her charms, for otherwise the friendship is over at once, and they are irreconcilably embittered with one another. This jealousy also has its basis in nature; if a woman is under the supervision of her friends in a household, or even in a society, she will try in every way to get away from the household, and thereby she becomes forced to entrust herself to the man's care.[a] The partiality of the sexes is always geared to the opposite sex. Hence one will find that the father favors the daughter, but the mother the son. The father severely disciplines the son, but the mother the daughter. But why does the mother prefer the son, and take more care with regard to his advancement, so that she often impoverishes herself thereby, than with the daughter? The braver and more vigorous the son is, all the more does the mother see her future support in him, and the father sees his future housekeeper in his daughter, if his wife should leave him.[b] Accordingly, a well-bred son will at all times have respect for his mother and respect her orders, even if he need not. Hence the saying is: that it is not good to have the man's mother in the home, however [it is good to have] the wife's mother [in the home]. For if the man has his mother in the home, then he will still obey his mother out of the respect which he has for her, but the wife does not like to see this; she has much to be worried about in this regard, lest the mother might say something to him which is detrimental to her. The man, however, does not have to worry about this with regard to his wife's mother, since when the daughter is married, she no longer obeys the mother. She thinks: now the covenant is done with,[c] now I am a woman[d] just as well. Therefore the man can take his wife's mother into [his] home without concern, but the wife always has something to be concerned about [if] the husband's mother is taken into the home, because the man is always still obedient to his mother. The man demands also in the marriage exactly the same abstinence which the woman manifests before marriage. The man is very delicate in this; he demands the strictest modesty and abstinence of his wife before marriage. But the woman is not so very particular about the man's abstinence before marriage. This has its basis in nature. The man wants to be assured that the children which he will have in marriage, for whom he is to look after, are his children. The woman is,

25:714

---

[a] *Vorsorge*, literally "provisions" or "precautionary measures"

[b] *abgehen*: presumably Kant means this as a figurative expression for "die," but as he has alluded to earlier, even under the circumstances of their times, it was not unheard of for women to leave their husbands.

[c] *Contract aus*, literally "the contract is broken"

[d] *Frau*, alternatively, "now I am a wife just the same [as she is]"; given that Kant in general uses *Frau* only for "wife," this version may better capture the psychological state he is imputing to the woman in this case.

however, always assured, since she cannot, after all, have any other children than those to whom she gives birth. Accordingly, the man is very particular about the woman's modesty before marriage, since he thinks this way: if a person dares before marriage, thus at a time when she is in danger of not getting a man, to have sexual relations, then she will do it all the more when she already has a man and is secure from the danger, and where all the consequences of her relations can remain concealed. It is always a highly daring matter for women to have sexual relations without the condition of marriage, for if such does not remain concealed, then she is in danger of not being provided for. Through marriage, a woman becomes free, but the man loses [his] freedom. An unmarried woman is very restricted;[a] she cannot go out where she wants, neither go to a comedy, nor anywhere else, without having an escort from her household. A lot [of things] are not seemly for them, neither to say nor to do; indeed they do not even eat until they are quite satisfied, because it is not seemly for an old maid to eat a lot. They are coerced both by the constraint of parents and guardians, as well as by the constraint of propriety, but in marriage they have a lot of freedom; there they are immediately more loquacious and presumptuous, they no longer have to fear anyone, for they have their man, they can go and do where and what they want, if the husband just allows them. However, the man loses a great deal of freedom through marriage; he is very limited and restricted, he can no longer undertake something so easily, he must adjust to his wife['s wishes],[b] he can no longer go as often to social gatherings away from home, but he must stay at home, he can no longer take up his friends as he likes, but he must conform to his wife's [way of] running the house.

25:715 If he then has no compensation through his wife, if he is not rewarded by something else, then he loses surprisingly [much] of his former freedom. Accordingly he would be a fool, if he is to lose his freedom thereby that he marries, and would not even be assured in the matter whether the children, whom he gets in marriage and for whom he is to provide, were his [own]. If they then are not assured in this [respect], that what they are to provide for belongs to them, and they marry nevertheless, then they lose much. Accordingly, the man demands the same abstinence of his wife in marriage as before marriage, and is very jealous in this. Women often jokingly ridicule men's jealousy, but they like to see that he is [jealous]. Jealousy is either intolerant or suspicious jealousy. Every man who shows a tolerant indifference with regard to his wife is held in contempt by others, also even by his own spouse. It is always to act ignobly and illiberally on the man['s part], if he has a person who is completely devoted to him, and he leaves her and is dissolute. He is

---

[a] *gebunden*, literally "bound"
[b] *sich nach der Frau richten*, literally "conform to" or "comply with the wife"

detested if he is dissolute, but held in contempt if his wife is dissolute and he is indifferent if others encroach upon his prerogative. He must endure ridicule if his wife is dissolute, therefore the man must not be indifferent with regard to his wife's behavior; if he were not jealous, then he should not marry, for were it all the same to him if he gave free rein to his [sex] drive,[a] then into what sort of state of affairs would women get? They would decline to the status of coquettes, where they would only have to wait until this or that person wanted to satisfy his drive. Therefore women are glad to tolerate all ridicule about their weakness, but not about marriage. For all are offended by ridicule about marriage, even old persons who will never marry. The reason is clear, for they get[b] their worth through marriage. The man would be a fool, if he is to marry and forgo other women, and thereby lose his freedom, if he were not even secure with regard to the matter of his children. If the men would not be jealous in this [matter], then the women would thereby lose their worth, but the man is derided if he tolerates such, and his indifference with regard to his jealousy seems very base even in the eyes of his own wife, because it is a sign that she is held in contempt by the man. Hence wives demand such of their husbands, and their ridicule about it is only in jest.

25:716

Young men dominate old women, and young women dominate old men. The reason lies in jealousy. If the man is old and the woman young, then the woman dominates, because the man has cause to be jealous; hence he must flatter her, through which she dominates him. But if the woman is old and the man young, then the woman has cause to be jealous, then she must flatter him and hereby he dominates her. Hence women gladly like to waive the man's age, and prefer to marry an older man because they can then dominate the man. Young people have to be very careful about this, that they do not later in marriage become a plaything[c] for the woman; accordingly they must not sacrifice their youth, but be very abstemious, for only under [this] condition can they be assured that they will assert domination.

As to what concerns the purpose of marriage, namely the upbringing of children, in the case of the unequal marriage, with a great difference in age it is thus better if the wife is older than the husband; the reason is naturally as follows. The man is seldom as abstinent as the woman, hence by age 40 his nature is much more weakened than the woman's in the same age. Therefore if the man is still older and the woman young, then they seldom have children, and if they indeed come, then they are very weak. But if the woman is much older, then it does not matter as

[a] *[Geschlechts] Neigung*
[b] *erhalten*: presumably the meaning here could also be "maintain"
[c] *Spiel*

much. If she has never borne children, then she has her full strength and is in this respect completely equal to the far younger man, because he could well have used his strength a lot; thus she surpasses him in this respect and the children are strong and healthy.[a]

In some countries it proves to be disadvantageous to the women if they remain unmarried, for the woman represents a civilian[b] through the man; in themselves they have no status in the civic constitution. In the Orient, the childless state is held in contempt, for there the woman does not have such equal authority with the man in the home as here, and if on top of that she has no children, then she is regarded as completely useless in the home.

25:717   If it is asked: who dominates in the home, the man or the woman, then with cultivated human beings in good marriages, where order prevails in the home, one finds that the woman dominates, but the man rules.[79] This seems to be one and the same, yet the difference will soon be evident. It seems as if the man has the right to dominate in the house; yet we find that he has the inclination to be dominated. If the wife makes the effort to dominate the husband, then she still loves him, and this is agreeable to the man. If a lover would know that his wife would later not dominate him just the same as before, then he would never marry. True, women accuse the men that they [may] well let themselves be dominated and [that they] flatter a great deal before the wedding, but do not even have a friendly word to say after the wedding. Yet we find in nature, that although he does not flatter so much after the wedding as before, which he now also may not do, the man nevertheless has the inclination to let himself be dominated, but the woman has the inclination to dominate. She torments the man like a favored lover, she shows him her love not from duty, but from goodwill. The man seeks to maintain[c] this, but in that case it is obvious, if her love is goodwill, then she is the one who dominates there, but if the man demands it, then it is a coarseness on his part. Domination in the home is the wife's affair,[d] but the rule [is] the man's [affair]. Domination can occur in accordance with mood, but rule in accordance with law. The wife must dominate over how something is to be utilized in the house. The wife is concerned with what the purpose is, the man must know how to direct [matters, so] that everything aims at this purpose. He must know his income, his scale, his expenditure, and he must have the law in his head according to which he is to rule, so that one agrees with the other. If therefore the wife wants to use something for decoration, amusement and sociability, then he must not

---

[a] This paragraph, taken from the Prieger manuscript, is missing in the Friedländer manuscript (400).
[b] *bürgerliche Person*
[c] *erhalten*: alternatively "get"
[d] *Sache*

immediately simply deny the wife such, but try to persuade her to [see] 25:718
this point through representations, since she cannot well tolerate [his]
commanding. He can say, that will indeed do, yet this would still be
better. He must therefore rule, but the wife must dominate. Just as in a
kingdom where there is a foolish monarch, the king dominates, but the
minister rules. When the king wants something which will not do, then
the minister must represent [the matter] for him and say: that will indeed
do; however, I think it would still be better to command this. The man
must not, however, be a commander and demand obedience, but it must
be [done with] kindness; if the man takes the gallantry too far, however,
then the woman is the commander and then the household goes to ruin,
since the woman does not have the law in mind,[a] also does not understand
the civil order, and does not know the sources of income. Then, however,
the woman is never at fault, but the man [is], for he must rule; if it does not
work by means of kindness, then [he must rule] by refusal. The woman's
reluctance will then no doubt subside, but not the misfortune of the
household. Indeed even the woman will afterwards understand that it was
the man's duty to rule, for when the misfortune has already happened,
then she says to the man: why did you let me have my way, after all you are
the man. A woman can sooner rule an entire kingdom than a household,
for in the land she does not rule, but only dominates, and the ministers
rule. But if there is no one in the household who rules, then she cannot
rule the household alone. The woman dominates the man, but the man
rules the woman, for inclination dominates and the understanding rules.
Inclination provides the purposes, but the understanding restricts them
to the purpose which agrees with the well-being [of the household]; it
directs and judges it according to its rules. Human inclination, however,
is love; therefore, the woman must begin to dominate the man from the
side of this inclination, but as soon as this inclination wanes on the part
of the man, then she also loses [her] dominance.

As to what concerns the specific difference of the virtues and vices of
the feminine sex, we must thus first note that nature had two purposes and
aims in mind, union on the one hand, but division on the other, so that
everything does not sink into inactivity; hence there are moving powers,
so that [things] do not go under like this. Human beings therefore have 25:719
an inclination for society, but also for war. It is an active and reactive
force, for otherwise human beings would fuse together through constant
unity, from which complete inactivity and tranquility would thereafter
arise. Therefore, in marriage there is also a predisposition to unity and to
war. The female temperament[b] occasions strife and war, which serves [to
effect] a new union, and even the peace which is established after such a
war, if no subservience but complete equality has just remained thereby,

[a] *Kopf*   [b] *Naturell*

serves to enliven the household. With regard to ills, masculine virtue is tolerant, but the feminine one [is] patient. The man tolerates ill, even if he could overcome it, but patience is a feminine virtue. With regard to ills, the man is sensitive, but the woman [is] susceptible. The man is immediately sensible of a person's discomfort and reluctance, which he immediately seeks to avert. With regard to herself, the woman is, however, more sensible of ill. If the man were susceptible in the case of every ill, then this would be womanish. The man's enterprise is earning a living, the woman's is to save. The man is master over nature, therefore he must also earn a living, but because the woman can enjoy nature only by means of the man, she must thus seek to save what the man earns. Because the woman earns nothing, thus she also disposes of nothing, her kindness extends only to an intercession and to liberality with leftover items; she gives nothing away except what she can no longer really use, for example, old dresses, because she cannot earn anything, for all wealth is acquired through the man, and although the woman can also inherit, it still thus comes from the man who acquired it. The man, however, can be magnanimous and liberal. Therefore the woman is more likely to be inclined to stinginess than the man, although the man is also often [so inclined]. There is nothing good to be said about the man who is already stingy in his youth. It is really contradictory [in his case], since he is in the position where he can acquire everything, but with women it is not contradictory; since youth they are already disposed to saving. With regard to taste, the man has the inclination to be satisfied in accordance with taste, but the woman likes to be the object of taste herself. Hence

25:720   the woman adorns herself and thereby she refines the man's taste. In the home, in her rooms, the woman is particular about that whereby she can please others, also beautiful furnishings. If she dines alone, then she dines poorly, because then there is no one for whom she can thereby become an object of taste; she prefers to save it and use it for clothing. The man is not, however, indifferent in this, and if he is already married, then he no longer dresses up for others, but has taste for himself; he prefers to use everything for the finery and splendor of the woman. The woman's honor is concerned with what people say, but the man's honor with what people think. Women do not care about what people think, if they just do not say it. The man's honor is the true honor, because it is a deep respect before another's inner judgment, but the women's honor is only a semblance of honor, because it only cares about the public judgment.[a] The feminine desire for honor is more [of a] vanity, but that of the man is more [a] desire for honor which can be called ambition. Honor with regard to what does not belong to our person is vanity, but with regard to what belongs to our person [it] is ambition. Accordingly the woman cares

[a] *Leute Urtheil*

more about the horse and carriage, clothing and furnishings, valuables and title; if the men also become enslaved to this, then they are also vain, and that is womanliness. The man seeks honor in what belongs to the worth of our person, although he also often seeks only to attain the semblance [of it]; for example, heartiness, magnanimity, strength, courage, that is all a [matter of] the man's love of honor. The women's principle is: what the whole world says is true, and what the whole world does is true; hence they refer to this in every case and say, the whole world in fact does otherwise and says otherwise. Such a woman who begins with a change of religion and thinks freely, already indicates great transgression of the character of her sex, but does not betray any weakness of soul. Before they concern themselves with such principles, they thus prefer to follow common judgment. To ignore others' judgment is not seemly for the woman. Even if a woman were only in a Platonic relation[a] with a man and people would judge badly, then it would not be fitting if she were indifferent about it; with the woman, the appearance[b] is something important, [but] the man is not concerned with the appearance. Therefore the woman seeks her honor in the appearance, because they are also the ones who are chosen; hence they must avoid all bad appearance, because they would thereby throw away their [good] fortune, since they would not be chosen. The way in which women assess objects is different from the way in which men assess objects. For example, Milton championed republican freedom. Then, when he was offered a post with much income serving the royal house under King Charles II, he thus did not want to serve the house against which he had previously written. Since then his wife urged him that he should do it, he said: my dear, you are right, for you and all your sex want to ride in carriages, but I want to remain an honest man. He saw that it was better to decline, than to belie himself, but the wife could not understand how the man could commit such folly to decline a position with such income because of his whims. One can also not reproach women for such, because it is in keeping with their nature; they are not capable of such principles, but aim at the maintenance of the household, and make light of the rest, [saying] that they were only whims. Hence they are also not very scrupulous with regard to the money which the man has earned and brought home; he may have come by it however he will, if he only dependably has it. The feminine vices are the vices of a weak creature, which carries out by cunning what another does by force; therefore, they will use craftiness in order to gain, [and] dissimulation, contentiousness, and grudgingness. They are especially begrudging toward their own sex; hence they are also jealous of such persons of their sex who could well have lovers, even

25:721

[a] *Gesellschaft*, literally "company"
[b] *Schein*, i.e. how it seems (literally, the semblance)

if they themselves do not love, while the man is only jealous of his sex then when he is in love. The cause already lies in the foregoing, because they, even when they are provided for, still try to please, which stands them in good stead after the death of the husband.

25:722   With regard to upbringing, the masculine sex is by nature more unrefined; therefore it must be more disciplined. The feminine sex is finer by nature; hence women need only school themselves through social intercourse, [and] therefore their upbringing must not ensue with such constraint. Their eloquence is a kind of natural ease of speech,[a] and not so constrained, dogmatic, and demonstrative as the man's. Their eloquence is the same as loquaciousness; speech sounds much finer in their mouth. Their understanding is not for investigating things and objects, but human beings. Because they are not destined[b] to dominate over nature and institutions in the commonwealth, but only over the man, they thus must also investigate only human beings. Hence women easily examine others, but they are not so easily examined. Therefore, they easily let out other people's secrets, but no one finds out their secrets, especially those concerning their person and their sex; not even their good friend gets to the bottom of those. Men are far less able to keep their secrets, and since they often accuse women that they are gossipy, they should thus rather look to their own failings. Nature has therefore ordered everything in such a way that what one might regard as a fault is a necessary condition of the preservation of unity and society. From this many practical consequences can be drawn with regard to the education[c] of women, which must be of a completely different kind than that of the masculine sex. With regard to morality, the instruction must be completely different, since because they do not like to hear about duties, and are incapable of these principles, the whole of morality must thus be presented from the point of view of honor and propriety, because the principle of honor is the only one of which they are eminently capable.

ON EDUCATION

There already exist many recommendations and writings by the philosophers concerning education. One has taken pains to investigate what comprises the main concept of education. The present-day Basedow institutes are the first to have come about in accordance with the complete plan.[80] This is the greatest phenomenon which has appeared in this century for the improvement of the perfection of humanity. All schools in the world will thereby acquire a different form [and] the human race

25:723

---

[a] *Wohlredenheit*, literally "well-speaking"   [c] *Erziehung*
[b] *bestimmt*

will thereby be freed from the constraints of the prevailing schooling.[a] At the same time, [the institute] cultivates many teachers.[81] Therefore it is worth one's while to give it due consideration.

Education is divided into the education of human beings as children and as adolescents. The education of children can be divided into four epochs, under which fall the development of nature, the guidance of freedom, the instruction of the understanding, and the development of reason and of character. As to what concerns the development of nature, the question thus is: how shall a child be reared so that its nature develops? This already begins at birth and [consists in] medical considerations. Many [considerations] may also be judged by means of philosophy. The child must be reared with the necessary health, with the proper use of its powers and sensory organs, with vivaciousness, eager activity and strength, with freedom to play and to exercise. One must give it the opportunity to toughen up and to endure hardships. With regard to the guidance of freedom, it must be noted that the human being is by nature wild and unrefined, [and] therefore must be disciplined. By nature, human beings want to follow their [five] senses and their inclinations. The child's initial cries are cries of need, but when it becomes older and sees that its crying has an effect, that one will grant it every favor just in order to prevent its crying, it thus employs this means at every opportunity to ensure being refused nothing. Thereby the child becomes accustomed early on to tyrannize and to give orders, from which malevolence and heated anger later arise. Discipline must therefore begin early and can only be negative at first. In no way should one concede to the child what it is insisting upon; one must ignore its screams, it surely must stop crying some time. One must refuse him everything and therefore discipline his will. With regard to the instruction of the understanding, it must be noted that the understanding must also be disciplined, just like the will. The education of the understanding may be negative when one is trying to prevent errors from invading the understanding. This is the plan of Rousseau, who is a subtle Diogenes[82] and posits the perfections in the simplicity of nature, and therefore education must be negative. Yet the discipline of the understanding can also be a positive instruction of the understanding. No animal requires instruction, but does what it should out of instinct. Human beings, however, who have understanding, must be given instruction. With unrefined individuals the instruction may only be simple, since they just have [a] few needs, but the greater the luxury, all the more must one be instructed. The

25:724

---

[a] "*Schulzwang*" normally means compulsory education. Since it is not the necessity for education as such that is in question, but rather the form that it takes, the passage (*aus dem Schulzwange gezogen*) is being interpreted as having an extended meaning consistent with Kant's criticisms elsewhere of the prevailing school systems.

25:725 suitable manner of positive instruction is one in which languages are acquired early and in an easy way, and so that [students] are not plagued for long [with learning] by the grammatical method, in order subsequently to gain time to utilize their industry for other things. Through a good manner [of instruction], by the twelfth year of age a child can have learned languages in such a way, that it can speak them as well as its mother tongue. The Basedow Philanthropin is an example of this [manner of instruction]. With regard to the schooling of reason and of character, what must be attended to is that the child cognize everything based on reasons and that it act from principles. It should have reason in its cognitions and character in its dispositions.[a] Education must here be in keeping with three elements, nature, the commonwealth, and society. In education one must proceed in keeping with the age [of the students] and not rush ahead of their years.

Youth must not be sacrificed in order to attain the benefit of manhood. One must not deny the youth [their] amusements, one must not teach them too early the knowledge they should have as men, so that they regurgitate a lot of science and can put on a show before the examiners. They lose their youth thereby, only for the sake of enjoying the later years. The child must be reared [to be] free, but in a way that it allows others [to be] free and does not, with its freedom, become detrimental to itself. Freedom is the sole condition where the human being can do something good [based] on his own disposition;[b] he who is a slave does nothing of his own accord, but [acts] from obedience and not from his own disposition. The child can therefore be free, but in such a way that it permits others also to be free; if it is restive in this, then it is not free. It must freely learn the esteem and force of the laws; all freedom notwithstanding, it must learn to obey, and to subjugate itself passively to the order, for example, the observances and customs of the school and household. If it becomes accustomed to the laws, then it can exist in harmony with the community. The child must be sensible of the weakness which it has as child, it must not become domineering and seek an advantage over others, it must not know of any advantage except the one the adult has over the small and weak person. That is really a bad upbringing[c] if children seek the advantage over others because of their understanding, and believe they also have the right to command adults[d] who serve their parents, and on top of that even strike them; if they do this, then they must be struck in return by the same person. *If they then come to realize* that they get nothing by force, then they will resort to pleas, and ask everyone for what they want to have, then it will not enter their mind to demand. They must be reared [to be] sufficiently

---

[a] *Gesinnungen*
[b] *Gesinnung*
[c] *Erziehung*
[d] *großen Leuten*

robust,[a] [of a] cheerful spirit, brave, vigorous, and active. It is very easy to rear a child on very little. Cake, milk and white bread are already delicacies for it. Softness is very harmful for them. In order that they are toughened up, one must let them go without caps, and let them go out in rain, snow, and cold. Locke wants that they should wear such shoes which are not water tight.[83] They must be ceaselessly active [and] like to be so. If they are thus soundly[b] reared, then they are reared in the way that Rousseau wants to have it. If his child is reared with great conscientiousness, then it is no different from what one otherwise takes to be a street urchin. Rousseau says: no one is reared as a brave man, if he is not first reared altogether rough[c] like a street urchin.[84] The delicacy of fine manners is later learned by itself, if the character has just first been developed. Nowadays however, the children are already dressed up since youth, and reared [in an] entirely trifling [way]; one teaches them to present all fine manners and compliments in society, on top of that even gives them watches and a snuff box[d] for their pocket; thus they learn to appear gallantly in human society, when neither their reason nor their character has been developed. Through such womanly things they acquire base, petty souls and are incapable of anything sublime and magnanimous. The child must not be compelled to dissimulate and behave affectedly. This happens thereby, that one asks it to do things for which it has no inclination at all. For example, one compels it to be devout. Since they cannot now be in a state of mind like this, they thus dissimulate, and their character is thereby corrupted. One must accustom them to manifest truthfulness when speaking. This happens thereby that one does not make it necessary for them to lie, and rather forgives them their mistakes, so that they do not later try to hide them. With every lie which they tell,[e] one must let disgust be evident, and only shame them in this one case; indeed it seems that the sense of shame has for this reason been instilled in us by God, that it should be a betrayal of the lie, for it otherwise has no use at all besides this. Therefore let us also use it for this. One must not make a child [turn] red on any other occasion, and shame it, for thereby children will blush and be embarrassed on every occasion; thereby they will become more embarrassed about the humiliation than about its cause.[85] Therefore if they, for example, lean on their elbows, or pick their teeth, or expose themselves, then one can

---

[a] *genügsam abgehärtet*, or "toughened up" (as translated elsewhere); also reading *genügsam* as *genügend* (given also the punctuation). *Genügsam* as a separate characteristic would be "easily satisfied."

[b] *wacker*, reading it as an adverb modifying "reared," instead of the characteristic achieved by the rearing.

[c] *roh*

[d] *Dose*, assuming that "snuff box" is what Kant has in mind

[e] *begehen*, literally "commit"

say to them [in a] completely cold [manner], they should not do this, it is not acceptable,^a and they must then obey. However, one must not shame them on account of this, for they do not understand the reason why they should be ashamed about it, as it then is also actually the case. However, if the child lies, then one must shame it and be contemptuous of it in such a way as if no human being would want to have anything to do with it, and one does not regard it as worth talking to. One must look at it in such a way, as if one shuns it, as if it were splattered with muck,^b and this having been often repeated, then the lie will stick in his throat; he will never again do it and remains an honest man for life. One further seeks to prevent the delusion of opinion, that he is not kept from doing something or refraining from it by means of opinion, but in accordance with the nature of the matter [in question].^c Others' opinion of him must not be [a matter of] indifference for him; thus propriety must begin to be actually [present] in him. If he would be indifferent to it, then he would not conduct himself in a way so that he pleases others. Further, the child must be kept [on the course] to humanity, that it not torment animals, for this results in hardened souls, and that it is also prepared to exercise humanity toward others; the latter [means] that it learns to esteem highly the right of human beings and the dignity of humanity in his person. These are the two things in the world which are holy. The word right must mean as much for him as a wall which cannot be scaled, and as an ocean which cannot be reached. If a human being has right, then he must not dare to raise a finger against it. The respect for the dignity of humanity in his person is the final level of education^d and already borders on the age of youth.

25:728   As a youth his instruction must be positive. He must first recognize duties which he has with regard to the human species, and then duties which he has in the civil order; there he must observe two items: obedience and respect for the law. The obedience must not be slavish, but out of respect for the law. Then he must be prepared for the love of honor and for merit in others' regard. With regard to the love of honor, the instruction is negative; he must only learn to be sensible of the worth of his person. Through [his] merits, however, he must seek to become worthy of honor. Finally he must learn to exercise magnanimity with regard to the duties of humanity. Last [of all] comes religion through the insight where he understands the true relation with God. Here arises the question: at what [point in] time must one begin with religion? At that point when the child can understand that there must be a creator. If children are accustomed earlier to religion, where they learn to repeat

^a *gebräuchlich*, literally "customary," "normal," "in fashion"
^b *Kot*: Kant may literally mean "excrement"
^c *Beschaffenheit der Sache*   ^d *Education*

prayers, then this has no effect. If they are to be saved[a] thereby, then the magpie, which one can also teach to parrot [one's words], could also be saved. However, if they learn to have insight into order in nature and traces of a creator, then one must tell them that a creator exists, and what this creator wants, what his will and his law are, and then one can instill gratitude toward God in them. Morality can only be negative in the beginning. The coldness human beings [manifest] with regard to religion stems from the fact that children have already been accustomed to it since youth, which later becomes for them a matter of complete indifference, because they have often enough heard a lot about it. The later such is made known to them, all the greater an impression will it make on them.

Finis

---

[a] *selig werden*, literally "become blessed"

Anthropology Pillau 1777–1778

Translator's introduction

This transcription, based on lectures given two years after the Friedländer text, is more fragmentary than Collins, Parow or Friedländer. Unlike the Collins and Parow texts, but like Friedländer manuscripts 399 and 400, it was apparently the work of a single transcriber. After an introduction of about five pages, it is explicitly organized around Baumgarten's paragraphs (§§ 527–655). It too follows the pattern of treating first the theoretical faculty, then taste and genius, followed by a discussion of the faculty of desire and human character.

The portions translated here include most of the introductory and methodological sections, selections from the discussions of the poetic faculty and genius, and selections from the discussion of desire and character, which discuss the human propensity to moral evil in a historical context. Also included here are selections that illustrate the racialist theories to which Kant subscribed, at least until the 1790s.

Lecture of the Winter Semester 1777–1778 based on the transcription *Pillau*

[Excerpts]

TRANSLATED BY ALLEN W. WOOD

[A] ANTROPOLOGIA. PROLEGOMENA.

There is no greater or more important investigation for human beings than the cognition of the human being. But this has been held by many to be very easy, and that from the following causes:

(1) It was believed that no discipline is needed for it, because this can be learned very easily in the ordinary course of things[a] and so it was held to be easy, although not unnecessary. It is the same with morals: It was believed that they are important, but it would be superfluous to make a science of them.

(2) It was not held to be all that important: For human beings are for the most part the greatest object we consider. All *passions* are even directed only at human beings. On the other hand, it was held not to be so necessary because it appeared that the behavior of human beings has no laws. Yet this consideration of human beings is one of the most pleasant matters.

We can consider this cognition of the human being in two ways:

(1) As a speculative cognition. There mere inquiry satisfies the understanding's desire for knowledge.

(2) As a pragmatic cognition that does not lead to further cognition insofar as it serves a utility already settled on.

If it is treated pragmatically, then it is knowledge of the world[b] and helps to form or educate[c] a man of the world.[d]

As the world, we take

(1) Nature, (2) human beings. One opposes these to each other, because the human being is the *sole freely acting* being on the earth's surface. Nature and freedom are opposed to each other. In physical

---

[a] *Umgang*
[b] *Weltkenntniß*
[c] *bilden*
[d] *Weltmann*

261

geography we consider nature, but in anthropology the human being, or human nature in all its situations. These two sciences constitute cognition of the world.[a]

25:734 The more one begins to consider the nature of a thing, the more one will begin to love the thing itself. Thus if one considers human nature, then we will be influenced by an ever greater love for it.

DISTINCTION IN COGNITION OF THE WORLD

(1) A local knowledge of the world, such as merchants have, which is also called 'empirical'. (2) a general[b] knowledge of the world, such as the man of the world has, and it is not empirical but cosmological. The local is bound to place and time and provides no rules for acting in common life. He who is acquainted with the world through travel has only this knowledge of it, which, however, lasts only for a certain time, for when the behavior at the place where he was alters, then his knowledge of it ceases.

How, then, will we best acquaint ourselves with the world, without traveling around it?

(1) Considering the human beings who are around us with strong reflection can take the place of an extensive experience, and it outdoes by far that which a thoughtless traveler receives. Human beings show the sources of their actions as much in this little space as in the larger world; for this only an attentive eye is required, and a traveler must first be provided with these concepts if he wants utility from his travel.

Civil intercourse.[c] What is essential to this is attentiveness to human dispositions, which often show themselves under many shapes.

Plays, novels, history and especially biographies.

THE UTILITY OF ANTHROPOLOGY[d]

(1) The better we know human beings, the better we know how to arrange our actions so that they are suited to the rest.

(2) It teaches how one should win over human beings.

(3) It teaches self-contentment, when the good one finds in others one has oneself.

25:735 (4) It provides us with the subjective principles of all sciences. And these subjective principles have a great influence

(1) in morals
(2) in religion
(3) in education.[e]

[a] die Welterkenntniß
[b] general
[c] Umgang

[d] Antropologie
[e] Erziehung

TRACTATIO IPSA*a*

No thought is greater or more important than that of our I. Every-thing is interesting for me only insofar as it has reference to me. This self of ours we seek to put forward everywhere, but for this reason it cannot always happen, since others are of the same mind. The fault*b* in accordance with which each gladly hears about himself, or talks about himself, we will call 'egoism'. The prudence in accordance with which one endeavors to suppress this egoism is 'modesty'. Authors and chil-dren always speak in the plural, in order likewise to show a modesty; for they want to give others to understand*c* that they want the subject mat-ter*d* they have treated, or that they want to treat, in such a way as to be judged in common. And great lords speak in the plural in order thereby to remove a certain coarseness from the orders they give: Through the 'we' they want to indicate, 'I and my advisors so order'. Montaigne is an author who seems to speak constantly about himself, for which Pascal and Malebranche blame him,[1] and they could also do it with right if that were the way it was. But that it is not so, we may glean from the fact that this author has such a general approval, which he certainly would not have if he spoke only of himself. No, he has adapted his book in such a way that in reading it, every reader is speaking of himself, and it is on account of this that he has received such general approval. For the human being takes gratification in becoming acquainted with himself, but not in examining himself.

The identity of the self is very imperfect. When someone has done some ill, after he has improved himself, which, however, takes no small time, cannot on this account have retributive punishments inflicted on him, because he is no longer the same (though he might have exemplary punishments).

25:736

In my self there is a twofold subject: for I am as a human being.

1.) An animal. 2.) *intelligens*. The human being often thinks that some-thing doesn't have to do with him when it is a matter of his animality, and hides himself under the *intelligens*. This also makes evident the con-tradiction which is often found in the human being. E.g. a man says, I fear death, and I do not fear it. As an animal I tremble before it, but as *intelligens* I cannot fear it, for I have insight into the fact that I must die someday, and I also see what misery it might be to live eternally in a miserable condition.

That is what the Stoics also meant when they asserted that pain is not sensitive, that is, that there would be no pain if one did not draw it into his mind. And [to achieve] this dominion of the *intelligens* over animality

---

a Treatise on oneself
b *Fehler*

c *tadeln*
d *Sache*

was the effort of the Stoics. For nothing can be an ill for me, unless it has to do with my *intelligens*, although it can be called a 'misfortune'. From this one sees that there is often a conflict between our self, where one often makes reproaches against oneself, that are the bitterest ones ever.

This expression 'I', or the faculty of representing oneself, is not only the most excellent thing in human nature, but it constitutes the entire dignity of the human being.

The faculty of a creature of intuiting itself, and to refer everything in creation to oneself, is personality.

All the greatest investigations in the psychology of human soul, about its capacities, freedom, etc., follow from the thought of the self. The consciousness of oneself one achieves through the observation of one's self, and through attention to oneself. We get the consideration of one's self if we become acquainted with

1) human nature

25:758 the individual ...

[Poesis]. The poetic faculty consists in voluntarily producing representations in our soul, and is distinct from fantasy and imagination. Fantasy enthuses and is involuntary. But to produce voluntary representations from the storehouse of the imagination, that is the authentic poetic faculty.

Words and expressions through which our language expresses this faculty.

To 'discover'[a] something. We discover something when we first encounter that which, however, is already given in appearance. E.g. The earth had already moved around the sun, but the first one who noticed it, discovered it. Thus America was also discovered. All these are not inventions,[b] the latter are not given. Thus the Pythagorean Theorem was invented. Franklin first discovered that storm clouds are electrical,[c] and invented the lightning-conductor.[2]

To 'bring something to light'[d] is as much as to discover once more
25:759 something that was lost, of which, however, one did not know that it was there. Thus one can bring to light a treasure that was buried somewhere. In the same way we can bring to light the perpetrator of a theft.

These expressions, regarding operations of the mind, refer to inventing, to the new production of thoughts.

To 'devise' is to invent a new practical knack[e] and especially through experiments. Thus someone can devise a new way of taking pleasure[f] and a new fashion.

---

[a] *entdecken*   [b] *Erfindungen*
[c] Editors' emendation; the transcription reads: "elastic."
[d] *ausfündig machen*   [f] *Art von* plaisir
[e] *Handgriff*

To devise something is to invent an apparent lie.

To *think up*: this appears to be a kind of invention of something untrue, yet with understanding.

To 'excogitate'. This corresponds to contriving,[a] and belongs to the understanding.

Poesis[b] is as much as the faculty of producing voluntary representations in the imagination.

That is poetically invented[c] which is not made recognizable[d] with sufficient marks. There are, e.g. kings in history who have not lived in the world at all, they are poetically invented. Everyone who wants to contrive a hypothesis must engage in poesis.

POESIS AS AN ART AND ITS PRODUCTS AS PRODUCTS OF THE SPIRIT

We will be able to call the harmonic play of the understanding and sensibility the 'beauty of the spirit'. A beautiful spirit thinks in such a way that understanding is there but stands in harmony with sensibility. In writings having wit, understanding must shine forth, but also a certain play of sense. In a beautiful spirit, the superior and inferior powers must also stand in agreement.

25:760

The humanities[e] are the arts and sciences which adorn a beautiful spirit from time to time, and are chiefly being well-read in the orators and poets. Through the humanities I understand

1) eloquence, the art of enlivening ideas of the understanding through sensibility.

2) The art of poetry, the art of giving the play of sensibility unity through the understanding.

In eloquence, the chief end is the understanding, insofar as it is educated through sensibility. In poems, sensibility sets the end and the understanding must only give it unity. Whoever gives an oration[f] first projects it from the understanding: here it could still be a logical treatment, but if in addition there occurs a play of sensibility, then only does it become an oration; but this play cannot go any farther than merely enlivening the ideas. A poet – takes a theme and depicts[g] it through sheer images, which, however, have to be so constituted that they are accompanied by conforming concepts. To enliven the powers of the mind harmonically are also the fine arts, and the powers of the mind are the understanding and sensibility.

---

[a] *ersinnen*
[b] *Dichten*
[c] *erdichtet*
[d] *kennlich gemacht*

[e] *Humaniora*
[f] *Rede*
[g] *schildert*

The fine arts are divided into

1) the material ones; these are further

1) the arts of lasting impression, painting is this. It deals only with shape. They are also appearances of the manifold in space.

2) The arts of transitory impression, music is this. It deals often with shapes, and are the play and are appearances of the manifold in time.

2) the spiritual; these are oratory and poesy.[a]

Under 'painting' we include painting proper, the art of sculpture, architecture and the art of garden landscaping.[b]

Under 'music', however, we include music proper and the art of dance.

Music is actually the pure play of sensations, for there are no shapes at all here. And it pleases us so much, even if the individual elements of it have nothing agreeable in themselves. Thus merely the harmonic in them is agreeable. Through the imagination they are enlivened. They make the greatest impression, but it is only transitory.

25:761

Eloquence has much similarity with painting; they coincide in this, that they are both concerned more with intuition than with sensibility.

The art of poetry coincides with music. For it also considers a measured tempo. Eloquence is a proper business of the understanding, but is enlivened through the play of the imagination. Poesy, however, is a business of sensibility, which the understanding orders. All fine arts are distinguished from the useful. Useful [arts] do not please immediately, but only by means of utility; but fine [arts] please immediately. The enterprises that please immediately are not businesses; the enterprise, however, that immediately displeases and pleases only by means of utility is labor. Everything that moves the powers of the mind harmonically pleases immediately.

Why is the art of poetry more agreeable than any other?

Because it is play, and thereby moves the imagination more.

Why is the poet happier in fable than in truth? Because his aim is not to promote the understanding but he takes merely the imagination as his chief end. Truth sets limits for him, and he does not love that at all. The orator, however, is happier in truth than in fable; e.g. poets are not happy in describing life, or if that is suitable, they mix a lot of untruth up with it. The same is not so with nature painting. In order to

25:762

paint nature, he must remain faithful to nature, and thereby he is indeed limited; but art will never attain to nature. By contrast, in mythology there live arcadian shepherds and he is happy everywhere where he can give the imagination free rein. Indeed, he can be happy even in didactic

[a] *Poësie*   [b] *Lustgarten-Kunst*

poems, for virtue is no object but he can portray it with all the beauty he can think up, so he has freedom enough.

Why do we need rhyme in our poetic art? Our language has no such determined syllabic meter[a] as the Greek or Latin; it does not even determine precisely the length or shortness of syllables: This has been replaced by *rhyme* so that harmony should not be adulterated.[b]

But why do poets have such freedom in poetic invention, in the choice of words as much as of images? Because their business is not at all to lend assistance to the understanding. If our aim is nothing but to converse, then nothing constrained must occur, for a constrained play is no play.

Why are most aphorisms[c] set in verse? Because meter and rhyme are the means of stamping them on the memory.

A mediocre poem is insufferable: for it is planned only to bring pleasure, and if it does not do this, then I have lost everything.

With age the poetic idea steadily decreases, but one can still be an orator. Poems about the foolishness of the world are best suited for that age:

The easiest question we can pose here is this: Why are the poets all poor?

**
*

Butler died of hunger in England.[3] And when one poet in Paris wanted to buy a house, the others found fault with him.

...   25:781

OF GENIUS

What is genius? Before one knows this, one must make a few preliminary remarks.

The talents for skill can be distinguished into natural aptitude[d] and spirit. The former is passive, the latter active. A human being has a natural aptitude to learn something, which is receptivity; but he has the spirit to invent something or to produce it, which is spontaneity. Mere natural talent makes one more skilled than his master. If one says, he has natural aptitude, then that appears to be the general ground of all talents; thus one speaks of natural aptitude only in the singular. And about spirit   25:782

---

[a] *abgemessenes Silbenmaß*   [c] *Sentenzen*
[b] *vermischt*   [d] *Naturell*

the same holds: for one does not say 'he has spirits', or 'the spirit', but 'spirit'.

'Spirit' signifies as much as 'genius' and expresses the thing almost better yet; the French had even used the word *esprit* for it. If with them this does not already mean the same as 'wit'; but we have two entirely different words for them.

In every human being lies some peculiar talent, which, if one could always seek it out, would be of great utility, and we would see more great people in all specializations.

Spirit is not a particular faculty, but what gives unity to all the faculties. Understanding and sensibility, or now better, imagination, are the human faculties; to give unity to these two is spirit. It is the universal unity of the human mind; or also the harmony between them. Spirit is the enlivening of sensibility through the idea.*ª* 'Idea' does not signify concept; for everyone can have concepts without the idea. The idea is really a concern of the understanding, but not through abstraction, since they are concepts.*ᵇ* It is the principle*ᶜ* of rules. It provides a double unity: a distributive and a *collective*. The idea always has to do only with the unity of the manifold in its entirety; thus it contains the principle of the manifold in its entirety.

Plato was the first who used 'idea', but later one took it mystically.

One must, however, necessarily make an idea first if one wants to manufacture*ᵈ* something. A sage and a spirit is nothing except an idea, and if I do not have this, how will I indicate what belongs to being a sage and a spirit?*ᵉ* There are arts of industry and of genius, the former are arts that may be learned, but the latter are of self-creation.

One can divide the formative arts into painting and music. Both are grounded on an idea, e.g. with the ancients, the human beings that one portrayed were such that one could not find such a person; but the image itself was made neither too stout nor too thin for this labor. This was an idea, for there was no such creature, hence he had to invent it out of his head. There is a *wit* without spirit, and that is a trite wit: But there is also understanding without wit, namely, when one shows everywhere too punctilious an order. This understanding and wit is a talent. A talent, however, is a predisposition to skill; and this skill is either natural aptitude or spirit.

25:783

ª *Idée*; other occurrences of the word in this passage also have the acute accent, suggesting that the word is intended to be in French.

ᵇ *Conceptes*; the Latin word is used, but capitalized, as if it were a German noun.

ᶜ *Principium*; the term 'principle' will translate this word through the remainder of the present passage.

ᵈ *verfertigen*

ᵉ Kant's question ends with a period.

In all human cognitions there must be something absolutely firm. There must be a use of our talents which is something new, and can be regarded as a principle of the new. But this principle is not to be found in all, and this is spirit, which can also be called the 'originality' of talent, that is, which is not derivative. There are arts *capable of spirit*, if spirit can be brought to bear, or where there is a principle of the new. There are also arts devoid of spirit, arts that are learned. But there can be no insight into that upon which the principle of novelty rests. Of course one appeals to a rich imagination: But the products of imagination are merely like a chaos; the products of genius foresee an idea, through which the imagination is enlivened.

Arts devoid of spirit are all handicrafts, for they follow only determinate rules and models. Arts capable of spirit are, as has already been said, those in which there is a principle of the new, because the essential cannot be learned, e.g. one should call someone. This cannot show us any rule, or any model, for if one knows it is imitated, then one regards it only as a machine and resists one's impressions. Hence eloquence is an art with spirit. The arts devoid of spirit one also calls mechanical.

The arts are thus also divided into: [1] formative arts, [2, those] that produce an object that can charm us. To the latter belong poesy and eloquence, to the former painting and music, to the first of which one counts the art of architecture, the art of sculpture, painting proper, the art of landscape gardening and the art of pyrotechnics (arranging fireworks), to the last the art of sound and dancing.

There must be a principle of the new, because one must begin from the new, the mind[a] that begins this is called a 'genius', or he has 'spirit'. This mind must have an originality of talent; now this can consist either in   25:784
the product itself and the materials, or in the form; genius really pertains only to the latter, for we ourselves cannot produce materials. Genius is only rare, for he takes a beginning, since he goes away from what was given, which, however, is extraordinarily hard, because we gladly adhere to what is given. It is this, but also very good; so that human beings use aright what they invent.

There is an aping of genius. Imitation is opposed to talent, but aping to mechanical imitation.

Genius is a freedom without guidance and constraint of rules. The dependence of the lazy on the guidance of rules is opposed to genius. The apers assume this freedom from constraint, as if a total absence of bounds and rules were the mark of genius. Genius is a principle of novelty in rules, because it gives new rules, as it were, and on this account does not follow the guidance of the old rules.

[a] *Kopf*

Sciences of genius and learning are philosophy and mathematics, of which the former belongs to genius and the latter to learning.

Genius belongs to invention, but the virtuoso to execution. The orator is a genius, but the sylist is a virtuoso.

It is especially*a* virtuosi who are *capricieux* and full of whims. Now a virtuoso excels in execution, and to this already belongs a precise accommodation, which is not always imposed on the human being, and it is hence that virtuosi are also so whimsical; for they always take account of every favorable moment.

AD § 655[4]

Feeling of pleasure and displeasure. This is a very important and indispensable matter, not only because it contains the principles of human passions, but also the maxims that teach against them, and besides, a book has just come out by an Italian, which treats this matter.[5] It is easy to understand something but not so easy to gain insight into it. What gratification is, we know. Aristippus says it does not depend on our sensations to say what is agreeable or disagreeable.[6] E.g. if someone calls something red, then he also asserts that this is always red for him; but he does not mean by it that this is universally red, but only for him. For it may be safely conjectured that someone does not sense as another does, and it is uncertain whether we have one and the same sensation. It can never occur that someone takes something agreeable for a pain. 'Agreeable' is: effort to remain in a state; and the effort to come out of this state is the disagreeable. So we can well understand what gratification is, but it is not so easy to gain insight into it, i.e. to cognize it with understanding, or to bring these concepts to others. Through gratification we can represent no object to ourselves; but the object is only a consequence of it; With gratification it is nothing objective, but subjective.

Wolff says that gratification is the intuition of perfection.[7] But 'perfect' really signifies nothing further than the completeness of a thing in its kind; thus one can also say that a crime can be perfect in its kind. But taken substantively, perfection is already an object of our desire. Perfection is the agreement of the manifold into one. But 'perfection' does not explain to me the source of the manifold in my gratification. One can have gratification in a deed. 1) from its end, e.g. the deed has something sublime in its goal. 2) From the deed's deliberation and execution, in which only the form gratifies. Is the latter a true perfection? Even though the agreement of the manifold into one causes a gratification, there is also gratification where one sees no agreement.

25:785

25:786

a *besonders*

There have been many and also the Italian author mentioned above, who have said that it is impossible to determine gratification and have insight into it.[8] But we are defining[a] it thus: Gratification is the feeling of the promotion of life. Not that the feeling of life is a gratification; we feel also through pain that we are living, and even far more. Also not the promotion of life, also the feeling of life does not promote pleasure; rather, the feeling of the promotion of life or of that which promotes life. Pain is the feeling of hindrances to life; Not everything that hinders life is at the same time a feeling of hindrances; e.g. Someone's lungs can be in bad circumstances, which shortens his life; but he does not sense it. Thus that is no pain. What promotes life altogether and not only partially, that is the essence tidied up, and cheerfulness of soul...

Pain is either a physical or an ideal pain. There is also a moral pain, which, however, is not to be set in this class, and a moral pain is always creditable and serviceable. A pain is ideal when it does not arise through the presence of the object, as fear and hope is an ideal gratification... Hope is a praegustus[b] of the future. All our ideal gratification and pain are such that they are on physical grounds. A human being who has done something good and yet is blamed by everyone can easily regard this, for he looks at the same time toward the agreeableness he will have in the future, when all of them will depend on him... 25:787

Of the species of pleasure and displeasure. 1) Something pleases;[c] 2) and gratifies; 3) Something is loved. That pleases to which we ourselves and our way of thinking give approval, e.g. virtue. – Gratification refers only to private sense, and it pleases in accordance with the form of sensibility; but what ought to please must be universal. What pleases the common sense[d] but does not gratify is beautiful. – But if I do something in accordance with the common sense, then I do it in accordance with taste. Taste thus depends on the judgment of the common sense. One cultivates taste when one makes it agree with the judgment of many.... 25:788

Of desires. It is a feeling in regard to what is future. But the effect of the representation of what is future on our feeling brings us into activity. The feeling of the present incites no activity, but when it means that it will endure, then an activity will soon be incited. Our activity is incited through the representation of what is future; the present is only a moment, so when we represent something present, that does not at all incite our activity, e.g. one drinks wine slowly so as to retain the taste for a long time. All our desires are really nothing other than to move the activity to pleasure or displeasure; what moves our activity to future 25:795

---

[a] erklären
[b] foretaste; the Latin word is, however, capitalized as if it were a German noun.
[c] gefällt   [d] gemeinschaftlicher Sinn

pleasure, that we desire,[a] but what it[b] moves us to future displeasure, to that we have aversion. The sensation of a merely idle pleasure is not desire; but the movement of our activity must be added; for this only is the end of nature.

Desires are 1) idle or inactive, 2) practical or active. Idle desires are mere wishes, desire,[c] longing; but they are called 'practical' from their objects: the first are mostly conversed about, through novels and novelistic ideas, they are such that one gets all too exaggerated ideas about the happiness of life. Idle desires are thus those that cannot move our activity, because one sees[d] that it is impossible to attain to such happiness.

All fruitless stimulations are harmful to the health of the mind; and the habit of filling the mind with empty wishes gives it a certain inactivity; if we represent to ourselves a happiness such that we can never hope to get it, then no desires are incited in us through this; but as soon as we 25:796 represent it as possible, then we get a longing for it. Thus we must ban from ourselves longing and wish directed to what we either cannot attain or what can be acquired only with much difficulty.

There is a longing without an object; this state is called ill *humeur*, or also a restless mind. We find this in women who have the *vapeurs*, and in male persons when they have whims. This is an unbearable state where one is always bored; this is a state of weariness with life, which has even brought many to suicide ...

Desires are 1) rational, 2) sensible; rational ones are 1) as regards matter, where the object is an object of reason; but if it is an object of the senses, then that is the sensible faculty as regards matter, 2) as regards form; if only the way we represent the object to ourselves is an agreement with reason, whatever the object may be. To sensible desires belong 1) propensity, 2) instinct, 3) inclination, 4) affect, 5) passion.

<u>Propensity</u> is distinct from actual desire. It is the possibility of desiring something, and is a predisposition of the subject to desire; thus one says of someone: he has a propensity to evil, without our having seen him do anything. Thus one says of the northlanders, they have a propensity 25:797 to get drunk. There is also a predisposition to insight, which one calls 'talent', or also a predisposition to desires, which one calls 'propensity'.

<u>Instinct</u> is a blind desire. It is a desire that we have when we are still not even acquainted with the object. The desire thus precedes the acquaintance with the object. Sexual inclination is of this kind. One also counts to it the love of parents for their children.

<u>Inclination</u>. It is an enduring subjective movement. The effect of instinct is momentary, but inclination is enduring.

---

[a] *verlangen*
[b] *Sie*; the capitalized feminine pronoun is hard to fit into the sentence.
[c] *Verlangen*   [d] *einsieht*

Affect. It really belongs not to desire but to feeling. Passion belongs to inclination and to the desires. Affect has its effect in a moment; affects do not endure. Passions, however, can endure through an entire life. Anger and terror do not endure, but avarice, haughtiness do.

Passions do not really move the mind, but they are an inclination, to the extent that they cancel the equilibrium of desires.

An affect cancels equilibrium through sensations. The preponderance occurs when the control of the mind is cancelled.

The affect is really a higher degree of feeling, and passion a higher degree of desires. One says about some human beings that they are full of affect, but not that they are full of passion; as about the French. There are people too who have no affects, but on this account are full[a] of passions, as the Chinese and the Indians,[b] who under all circumstances show no affect, and thus seem to play the role of a philosopher, even though they have insatiable desires . . .   25:838

Character of the Human Species or the concept of human nature in general. There are many difficulties with this problem. For the appearances in different ages do not show how the human being is constituted, but only how he will be constituted at the time and under these circumstances. They do not allow us to cognize what kinds of germs lie hidden in the soul of the human being. – The predispositions for morality that lie in human nature are discovered by us through education,[c] but we cannot know whether a far better education might be thought up, through which the predispositions to morality might reveal themselves even better. What is authentic to the human being is hard to make out from the present and past appearance; for we find only the constitution of the predispositions that are there now.

I attempt to find the character of the human species by comparing one age of the human beings with another, and seeing what the determination of the human being is. For we cannot say that it will constantly remain as it now is; that is just as if the ancients had said that it will remain for all times as it was in their time; for the condition now is entirely unlike[d] the ancient one.   25:839

We find that here a right concept of the human being is to be made from the phenomenon, or also from history. – From various circumstances, however, we can discover certain predispositions from time to time and infer from them what nature's goal for humanity is.

---

[a] reading with the editors, voller; the text reads völlig.
[b] Indianer, a term which now refers to native Americans; but it seems more likely that Kant is referring to inhabitants of the Asian subcontinent and the East Indies, since he uses Amerikaner for native Americans (cf. Ak 25:1187).
[c] Erziehung   [d] ungleich

With the sexual drive we find something contradictory. A human being is a child as long as he cannot feed himself, and he is a man when he is in a position to procreate what is like him. But manhood is found already at the time, as in the 16th year among northerly peoples, when they are not yet in a position to preserve and feed themselves. But is this not a contradiction: to be able to procreate and yet not to be permitted to? In the estate^a of nature we do not find this; savages^b will not breed unless they know that they can feed their children. In the cultured^c estate, this partly arises from civil laws. Thus there will come a time when this contradiction will no longer occur.

Every individual animal reaches the vocation of its nature; by contrast, every individual human being does not achieve the vocation of human nature, but only the entire human species is predisposed so that it can achieve this vocation.

Does the savage achieve his vocation? No, not even the vocation of an animal. Human beings in Germany, do they achieve theirs? No, they don't either. Every animal, however, achieves it, but the entire species is not altered; the human being alone does not achieve it, but his species approaches ever nearer to its vocation.

E.g. Every bee is born, learns to make cells and prepare honey, and dies, and has come to the highest degree of its vocation. But the bee has done that just as well from the beginning of the world up to now; thus it does not alter at all.

With the human being it is entirely different. The ancients and the first times were farther distant from their vocation than the following ones, and in recent times it seems to have been reserved for the human being to have achieved his vocation. But no human being can complain on this account against providence that it has not made him so fortunate as to achieve this vocation. For he is just as fortunate; for since the concept of happiness alters in precisely this way, human beings come that much nearer to their vocation.

We find nations that do not appear to have progressed in the perfection of human nature, but have come to a standstill, while others, as in Europe, are always progressing. If the Europeans had not discovered America, the Americans would have remained in their condition. And we believe even now that they will attain to no perfection, for it appears that they will all be exterminated, not through acts of murder, for that would be gruesome! but rather that they will die out. For it is calculated only a twentieth part of all the previous Americans are still there. Since they only retain a small part, while the Europeans take so much away

25:840

^{a} *Stande* ^{c} *gesitteten*
^{b} *Wilden*

274

from them, there will arise internal struggles between them, and they will be in friction with one another.

China and Hindustan is a land in which there is much art and also an analogue to science; indeed, we are much indebted to this land. If we consider this people, then we ask: has it come to the bounds of its destiny? We have conjectured that it will not proceed further, since it lacks spirit.

The Greeks, by contrast, were a nation that came ever nearer to its vocation; the Romans, and further the Gauls, and thus also Germany have received it through them. From the fact that every individual human being has not achieved his vocation here, nothing has been subtracted from his good fortune, as has already been shown; but from this another life may be inferred with much certainty. One sees, to be sure, that human beings together come ever nearer to their vocation, but no less it is shown that they often fall back again in their vocation. What is one to make of this? This is only an apparent fall, for it is always a means to an increase that is all the greater. 25:841

There are some who have believed that there has already been a fully perfect condition in the world, which, however, began to be subtracted from; but this has no probability; for how is it possible that barbarism should creep in again, when a nation has once been cultivated?

In a letter *d'histoire ancienne*, a member of the Paris Academy provides the cause that the sciences have not come from China and India but from lands lying in the north; about which astronomy gives him the opportunity to conjecture.[9] He says the nation from which China and India have learned everything must have lain in or near Siberia, which he conjectures from the Zend-Avesta.[10] 25:842

From the Greeks one can see that they were civilized from their northern nations, the Thracians.

In all nations we find some concepts of threefoldness (*quod notandum est*)[a] for all have represented God as lawgiver, as a kind governor, and as a just judge.[11] The Indians have their Brahma, Vishnur and Ruttren Shiva. Because there are four elements, Brahma has recreated the world four times, and now we live in the last one.

The Persians once again have their Ormuzd, Mithra and Ahriman; the ancient Celtic nations always prayed to only one God, and destroyed all the temples of idols.

If a human being investigates himself precisely, it appears that he should go on all fours, which is shown in particular by the position of his heart and even better by the position of the embryo in the mother's body.[12] 25:843

---

[a] which is to be noted

The Americans have such relations in their nature that they now should become no more perfect.

The Negroes, however, are also no longer susceptible of any further civilizing; but they have instinct and discipline, which is lacking in the Americans. The Indians and Chinese appear now to be at a standstill in their perfection; for their history books show that they now know no more than they have known for a long time.

On what, then, rests the achievement of the ultimate vocation of human nature? The general foundation is the civil constitution; the union of human beings into a whole, which serves to achieve the cultivation*a* of all talents, and also for one person's giving the other the freedom for that cultivation – through this it happens that the predisposition to talents is developed; through this the human being is elevated out of his animality. Here, however, one member already influences a perfection of the other, which the other can cultivate all the better.

If human society becomes more perfect, then humanity will come along with it, until the civil constitution has attained to its greatest goal; then the highest development of the predispositions in humanity will also show itself. That humanity will someday achieve this goal, for this we have the greatest conjecture; for we find in ourselves an ideal to which we always take the effort to come nearer, but which we have still not now achieved; because we always reproach ourselves, this shows that we can become perfect, for were this not so, we could not accuse ourselves.

On the origin of good from evil. Ill is that to which we physically have an aversion. But evil is that to which the understanding has an aversion, and the vices alone are evil, whereas all pains are an ill. Everything begins from ill, and with it some evil is also mixed in. This evil, however, is the occasioning cause through which something good is awakened. If human beings had remained under the care of nature, if it had offered them everything voluntarily, then all of them would have remained in a state of stupidity, and would at least only somewhat refined their animal enjoyments. Providence, however, has willed that we should live in a

25:844 world where we are able to obtain something for ourselves only through effort. From this point of view the fall of Adam has something useful about it philosophically considered; for earlier the human being misused his reason because he had everything in superfluity. In the state of superfluity the human being must be looked upon as a spoiled child, who knows no hardship at all. It was said to the human being that he should labor and also die, in order that he might let his hardships appear.[13] With a very long life, some who now tremble before vice because they are near to the grave would practice far more vices.

---

a *Ausbildung*

Here, then, is an ill from which good arises. The hardships of life are the incentives to the full development of talents.

Ills still do not serve fully for the development of talents. The human being must therefore have something evil in him, that he inflicts on others, and provides an incentive to the development of talents.

Evil in the human being is nothing other than animality combined with freedom, to the extent, namely, that freedom is not brought under any law. Animals are merely under natural laws; the human being also has animality, but he is also free; hence he is under no law; Now because his choice cannot possibly agree with that of others, there arises disunity and quarrels. Now if human beings were with one another in the social condition, then there must soon arise a fear among them each of the other; from this might first arise violence and war. But because each is afraid of the other, human beings are spread all over the surface of the earth. For we find there are human beings on all the islands, separated by the broadest seas, and we do not know how they got there. Thus since human beings have distrust one toward the other, they have populated the earth.

The chief success that the evil of unsociability had was the beginning of civil societies. Since human beings could not stand one another, and also had no safety one from another, the most proximate means was to combine with one another; and since in this way they could be safe on account of their property as well as their persons, they laid aside their freedom and assumed a social constraint; they chose one human being who is to give laws and act as judge, and constrain us to hold to the law, and thereby obtains security for us.

25:845

With this the development of all talents and the grounding of a good character were combined.

Development of the species of the arts. One can well regard language as something that arises gradually, for only through it are we in a position to make concepts for ourselves.

Of great advantage and increase of the human race is domestic livestock; from it human beings have the utility that besides the labor they do for us, they are also useful for food. It is to be conjectured that, as some would give it, one makes the sheep into the beginning, and, on account of Jupiter, one has imagined Ammon with a sheep's-head, as a memorial to the invention of the sheep, as likewise Apis with an ox head as a memorial to the invention of beef cattle. What is most probable is that one began with the dog, because it already has an inclination for it, and once the human being has this one, then at the same time he has others too; the dog appears always ready, as it were, to fulfill the commands of its master; and by means of its sense of smell it tracks other animals out too, and shows them to its master.

When the human being began to build,[a] he seemed better determined to have his property; he had to make boundary stones; and among the consequences of this, the finest is <u>agriculture</u>.

<u>The division of labors</u> one from another. The cruder the human being is, the more he will take all labours on himself, but then these labors cannot console themselves with any great progress when they are divided; thus each can work on his particular part.

<u>The invention of writing</u>. This is connected with lineage and a com-

25:846 munity in the distance.

<u>Postal services</u>. From the lack of postal service it happened that one did not hear very much about foreign regions, since it took a very long time before it came back from there, now this is no longer lacking and one can also take the newspaper.

<u>The invention of money</u>. By this commerce is greatly promoted. Likewise[b] exchange. (This is supposed to have been invented in Venice.)

<u>Printing of books</u>. This was a means of the multiplication of means, and also correct at the time, except that it is now more suspicious, since too many writings see the light.

<u>The compass</u>. It is the means of connecting[c] the countries separated by seas.

<u>The security of the civil condition</u> through standing armies.

<u>Cannons and powder</u>. Which are a hindrance to nations not being driven out of their security.

<u>Thoughts of Rousseau</u>. He wrote a book[14] which made a great stir: titled about the inequality of human beings; in which rules much misanthropie[d] but from benevolence. He shows what is terrible and unbearable in the civil condition, and on the contrary, what is agreeable in the crude condition. But one must not understand this as if he prefers the crude condition to every civil constitution; but rather he shows only that our present civil constitution is less well suited to human nature than the crude condition in which we were previously, and if we did not have the hope of going further, he advises that one should turn around and go back into the estate of nature. Thus he did not assert, as some believe, that it is the vocation of the human being to live in the woods.

Is the cultivated[e] condition, then, suited to the human being? If we consider the talents lying in him, and that have been developed up to now, then we can always assert with right that the human being in the

---

[a] *schlagen*

[b] The text reads *Glückfeld* ("field of good fortune"), or possibly a proper name; the editors suggest *Gleichfalls*.

[c] *verbinden*

[d] The word is spelled as in French, but capitalized as if it were a German noun.

[e] *gesittete*

state of crudeness has not yet come to this cultivation.[a] But if we consider   25:847
the human being from the other side of his animality, then we infringe
nature.

Rousseau shows how a civil constitution must be in order to achieve
the entire end of the human being.[15] He shows how youth must be
brought up in order perfectly to fulfill this end of nature.[16] He shows
into which constitution various peoples must enter so that barbaric wars
might pass over into friendly disputes.[17] Thus he shows in general that
in us lie the germs for cultivation toward our vocation; and we have need
of a civil constitution on this account, in order to fulfill the end of nature;
but if we stop with the civil constitution we have now, then it would be
better to return to the estate of wildness.

The human being was obviously not made to roam about in the woods,
but to live in society. Apart from culture, society also has this, that one
disciplines the other and through that we curb the ills that can hold up
our progress toward perfection.

The civil constitution arises from freedom, laws and authority.[b] Freedom without laws is *anarchy* (the estate of wildness). Freedom and laws
but no authority; that can take place only with purely good-natured
human beings. – Authority and laws without freedom is despotism. –
Authority with laws and freedom is tyranny.

If the human race is to come nearer to its vocation, then to this belongs
a perfect civil constitution, good education[c] and the best concepts in
religion.

Finis Anthropologiae.[d]

---

[a] *Ausbildung*
[b] *Gewalt*

[c] *Erziehung*
[d] the end of anthropology

Menschenkunde (1781–1782?)

Translator's introduction

The *Menschenkunde* transcription is unique among all of the anthropology transcriptions included in this volume in that it was not first published in 1997 as part of volume 25 of the Academy Edition of *Kant's gesammelte Schriften*. Rather, as Allen Wood notes in his General Introduction, it was first published in 1831, under the title *Immanuel Kant's Menschenkunde oder philosophische Anthropologie. Nach handschriftlichen Vorlesungen herausgegeben von Fr. Ch. Starke* (Leipzig: Die Expedition des europaischen Aufsehers, 1831). A new edition (*neue Ausgabe*) followed in 1838 (Quedlinburg und Leipzig: Verlag der Ernst'schen Buchhandlung, 1838). "Fr. Ch. [= Friedrich Christian] Starke," the editor, was a pseudonym for Johann Adam Bergk. Bergk (1769–1834), who was born in Hainichen and died in Leipzig, was professor of philosophy and jurisprudence at the University of Leipzig, and also a prolific author, editor, translator, and publisher whose works appeared not only under his own name, but also under the pseudonym Fr. Ch. Starke, and at least two additional pseudonyms: Dr. Heinichen and Justus Freimund. Among Bergk's own works are a defense of the French revolution (*Untersuchungen aus dem Natur-, Staats- und Volkerrechte, mit einer Kritik der neuesten Konstitution der französischen Republik* [1796]), a treatise on punishment (*Die philosophie des peinlichen rechtes* [Meissen, 1802]), a monograph on critical reading (*Die Kunst, Bucher zu lesen* [Jena, 1799]), and two commentaries on Kant's *Metaphysics of Morals* (*Briefe über Immanuel Kant's Metaphysische Anfangsgründe der Rechtslehre, enthaltend Erläuterungen, Prüfung und Einwürfe* [Leipzig, 1797], *Reflexionen über I. Kant's Metaphysische Anfangsgründe der Tugendlehre* [Gera, 1798]).

An energetic popularizer of Kant's work, Bergk also edited (under the pseudonym Fr. Ch. Starke) three additional books that contain transcriptions of Kant's classroom lectures. The first, an anthropology transcription, is entitled *Immanuel Kant's Anweisung zur Menschen- und Weltkenntniß. Nach dessen Vorlesungen im Winterhalbjahre 1790–1791 herausgegeben von Fr. Ch. Starke* (Leipzig: Die Expedition des europaischen Aufsehers, 1831). The second, which contains a transcription of Kant's physical geography lectures given "during the summer semester 1791 from May 11, in Königsberg," is entitled *Immanuel Kant's vorzügliche kleine Schriften und Aufsätzte*. Mit Anmerkungen herausgegeben von Fr. Ch. Starke. Nebst Betrachungen über die Erde und den Menschen aus ungedruckten Vorlesungen von Imm. Kant. In zwey Bänden (Leipzig: Die Expedition des europaischen Aufsehers, 1833). And the third, an anthology of anthropology writings, the Kantian contributions of which stem primarily from the *Menschenkunde* and *Anweisung zur Menschen- und Weltkenntniß* texts, along with some earlier material from the 1770s, is entitled *Taschenbuch für Menschenkenntniß und Menschenbesserung nach Hippel, Wieland, Sterne, Helvetius, Shakespeare und Kant*. Mit einer Abhandlung über Menschenkenntniß von Dr. Heinichen. Neue Ausgabe (Quedlinburg und Leipzig, 1838 – a first edition was probably published in 1826, but no copies survive).

In 1976, "because of the slow progress of the Academy Edition of Kant's works,"[a] a photomechanical reprint of the two main Kant anthropology texts edited by Bergk was also published by Georg Olms (*Immanuel Kants Menschenkunde*. Nach handschriftlichen Vorlesungen hereausgegeben von Fr. Ch. Starke. Im Anhang *Immanuel Kants Anweisung zur Menschen- und Weltkenntniß*. Nach dessen Vorlesungen im Winterhalbjahre 1790–1791 herausgegeben von Fr. Ch. Starke. Mit einer Vorbemerkung von Giorgio Tonelli [Hildesheim/New York: Georg Olms Verlag, 1976]). Olm's one-volume reprint edition of Bergk's two texts, though no longer in print, is still widely available through major research libraries.

It is also worth noting that an English translation of one of Bergk's essays has also been published previously: "Does Enlightenment Cause Revolutions?,"[b] translated by Thomas E. Wartenberg, in *What is Enlightenment? Eighteenth-Century Answers and Twentieth-Century Questions*, ed. James Schmidt (Berkeley: University of California Press, 1996).

In his own writings, Bergk frequently draws much more radical conclusions from Kantian doctrines than Kant's more orthodox followers have done. For instance, in "Does Enlightenment Cause Revolutions?," after comparing (in a manner quite similar to Heinrich Heine's

---

[a] Giorgio Tonelli, "Vorbemerkung," *Immanuel Kants Menschenkunde*. Nach handschriftlichen Vorlesungen herausgegeben von Fr. Ch. Starke. Im Anhang *Immanuel Kants Anweisung zur Menschen- und Weltkenntniß*. Nach dessen Vorlesungen im Winterhalbjahre 1790–1791 herausgegeben von Fr. Ch. Starke. Mit einer Vorbemerkung von Giorgio Tonelli (Hildesheim/New York: Georg Olms Verlag, 1976).
[b] Originally published as "Bewirkt die Aufklärung Revolutionen?" *Deutsche Monatsschrift* (1795): 263–279. The essay was republished in Bergk's 1796 book on the French Revolution, mentioned earlier.

remarks nearly forty years later)[a] the political revolution in France
with the intellectual revolution "that a German man brought about
in the realms of knowledge, belief, and opinion, and that will cause
incalculable alterations for the betterment of humanity in all that people think and do," Bergk goes on to argue that a "merely speculative
Enlightenment is, at most, cunning, clever, refined, selfish, and still cowardly." Rather, what is needed is a "moral enlightenment," one which
demands that external social, political, and legal arrangements "correspond with the pronouncements of conscience." And "if the nation recognizes or senses the injustices that burden it and mock its humanity,"
he adds, "then a revolution is unavoidable." Enlightenment thus stands
"justly accused as the cause of revolutions," and we should stop trying to "falsely absolve writers" of this charge. Rather, Enlightenment
authors "are the salt of mankind since they guard against stupidity and
lethargy."[b]

Similarly, in an 1801 essay entitled "Ueber die Einschrankung der
Freiheit zu studieren durch den Staat" (On the Limitation of the Freedom to Study by the State), Bergk argues that everyone should have
unrestricted access to a university education. It is the duty of the state to
protect "the freedom of all according to the same laws," and to exclude
potential students from universities because of their social backgrounds,
financial resources, or any other reason is inconsistent with this fundamental obligation. "All right (*Recht*) rests on equality of action. What
one citizen as such is allowed to do, all must be allowed to do." As he
declares later in the essay, "Money and class (*Geld und Stand*) are the most
inappropriate and ignoble conditions that the state can choose for conferring permission to study."[c] Furthermore, when governments impose

[a] "On each side of the Rhine we see the same breach with the past; all respect for tradition
is withdrawn. As here, in France, every privilege, so there in Germany, every thought,
must justify itself..." (Heinrich Heine, *Religion and Philosophy in Germany*. Translated
by John Snodgrass. With a new Introduction by Ludwig Marcuse [Boston: Beacon Press,
1959], p. 102). First published (in French) in 1834; in German, 1835.

[b] Bergk, "Does Enlightenment Cause Revolutions?," in Schmidt, ed., *What is Enlightenment?*, pp. 228, 229, 231, 230, 231. See also Schmidt's "Introduction: What is Enlightenment? A Question, Its Context, and Some Consequences," esp. p. 14.

[c] Bergk, "Ueber die Einschränkung der Freiheit zu studieren durch den Staat," *Montats-
schrift für Deutsche; zur Veredlung der Kenntnisse, zur Bildung des Geschmacks, und so froher
Unterhaltung* 1 (1801): 3–16, at 7 and 10. The article is dated April 23, 1800. I would
like to thank Niko Strobach for obtaining a photocopy of this essay for me. See also my
discussion in Chapter 2 (Education) of *The World We Want: How and Why the Ideals of the
Enlightenment Still Elude Us* (New York: Oxford University Press, 2007), and Anthony
J. La Vopa, *Grace, Merit, and Talent: Poor Students, Clerical Careers, and Professional
Ideology in Eighteenth-Century Germany* (Cambridge: Cambridge University Press, 1988).
La Vopa, however, reads too much Smithian economics into Bergk's argument. It is
primarily intended as an application of what Kant calls "the universal principle of right":
"Any action is *right* (*recht*) if it can coexist with everyone's freedom in accordance with a

limitations on the number of university graduates, they are also stifling the search for truth. Open competition and the free exchange of ideas are the best means of achieving maximum progress in the search for truth and new knowledge.

The dating of the *Menschenkunde* transcription is not certain. Bergk, in his Preface, says rather vaguely that "we present here the printing of lectures that he [Kant] probably delivered in the second half of the previous century, because the contents reveal that the *Critique of Pure Reason* (1781) had not yet appeared."[a] Subsequent Kant scholars have reached a variety of conflicting conclusions regarding the dating of this transcription. Benno Erdmann assigned a date of 1773;[b] Paul Menzer, 1778–1779;[c] Fritz Medicus, 1787–1788;[d] Otto Schlapp, 1793–1794.[e] Reinhard Brandt and Werner Stark, the editors of Academy Edition volume 25, assign a probable date of 1781–1782, based in part on the appearance of specific terms and phrases in the *Menschenkunde* that in their view were not used by Kant before the *Critique of Pure Reason*.[f]

The translated selections from the *Menschenkunde* transcription that follow are based on the Academy Edition of the text. However, the Academy Edition of the text is not a reprint of Bergk's edition. The Academy editors have occasionally supplemented Bergk's text with material from a second transcription (*Petersburg*), which is stored at the Russian National Library in St. Petersburg. Material taken from the *Petersburg* transcription – both in what follows and in Academy Edition volume 25 – appears in italics. In preparing the translation, I have also made use

---

universal law" (*The Metaphysics of Morals* 6:230). Johann Gottlieb Fichte, in his *Addresses to the German Nation* (first presented as public lectures in the amphitheater of the Berlin Academy in 1807–1808), later defended a position quite similar to Bergk's: the state has an obligation to make "education universal throughout the length and breadth of its domain for every one of its future citizens" (*Addresses to the German Nation*. Edited with an Introduction by George Armstrong Kelly [New York: Harper & Row, 1968], p. 166; cf. 12–13).

[a] Bergk, "Vorrede," *Immanuel Kant's Menschenkunde*, Neue Ausgabe, p. xii.

[b] Benno Erdmann, *Reflexionen Kants zur Anthropologie* (Leipzig: Fues's Verlag, 1882), p. 58 (as cited by Reinhard Brandt and Werner Stark in their "Einleitung" to Academy Edition vol. 25, p. lix n. 5).

[c] Paul Menzer, "Kants Vorlesungen über Metaphysik," *Kant-Studien* 3 (1902), pp. 58–59 (as cited by Tonelli in his "Vorbemerkung" to *Immanuel Kants Menschenkunde*).

[d] Fritz Medicus, "Kants Philosophie der Geschichte," *Kant-Studien* 4 (1902), p. 5 (as cited by Tonelli in his "Vorbemerkung").

[e] Otto Schlapp, *Kants Lehre vom Genie und die Entstehung der "Kritik der Urteilskraft"* (Göttingen: Vandenhoeck & Ruprecht, 1901), pp. 8–9 (as cited by Tonelli and Brandt and Stark).

[f] Brandt and Stark, "Einleitung," pp. xxxv, cxi–cxiv. Their dating is also based on some additional factors.

of Tonelli's 1976 reprint of Bergk's 1831 text, as well as of a copy of the 1838 edition of Bergk's text, held at the New York Public Library.[a]

[a] I would like to thank Thomas E. Wartenberg, James Schmidt, and Zip Kellogg for their help in securing information about Johann Adam Bergk; and Manfred Kuehn, Heiner F. Klemme, Jens Timmermann, Allen Wood, and Robert Clewis for their suggestions and advice on my translation.

Lecture of the Winter Semester *1781/82* *[?] based on the transcriptions* Menschenkunde, *Petersburg*

[Excerpts]

TRANSLATED BY ROBERT B. LOUDEN

INTRODUCTION[a]

One must distinguish two kinds of study: there are brooding sciences,[b]   25:853
which are of no utility to the human being, and there were formerly
philosophers called *scholastics*, whose entire science consisted of surpass-
ing each other in shrewdness; their art was science for the school, but
one could not obtain any enlightenment for common life from it. One of
them may be a great man, but only for the school and without the world
having utility from his knowledge. A second kind of study consists not
merely in gaining esteem for oneself from members of the school but
also in extending knowledge[c] beyond the school and trying to expand
one's knowledge[d] toward universal utility: this is study for the world. A
science is scholastic[e] when it is in accordance with the standards of the
school and of the professions. This is a perfection not to be despised;
for all sciences must be scholastic at the beginning, later they can also
become popular in order to be accepted and made use of by mere admirers.[f] Initially science should give satisfaction to the student of the craft,[g]
and then afterward we will see how it can best be grasped by common
people.[h] He who makes a scholastic use of his knowledge is a pedant, he
knows how to describe his concepts merely with the technical expressions of the school and speaks merely in scholarly phrases of expression.
He makes a use merely of scholastic cognitions in the world, but here
one must understand simply how to apply one's knowledge popularly,

---

[a] The section title 'Introduction' ('*Einleitung*') does not appear in the Table of Contents
   listed in Academy volume 25, but it is listed in the original published version of the
   Menschenkunde lecture (1831).
[b] *grüblerische Wissenschaften*   [e] *Schulgerecht*
[c] *Wissen*   [f] *bloße Liebhaber*
[d] *Kenntnis*   [g] *Studierende von Handwerk*
[h] common people: *Menschenkunde*; the community: *Petersburg*

289

so that others also understand us, not merely professional scholars. One laughs when pedants display their knowledge so inappropriately[a] that they make a scholastic use of it in the world, for nothing is more laughable than when one shows no power of discrimination (*judicium discretivum*) and does not see what is fitting for the circumstances. Thus the pedant, who in other respects can be a man of merit, often gives us occasion to laugh. It is therefore necessary that we learn to make a popular use of our knowledge acquired in universities, so that we know, in our dealings with human beings, how to educate[b] them or make ourselves be liked by them. We should be concerned not with the school but rather with the world; we must therefore study the world. A human being has knowledge of the world[c] often when he knows little but can teach that little [part] well to others. Someone can be very scholarly, but because he has no knowledge of the world[d] he is unable to make advantageous use of his scholarship and by means of it promote his utility and that of the commonwealth. Knowledge of the world also sometimes means knowledge of nature, but this is not the meaning of popular speech, there it merely means knowledge of the human being. –

25:854

The human being knows the world;[e] that is, he knows human beings in all walks of life.[f] Knowledge of the world according to its common meaning is called knowledge of the human being. The French say the human being "has world";[g] that is, he has knowledge that consists not merely in speculations, but he knows well how to apply them.[h] We need the assistance of other human beings for the attainment of other things; that is primarily why one calls knowledge of the world knowledge of the human being. Now what is to be done in order to get to know the world? In order to acquire knowledge, one person goes on journeys, another steps out of his family circle and broadens his social intercourse[i] up to the part of human society that is most educated;[j] that is, to the distinguished part. At the beginning his dealings were limited to his family and to his *peers*[k] in school, and then he proceeds on to more refined people. Practice and experience give us the best school for getting to know human beings, but they alone do not suffice to complete our knowledge of the world and make it practical. Unless one learns to think about human beings, one will not become very learned through social intercourse. That is why from the start one must point the other to that which he must pay attention to

---

[a] *Petersburg*: unskillfully   [b] *bilden*

[c] *hat Welt. Petersburg*: has little knowledge of the world, when he knows little, that he can make known to a person.

[d] *Weltkenntniß*   [e] *kennt die Welt*

[f] *in allen Ständen* (or "in all social classes"). *Petersburg*: all kinds of estates.

[g] *hat Welt*   [i] *Umgang*

[h] *an den Mann zu bringen weiß.*   [j] *am meisten gebildet*

[k] *Menschenkunde* reads: his contemporaries

when observing human beings. Of these matters one must assign basic ideas, in accordance with which one can acquire knowledge of the human being: if one is not well-informed, one can deal with human beings for a long time without noticing anything about them. But if someone has shown us the main points that we have to keep an eye on, then we know what we must pay attention to. A complete instruction in the varieties and characteristics in the human being thus belongs to cognition of the human being. Both are of great importance and must always precede cognition of the human being and that is why experiences must be broadened. Armed with these instructions, one can in a short while learn more than another can learn in his entire life. For once the foundations are laid it is easy to extend them, and as a result one also receives more gratification from one's social intercourse, because generally speaking the most important aspect of them consists in reflection. Often a bad tone[a] can cause deadly boredom, but a thoughtful person always finds material for his considerations in such unsociableness; as a result he learns and has not spent his time unpleasantly. This preliminary knowledge will be what is necessary in order to make progress in knowledge of the human being.

25:855

There are three kinds of doctrines, all of which contribute to our perfection. The first kind makes us skilled, the second prudent, the third wise. All sciences of the school help one to become skilled: thus one learns history, for instance, in order to become skilled in *respect* to[b] the things of experience. But if we wish to take a step into the world, we must learn how we are to become prudent.

The highest level of wisdom is *the greatest*[c] perfection, but it is rarely reached. The skilled person is the theoretical one of the school,[d] but the instruction that makes us prudent is instruction in the practical, which shows us how we should make use of our skill. Skillfulness is directed toward things; prudence, toward human beings. The watchmaker is skilled if he makes a perfect watch; but if he knows how to bring it to the customer quickly because he repairs it according to fashion, then he is prudent. Only when we are able to acquire influence on human beings do we also have an influence on things, because human hands produce everything out of raw nature. Prudence is therefore based merely on knowledge of the human being, by virtue of which we are in a position to direct others according to our purpose.

Knowledge of the human being is twofold. Speculative knowledge of the human being makes us skilled and is treated in psychology and

[a] *ein übler Ton*
[b] *Petersburg*: in respect to; *Menschenkunde*: in confirmation of
[c] *Petersburg*: the greatest: *Menschenkunde*: the spirit of
[d] *das Theoretische der Schule*

physiology, but practical knowledge of the human being makes us prudent; it is a knowledge of the art of how one human being has influence on another and can lead him according to his purpose. One calls all practical knowledge of the human being 'pragmatic' insofar as it serves 25:856 to fulfill our overall aims. Every doctrine of wisdom is moral, and every doctrine of prudence is pragmatic. A doctrine*ᵃ* is pragmatic insofar as it makes us prudent and useful in public matters, where we need to have not merely theory but also practice.*ᵇ*

Knowledge of the human being we designate with a general name 'anthropology', which is not taught at any other university.*ᶜ* Platner has written a scholastic anthropology.¹ But our purpose is merely to draw up rules from the multiplicity that we perceive in human beings, for however incredibly different the human moods appear to be, still there is more regularity here than one would think. We will attempt to bring this play of human actions under rules. Every human being is delighted over a rule; for example, Sharp, an English physician,² says somewhere that in England everyone is coarse except for the innkeepers, while in France everyone is refined except for the innkeepers. The reason is that in England there are many innkeepers, in France few. This rule pleases, even though it may not be grounded in a thoroughgoing way.

We will give no *other*ᵈ explanations of the rules in our anthropology except those that can be observed by everyone, without making the theory complete. We will search out the rules in the manifold experiences that we observe in human beings, without inquiring after their causes.*ᵉ* But scholastic anthropology deals with the most universal rules and their*ᶠ* causes; thus as soon as we have inquired after the causes of rules, we come 25:857 to scholastic anthropology. Our anthropology can be read by everyone, even by women at the dressing-table,*ᵍ* because it has much that is engaging when one everywhere comes across rules that give information, and when one always finds a guiding thread where there is apparent disorder.

Now what are the sources of anthropology? When the incentives of the human being are active, he does not observe them; for example, if he is in the throes of affect,*ʰ* then due to the play of his incentives he cannot observe them. But if he observes himself, then all of the incentives rest, and as a result he has nothing to observe. It is therefore difficult to observe*ⁱ* the mind of the human being, as soon as his incentives are in play. However, this difficulty is diminished once one begins

---

ᵃ *Petersburg* reads: a narrative
ᵇ *Petersburg*: if we need to learn not merely the theory of history [*theorie der Geschichte*], but rather learn it as a principle of prudence.
ᶜ *auf keiner anderen Akademie*
ᵈ "other" is missing in *Menschenkunde*
ᵉ *ohne nach ihrer Ursache zu fragen*
ᶠ "their" is missing in *Petersburg*
ᵍ *sogar von Damen bei der Toilette*
ʰ *wenn er im Affect ist*
ⁱ *Petersburg*: Therefore it is not possible at all

to observe others, because one can be very peaceful near by, and from time to time one can apply these observations to oneself. For since one is already in possession of some knowledge, as a result one can also observe oneself more correctly when the mind is active. Association with many social classes and with cultured human beings[a] is a very fruitful source of anthropology. With uncultured human beings[b] complete humanity is not yet developed, because they do not have the opportunity to unfold all of the attributes of humanity. But if I go to the civilized part[c] of human beings, then I run into the difficulty that the more cultured the human being is, the more he dissembles[d] and the less he wants to be investigated by others. The gentleman does not want to be studied, and in order to *conceal*[e] this cunning he advances with the growth of culture, where one does not simply dissemble but also shows the opposite of oneself.[f] We must therefore observe human beings so that we do not in the least give the appearance of being an observer, and we must also dissemble. One must position oneself as though one would speak entirely without caution and is thereby able to pay attention to everything that others say. Still, it is always difficult to get to know human beings while one is observing their actions, because this demands an educated and acute observer.[g]

Another source of anthropology is history, but of course an anthropology must be there beforehand: for if I do not know what I have to give attention to, then through the historical narrative alone I will not know what I should observe. Can novels, comedies, plays, tragedies (for example, Shakespeare's) deliver anthropological knowledge? Plays and novels always exaggerate that which would otherwise be an attribute of a human being. To be sure, the authors lay the foundations of correct observations, but they produce distorted images; that is, exaggerated characters. By contrast, anthropology will judge plays and novels to determine whether they agree with human nature. Of course there are human beings, but only a few, who know immediately how to establish their knowledge of human beings in comedies and tragedies in a way that is fitting.[h] All morals require knowledge of the human being, so that we do not chatter empty exhortations to people but know how to lead them, in order that they begin to hold moral laws in high regard and turn to their principles.[i] I must know which avenues to human dispositions I can

25:858

---

[a] *Der Umgang mit vielen Ständen und mit gebildeten Menschen*
[b] *Bei rohen Menschen*   [d] *er sich desto mehr verstellt*
[c] *zu dem gesitteten Theile*   [e] *Menschenkunde* reads: dissemble
[f] *Petersburg*: dissimulates, rather than simulates, and this shows the opposite of oneself.
[g] *einen gebildeten und scharfen Beobachter. Petersburg* reads: for this demands that one is a civilized observer.
[h] *Petersburg*: but of which there are only a few, and not all of such keen understanding.
[i] *zu ihren Grundsätzen zu machen*

have in order to bring forth resolutions; knowledge of the human being can give us the opportunity for this, so that the educator and preacher do not produce mere sobs and tears but are in a condition to produce true resolutions. Knowledge of the human being is just as indispensable for politics, for in order to be able to rule human beings one must know human beings. Without knowledge of the human being the sovereign cannot lead such a multitude of social classes; they will all oppose him and he cannot lead them according to his will.

A great utility of anthropology consists in social intercourse,*ª* for anthropology makes us skilled with respect to it, and also gives very beautiful material for conversation. Many materials are not appropriate for social gatherings:*ᵇ* women do not inquire about affairs of state, but nevertheless want to converse, and so one finds that certain observations about the human being please, because every human being can employ them. Because this study is so engaging and so important for everyone, it therefore must rightly be held in high regard. Many authors maintain that it is difficult to cognize oneself. If I am to know myself in comparison with others, and the question is whether I know myself better than others do, then it is evident that each human being must be able to know himself best; because he can search out the ground of all of his thoughts and incentives, and with regard to himself or his own cognition he can

25:859 give no dissimulation or concealment. So I do not know who should know me better than I know myself. But if this means the same as: cognize the human being in general,*ᶜ* then cognition of the human being is admittedly difficult, because if I want to cognize the human being I am unable to compare him with any other being. If I am to know myself according to how I differ from others, I can compare myself with others and therefore know myself more exactly. But if I ask, what is the human being? then I cannot compare him with the animals, because it is a privilege*ᵈ* for him not to be an animal, and we do not know other rational beings. Knowledge of the human being in general is therefore difficult, particular knowledge of a single human being is much easier, and easiest of all is self-cognition, because I cannot conceal myself from myself, and as a result all veils which other human beings hang before us fall away here.

Because there is no other book on anthropology, we will select Baumgarten's metaphysical psychology³ as a guide; the text of a man which is very rich in substance and very short in execution.

. . .

ª *Umgang*
ᵇ *sind nicht für die Gesellschaft*

ᶜ *überhaupt*
ᵈ *ein Vorzug* (or "a sign of superiority")

ON THE CHARACTERISTIC*ᵃ* OF THE HUMAN BEING.

'Character' has a twofold meaning: either it means the character of the thing, or it is a distinguishing mark of a rational being. Thus there can be human beings who as human beings have no character, but nevertheless do have character as things. 'Characteristic' shall here be meant to signify that which marks what is peculiar to the human being; and, more explicitly, according to certain rules and principles. But since 'character' is also used of things, we shall call this character simpliciter.ᵇ Characteristic is either inner or outer; to inner characteristic belong talent, temperament, and character; that is, natural gifts, the way of sensing, and the way of thinking. Talent has so to say a market price, temperament a fancy price,ᶜ and character a moral worth.⁴ The human being is formed according to talent, he is made polite (civilized) according to temperament, and he is moralizedᵈ according to character. To talent belongs natural aptitude,ᵉ or the capacity to learn, and spirit or genius; that is, the faculty of invention. *The word 'natural aptitude' is also used of lifeless things. But with human beings and animals one uses this concept so that it signifies the natural vocation of talent,ᶠ the end for which nature has equipped one subject more than another. Therefore with the human being it depends on taking his natural aptitude into consideration, and so one must track down his inclinations, by which he makes use of his talents. Many a human being has inclinations for which his talent has not grown; however, he cannot allow them to spoil him, which presumably happens through a propensity of the power of imagination. But at bottom we must say that the natural vocation opens up the talent in us for which inclination has inspired the calling.ᵍ But to find this is difficult, so much that many a human being does not himself know his talent. Sometimes something is added to natural aptitude, which is habitual disposition.ʰ Natural aptitude is used by the capacity to learn, whereby one does not invent, and in this way it is distinguished from genius, which is a talent of invention. This is why we help pupils with their expression, because they are still apprentices. The particulars of the natural aptitude of a human being we take from the particular manner by which he acts. Even affectationⁱ is with many a human being a particular manner, which is natural to him. Reason should teach the human being to constrain his facial expressions;ʲ but nature nevertheless gets the upper hand. Natural aptitude is primarily called the passive quality of a human being, to which no hindrances are opposed, and with which*

25:1156

25:1157

ᵃ Charakteristik
ᵇ Charackter schlechthin. The italicized sentences are taken from *Petersburg.*
ᶜ Affectionspreiß
ᵈ formed: *gebildet*; made polite (civilized): *versittigt (civilisirt)*; moralized: *moralisirt*
ᵉ Naturell   *ʰ habituelle disposition*
ᶠ die Naturbestimmung des Talents   *ⁱ Affectation*
ᵍ Beruf   *ʲ Mienen*

one can do what one wants. For instance, if one is called docile, patient, pliable, or agreeable, etc., this means simply, being a dupe for the deceiver.[a] It is the so-called good mind,[b] which, however, does not belong to the way of thinking. The negative good mind is something entirely different from the good heart, which is positive. Nevertheless, the good heart is also distinguished from good character, because the latter acts according to principles of reason. The good mind represents a thing as possible in thoughts, and seeks to make more possible than it can achieve, namely, from pure temperament.[c] We include mind and heart with temperament. He has a good mind who carries out no revenge, and who is not capable of offending. Properly speaking, of women one must not say they have a good mind; in general it is more difficult for men to lead women than women to lead men, because women as dependants[d] often insist on their rights. Not a lot hides behind a good mind, for it can become a scoundrel under the hands of a deceiver, since it exists only through the manageability of others.[e] However, a human being who does not always want to remain a child must have a particular sense.[f] A good heart consists in the actual activity of doing good, though only according to a certain instinct; which distinguishes it from character, which is the activity of doing good from principles. With the good mind no incentives are necessary; because it is only passive, only with the good heart is there always an impulse, if these are also not true principles. Parents and superiors always inquire into the natural aptitude of the child and of the pupil, in order to see which impression they take on best. The Russians have an extremely varied natural aptitude; that is why they are able to do all kinds of things, but not excellently. Subordinates, however, inquire into the temperament of their superiors, so that they know how to accommodate themselves to them.[g]

25:1158

A) THE TEMPERAMENTS.

There cannot be more than four temperaments: these are the sanguine, melancholic, choleric,[b] and phlegmatic; that is, the light-blooded,

---

[a] *kurtz daß, was der dupe für den Betrüger ist*   [b] *gute Gemüth*

[c] The italicized sentences are taken from *Petersburg*. *Menschenkunde* reads: First one must discover the natural aptitude of the human being. It is actually the calling of nature to be one person more than another, and it is more suffering (passive) than doing (active). Properly speaking, he has a good natural aptitude who places no hindrances in our way, gladly undertakes everything, is capable of being led, and has a so-called good mind. However, a good heart is not merely passive, but also active.

[d] *Untergebenen*

[e] *Petersburg* reads: since it exists only in the manageability of the mind through the will.

[f] *einen eigenen Sinn*

[g] *Menschenkunde* reads: subordinates seek to ascertain the talent of their superior, so that they can accommodate themselves to him and be willing to serve him.

[b] *Menschenkunde* reads: choleric, melancholic

the heavy-blooded, the warm-blooded, and the cold-blooded. Because temperament is the source of all sensible desires,[a] all temperament therefore rests on feeling and inclination, thus: 1) the temperaments of feeling, to which the sanguine and melancholic belong; and 2) the temperaments of activity, these are the choleric and phlegmatic. Temperament can be considered, first from the point of view insofar as it is brutish[b] and insofar as it depends on complexion[c]; secondly from the standpoint of an anthropologist, insofar as one considers the sensibility of human beings, or the temperaments of the soul. The mental life[d] contains two parts: 1) sensation and 2) movement. Some examples prove that it may be quite possible that a human being could have sensations but no movement. The temperaments tend to be determined through propensity toward a thing, *however there can be temperament where there is only propensity, and the propensity can be stronger or weaker.*[e] One can make out four[f] composite temperaments, namely: 1) the sanguine-choleric, 2) the melancholic-phlegmatic, 3) the sanguine-phlegmatic, and 4) the melancholic-choleric. A more diverse mixture of temperaments is likewise not possible, because the temperaments that are under one name cannot be placed together, for they are directly opposite. The sanguine is the temperament according to which sensation is very much affected, but little penetrated; melancholic, where sensation is not so much affected but deeply penetrated. Easy irritability and its instability therefore constitute the sanguine person. That is why a sanguine person will, for instance, be heated in anger but not[g] bear a grudge or be intent on vengeance, like the melancholic person.

25:1159

The sanguine person usually has a good mind, but he takes nothing to heart, and does not once take it to mind when he does something vile, since he makes highly favorable representations of the good-heartedness of his mind. He is a person of nothing but good resolutions and decisions, but very unsteady and usually very merry. This mental constitution of the sanguine person is a happy and therefore also a good temperament, because nothing penetrates deeply into it. Sadness with him will never be grief, and anger never vengeance or a deeply rooted rancor. The sanguine person also is not affected; he is good company, but a bad citizen. He is polite without friendship, and loves without being in love. Furthermore, he has a very capable but not an exact memory, and because he is devoted to wit, that is, to a careless but nevertheless conspicuous

25:1160

---

[a] *alle sinnlichen Begierden*   [c] *Complexion*
[b] *thierisch*   [d] *Das geistige Leben*
[e] The italicized phrase is taken from *Petersburg*.
[f] "four" has been inserted by the Academy editors. *Menschenkunde* reads: many.
[g] "not" (*keinen*) has been added by the Academy editors. *Menschenkunde* reads: bear a (*einen*) grudge.

intellectual judgment, he will thus love inspirations much more than insights.[a] He is loved, but not highly esteemed, and he is a bad debt-payer; because he is carefree. He feels little afterwards, because nothing clings to him. (In France there are a lot of sanguine people.) The sanguine person promises everything and keeps nothing, but not from resolution, he also does not in turn regard it as bad in return when one does not keep his word with him. He makes the most important things laughable, and the least important things important for a moment. He does not worry about his fate. He is hard to convert, for the remorse does not last long. He is capable of compassion, or whatever he can do immediately in order to relieve the unhappiness of another, this he does; but it is not his business to think about means.[b]

25:1161   Apart from this one generally understands by the sanguine tempera-ment that which is inclined to fun, and by the melancholic temperament someone who is inclined to sadness, but these are much more the effects rather than the character of temperament; for with the melancholic tem-perament joy enters into the mind just as much as sadness; on the other hand both affect the sanguine temperament only *lightly*.[c] The fact that in the melancholic person joy is greater than in the sanguine person, but sadness with him is greater than joy, is because a human being in the world always finds more opportunity to grieve than to be glad, and through reflection it is compounded in a kind of seriousness. Pleasure does not allow itself to increase as highly as sadness.

---

[a] *weit mehr Einfälle lieben, als Einsichten*
[b] *Petersburg* reads: The sanguine person is thoughtless, careless, hopes [*hoft*] easily, is cheerful and in good temper, because grief arises from reflecting on a sensation. This carefreeness carries hope with it, for nothing disturbs our cheerfulness more than atten-tiveness tied to sorrows. Because no impression goes deeply into the sanguine person, he grants nothing important for more than for a moment. Consequently, he is unsteady, is good-natured, has the best intentions, promises easily, but does not keep his word. He always sees no difficulties, and when they are there he can endure them the very least; however he also assumes there is no further ill, if he does not keep his word. He is friendly, but he will not at will give himself over to a sympathetic grief. This happens not from enmity, but he would rather quickly cheer himself up again. Such an ease does not come into the mind of the melancholy person, for this one always has all kinds of dif-ficulties in his mind. He is unsteady, grants a proper importance to nothing, and makes it a subject of ridicule; to unimportant things on the other hand he grants a comical importance. He has the spirit of bagatelles, which is always very welcome in society. He is sociable, and is also suitable for society; he needs it, for it is his element. He is not a man of evil intentions, but a difficult-to-convert sinner, for his repentance never lasts long. He is the friend of compassion, for compassion affects one quickly, and he also does whatever can be done. But to reflect over it afterwards is too boring for him. He does evil more from willfulness than from malicious gloating, for his mischief consists in a joy over the embarrassment of another. In France there are a lot of sanguine people.
[c] "lightly" is missing in *Menschenkunde*.

The melancholic temperament is not as happy as the sanguine temperament. *Sensation does not strike a melancholic person strongly at all, it is true, but it penetrates all the further, and is felt longer afterwards. He interweaves*[a] *imagination into the middle of everything and reflects on the consequences*[b] *of the thing, gives things an imaginary weight that they do not have, and gives all things an excessive importance. But there is no better means to think about the feeling of the trouble of life than if we deprive things of their importance, and take life for a game that contains little that is satisfactory and lasts a short time. Since we are fitted to lead a peaceful life, we place no great worth in everything, and nothing is important for us except honesty. The melancholic person has a propensity to sadness; he is always full of caution and concern: he cooks up difficulties where other human beings would not notice any at all. As a result, he is a good advice-giver and does not promise easily, but one can rely all the more on his promises. He is not easily satisfied, but he is thankful toward acts of friendship in a lasting way. He is enthusiastic*[c] *in religion, friendship, and patriotism, this fancy*[d] *occurs with a temperament that is always accustomed to brood; that is why he comes into fanaticism,*[e] *for it always depends on the difference of concepts among human beings. There, where one reflects, the sensations penetrate deeply; he dwells on his condition and soon takes something to heart, and is inclined toward depression about it. He is always worried; but nothing frees*[f] *us more from sorrows than if we pass over each point of life with a certain lightness; for the prospects of the future are always adverse. He gives all things a great importance, and this makes him* 25:1162 *always apprehensive about losing them. The melancholic person is often inclined toward stinginess, because he cares, and because he is not satisfied with the cares for the present moment, and sensation penetrates so deeply with him. Sadness does not come from the sensation of ill, but from reflection concerning the state in which one finds oneself. As a result the melancholic person is also called pensive;*[g] *for he gets lost in anticipation of the future. He will always have more sad prospects than pleasant ones, and reflection is in itself a seriousness, and takes away liveliness from the mind; and a human being who is disposed to care also has a propensity to sadness.*[h] The melancholic person is steadfast in friendship; to be sure he demands much from a friend, but he is also ready to render much to him in return. He sticks to that which interests him; he is full of suspicion, and raises difficulties about everything. With regard to promises, the claims to friendship of others, and thankfulness, he is the direct opposite of the sanguine person. He is firm in his resolutions,

---

[a] "interweaves" added by Academy editors.
[b] *Petersburg* reads: consequence.　　　　[c] *enthusiastisch*
[d] *Phantasterei* (added by Academy editors). *Petersburg* reads: *phantasterie*.
[e] *fanatisme. Menschenkunde* reads: He is enthusiastic in religion, in friendship, and in patriotism, out of which ultimately fanaticism springs.
[f] "frees" added by Academy editors.　　　　[g] *tiefsinnig*
[h] The italicized sentences are taken from *Petersburg*.

and does not promise a lot, because to him all things seem very difficult; as a result he also appears to be not as compliant[a] as the sanguine person, because he always wants to keep his promises willingly, and compliance is an excellent quality of social intercourse, but no virtue.

Melancholicus est tenax vir propositi,[b] however this firm resolution can also ultimately become stubbornness and obstinacy. The melancholic person enlarges everything, while the sanguine person diminishes everything. Every [matter of] importance borders on melancholy; the sanguine person is in this case also completely contrary to the melancholic person. After he, so to speak, has lied to himself many times, in the end he no longer believes himself, but it is of great importance that he may trust his resolutions. Because the melancholic person is not as compliant as the sanguine person, he is also not loved as much. His mistrust may well derive in general from the fact that he has a propensity to always fear ill; because the unhappy person, who now may be unhappy owing to external causes or owing to his natural aptitude, also[c] does not begrudge others their happiness. *He is a good patriot.*[d]

25:1163

Depression[e] can pass, but sadness is persevering; for all sadness springs from reflection, and reflection always doubles our feelings. Now the melancholic temperament is disposed to such reflection, and therefore with the melancholic person sadness exists, which with the sanguine person is depression.

The temperaments in respect to activity are the choleric and phlegmatic. Choleric is the temperament by which the powers are set quickly in movement, but do not continue; however phlegmatic is that temperament where the powers are set slowly in movement, but they continue for a long time.

The choleric temperament is the temperament of energetic activity. He (the choleric person) is full of affect, and his activity is set quickly in motion, but it does not continue long. He has strong incentives, which however do not incite continuously, rather, without stopping, they jerk away. He has a propensity to love of honor; he is consumed by a fierce burning fire, but it does not last long. Honor is an incentive where the human being is moved merely through desire, without it there would not be so much natural drive toward actions of general utility: for he who is to be brought to act by means of it must have an uncommon sensitivity toward activity.[f] The choleric temperament also is present with those who have honor in love. Through them great things are accomplished. Because

---

[a] *willfährig*

[b] Trans.: The melancholic person is firm in his resolutions. Cf. Horace, *Carmina* iii.31. "Iustum et tenacem propositi virum." See also Kant, *Lectures on Pedagogy* 9:487, 15:766.

[c] *Petersburg* reads also (*auch*). *Menschenkunde* reads indeed (*doch*).

[d] The italicized sentence is taken from *Petersburg.*

[e] *Betrübniß*   [f] *ungemeine Reitzbarkeit zur Thätigkeit*

the choleric person is busy, he gladly intermingles in everything; he has, if he is a clergyman, the πολυπραγμοσύνη;[a] *he is slightly pugnacious;*[b] *his element is quarrel, and he wants to sink into lifelessness as soon as everything is peaceful. He is more inclined to be magnanimous than just; he does not enjoy doing something from duty, rather he wants to do everything from magnanimity. But if he does me an injustice, to be sure he acknowledges that I am in the right, but he does this under the talent of magnanimity, for if I can nevertheless demand it by right, what in his actions is unjust?*[c] *And we really do find such people, who do this merely from magnanimity. However, such a frame of mind has much that is seductive, and for others it is unbearable. An upright human being must* 25:1164 *already tremble for laying his hands on the rights of other human beings. With such troublesome noble-thinking people, every rogue ultimately finds protection, so that one would like to say, one can protect oneself from a rogue, but not from an honest man, if he has excessive pride. In business the choleric person is always very orderly and energetic, but not hardworking; for patience is not his thing. With him, order rules. He thinks that he is smarter, and also appears smarter to others, than he in fact is. Tone with him is* arrogant,[d] *he is polite, but ceremonious.*[e] *The matters that he brings forward are brought forward with such a decisive manner that one cannot endure the superiority he shows. It is difficult for a human being to know his own tone, and as a result it is also difficult for him to get rid of it. The choleric person speaks oracular wisdom; he is always in need of company*[f] *that has rivalry with him; he entertains company with things that concern common life;*[g] *in all things he searches more splendor than enjoyment, more bombast than content. He dissembles, in order to give an advantageous view of himself. In religious matters he is orthodox, because the orthodox dominate.*[h] *He accommodates himself least of all to orthodoxy, because he continually wants to stick out, and because he finds a great deal of resistance to it. As a result proud people always search for company that is inferior. As a scholar, he is very methodical; but without genius. He is a better relative than friend, because he* promotes[i] *the former from pride. However, as a friend he does not have enough open-heartedness. He has the shortcoming that he does not want to permit others to do toward him that which he permits toward them. As judge he does not allow himself to be bribed, but through humility and mercy*[j] *he easily allows himself to be brought over to the other*

---

[a] Trans.: meddlesome character. (In the manuscript this term is written in Greek letters.)
[b] *er ist leicht händelsichtig*
[c] *in seinen Handlungen ungerecht ist.* (The text is corrupt here.)
[d] Added by the Academy editors. (*Petersburg* reads: *arregant*.)
[e] *feyerlich*   [g] *das bürgerliche Leben*
[f] *eine Gesellschaft*
[h] *Menschenkunde* reads: He almost always entertains company, and in all things searches more for splendor than enjoyment. He is generally orthodox.
[i] Added by the Academy editors (*protegirt*). (*Petersburg* reads: *protgirt*.)
[j] *Dehmuth und Gnade*

side. If he himself is in a dispute with someone he fights vehemently against him, until the other implores him to give up.^a Two or more choleric people do not accommodate themselves well in company: for they all want to assert their judgments, and in this way a dispute often arises. The choleric person is inclined to dissimulation, in general one characterizes him through the propensity to quarrel and pride; but these are only the results of temperament. He expresses everything with much pomp, and he talks too much; the drive to honor is his ruling passion. He is very vehement; generally speaking he is reasonable.^b It is the temperament of the greatest dissimulation; on the contrary the phlegmatic person believes he is less than he really is.^c The gait of the cholerics is always

25:1165

somewhat stiff, they walk, so to speak, always on stilts, and their language is somewhat pompous.^d They always desire to have people around them to whom they can show their wit. They are usually very orderly. But where a very forced order occurs, there is also always a weak mind. The choleric person often is wrong in tone, although at the same time in the thing itself he is right. As a result, he is not good company, but he is a good master of the house; he is very methodical and seldom a genius. As a result of the vehement incentives that are located in the choleric, it follows that he easily gets angry. From this irritability of activity^e it follows that a choleric is created for great things, because greatness always requires courage. Precisely for this reason such a human being also has many shortcomings; for instance, he enjoys interfering in all kinds of matters, as a result he is also inclined toward quarrel and conflict. Such a human being does not enjoy hearing of duties, rather he very much enjoys accomplishing everything out of his own free movement,^f as if from magnanimous beneficence. He gladly takes people under his protection without interest, merely in order to confer protection. He works energetically, but not diligently. He is polite, but nevertheless, because he asserts everything as something incontestable, one finds in him a desire to contradict. Two or more cholerics are not good in company,

---

^a *Menschenkunde* reads: If he is a judge, he does not allow himself to be bribed, but through humility and petition for mercy he allows himself to be brought over to the defendant's side at once. If he himself is in dispute with someone, he fights vehemently against him; if he is implored, then he gives up at once.

^b *verständig*

^c The italicized sentences are taken from *Petersburg*. *Menschenkunde* reads: In general one characterizes the choleric person by the propensity to anger and pride, however these are only the results of temperament. The choleric person expresses everything with much pomp, and he talks a great deal; the drive to honor is his ruling passion. As a result he is very vehement and generally reasonable, however he always appears to be more than he really is. On the other hand the phlegmatic person tends to appear to be less than he in fact is. The choleric temperament is a temperament of the greatest representation (*Vorstellung*).

^d *hat etwas Gedrechseltes*   ^f *aus frier eigner Bewegung*
^e *diese Reizbarkeit der Thätigkeit*

for both want to assert their judgments, and in this manner dispute often arises.

– The phlegmatic temperament consists in the fact that the movements of the mind begin slowly and weakly, but continue for a long time. The phlegmatic person is cold-blooded, and his character is apathy or dispassionateness.[a]   25:1166 *One can consider all temperaments as weakness or as strength. The sanguine temperament can be considered as weakness, insofar as the impressions do not last long; and as strength because the sanguine person is affected very easily. The choleric temperament is weakness, insofar as the mind is easily disturbed;*[b] *strength, insofar as the human being is vigorous and resolves easily. Phlegma as weakness is insensitivity, laziness, uselessness, or vileness, since one never earnestly presses after something, so that one also does not once grasp something with zeal either; it is complete uselessness and action without incentives; the* South Americans *have something like this, so that with them even the sexual drive is weak. Phlegma is almost never considered as strength; rather it consists in the fact that the mind is not subjected to any violent movements, so that the movement continues all the longer. Such a human being is on his guard. Here phlegma is a power, namely, one that depends more on mass than on velocity. The phlegmatic person becomes warm slowly, but retains the warmth for a long time. Phlegma is one of the most glorious properties of a human being; for it makes good on resolution,*[c] *and that is why such a person is of unchanging disposition. Phlegma in temperament makes one very happy; for it always considers the vanity of things;*[d] *and if one begins to consider a thing according to its lasting quality one will be very indifferent toward a great many things, and thus we can actually be happy through a defect of sensation. One can therefore call it the happy temperament; since the sanguine temperament, which is also cheerful, has just as much opportunity to grieve. The cold-blooded person has little to regret. He has a cold-bloodedness through principles, which becomes habitual through inclination. Nature has given self-rule to many a human being through happy phlegma, whereby he carries out actions that come close to wisdom. It gives the human being a special superiority over others, and an irritable human being loses all composure through an opponent with phlegma. And he immediately feels his inferiority. If the conversation gets heated (where usually the tone is to blame), and one person is angry, and where it is difficult to get into good tone again, there phlegma is preferable; for such a human being shows an evident superiority! He*[e] *is not brilliant, arouses no jealousy; and precisely because of this he advances the furthest of all. Moreover, here there*   25:1167 *is true domestic bliss in marriage. He rules there with a certain good humor that never goes away. A human being who has phlegma is occasionally taken for a philosopher; and insofar as he is inclined toward reflection he can actually*

---

[a] *Affectlooßigkeit* (or "freedom from affect")   [d] *der Sachen Nichtigkeit*
[b] *leicht aus der Faßung gesetzt wird*   [e] *Petersburg* reads: it.
[c] *beweiset fest den Vorsatz*

accomplish by himself what philosophy accomplishes through much reflection.[a]
The phlegmatic temperament is most subject to bad repute, but because
phlegma, provided that it should be a temperament, consists precisely in
the temperature or moderation and relaxation of the heat of the affects,
it is therefore happy, as much for those who possess it as for others, and
the phlegmatic temperament can with average reason reach the purpose
that great heads miss, since they give themselves up to rapturous affects.
It carries with itself a great reliability; because here *nothing*[b] is attempted
suddenly, thus *also nothing*[c] is carried out hastily. The phlegmatic person
does not frighten easily, and has *uncommon perseverance with weighty matters.*[d] To be sure, in friendship he will show nothing glimmering, and as
a result he is not greatly loved, but he is nevertheless always very steadfast and loyal. He is diligent toward work, although at the same time he
always has a propensity toward laziness, and usually manages only with
desires.[e] He is seldom bored, but he is boring for others. As a scholar he
will be a good compiler. In his domestic state he easily allows himself to
be governed, because it is easier to allow oneself to be governed than to
govern oneself, though the choleric is of an entirely opposite opinion. If
one wants to call him good, he is of course only negatively good, namely
harmless.[f]

*A habitual disposition that depends on education is often passed off as tem-
perament, and it is hard to distinguish from temperament. Still, no single
circumstance can entirely suppress temperament, rather it surely always breaks
through. For instance, women should be freely educated,[g] and yet many are not
choleric. Misanthropy is not a temperament under which, as is believed, enmity
toward human beings is understood (which is actually signified according to the
word), rather it occurs when one regards all other human beings as evil.*

25:1168   *The Indians say:*[5] *the way of life makes a businessman phlegmatic, a scholar
and clergyman melancholic, the soldier choleric, and the craftsman sanguine.
Craftsmen are usually cheerful people, for their cares usually go on for only a
day.*[b]

---

[a] The italicized sentences are taken from *Petersburg*.
[b] *Menschenkunde* reads: something.   [c] *Menschenkunde* reads: something.
[d] *Menschenkunde* reads: of uncommon gravity toward weighty matters.
[e] *Wünschen*   [g] *soll frey erzogen werden*
[f] *unschädlich*
[b] The italicized sentences are taken from *Petersburg. Menschenkunde* reads: If one wants to
call the phlegmatic person good, then he is only negatively good, that is to say harmless.
The phlegmatic temperament is that wherein the sensations begin slowly and weakly, but
increase and last a long time. The character of this temperament is apathy, which is not
lack of feeling, but rather a certain patience. Phlegma can be considered as strength and
as weakness: considered as weakness it is an art of insensibility, inactivity; considered as
strength it consists in the fact that the mind is capable not of vehement but slow sensation.
It is a power that flows from the natural aptitude. It is warmed slowly, and is set in motion,
but it lasts very long; the phlegmatic person therefore reflects on everything, has a firm

With regard to religion, the choleric person belongs to the ruling church, *which is*[a] orthodox, the sanguine is inclined toward free-thinking,[b] the melancholic toward enthusiasm, and the phlegmatic toward superstition, which is servile and must be completely distinguished from enthusiasm; in spite of the fact that both of the latter have a religious delusion.[c] In public office the choleric is inclined toward domination; the sanguine would be *absent-minded*,[d] the melancholic very meticulous, and the phlegmatic would be a yes-man,[e] and gladly leave everything as it was before. In the sciences the choleric is thorough but unimportant,[f] the melancholic profound, the sanguine generally intelligible, and the phlegmatic very detailed, but nevertheless without much content. As a writer the sanguine person is witty, the choleric stilted,[g] the melancholic is an original, perhaps also humorous, but dark; the phlegmatic shows much book-learning and cites a great deal.[b]

25:1169

B) CHARACTER IN GENERAL.

There are in fact human beings who in respect to their actions and their intentions are not determined at all, and who do not act according to any maxims at all, thus they also have no character. Still, a human being is nevertheless praised if he has a definite character, even if this character is an evil one, because here more capability[i] is found than with a human being who has no character at all, though the latter may have a good mind and heart anyway. Character actually rests on the power of the

resolve, and an unchangeable way of thinking. As a result one can rely on him. Phlegma in temperament is happy. A human being who has phlegma is occasionally taken for a philosopher, and insofar as he is inclined toward reflection he can actually bring about by himself what a philosopher brings about through much reflection. This temperament is not illustrious, and one often advances the furthest with it. For the household phlegma is very happy, for it is a continuous good humor there. It is difficult to distinguish what education or natural aptitude brings forth in the human being. The Indians remark that the way of life can make the businessman phlegmatic, the scholar melancholy, the soldier choleric, and the craftsman sanguine. Habitual inclinations can often appear to be false temperaments; as, for example, misanthropists, under which one understands not enmity toward human beings, but rather when one regards all other human beings as evil.

[a] "which is" added by Academy editors.
[b] *Petersburg* reads: is easily a ridiculer.
[c] toward superstition … delusion: *Menschenkunde*. *Petersburg* reads: is indifferent.
[d] *zerstreut*. The Academy editors suggest: disorderly. *Menschenkunde* reads: orderly.
[e] *ein Ja-Herr*. *Petersburg* reads: mechanical, and a yes-man.
[f] *unwichtig*. *Petersburg* reads: incorrect (*unrichtig*).
[g] *Stelzen*. *Petersburg* reads: prideful (*Stöltzen*), is thereby methodical and clear.
[b] *Petersburg* reads: shows his arduousness in a great book-learning, for which one, e.g., lays the blame on the German.
[i] *mehr Tüchtigkeit*

understanding, and also can often be stimulated through self-love; on the other hand mind and heart rest simply on feelings, and belong to temperament. One should be sensible with regard to the education of children to bring forth a character in them, even if this would not always be directed toward the good.

Character is that which marks a resolution in principles in the human being. A caricature is an exaggeration of character; thus there are, for example, comedies. In character lies the ground of all formations[a] of the human being. Character has an inner moral worth. For character a will is required on which one can definitely rely, a settled way of thinking and not merely a feeling; because he who does not have a definite character is overcome by moods. A human being of genuine evil character is terrible, but is nevertheless admired.[b]

25:1170 The first marks of a character consist in the fact that the human being fulfills what he himself promises. He who does not do this cannot trust himself. One must practice, so that one has firm resolutions. If nature has given no predisposition toward a character to someone; that is, no firmness in principles, then it is extraordinarily difficult to acquire a character. A human being without character never makes a definite person, with each opportunity he is another human being; thus a human being must take hold of principles with regard to his expenses.[c]

A bad character is distinguished from an evil one. Under a bad human being one understands a human being without honor; for example, he who lies. Bad character consists therefore in a lack of love of honor, and, what is more, in the relations in which we stand toward each other; however, falseness and faithlessness in friendship is a malicious character if one plans something evil, and, what is more, does so according to principles.

One calls a human being wild who has obtained no training,[d] which consists precisely in the taming of our natural animal independence. But if someone has not received any culture or instruction, *which is something positive*,[e] then he is crude;[f] on the contrary if the same person is not capable of culture with regard to the understanding, he is coarse[g] when this occurs with regard to morals.

The good-naturedness of a human being from instinct, feeling (sentiment), and from character are very different. With a human being of the first kind there is no security; sentiment shall consist in the feeling for the good, and what character is has already been said above.[b] With

---

[a] *alle Ausbildungen*
[b] *bewundert*
[c] *in Ansehung seiner Ausgaben*
[d] *Zucht*
[e] The italicized phrase is taken from *Petersburg*, and is missing in *Menschenkunde*.
[f] *roh. Petersburg* reads: stupid (*dumm*).　　[b] See the beginning of this section.
[g] *grob*

the fair sex one must primarily try to ground a good sentiment, but they may never bring it up to good character, which on the other hand one must demand from the male sex. With woman feelings of honor must take the place of principles. Education must ground this with woman, and it must ground principles with man.

A human being of character has his maxims in all things, in friendship, actions, and religion.[a] A human being who wants to claim that he has a character because he does not do anything from fashion does not nearly have a character, for it can simply be a principle to follow fashion.

The maxims of a true character are:

1) Love of truth. All lies make one contemptuous, and a liar has no character.

2) If someone promises something, then he keeps his word; that is, faithfulness toward one's enemies.[b]

3) He does not flatter, for a flatterer has too little worth, since he allows the influence of others to make far too much an impression on him.[c]

A noble character is he who does something meritorious; all of his maxims are principles, where the private good is placed after the common good. Such a human being sees with his good intentions that he never presents a scandal to anyone that an imitator could find.[d] He does not repeat something to anyone that has been said to his disadvantage, while the other likes to be indiscreet or very vulgar. In general it is already somewhat vulgar when a human being gladly wants to know what others say of him, for it is uncomfortable to everyone to hear what others have said about him that is unfavorable, and this cannot fail to become evident. A noble human being is impelled by true love of honor, so that he is not enticed to call good that which is in fact unworthy, even when it is privileged by his actions.[e] If this were to take place universally among all human beings, it would be an immediate punishment for baseness. A human being has no character if he is directed by what other people say, and if what others say is of great importance to him. A human being who is good, but only insofar as the judgment of another human being determines him to act, can be a good common man, but not an excellent character. Our moral doctrines spoil character badly

25:1171

---

[a] The Academy editors have deleted a short sentence from *Menschenkunde* after this point.

[b] *Treue gegen seine Feinde*

[c] *Petersburg* reads, in place of "The maxims … on him": The general marks of a morally good character are as follows. The first maxim is truthfulness. A liar has no character. All lies make one contemptible, even if one were also still so innocent; when one makes a promise one must keep one's word. The liar does not crawl. Hypocrisy goes against the dignity of the human being himself, and inner character presupposes a certain pride. But the good-naturedness of character is most contrary to falseness; a false human being is not only a bad human being, but also evil.

[d] *daß Nachahmer finden könte*

[e] *nicht in prolection nimt, noch durch seinen Umgang privilegirt.*

in this way, because they are all based on sentimentality.[a] For we can do what is good from love or from duty. Duty has its definite principles, but love has allurements that we can seldom explain, and which do not last.[b] Additionally,
25:1172 *a religion that is grounded on[c] fear of punishment contributes much to the spoiling of the foundation of character. However, certain conditions[d] contribute to grounding a character, or even to eradicating it. Poets are usually without all character, because they can go into every character in imagination. The speculative scholar, Hume says,[6] has a good character, because he abandons entirely the incentives that move the rest of the world to depart from natural rules. The <u>soldier's profession</u> gives rise to an open-heartedness in character. The clerical profession has a strong propensity to dissimulation. Deficiency in character is not yet an evil character. Something that corrupts character can arise from natural instincts, and there character finds only many hindrances springing up. As far as evil in character is concerned, one distinguishes it as follows. A human being is a bad human being and an evil human being. Bad, depraved, is baseness of the way of thinking and duplicity. Wickedness in the character of the human being is hate and pleasure in others' misfortunes. The source of these different predispositions is very hidden.[e] People of the first kind are incurable, one could sooner bring an enemy of humanity to what is right than a dissembler.[f] Evil in character must rest on principles according to which, if they were to be set going, there would have to be evil in the world universally. For instance, the common man must have nothing, for he can be more easily ruled. Buyers beware,[g] all human beings are secretly villains, and virtue is a false pretence, and so forth. Good character does not come from nature, but must be acquired. To be sure, one has the predisposition for it, but these seeds of nature must be cultivated through understanding and reason, so that principles emerge. The acquisition of good character in the human being occurs through education, and just as male[h] character rests on principles, so the grounding of female character is the feeling of honor. The man says always, "What will people think?"; the woman, "What will they say?" Man must have a firmness*
25:1173 *according to rules in character, in order not to bring contempt upon himself, for this one's own reflection must come in, in order to eradicate mistakes which have crept in by means of education. One must reflect on principles and thereby remove mistakes from one's undertakings; once one has grasped principles, then one must make these engagements very gravely and solemnly. One must always be aware of principles once they are adopted, and then one must try to bring it about that the human being does not despise himself.*

---

[a] *Empfindsamkeit*
[b] *die sich* nicht *conserviren*. (*Nicht* – not – has been added by the Academy editors.)
[c] Reading, *per* the Academy editors' suggestion, *auf* instead of *aus*.
[d] *Stände* (this word is missing in *Petersburg*).   [f] *als eine faussete*
[e] *sehr verborgen*   [g] *Käufer thun die Augen auf*
[h] "male" added by Academy editors (*Petersburg* reads: natural).

One must distinguish modesty according to instinct from modesty according to principles. The former type of modesty shows itself in this way, that for the sake of a friend one is honest, but also deceitful. But it is called Amicus usque ad aram.[a] *One can also distinguish the good-naturedness of instinct from the good-naturedness of character, in benevolence, compassion, and the like. A maliciousness of instinct*[b] *is no doubt innate, but not an evil character.*

One and the same human being can have a good private character and nevertheless be useless in public life, and this indicates a narrow-minded human being.[c] *Even in religion conscientiousness is the actual religion of the way of thinking, devotion lies often only in the manner. Simplicity is ordinarily only an external decorum;*[d] *but good character, without which everything is affectation, occurs only with people who are well aware of their inner worth. If nature has not given one the predisposition to character, then it is extraordinarily difficult to acquire one. A human being without character never constitutes a person, rather with each opportunity he is a different human being. Therefore a human being must grasp principles; for instance, with regard to his expenditures.*[e]

One also frequently finds human beings who affect a character. One is honest from honor, upright from conscience, and just from principles. One also more often calls character the funds (it is actually the natural predisposition toward character), that is, the ground of the soul. A refined or well-understood honor, or a proper concept of honor, can be the greatest analogue of a good character, although it itself is nevertheless not a good character.

25:1174

The natural predisposition of character is innate, but it demands a great deal of activity and attention in order to develop into the true character of a human being. There are certain defects in character which, if they are not corrected in youth, also remain in old age; *but a deceitful temperament is not easily altered.*[f] True character very rarely manifests in the human being itself before the fortieth year, *at that time all acts of thoughtlessness cease, and the human being has thereupon acquired enough strength to attend to them.*[g] *Before this age,*

---

[a] Trans.: being a friend as far as the altar. See also 15:488.

[b] *Eine Bosärtigkeit des Instinckts*   [d] *nur ein äußerer Anstand*

[c] *ein bornirter Mensch*

[e] *in Ansehung seiner Ausgaben.* The italicized sentences are taken from *Petersburg. Menschenkunde* reads: A noble character is the way of thinking when one sets less value on the private good than on the common good; further when through one's example one never gives rise to evil. It is something base to always inquire what human beings say about one, and it is also just as base to report to others what is said of them in society. To conceal this is something noble. Still nobler is the way of thinking where one does not call good that which is evil, and does not grant privileges to base conduct. Education and one's own reflection are the means to acquire a character. Moral discourses and seizing hold of good, well-grounded principles can also be added to the means.

[f] *but . . . easily* taken from *Petersburg.*   [g] *darauf zu attendiren*

insight is not mature enough to distinguish true interest from apparent interest.[a]

Character is not, like temperament itself, a predisposition to happiness; it merely determines the worthiness to be happy[7] – that is why one also says not a happy character but a good character. Because character is a matter of free choice, we also do not view it as a natural gift, but as our own merit. By virtue of a good character the human being is not always *invariably*[b] happy, but worthy of happiness. If the good that we have in us does not rest on principles, then it is transitory and of no use.

We characterize a human being either through that which is not attributable to him himself but is a gift of fortune, or we can also characterize him through the innermost part of the human being which constitutes him. One calls the former merita fortunae.[c] *But the real character of the human being consists in the relation of the human being through that which properly belongs to him, and is ascribable neither to nature nor to fortune. This character consists in the fundamental predisposition of the will to make good use of all talents, and*[d] *to command them well with one's temperament. By virtue of a good character the human being is author of his own worth; he can also replace lack of talent with industry, and this must arise from character. In character lies the foundation of the improvement of all of our talents; one calls this the will, and it is the*

25:1175 *predisposition to use one's talents towards the best ends. With the human being it depends on whether he has a character, or whether he has a good or a bad character. Talent determines the market price. Temperament determines the fancy price, and character determines the inner moral worth of a human being.*[8] *A great ruler judges his subjects according to the market price, and this also happens in other cases. We love human beings according to the fancy price, according to the way we see that their inclinations are affected. Temperament is the foundation of good and bad humor,*[e] *but character constitutes inner worth. Character is that by which we can always distinguish a human being. There must be a definite way of thinking, on which one can always safely rely. "Ill-humored" comes from "lunatic"; that is, changeable according to the quarter of the moon, fickle.*[f] *But character alone fixes in the human being the concept of his person.*

The question arises, whether a human being everywhere has a character? It should be attended to beforehand, without yet looking at his constitution. A human being of true evil character is a terrible thing, but if he simply

---

[a] The italicized passages are taken from *Petersburg*.
[b] *allemahl* (*Petersburg*). *Menschenkunde* reads: *einmal* (once).
[c] Trans.: the merit of fortune.   [e] *Laune*
[d] *und. Petersburg* reads: *um* (in order to).
[f] fickle: *wetterwendisch* (literally, "as changeable as the weather"); lunatic: *lunatisch*; ill-humored: *launisch*.

has a firm evil character he nevertheless acquires admiration. The quality of character therefore rests on the firmness of principles. Many human beings are such that they can never settle on a principle, but wander about as directed by mere circumstances^a and never reflect on principles. But one can commit all vices from pure kindness,^b the firmness of principle takes place only where the human being can firmly forsake the promise that he has made to himself. But if a person has often lied, then eventually he no longer believes himself. A human being who loves procrastination[9] *is so weak that in the end he has no more real resolution, for he does not trust himself, if a firm resolution will not produce a change in him.^c* If nature has not given a predisposition or an inner fund toward character to a person, but he is a game of instincts and impulse, then it is difficult to reach him through art. *Character is therefore the firm attachment to principles once they have been grasped.^d* Each person must therefore from youth onward begin to fulfill his principles that he has grasped once. Because a human being who loses confidence in himself is for that reason miserable. To attain that end one must point out the contempt of a human being without character, for without character the human being is always another person. A continuous effort towards the determination and observance of principles must therefore be exercised.

25:1176

Good-naturedness of temperament does not yet make the good man. A human being is good-natured if he promises compliance and friendship, but the good must be located in character. Much is needed in order to be a good man, and to cultivate principles that the will has most tenderly adopted. A man of principles has maxims, and the grounding of maxims presupposes a strong soul. Even wickedness in temperament can nevertheless be a good character, therefore it is difficult to distinguish wickedness in temperament from the predisposition to a good character. If a human being simply has reason, then usually the predisposition to good character is there. We love a human being because of his heart, we value^e him because of his character. *Good-naturedness in temperament is a painting in watercolors, and looks beautiful but does not last long. A rigid disposition^f often looks like character but it is not, because character must come from reason and be attachment to principles.* Thus, for instance, Charles XII's rigid disposition[10] was not character. There is also an emulation of character, where the human being displays himself as an eccentric, without conforming to the changes in public taste.^g *He chooses certain habits, which he remains firm about.*^h

---

^a *unter lauter Anwendungen*   ^b *aus purer Gefälligkeit*
^c *ob ein gefaßter Vorsatz sich nicht bey ihm ändern werde*
^d *Anhänglichkeit an einmahl gefaßte Grundsätze*
^e *schätzen*   ^g *Veränderungen des Geschmacks in publico*
^f *Ein steifer Sinn*
^h The italicized sentences are taken from *Petersburg.*

JUDGMENT OF THE INNER HUMAN BEING THROUGH THE OUTER HUMAN BEING, OR OF PHYSIOGNOMY.[a]

25:1177 *Physiognomy, which provides the material to this science, considers the structure of the body, the shape of the face, and the features of the face. Although body and soul make up a complete unity, nevertheless here, so far as we know, no natural connection can occur. However, Shaftesbury notes in his philosophical writings[11] that in the face of every human being, even the ugliest, there is such an originality and regularity that, as soon as we would want to change only something in it, we would ruin everything. This also appears to be confirmed by the fact that if one looks at many paintings, one can easily distinguish which portrait is derived from a living human being, and which merely from fantasy. So much peculiarity[b] lies in the features of the face of each human being. Nevertheless, physiognomy is very deceptive.[c] With the human being we can point out:*

1. The shape of the body, the regularity of the structure is like harmony. A strong, robust human being who feels superiority in himself often misuses his powers, and that is why often a human being is merely peaceful, because he feels too weak to rise above others.

2. Posture and looks are merely modifications of the shape of the body. In a face one can justly distinguish the shape of the face and the features of the face. Lichtenberg,[12] the great rival of Lavater,[13] believes that the features of the face are not at all original, but depend partly on education, partly on habit. However, if one considers the matter carefully, one will[d] find that he is incorrect about this. Because then physiognomy will not be able to be brought under rules, it would not be able to be propagated or communicated to others, this acuteness[e]

25:1178 *would also not be of utility to the human race. Gesticulation, articulation, and modulation[f] determine speech. In gesticulation the facial expressions[g] are the chief thing, which in the whole world signify one and the same state of mind.*

Very great regularity in structure indicates an average human being who is proficient in all fields but excels in none; this also agrees with our concepts of the beautiful; for the beautiful must lie more in fantasy than in

---

[a] The following section is taken from *Petersburg*, but similar material – arranged in a different order – can be found in *Menschenkunde*, pp. 349–352. The section title in *Menschenkunde* reads: Can we recognize the inner from the outer in the human being? See also 15:876.

[b] *So viel eigenthümliches*

[c] *Menschenkunde* reads: So much lies in the physiognomy of each human being, but it is also very deceptive.

[d] *Menschenkunde* reads: will; *Petersburg* reads: would.

[e] *Scharfsichtigkeit* (*Menschenkunde* reads: *Scharfsinnigkeit* – sagacity).

[f] *Menschenkunde* reads: Gesticulation (conversation by gestures), articulation (the manner of pronunciation) and modulation (the manner of delivery).

[g] *die Mienen*

nature, and more concepts of beauty lie in the average of the proportion of the parts and members of the body. One has in one's imagination a middle height (which one abstracts from the height of some 1,000 human beings), whereupon one misses all human beings, and the Greeks appear to have had this proper ideal of beauty; nevertheless this average of beauty must be different in each nation.

Concerning human beings who characterize geniuses by means of their size, mainly with genius of the power of imagination, one finds that they have something disproportionate in their body; for example, Socrates, Pope.[14] Hay,[15] in his book on deformity, in which he describes the good-naturedness of a deformed person and the wickedness of people of good structure, proves that faces which one would like to explain as deformed have such a proportion that one sees immediately that this depends on the originality of nature. It has been observed that the proportion of each human being lies in germs,[a] and thus a true proportion is always there, because one cannot change something in any painting without producing something unnatural for an expert. Hogarth[16] has made copper engravings of the character of the human being that are the best the art of copper-engraving has ever produced. This came from the fact that he went through nature, took everything out of it, and fabricated nothing. One can change nothing in the face of a human being without giving him an entirely different face. There is no true beauty in nature. What we call beautiful is in the concept according to proportion.[b] The properly beautiful has a hidden proportion. By means of this principle we will move on to love of human beings, and there all seeming deformities vanish. True deformities are remnants[c] of vice.

An entirely regular face says nothing at all.

25:1179

In women the foreheads are all more spherical than in men, where they are flatter. If the hairs of the human being are so overgrown that the side hairs go together with the eyebrows, then there is little spirit.[d] A rhinoceros nose;[17] that is, a gable on the nose, should indicate a mocker; if it points upward, a proud human being.[e] The features of the face must be distinguished from the expressions, which are attitudes.[f] Should one say: expressions are facial features set in a game; or are facial features fixed expressions? Nature has not equipped us with facial features for expressions; instead, expressions fix facial features. Lichtenberg[18] is for the most part right in his opposition to all physiognomy, but one cannot dismiss it altogether. He says among other things that through facial expressions one can indicate the wickedness of a human being, not natural wickedness, but rather depraved wickedness, for if one has indulged in excess

---

[a] *Keime*
[b] *ist im Begriff nach proportion*
[c] *Überreste*
[d] *wenig Geist*
[e] *Menschenkunde* reads: A little pit in the middle of the nose indicates a ridiculer; if it is at the top, a proud person.
[f] *Gebährden*

for a long time, then one assumes such expressions, and these ultimately become persistent facial features. In each human face there are incontestably original features, but in upbringing ᵃ the features get distorted ᵇ according to the diversity of temperament. Still, he says that we are in need of an art of interpretation of these characters. All affects produce certain expressions; and these are the same with each nation. They are natural signs of our emotion,ᶜ and just as there is diversity in temperaments, so also facial features are predisposed more for one affect than for the other. If facial expressions did not arise through temperament, then it could come about that a human being could have an expression of sadness with the most cheerful incident. Upbringing ultimately produces expressions which turn into facial features. Country people are instantly recognizable by their faces. The face puts on different wrinkles when one converses with one's equals than when one converses with farmers. One can also perceive a difference

25:1180 *between a literary person and a townsman, for study gives the mind a habitual direction, which is revealed in expressions and which determines many kinds of facial features.*

One says of a human being that he has a common face; many a face resists refinement completely, and this indicates rudeness.ᵈ Where devotion to certain religions is observed, human beings through diligence in observation of the religions can receive a facial feature which makes them recognizable, for the pious expressions and downcast eyes disguise them, this holds particularly with women, who easily retain the expressions that they assume in church.ᵉ There are human beings who normally do not squint, but when they explain something that it is a lie they look at their nose. Painters distinguish character and caricature. These caricatures are exaggerations of character, but they are not to be sneezed at. Hogarth's copper engravings are like this, and so are the characters in all of our comedies.

Certain human beings have distorted faces, because they express a character until it has been exaggerated.ᶠ –. Physiognomy *is something natural and is practiced by everyone, because it often proves true. If it fails, then one forgets this like the prophecies of the calendar. There is something obscure in it which has been given to us as a warning,ᵍ but from which we are not yet able to grasp the whole way of thinking of a human being, for there is no universal mark in it. Physiognomy is useful in marriages, because by analogy from the way of thinking of the relatives one can infer to the way of thinking of the beloved. However, one must not judge people immediately by facial features, if*

ᵃ *Erziehung*   ᶜ *Gemüthsbewegung*
ᵇ *verziehen sich*   ᵈ *Grobheit*
ᵉ *Menschenkunde* reads: As concerns devotion to religion or observances, one can always discern which religion people belong to according to their expressions; particularly women, who easily retain the expressions that they assume in church.
ᶠ *bis ins übertriebene*
ᵍ *Es ist uns darin was Dunkeles zur Warnung gegeben.*

one has not already examined them. For imagination sometimes does the most work.[a]

Physiognomy is extremely deceptive if one only wants to consider it for the evil that malicious faces have. It is dangerous when judges want to derive guilt from the expressions of the delinquent; for expressions normally tell[b] *nothing of the most abominable villain. A certain physician remarks, in his book Travels through England,*[19] *that all criminals have strongly angular bones, so that a certain self-confidence may have led them to depart from straight paths, also they were normally brunette.*[c]   25:1181

If one wishes to practice physiognomy, then to be sure it is an advantageous undertaking; however, we have almost entirely closed our eyes on the matter. If one hears of an evil deed from someone, one believes right away one can see it in his face, so great is the deception here. When someone is led to the place of execution,[d] *everyone notices roguish expressions on him. But if you were also only to feel such fear of death, the laughing in your expressions would no doubt become distorted, too.*[e]

THE CHARACTER OF NATIONS[f]

The variety of natural gifts among the many diverse nations cannot be explained entirely by incidental causes,[g] but must lie in the nature of the human being himself, because this variety also often occurs under identical circumstances. The incidental causes are 1) physical; to these belong the climates (climatic zones) and domestic products, and 2) moral.

If a people in no way improves itself over centuries, then one may assume that there already exists in it a certain natural predisposition which it is not capable of exceeding. The Hindus, the Persians, the Chinese, the Turks, and in general all Oriental peoples belong to this group. However, we can follow here merely the speculative interest of our reason, and must give up the practical interest.

The sources from which one can characterize all peoples are the following: 25:1182
natural aptitude, spirit, instinct, and discipline. Natural aptitude and instinct belong to character proper, from which affects rise, but spirit or discipline or

---

[a] *macht zuweilen das mehrste. Menschenkunde* reads: In marriage physiognomy is really good, for from the parents one can draw a conclusion about the daughter, if she resembles them. However, one must not immediately judge people according to facial features, if one has not already examined them, for the imagination sometimes constitutes the most in it.

[b] following the Academy editors' suggestion of *sagen. Petersburg* reads: *sorgen* (care).

[c] *Menschenkunde* reads: A physician published a book under the title "Remarks on a Trip through England." He says in it that when he has visited prisons he has found that the criminals have large bones and had become brown.

[d] *Gerichtsplatz*

[e] The italicized sentences are all taken from *Petersburg*.

[f] This section title is taken from *Petersburg*.

[g] *gelegentliche Ursachen*

training do not, for these are merely negative and are properly that which set limits to the dynamic powers.[a] The character of the lowest rank is: a great deal of natural aptitude and a great deal of discipline. This is characteristic of the German nation, which, however, nevertheless also has spirit. Character of a higher kind would be: a great deal of instinct and spirit, only a great deal of instinct without discipline destroys everything, on the other hand for natural aptitude [and] docility,[b] it does not appear necessary to have a great deal of discipline. Spirit; that is, the originality of talent added to natural aptitude, makes a great mind. All Tartarian nations have a great deal of instinct, but little discipline, and as a result they always remain wild and uncultivated. It may also be that natural aptitude is not missing in them, but great instinct hinders them at it. The French do not have as much discipline as the Germans, but they have somewhat more spirit. The people of India[c] have very little instinct but a great deal of natural aptitude and discipline. However, they have given us the most important and most numerous discoveries; for example, the art of writing, the art of counting with ten numerals, and even gun powder, which was known earlier in Hindustan than in Europe. The Greeks have little discipline.[d] France is the land of taste in social intercourse; that is, of good manners (der Conduite).[e] Liveliness for them is what affect is for peoples. With them levity[f] is completely at home; that is, they do not like to persevere in a condition, they like to talk a great deal, as a result they often say something that is entirely irrelevant; *the excesses which their own authors accuse them of are preeminently frivolité,[g] which is a certain willfulness to exaggerate or understate things.[h]* The Point d'honneur[i] and gallantry are two inventions of the French. The latter is mainly the delicacy of feeling of the woman. Etourderie[j] is an art of boldness, and with the French the effect of liveliness. Good manners are nowhere as universal as in France; the French particularly praise gentle manners. Woman is not domestic at all, but she is also nowhere as cultured as in France. The French are not hospitable, but they are extremely willing to show small favors to a stranger. They have a great deal of natural aptitude and spirit, but little instinct and even less training[k] (discipline). The Point d'honneur (the point of honor), which with them gives rise to innumerable duels, is not

25:1183

---

[a] *bewegende Kräfte*   [b] *Gelehrigkeit*

[c] Reading (with the Academy editors) *Inder*. (*Petersburg* reads: *Indianer* – Native Americans.)

[d] The italicized sentences are taken from *Petersburg*. In *Menschenkunde*, the section on the races follows here.

[e] trans.: conduct, behavior.   [g] trans.: frivolity.

[f] *Leichtsinn*

[h] The italicized remark is taken from *Petersburg*.

[i] trans.: point of honor.   [k] *Zucht*

[j] trans.: thoughtlessness.

a true concept of honor, but rather something by means of which one wants to win reputation.

Titles, which serve as a distinction of things, give rise to a language which is very extensive and has a great richness of words for intellectual concepts, wherein consists precisely the greatest beauty of the German language. The spirit of order is characteristic of the Germans; as a result they also have many titles and names. With the Germans there is more natural aptitude than genius, and more discipline than instinct. The German always shows more power of judgment than spirit, or power of discovery; on the other hand with the French the opposite occurs more. The Germans have more of a tendency toward useful things;[a] the French toward fashion. Something first catches on as a useful thing when it has already stopped being fashion. The German is very hospitable.

One could call Spain the land of ancestors, in the same way that France is the land of fashion. It is difficult to sketch a character of the Spaniards. They do not gladly descend from the Moors but from the Goths, although they may not value the latter a great deal. They are full of ceremonies; as a result they are the greatest enemies of the French. They are still several centuries behind in the sciences,[20] because they do not accept anything from other nations. They are true antipodes of the French, because they are great enemies of all changes, both with regard to religion and in the mode of life;[b] nevertheless they do have many passions[c] and almost always a dance,[21] which is called the fandango. They are certainly not lacking in spirit; however, from their pride, according to which they regard themselves as the most distinguished and most skillful nation, springs also at the same time the laziness, *which generally speaking is linked to each person.*[d] However, in respect to this a great deal depends on the different regions of Spain; for in those districts which border France, many characteristics and customs of the French have already been taken up, as in Madrid, where the courtyard[e] is; but in New Castile and in the Asturian mountains[22] one still finds proper Spaniards who pass themselves off as descendants of the old Goths *(because they all believe they are of a noble origin),*[f] and this is exactly why they walk along quite solemnly in black clothes *and with glasses.*[g] Only a very few of the Spaniards learn foreign languages.

In England knowledge reaches out to the most common man, the causes of which are supposed to be newspapers, which are superb

25:1184

---

[a] *Gebräuchen*
[b] *Lebensart*
[c] *Petersburg* reads: liveliness.
[d] The italicized phrase is taken from *Petersburg.*
[e] *Hof*
[f] The italicized phrase is taken from *Petersburg.*
[g] The italicized phrase is taken from *Petersburg.*

products of wit. Even the servant reads the newspapers. The hatred of imitation, and the propensity to originality, are very characteristic of the English people, and make them headstrong and the enemy of ceremonies and politeness. The Englishman despises the Frenchman, because to him he is too fickle.*ª* The English are hospitable, and proud of their freedom.*ᵇ* They travel a great deal, yet they nevertheless always despise foreign lands; *they have no taste, but they are also the only ones who bring each work to perfection: they make nothing except that which is appropriate.ᶜ* England is the land of moods.*ᵈ* The Englishman is witty in his writing and this wit is especially valuable because of its great content, *because of its great content and not so much on account of its facility.* It is the land of moods.*ᵉ*

25:1185

The Italians appear to hold the middle road between the French and the Spanish; they have more affect than the French, and more true strength of spirit. They take delight in the fine arts, in which they particularly specialize. The objects of public admiration are painting, architecture, and sculpture. Italy is the land of sly heads.*ᶠ* The inventions of the Italians must always agree with the taste of the nobles and the civilized peoples.*ᵍ* The Italian nation has a great deal of spirit and talent.

Some place the character of the Germans in their phlegma. The German is not attached so much to his fatherland, and this indicates already *an enlightened people. He shows his composureʰ particularly through patient efforts; he accommodates himself well to reforms, and easily allows himself to be ruled despotically. Germany is the land of compliments.ⁱ*

Poland, the land of braggarts, and Russia, the land of spite, are both of Slavic origin. They do not appear to be properly capable of civilization. The inhabitants of Poland want freedom and law, but no executive power,*ʲ* a demand that is completely absurd. They have something of the Spanish and the French; with them something begins with pomp and ends very ordinarily.*ᵏ* The Russians are still too unknown, and it is not advisable to judge the nation from some little things. The Poles and

---

ª *flüchtig. Petersburg* reads: light, and imitates too much.

ᵇ *Petersburg* reads: proud of their independence, and the French are proud of the power of their king.

ᶜ *zweckmäßig.* The italicized phrase is taken from *Petersburg.*

ᵈ *das Land der Launen*

ᵉ The italicized phrases are taken from *Petersburg.*

ᶠ *das Land der Schlauköpfe*   *ʰ* *Gelaßenheit*

ᵍ *die Versittigten*

ⁱ The italicized phrases are taken from *Petersburg. Menschenkunde* reads: an enlightened people, they particularly distinguish themselves through patient, industrious composure, they do not accommodate themselves to reforms, and they can be ruled despotically.

ʲ *keine vollziehende Gewalt*   *ᵏ* *sehr gemein*

Russians have more of an oriental character mixture than all of the other nations of Europe.

To be enlightened and of broadened concepts are great expressions of praise for a people, but are also very much to be distinguished from each other, for a human being who has learned much can also be very narrow-minded in his concepts; many people to be sure acquire knowledge, but few acquire concepts. History and geography help us to obtain broader concepts, and a human being who is very limited in geographical knowledge is also usually very limited in concepts. People of limited concepts are proud and full of self-love.[a] The English have the most broadened concepts of all peoples. A human being of such broadened (extended) concepts always attends to the universal best for the world,[b] and is not simply content with the welfare of his family and the narrow district of his fatherland; he will care for the salvation of the entire human society,[c] and for just this reason not be a stern patriot, whose glory in fact is not very significant. "*In the Gospel,*[d] if it is correctly understood, lies the most broadened concept, to make all human beings happy, and for this reason it earns respect from all."

An enlightened people is one in which individual persons think for themselves, and do not allow others to think for them.[23] One finds in fact that those nations in whose language Latin has a strong influence have a great deal of education.[e] This comes primarily from the Romans. These peoples are particularly the French, Italians, English and Spanish. When the public begins to pay attention to what its real interest consists in,[f] then this is the true sign of an enlightened people, of which the superb example is the French. On the other hand, the Russian nation is perhaps well disciplined, also in some degree cultivated, though more as concerns capacity rather than faculty; *on the other hand, it is not yet civilized at all, and even less moralized than any other people in the world.*[g] Precisely because its concepts are not broadened at all, the Russian nation hates all nations, with the exception of the English.[h]

25:1186

---

[a] *Eigenliebe*

[b] *das allgemeine Weltbeste*. *Petersburg* reads: decide for the entire world, and seek to promote its best.

[c] *Petersburg* reads: of the human race.

[d] The italicized phrase is taken from *Petersburg*. *Menschenkunde* reads: In the nature of the Gospel, ...

[e] *viel Bildung* 	[f] *was für dasselbe Interesse hat*

[g] The italicized phrase is taken from *Petersburg*.

[h] *Petersburg* reads: It is still peculiar that certain nations distinguish themselves above others, in a manner that is hardly advantageous, and mainly due to the fact that their servants have a deceptive nodding (*Nicken*). They indicate a malevolent and base way of thinking, and consist primarily in the aversion to a command, but they are not nearly as bad as the spite which is nothing else than a resentment against someone who has power over us.

25:1187 ᵃShould one assume different human races (human kinds) that have different phyla?ᵇ If this were the case, then God must have created different first human beings, a specific pair for each race; we have no reason to assume this. If we plant a speciesᶜ of flowers or fruits in a different soil in a different manner, then we get different kindsᵈ of flowers and fruits. So a [single] human phylum can also have populated the entire earth, and incidental causes could have altered human beings. All kindsᵉ of human beings are fertile with one of another race when they have copulated with one another. This also makes it credibleᶠ to us that they descend from a single phylum.

*There are Four Races on Earth; these are*ᵍ

1) Theʰ American people acquires no culture.ⁱ It has no incentives; because affect and passion are absent in it. They are not in love, thus they are also not fertile. They hardly speak at all, do not caress one another, also do not care for anything, and are lazy, *they paint their faces in an ugly manner.*ʲ

2) The Negro race, one could say, is exactly the opposite of the American; they are full of affect and passion, very lively, talkative and vain. They acquire culture, but only a culture of slaves; that is, they allow themselves to be trained. They have many incentives, are also sensitive, afraid of beatings, and also do many things out of honor.

3) It is true that the Hindus have incentives, but they have a strong degree of composure, and they all look like philosophers. Despite this, they are nevertheless very much inclined toward anger and love. As a result they acquire culture in the highest degree, but only in the arts and not in the sciences.ᵏ They never raise it up to abstract concepts; a great Hindustani man is the one who has gone very far in deceit and who has a lot of money. The Hindus always remain as they are, they never bring culture further, although they began to cultivateˡ themselves much earlier.

ᵃ At this point the Academy editors write: "Beginning of the moved (*verschobene*) passage. Cf. 15:793, 18–19." The following material on races is taken from pp. 352–353 of the original published text of *Menschenkunde*, and occurs six pages earlier than the preceding paragraph.

ᵇ *verschiedene Stämme*   ᵉ *Alle Arten*

ᶜ *eine Art*   ᶠ *glaublich*

ᵈ *verschiedene Arten*

ᵍ The italicized section heading is taken from *Petersburg*.

ʰ In *Menschenkunde*, the word '*Anmerk.*' [= Remark] precedes '1).'

ⁱ *nimmit keine Bildung an*

ʲ *ins häßliche*. The italicized phrase is taken from *Petersburg*.

ᵏ *Petersburg* reads: not in the arts, only in the sciences.

ˡ *bilden*

4) The white race contains all incentives and talents in itself; as a result *it must be considered in a bit more detail. Information concerning it is given above.*[a]

All of Europe, the Turks, and the Kalmucks belong to the white race. 25:1188 Whenever any revolutions have occurred, they have always been brought about by the whites, and the Hindus, Americans, and Negroes have never participated in them. Under the whites one could make the division of the Oriental and Occidental kinds.[b] Thirdly one can also count the Finnish nation here.[c]

OF THE CHARACTER OF THE SEXES.[d]

It is a principle of lazy reason to assume that everything is one and the same, and many people even do so with the two so very different human sexes.[e] The more we study nature the more we find diversity, but at the same time we also find the most perfect unity of connection. Upon closer consideration this is also obvious to us with respect to the two sexes.

In order to study the whole human being, we are allowed to set our eyes only on the female sex; for there, where the power is weaker, the instrument itself is all the more artistic.[f] We must say: everything that lies in nature is good, for nature is the measure of the good.[g] Nature has laid a natural predisposition toward art in the female sex. Man is created in order to rule over nature; and woman, in order to govern man.

To the former belongs a great deal of power; to the second, a great deal of skill. One can say, man was made to have authority over nature, and woman, authority over man, and through man authority over nature. The seeds that lay in nature develop only according to the occasions given by circumstances; that is why we can see nature properly unfold only in the condition where all *merely imaginable charms*[h] lay hidden. Therefore, in order to get to know female nature precisely, and in order to determine her incentives, we will also need to consider her in none other but her

---

[a] The italicized phrase is taken from *Petersburg*. *Menschenkunde* reads: we will have to consider it a bit more exactly. The Academy editors add: "Apparently the remark [from *Petersburg*] refers to the treatment of the different European nations [a few pages earlier] in the *Menschenkunde*."

[b] *Schlages*

[c] Here the Academy editors note: "End of moved passage; cf. 15:793, 18–19."

[d] This section title is taken from *Petersburg*. In *Menschenkunde* the section title reads: Of the Character of Humanity and the Sexes.

[e] The italicized sentence is taken from *Petersburg*.

[f] *um so viel künstlicher* (also "ingenious," "clever," "artificial").

[g] *der Maasstab des Guten*

[h] *nur denkliche Reitze*. The italicized phrase is taken from *Petersburg*. *Menschenkunde* reads: orderly impulses.

25:1189 civilized condition; for in the crude[a] condition of the savages women are not at all different from men, because here even their great influence on the male sex ceases.

Among savages the female sex is held very much in contempt; however, among cultured peoples the female sex can make use of its arts with men more; in the civilized condition, the situation is exactly the opposite, because here the female sex is also at the same time the cause of the refined condition. *Feminine qualities*[b] are called weaknesses when the man has them; on the other hand in woman these weaknesses are not a reproach at all (if in this respect one still has the right to call them weaknesses); *rather they are precisely the instruments by which woman dominates over man. On the other hand,*[c] in women masculine qualities are always something unseemly. *The female sex is timid in respect to danger, and this is purposely put in her by nature; for nature has entrusted to woman her dearest pledge, the child.*[d]

However, these feminine qualities are weaknesses concerning which a woman should not *at all*[e] be ashamed. To ridicule these weaknesses is in fact to mock oneself, namely because through these weaknesses one charms oneself, through them one lets oneself be easily enticed and persuaded of something.

The end of nature in the most perfect unity of connection between two so very different sexes was: 1) to maintain the species,[f] and then also: 2) to promote the social condition in the human sexes. –

After this preparatory report we proceed to the character of these two sexes. Forgivingness[g] is more characteristic of man than of woman. Man is easy to fathom, but the female sex can completely conceal its secrets, *only*[h] not easily the secrets of others.

Man is quite inattentive with respect to the observation of others and easily defers to the judgment of others; he also lets himself be easily persuaded to give up his resolve; on the other hand, with woman exactly the opposite occurs.

25:1190 Man always loves domestic peace, however quarrelsome he is outside of the house, and that is why he concedes everything; but woman does not shy away from domestic quarrel, rather she looks at it as a pleasant commotion.

---

[a] *roh*

[b] *Weiblichkeiten*. The italicized word is taken from *Petersburg*. (In *Menschenkunde*, the same word appears, but in the singular rather than the plural.)

[c] The italicized phrases are taken from *Petersburg*.

[d] The italicized sentence is taken from *Petersburg*.

[e] The italicized phrase is taken from *Petersburg*.

[f] *die Art* [g] *Die Versöhnlichkeit*

[h] The italicized word is taken from *Petersburg*. *Menschenkunde* reads: only it cannot.

The reason why man loves domestic peace probably comes from the fact that he maintains the house as his place of rest, but because of this he loses a great deal with woman.

It is also a characteristic of women to be eloquent; they can chatter a great deal about things that they scarcely understand. The inclination *to pleasure*[a] and to domination is, as Pope says,[24] the greatest inclination of woman. Experience also confirms that this sex has the most inclination to dominate; but it would lose all of these advantages if it were dominated. That is why we [men] also willingly concede to be dominated by the other sex, and gladly demand this from it, indeed we also often affect an inclination toward a woman, in order to empower her to dominate us.

Flirtation (gallantry) is the first beginning toward a refined and civilized condition; but here we must perhaps distinguish morals[b] and virtue well. The principle of male morals is virtue; of female morals, honor, and what the world does, woman does too. – Among the Germans women have always had a very great influence on men, even those who still lived in forests. From this we can infer that they must not have been nearly so crude and uncivilized as the savages at present are in America and elsewhere, *as also in general people who live in cities always prove to be more civilized than nomadic nations.*[c]

Man is pleased [and] always completely satisfied with the woman's kind of pride, in virtue of which she displays confidence; hence politeness toward woman, too, strengthens this pride.

The merits of man do not produce as much respect with woman as do the merits of woman with man. The female sex can only have an influence on men according to the measure by which men are refined and civilized. As long as man is not yet accustomed to companionship[d] with woman, he continually cultivates a lower opinion of himself in respect to her[e] judgment, because he believes that nothing could remain hidden from her critical eyes. *On the other hand, women are always very free with men in companionship,*[f] *because they do not fear their harsh judgment at all, and precisely through this they elevate their weaknesses, which otherwise could easily be obvious to a careful observer. In general, the merits of man do not give rise to as much respect with woman as do the merits of woman with man.*[g]

25:1191

---

[a] *zum Vergnügen*. This phrase is added by the Academy editors. Here they also draw readers' attention to a similar passage in *Anthropology from a Pragmatic Point of View* at 7:305. *Menschenkunde* reads: to change (*zur Veränderung*).

[b] *Sitten*

[c] The italicized phrase is taken from *Petersburg*.

[d] *Gesellschaft*

[e] The italicized word is added by the Academy editors. *Menschenkunde* reads: the judgment.

[f] *in Gesellschafft immer sehr frey*

[g] The italicized sentences are taken from *Petersburg*.

The point of view from which we consider all weaknesses of woman (which nevertheless are arranged according to the great wisdom *of nature)ᵃ* is the following: nature has implanted in the womb of the female sex the preservation of the species or humankind;*ᵇ* in order to guard this gift faithfully a fear of all that brings danger is also at the same time laid in her, which makes her cautious and prevents her from risking something which would be connected to danger, [and might] *destroy the species.ᶜ* As a result one will never see woman pulled into war, not even among the savage peoples; and that is why everything said by the Amazons in this respect is a fantasy of a writer of fables.

Concerning taste, woman has a great deal of judgment about it but little inclination for it, so that one can justly say that man is much more refined and more censorious*ᵈ* in choice than woman is. The reason for this lies in the thing itself; for since the female sex must be sought after, it must also not be as sensitive*ᵉ* as the male sex, which can select out a person that pleases it.

Each sex is determined*ᶠ* for the taste of the other; now since man is created more coarsely, woman therefore has a coarser taste, man a finer taste. Woman is an object of taste, as a result she takes pains only to please, but she searches not so much for what pleases him. Woman is not generous, and even when she is, she will not admit it.*ᵍ* Man earns, woman saves. Woman searches for domestic advantage, man is capable of searching for the public good. *Job and Socrates' wives, who were reputed to be so evil, appear to have been a pair of honest women who were dragged into domesticity and wanted to know how to adjust to useless complaints and studying.*²⁵

So one also maintains with justice that man is actually more tender than woman, since this demands of him that he should expose himself to adversities on her account. Man also gladly undertakes this in order to *please*ʰ woman, as a result the male sex must in fact have an advantage over the female sex in respect to tender affection. *On the other hand, in respect to pampering*ⁱ *the female sex maintains rank over the male sex. We have already seen*²⁶ *that*ʲ sensitiveness is a weakness, but sensitivity is a strength. Women possess the former; men the latter. On the other hand,

ᵃ The italicized phrase is taken from *Petersburg.*
ᵇ *die Art oder das menschliche Geschlecht*
ᶜ The italicized phrase is taken from *Petersburg.*
ᵈ *krittlicher. Petersburg* reads: more delicate.
ᵉ *feinfühlend*   ᶠ *bestimmt*
ᵍ *und es läßt auch nicht, wenn es dasselbe ist.*
ʰ The italicized word is taken from *Petersburg. Menschenkunde* reads: free.
ⁱ *Verzärtelung*
ʲ The italicized phrase is taken from *Petersburg*, but part of it is found a few sentences below. *Menschenkunde* reads: The.

in respect to pampering the female sex maintains rank over the male sex. The female sex is refusing, the male sex is wooing; *the ground for this lies in the fact that the one searches, but the other should be sought.*[a] The refusing sex must be bold,[b] and this is counted as gallantry.

Man is only jealous when he is in love, but woman is also jealous when she is not in love.[27] Woman must generally still seek the married state to be happy, and about this no man can also be jealous; since this is unjust.[c] Jealousy also often appears because of reputation and social position, but it also often appears from love. Among themselves, women are not nearly as agreeable as men. A tolerance in marriage always causes the man to grumble, and he is also burdened with ridicule when he is the offended party, because in both cases he still always has guilt.

25:1193

One must lecture to the female sex about something not as duty, but always from the point of honor. The reason that women do not like to hear about duty is because they have an inclination to dominate.

Woman dresses herself up generally for the judgment of other women. With man it is usually the opposite.

The tenderness of men is *magnanimous,*[d] but the tenderness of woman is sensitive.

The honor of man consists in what people think, but the honor of woman consists in what they say. *Male understanding goes to what things are, female understanding to how they appear; and to how they are current.*[e] Woman should dominate, man should govern; for inclination dominates and understanding governs.

Domination permits moods,[f] which however do not occur with understanding. Man prescribes the domestic laws, whereby he however must always arrange everything so that woman retains the appearance of domination. Thus most princes dominate, but the ministers govern.

One must leave enjoyment in the house to woman, but honor and peace in the house is the concern of man. Woman always thinks that the inclination toward the other sex will not go away, but perhaps that the desire to marry could go away, and if no wedding were to take place she would then be seen as an illicit lover. – Hume remarks[28] in his philosophical inquiries that woman would very probably endure a satire of her sex, but never a mockery of the married state, *and even old maids think this.*[g] The reason lies incontestably in the following: through marriage woman is all at once free, while earlier in the unmarried state she was tormented

---

[a] The italicized phrase is taken from *Petersburg*.
[b] *dreust*   [c] *ungerecht*
[d] *großmüthig*. The italicized word is taken from *Petersburg*. *Menschenkunde* reads: capricious (*grillig*).
[e] The italicized sentence is taken from *Petersburg*.
[f] *Launen*
[g] The italicized phrase is taken from *Petersburg*.

25:1194 dreadfully by propriety. Man by contrast loses his freedom through just this condition. Therefore one also assumes that it is not bad[a] for the man if he is not married. On the other hand, for us an already grown female who is unmarried is a great discredit, and similarly in the Orient with the childless condition. – Because the married state is an exclusive possession of the object of sexual inclination, so also jealousy, which is opposed to forbearance, is entirely natural; indeed a woman will even hate the man who is not jealous, because this is a sure sign that he does not care much for her. The intolerance of men is the entire advantage of marriage, otherwise the purpose[b] is missing; for man wants to be the possessor of a woman, and if there were no jealousy in the male sex, then there would be no marriage; for certainty concerning the true paternity of children is the first prerequisite for the care of their preservation; of this the man must be completely convinced.

OF THE CHARACTER OF THE WHOLE HUMAN SPECIES.

Does the human belong to the four-footed animals or not?[29] There are many reasons to assume that at the beginning he walked on four feet (according to anatomy), but nevertheless this is not entirely believable, because the arms are shorter than the feet, and the knees are bent forward, while with other animals they go backwards.

25:1195 The embryo of the human being has calluses[c] on the soles of the feet, like all four-footed animals, but they are entirely missing from the hands. Therefore he is not a four-footed animal. Is the human being related to the orangutan?[30] From the outside he seems very similar to him; however, the human being's bone structure is entirely different from the orangutan's, and similarly with all the rest; as a result one can[d] set aside such suppositions entirely.

Is the human being a herbivorous or carnivorous animal? Like other carnivorous animals, the human being has a membranous stomach, and the herbivorous animals have a muscular stomach; according to the stomach, therefore, the human being is a carnivorous animal; however, he also has long intestines, like the herbivorous animals. One finds a very great weakness with the peoples who eat a pure vegetable diet, and also with the animals who eat herbs. An English physician[31] has ascertained through long observation of the teeth of all kinds of animals that the human being is destined[e] to eat a one-third flesh and two-thirds vegetable diet. Therefore the human being could actually be the mean between herbivorous and carnivorous animals.

[a] *nicht übel*
[b] *Zweck*
[c] *das Callum*

[d] *Petersburg* reads: could.
[e] *bestimmt*

The discovery of what kinds of seeds lie hidden in humanity gives us at the same time the means that we have to apply in order to hasten the unfolding of these natural predispositions. Despite the unity of the human species, there is still a difference of races to take up, whose special character belongs to physical geography.[32]

If the human being were himself destined through the development of his inner predispositions to be the author of all of his skill, indeed even of [his] good nature, then we must, so far as we can, go back in the previous[a] time, in order for us to think the crudest condition, as the[b] first condition. Naturally this must *now*[c] be the one that simply contains the smallest portion of human needs. The first skills, which we also come across with the crudest human beings, are walking and speaking.

How did the human being learn to speak? He could not have been placed in the world endowed with this capacity; because he also would already have had to have all concepts, of which words are merely signs. If speech was also imparted by birth to the first human being, he could still come in circumstances to lose it again and he must have possessed the skill to invent it again when it had been lost. The human being therefore invented speech gradually, as birds have learned to sing, and dogs have learned to bark; for just as little as singing is imparted by birth to the bird, because it would also then have to have been innate, which contradicts experience, just so can this also not be valid for the speech of the human being. The speech of the human being therefore appears to have arisen because he wanted to express his feelings[d] through sounds; that is why one finds that sounds agree with feelings. As soon as the human being could walk and speak, he went out hunting, after that came the acquisition[e] of domestic cattle, when he began to tame the still wild animals, by means of which he took a mighty step toward his perfection.[f] After this followed the discovery of metals, especially iron, which must have made a very great commotion among human beings and animals. Afterward the art of writing and finally money were invented.

In the animal species[g] each individual reaches its destiny,[h] but in the human race a single individual can never do this, rather only the whole human species can reach its destiny, despite the fact that the human being is furnished by nature like an animal. – In the human species it is inappropriate,[i] that never the individual, but rather the species, reaches its destiny. This is an additional cause toward society,[j] for which the

25:1196

---

[a] *Petersburg* reads: first.
[b] *Petersburg* reads: in the.
[c] The italicized word is taken from *Petersburg. Menschenkunde* reads: only.
[d] *Empfindungen*
[e] *Petersburg* reads: rearing.
[f] *Vervollkommnung*
[g] *Petersburg* reads: animals.
[h] *Bestimmung* (also "vocation" – when used with respect to human beings).
[i] *zweckwidrig*
[j] *Mitursache zur Gesellschaft*

human being is expressly created. All work for one, and one works for all, for then each animal can itself search for its nourishment without the help of others. But *precisely from this inner*[a] predisposition in the human being, as in the animal, arise also all hindrances that are opposed to the development of his humanity, a development, however, which should be his foremost end and his destiny. In order to arrive at the true destiny of the human being, it should be noted that the human being is an animal that can perfect itself, but that animals are not able to do this. But this is still the least,[b] the whole human species should perfect itself, and this is far more important.

25:1197 Everything always increases in *invention and perfection*;[c] everything comes nearer to its destiny, and we can hope that it will at some point happen, that everyone will perfect himself and reach his destiny, where no changes take place,[d] no states fall, no conflict and no more unrest will emerge. This has a great similarity with the ages of the human being, and the interim until perfection is like the interim of the maturity[e]33 of nature and of the *civil*[f] maturity of a human being; that is, adolescence.

In order to make this clearer, it is necessary here to state the divisions of the ages of the human being together with his explanation. A child is one who can neither support itself nor reproduce its species. A youth can certainly reproduce his species, perhaps also support himself, but not his family. Nature makes no distinction between the youth and the man, but civilizing[g] and the civil condition make the distinction all the greater; hence in the uncultivated condition no marriages are necessary. The human being who is in a position to do all of this is a man. Civil maturity begins not until approximately the thirtieth year; the maturity of nature enters in already in the fifteenth year. – Before the human being was reared (that is, disciplined), thus when he was still in the first condition, he was savage; *before he developed himself, that is, before he cultivated his talents, he was crude,*[h] before he was civilized, and entered into a human society, he was coarse, and before he was morally good (moralized), that is, until his actions arise from moral incentives, he is evil.

The crude human being regards every stranger as his enemy. Hence, among the savages he who is the bravest has the highest standing; but

---

[a] The italicized phrase is taken from *Petersburg. Menschenkunde* reads: just as much from this inner.
[b] *das Wenigste*
[c] The italicized phrase is suggested by the Academy editors. *Menschenkunde* reads: inventions and perfection of its shelter. *Petersburg* reads: in sensation and perfection.
[d] *wo keine Veränderungen vorgehen*   [e] *Mündigkeit*
[f] The italicized word is taken from *Petersburg*.
[g] *Versittitgung*
[h] The italicized phrase is taken from *Petersburg*.

in this, fear is blameworthy. Actually the intention of nature appears to have been this, that the human being might disperse itself around the earth, which would not have occurred if human beings had lived together peacefully.

The human being has by nature a propensity to dissemble. This reveals itself with^a the savages; for every human being still has certain special secrets of his own that not everyone should know.

Up to now there is still no moral constraint among human beings other than the constraint of decency, but we have reason to hope for it.   25:1198 *Culture actually concerns only the person, civilization concerns society; moralization concerns what is best for the world in general.^{b} These are three kinds of progress that nature has laid in human beings. We have already come far in culture, in civilization we have not done much, and in moralization we have done almost nothing.*

As regards culture, one can ask:[34]

1) What can I know? Metaphysics and philosophy teach this.

2) What ought I to do? Ethics teaches this.

3) What can I hope? Religion teaches this.

All of these sciences, which are already widely disseminated, are not yet applied at all to the universal.^{c} As regards civilization, to be sure we are refined as human beings, but not as citizens. We have manners,^{d} but the further one comes in manners, the less he concerns himself about true civilization. The human being is not made to be a landlord,^{e} but rather to be a member of the universal.^{f} Regarding moralization: to be sure we have refined manners,^{g} but not [a] true, real way of thinking. Nevertheless, manners also are always good. The three means to these kinds of progress are:

1) Public education. This presupposes that the child is good by nature, therefore one must protect it from prejudices and develop its talents.

2) Public legislation. Negative legislation is very necessary. For if what is forbidden is what can harm others, then all is well.

3) Religion. This must also be negative; for it must separate what is contrary to morality, then positive development^h can follow. All of this must be negative at first, for one must separate what is contrary to morality. The human being is immature in all [of these areas]. With respect to culture he is a child of the house-father. With respect to moralization and religion he is a child of the father confessor. The prerequisite of all of these kinds of progress is freedom. But human beings are not yet capable of 1) a free educational method, 2) a free divine service.

---

^{a} *Petersburg* reads: not with.
^{b} *das allgemeine Weltbeste*
^{c} *aufs allgemeine*
^{d} *Sitten*

^{e} *Hauswirth*
^{f} *Glied des Allgemeinen*
^{g} *verfeinerte Manieren*
^{h} *Ausbildung*

25:1199 *Small states and kingdoms can bring culture to its furthest, since even big kingdoms often break up. Nature has willed that the human being should live in a civil society, as a result the incentives for this lie in him. The human being unites with others in order to protect himself against the excessive force*[a] *of others, out of this emerge families, societies, and so forth.*[b] The human being is destined to live in society, and all mistrust that still now prevails with human beings among one another has its ground in their animality. Taken as a whole, progress goes always from evil toward good, but not the reverse; for evil clashes with itself every time,[c] and urges us to look for a means in order to remove this antagonism. For this reason there is also in fact an incentive of the good; on the other hand, since the good perfectly harmonizes with all existing things, it can never move us to do something else that is not good; that is, to bring forth something evil, and it is consequently a persistent condition, if only it has first properly taken its start. In the same way, just *as*[d] moral evil is an incentive of the good, so also is physical evil a spur to activity, which is all the more necessary since the human being by nature is lazy.

In the crude condition a great unsociability also takes place with the human being, which springs from fear, a fear which prevails over each person within; hence the point in time when the talents of the human being can properly develop actually only arises in a civil constitution. Nevertheless improving manners (civilizing)[e] is not nearly the proper degree of improvement, rather for the destiny of the human being it is also absolutely necessary that he improve his character and that he be moralized, the incentives for which also lie in civil society, so that the true worth of a people appears to consist only in that it comes near to this, its final destiny.

Animality and instinct taken together occur with animals and are entirely good, because here everything is in harmony. Freedom and reason, both of which should occur with the human being according to his true destiny, are also good. On the other hand, animality and freedom, which present themselves in the human being in the savage condition, are the sources of the incentives of everything evil and the origin thereof.[f]

25:1200 The human being is a creature that is necessarily in need of a master, which the animals do not ever need.[35] The reason[g] is freedom and its misuse; the animal, on the other hand, is confidently led by its instincts. Now the human being can get this master from no other race than his

---

[a] *Obermacht* (also "predominance")
[b] The italicized sentences are taken from *Petersburg*.
[c] *widerstreitet sich jederzeit selbst*
[d] The italicized word is taken from *Petersburg*. *Menschenkunde* reads: if.
[e] *Versittigung (Civilisirung)*
[f] *Petersburg* reads: incentives, and the origin of evil.
[g] *Ursache*

human species, which is a real misfortune for the human race, precisely because this master, whom the human being chooses over himself, is also a human being, who likewise is necessarily in need of a master.

Herein also lies the reason[a] why a perfect civil constitution from human beings is not at all able to be produced. – One can call a human being who has no master *a completely*[b] free human being; but because he would then certainly misuse his freedom one could also call him a savage. If the human being is in society, then the right of the other comes in the way, which is why judges are necessary;[c] the inconveniences here begin to become greater, since one person always believes he has need of the other; then the inequality of worldly possessions arises; and of prestige. An inequality of social ranks[d] occurs; the one that is higher-ranked commands, and the lower-ranking one serves. Now there is still no judicial power and no law there. Nations fall into jealousy, one is stronger than the other, and they fall into war. Here they must enter into a civil constitution; that is, into a constitution, which takes law and authority as a foundation.

A people is more in the condition to protect itself from others than to govern itself. However, a commonwealth already governs itself, and consists in a systematic constitution of the people, whereby a distinction of social ranks occurs. – A people united in a commonwealth is called a state insofar as it has power. The relationship of states towards one another is the relationship of savages; for as the latter stand under no lawgiver, and are free from all constraint between each another, so this also holds for the former, because each state cares only for its own welfare, without therefore having to give an account to another. However, this clearly reveals a barbarism that is still at hand.

The chief requirements for a civil society are freedom, law, and authority. Freedom and authority without law constitute the state of nature, which human beings should come out of because they have reason. One could call the Polish government[e] freedom and law without authority; a marvelous whim about which the nobility in this land is pleased, and the whole thing contains something absurd and contradictory.

25:1201

This is the first rough sketch for a civil constitution. Law and authority without freedom are despotism. This is in fact barbaric authority without law; however, it is still better than barbaric freedom, because in the former case culture is still possible. The genuine civil constitution is very ingenious,[f] and consists in the human being having as much freedom as

---

[a] *Grund*

[b] The italicized words are taken from *Petersburg. Menschenkunde* reads: completely a.

[c] *Petersburg* reads: from this judges arise.

[d] *Stände*   [f] *künstlich*

[e] *Petersburg* reads: way of government.

can occur and that is compatible with the limitation of the freedom of all in accordance with (just) law. Here there must be a law, and as much authority as is necessary to execute the law.

A perfect civil constitution is not possible before cultured subjects[a] exist who allow no other constitution and government. That is why one must enlighten the people, and try to establish international law better. The civil constitution of the Romans appeared to be better than that of the Greeks, but there was still much in it that was not just, particularly concerning the conflict between the patricians and the plebeians. One sees from this that much of which one believes to have reversed development[b] was in fact beneficial to it. Freedom under a law and bound with *authority*[c] consists in the laws being given as if they arose through the universal voice of the people. These laws must go out to all, be valid for all, and be able to be given by all; not until this happens will they earn the name of just laws. Therefore, whenever freedom, law, and authority occur together, the civil constitution is the most orderly and the best. Additionally, in each state there must be a head of state. Now this can be viewed either as a supreme lord[d] (sovereign) or as a regent. According to the nature of things only the people can legislate a law; for what the whole people decides is certainly always justice, because it is its own will. But only he can be legislator who is in a position to give just laws; as result the sovereign power[e] (sovereignty) can only be with the people, but the government can be with someone else. One can also call sovereignty supremacy,[f] which is either despotic or patriotic. It is called patriotic when the head of state governs the state not as his good but as his fatherland; that is, a government that takes care of the state as a whole, whose weal[g] should last not only during the lifetime of the regent but always. A state constitution is despotic when the head also has authority in his hands.

A *way of government*[h] can be either despotic or aristocratic or democratic. A monarch is a negative concept, and actually signifies one over whom there is no greater authority in the state; therefore one who himself has been subject to no authority. *But the sovereign is he who also at the same time can exercise authority.*[i] With us there is no considerable difference now among all of these ways of government, neither with regard to the temporal welfare of nations, nor with regard to morals.

25:1202

---

[a] *gebildete Unterthanen*　　　　[b] *Ausbildung*
[c] *Gewalt*, which is an interpolation of the Academy editors. *Menschenkunde* reads: law (*Gesetze*).
[d] *Oberherr*　　　　[f] *Oberherrschaft*
[e] *oberherrliche Macht*　　　　[g] *Beste*
[h] The italicized phrase is taken from *Petersburg*. *Menschenkunde* reads: government.
[i] The italicized sentence is taken from *Petersburg*.

But whether a more perfect civil constitution will not some day with time come into being cannot be hoped for until human beings, and their education, have improved; however, this improvement does not appear to be able to happen until governments themselves become better. Which one will begin cannot be guessed; perhaps both will meet each other, a point in time, however, that is still very far away.

The point of view from which particularly princes should consider states must not be merely patriotic, but also cosmopolitical; that is, it should rise to the universal good.[a] Citizens of a state cannot and may not have cosmopolitan purposes, with the exception of scholars, who can be of use to the world with books; rather, it is the concern of the prince, who has neglected it so much that up to now there has not yet been a monarch who has done something in which he has taken what is best for the entire world[b] in view: for example, the battle of Miltiades,[36] one can say, almost decided the whole culture of human beings. If Greece had come under Persia's domination, then the sciences would have been crushed. Now in order to stimulate the princes' desire for honor to strive after such sublime ends and to work for the welfare of the whole human race, a history, which would be written solely from a cosmopolitical point of view, would be of considerable use. Such a history would have to take as its standpoint merely what is best for the world, and make worthy of remembrance by posterity only those actions that concerned the welfare of the entire human species.[c]

25:1203

---

[a] *Petersburg* reads: to the best for the world.
[b] *das ganze Weltbeste*
[c] *Petersburg* reads: Now in order to stimulate princes' desire for honor to strive after such sublime ends and to work for the welfare of the whole human race, a history, which would be written solely from a cosmopolitical point of view, would be of considerable use. Although for now it may certainly be quite small. Such a history would be allowed only to take what is best for the world as its standpoint, and make worthy of remembrance for posterity only those actions that concern the welfare of the entire human species. For example, the battle of Miltiades, one can say, almost decided the whole culture of human beings; for if Greece had come under the Persians, then the sciences would have suffocated.

Anthropology Mrongovius

Translator's introduction

This translation of the anthropology lecture that Kant delivered during the 1784/1785 winter semester is based on the so-called Mrongovius lecture in the Academy Edition (AA 25:1207–1429), prepared by Richard Brandt and Werner Stark (1997). Brandt and Stark edited the Academy Edition lecture on the basis of two transcripts: one written by Christoph Coelestin Mrongovius (1764–1855) (although occasionally there is handwriting by an anonymous writer), and another written by an unknown transcriber (hence called the "anonymous-Marienburg" transcript).

I have closely followed as much as possible the translation principles summarized in the General Editors' Preface reprinted at the beginning of each volume of the *The Cambridge Edition*. Special care has been taken to reproduce the appearance of the Academy Edition, and particular attention has been given to using the terminology listed in the glossary of the present volume and other volumes in *The Cambridge Edition*. Since the Academy Edition lecture imitates the transcripts' frequent omissions of commas, periods, quotation marks, etc., I have needed to add punctuation to make the text more readable or grammatically correct. These additions of punctuation are so frequent that I make note of them only when deemed relevant or significant. I have done so by using linguistic notes at the bottom of the page, where the Mrongovius transcript is abbreviated "Mro" and anonymous-Marienburg "Mar." Important terms and words translated in a special fashion are indicated using linguistic footnotes.

The transcribers' parentheses ( ) and their underlining have been reproduced. It should be noted that the German transcripts do not underline in a consistent manner, particularly in the case of chapter headings. Angular brackets < > designate interlinear or marginal insertions likewise made by the transcribers. However, square brackets [ ] indicate the translator's insertions.

Foreign words have been written in italics when it is clear that Kant is using them as foreign words, as he does with French, English, or Latin phrases. In order to assist the reader with Kant's references and sources,

I have also created endnotes, making extensive use of the annotations offered by Brandt and Stark in the Academy Edition.

This lecture has not been previously published in English. I am very grateful for the editorial assistance of Rachael Fitzgerald and express sincere thanks to Brian Jacobs, Henry Pickford, and Holly Wilson for allowing me to consult their translations of several passages. I would like to thank Robert B. Louden for his comments on a late draft of my translation. This translation, including preparation of notes and endnotes, was undertaken by Robert R. Clewis.

Lecture of the Winter semester 1784-1785 Based on the Transcription Mrongovius, Marienburg

TRANSLATED BY ROBERT R. CLEWIS

Contents

a   *Erkentniße*   *b*   *Caput*

a Gemeinschaft   *b* Vom Naturell

FIRST CHAPTER

INTRODUCTION TO ANTHROPOLOGY

There are two ways to study: in school and in the world. In school one studies scholastic cognitions,[a] which belong to scholars by profession; but in social intercourse with the world one studies popular cognitions, which belong to the whole world. –

Now whoever wants to apply scholastic cognitions, which one uses only in the school and in scholarly writings, for use in the world without seeing whether or not they hold interest, is a pedant, namely, a pedant with regard to the subject matter; but if he actually has a great deal of knowledge and merely does not know how to make his knowledge understandable except in methodical[b] form, then he is a pedant with regard to the manner.[c]

The word "pedant"[d] originally comes from Latin,[1] for in Italy one called the domestic tutors *magistri pedanei*. The Italian word *pedanto* came from this, as one left off the *magistrio* and changed *pedanei* into *pedanto*; hence today the German word *Pedant*. These people were supposedly not to be received outside of their study rooms; they thus applied only their school knowledge when they were in social intercourse and therefore gave people the occasion to call a person who did not know how to conduct himself with human beings a "pedant." A pedant can make only a scholastic use of his knowledge because he does not know how to apply it any better and does not know any other use for it.

School is the acquisition[e] of cognition that one must apply in the world, for school teaches us the skill of acquiring knowledge, but not of making any use of it for the world.

A cognition is methodical if it is appropriate for the method of the school, i.e., when thoroughness, completeness, appropriateness, and clarity are the essence of a cognition. In order to make use of one's skill for the world, it is necessary to have yet another [kind of] knowledge, which for the most part one learns to use through social intercourse and experience. This knowledge is called knowledge of the world: not the knowledge of all of nature, but of the human being. For every science certainly refers to the human being, and if one gathers together all of our purposes, they surely boil down to the human being.

One acquires knowledge of the world or the human being more from experience than precepts; however, there are a few of them after all.

---

[a] *Erkenntnisse*   [c] *Manier*
[b] *Schulgerechter*   [d] *Pedant*
[e] Following the Academy Edition editors Brandt and Stark, reading *Erwerbung* (acquisition). Mro: *Anwerbung* (enlistment).

Skill is very different from prudence, for skill is a proficiency in the use of means in nature. But prudence is a proficiency or knowledge in reaching one's aims, and making use of this skill or using other human beings for one's aims; but to do this I must avail myself of what everyone understands and what interests everyone. Every pragmatic instruction[a] thus makes one prudent. Knowledge of the world thus does not aim at knowledge of nature or skill, but in the proper sense at prudence.

One can arrive at prudence in various ways; either:

1.) through one's own experience, although to an extent this is too late; to an extent one must learn this through one's own troubles; or
2.) through observations of others; this is the most advisable; or
3.) through learning certain precepts that can be of service to us for preliminary practice and that are [the results of] the experience of other human beings.

Cognitions of the understanding[b] are practical if one can make use of them at all; but they are pragmatic when one generally uses them in society, and here they must 1. be generally understandable and 2. interest everyone. Practice[c] makes us fit for all contrivable purposes, whether they interest us or not. – But prudence is determining an actual purpose.

The knowledge of the human being in general is called, under another name, anthropology; but it is further subdivided in two ways; either:

1. *Anthropologia pragmatica*, when it considers the knowledge of the human being as it is useful in society in general; or

2. *Anthropologia scholastica*, when one considers (treats) it more as a [kind of] school knowledge; the former is the application of the latter in a society. In recent times Platner[2] has published an anthropology of the latter kind that describes the constitution of the body and the soul, e.g., the cause of the power of imagination, dreams, and so forth; but here we have nothing to do with this, but only wish to deal with pragmatic anthropology, or anthropology as a knowledge of the world; and it has never before been treated in this way. In scholastic anthropology, I search for the causes of human nature. In pragmatic anthropology, I merely look at the [human] constitution and attempt to apply it. Anthropology is called pragmatic if it serves prudence rather than erudition.

25:1211

If one uses anthropology for social intercourse, it becomes knowledge of the world. We can use it every day in conversations, practical affairs, and with regard to ourselves,[d] and through new observations we can illustrate it more and more. No one has yet treated anthropology

---

[a] *Anweisung*
[b] *Verstandes Erkenntiße*
[c] *Praxis*
[d] *in Ansehung unser selbst*

344

from such a perspective, namely, as knowledge of the world, and Herr Professor Kant is the first to have made a plan of it and to have lectured on it in his courses.

The uses of anthropology are diverse:

I. With regard to the sciences.

a. With regard to morals and homiletic theology.

Here we must state the following in advance. There are three doctrines:

1. The doctrine of skill, which one teaches even to children and through which one learns how things are.

2. The doctrine of prudence, which one first learns with a growing power of judgment*a* and which teaches how to apply skill.

3. The doctrine of morals,*b* which adds to all the ends of the human being and through which one becomes wise. Skill is scholastic, prudence is pragmatic, and wisdom is moral.*c*

Anthropology is pragmatic, but is of service for the moral knowledge of the human being, for one must create the motives*d* for morals from it, and without it morals would be scholastic, not at all applicable to the world, and not agreeable to the world. Anthropology stands to morals as spatial geometry stands to geodesy.*e*

In this way anthropology provides very great benefits for homiletic or doctrinal theology.

b. with regard to history.

History is of two kinds:

1.) scholastic, when I only know what occurred; and

2.) pragmatic, when I investigate the private aims of the human being and the public aims of the commonwealth.

Pragmatic history really provides a benefit; for if I know history only scholastically, it serves me just as much as a fairy tale or novel does.

Now anthropology is indispensably necessary for pragmatic history. For how can we reason about a history if we do not know human beings and are not able to explain through their inclinations and passions the causes of events? Indeed, without an anthropology we cannot even make the sketch of a pragmatic history.

Everybody[3] now demands that a history be pragmatic, but there still are extremely few history books that are written strictly pragmatically. For, because the authors of many history books possess little knowledge of human beings, they cannot even create a correct concept of a pragmatic history, much less carry it out.

25:1212

---

a *bei zunehmender UrtheilsKraft*
b *Sittlichkeit*
c *moralisch*

d *BewegungsGründe*
e *Geodaesie*

However, anthropology is again also extended by history and clarified by new remarks. For I can take examples from history, and both sciences are thus mutually bound up with each other.

2. With regard to social intercourse

1.) Anthropology educates human beings for social intercourse and is a preliminary practice for the extended knowledge of the human being that one attains through traveling. It is true that many people, if they enter into good societies, will train their initially crude social intercourse[a] little by little. But again many do not have the occasion to do this, and then the knowledge of the human being that I attain through the social intercourse is merely ephemeral and consists merely in ways of complimenting and colloquialisms. It has no true content and also does not interest everyone; hence the most garrulous people often have the emptiest heads.

2.) But a solid knowledge of the human being interests everyone and provides material for conversation, even for a woman;[b] as Chremes in Terence⁴ says: "I am a human being, what relates to human beings concerns me, too," for here every human being can examine it; all that is abstract, namely, what one must for the most part examine [only] with great effort, thus does not belong here, yet it must not be completely commonplace[c] either.

3.) It also teaches us to know ourselves properly. The knowledge of the human being, or anthropology, is necessary for every human being. For through it he can make proper use of his skill, and thus produce many benefits, but also protect himself against a great deal of adversity.

THE SOURCES OF ANTHROPOLOGY ARE SELF-OBSERVATION, HISTORY, AND TO AN EXTENT NOVELS AND PLAYS AS WELL

We already spoke above about self-observation and history. Novels and plays are also of service for anthropology and quite often provide an occasion for some pleasant remarks, but only he who already has some knowledge of the human being can use them, and only such a person can make them up; indeed, the knowledge of the human being that they more or less contain is also their sole attraction. Hence, for example, the plays of Shakespeare are masterpieces because he had a deep understanding[d] of the human being. However, both novels and plays have a fault in that they mislead. For novels heat the passions and represent humanity with exaggerated features.[e] Even plays must use exaggerated features, and if one says that a caricatured portrayal is silly because

25:1213

---

[a] *Umgang*, social relations or dealings
[b] *Frauenzimmer*
[c] *vulgaer*
[d] *Erkenntniß*
[e] *Zügen*

346

the event that occurred over several years is then represented in a few hours, then one must attempt to make this fault, which would otherwise appear to us as unnatural, invisible by using exaggerated features 25:1214 that stir our power of imagination. Thus anthropology is also necessary for authors of novels and comedies. Because of its order, Baumgarten's empirical psychology is the best guide, and only the order of the materials and chapters will be retained in this anthropology, although many other considerations will enter in, since his book only concerns what is scholastic.

Now there still remains another question with regard to learning anthropology from experience.

Question:[a] Is it more difficult to become acquainted with oneself or with humanity? Response:[b] Both have their difficulties. However, it is still easier to become acquainted with oneself and with others than with humanity in general, for if I want to become acquainted with myself, I may only compare myself with other human beings, but I cannot compare humanity with any other rational creature because we are the only ones on earth. However, they both also have their own difficulties in themselves.

1. It is true that observing oneself appears to be easy because one always has oneself at hand and is most conscious of one's incentives with every action; however, it is still difficult in reality because the incentives of the human soul, the inclinations and passions, are either in <action> movement or in repose. If they are in movement, one does not think of observing them; but if they are in repose the occasion is gone and the power of memory[c] is also already somewhat extinguished or incomplete. In order to know oneself a series of observations is needed, and this is even more difficult.

2. Observing others is even more difficult, for human beings conceal their true character when they notice that someone is observing them, and no one wants to let himself be observed; and the more civilized the human being is, the more he misrepresents himself.[d] They are corrupt. But knowledge of the human species in general is the most difficult. 25:1215

SECOND CHAPTER

ON THE INVESTIGATION OF THE I

Our author[5] here begins with the investigation of the I, and we wish to follow him in this.

---

[a] *Quaestio*
[b] *Responsio*
[c] *Errinnerungskraft*
[d] *verstellt sich*, as in "dissembles"

Of all the creatures[a] on earth, the human being alone has a representation of his I or of his person.[b] This also makes him a rational being. Animals indeed have representations of the world, but not of their I; thus they are also not rational beings. Very small children speak of themselves <not through I—rather, they say their names> more in the third person than in the first person. This happens because they are called that and because they cannot grasp the difference between when one speaks of oneself and when one speaks of another. Likewise, a child of two months only sees with his eyes fixedly and does not follow any objects; thus he does not [really] see. But in two months he already sees properly and then he also begins to cry and laugh. Why this is the case is as obscure as the former. Whatever designates our person, our I, draws our entire attention. For instance, if we are in a conversation in society and we are not paying attention and then suddenly hear our name, we awaken as if from a dream, as it were, and our entire attention is aroused through it. Thus it can also happen that, as one says, the sleepwalkers or night-climbers awaken from their deep[c] dreams upon the mention of their names, and if they have climbed up into dangerous places, they are in danger of falling down, for the mention of our person arouses the greatest attention in us.

If a human being is concerned only with himself and directs all of the attention only to himself or at all occasions has incentives to speak about himself, he is called an egoist (conversation egoism).

25:1216   A moral egoist values his worth the most. An egoist in social intercourse, however, speaks and occupies himself always with his most beloved I. The latter possesses a certain vanity, and his egoism indicates a lack of culture, conduct,[d] and knowledge of the human being.

Every human being has a kind of egoism in himself, as he does not think that he is the center of the world, to be sure, yet he certainly wishes to be.

1. Hence if a person finds an occasion to speak about himself, he or she views as clever the person who offers the opportunity to do so. Thus Helvétius[6] tells a pleasant story of a lady: When he was in Paris he entered into a social gathering in which a lady was conversing with a man for a rather long time. Afterwards she praised him as a man with a great mind; in the end it turned out that he was deaf, and that she had been speaking only to herself, and that naturally he had just kept saying "yes" to her.

---

[a] Reading, as in Mar: *allen Geschöpfen* (all the creatures). Mro: *allen vernünftigen Geschöpfen* (all the rational creatures).

[b] *Person*

[c] Marginal notes, similar to the passage at Collins 25:10 in this volume, are inserted here: "The first thought that strikes us ... for the I is not an external thing." Brandt and Stark indicate this, but do not reproduce the insertion here.

[d] *Conduite*

2. The human being is kind to his neighbor not because he has good qualities, but because he finds an occasion to show off his own good qualities. Hence one often becomes fond of those for whom one has done good deeds. From this it follows that in society we must speak of ourselves the least, since everyone else also always wants to speak of himself; hence in the end everyone <u>would</u> speak of himself, and through this in the end all society would at last be abrogated. One must therefore constrain this impulse of self-love so that partiality toward ourselves is not so prominent. The finer the human being, the more he yields to the egoism of others and denies his own. However, it is still very entertaining; for example, Montaigne's *Essay*[7] is a very entertaining book, and even if it is already 200 years old, its reputation still remains undiminished. But this is because he manages to speak of himself in most occasions, and this is the most entertaining part of the whole book and not at all a fault, as some[8] believe. For if one speaks about himself, one talks about the human being, and the knowledge of the human being interests everyone indeed.

25:1217

If one speaks about himself, however, he must not record what differs from other human beings, unless it is peculiar and can be useful for the knowledge of the human being. For example, *Magister* Bernd[9] wrote a book about hypochondria in which he recorded all the peculiar whims[a] he had while in a paroxysm.[b] <We disapprove of something if we consider it unseemly in general relations.>

A moral egoist is one who lets himself become so blinded that he attaches little value to everything except himself. – Through the self-esteem that he ascribes to himself,[c] the human being perhaps receives a value from others, but self-esteem must not go so far that it is not considered an attribution.[d] Concerning his attentiveness, each human being has himself as the main objective. The I constitutes the ground of all affection.[e] That is why, for example, one does not impute guilt to a fired bullet if it kills someone, but to the I that fired it.

Many people, especially kings, writers, and preachers on the pulpit, prefer to speak of themselves as "we" rather than as "I," and indeed they do this out of prudence so as to avoid the appearance of egoism.

For kings in earlier times it was an expression of modesty, for when the king wrote "we" in his writings, he always included the estates. Now, however, it has become a concept of majesty. It is also a concept of modesty for an author, for he regards his listener or reader as his associate. On the pulpit, one must also use "we" out of modesty. The plural as a

---
[a] *besondre Grillen*
[b] *Paroxismo*, i.e., periodic convulsion or attack brought on by disease
[c] *sich beymessende Selbstschätzung*   [e] *Zuneigung*, as in "sympathy, fondness"
[d] *Attribution*

form of address is in use only in the Oriental[a] countries, and the Germans, among whom this [use] varies widely, have thereby made social intercourse much more cumbersome. It should indicate an honor. One does not come across this in any living or dead language; instead, one uses the familiar "you."[b] "He" actually must be used for someone absent.

25:1218 If it is used for someone present, it is ridiculous.

The familiar "you," "he," the plural familiar "you," and the formal "you"[c] are the grades of honor for the Germans; they have made their social intercourse very wearisome through these courtesies.

Just as much as I consider things outside of myself, I can also consider myself. The habit of observing oneself is unnatural, for through this one's mental powers become bound[d] and cannot produce naturally.

Giving attention to other objects is more natural.

A consistent observer of oneself is much more harmed by this than is the most melancholic mathematician; in the end he becomes a fanatic <mystic> and fantast <as he wants to brood about himself and dig for buried treasures in his mind. Such people tire themselves out with their own selves and grind themselves as one whets a sword. In order to be happy, one must forget oneself.[e]>

To the human being observation of oneself is unnatural, not because one does not get enough entertainment nor because he does not find himself sufficiently likeable; rather, the cause is that self-observation tires the mind[f] exceedingly and ultimately renders it confused. The observation of other objects therefore helps us toward recovery – the philosopher's occupation with the analysis of concepts is also rather unnatural, but he still has objects that he thinks by using his understanding. But as soon as he finds an example the mind is instantly relieved. Therefore, when active the human being must be occupied with himself the least, but instead should be occupied with other objects, and only occasionally cast a glance at himself. Indeed, nature wanted us often to occupy ourselves with thoughtlessness. A human being who always considers himself while in a society is either forced [or] bashful, for he believes that he does not demonstrate his own qualities sufficiently <out of fear again of breaching good decency. In his behavior he is timid, oafish, and stiff, and he thereby falls quite short of his purpose. This is an error in education, as one continually calls upon the child to be well-behaved, etc., which is a delicate[g] concept, and then he becomes anxious, timid, and

[a] *bei den Morgenländern*. To refer to Asia, Kant usually uses *orientalische* and words related to it (e.g., 25:1232), sometimes capitalized; in such cases the capitilization is reproduced. Kant uses *asiatische* only once in Mro (25:1412).
[b] *Du*
[c] familiar you: *Du*; he: *Er*; plural familiar you: *Ihr*; formal you: *Sie*.
[d] *gebunden*, as in "tied, linked"   [f] *Geist*
[e] *sich Seiner Selbst vergeßen machen*   [g] *delicater*

loses all self-confidence. Good behavior is entirely a task of education. Here society contributes the most. The English youth is well-raised.> or acts affectedly,[a] for he believes that he demonstrates his qualities too much or too markedly, since through that consideration he demonstrates that he likes himself. In a word, a human being acts affectedly if he endeavors <in order to please the eyes> to demonstrate an attractive decency and therefore misrepresents his attitudes <and modulates his tone accordingly>; this is contrary to nature and one seems forced when he worries about appearing to lack good decency. <An affected human being loses a great deal in the eyes of others, as he deceitfully attempts to acquire his worth through outward semblance. No great man is able to act affectedly, for example, to speak as if from a book. The way of writing in texts is, as it were, like a gala costume and, as in society, one cannot arrive in a nightgown and nightcap.>

25:1219

He who pays no attention[b] to himself or appears not to have any attention, shows himself in a natural ease (*air degagée,[c]* naïveté), which pleases everyone.

But one must pay attention to the posture of the body, or ought to have already acquired dexterity during [one's] youth. An affected human being hears himself, as he pays attention to the tone and choice of his words.

Hence the human being who always pays attention to himself is scarcely cultivated.

This egoism is also the cause of hypochondria, as in that case one always pays attention to himself, and if one hears of something happening to others he also believes it is happening to him as well. Raptures, or fanaticism,[d] also derive from this source. From all this one concludes that one ought not relinquish very much to egoism, but restraining this egoism in social intercourse also requires a great art.

We can divide our consciousness into subjective and objective consciousness. Our consciousness is subjective when we direct our thoughts to our existence and to our understanding itself; it is objective when we turn them to other objects.

The objective consciousness is entirely natural to all sciences and to us. Hence the human being who does not feel his body at all is properly healthy. It is therefore bad advice if one suggests that the human being should examine the condition of his soul. But I can find this out just as well through attentiveness to my actions. Therefore, Lavater[10] was wrong to have written a journal containing observations of himself. He should

25:1220

---

[a] *affectirt,* as in "feigns, pretends"   [b] *Acht*
[c] Trans.: easy manner. Kant explains "naïveté" below.
[d] *Die Schwärmerei oder der Fanatismus*

have let this be and instead should have written a journal describing his actions.

Thoughtlessness with regard to the subject is a [kind of] recovery for us. –

Nature gave us a drive to occupy ourselves with different objects always, so that we might not stay calmly with one object for too long.

We go into society, hunting, etc., and with what aim? In order to distract^{*a*} ourselves. Now one distracts oneself in two ways.

1. When one turns his attention from himself to other objects and

2. The other way around, when one turns his attention from other objects to himself.

The first distraction occurs in society and is beneficial to us and also constitutes the proper use of society, but the second is harmful to us. The former is agreeable to our soul, but the latter is annoying and painful. The former serves to strengthen our mental powers and to recover, but the latter to weaken them.

Hence the occupation and observation of oneself also leaves one unnatural. One observes oneself as it is left to another [or] as one appears to others, and through this one becomes either forced or affected.^{*b*}

Every human being is always ready to conceal himself and to show his most advantageous side in order to conduct himself in a way befitting outer prosperity.

But we act then in an artificial, forced manner and not naturally. The natural behavior of a human being, if one shows oneself as one is, without paying attention to outer appearance,^{*c*} is naïveté.^{*d*} Naïve is what is actually artificial but appears to be brought forth entirely naturally and becomes [so]. Hence it also pleases everyone because it is natural and shows a human being's true disposition, which one after all so much likes to conceal.

25:1221

THIRD CHAPTER

ON REPRESENTATIONS

We turn now from the subjective consciousness of ourselves to the objective consciousness of other objects.

We have either clear or obscure representations of things.

We wish to consider obscure representations a little here. I am not conscious of my obscure representation; but how, then, do I know that

---

^{*a*} *zerstreuen* ^{*b*} *genirt oder affectirt*
^{*c*} *Schein*, usually "illusion, semblance," but here used in the sense of "look, appearance."
^{*d*} *Naivitaet*

I have them?[a] I do not know them immediately; however, from their effects I can conclude that I must have them; for example, it is true that I cannot see the air, but I can conclude from its effects that it must be there. In this way, for example, the ancients already explained the glimmer of the Milky Way as the light of a multitude of stars, although for lack of telescopes they could not see these stars. <A musician, without thinking, would not produce any harmony.>

The human soul is occupied mostly with obscure representations, and these are also the basis for clear representations and for all discoveries and inventions. They play so great a role in the actions of the human soul that, if a human being could become conscious of all these representations all at once, he might be astonished at their inventory; but the capacity to reproduce these representations is so limited that they see the light of day only individually and on certain occasions. When we remember a thing, we bring forth the obscure representations in the thing and make them clear; thus a man who has seen and read a lot cannot recount anything and becomes silent if one asks him to do so. But if one points him toward a topic, he knows right away what to recount from it. This occurs because he has such a multitude of obscure representations in his soul that he cannot instantly choose any of them. It is as if he could not see the forest for the trees. One could represent the human soul as a map whose illuminated parts [and] the clear, certain, particularly bright parts signify the distinct representations, while the unilluminated parts signify the obscure representations; the latter occupy the greatest space and also underlie the clear representations and constitute the majority of our cognition.

In analytic philosophy,[b] I simply make obscure representations in the soul clear. For all propositions of philosophy are known to everyone, although only in obscure representations that are made clear and distinct through philosophy [so] that he becomes conscious of them and so to speak remembers, as he feels that these are the same propositions of which he was also previously conscious, albeit indistinctly. For example, if I speak about right to someone who is not a legal scholar,[c] he will concede [something] to me insofar as it appears to him that he had also previously known it, but he will not consider it to be right, at which [point] he will remember[d] that he had also thought or suspected it thus. – Previously obscure representations underlay most inventions. The knowledge of the human being can be seen as a large map, where only a few points are illuminated.

25:1222

---

[a] The Academy Edition has a period here rather than a question mark.
[b] *Analytischen Philosophie*
[c] *der kein Rechtsgelehrter ist, vom Recht sage*
[d] *für Recht halten, von dem er sich erinnert*

The soul thus works for the most part in obscure representations, and it takes some time before one makes them clear. Hence Socrates rightly says: "I am not the teacher of my listeners, but only the midwife of their thoughts."[11] For, as a midwife during the birth of a child brings the latter into the light, so, too, the philosopher brings the obscure representations of his listeners into the light and makes them clear. There are two things to note from this:

α.) 1. The human being is often a play of obscure representations, as by obscure representations he lets himself either be brought toward a thing or held back, against his intention and against the voice of reason. For example, if I traverse a rather dangerous place – such as [a body of] water over which a plank is set down – and I also see many people traverse, and my understanding tells me that I can traverse without danger if I use caution, some obscure representations will nevertheless stir within us that hinder us from traversing. Many indeed who have fallen down in such dangerous places have also had such obscure representations, as if they were already falling down; and through this they ultimately got dizzy and actually fell down, too. Thus some people also fear death, although their lives are not at all enjoyable.[a]

We also mourn a deceased person in this way, for after all our understanding tells us that instead we should be pleased in this case because he goes on to a happier life. However, the obscure representation of resting in the grave is still repugnant to us; hence many people also have themselves buried in the mountains under trees, etc. <not in humidity; they think that they will catch a cold> although their understanding tells them it does not matter where their bodies lie. However, they have obscure representations that it nonetheless might perhaps be better there than elsewhere, as if while still dead he[b] could look at the agreeable and amuse himself with it. Similarly, everybody, even if one is still very poor, attempts to accumulate enough money for an honorable funeral.

Expressions that are used in a shallow joke lose their beauty and dignity as a result. – <The miser sees the enjoyment in this.>

According to Buffon,[12] the particular taste in love depends on the following: the first person one sees when one reaches his virile age becomes his[c] archetype. Now if there is another woman who is rather similar to her, even if it is also a mistake, then our imagination[d] adds to the archetype in obscure representations what is left over, and the person thereby becomes likeable even if she is not.

---

[a] *gar nicht lieb*
[b] *er*. This is one of several cases in which the transcriber switches from plural pronouns or verb forms to singular ones.
[c] *unser* (our) [d] *Imagination*

β.) 2. By contrast, the human being also talks in a roundabout way with obscure representations. Hence, for example, every trope and every figure of speech is a detour, as one suddenly makes an obscure representation clear, and its agreeableness consists in that. Every witty gag must initially be obscure and then suddenly clarify itself; otherwise it is bitter. Nature has certain secrets, such as the natural needs and the difference between the sexes, which she always wants to have hidden[a] though obscure representations. These appear to be below the dignity of human beings, for in these respects he agrees with[b] the animals. Hence we always speak of these things in obscure representations, and the more obscure they are, the better and more agreeable they are; but if one speaks about it such that everyone understands it without the slightest ambiguity, this is viewed as crudity. Hence one sees that the human being possesses an art of obscuring, so to speak; these obscure representations are all the more agreeable, the more obscure they are and the more suddenly they become clear.

There is currently a contemplative <mysterious> way of writing in which obscure representations are found; this is an artifice of writers who want to convince the public of the opinion that a great deal of wisdom remains hidden in their writings. For obscure representations sometimes appear to contain more than they actually contain.

25:1224

FOURTH CHAPTER

ON THE PERFECTION OF COGNITIONS, IN PARTICULAR ON THEIR TRUTH, DISTINCTNESS, USES, MAGNITUDE, AND ORDER

The perfection of a cognition can be distinguished in three ways:[13]

a. With regard to the object, and here it is truth, magnitude, and distinctness. This is logical.

b. With regard to the subject; here it is ease, liveliness, and interest; this is aesthetic.

c. With regard to the connection of cognitions with one another; here it is diversity, order, and unity.

Truth is the greatest perfection of cognitions, since it is demanded that every cognition in the first place be true; if it is not true, it lacks everything and it is no cognition at all. But it is the greatest perfection only for the understanding, and not for inclination. The latter prefers to occupy itself more with the fable than the truth. Hence it is not advisable to tell a human being the truth, since one offends his inclinations. In

---

[a] *immer bedeckt haben will*   [b] *überein komt*

poetic representations, cognitions are untrue but are not errors, for one knows that they are untrue.

Error and ignorance are set in opposition to truth. Ignorance is set in opposition to truth as a privation[a] and [is] a mere lack of cognition. Error, however, is set in opposition to truth as a contrary,[b] for it is not a mere lack of cognition and of truth, but a hindrance to these as well. Ignorance is, as it were, an empty space in the soul that is not yet filled with cognitions. Error, however, is a space that is filled with erroneous cognitions. Error is therefore much more harmful than ignorance and also much more difficult to eliminate.[c] The removal[d] of errors provides a negative use that is much greater than the positive use, and without which the latter is not even possible. Thus it almost seems better to be, to remain, ignorant than to put oneself at the risk of committing an error.[14] But it only appears this way, for in order never to err we also must never venture a judgment; we would remain in lethargic ignorance and would then need to do away with every employment of our understanding, and even if we often err in our judgments, surely this cultivates our understanding. For error arises out of unreflective activity, but ignorance out of inactivity. The more extensive the cognitions are, the more we run the risk of erring. Hence a society of scholars is more prone to error than an entire village of peasants. (Truths receive importance first through their fruitfulness in application, through their magnitude, and through their interest; otherwise, they are insignificant.)

A judgment ventured with an understanding of the risk of error is called a paradox. The French love these judgments and name it *audacity*.[e] But the Germans proceed cautiously with these. It is true that a paradoxical man runs the danger of being laughed at, but he is also thereby useful to others, as he thereby considers the matter from a completely different angle. Paradoxical judgments are, so to speak, counterintuitive[f] because they run counter to the first appearance of the senses. He who shies away from the paradox is cowardly in judging, for with regard to truth one runs just as much risk with paradoxical [judgments] as with everyday judgments, except that with the latter one is more sure of approval. Because the paradox shows us an expansion of our cognition, it delights us and is agreeable to us. But one must not attempt always to judge [by] paradox, otherwise one becomes an adventurer in the sciences; Berkeley, Bishop of Cloyne in Ireland, was such a person. All paradoxes open up new perspectives for us. There are also paradoxical propositions that are

[a] *privative*
[b] *contrarie*
[c] *heben*
[d] *Aufhebung*
[e] *Hardiesse*, from the French *hardi* (bold, courageous, audacious)
[f] *wiedersinnisch*

actually true: for example, Copernicus's proposition about the orbit of the earth around the sun.

The popular criterion*a* of truth in anthropology is the approbation of other human beings, and is quite different from the logical one. To court the approval of others is vanity, but it is certainly important for us and we are in need of it.

We all have a drive, implanted in us by nature, to make our judg-   12:1226
ments known to others; should we thereby also bring shame and annoyance upon ourselves and our knowledge seem to have a value for us only insofar as we communicate it to others, nevertheless this occured intentionally so that, if our judgments remained locked up inside ourselves and were false, we did not always remain stuck in error, and so that a human being had the occasion to extend his knowledge through the judgments of others. Thus in some sciences one invokes other men who are of the same opinion, particularly in jurisprudence, because there is such a multiplicity of court cases here that some are difficult to distinguish from one another, and thus one invokes others to strengthen one's opinion.

One has*b* raised the question:[15] Whether in some cases one could not favor errors in order to draw utility from them? And the Jesuits actually assert this.[16] But this is never acceptable. For the utility of errors is only accidental and can quickly cease, and it is also always far too small to outweigh the harms they bring about.

An enlightened*c* age is one in which <one questions with clear concepts> the dissemination of truth meets no obstacles, even if the sciences in that age have not yet climbed very high. An enlightened age is where one sees with one's own eyes, but a blind one is where one is immature, so to speak. To some extent our age can be put here; however, religious and governmental coercion has not yet been eliminated. But with the current condition of Europe, since every monarch and every state has a large standing army, they could perhaps allow a general freedom of conscience because they have nothing to fear. An enlightened or bright mind is one that sees cognition clearly and distinctly <and also yields itself to no other>, but therefore cannot always make it easy and comprehensible to others. For the brightest minds are often able to do this the least. Some writers love the obscure way of writing, so that their cognitions might appear to contain a great deal of content.[17]   25:1227
One calls this: the author "gives cues."[18] But one must not trust these cues because often nothing is hidden behind them, and it is frequently an artifice used by the author to cloak his ignorance. <A human being

---

a *Populaere Criterium*
b Following Mar: *hat* (has). Mro: *hat zu manchen Zeiten* (has sometimes).
c *Erleuchtetes*

who, like the Roman praetor, etc., always says *non liquet*[a] is on a good path to enlightenment.[b]>

The actual extent of knowledge[c] is based on its comprehensiveness of application, not on its amount. All polyhistors[d] have vast knowledge.

The distinctness of cognition is either:

1. scholastic distinctness, where the work and the process through which the distinctness is produced must be evident; and 2. popular distinctness, where just the opposite must happen and the labor must not be conspicuous at all. This latter makes a cognition that is difficult in itself appear to require no effort and [makes it] easy to comprehend; this is a great feat for a writer, and here Voltaire has a great deal of uniqueness.

Order is required for the distinctness of cognition. One must observe order in all things, and order is also agreeable to everyone. If, concerning distinctness, there is order, and if at the same time the order is not conspicuous, it is agreeable. The Germans attempt to be distinct through order, but they let the latter be conspicuous in doing so, hence it does not work. But the French possess this [ability]. On the one hand, we love order, but on the other hand, we shy away from it because of its rules. Hence derives the expression "agreeable inattentiveness,"[e] when it appears to be effortless and the rules of order are not conspicuous. For example, in a garden the inattentivenss to order, imitating nature, is more agreeable than a strict order that is noticeable everywhere.

25:1228 Every cognition is useful in that it cultivates our understanding and extends our knowledge. But it also has its particular uses that we learn to appreciate sooner or later, even if at first it seems to us to be useless.

The practical worth of cognition is the one that puts us in a position to exercise our advantages.

The aesthetic worth of a cognition is entertainment, for example, well-written novels, poems, and the like, entertain us while we read them. Even titillating poems have a moral use. For the more I learn to see what is refined in action and not find taste merely in crude enjoyment, the more the mind is able to be influenced by moral principles. But in such poems, the refined and charming in love is treated, not animal needs; consequently, etc.[f]

---

[a] Trans.: it is not clear. *Mihi non liquet* ("The matter is not clear to me") was a technical term in Roman law.

[b] *Aufklärung*

[c] In this paragraph, *Erkenntniß* is translated with "knowledge" rather than "cognition."

[d] *Polyhistors*   [f] The sentence appears to break off here.

[e] *angenehme Nachlaßigkeit*

In some cognitions, logical and aesthetic worth are found together. Thus Horace says: *Suaviter in modo, fortiter in re,*[a] "Pleasing in manner and important in content."[19] One also calls the latter hypostatic, independent, and the former emphatic.[20]

Appearance,[b] diversity, is the most entertaining when it comes to cognition. Unity in diversity is the most difficult, but at the same time an important purpose for all our cognition.

FIFTH CHAPTER

ON SENSIBILITY

To this belong not only the senses but also the lower powers of the soul, in short, everything that draws us involuntarily to a thing. It is set in opposition to the understanding. The understanding belongs to concepts, sensibility to intuition and sensation. One blames a human being when it is said that he is sensual.[c] We consider what is dominated to be base, although not as indispensable as what dominates; the understanding is nobler, but not more useful.[d] Sensibility is held responsible in two ways:

25:1229

α it allegedly deceives the understanding

β it allegedly obscures and confuses the understanding.[21]

We now want to make an apology for it and attempt to absolve it of these crimes,[e] although we do not want [to offer] a panegyric. Note: Apology means to present a thing as it is, yet neither to elevate nor, through imputed deficiencies, to lower it, but certainly to free it from prejudices.[f] Sensibility does not deceive the understanding, not because it does not judge falsely, but because it does not judge at all. The understanding thus has to blame itself if it judges falsely. <It should be attributed merely to the errors of commission and omission [on the part] of the understanding, and the lack of attentiveness. The fair sex is primarily sensible,[g] and children are as well. The former do not have that much skill in sculpture, etc.>

We can have neither mere understanding nor mere sensibility.[22] For through mere sensibility we cannot judge at all; it is true that we could judge through mere understanding, but it would result in sheer figments

---

[a] Trans.: gentle in manner, resolute in execution. Or: gentle in manner, strong in the matter.

[b] *Einkleidung*, more literally, "dressing, outfit, garb, clothing"

[c] *sinlich* (usually rendered as "sensible")

[d] Reading, as in Mar: *nützlicher* (more useful). Mro: *höher* (higher).

[e] Reading, as in Mro: *diese Verbrechen zu befreyen* (to absolve it of these crimes). Mar: *diese Beschuldigungen los zu machen* (to release it from these accusations).

[f] This note is found in Mar, but not Mro.

[g] *sinnlich*

of the mind; hence both [faculties] have to be conjoined to each other. <For it furnishes the materials, etc.>^a

In general, one can divide the faculty of the human being into a sensible^b and an intellectual faculty. Sensible is everything that belongs to the modification of the subject; intellectual is whatever concerns the object. If I consider a speech according to the effects it has upon me it is sensible for me, but if I look at its properties it is intellectual. Sensible feeling is based on the consciousness of the modification of our condition; intellectual [feeling rests] on the knowledge^c of the objects. All types of metaphors are sensible representations. Sensible pleasure is if my condition is affected;^d intellectual [pleasure], if I am conscious of the change in my condition. Sensible desire arises out of stimuli;^e intellectual [desire] out of motivations.^f Sensibility supposedly confuses understanding, but the understanding does that on its own if it collects too many concepts without separating them from each other properly. Sensibility also does not obscure the understanding, for on the contrary it makes the understanding even clearer because it gives the understanding examples. Sensibility produces the clarity of intuition, but the understanding [produces] the clarity of concepts. The clarity of intuition is nevertheless much greater than the clarity of the concepts <It is a delusion, to attribute deficiencies to sensibility as if that were a remnant from the fall of man.>

One blames some for being abstract minds because they do not take any examples from sensibility; on the other hand, one calls others who use sensibility rather than understanding superficial minds.^g Both [types] go too far because they do not properly conjoin understanding and sensibility with one another. If sensibility is in play, it can be somewhat of a hindrance to the understanding and disturb it; but it is infinitely more useful to the understanding. The understanding gives concepts. However, sensibility gives the intuition. It gives examples and thereby realizes the concepts [so] that they become distinct. Hence we demand everyone to represent the matter^h sensibly <make sensibleⁱ>. If we did not have sensibility, our understanding would not at all have cognition of things,^j for then it would have no object.^k Indeed, we could almost sooner do without the understanding than sensibility. For if we only had

25:1230

---

^a Mar reads: "Sensibility also does not obscure the understanding, but on the contrary enlightens it even more because it gives the understanding examples." A similar line is found in the next paragraph (25:1230).

^b *sinnliches*

^c *Kentniß*

^d *afficirt*

^e *aus stimulis*

^f *aus Motiven*

^g *seichte Köpfe*

^h *Sache*

ⁱ *versinnlichen*

^j *von Dingen erkennen*

^k *Gegenstand*

mere sensibility, then to be sure we would not be human beings, but we would still be animals. But if we had only understanding, we could be neither human beings nor animals. Sensibility is therefore actually more useful to us than the understanding.

But why, then, does the understanding have a higher rank? Because it governs and gives rules; hence everything must be subordinated to it. For example, the scholar has a higher rank in human society than the farmer, although the latter is more useful.

Because the impressions of sensibility are greater than those of the understanding it occasionally happens that sensibility, when it is in play, makes it more difficult for the understanding to be conscious of what it is doing. But sensibility richly compensates the understanding for this, as it gives the understanding material for its considerations and thereby makes its concepts clearer. Hence, if we want sensibility not to hinder our understanding, we may take from it only one example and thereby draw sensibility in our interest; thus this [concept] will keep all other concepts out of sensibility. <Sensibility can individuate universal concepts, as it were. But there are nevertheless also cases, for example, [in] metaphysics, 25:1231 where one cannot exhibit*a* something *in concreto* without damaging thoroughness, and in this, aiming for popularity, many ancients went too far.>

The habit*b* of concepts is a great advantage for the understanding, as concepts then return without being summoned. But the habituated way*c* is the great hindrance for human understanding. False concepts, once they become habituated, repeat the same play of sensibility and thus let the understanding take no other course at all. For example, if a preacher in the pulpit soundly speaks of pleasure*d* as a high degree of self-satisfaction, then his listeners will not find it sufficiently evident and understandable because they will always connect it with their habituated concepts of an animal pleasure. In such a case, one must then attempt to draw them into one's interest through an example from sensibility. But the greatest ill that sensibility does is this, that it often draws us against our power of choice in the direction where the understanding did not want to go. Here sensibility actually does deserve blame, and this is also the reason why the ancients vociferated so strongly against it.[23]

For the greatest perfection of man is that of being able to act according to his power of choice, to direct his cognition to an object and again turn away from it. This is also the first condition of all rules and precepts that I should uphold and practice; for if this is missing, I am also not able to direct myself according to rules. –

---

a *darstellen*   *c* *Angewohnheit*
b *Gewohnheit*   *d* *Wollust*

We must therefore always take care to have our mental powers under our control, and this must already occur in early youth. We must thus not let sensibility dominate, but rather discipline it through the understanding, [so] that we can use it if and however it is conducive to our understanding. For if sensibility gets the upper hand, it will be with us as it is with those republics where anarchy creeps in.

On the contrary, we must not weaken sensibility, but sharpen and cultivate it; but the understanding must always remain master over it. Now governing this sensibility is the first and greatest perfection, which, however, one has still developed [only] to a slight extent, unfortunately.

25:1232

In our soul, the understanding is the guide and sensibility the motive force, as Pope rightly says.[24] Without sensibility, the concepts of understanding would have no meaning, for they would have no object to which they could be applied. It is thus an instrument of the understanding. Hence every concept of the understanding, however clear it may be, does not have as much intensity[a] as a concept from sensibility, and these latter stimulate the will more than the concepts of the understanding, for the understanding is directed only at objects;[b] but sensibility is directed merely at the subject, that is, at ourselves; hence it also interests us more than the understanding.

Every human being has at times a greater, at times a slighter, degree of sensibility. One can regard this sometimes as useful, sometimes as harmful. Because sensibility is a hindrance to the understanding, a great degree of sensibility can significantly harm the understanding. But, on the other hand, because sensibility is extremely useful to the understanding, it can also be of great use to him <(him, i.e., to the human being)>. And this is also how it is for someone who has a slight degree of sensibility.

The play of sensibility is much more lively in the female sex than in the male. Hence they become vexed[c] over things and beside themselves much sooner than men. They would like to have everything represented in examples and fables. In their desires they are also very sensible.[d]

Musicians, gardeners, cooks, master builders, orators, poets, painters, etc., are the virtuosi of sensibility.

It is not the case that one has a greater degree of sensibility in childhood than he does later; rather, the understanding is weaker then and sensibility is thus proportionally greater. – In old age, our understanding is not greater than in our youth; rather, sensibility is weaker, etc.; hence in comparison with sensibility the understanding is great in old age; the power of judgment,[e] it is true, grows with the years and is strong in old

[a] *Stärke*
[b] *geht nur auf Obiecte*
[c] *alterirt*
[d] *sinnlich*
[e] *BeurtheilungsKraft*

age, but it does not at all contribute to the suppression of sensibility, but rather helps one to resist sensibility better in old age than in youth.[a]

The sensibility of cognition is very common among all the oriental[b] peoples, for there they all speak with pictures[c] and do not have spiritual[d] and abstract words such as we have; but this indicates a weak cultivation of their spirit, for in this respect they are like the first human beings who also used pictography.[e] Meiners[25] here makes the good remark that one wrote in verse before one wrote in prose and that in the beginning one taught in verse all of the sciences, indeed even philosophy. But that happens because the first human beings always spoke in sheer pictures and still did not have any words for abstract concepts because they are not found in common life. Now only verse is suited to this pictography, and through syllabic proportion the power of imagination is all the more entertained. Thus Orpheus and others sang the first philosophy in verses.[26] Heraclitus was the first to speak in prose; hence he was also incomprehensible to the Greeks, for he could find no words for the expression of abstract concepts. But as soon as people began to speak with concepts, prose was introduced. In this way Parmenides, Anaximander, and Pythagoras later availed themselves of prose for their philosophy. Because philosophy ascended among the Greeks, they enriched their language with a multitude of abstract concepts. The Romans later began to pursue philosophy and other sciences, and in doing so they did not bring it as high as the Greeks. Hence in their language they do not possess so great a multitude of abstract words.

From this short survey of the history of human languages, one can see that the Oriental peoples still have a child's language of humanity, and that the Westerners abandoned sensibility much sooner and have raised themselves up to the concepts of the understanding. Hence it would be ridiculous for us, who have a more masculine language, to exchange this for the child's language of the Oriental peoples and also to start speaking in sheer pictures, as some writers urgently admonish us to do.[27]

25:1233

25:1234

CHAPTER 6.

ON THE USE OF SENSIBLE REPRESENTATIONS

ON EASE AND DIFFICULTY

Actions in which we use our representations and powers voluntarily are either easy or difficult.

---

[a] This period replaces a comma at the end of the sentence found in the Academy Edition.
[b] *orientalischen* (not capitalized)
[c] *Bildern*
[d] *geistige*
[e] *BilderSchrift*

An action is difficult if a large part of our powers must be applied to bring it about, and easy if I perform it with a small part of my powers. <If I thus still retain a great surplus of my powers: for example, if a child of nine years lifts up a stone that weighs 33 pounds, it is difficult for him, but not for a laborer because he still retains a large surplus of his powers. One calls whatever is difficult in terms of the capacities of most people, difficult in and of itself.>

With regard to the diversity of the capacity and the powers of a human being, ease and difficulty is also different[a] with each person. Hence what is easy for one person is difficult for another. All that is easy and difficult is thus easy or difficult in comparison with the powers of the subject.

The difficult[b] is distinguished from the burdensome;[c] the former concerns capacity, the latter pleasure. At *1 John* 5:3, Christ says, "My commandments are not difficult":[28] this should say "burdensome," for the duties are perhaps difficult but not burdensome, not tied to useless ceremonies and drudgery <vexation> as the Jewish [duties are]. But why then is the difficult disagreeable?[d] Because we must direct a large part of our powers to an object [and] thereby deplete our powers and are not able to apply them to other objects. Because with the easy, by contrast, we can also direct our attentiveness and powers to other objects, it pleases us.

But if the difficult is an attempt to reveal the degree of our powers and cognition, it is agreeable to us; the difficulty of a thing is either internal, if its ground lies in the thing <and the purpose or its true content is of greatest importance>, or external, if external circumstances hinder the performance of a thing. What is easy can still become burdensome, either if one has many easy things to do, or if it seems to us to be unnecessary and vacuous and we have no desire to do it. The many compliments and visits that one must make to reach an office or a higher level of good fortune [are] otherwise customary in social intercourse, and thereby make it very tedious. These are utter vexations and unnecessary things. For that reason one prefers to take pains to do something difficult, yet also important.

Everything appears easy to a man who imagines that a thing[e] has only a small purpose. However, for a person who resolves that every thing has a great purpose, every thing becomes difficult. For instance, to a man who resolves, in the education of a child, to imprint on the child only things to memorize, it appears easy. (It seems that human beings invented these

25:1235

---

[a] *ist ... unterscheiden*

[b] *Das schwere*

[c] *beschwerlichen*

[d] This question mark replaces a semi-colon found here in the Academy Edition; the *B* at the beginning of the next sentence is capitalized accordingly.

[e] *Sache*

vexations in order to really spoil the good fortune a person has attained.)
<For instance, the hazing of freshmen[a] at universities, earning a doctorate, marrying. So, too, in religion, fasting, as with the Mohammedans, [and] the five great commandments;[29] the more reasonable a man is, the more annoying it is to him. The so-called bantering[b] among traders is also included here: *Hansa* means bantering and *Hans* merchant, hence Hanseatic cities.[c][30]> Doing something easy is no art, but making something difficult easy is a great feat. One makes difficult burdens easy by means of certain machines, but difficult cognition [easy] by means of certain pedagogical methods. Revealing difficulty is not charlatanry.

If I replace difficult cognitions with easy ones and thereby represent them [as] easy, I am engaging in a deception. For I then offer the easy instead of the difficult, as well as the superficial instead of the fundamental. Many writers make their cognitions easy in such a way, as they touch only the surface of the cognitions and thereby become superficial. Voltaire[31] was like this and made the philosophy of Newton easy   25:1236
<(Lawyers often try to dupe judges in this way when they commence with a clause that they hold to be agreed upon and say, "It is agreed upon, it is self-evident.")> by leaving out everything difficult; but that is charlatanry.[32] Algarotti[33] also wrote Newtonian philosophy for ladies, and here he met with better success. Voltaire's hobby-horse is tolerance,[34] but that is also in itself an easy matter; only a few have succeeded in making the difficult easy; for example, Fontenelle,[35] author of dialogues on a plurality of worlds, edited with notes by Bode, gives proof of this.

Hence, in order to scare off such superficial minds, one must reveal the difficult in a cognition <and geniuses will embrace science precisely for the sake of the difficulty. Revealing difficulty is good>.

A human being who thinks everything is easy[d] is thoughtless,[e] but he who by contrast thinks everything is difficult is punctilious.[f] A thoughtless human being often promises much and thereafter does not hold his word; but this occurs not because he wants to deceive us, but rather because he really thinks the thing is easy and neither understands nor thinks about its difficulty. One must therefore not trust such [a person] very much; on the other hand, it is better to trust a punctilious [person], for the latter thinks about the internal and external difficulty of a thing and does not promise until he is certain he can deliver on it. Yet such people also do not undertake anything at all, but instead always dissuade everyone from it. A punctilious human being always looks first at the

---

[a] *Pennalismus. Pennälen*, analogous to first-year students, performed menial tasks for older students.
[b] *Hänseln*, as in teasing, mocking
[c] *HanseStädte*
[d] *leicht*

[e] *leichtsinnig*
[f] *peinlich*

difficulty in every thing, but a thoughtless human being always looks at the ease.

Those who think everything is easy are often very weak minds, for their concept accommodates itself to the power of their capacity. They can never see the importance [of something]. The punctilious [person] partly places too much distrust in his powers, partly is concerned about obstacles or even sees some [obstacles]. Whoever has often met obstacles while carrying out things that appear easy becomes punctilious as a result. <The sanguine human being is always thoughtless, but the melancholic is punctilious.> The sanguine temperament is in this regard in and of itself happier; the melancholic [is] of more use to the state. Whatever one finds easy is pleasing to onlookers, and this is the well-known *air degagée,*[a] to which one's natural aptitude contributes most. Whoever finds everything difficult is rigid.[b] Social intercourse should be seen as entertainment and as a game; hence no punctiliousness and no affected manner[c] must be found there, for otherwise it might have the look of [being] work, and the *air degagée* is thus of great use here. It is excellent because it has a great influence on other human beings, who believe they can also do it immediately, and hence feel delight in the thing, and thus also [feel delight in] the human being who has it.

Work that lasts only a short time but that requires a great deal of power is called difficult; but if it is continuous yet requires only a small amount of power, it is named arduous[d] work.

The difficult is constituted as follows: either 1. the endeavor is continuous, and in that case it requires industriousness[e] [and] diligence; or 2. exertion is required, even if it is continuous. If one has to work on difficult things, one tries to be free from them soon and so works with all [of his] powers. But if one has easy things to carry out, one prefers to labor more slowly and more continuously.

It is thus correctly said:[36] "A lazy man works himself to death, for he wants to be rid of the work, and therefore works so hard that it exceeds his powers." This is a characteristic of the Prussians, that they like to work hard, whereas by contrast the people from Salzburg[37] who have come into the country, as well as other foreigners, prefer to work less and more continuously.

However, arduous work is boring and burdensome. A lazy man therefore works hard in order to be able afterwards to rest longer. For he finds a period of repose that is rarer yet longer [to be] better than one that is more frequent yet shorter. But it is more beneficial for our body if

25:1237

25:1238

---

[a] Trans.: easy manner
[b] *steif*
[c] *affectirtes Wesen*
[d] *emsig*
[e] *Emsigkeit.* The number "1." is absent in the Academy Edition.

work and repose alternate with one another often. And repose without alternating work is an absurdity, for one gets bored by this.

The choleric always chooses diverse [work], the phlegmatic arduous [work], the melancholic difficult [work], and the sanguine easy and long work. Habit[a] makes everything easy; our powers grow through this and discontent with a thing continually decreases. The more burdens we have or bear, the stronger we also become. However, this does not proceed to infinity, for otherwise (who knows?) we could learn to not bear something; rather, our powers grow only up to a certain age. If we have reached this age, our powers begin again to decrease, the older we become. Through habit one becomes practiced in no longer turning as much attentiveness to a thing; that makes it easy. How this happens belongs to speculative philosophy. Things that are practiced according to a certain habit are nevertheless such that they do not happen completely perfectly. One must never do moral actions out of habit; we have to carefully distinguish a habituated way[b] from habit.[c] For the former makes it necessary for us to do something, and through this one makes oneself dependent on things. Thus, for example, one can accustom oneself[d] to words and curses that always come out of one's mouth and to which it is afterwards difficult to become unaccustomed. One can even accustom oneself to sensations. Like tobacco, brandy, indeed even poison; for example, [it is like this with] the Turks [and] opium. These are pains, but one can nevertheless accustom oneself to them in that, through frequent repetition, one's attentiveness is less and less directed at it, and we grow indifferent to it, and in the end it becomes agreeable to us.

Hence one must not in the least, indeed not even once, accustom oneself to something good, for otherwise one will always do it, without considering[e] whether or not it is suitable at this place and in these circumstances.

25:1239

CHAPTER[f] 7.

ON ATTENTION AND ABSTRACTION

We can make our representations clear and we can also obscure them. The former is called attending,[g] the latter abstracting.[h]

All attention is either positive or negative.

[a] *Gewohnheit*
[b] *Angewohnheit*
[c] *Gewohnheit*
[d] *sich angewöhnen*

[e] *erwägen*
[f] *Caput* (rather than *Capitel*)
[g] *attendiren*
[h] *abstrahiren*

367

It is positive if I direct*ª* my thoughts to something and make them clear, that is, I intensify [them] up to the consciousness of my representations; but [it is] negative if I avert my thoughts and weaken the consciousness of my representation of it. Now this last latter is abstraction; here the purpose is purely negative. Accordingly, abstraction is a merely negative use of attention – for if I avert my thoughts, I must direct them to another object, and we must employ just as much power to keep something away from us as to arrange something. Thus the same attention is present in abstraction, only the objects are different. Abstraction is still more difficult than attention, since if I attend to something I follow sensibility and the natural propensity of my mind always to occupy itself with objects. But if I abstract, sensibility always gets in my way. Hence sciences that require a great deal of abstraction are much more difficult than those that require attention. I cannot attend to a representation without abstracting from the other [representations] or making them obscure. Hence abstraction and attention is*ᵇ* always connected. I can make my representations clear in two kinds of ways:

1.) If I raise these representations to as high a degree of clarity as possible. Attention does this.

2.) If I extract from all the other representations in the vicinity so much clarity that they become completely obscured and only the one [representation] remains. That is abstraction. Abstraction is not a lack of attentiveness; its purpose is merely negative – it is an activity, as I keep away other representations [so] that their impressions do not act on my consciousness. – All attention and abstraction can be voluntary*ᶜ* and involuntary. Voluntary abstraction and attention constitutes the principle of self-control. – A human being abstracts involuntarily when he pushes away all ideas that run through his head and he clings to one so strongly that he cannot let it go. <Hypochondriacs are this way; the human being has control over these follies only in a healthy condition.> It is a cruel hindrance to thinking. Involuntary abstraction reverberates for a long time, although this reverberation consists of obscure representations. The human being is ill over whatever abstraction it is clinging to, for it weakens the powers greatly. The best means against it is society; the condition of [being in] thoughtless abstraction is a [kind of] thoughtlessness. For instance, empirical people do not sufficiently abstract from certain secondary things to attend to principal things. If one makes a plan, one must abstract from the means of implementation. Speculative minds abstract too much. They do not think at all about how things are *in concreto*; rather they consider them only *in abstracto*. Many human beings

25:1240

ª *worauf richte. Aufrichten* means "to straighten up, erect, lift up."
ᵇ *ist*   *ᶜ* *willkührlich*

become unhappy when they [abstract] too little, many [are unhappy] when they abstract too much. For example, if someone wants to marry and [finds] all the virtues in a woman yet cannot get over her damned pockmarks, he abstracts too little. A human being who finds the beauty of a girl offensive because he fears becoming a cuckold, abstracts too much. Their unhappiness stems from their not being able to abstract at will. The greatest fortune in life is to get troublesome thoughts out of one's mind[a] and replace them with more agreeable ones. The Stoics preeminently inculcated this and had this chiefly in their control, too. It seems that every deviation from the rule involuntarily fastens human beings to an object. For example, if someone falls, our eyes are involuntarily drawn to the place. The words "to attend" and "to abstract" have a meaning similar to that of the words "to dissipate"[b] and "to distract."[c] One dissipates or distracts[d] oneself if one fastens his attentiveness on nothing special, but instead occupies himself fleetingly with diverse objects. This happens in society. It is the opposite of intense work and, if it follows the latter, is of service for recovery; through this dissipation the thing we were previously pursuing appears completely new and in a different perspective, when we return to it again afterwards. – Often one also dissipates oneself in order to be rid of the object. For example, with grief, mishaps, etc. From youth onward, one must train oneself in this, and one is very fortunate if one has it in his control. Dementia[e] thus often arises if one always directs his attentiveness to an object for a long time. If one is distracted[f] involuntarily, then he is distracted[g] (*distrait*, *absent*[h]). Melancholics are like this. But it is not allowed in societies at all and is blameworthy. For example, when I speak to someone and he does not hear me and is thinking about something else. – Women are rarely distracted, and less so than men. Scholars who are very occupied are also often involuntarily distracted; for example, Newton was visited by his friend; the latter entered his dining room, and, since he discovered covered dishes with food inside, he ate what they contained, in order to test Newton. – Newton came down and his friend asked him to go for a walk with him. Newton agreed, but wanted to eat first. But when he found nothing in the dishes, he thought that he had already eaten, became very ashamed of his forgetfulness, and said to his friend: "We scholars are very forgetful indeed."[38] – This is a deadly[i] distraction from which one can escape [only] with difficulty.

25:1241

---

[a] *aus dem Sinn*
[b] *Dissipiren*
[c] *Distrahiren*
[d] *zerstreut*
[e] *Wahnsinnigkeit*, or "delusion of sense"
[f] *zerstreut*
[g] *distrahirt*
[h] Trans.: distracted, absent
[i] *todte*

CHAPTER 8.

ON THE SENSES IN PARTICULAR

Sense[a] is that through which we represent an object as present, or the faculty of representations insofar as the presence of the object is produced through it. The senses are either outer or inner senses, or the power of imagination; the latter is an intuitive[b] representation that is produced without the presence of the object. There is no more cognition through sensibility than just this, that the object is either present or [is] not. – In all our sensible representations, there is a.) the <u>matter,</u>[c] the impressions that the objects make on us; b.) the <u>form,</u> the combination of the impressions; this is the way in which the object is determined in a space; the impressions consist in the effect something has on me. The power of imagination has in its power [the ability] to represent the form of things to us, but impressions to a much lesser extent; rather, the power of imagination falsifies them. Thus, for example, in a dream we represent the form of things entirely correctly, but their colors in semi-darkness. The outer senses always require impressions, but the power of imagination does not. The senses always need an object. They are:

25:1242 a.) outer for the body, through which I cognize objects

b.) inner,[d] that is, the power of imagination, through which my own condition is affected.[e] With the former, first our body is affected; with the latter, first our interior[f] is affected, and then our body.

The outer senses are 1. the sense of vital sensation[g] 2. the senses of organic sensation. – With the first, I find myself completely affected, but with the others only in one organ or another; through the vital sense the entire nervous system is vibrated, as for example with horror, which is elicited by ideas as well as outer objects. – We could call the vital sense *sensum vagum,*[h] the other ones *sensus fixos.*[i] Through the vital sense I have a sensation of my entire life. These organic senses, in turn, are of two kinds:

α.) Objective senses, which represent to us the objects[j] more than the way in which we are affected by them, and

β.) Subjective [senses] – which represent to us more the way in which the objects[k] affect us than the objects[l] themselves.

---

[a] *Der Sinn*
[b] *anschauliche*
[c] *Materie*
[d] *innere*
[e] *afficirt*
[f] *unser Inneres*

[g] *Empfindung*
[h] vital sensation
[i] organic sensation
[j] *Gegenstände*
[k] *Objecte*
[l] *Gegenstände*

To the first genus belong the sense of sight, hearing, feeling, which are more objective than subjective; to the other [genus belong] taste and smell.

A.) Feeling*a* is of two kinds: a. the feeling of pleasure or displeasure, and b. the sensation of an object through touch. Feeling is the crudest sense and is closest to [being] objective. It is also the most accurate sense. It is the surest and the best means to acquaint oneself with the object. For without feeling and through sight alone we would not take objects to be substances, but rather made-up figures. If I notice an inverted rose in a concave mirror, I see one hovering in the air. I can find out only through feeling whether it really is a rose. This sense perhaps gives us the elements of our cognition, but it does not give any new concepts. It is found chiefly in the fingertips. Contact occurs only on the surface. – The sense is an immediate sense; we cognize the substance through it.

B.) The sense of hearing. With hearing the object does not have an effect on me immediately, but only through the air, and I do not have an effect on it at all. It is the sense that is best suited to communicating thoughts, [and is] much more important than the sense of sight, for without it we cannot receive any representations or ideas; the sense of sight is the most dispensable of all the senses. – We feel whether something is rough or smooth. Blind people can even distinguish colors in this way.[39]   25:1243
Thus blue seems the smoothest to them, white rougher, and black even rougher still. Hearing does not represent to us the shape of an object, but rather only that an object is there. – Hearing is the fastest means of representing or communicating one's thoughts to many people all at once. Sound is temporary and does not reveal any objects; hence it can best be taken as an arbitrary sign of objects. Writing is, like thinking, an immediate [kind of] hearing. Hearing is primarily occupied with objects, but nevertheless [is] also [occupied] with our own condition. It is penetrating and shares in the feeling of one's entire life. That music moves us so much comes from this: with every movement, the oscillations of the notes are all simultaneous, and this causes a great vibration in the nerves, even greater than [would occur] from a non-simultaneous movement; thus an orderly march of an army across a pontoon bridge causes the pontoons to separate from each other – which does not happen in a disorderly crossing; hence this always occurs [because] of an army.

C.) The sense of sight. Here we sense objects through light. Hence the sphere of sight is the greatest, for one can see all at once a larger amount than [one can perceive] with any other sense. The impressions of hearing and of seeing do not distort themselves or blend into each other. In playing and speaking, namely, one can well discern if mistakes are made. The sense of sight is more objective than subjective. For one

---

a *Gefühl*

cannot look at something without observing it. (When seeing, one does not have a sensation of his own condition at all. Only after looking for a long time does sight become imperceptibly fatigued.) Sight has a special freedom. For example, if one sees something for which one feels disgust, one can turn one's sight from it. By contrast, this cannot be done with hearing. The entertainment of sight is the most noble, for there one has freedom. One can consider an object for a long time, and when one has considered it long enough one can turn away. The more enjoyment someone gets from forced sensations, the more incorrect is his taste. With regard to shape, sight bears a similarity to feeling. One believes that the rays do not go from the object into our eyes, but from our eyes

25:1244 into other objects. This happens because it seems to us as though rays from our eyes fall on the object. Hence the common man's belief that so-called witches could cause harm through their gaze. Hence in Spain one prays in churches that God might protect them from the evil eye, and Virgil also says: *nescio qui oculis teneris mihi fascinet agnos.*[a] With regard to colors, sight has something similar to hearing, namely, with regard to notes, or [in other words]: colors, if they are to please, must have just as much harmony as notes do. For example, if someone has a blue coat and a blue vest, this would not stick out; however, a yellow vest under a blue coat perhaps would, but not a blue vest under a yellow coat. In the former case, a green color would arise in the eye, in the latter case, a dirty yellow color (the eye thus seems to judge according to the mixture of colors). This is like harmony with notes. One also notices that many who wear yellow do not wear blue, and many look quite bad in certain colors; why that happens has not yet been properly determined. Young people wear bright colors. Those who have [on] a lively[b] color seem even ruddier by doing so, and those who look pale look even paler because of

25:1245 the bright colors. There are certain contingent colors.[40] For example, if one looks at a red paper in the sun for a long time and then immediately takes a white one, he will see it as green. For in white lie all the primary colors, namely yellow, red, and blue mixed together. Now the red color is extinguished.[c] But from yellow and blue comes green. If one takes a yellow paper and then a white one, one sees the latter as violet. For red and blue yields violet. If one takes blue and then white paper, one sees the latter as orange-yellow.

There are people who are not affected at all when hearing, who also cannot distinguish notes, and thus a family was recently discovered in

---

[a] Virgil, *Eclogues*, III, 103: *nescio quis teneros oculus mihi fascinat agnos* (Trans.: Some evil eye bewitches my tender lambs).
[b] *frische*   [c] *ausgelöscht*

England that could not distinguish any colors at all and to which every-thing appeared to be light and shadow.[41]

The senses that are more subjective than objective are smell and taste. Both kinds of sensations [are communicated] mediately by means of salts. Smell [is communicated] by means of fleeting salts, that is, salts that are dissolved in the air and delivered to us. Taste [is communicated] by means of fine salts.

Smell.[a] If there are many smells at the same time, one does not know how to distinguish what one is smelling – for example, when one smells many flowers all at once in a garden. Smell and taste differ here from the impressions of hearing and sight: these latter occur by means of straight lines. Smell and taste do not act in straight lines, but rather in curved lines and in an entire space (hence various smells intermingle).

If many smells come together, they smell like something at first, [but] after that like nothing. (When [eating] in the dark we cannot taste as much as when we see, and we cannot distinguish beef from mutton. Likewise, tobacco does not taste good in the dark.) Moreover, one can become satiated just from mere tasting. Thus, if I taste various wines and spit them out immediately, in the end I can still become dazed. Smell acts at a distance, taste [acts] through direct contact, as it draws the moisture out of the tongue by means of the salts. The previous objective sensations of touch, hearing, and sight are senses of perception. But these subjective ones are senses of enjoyment. For I actually enjoy something through both;[b] smell actually satiates; that is why we are disgusted by an offensive smell and even vomit because of it, the latter of which nevertheless always presupposes a previously enjoyed meal. Both of these senses are thus much more penetrating. The sense of smell passes more frequently into the vital sense than the sense of taste does, for more disgust arises through smell than through taste. (Of all the remaining senses, the sense of smell causes the greatest vital sensation. A smell that is long and pervasive is harmful, particularly from flowers, and this chiefly in the evening when the sun is no longer shining on them. Smell acts so strongly upon the animal spirits that it can cause us to faint and then awaken us again. One must thus guard oneself from all strong-smelling things. For the finer the vital sensations are, the more harmful they are, for they weaken our bodies.) The senses are affected by either mechanical or chemical influences; the latter are more penetrating. For the former affect[c] only the surface, as it were.

25:1246

---

[a] The Academy Edition here reads "1.)" but it has been omitted since no corresponding numbers follow it.

[b] i.e., smell and taste   [c] *afficiren*

Some senses can be called social senses, such as sight and, in particular, hearing. Losing these in one's adult years is thus very grievous[a] for human beings.

NOW SOME ADDITIONAL GENERAL REMARKS
ON THE SENSES

If the vital sense is very strong in a human being, the human being is very unhappy. The basis[b] of well-being in a human being therefore must always be the same. He can indeed from time to time add something to it, but if this is too great, it results in an overextension of the vital sense, and this often repeated exhaustion [results in] the human being's ill condition. Sensation is very good for human beings, but excitability[c] exhausts the nerves. If someone is enchanted by the sight of a beautiful region, melancholy immediately follows, for one's mind is then too exhausted. An excitability that is too great arises after exhaustion. A dull sense is one that, though it has a sensation, does not have much of one or is not affected by it at all. Men have this. Women, by contrast, have too great an excitability; hence at every small scare they make a loud cry; nature teaches them the latter and it is actually salutary for them. For through it they are relieved of their fear and are directed to another object, namely, their cry. Fineness of taste is rarely found alongside excitability.

25:1247

Likewise, whoever is very much excited[d] by a thing can never judge it truly impartially.

Some senses teach little, but affect[e] [us] a great deal more, and those [senses] that teach more, in turn affect less. For example, a meal affects more than a painting, but teaches less. For the more attention[f] we pay to the subject, the more we are diverted from the object, and yet only the cognition of the object grants us knowledge. Certain senses are very unthankful.[42] Thus it is said:[43] the sense of smell is given to us more as a punishment than a benefit, for through it we have more sensations of disagreeble odors than agreeable ones. But smell is actually not made to do this, but rather to recognize from a distance things that are harmful for us. – Fineness of the senses for judgment is to be sharply distinguished from tenderness of the senses or the share[g] we take in things. The savage certainly has much stronger and finer senses than we do, for he can smell fire from a very great distance, for example; indeed, he is even said to be able to recognize the footprints of his enemies. But his senses are not as tender and excitable as those of the European, for he can smell

---

[a] *empfindlich*
[b] *Fond*
[c] *Reitzbarkeit*
[d] *gereitzt*
[e] *afficiren*
[f] *Acht*
[g] for judgment: *zum Urtheil*; share: *Antheil.*

374

the most disagreeable things without feeling great displeasure from it. Savages have a sensation of smell only with edible things. (Hence an Indian sachem in Paris liked the cookshop the most.[44]) Thus children are rather indifferent to smell. Smell seems to be given to us preeminently to notice foul air, for the latter corrupts the blood – but does our taste have a use as well, or [is it] merely for amusement? [It is] primarily for the former, for, if one considers the pharynx, this long canal is filled with one type of gland all the way to the stomach; now, according to the characteristics of the ingested foods and according to the characteristics of the digestion, these glands are filled with juices that are either present in the necessary proportion or are there gratuitously and are found to be corrupted. If they are corrupted, this derives from the enjoyable foods. Sweet things produce a lot of acid and fill the glands with it. Alkaline things produce a great deal of alkali. According to the characteristics of this thing, taste now makes general demands. If the glands are filled   25:1248 with too much acid, it requires alkaline things such as dried cod. If they are filled with too much alkali, it likes sweet or sour things. In general, the stomach of every human being contains either too much acid or too much alkali.

Taste thus teaches us always to enjoy what is good for us. Of all the senses, taste samples the most. – In drinking, it is social. – Sweet things do not taste good in the throat afterwards, but sour things have a good aftertaste. A variety of dishes is more beneficial to the stomach, for it requires a variety of juices. One can also eat more when it is a variety of dishes than when it is just one kind. – For patients, it is a sign of health if they get an appetite, and one must satisfy it. Some dishes are particularly nutritious in that they are of service for the preparation of various juices, e.g., sugar, bread, which perhaps almost all animals enjoy.

ON THE MEANS OF MAKING REPRESENTATIONS CLEARER OR MORE DISTINCT

Our representations are elevated:[a]

1.) through contrast or dissimilarity[b]

2.) novelty[c] and

3.) through change

1. Through contrast. Contrast is a representation of an object with its contrary[d] in another object. The opposite of a thing gives a contrary in another thing, and that is a contrast. For example, when someone from

[a] *gehoben*

[b] contrast: *Contrast*; dissimilarity: *Abstechung*. Kant uses these as synonyms here; cf. ApH 7:162.

[c] *Neuigkeit*   [d] *Wiederspiel*

Westphalia, where there is the greatest impurity, comes to Holland, where there is the greatest purity – this makes for a contrast.[45] Or, if one sees a bit of leftover food stuck on gilded dinner service, this is a contrast. Thus, for example, when Rabelais[46] had come to the French court for the highest honors [and] appeared at a brokerage with a black coat, [he] directed the eyes of all the courtiers towards him. Contrast thus elevates a representation and makes one direct his attentiveness to the object more.

12:1249

2. Newness.[a] When we see or hear a thing for the first time, it is much more agreeable to us than when we see or hear it the second time. Novelty[b] is a new acquisition, at it were, and this is always agreeable. One does not in this case ask whether it is in fact true, but rather tries to convince oneself of the truth, and to reveal its truth in all possible ways. The representation of something that we already see as old, is very weakened, for it is already familiar to us and we are accustomed to it. If one has already trumpeted a novelty to others, they develop so great an expectation in their power of imagination that the thing itself never matches the expectation. Because the other [person] is thus disappointed, he represents the thing as worse than it is. Hence one does a man no favors if one greatly elevates him in a social gathering into which he is supposed to enter for the first time. In so doing, one creates great expectations among the people; they notice the slightest trivialities about him, and how easily they notice something that contradicts their ideals. But if we say nothing of such a man and he enters the social gathering for the first time, then, if he is a skillful and polite person, he will gain so much from the charms of newness that the social gathering, since they had not expected or suspected it at all, will hold him to be far more polite or skillful than he is.

3. Change is the successive alternation of being or not-being.[c] There must be interruption; hence no one can endure a repose for a long time, and it is a burden if it does not alternate with work. Repose is, so to speak, a null[d] in the work. All representations are much livelier in the morning, which happens because I was deprived of these representations for awhile; liveliness arises through this change. An uninterrupted enjoyment awakens weariness,[e] and he who has never been hungry can never really enjoy food. – The comfort of traveling arises from this change. The ending[f] to things here creates, through the change, the greatest comfort. So, for example, if the concluding verse of a poem is of exquisite goodness and beauty, then the entire poem, which can often be rather mediocre, frequently pleases on account of this verse. Hence it happens that the

25:1250

---

[a] *Neuheit*
[b] *Neuigkeit*
[c] *das auf einander folgende Sein oder Nichtsein*
[d] *Null*
[e] *Ueberdruß*
[f] *Ende*

preeminently agreeable and humorous chats[a] with which the entertainment of a social gathering concludes please us for a long time afterwards,
and we thus represent the whole earlier entertainment as having been
agreeable, as notes reverberate as it were for a long time: – hence also
the advantageous judgment, the exquisite liking, and the impression, of a
sermon or speech that has a beautiful conclusion. And all of this because
a deprivation follows the ending and a change thus arises out of this. It is
like a weak[b] color against which all colors appear livelier and brighter. –
In like manner, we hold the life of a human being to be thoroughly good
and pious if he performed a pious act in the last days of his life. – And
when someone undergoes a misfortune at the end of his life, he is held to
be more unfortunate than if he had encountered the misfortune earlier
and had been fortunate toward the end.

Just as we now sometimes need to enliven our sensations, so too we
also sometimes need to make our sensations dull or weaken them. The
first means for doing this is to redirect[c] one's attentiveness from the
sensations and turn [it] to something else. This is thus a diversion[d] that
I make with the sensations.

Intoxication, which is caused by drink and narcotic substances, serves
to weaken the intensity of the sensations. Actually, it does not weaken the
sensations, but the faculty of sensations. Love of drink is to be sharply
distinguished from an inclination toward drunkenness;[e] whoever possesses this is a detestable person who is capable of all vices. But this
drunkenness has become very unfashionable among civilized persons; at
least one extremely rarely sees human beings in the condition where they
are completely intoxicated. The effect of intoxication is that the condition averts one's attentiveness away from every unpleasant thing, and
makes one talkative. – All savage nations love the condition of intoxication very much. When one has so many occasions for it, true resistance,
either of reason or of religion, is required to avoid this condition. Hence
this condition must nevertheless provide great comfort to the senses.
To this end they have many kinds of special drinks. The Africans have
rice beer, the Americans [have] root manioc, which their women chew
in a disgusting way and in so doing remove from the root the poisonous   25:1251
juice, which they also spit out into a vessel, whereupon it then ferments
from the spit and hence becomes beer.[47] The Koryaks pay very dearly
for a kind of fly fungus[48] that contains a real poison and with which they
intoxicate themselves almost to the point of senselessness.[f] The Turks
use opium almost daily and here as well the common man customarily

---

[a] Reading, as in Mar: *Schnaken* (chats). Mro: *Schwenken* (turns).
[b] Following Brandt and Stark's suggestion: *schwache* (weak). Mro: *schwere* (hard).
[c] *ab zu lenken*   [e] *versoffener Neigung*
[d] *Diuersion*   [f] *Unsinn*

puts wild rosemary[49] in his beer, which also has a numbing power. Thus Bayle says of Augustine that he asked God to protect him in the morning from a hangover[a] when he had drunk wine the previous day.[50] How this intoxication has an effect on the nerves is for the doctor [to describe]. But the accompanying condition of the mind, which we want to consider here, is for anthropology. It seems that human beings in society feel an extraordinary kind of compulsion to have a constant attentiveness toward oneself. Now, one drinks in order to relieve oneself of this compulsion, to excuse oneself of this attentiveness to propriety, and thus to say out loud entirely frankly whatever crosses one's mind; from this arises frankness and garrulousness, for no one takes notice of the other person, and the other is thus not allowed to restrain himself. Therefore, in drinking parties it is never permitted for someone to be sober, for that would make it necessary for the others to pay attention to themselves, and for the most part they do not want to do that. People who, except for circumstances of health, very adamantly shy away from drink do not seem to be completely frank. By contrast, people who like to drink in society have nothing to hide. Drink actually seems to be only for societies;[b] for to get drunk on one's own is completely foolish, for in that case I have no purpose, but in society I have the purpose of conversing with complete frankness. Brandy[c] is thus a peculiar swill, for it intoxicates quickly; in society one tries to intoxicate oneself gradually. Brandy makes one suspicious and reserved; wine, by contrast, [makes one] frank and garrulous. –

25:1252

That was drink considered from its good side, as it serves to make human beings frank with one another. All kinds of absurd things very often run through the head of even the most reasonable man, [and] he thus has to refrain from speaking these aloud. One very much wants for once to be free from this compulsion, and thus one inebriates oneself. – Furthermore, it also produces something good [in] that it gives a man the courage to carry out daring and great decisions. Of the ancient Germans it is said: "They arrived at their counsels with drink, and thought them over in the morning with reason."[51] Since they were a warlike nation, it was necessary for them to do so, in order to enliven their stoutheartedness even more. – Seneca says of young Cato:[52] *virtus eius incaluit mero.*[d] – It seems in general to have been a habit of great and active men to love

---

[a] *crapula*: hangover, but it can also mean inebriation, overindulgence.

[b] In Mar this clause reads: "Drink actually seems to be only for young people and to belong in those social gatherings where a person is not allowed to constrain himself for the sake of prosperity."

[c] *BrandWein*

[d] Trans.: his virtue was enkindled by unmixed wine.

wine, as it gives them more fire and activity. Drink and intoxication is much less harmful to the northern countries than to the southern ones; indeed, it seems that a warm beverage, consumed in moderation, at times is of service for their health. By contrast, in the Southern countries, for instance in Upper Egypt, the people often tend to become frenzied from intoxication.

Some nations love drink preeminently, for example the Turks, although wine-drinking is forbidden to them. The Greeks even see drinking a lot or being able to tolerate a great deal as something glorious,[a] and this always reveals a certain strength of body.

Among the civilized Europeans the love of drink seems to have subsided considerably, namely, 1. on account of the improvement in morals in this century, and 2. on account of the societies, now mixed with women, who cannot keep up in drinking.

25:1253

But the more this polishing[b] progresses, the less common the societal virtues become. Whereas one wants to appear so refined, frankness and true friendship fall by the wayside, for since others appear to keep a great deal concealed through the condition of sobriety, so too one becomes reserved – nonetheless, it is good that the condition of drunkenness, where one considers no meal to be genuine unless all the guests have gotten themselves heartily drunk, has subsided.

ON DECEPTION AND SEMBLANCE OF THE SENSES

With our sensations, we reflect[c] without consciousness. Deception[d] and semblance[e] with sensations should not be blamed on the senses, for these do not judge at all – for reflection[f] is what makes the senses appear to deceive us; but understanding reflects, so when it is deceived, the blame is due solely to understanding itself. In this mirage[g] of the senses, we must carefully distinguish illusion[h] and deception from each other. With illusion, we often do not want to know the truth. But with deception we do indeed want to know the truth, but are not always acquainted with it. The objects of the senses always lead us to reflection, whereupon we want to judge. If I now find that the judgment is erroneous, but the semblance of its truth still remains although we are persuaded of the opposite, then that is illusion. For example, when a hand in a painting seems to protrude beyond the painting itself, it is an illusion, for we know

---

[a] *einen Ruhm*
[b] *Polirung*
[c] *reflectiren*
[d] *Betrug*
[e] *Schein.* In this passage *Schein* is translated as "semblance," and *Illusion* as "illusion."
[f] *reflexion*
[h] *Illusion*
[g] *Blendwerk*

that the hand does not protrude and we can easily convince ourselves that it does not, and nevertheless it still seems to us to protrude. We often want illusion, but never deception; hence the former pleases, but the latter does not. A deception is an erroneous judgment in which, as soon as I discover it, all semblance disappears just as quickly. The more we are compelled to believe the illusion in a thing, the more it pleases us. – Thus good decorum[a] is a semblance of an inner dignity. Now although I know that this human being possesses many follies, nevertheless his decorum pleases me, and because of this he seems to be a worthy person. The more human beings make the semblance natural, the closer it borders on deception. The semblance of politeness and friendship is politesse, but is no deception. For it pleases, and although one knows that they are merely empty compliments, the semblance still remains that they actually indicate something. – Illusion and deception occur in various ways in a human being, and we do well if we attempt to learn to recognize certain duping inclinations. The understanding will otherwise be led astray and deceived.

25:1254

Understanding cannot overcome this seduction. It must therefore avail itself of certain countermeasures. We can think of ourselves in societies as actors. Everyone there shows his best side, decorum, etc. But through this kind of theater, through this semblance of politeness, the human being will nevertheless be disposed[b] to adopt true politeness in the end – hence one must not always be predisposed[c] to deception. For one will be brought so far through this practice that truth will often arise out of this semblance. It is thus not good to brood over a false semblance, for semblance is still a step toward the truth, and if semblance indeed fell away, very likely nothing would remain for us at all. The semblance of the good often causes us to become fond of the good itself. Modesty is an external semblance of complete renunciation of the judgment[d] of others. This self-control is almost always semblance, but since it is [like this], one is already working on it, and habit can bring it into actuality. If one wanted to brood so much about semblance, in the end all delight in human society would disappear, and in so doing one would become a misanthrope, just as a human being who broods too much about the virtues of women thereby becomes a misogynist. – We must thus not look too profoundly behind this curtain; otherwise we will return from there with a great deal of unease. We prefer to say, as Swift[53] said, *Vive la bagatelle*;[e] long live semblance as well. –

[a] *Anstand*
[b] *disponirt*
[c] *angelegt sein*
[d] Following Brandt and Stark's suggestion: *Urtheil* (judgment). Mro: *Vortheile* (advantages).
[e] Trans.: long live the trifle.

How excellently would the rulers thus act if they allowed their subjects merely the semblance of freedom![a] For then the subjects would believe that they actually were free. And this semblance of freedom greatly ennobles the mind. Many free states pester and break up their citizens more than do other sovereigns, but through this they have a semblance of freedom and believe themselves to be fortunate, and are [so] as well. But the freedom of a choice that consists of mere semblance is called a "Hobson's choice." The latter was a famous horse swindler in London who always had a great number of horses in the stables to rent out. Now when someone arrived at the end and wanted a horse, he said [of one horse] that it is tired, of another that it is sick, of a third that it hurt its leg, etc. In the end, no horse remained that did not have something objectionable, except for the horse that was standing on the lefthand side of the stall. – He thus allowed free choice, and yet one had no free choice, but rather the mere semblance of it. That is how the aforementioned saying arose.[54] 25:1255

Semblance gives the human being a certain well-being and – what is peculiar – it brings forth that which truth brings forth. The semblance that compliments have has something agreeable, although no one believes in their being true. – Semblance 1. indicates culture 2. is a means of winning hearts until it finally becomes reality. – With regard to cosmopolitan government, semblance is necessary and is also interwoven [with it]. In nature there are plants that have more semblance than utility, and here it is also agreed that the more semblance they have, the less utility, and vice versa; e.g., tulips and corn ears. But with assertions suited for the school, semblance must not be tolerated – we must thus accept external semblance in the absence of truth. Even our clothes have a semblance, for they conceal our true shape. – We must therefore present ourselves in a good semblance; otherwise we will quickly lose every comfort. But when we examine ourselves we must brush aside all semblance. But too often the human being deceives himself in judging himself and others, for when he sees only the semblance of a good heart, he already believes it actually is a good heart.

ON PRINCIPAL AND ADHERING REPRESENTATIONS 25:1256

A *perceptio complexa*[b] is where a principal representation is accompanied by secondary representations, so that in the end the main representation is thereby completely absorbed.

---

[a] This exclamation point replaces a period in the Academy Edition.
[b] Trans.: complex perception

Thus to every representation belongs the principal and the adhering[a] in the representation. In oratory, the former is commonly preferred to the latter. When Cicero orated, people praised the beautiful style, the antitheses. But when Demosthenes spoke, people said one had to reach for one's weapons.[55] This means that Cicero neglected the principal and brought into play merely adhering representations. But Demosthenes inculcated the principal representations more. Thus in sermons where the human being is supposed to be brought more to act than to admire, the style of Demosthenes is to be preferred – the adherence[b] of the representation must merely be a *vehiculum* for enlivening the principal in the representation, to make it easier to produce and more striking. – But one must not prefer the adherent[c] to the principal and pursue it alone; yet this often occurs. – One makes wit and folly into the principal, but the understanding into the adherent; thus Rabelais[56] says quite correctly: "Sound reason and understanding are like a dish of beef and mutton and are fit only for the table of the common man; but a ragout of folly with a sauce of wit is fit only for an imperial table." The enlargement of the representation is often very useful and necessary – for the effects of the representation are attributed to the principal representation and these [effects] are thereby elevated and made livelier. But it is a misuse when one allows the adherent[d] representations to stand out so much that the principal representation thereby becomes completely obscured and one is entirely diverted from attentiveness to it.

<u>On the delusion of inner sense.</u> – Here the mind has a sensation of its own state itself. But here we can delude ourselves if we do not know the cause of what arises in our mind and then believe that something

25:1257

else is acting on our state. Thus poets were seen as inspired, that an unknown power had given this to them; the poet himself does not even know why something at one point occurs to him, while at another time, with the greatest exertion, nothing comes. He thus believes that he has acted like a machine. When an involuntary state of mind overcomes someone, that is a mood. – A human being, when he meditates deeply, often gets into such disorder that thoughts run through this head whose origin he cannot explain to himself. Now because they can discover no cause within themselves, they look for it in other things. All the fanaticisms of the fanatics[e] of inner sensations of a divine light, for example, the cobbler Böhme,[57] come from this delusion. They are theosophists,

---

[a] *adhaerirende*. Although Kant uses several related terms (*adhaerirende, Adhaerenz*, etc.) and they appear to be synonymous ("ancillary, accessory"), the translation attempts to reflect the variety of words employed.
[b] *Adhaerenz* [d] *adhaerenten*
[c] *Adhaerens* [e] *Schwärmereyen der Fanatiker*

and it is peculiar that such human beings believe that they understand themselves although they do not understand themselves in the least. In philosophy, too, one often comes close to fanaticism, for example, when one represents the moral feeling as something particular in the soul, as Hutcheson[58] does.

We now come to the power of imagination, or the faculty of the power of imagination without the presence of the object. It is more skillful at representing the forms of the object than at representing the sensation; for example, I can always represent the form of a set table, but cannot do this as correctly for the taste or enjoyment I had. There is only one kind of sensation, namely sound, that can be restored well in the power of imagination. Our imagination[a] cannot create anything, and it is true that it cannot produce any sensations in us that we have not already had, but it can create new forms. Someone who was born blind cannot represent light and darkness to himself. Our imagination is reproductive when it makes intuitive to us an object that we have previously perceived. [It is] productive when it portrays for us an object that is not[b] present in our senses. The latter is found particularly among poets, painters, etc. They[c] are different for each human being. Both kinds of power of imagination are either voluntary or involuntary.

1. The reproductive [kind] is involuntary. It gives certain impressions that one can never be rid of. Hypochondriac persons, and in general people that have delicate[d] feeling, are particularly subject to these impressions.

25:1258

The power of imagination progresses in us involuntarily in an incessant course, without our being able to do anything about it other than give the imagination[e] another direction. In solitary moments every human being occupies himself with castles in the air. However, it is true that we like to occupy ourselves with certain objects the most. But here, too, we merely set the power of imagination going; afterwards it progresses involuntarily. In this way the power of imagination always seems to be active in dreams, for when one awakes one finds oneself surrounded by many foolish images.

But we must always try to keep the power of imagination so much in our control that we can also cease giving it another direction. Otherwise we are in a state of distraction.[f] – The voluntary power of imagination[g] is

---

[a] *Einbildungen*
[b] Brandt and Stark added the "not," which is missing in Mro.
[c] presumably, the two kinds of imagination
[d] *zart*
[e] *Imagination*, not to be confused with *Einbildungskraft* (power of imagination).
[f] *Distraction*   [g] *EinbildungsKraft*

called imagination,[a] and the involuntary is called fantasy.[b] With fantasy we often play our game, as we intentionally direct it, but it also plays its game with us, as it carries us away involuntarily toward ideas – this is especially so in the case of pain suffered over a great loss; in that case one tolerates no reasons for consolation, as one gets angry that another person believes that one could so easily divert oneself away from the pain. One thus sees that it is folly to agonize over worries for the future about things over which one has no control; but one still cannot dismiss them. It is thus very useful and necessary to accustom oneself to keeping the power of imagination fully in one's control. If one tries to stop the power of imagination often, it will become more and more manageable in the end. Some people consider themselves geniuses if they have an unruled power of imagination, but that is like riding a staggering horse. In writings, the imagination must be organized according to rules at all times. The imagination is stronger in the evening than in the morning, for my senses are more occupied in the morning because they have rested for so long; in the evening they are already fatigued, hence one thinks of death and eternity, etc., then. Some people enjoy this so much that they like to stay awake into the night, but the mind becomes very worn out through this and the understanding is also already tired. – Hypochondriacs thus like to stay awake at night.

25:1259 Fantasy is entertained through very insignificant things if they merely provide some material for images; for example, the fire in the fireplace through its various shapes arouses a gentle motion in the mind and gives it ever new material. Likewise tobacco, with the different indefinite shapes of smoke. Thus if one smokes in the dark it never tastes good, and the comfort of the tobacco derives from the fact that it gives our imagination nourishment. So, too, the imagination is served by broad vistas, where I cannot think anything definite about the objects and my fantasy can thus swarm[c] as it pleases. People who do not understand much about music can occupy themselves with objects better if gentle music is playing. It is inexplicable how it happens that, by occupying oneself with insignificant things, one can better sharpen one's attentiveness. Thus Euler made his best inventions when playing with his children.[59] It is good to study while spinning wool, for the even motion keeps the mind in an even tension. The imagination[d] greatly embellishes the past and the future. That is why one finds one's childhood years so agreeable when they have passed. But when one thinks about it, they are actually more troublesome than the present years. In one's youth one is under compulsion; through

[a] *imagination*. Like typical German nouns, *Imagination* is usually capitalized in the transcript, but it is not capitalized here.
[b] *Phantasie*   [d] *Einbildung*
[c] *schwärmen*

the spur to activity the mind is anxious first here, then there, and our desires are then untamed and make us unsettled. With more years one becomes calmer. But one forgets the discomfort and remembers only the comfort one enjoyed. It is like this for the Swiss with their homesickness.[60] – It is peculiar that nations where luxury clearly predominates lack homesickness; but the poorer the nation, the more homesickness there is. – Imagination often becomes so strong that it seems as if the object were present, and it also has just that effect. For example, if one represents to himself the great danger of falling into a chasm from a height – the fantasy, which precedes the present, greatly weakens the sensation that one afterwards has in the present. A comedy that one has already read will not please very much when it is on stage. – Hence gardens are designed so that one does not see everything at once, but rather always sees unexpected things. – The imagination directs itself according to the inclinations. If one feels hatred, then the imagination shows everything from its most detestable side. For example, if a delinquent is executed, then for the most part according to the judgment of human beings he looks very treacherous; this happens because we know for the most part that he is a vicious man. Lavater[61] recognized faces well when he knew the persons; in short, everyone believes he sees that of which his head is full. With the imagination, the productive [kind] is also voluntary and involuntary – one must not reproduce thoughts that bear a similarity to some thoughts that are contrary to another representation; otherwise he will reproduce it[a] according to the law of association.

The French say: "One should not speak of rope in the house of a hanged man."[62] If one has eaten rhubarb with coffee, then afterwards the thought of rhubarb will always occur to one when drinking coffee.[63] This is a good way of giving up coffee. Even *opposita*[b] reproduce each other, since they are related in that by positing one, the other is preserved;[c] for example, the cares of old age recall the joys of youth. Reconciled enemies[d] think more about their enmity than friends who have separated think of their former friendship.

The imagination is aroused by miens.[e] I represent to myself the same affects that the other expresses through miens – it is peculiar: when one person who is in the throes of affect[f] makes all kinds of miens to another, the spectator imperceptibly imitates them. – When someone falls in the street, all the spectators make a movement to hold themselves upright, as though they too were going to fall. When I yawn, the

---

[a] *sie*
[b] Trans.: opposites
[c] *aufgehoben*
[d] Following Brandt and Stark's suggestion: *Feinde* (enemies). Mro: *Freunde* (friends).
[e] *Mienen*
[f] *im Affekt*

other person is often forced to yawn, too. These are kinds of convulsive movements, and of these it is known that they are communicated involuntarily. –

The power of imagination can be very harmful. – It embellishes the object of my love, and such love is very hard to eradicate; it is strengthened even more by absence. We commit vice because the power of imagination embellishes it for us and adds a false charm to the thing. So if one wants to be fortunate and virtuous, one must never let the power of imagination go without the reins. He must avail himself of the power of imagination merely for his advantage and enjoyment. Among our mental powers, the power of imagination seems to be the one that is least able to be tamed. One calls a fantast someone who becomes fanatical in his fantasies, and whose fantasy is unreined. The power of imagination's being unruled is far more worrisome than its being unreined.[a] The former is found among all oriental peoples, as with them everything is based on a play of images, and as far as these images reach, so too their concepts reach, but where the images are missing, so too are their concepts. The power of imagination is the servant of all other powers of understanding, wit, etc.

For it provides for the use of understanding and reason the intuitions that give a meaning to their concepts. The power of imagination can, as it were, carry us out of this world and transfer us into another one. When it industriously plays its game, one hears nothing, sees nothing, and one can thus also drive away pain and procure enjoyment. It is the most necessary of all our powers, because, for instance with regard to the understanding, it provides us with an image, to which our abstract concepts can be applied *in concreto*. But the power of imagination does not substitute for us a lack of the senses. For if someone is blind from youth, for example, he will not be able to represent to himself, by means of fantasy, images that only the eye can see. But if someone had his vision and lost it later, he will be able to make enough images. For fantasy is much richer than the entire field of intuitions, indeed not in materials, but nevertheless in forms; fantasy is our good genius, but also our evil demon. It is the source of our most enchanted joys, but also of the bitterest sufferings. Thus, for instance, the enjoyment a miser takes in his money is merely the enjoyment of his fantasy, and all his agonizing worries are mere effects of his fantasy. Fantasy extends to the grave, for human beings are very worried that after death their body will lie in a good, comfortable, and safe place. If we had no fantasy, we would have to do without a multitude of pleasures.[b] Since we cannot always enjoy

---

[a] unreined: *zügelloß*; being unruled: *Regellosigkeit*; being unreined: *Zügellosigkeit*. Cf. Mro 25:1373.

[b] *Vergnügen*

sensible joys, the imagined ones are thus of service for filling in idle hours. This aim is served by novels, stories, travel books, in the reading of which our imagination always plays along, as it always transfers us to the places and into the situations themselves.

Whoever habitually occupies himself with the idea of the good in fantasy is a fantast. For whoever is so taken in by the idea of a perfect good up to the point of passion that he forgets that this is a mere idea and believes that it could actually be realized, is such a fantast in the good, or enthusiast.[a] Thus there are enthusiasts of patriotism, friendship, etc.[b]64

But someone who is so taken in by his ideas that they become unruled, is called a dreamer. With enthusiasts, the power of imagination is no doubt unreined, that is, without limits, but not unruled.[65] With the dreamer, the power of imagination is unruled. The imagination, when it is involuntary, is fantasy, and this alone is both unreined and unruled – a fanatic is someone who in intuition exhibits to himself (and wants to do so) spiritual[c] representations that are merely in the understanding. Those who see spirits at every step are <u>visionaries</u>.[d] – The power of imagination forms[e] all representations out of the material presented to us by the senses. This is also why it has the name [it does].

ON WIT AND POWER OF JUDGMENT

That representation which offers up the power of imagination's representations to the understanding to be worked on is called the power of comparison. It is twofold: 1.) the power to compare the representations is called wit; 2.) the power to connect the representations is called the power of judgment.

25:1263

Where both are together, that is acuity.[f] The power of judgment has a negative use. That is to say, it is of service for the distinction of one cognition from another and thus for the prevention of errors. Wit has a positive use, and that is to extend our cognitions and to give them an extended application.

One can already glean from this that wit will be liked, but not the power of judgment; for the latter limits, but the former extends. Wit enlivens the mind via comfort; the power of judgment delights the mind via thoroughness.

---

[a] enthusiast: *Enthusiast*. passion: *Leidenschaft*.

[b] Using reddish ink, the transcriber Mrongovius later inserted: "Enthusiasts of freedom 1793."

[c] spiritual: *geistige*; exhibits to himself: *sich darstellt*.

[d] dreamer: *Träumer*; fanatic: *Schwärmer*; visionaries: <u>*Visionarii*</u>

[e] *bildet* (as in *Einbildungskraft*, power of imagination)

[f] *Scharfsinn*

Wit is fleeting. The power of judgment is slow and serious; the former delights, the latter gains respect.

Wit is an attribute of youth. The power of judgment is an attribute of mature age; he who makes poetry into his chief métier thus makes an unfortunate choice, for wit vanishes with age and with it his art as well, the beauty of his poetry. – A cognition of the understanding, insofar as wit is noticeable in it, is perspicacious; insofar as the power of judgment is conspicuous in it, it is acute. Wit is the source of inspirations[a] and witticisms,[b] but the power of judgment gives rise to insights. Inspirations are thoughts that are not sought after, and when these are witty they are called fortunate. But insights are prepared thoughts that must be acquired through industry. Wit concerns the secondary,[c] while the power of judgment concerns the principal, or the nourishment for the understanding. There is certainly a quota[d] concerning spreading wit, [or] the secondary, in addition to the principal, throughout one's discourse.

Witticisms are the fruits of wit and are brought forth through the play of the power of imagination. They must be intermittent; going after witticisms is a disgusting occupation – he who lets his wit show is a joker. He who parades his power of judgment is a smart aleck. The latter is the most disgusting of the two. For, because the power of judgment is something serious, it is unbearable to see it played with.

Wit gives rise to fashion, or an object of imitation for the sake of its being new. Fashions are thus witty because they delight through the representation of novelty. Hence fashion stops being fashion as soon as it becomes a custom.[e] Custom is an object of imitation for the sake of its being aged. Custom is found among the English and Germans, fashion more among the French. – One mental ability suits one nation better than another; for example, wit suits the French, the power of judgment better suits the English and Germans.

25:1264

The witty person is free in judging, hence his judgments are called audacious,[f] because he decided to judge for the sake of a small similarity. He who possesses the power of judgment is cautious in judging, but also therefore must not take back his judgment easily. The genius takes risks and judges swiftly, but also has to take back his judgment often. Cromwell, or rather the witty Swift, says: "Caution is a mayor's virtue."[66] Wit is popular, but the power of judgment always has something scholastic to it. Wit is insipid when it has nothing of the understanding. The power of judgment is brooding when it has nothing of wit, and therefore when it has nothing for the senses.

---

[a] *Einfälle*
[b] *bon Mots*
[c] *das Secondarium*

[d] *ein Contingent*
[e] *Gebrauch*
[f] *hardi*

Wit enlivens the social gathering; but the lack of the power of judgment makes the social gathering tasteless. Since wit is insipid when it contains nothing of the understanding, all word play is insipid because it also contains nothing of the understanding.

The French have two words, *sot* and *fat*,[a] which we use for almost the same thing, for *sot* is translated as "fop"[b] and *fat* as "fool,"[d] but the first means a young fool and the second means an older one. With regard to the Germans, Kaestner[67] explains this as follows: *sot* is the man who travels to Paris in order to learn wit and how to live, *fat* is the man who returns from there with evidence of folly. A wit is called humorous[e] when a mental disposition that is uncommon underlies it. In general, everyone has a characteristic mental disposition, but it is nevertheless often moved by the circumstances and rarely remains in its place. The humorous wit is based on an original disposition of mind, and one finds it among the English, and indeed because the court does not itself set the tone; the wily mood is an entirely peculiar part of some people. Swift had such a mood: for example, he once gave a speech in church before parliament 25:1265 (which always occurs before parliament opens its meetings). He spoke of the advantages of understanding and wealth, etc., and when at last he came to the advantages of understanding, he said: "Since in this most highly-regarded assembly surely no one will lay claim to this, I therefore conclude, etc."[68]

A light wit is one that requires little effort from the understanding while it is being produced. Swift preeminently has this. Wit that is conceived profoundly is especially found in Young's and Pope's writings. The English call it *bull* when one contradicts oneself while speaking, for example when someone says, "I went on a walk with someone completely alone."[69] The Germans do this often. Popular wit is wit in the vernacular,[f] to which primarily proverbs belong. Proverbs are[g] the language and wisdom of the rabble, and cultivated persons do not avail themselves of them, for when one hauls out the thoughts of others, it indicates an empty head and a lack of thinking for oneself. Aphorisms[h] are learned 25:1266 proverbs, and to produce them, and indeed to do so often, is also a mistake. – Proverbs are a special way of expressing rather concisely or allegorically an otherwise quite common cognition. Aphorisms at times exceed common cognitions. Proverbs are good for getting to know the national character of a people. Wit belongs to invention and the sciences,

---

[a] A *sot* is a stupid or idiotic fool or simpleton. A *fat* is a vain or smug fool.
[b] *Geken*. Cf. *Gek* (cockscomb) and *Laffe* (dandy) at Mro 25:1306.
[c] Following Brandt and Stark's suggestion: *fat*. Mro: *fou* (fool).
[d] *Narren*
[e] *launigt*, from *die Laune*, "mood" or "humor"
[f] *Volkston*   [h] *Sentenzen*
[g] *ist*

but truth must still be present. Some great men have often obtained their supposed fame merely by their wit. For wit shows something new, and this dazzles and pleases. In particular, one can no longer arrive at the proper understanding when explaining the ancients, and wit thus has free play there. Much erudition is therefore the mere amusement of wit. Wit serves the designs, the power of judgment the execution. Colbert said he remunerates all projects, for if just one out of 100 succeeds, they are all paid for.[70] The designer of a project is often unfit for its execution. For the former involves vivacity, easiness, and execution involves industriousness, patience. – There are nations that are more able to execute plans than to make them, for example the Germans. Wit often fails in the execution [of a plan], hence the power of judgment must enter in. Wit combined with naïveté pleases. But when art is obvious, it displeases. Wit is a game; thus it must not be laborious. The power of judgment is the latter. With wit, the mind recovers. With the power of judgment, the mind is indeed strengthened, but also fatigued. Similarities are found easily, particularly with a lively power of imagination. And this happens because our understanding is oriented toward genus and species, which are based on affinity.[a] But the power of judgment is difficult because here one must perceive the smallest differences. For here I must fix my attentiveness at a single point and in doing so we become riveted, and this is wearisome. It is as if one wanted to stay entirely motionless. That is why, as Tschirnhausen[71] affirms, when a human being lays down and remains in a completely immovable position for awhile, he begins to perspire all over from it.

25:1267
But when I direct my attentiveness to various objects, it enlivens the mind. The play of wit pleases us very much indeed, but when it is over we are not satisfied with it. The understanding tries to make for itself an idea from the whole and the manifold. If it cannot do this, it is unsatisfied. It is like this, too, in a social gathering. When the conversations are not conducted in a coherent way, but everyone speaks at odds with each other, then, when we come out of the social gathering, we are completely confused and as if drunk, and the social gathering does not please us, for in our mind nothing remains but an indiscriminate noise. As one of Plato's friends from his symposium said, a social gathering must be such that it delighted him not only at the time he first enjoyed it, but also every time [and] as often as he thought about it.[72]

An Englishman wanted to go with another into the madhouse, but the other was speaking in Lloyd's Coffee House.[73] The latter saw a great melee of human beings and said to his comrade, "Let's go. I see that the

---

[a] *Verwandschaft.* Kant identifies *Verwandtschaft* with the Latin *affinitas* at ApH 7:177.

delirious[a] human beings have now been released." He believed that it was the madhouse.

Subtlety occurs in wit as well as in the power of judgment, but it is still better suited for the power of judgment, for it is difficult. Love of subtlety is micrology. It is better suited to the power of judgment. The laws of the Romans are micrological and are based on the most minute differences; hence they are the cause of much chicanery. When wit judges, it judges *en gros* and not *en detail*[b] – *Madame* Geoffrin,[74] who maintained a *bureau d'esprit*, that is, a meeting of beautiful minds, said one must judge human beings not *en detail* but *en gros* – however, in that case I am not making a judgment of a thing at all. In funeral sermons, it is often good and even necessary to judge *en gros*. – Reviews often judge *en gros*. Wit and power of judgment serve for the combining of the power of imagination and the understanding. Wit brings the power of imagination closer to the understanding, insofar as the understanding aims at the universal – the power of judgment must see whether what one imagines is applicable *in concreto*. The power of judgment is required in order to be able to apply universal concepts. All acts of wit are called play, and wit and play are dull when wit produces a false similarity, and then it is very disgusting. This dull wit consists of word play. It was once very fashionable in France. Thus a servant said to the chancellor of France, when he spilled soup on him: *Summum jus, summa iniuria.*[c] For the chancellor, this was witty. One often finds something witty in another person when the other does not even think of coming up with something witty; for example, to honor Louis XIV,[75] an honorary gate was built on a bridge across which he had to cross; on the gate was an angel holding a crown in his hand; a Gascon man said: "One can't tell whether he is giving him the crown or taking it away." This sounds witty, and everyone praised it very much. Wit is applied while one is teasing somebody, and it occurs if it is refined and the other replies.[d] If the latter does not happen, it is offensive. Wit is the most excellent of the amusements in society. Wit is the most essential part of satire. Satire is roguish and wily when one appears to praise the thing and speaks totally earnestly and thus appears simpleminded in the process, so that one does not believe he is thinking of it. Swift in particular writes such satires. The French are full of wit, but original jokers are particularly to be found among the English, for example Swift, especially *The Tale of the Tub*[76] and *Anti-Longinus*,[77] and Butler in his *Hudibras*, of which Hume[78] says that no book ever written contains so much erudition as this

25:1268

---

[a] delirious: *Toll*; madhouse: *Tollhaus*.
[b] Trans.: *en detail*: in detail; *en gros*: in gross (in bulk, loosely).
[c] Trans.: Extreme right is extreme injustice. See also Cicero, *De Officiis*, 1.10.33.
[d] *replicirt*

one – and this is also true. It is a satire of the religious fanaticism of the time. It is a counterpart to *Don Quixote*.

25:1269 Some examples of Butler's wit are, for instance, that his knight-errant at one point tells someone that he wants to make him into a pendulum according to which all of the tailors' yardsticks in England would be rectified.[79] The first means he wants to hang him; the second refers to the fact that in England at that time one wanted to make the length of the pendulum's oscillation at each second into a general standard, for it would remain a constant. – Thus Ralpho, this knight's squire, says: "Human mental diseases are like the courts, which sometimes hold trials and sometimes go on vacation. My conscience is currently on vacation and lets no one come before it."[80] – When the knight was once in danger, Ralpho advised him to flee and proved to him with reasons that flight is something praiseworthy. That is to say: since the Romans had promised a crown to the man who saved a citizen, he thus earned a crown when he fled, for he saved a citizen's life, that is to say, his own.[81] Furthermore, if he took flight, then the others would run after him and he would be everywhere earlier, etc.[82] What convinces someone of the truth and goodness of a thing? 200 pounds sterling. And what in turn convinces someone of the opposite? 200 pounds sterling more.[83] The strength of the joke consists in the fact that one puts forward quite unexpected things. It is useful for a magazine of aphorisms. A third Englishman is named Sterne, whom many have imitated and aped. Does wit make a person fortunate or unfortunate? Unfortunate. Butler died of starvation, although his writings greatly pleased Charles II, who nevertheless forgot to support him.[84] Sterne shortened his life through the frequent

25:1270 societies to which he would be carried away. Swift ultimately went mad, presumably because he had exerted himself too much – this happens because they neglected the power of judgment.[85] Wit must be merely a *vehiculum*, and the power of judgment must be like reality. He who has no wit has an obtuse mind.[a] He who has no power of judgment has a stupid mind;[b] mere ignorance is no stupidity. Actually only he is stupid who does not know how to apply a rule that someone gives him. Servants are stupid when they follow rules merely to the letter. The Russians are often without the power of judgment when the Neva is frozen;[86] thus a canon is fired in order to announce it to the people. Now when someone from the opposite bank of the river comes over and the canon is just then fired, then he is forced to go back over [to the other bank]. Whoever has practical power of judgment is shrewd,[c] and one also becomes this way through adversity. He who becomes shrewd through the deception of others is made wise.[d] A human being who is young and who does not

[a] *stumpfer Kopf*   [c] *gescheut*
[b] *Dummkopf*   [d] *Gewitzzicht*

have much power of judgment must be cheated often. The lack of understanding is simplemindedness and is distinct from stupidity. Thus there are peoples who can count only up to five, for example near the Amazon River. It is said that through one's stupidity a human being makes progress; this happens because the stupid person makes nobody jealous, cannot ignore anyone, and is thus tolerated among human beings. He who displays more insight and understanding makes others jealous. The stupid person also does not realize how much he needs, hence he begins everything with presumptuousness, and this already helps a great deal towards his success, and with time he also acquires a moderate, small amount of skill. But the insightful person has insight into the greatness of his duties and does everything timidly. Patrons were always ignoramuses; they may indeed be aficionados, but are not experts of erudition. Colbert[87] was one of the greatest patrons, but not a scholar. Under a scholarly expert of the sciences, no erudition will blossom in a state, but it probably will do so under a non-scholar and an aficionado, for a non-scholar esteems the scholars. But a scholar himself organizes everything according to his own expertise. 25:1271

One perhaps sees that one has a weak memory, but never that one is stupid. – For in order to see the level of power of judgment and understanding in oneself, these faculties are themselves first needed.

Lack of the power of judgment, with wit, is silliness;[a] without wit [it is] stupidity. He who possesses the first is not quite shrewd; he who has the second is stupid. A human being is more bearable when he is stupid than when he is not shrewd or silly. But in ordinary life these words are not customarily used for this, for they convey an aversion or resentment since they indicate mere infirmity. When a human being is stupid and yet imagines that he is clever, one feels aversion to his arrogance and one then actually calls him stupid. – One calls a person a simpleton;[b] this happens because someone who exerts so much punctiliousness on letters, and hence does easy things very slowly, indicates a lack of power of judgment. – Lack of power of judgment alone is simplemindedness. Being shrewd comes from experience, not through capacity and understanding. Hence a person suffers more easily when he is told that he is not shrewd, than when he is told that he is not clever. For in the latter case he is being told that he lacks ability, in the former case that he has not made use of it. People often confuse and combine honesty and stupidity. – This occurs because when human beings have some superiority in cleverness vis-à-vis others, they immediately use it for evil. But one can be sure that someone who lacks talent would still do something evil. However, no human being will let it be said of him that he has no capacity for evil. Many proverbs touch on this. For example: "He will not betray the fatherland." "He is

---

[a] *Albernheit*

[b] *Pinsel*, literally, "paint brush"

25:1272   no wizard." Georgi[88] tells of the Tungus, that they are very honest, but he adds that when they do want to lie they produce such absurd rubbish that one has to laugh, for they are honest merely because they have no talent for doing the opposite. The deceiver is not always more clever than the deceived. The latter often withstands the former, but when he acts according to principles of the love of humanity, he suspects nothing evil. And when he uncovers the deceiver once, he certainly will not be deceived by him again. The deceiver is often more stupid than the deceived. Even the cleverest minds can often be deceived; for example, as Abelard[89] was riding in a carriage with an abbot, the latter said: "My good sir, there's an ox flying." "Where? Where?" Abelard asked. The abbot responded: "I would not have thought that such a scholarly human being could believe something like that." But Abelard paused, then retorted: "I would sooner believe that an ox could fly than that a clergyman could lie."[90] It is therefore very unjust when an honest man is thought stupid.

ON MEMORY

The power of imagination is productive and reproductive. – We are here speaking of the reproductive power of imagination, where a representation is reproduced according to the laws of association; this also happens with dogs, where, if they have received food from people once,
25:1273   they appear again for more. Through the law of association either similar ideas, according to instinct, or ideas that were often connected with present ones, are produced. Memory is the capacity to avail oneself of one's reproductive power of imagination voluntarily. –

It is assumed that the power of imagination has a repository,[a] where all previous representations are located in obscurity and are not extinguished. We cannot have insight into how that might work. Memory is like an *archivarius*.[b] A memory can be artfully organized if one places all representations in certain scientific fields where they belong; this is *memoria localis*.[c] With memory the benefits are: 1. grasping easily 2. retaining for a long time 3. remembering quickly. The human being always has only one of these three. He who easily grasps something tends not to retain it for a long time. These are the witty persons. He who slowly grasps something retains it for a long time; this is how it is with phlegmatic people; he who retains something for a long time does not[d] know how to recall it quickly. Judicious persons[e] grasp slowly and

---

[a] *Magasin*
[b] Trans.: archivist
[c] Trans.: memory of places
[d] Following Brandt and Stark's suggestion: *nicht* (not), which is missing in Mro.
[e] *Iudicioese Personen*

also retain it a long time. A memory is unsure, unfaithful, if instead of one thing, one remembers another thing – this is a great mistake, which we can remedy merely by suspending our judgment. – Judicious people for the most part have a sure memory. Memory and wit are called fortunate, [but] the power of judgment [is] not. For I can take steps to exercise it and thereby enlarge it. When one strongly exerts his memory, he weakens it. One must thus be very cautious in this area. Memory is a gift of nature, and for that reason it is called good fortune.*a* The power of judgment is merit. One disdains the memory, especially when one possesses it only to a small degree. But sciences cannot at all be learned without memory, and understanding itself cannot subsist without memory. Memory is the repository of materials for thinking.

Memorizing is either mechanical, through frequent repetition, or [it is] methodical. The former constitutes the basis [of memorizing] and must not be avoided, and is thus the best means of retaining something for a long time. Religious truths must not be learned mechanically. For if the learned formulas disappear, their sense also disappears. – When it comes to names, mechanism is good. – But not when it comes to the explanation of concepts. Methodical memorizing is ingenious*b* or judicious.*c* In his history of images, Buno[91] has a kind of ingenious memorizing, but it is ridiculous. For example, to remember Erasmus, he paints a mouse because *eras mus* makes up the name. Or he says: One should think of a "must" as follows: *Er aß Muß.*d In order to remember Julius Caesar, he paints an owl and cheese.*e*[92] In order to recall to memory the chapter heading, *de haeredibus suis et legitimis,f* he painted a box, with curtains, castles, a sow, and a scale.[93] Ingenious memorizing is without power of judgment and shows similarity which is merely contingent; it thus neglects the power of judgment; it is also harmful. It also creates a deceptive memory and bothers more than relieves it. Judicious memorizing shows the application of things through examples, etc. It is believed that persons with great power of judgment have little memory and vice versa. This is perhaps somewhat true. The memory of many human beings is merely mechanical, and is thus generally the vastest*g* memory. Here the *iudicium*h is thus not cultivated at all, but neglected. But when a human being has a good memory, he can thereby cover up the lack of power of judgment and understanding, as he produces the understanding and power of judgment of others by spouting aphorisms; nevertheless,

25:1274

---

a *Gluck*   *c* *iudicioese*

b *ingenioese*

d Trans.: He ate a must. mouse: *Maus*; a must: *Muß*. i.e., because a "must" (necessity) sounds like "mouse," it serves as a mnemonic device.

e owl: *Eule*; cheese: *Käse*. In German these sound somewhat like "Julius Caesar."

f Trans.: of his legitimate heirs   *h* Trans.: the power of judgment

g *vasteste*

he must have power of judgment to apply these aphorisms, otherwise it will become absurd. The ancients said: *tot scimus quot memoria tene-*
25:1275 *mus.*[a][94] One of the ancients[95] also says: books have destroyed memory, since we can write things down now, or have books where we can find anything, hence we do not trouble our memory with it. And when one writes it down, one is glad and it is as though one were relieved of a great burden. We must thus record little and resolve to retain many things; in so doing we actually shall retain them. For the memory is like a magnet whose power is strengthened by always taking on new weight. (Often people who cannot write have a wonderful memory, for they exercise their memory by trying to retain everything that they read, and writing spares[b] the memory.) – We must not read with the aim of forgetting it in the future. For thereby we acquire a propensity for forgetfulness. Novels are such writings. They cause more harm than good, for they stimulate the nerves and tweak our heart ceaselessly, so that it becomes lukewarm and ultimately dissatisfied with everything, and then they also have the disadvantage that one does not even read them with the aim of retaining them, but simply to amuse oneself. One thus gives them scant attentiveness and therefore retains nothing from them. Hence it happens that afterwards when one reads other books, one gives just as little attentiveness to them, and forgets everything. Wallisius,[96] one of the great mathematicians of previous centuries,[c] became dangerously ill in his youth. But when he was slowly recovering, he was given calculations to read, which also pleased him since he had to give them only scant attentiveness. But when he later read other writings again, he noticed that he forgot everything he read. Thus with much effort he forced himself to calculate the square of a ten-digit number until he once again had strengthened his memory to the point where he retained what he read. Common people have an unfaithful memory; hence they often lie without even resolving to do so. They do not consider it that important whether they speak entirely accurately or add something to
25:1276 the story. Hence no writer should readily trust the stories of common people. On the contrary, Pontoppidan made a mistake when he wrote so much about the kraken[97] and presented it as certainty.[98] To recollect[d] is an action whereby we clarify our memory. Whoever remembers without previously recollecting has an adroit memory. To recall[e] is when I first see whether I even know it. In the case of recollecting, I know that I certainly have known it. There are marvels[f] of memory, such as Pico,

---

[a] Kant seems to be loosely quoting: *Tantum scimus, quantum memoria teneamus.* (We know just as much as we remember.)
[b] Mro: *bespart* (spares). Brandt and Stark suggest: *schwächt* (weakens).
[c] *Saeculi*
[d] *Sich besinnen*
[e] *Entsinnen*
[f] *Portenta*

Bishop of Mirandola,[99] who was able instantly to repeat 2,000 names that had been said to him. Julius Caesar Scaliger,[100] Angelus Politianus[101] were also such [marvels], but the greatest of all of them is Magliabecchi,[102] librarian to the Duke of Florence. He was a poor young man who could neither read nor write. He worked for a gardener, and he dragged together all [kinds of] printed and written books and tried in every possible way to understand them; since he was always occupied with them and did not properly wait on the people who came to buy something from the gardener, the gardener chased him away; then a printer, who knew him from his great love of writings, took him in as an apprentice. He allowed him to learn how to read, and as soon as he could, he read all the books in the bookshop, and whatever he read he knew by heart; by doing so, in a short amount of time he became the greatest polyhistor of his time, and when scholars wanted to locate a passage from a book, they just wrote to Magliabecchi, who immediately knew the whole passage by heart, as well as where it was located, down to the exact page.[a] He lived in the previous century. All the great polyhistors who [had] a vast memory also did little in other sciences. Sanguine people have an adroit and vivid memory, phlegmatic people have a slow and lasting (tenax[b]) memory. Choleric people have a memory that is faithful but does not grasp easily (non capax[c]). Melancholics have a vast and faithful memory.   25:1277

ON THE PRODUCTIVE FACULTY

The author[103] now speaks of a productive faculty.[d] The mental powers should be divided in an orderly fashion into those directed at the present, that is, the senses; at the past, that is, the power of imagination [and] the memory; and at the future, that is, forsight.[e]

One can also divide them 1. into those where the objects[f] are given, as senses, the power of imagination; and 2. into those that create the objects themselves, that is, the productive faculty. We cannot indeed create any materials <(hence the power of imagination cannot be called creative)> but we can modify them in very diverse ways and assemble them in all kinds of ways. When we are composing,[g] nature must give us material; the productive power then creates new forms for us by adding or removing something to the sensible representations; for example, the gods of the Indians are such monsters of the power of imagination.

---

[a] *Paginam*

[b] Trans.: tenacious

[c] Trans.: not capacious

[d] *DichtungsVermögen*, the faculty that composes, fabricates, constructs, or engages in poesis.

[e] Praevision

[f] *Objecte*

[g] *beim Dichten*

One has ten heads that are positioned such that only [one] comes to sit on top, and it has infinitely many crowns.[104]

The true poet must compose only such things that can actually occur in the world. But the philosopher even composes things that, given the current organization of nature, cannot occur in the world.

Composition[a] is actually [carried out by] the power of imagination, for here one fancies something that does not exist. The productive faculty is the productive[b] power of imagination, but merely voluntary and not involuntary. Composition includes inventing,[c] in that here one produces a new cognition. Inventing and discovering[d] are different. The former is to first produce something that did not yet exist, whereas the latter is to first find something that already existed. For example, in Germany gun-

25:1278   powder was not invented but discovered. For, fifty years before Berthold Schwarz, the Moors fired upon the Spaniards with powder and canons when they were besieging Algeciras.[105] It was invented much earlier in China.[e]

Schwarz perhaps got the powder and discovered its properties through chemistry. – To find something out[f] is to bring to light something that is known but that was hidden. For example, Barthélemy[106] assembled the many Phoenician inscriptions found in Malta and Phoenician coins found in Spain, and thus he found out the Phoenician alphabet. To devise[g] is to invent the means of bringing about a certain purpose. One devises compendia. – Thus Savery[107] invented his fire machine, in which a number of pumps are moved by a vat of water, whereby all of London is supplied with water. But he also required two people for it, and for the next 23 years he reflected on how to get rid of one of them, which he for-

25:1279   tunately accomplished in the end. To think up is to fabricate something. Excogitating[h] is distinguished from thinking up in that it is directed at a certain purpose.

To compose is to determine the power of imagination voluntarily, in part in order to contrive[i] new cognitions, in part merely to entertain. Through his making of plans, a *projecteur*[j] has the intention of attaining several purposes. Strictly speaking, he who produces new representations not in order to make the objects actual (the project maker does this), but in order to play with his power of imagination and thereby to entertain himself, is a poet. But this play of the power of imagination

---

[a] *Dichten*   [c] *Erfinden*
[b] *productive*   [d] *entdeken*
[e] Instead of Mro's lines from "For example" to the end of this paragraph, Mar has: "Thus, for example, Columbus did not invent the new world, but discovered it. By contrast, lightning rods are invented, but the electricity of the weather clouds is discovered."
[f] *Etwas ausfindig machen*   [g] *Aussinnen*
[h] Excogitating: *Ausdenken*; To think up: *Erdenken*; to fabricate: *Fingiren*.
[i] *ersinnen*   [j] Trans.: designer

must be harmonious with the understanding, otherwise it cannot entertain; for example the hunter, when he imitates the sounds of animals with a whistle, has the aim of luring these animals and shooting them. But he who plays himself a tune has the aim of simply enjoying himself.

Poetry and eloquence are called beautiful[a] sciences. One distinguishes beautiful arts and beautiful sciences. But this is false, for the latter are actually beautiful arts as well, because they do not have rules *a priori*. Critique of taste: this alone can be called a beautiful science. Eloquence is the business of the understanding, illuminated by the power of imagination. Poetry is an occupation of sensibility, arranged by the understanding. With the latter, the sensibility sets the purpose; with the former, the understanding does. However, in a speech it must seem as if the power of imagination has a free play. With poetry, by contrast, the understanding must shine through. Poetry, when it represents ideals, does not trick, for its aim is directed not at the understanding but at entertainment, and in the case of poetry I even want to be tricked. In the case of eloquence, one wants to engage the understanding through the illusion that is given by the power of imagination; but when I notice this, it displeases. – Loquacity,[b] eloquence[c] and well-spokenness[d] are different. Garrulity[e] is   25:1280
when I always talk away, without asking whether the other has an interest in what I am saying or not. But this is considered a weakness. Loquacity is considered a skill, namely, one teaches children that with few thoughts one can make many words. – Bacon of Verulam[108] had this fault. Eloquence is actually the art of persuasion, making black into white with the help of the power of imagination. Cicero avails himself of such eloquence, and at several places Quintilian[109] also provides instruction in it. But such eloquence can lead to errors and thus it is not permitted. Well-spokenness consists in the expression's suitability to the object and then [suitability] to the speaker's person and the listener's person, the last of which is actually propriety.[f] Eloquence flourished only in the period when the states were in the greatest luxury and vices, and were leaning towards their downfall. Eloquence flourishes only in a democracy, where everything is unordered and justice is administered by the people, who cannot clearly see through the mirage of eloquence. In the English and French parliaments, eloquence is still customary. In the French parliament, the lawyers give long speeches in court. Once, when one such lawyer was speaking, the president of the parliament, Harley,[110] summoned him and said to him: "You have brought forth a lot of quite weak arguments and even several sophistical ones." He answered: "One set is for these people, and the other for those people." When it came to a vote

---

[a] *schöne*
[b] *Beredtheit*
[c] *Beredsamkeit*
[d] *Wohlredenheit*
[e] *Redseeligkeit*
[f] *Wohlanständigkeit*

the lawyer won, and the president said to him: "My sir, your packages all arrived at the proper destination." – In pulpits, eloquence is exceedingly harmful. Eulogies to ruling lords can never be true.

The Oriental style[111] aims at the mere play of the power of imagination, where there is no cooperation from the understanding. He who has recommended the Oriental poets as models should thus be sharply rebuked. Rhetoric appears to want to entertain merely the understanding, yet at the same time it entertains sensibility. Poetry appears to want to entertain nothing other than sensibility, but it occupies the understanding at the same time. Eloquence appears to be a difficult business, 25:1281 yet it is a play. Poetry seems to be a play, but in the end is a business. – The orator can deceive, the poet cannot. If the former leads sensibility astray at the cost of the understanding, he delivers less than he promised. From poets, I want only entertainment, but whether the thing is true or not does not concern me. If the poet bestows, in addition to entertainment, nourishment to my understanding (which is the case with all good poets), he delivers more than he promised. Poetry provides only a pure enjoyment. Even if rhetoric does not always deceive, nonetheless it always arouses <awakens> suspicions against it and the one who practices it, as he could at some point let himself be seduced into applying it harmfully.

Massillon[112] had so moved his listeners with a speech about the Last Judgment that they stood up and sobbed; but were they also all improved by this? In the courts, rhetoric is also exceedingly harmful; the lawyers there imperceptibly try to attack the judge on his weak side and thus try to win him over through cunning. Mauléon edited Pivital's *Select Causes*,[a] which may indeed be good to read on account of the particular lawsuits, but which still have a great deal of seductive eloquence.[113] One could also produce an eloquence of doctors, which one could learn from the charlatans, who enjoy such great trust for that reason. Why is poetry more agreeable than rhetoric? Because the former goes from sensibility to understanding, but the latter from understanding to sensibility. Waller[114] had written a poem about thunder, and he therein alludes to Cromwell with great exaltations of praise; and when Charles II came upon the throne, he also produced a poem for him. When he presented it to Charles II and the latter said it was not as fiery as the one for Cromwell, Waller said: "We poets are more fortunate with fables than the truth."[115] This is also true. For with the truth, the poet cannot compose, but must remain faithful to the truth. Hence none of the poets' depictions of nature is ever hammered out very perfectly. For example, 25:1282 Brockes' *Earthly Enjoyment in God*,[116] which also perhaps contains much that is good; and Haller's poem to the Alps,[117] which is nevertheless rebuked, and I believe, for the same reason. But: Milton's *Paradise*;[118]

---

[a] *Causes selectes*. Kant seems to have meant *Causes célèbres*.

the life of the Arcadian shepherds.[119] One can compose without syllabic measure and rhyme: this is poetic prose. But why does syllabic meter please? Because it is a bar,[a] a song, and it always keeps the power of imagination equally strong and in motion. A bar of language without poetic motion can be called prosaic poetry, and this displeases greatly, for the syllabic measure is here without any aim. A bad poem displeases much more than a bad speech, perhaps because with a bad poem, one's expectation is always let down. Rhyme is a melody, but only in the West. It was first disseminated by the Northern peoples in the West and is now indispensable, for we have no orderly prosody, but instead can arbitrarily use various words. Hence rhyme serves to give our verses more inter-connection. Rhyme also helps the memory – hence an epigram in verse is more pleasing than in prose, because it can be retained more easily on account of the rhyme. But it is not permissible to make feeble rhymes. – It is peculiar that a rhyme in a speech is very unpleasant. The poets have *licentiam poeticam*[b] in that they can invent new words and use audacious[c] expressions. They are allowed to do this in order to compensate them for the coercion that the syllabic measure imposes on them, but only for the purpose of actually enriching, and not ruining, the language. Klop-stock[120] here makes the error of powerfully contorting the language, but he did not have a literary gift, for he mostly speaks the language of one who is astounded or terrified, and he arouses admiration through sym-pathy rather than arousing admiration through the depiction of objects, as Milton does.

When Klopstock does not arouse admiration through affects, he there follows Milton precisely. Poetic language is earlier than prose because the former is more directed at sensibility than is the latter, and ordinary human beings were still sensitive only to sensibility. Hence Orpheus recited even philosophy in verses. The poetic fire is lost in old age, just as a beautiful woman loses her beauty. Voltaire still possessed it in old age. – Youth likes plays that are risky and that arouse affects; old age likes something comical. This happens because: 1.) youth likes to test its power and therefore finds delight in all exertions of power, and 2.) with youth the impression that the affects of others make upon them quickly dissipates. Old people, because they know that in the world affects are not in fact aroused so strongly or at least do not last very long, and because when they look at such affects, the impression stays put and afterwards causes them discontent, prefer to go to comical plays.

25:1283

---

[a] *Tackt*
[b] Trans.: poetic license. Quintilian, *Institutes of Oratory*, II.4.3: *in quas plerique imitatione poeticae licentiae ducuntur* (in which many speakers indulge with an emulation of poetic licence).
[c] *hardies*

ON DREAMING

Composing[a] while sleeping is involuntary; but here that must mean power of imagination, namely the productive power of imagination, and from this one can say that it swarms when we compose while dreaming, or that it composes. The power of imagination is constantly busy and for the most part involuntary. In any work, our power of imagination silently continues to have an effect, and it is a great benefit for us, as it takes away the disgust of monotony that we sense in the present world, its uniformity, and the events within it, since we can create worlds at will. In sleep we are not disturbed by the senses, hence the power of imagination is stronger. One dreams when one is conscious of the effects of the power of imagination at night. Some human beings pretend never to have dreams. But every human being dreams; however, when he first sleeps he does not know it, and when in the morning he does not encounter anything similar to his dreams, he cannot remember it. One can also see this from the fact that when one suddenly wakes up during the night, all kinds of images occur to him that he must have been thinking shortly before waking up. But for what are dreams useful? We have all kinds of mechanical motions that are involuntary, for example, the intake of breath, laughing, in which the diaphragm is vibrated. Dreams are of service in that, through the vehemence of the power of imagination and through the affects, the body and one's entire life is vibrated. When we awake from a dream, we are all the fresher. Animals also receive the effect of dreams. There are dreams of a special kind where one sees oneself transposed into a completely different condition. There are also dreams that are very general. Very frightening and interconnected dreams make one merry the following day. It is peculiar that in a dream we pass through so much time in so short a time. But we do not pass through all the events, rather our mind simply takes such great leaps. In our dreams, we pass through some [events], but we skip over a great deal. For example, when we read a poem in a dream, it seems to us to have been very beautiful, but when we want to write such a poem afterwards when awake, we cannot do it. But this happens because in the dream we do not read a poem word for word, but only the beginning and the end of a verse, so that an interconnection results and we skip over the rest. It is just as if we quickly skimmed a printed poem. When dreaming one imagines[b] his own entire world, and if we were constantly fully conscious of our dreams, it would be almost as good as living in two worlds;[121] often things occur to one in dreams that one never thought when awake.[c] Hence the Greek emperor was wrong

25:1284

---

[a] *Dichten*   [b] imagines: *sich denkt*

[c] Instead of this sentence, Mro has: When dreaming, one thinks of his own entire world and his things.

who, when he heard that someone had dreamed he had murdered the emperor, summoned this man and said to him, "You would not have dreamed that if you had not thought of it while awake," and thus had him beheaded.

The productive power of imagination has three phenomena when it is involuntary. 1.) dreaming 2.) fantasy[a] 3.) insanity. In all these cases, the power of imagination is involuntary; and we say and believe that we do not think anything when our imaginings are involuntary. – More about dreams. The images in dreams all appear to us in a shimmer, as with the Northern Lights. Dreams are useful in that, via the aroused affects of the mind, they from time to time agitate our body, which is almost completely inactive during dreaming; this is a motion that is agitated by the mind, and it is much more useful than the motion aroused by the body and has more of an effect. Conversation with good friends perhaps does not move our lungs very much, but in the process it agitates our life much more than a bodily motion. Moreover, the latter is,[b] for people who are not accustomed to it and do not need it, for example, lumberjacks, etc., completely without use because their mind cannot enjoy itself in the process.

25:1285

Going for a walk often exhausts more than it strengthens. One should promote the transpiration, but this is either an imperceptible perspiration or a sweat. The latter is unhealthy. When one therefore walks so vigorously that one sweats, all benefits are lost. Sanctorius,[122] a doctor in Italy who started to weigh the *Medicinam Staticam* of human beings in various conditions, once weighed someone who had been playing cards, and he found his imperceptible perspiration to be very great. Sanctorius found that only imperceptible perspiration cheered a person up, while obstructed perspiration had the opposite effect.

One who dreams while awake is a fantast. [He is] a human being who, by the liveliness of his power of imagination, is misled to take an object of the power of imagination to be actual. If the fantast believes that his power of imagination derives from his senses, he is a demented person[c] (*delirus*), if this imagining is habitual.

The fantast does not create new things, but represents to himself the images of the senses differently than they are; the demented person creates for himself in his power of imagination objects that he had not previously had in the senses. One can see, from the fact that physiognomists are often fantasts, that they judge falsely when they do not know a human being. Lavater,[123] on the basis of the facial features of a painting

25:1286

[a] *Phantasterey*
[b] Reading, as in Mar: *überdies ist letzteres* (moreover, the latter is). Mro: *Alle körperliche Bewegungen* (All bodily movements are).
[c] *ein wahnsinniger*, more literally, "one with delusional sense"

of a certain Rütgerodt that had been sent to him, judged that he had a malicious mien, for this man was indeed a great murderer who killed many people simply out of avarice, as he himself had wealth. He was in Hannover. When they already know what kind of man he was, they imagine they can find everything in his facial features. – But not every face portrays the constitution of the soul. Newton was a man with a lifeless, languid look and a face of simplicity and simplemindedness.[124] Those who are enamored are also fantasts. It is right to love, but to become enamored is foolish, and he who has become enamored once will always regret it. Poets can never write poetry about a beautiful woman any better than when they are alone. When Petrarch[125] presented to the Pope

25:1287

his masterpiece, "Laura," whom he had depicted so splendidly and even compassionately that the Pope told him he wanted to help him win over this person, Petrarch said to him that he did not want her, for otherwise his poem would lose a great deal of its splendor. There are fantasts in morals. All practical ideas can be thought to the greatest degree of perfection, and to do this the power of imagination must cooperate. It is correct when I think merely of an original, e.g., of friendship, then try to come as close as possible to it; but he who flees human beings because they are not all perfect friends with each other is a fantast. A completely perfect friendship, where the one confesses to the other all his faults and shortcomings and as it were reveals his whole heart, would not last long in the world. We must always be somewhat reserved. – Fantasts in principles are enthusiasts.[a] There are enthusiasts of patriotism, etc. But such people always do not do well, for when they have sacrificed all their wealth for the home country and in the end are unfortunate, the home country will not grieve over them. Everybody refers[b] him to the rest of the public. But in what, then, does the public consist? William Dyck,[126] a rich businessman, was an enthusiastic patriot of this sort in that he advanced his home country 60,000 pounds sterling for the war. When he later lost the rest of his wealth in trading and acquired debts, he had to starve in prison, and the entire nation to which he had lent his money did indeed return 1,000 pounds sterling to him in response, but that could not help him; he had to die in prison. Nowadays enthusiasm is praised so much, but one must intuit principles not with affect, but with cold reason. The author[127] conflates enthusiasm with fanatics[c] or

25:1288

visionaries.[d] The visionary believes inner intuition that he actually has a sensation of the objects of his power of imagination in themselves. It is easier to improve the enthusiast than the fanatic. The visionary believes,

---

[a] Fantasts: *Phantasten*; enthusiasts: *Enthusiasten*
[b] Following Brandt and Stark's suggestion: *verweist* (refers). Mro: *sagt und verwendet* (speaks and disposes of).
[c] *Schwärmern*   [d] Mar: *Visionairen*. Mro: *Visioneur*

for example, in community with God, revelation. Love is practical when I do justice to God's commandments, as it says in the Bible;[128] love is physical when I believe I am actually enjoying God and thereby have a sensation of blessedness; it is also called mystical and is fanatical. Such visionaries especially existed among women, for instance Antoinette de Molignon believed she had had an immediate divine revelation, and Antoinette de Bourignon as well.[129] When one affectedly feigns such fanaticism, it is fantasy.[a] But if a person actually is such a fanatic, he is like[b] the demented person. It is peculiar that nowadays many such fanatical writings are again coming out, e.g., the book, *Of Truth and Error*.[130]

One who dreams while awake can be awakened. But a demented person cannot be awakened, no matter what one does with him. Many kinds of mental illnesses are hereditary, but dementia[c] is not; rather, it is like a sickness. Insanity,[d] which consists in ratiocination,[e] is probably hereditary. The demented person believes he sees something and he cannot be talked out of it. – There are peoples who have considered insane persons to be prophets. The Turks consider insane persons to be holy; for they believe that the soul of the demented person[f] is in heaven and another   25:1289
spirit currently speaks out of him.

7. ON FORSEEING[g]

The entire power of cognition, with regard to time, is: 1. with regard to the past, recollection[b] 2. with regard to the present, sensation through senses and 3. prevision or foresight.[i] The power of imagination can be divided into 1 recollection; 2 prevision; 3 the faculty of designation.[j] We would like very much to be able to remember the past, or to have a memory, for that gives us an aftertaste, which, however, does not interest us very much; but knowing the future gives us a foretaste, which awakens in us a desire for the thing.

We have very limited ability to foresee, and we have a great desire to possess it; we can perhaps foresee the future of nature through astronomy, insofar as it unfolds according to nature's laws. But we can do no more than surmise the future on earth, insofar as the future depends on human influences, and often cannot even do that, and that interests us

---

[a] *phantasterei*
[b] Reading, as in Mar: *gleich* (like). Mro: *viel einerlei* (much one and the same as).
[c] *Wahnsinn*
[d] *WahnWitz*, more literally, "delusional understanding"
[e] *Vernünfteln*   [g] *Vorhersehen*
[f] *des Wahnsinnigen Seele*   [b] *Erinnerung*
[i] prevision: *Praevision*; foresight: *Vohersehung*.
[j] *Bezeichnungs Vermögen*

the most. The Turks value astronomy only insofar as it can give them information about human fates. Hence they do not respect all of the astronomy we have. The Great Sultan once sent an emissary to a great king in Europe, and gave the emissary, among other things, the secret assignment of asking the king by what means he had calculated the fortunate days on which he won so many battles. We do everything with an aim toward the future, hence the future also interests us the most. Indeed, when the future is so distant that it cannot be of any use to us, it nonetheless interests us, [e.g.] when we hear from astronomy that over the span of 140,000 years, the entire year, day, and night will be the same and there will be a perpetual spring.

25:1290

Prevision includes: 1. premonition 2. dream interpretation 3. the secret meaning of certain numbers 4. prophecy from facial features 5. [prophecy] from the constellation of the stars 6. chiromancy 7. prophecy from the movement of animals and their entrails 8. drawing lots, etc.

1. Premonition is not when we distinctly know what is to come, but rather a warning about an impending misfortune or a hope concerning an impending fortune, without knowing exactly what kind of fortune or misfortune it is. We can adduce no reason that premonitions are possible and also no reason as to how they should benefit us. If I can learn from them what will occur, I can prevent the thing, and then the premonition is false. Premonition is fear or hope through an obscure representation of danger or fortune. They are simply misinterpreted mental indispositions that we do not represent as effects of something present, for example, flatulence, constipation, but rather we represent them as meaningful indications of something in the future. Premonitions about her beloved come to a woman in particular. But when their premonitions are not fulfilled, they forget them. But if they are fulfilled, they retain them. Thus they know how to remember nothing but fulfilled premonitions, and therefore believe that premonitions actually indicate something.

2. Dream interpretations. The most savage peoples, especially the North Americans, believe that dreams are oracles, and this occurs because our dreams often are so interconnected, that we cannot represent to ourselves how we should have been able to make them. However, it is really ridiculous to believe that at night, during the swarming of our fantasy, we will be able to have a sensation of what we cannot have a sensation of during the day with the greatest exertion of our minds. Someone traveled around Asia, listened to the dreams of women and what happened after that, and collected them into a dream book.[131] The dream interpreters for the most part say the opposite of the dream. Some dreams are also fulfilled when they arise from physical causes. For example, when at night the gall overflows into the blood and then in a natural manner I have an anxious dream, for example, that dogs are barking at me, I get up in the morning with whimsical ideas, and whoever has

25:1291

whimsical ideas easily gets lawsuits. – People often dream that they are going to die and it happens; this can occur because during the night the body, when it is resting, feels its condition and even its affliction more than during the day. Foresight is the foundation of our activity. The common man asks only about what interests him; he thus asks especially about success and does not worry about the cause. Intellectual desire concerning things that do not interest us is curiosity.[a] The common man has this. When, for example, the Northern Lights occur, the common man does not ask where it comes from, but rather what it means, that is, what consequences it will have. Foresight arises for the most part from fear. It is natural only if I actually have it in my control and thus can derive benefits from its use. The opinion that there is an absolute fatality is also for the most part the cause of the human being's propensity[b] toward the future. – Thus the premonitions already presuppose a fate,[c] as they do not predict for us any definite misfortune, so we cannot avert the misfortune. – Dreams are also indeterminate. All ancient prophecies and oracles were always ambiguous. If one presupposed a fate,[d] no foresight was possible. Hence the Turks, who strongly believe in previsions, also have the doctrine of fate.[e]

When Mohammed was once defeated and had lost the core of the Arabian nobles who were with him, he said to the survivors: "According to the will of God, these men were destined to die today; now they have died in a praiseworthy way for a good cause and are rewarded, since otherwise they would have had to die in their beds."[132] – Careless[f] is he who does not ask about the future, even when it is in his control. Such are the Caribbeans, who in small numbers can still be found in Dominique and somewhat more frequently in Guiana; the Caribbean sells his hammock in the morning, and when he wants to go to sleep in the evening he wonders where it went.[133] Carefree[g] is when one does not think of the future that does not lie in our control. – Precaution[h] is when I foresee the future that lies in my control. Care[i] is when I foresee the future that does not lie in my control. One must not fear childishly, but also not childishly hope; the latter perhaps seems to be agreeable, but it gives one a fickle state. Whoever neither hopes nor fears childishly is in a steadfast state. –

25:1292

Fortune-telling concerns the past, the present, and the future, and things that cannot at all be explained by natural means. – Moreover,

[a] Intellectual desire: *Wißbegierde*; curiosity: *Curioesitaet*
[b] fatality: *Verhängnis*; propensity: *Hang*
[c] *Fatum*
[d] *Schicksal*
[e] *Fato*
[f] *Sorglos*
[g] *Sorgenfrei*
[h] *Vorsorge*
[i] *Sorge*

the *astrologia iudiciaria*^a also belongs to the kinds of foresight. Fortune-mongering^b from the constellation of the stars. It has already been banned from Europe, but in Asia it still very much reigns, especially among the Turks. –

Thus there is also chiromancy, pyromancy, etc. [There is] also interpreting from the features of the face, which in the Prussian era the Privy-Councillor von Brenkenhof and the Minister von Ilgen purported to Frederick I to know.[134]

One commonly chooses ignorant people to be fortune-tellers, [such] as gypsies, old women, etc. The *auspices* and *augures* among the Romans were stupid people, yet no writer at that time was completely free of belief in them. A Spaniard who came from Goa once was robbed in the Syrian desert. But when the Arabs saw that he stuttered severely and made all sorts of grimaces while doing so, they thought he was crazy,^c and thus holy. They brought him to the French consul in Aleppo. – At times the gift of prophecy is attributed to poets, and perhaps they attribute it to themselves as well, especially when they are in the midst of inspiration. It may perhaps seem to them that they were really inspired at that time, as they cannot always make themselves that way. *Mantis* was the fortune-teller among the Greeks, but he merely uttered incomprehensible words that another always interpreted – from this come *chiromantica*, *hydromantica*, etc. Prophesying^d is when I merely predict something in the future which cannot be explained from the present at all. Prophecy^e is also commonly directed at an entire age and not merely at individual persons. When it concerns the improvement of the age, it is called prophesying.^f

8. ON THE FACULTY OF DESIGNATION

This is the capacity to produce representations that are the means of producing other representations – these are called signs, and are either accompanying^g or representative.[135] The former are called words, the latter images. As miens, signs are natural; as words, signs are arbitrary. Signs are either signs of cognition or signs of things. The former are signs of sensation or of concepts. Signs of sensation consist either in sound or in gestures. All these are of one kind for all human beings. Signs of things are either immediate or through the designation of the sign, that is, mediate. We designate the wild^h through words. We also designate

---

^a Trans.: judicial astrology
^b *Wahrsagerey*
^c *verrükt*
^d *Weißagen*
^e *Weißagung*
^f *Prophezeyung*
^g *begleitende*
^h Mro: *die Wilde*, possibly in the sense of wild game. Brandt and Stark think the text may be corrupt and instead suggest *Sache* ("thing, matter") or *Begriffe* ("concepts").

the thing by painting it, through pictures that naturally are visible. The Canadian savages cannot write, and they therefore paint things. Hence some nations are called the Foxes, Bears, etc., and the people also have plain[a] names for things. When they want to name the nation of Foxes, then they paint a fox. When one expresses, through an *analogon* from sensibility, things that are not sensible, it is a *symbolum*; e.g., when the Egyptians paint a snake that is biting its own tail in order to indicate the year. For where the year ends, there it begins anew. Lastly, one also has arbitrary signs of things that have no connection with the things at all. Hence the Egyptian divinities in the temple at Heliopolis were probably emblems for the cities in Egypt; over time they were taken to be gods. Thus, due to the lack of the art of writing, many images may have arisen. Oxen and sheep are the most useful animals; hence in ancient times they yielded *symbola* of the divinities. Thus Moloch was painted with the head of an ox, and Apis was represented by a steer. Thereafter these signs were taken for the things themselves. Egyptians paint even their kings with the heads of cattle. Thus the Indians, too, consider cattle to be a special gift of God, and therefore holy. There are signs that relate to a certain time, namely: to the past, *rememorativa*; to the present, *signa demonstrativa*, and to the future, *prognostica*; the first [kind of sign] is something we have for remembrance. The doctor knows and concludes from the representation of the face that the sick person will die (*facies hippocratica[b]*). Barometers are *prognostica*. There are signs that we take for something meaningful in itself. This applies especially to numbers. For example, the number ten is just like this, perhaps because we have ten fingers and because it is quite perfect for counting. Some peoples count only to five, others only to three. A dozen is also like this, perhaps from the twelve zodiacs, months. We find that, already among the ancient Goths, there were always twelve persons in the courts. Thus, too, the jury in England consists of twelve persons. – They chose to do this because they believe it is not complete if a dozen people are not there. – Perhaps this also explains the superstition that, if there are thirteen persons who are guests, one will die, a superstition found not only in Germany, but also in Italy. This also explains why people collect until they have a round number. Philo says, according to Marquis d'Argentean: "The number seven is so excellent not because there are seven days in the week and seven planets, but there are seven days in the week and seven planets because the number seven is so glorious."[136] Thus historical things, too, were often organized according to the numbers, for example, the seven kings of the Romans. Romulus means "force" and Numa "law," and who knows whether these kings ever existed.[c] Hence, too, the *annus*

25:1294

25:1295

---

[a] *lauter*   [b] Trans.: the Hippocratic face
[c] force: *Gewalt*. In Greek, *rome* means "force, strength" and *nomos* "law."

climacterius,[a] the great step-year[137] that derives from the multiplication of seven, which was so holy to the Egyptians, and the number nine, which was holy to the Tartars and Goths, and from which comes 63, the year in which the fewest people survive. Thus the Chinese, too, take the number nine to be something special, and the emperor therefore possesses no more and no less than 9,999 ships; this sounds so dramatic when one utters it. With all of this, it comes down to the fact that we consider the things that are designated by the named numbers to be perfect because the numbers have a certain perfect harmony.

25:1296

9. ON THE HIGHER COGNITIVE FACULTY

Up to this point we have spoken of the lower cognitive powers or the ones that furnish us with materials for our representations. The higher cognitive faculty is the faculty of thinking and is threefold: understanding, power of judgment, and reason. Their differentiation is fine, but important. Understanding is the faculty of rules. The power of judgment [is the faculty of] applying them. Reason is the faculty of making rules from its own principles, of creating universal rules by itself. Thinking, grasping, and comprehending are due to understanding; applying it is due to the power of judgment, and thinking for oneself due to reason. <Skill[b] consists in knowledge and ability and is learned. Prudence[c] is the manner of disposing of one's skill. Skill is found more frequently than prudence. Skill is needed in dealing with things, prudence in dealing with human beings, with things where it is not in my control to guide them according to my aims. Wisdom is the ultimate purpose, the aim for which one does that. Women do not have it. They surely have all kinds of aims and also know how to carry them out, but they do not know how to choose them well. Through understanding we acquire concepts, through the power of judgment we make them usable, and through reason we extend them.> Skill requires understanding, prudence requires the power of judgment, and wisdom requires reason. Thus the general must have reason, but the subcommander understanding and power of judgment, and the common man must have understanding or mere mechanism.

The power of judgment cannot be learned, and when it is missing it cannot be substituted either.

One can merely exercise it, but not learn it. For in that case one would have to have rules of application, but these would again have to have new rules since their application always presupposes the power of judgment, and it would progress like this to infinity. If one lacks understanding, it can be substituted fairly well by wide reading. Jurists need excellent

25:1297

[a] Trans.: climacteric year. Step-year: *Stuffen Jahr.*
[b] *Geschicklichkeit* [c] *Klugheit*

power of judgment, for there can be fewer *casus in terminis*[a] and more *casus discretivi*,[b] that is, the law contains fewer cases according to the letter and more according to the spirit.[138] Even when someone has the theory, he can still lack the *praxis*, and very often it is missing in the beginning until one has first exercised his power of judgment. However, theory is nevertheless more necessary than *praxis*, for it underlies the latter. The power of judgment, without understanding or acquaintance with the rules, is nothing; but understanding without power of judgment can still subsist, although something is missing. – It is thus foolish when the practitioners put down the theoreticians. They do not keep in mind that they draw their knowledge from the theoretician. – Reason is the faculty of the cognition of the principles from which the understanding derives its rules. It is the highest mental capacity for human beings. Reason, too, cannot be learned. Whoever learns science without being acquainted with the principles can perhaps teach it to others afterwards, but only in the manner in which they learned it. They cannot extend and alter[c] it. The Russians, it is said, may indeed have a great desire to learn everything, but few have the ability to teach. – <Jurists are narrow-minded. They take the laws to be oracles. To ratiocinate[d] is to draw from things consequences whose principles are not known; it is easy. Reason is the legislator, understanding teaches laws, and power of judgment applies them. Reason only provides laws of the way of thinking. Philosophy is teaching to cultivate[e] reason. It is legislation. Mathematics and physics are arts of reason.> A human being is narrow-minded <limited> who does not judge independently, but according to the precepts he learned: – The diversity of the laws comes from the fact that they were always given to deal with various cases, but one was not thinking according to the laws' principles. If one had established the principles, many laws would be superfluous. – The systematic part of our cognition is based on reason, makes our cognition stable and secure, and elevates it above common cognition. – A pupil can and will surpass his teacher when he knows the principles of thoughts. – A human being possesses extended[f] concepts when he judges according to his own principles, and possesses extended attitudes when he loves not merely his home country but all of humanity, when he finds other religions tolerable. – He is the opposite of the narrow-minded person. – A people can extend its concepts or alter[g] them. Toleration arises from concepts that are already extended. Erudition increases concepts but does not extend them. – Understanding

25:1298

---

[a] Trans.: case[s] in the terms   [b] Trans.: discriminating case[s]
[c] Reading, as in Mar: *verändern* (alter). Mro: *erwegen* (ponder, consider).
[d] *Vernünfteln*   [f] *erweiterten*
[e] *excoliren*
[g] Following Brandt and Stark's suggestion: *verändern* (alter). Mro: *erregen* (arouse).

abolishes ignorance, the power of judgment error, and reason the source of ignorance and error. – Reason is legislator, but it teaches us thinking, not thoughts. That is: not materials, but forms. – In learning the thoughts of others a great deal, one loses one's own thoughts.

Immaturity*a* is the inability to use one's own understanding without guidance from another.[139] With regard to years in childhood, it is first. In natural life we are mature earlier, but in civil life everything is artificial, hence here we become mature later. There is an immaturity of sex, namely, of woman. Lastly, there is an immaturity of sickness or of natural inability. This is a [kind of] idiocy. – But human beings are immature in other aspects, even if it goes unnoticed, for it is universal. Here the scholars have often raised themselves up into guardians of the people. The theologian, jurist, medical doctor, and so on, often command without giving the reason for their command. – It also pleases human beings terrifically to leave themselves to the care of others: his soul to the preacher, his body to the doctor. Using their own reason is
25:1299 too laborious to them. They have thus often been dominated by those who crave for dominance. Lord Bolingbroke thus says that a mass of human beings is always a mob over whom one person prevails.[140] – If the regent makes the subjects immature, they are indignant. Denmark therefore did not do well when it introduced the order governing dress. Smith, in the book on national character, says just this.[141] – Pauw,[142] in *Inquiries concerning the Americans*, says the comparison of a prince to a father, where the subjects are like immature children to whom he can give whatever he wants, is an unfortunate one. – It is peculiar that those who are made to be immature also actually become immature, and
25:1300 then give their oppressors the excuse to think they could not avail themselves of their freedom and thus that they had to make them slaves even more. – This is the case with serfdom, which is especially great in Courland and Livonia. – But when one liberates him, he will surely learn to use his powers, just as someone who is bound cannot walk so long as he is bound, yet when released is able to walk. – Another unfortunate comparison is that of the clergyman with a shepherd, where his subordinates are to be seen as his beloved livestock. The immaturity of the second sex is in public affairs, whereas for the most part the man is immature in domestic matters. But this is true only in Europe, for in the other parts of the world the women are held in the greatest contempt and subjection by the men.[143]

In the case of the higher cognitive faculty, I cognize by means of general concepts, and this is what distinguishes it from the lower faculty. We often lack reason. – But one often thinks without being conscious of the principles of thinking. If someone discovers general rules, he must

---

a *Unmündigkeit*

know the principles of thinking. A rule without power of judgment is of no help. One does not need power of judgment in a public speech, but does need it in conversations and social gatherings. A human being can possess much erudition and still be very stupid. A great deal is imputed to sensation that belongs to understanding, and vice versa. For example, when the ignorant judge of something, they appeal to an inner feeling. But this is valid only for sensations and not for cognitions of the understanding. Moral judgments are judgments of the understanding, not of sensation. If the latter were the case, one would not need to judge at all, but merely have a sensation. Understanding can be speculative and occupy itself merely with thinking; or practical, to invent and use the rule as a means to application; this is active and is based on experiences. The speculative [understanding] needs no experience. One says: "Understanding does not come before years." But this actually applies to the power of judgment. For one can learn the rules of the understanding early on.

The common understanding, *communis, non vulgaris*, which judges in common with all human understanding, is also called sound understanding.[a] Every human being is satisfied with his understanding. For he uses his own understanding as a standard of the understanding, and there the measured will always be equal to the measure. – The average of the understanding of every human being serves as the standard, but we cannot determine it.[b] An adroit understanding is superficial. The Frenchman who merely aims at the surface is like this. Because he grasps something quickly, he is content with that. The deceiver is not always more clever than the deceived. This latter can be the cleverest man; he simply does not suspect anything bad. The Negroes have a proverb: they can understand their masters easily, but their masters cannot understand them at all.[144] This occurs because their masters do not make the effort to find out about them. The honest man is not stupid; he has sound understanding. Inexperience can often give one an appearance of honesty, namely when one does not understand the artifices of deception. – Malice and stupidity are often connected, but uprightness[c] and stupidity are not connected at all. Honesty can be thought of with stupidity, but probity[d] i.e., honesty out of principles, cannot, and only a reasonable man can have this. Human beings have a great deal of understanding and yet little reason. Some people can brood well about little things but cannot expand their concepts. Limited minds can excogitate individual materials well, but not put together the whole. They perhaps have fine concepts, but not extended ones. For example, Lessing's[145] plays in themselves are very beautiful, but do not have the interconnectedness of

25:1301

---

[a] *gesunder Verstand*
[b] i.e., the average

[c] *Rechtschaffenheit*
[d] *Redlichkeit*

the whole. Reason is a higher understanding, which again gives rules to the understanding. In order to cultivate reason, one must always seek out the principles. The talent of reason is speculative and practical. Logic and metaphysics cultivate both, yet understanding has to do with objects of the senses. But reason [has to do] merely with the understanding. I cannot adopt as a principle what is possible and actual only in individual cases.

25:1302

Many people are immature for their entire lives. Their understanding is not suited to the business of living. We have a certain measure of years during which we cannot do anything without the guidance of others, because we still lack experience and are unfamiliar with the world's deception. Women acquire their understanding earlier than men. This notwithstanding, they are surely immature in civil life for their entire lives and always have caretakers.[a] Scholars are often immature in civil affairs, but this cannot redound to their dishonor. A professor in Halle once was in the middle of writing. A fire broke out in the house. Someone ran to him but, annoyed, he answered: "Didn't I tell you that this is a matter for my wife?"[146] All hereditary kingdoms are governed better than elected kingdoms, for here the people are immature and therefore cannot be governed very well.[b]

– One must always examine oneself as to whether and in which areas one might be immature.

ON THE IMPERFECTIONS OF THE MIND

We can distinguish mental illness and mental frailty. One is born with the latter. It is otherwise with mental illness, which concerns either the state of the mind or its constitution. – The first is the fantasizing in fever, which, however, is really a corporeal illness. But there is also the question as to whether genuine dementia is not also caused by a bodily illness. – Rousseau was one of the greatest eccentrics, since he was an extreme misanthrope, but in so doing he had a great genius. But after his death a great amount of water was found in his head.[147] This could have perhaps been the cause of his eccentricity. – Swift, who fell into a stupid dementia before his death and in whose head they also found water, was like this as well.[148] –

Genuine mental illness concerns merely the state of the mind, the wrong use of the powers, even if in themselves they are good. Mental illness includes hypochondria, [and] considered from the perspective of the mind, melancholia. – – There the doctor might perhaps be able to help, but there is still no certain means against illnesses of the nerves. – The

25:1303

---

[a] *Curatoren*
[b] *läßt sich deßwegen nicht so gut regieren*

hypochondriac must leave himself to his nature, live on a diet, <u>never be in bed longer than he sleeps</u>, his spirit is unfree,[a] eat no fortifying things, for example wine; for it is true that they stimulate, but they also weaken in the process, and they arouse in us more appetite than is useful to us. – Medicines always weaken the body; for they do not place it in its previous state, but in another one. – The hypochondriac fancies that he has all kinds of illnesses, likes to read medical books, and worry alternates in him with cheerfulness and often with exuberant joy. –

It is hard to define a disturbed mind and to distinguish it from a silly person and from fools. <Idiocy and simplemindedness are a lack of understanding. It is a lack of the ability to check one's judgment against others, [to see] whether one's beliefs are equal to the touchstone. The cretins in the canton of Valais,[b] people with enlarged goiters, are idiotic.[149]> For there is a specific difference. An idiocy is a mental frailty, and should be distinguished from the disturbed person. The disturbed person acts against the rule, <u>and does not concern the lack of the mental powers, but the incorrect use of them insofar as it is habitual.</u> But the idiot is crippled in the mind; he can hardly use his mental powers; he has an innate stupidity. – <u>The doctors cannot define the state of a healthy person, for, it is true, they say it is</u>[c] <u>when all of the animal functions operate regularly, but we do not know whether any human being has ever been so healthy that he does not lack the least thing. – It is just as hard to characterize the disturbance.</u> – A person has sound understanding when he compares his judgment with others and his judgment is objectively valid. But the disturbed person has neither the ability nor the drive to compare his judgment with the judgment of other human beings, but rather believes that everything he thinks actually is so. <It is as if the disturbed person were drunk. He does not listen to others. When we speak, we always attend to whether others hear us. Hence whoever speaks aloud to himself without anyone else around, probably no longer has everything quite right with him.> – Disturbances include: dementia, insanity, and lunacy.[d] – Dementia is either internal, when people believe they see an inner light, or external. The former is fanaticism, the latter is spirit-seeing.[e] – In judgments of the senses the demented person does not at all ask others, whereas in judgments of the senses we give a decisive worth to approval from others. – He is in the midst of whims. – Dementia is actually a false sense. If the demented person doubts, he will be a

25:1304

---

[a] This sentence, though comprehensible, is grammatically incorrect in the German, too.

[b] *Walliserlande*, or "Valais" in French.

[c] Reading, as in Mar: *denn sie sagen zwar es sey der* (for, it is true, they say it is). Mro: *denn sie sehen wol* (for they perhaps see).

[d] dementia: *Wahnsinn*; insanity: *Wahnwitz*; lunacy: *Aberwitz*.

[e] spirit-seeing: *Geisterseherey*; fanaticism: *Schwärmerey*.

415

mere fantast. – Insanity is based not on the judgment of the senses, but that of the understanding. <He concludes, from false grounds, correctly and truthfully. But the lunatic concludes falsely from true grounds. He uses correct rules in a backwards fashion.> Delusion*a* is a semblance,*b* a representation the ground of which lies in the subject, but which we take to be in the object. – Insane persons rely on a hypothesis that is imagined. The understanding orients itself according to this hypothesis, and he is properly clever and witty. He sees something, and he interprets it according to his delusion, and cannot be dissuaded of his view. – He is an egoist of the power of judgment, just as the demented person*c* is an egoist of sensibility. – There are many species of insanity. – It is believed that it arises largely out of arrogance and love. – But it appears to be innate and inherited; [it is] just that this or that was the trigger, so that his insanity completely broke out. That is also the object with which he is always occupied in his folly. One says that so and so was always arrogant, already in his youth. But at that time he was already foolish to a slight degree. – It is believed that one can become delirious*d* by studying too much. – But through too much exertion of the powers, they become weakened, not overextended. – Sitting up late at night and occupying oneself with materials that are unsolvable are already effects of hidden folly. – One says that he who "crosses the line" becomes insane. But it already indicates a degree of folly that it even occurs to someone to go to East India, with which he has nothing to do. – With insane persons, understanding and reason are*e* correct, [they are] just built on an incorrect ground. – But in the case of lunacy, it is not just delusion that underlies the human being; rather, something correct can also be underlying; but his understanding does not judge according to rules. – Such are all the theoretical writings of Böhme: they seem to be reasonable, but are not. [The same holds for] the Kabbalah, or producing something by numbers, and theurgy, or the art of listening to spirits and availing oneself of them for one's judgment. This is insanity. Such a thing seems to arise again every once in a while, for example, *Of Errors*f *and Truth*,150 and *The Relations that Exist among God, Man, and the World*,*g*151 two books full of fanaticism and lack of understanding. – Disturbance in affect is delirium.*b* – One says that human beings, when they slip unawares into

25:1305

---

a *Wahn*   *b* *Schein*

c *der Wahnsinnige*, more literally, "one with delusional sense"

d *toll*   *e* *ist*

f Two sheets, the second of which was blank, were inserted here. The first sheet reads: "Destiny [*Destinée*] is an entirely invariable necessity that is wholly brutal, where it must go the way it goes on."

g The transcriber wrote the titles as: *Des erreurs et de la vérité* and *Les rapports, qui existent entre le Dieu, homme, et le monde*.

b *Tollheit*

a completely repugnant mental disposition, have whims or raptus. They are moody, like dogs. – They are people who have an ungoverned affect, and that is very closely related to delirium. – There are errors of understanding, power of judgment, and reason that do not belong to disturbance, yet still are defects: such as folly, silliness, foolishness.[a] – All human beings digress from the rule of reason, and often no one can acquit himself of folly. Folly is deviation from the rule of reason through the seduction of the inclinations. – Everybody has his hobbyhorse towards which he is inclined and from which he cannot be pulled away. – But one just has to leave that to him. –

A dolt[b] is someone who lacks the understanding for appraising things according to their true worth. – In a game, I place the greatest importance here. – The dolt can be liked; the fool[c] is always an object of hatred for us, for foolishness conveys with it the concept of arrogance. A fool is someone who has a great opinion of his own worth. The fool prefers evil over the good. – Foolishness is an object of biting ridicule. Foolishness is a delusion of one's own merits to the detrimental appraisal of others. A delusion that is detrimental to everyone in society is foolishness. Arrogance, too, belongs here. – Thus avarice, too, is considered a foolishness, but merely greedy avarice, not frugal[d] avarice, which is merely a [kind of] folly. – A person with greedy avarice commits a host of foolish acts.

<A few ridiculous examples of avarice are the following.[152] A preacher once was preaching a quite good sermon on the worth of giving alms. A friend of a miser wanted to make this sermon very useful for him, but his friend told him: "It's a lovely thing, giving alms, so I will ask for some myself at the next opportunity." Another one heard a beautiful sermon about the shamefulness of money-lending. He went immediately to the priest and asked him to give the sermon again. The priest, who knew him, answered him that he already had explained the matter well. "Yes," said the money-lender, "but there is still another money-lender here on the street. Perhaps he would like to convert, then I'll be the only one on the street." – An avaricious person bequeathed 1,000 guilders to a hospital. Before he had died, the [amount of] money had diminished. In a short while he had the director of the hospital summoned, and said to him that if he wanted to receive the *legatum*[e] in a diminished [amount of] money, he would pay it out to him right away; if not, he would have to take it back. – The director naturally accepted the offer.>

25:1306

If I take something to be an end that is merely a means, it is a delusion. But this occurs in the case of avarice. – Thus a delusion of honor[f] also

---

[a] folly: *Thorheit*; silliness: *Albernheit*; foolishness: *Narrheit*.
[b] *Thor*
[c] *Narr*
[d] frugal: *karge*; greedy: *habsüchtige*.
[e] Trans.: bequest.
[f] *Ehrenwahn*

exists. It would be good if one made vice out to be a [kind of] foolishness, for: 1, if one ridicules a person one humiliates him, but by earnest refutation I still make him important; 2, if I laugh, it is better than when I show him my bitter hatred. This last thing can mislead one into misanthropy and is a mental disposition that others cannot take part in. By laughing at [something] I at least make a vice human, but by hatred I make it diabolical. One makes a vice ridiculous when one shows that through it one brings about precisely the opposite of one's aim. – That therefore holds true of arrogance: for the arrogant person causes other human beings to be contemptuous of him, not honor him. – Foolishness is a misuse of things in one's memory, when it is conjoined with self-conceit. – Foolishness still requires culture. – – –

A cockscomb is a person who believes anyone, and a dandy[a] is a person who can be deceived by anyone. – Old people are for the most part called cockscombs, and young people dandies. – A cockscomb is also someone who thinks the best of himself in all cases. – One becomes shrewd by having many experiences. – One becomes cunning,[b] when, through experiences, one has not only become skillful at averting one's troubles, but also skillful at outwitting others.

25:1307

People have idiotic children, but never have disturbed ones. In the case of the latter, the germ of craziness already lies in the child, when they later become crazy, and when the understanding becomes developed, then this too breaks out. – Grimm, who wrote *Notes of a Traveler through Germany, England, and France*,[153] observed human beings in their mental sicknesses and in their errors of the heart, that is, in the hospitals for nervous disorders and prisons, and there he made many kinds of remarks, for example, that for the most part there were strong persons in the prisons. Hypochondria, so very common among scholars, can to some extent be counted here. It seems to express its effect excellently with frequent use of warm beverages and stimulating things, for example, tobacco. Hypochondria comes not so much from studying as from disorderly studying, from the transition from idleness to a suddenly overextended and highly strained work. When one needs certain mechanical means in order to brighten up the mental powers, for example, drinking coffee late [hypochondria can result]. One can also count here all the sensation-straining writings, and in general all the irritating and stimulating things. One probably cannot say that sitting is the chief cause of hypochondria; otherwise all cobblers and tailors would have to be hypochondriacs. – But sitting, together with the strain of thinking, can contribute greatly to hypochondria. The structure of the body contributes greatly to hypochondria, notwithstanding that the main source of it is an unruled power of imagination. Rousseau was an

---

[a] dandy: *Laffe*; cockscomb: *Gek*.   [b] cunning: *Abgewitzt*; shrewd: *gescheut*.

astounding hypochondriac, which one can see from his soliloquies on   25:1308
solitary walks.[154]

ON TALENT 20[a]

One distinguishes talent of mind[b] from genius. What is characteristic
of the human being in the faculty of cognition is called "mind," in the
faculty of desire "heart." Mind is opposed to the simpleton.[c] Under the
mind, one thinks of the ability to think for oneself, and this includes
sound understanding,[d] and the faculty and possession of a correct power
of judgment.[e] He can lack familiarity with the rule itself, but he knows
how to act in a practical manner without this theory.

Talent is an ability insofar as it is considered a cognitive power in the
application of a certain kind of object. With talent, it is based not so
much on the degree as on the proportion. A human being with a small
degree of wit and a greater degree of the power of judgment can be a
reasonable man; but if, with the same degree of the power of judgment,
he had an even greater degree of wit, then he might babble. Hence one
must attempt to cultivate all the talents mutually, so that a proportion
remains. Disproportion in talents stands out and makes one monstrous.
Should one try to do away with this? With regard to the human being,
yes. With regard to society? No, for there what is striking is agreeable
and serves for variety.

The pupil requires natural aptitude in order to learn, the teacher talent, and the inventor genius. The pupil needs only to learn and to retain,
the teacher must already know how to teach what he has learned and in
turn to instill it in the most comprehensible manner. Many teachers are
pupils; that is, they teach merely as they have learned. – But they must
not merely [teach] the letter of science as it is found in books, but also the
spirit of the science; they must try to have insight into its principles – the
teacher must know this latter more, in order to form his knowledge in
accordance with the characteristics of the subjects[f] as the circumstances
require it.

The talents are diverse: there is a critical talent, an historical one, a
philological one, a philosophical one, a mathematical and mechanical
talent, etc. Whoever is excellent in one talent, is not necessarily for that
reason excellent in all of them.

---

[a] It is unclear why the numbering of this and the next section appears like this in the
transcription.
[b] *Kopf Talent*   [e] *BeUrtheilungsKraft*
[c] *Pinsel*   [f] *Beschaffenheit der Subiecte*
[d] *gesunde Verstand*

25:1309   For the kinds of cognition involved are diverse. He who possesses a great degree of all the talents is a universal mind. A mind[a] for the superficial, who knows the titles of everything but not the contents, often seems to be a universal mind but is not; for example, the French [are] like this.

Anyone who applies himself to a science can attain the mind of universality in a short while. –

One must see science in terms of universal purposes, how everything is interconnected with a principal purpose. This is an architectonic talent and the source of systems. Did nature give the human being the inclinations he has toward an art? – One does indeed have inclinations by nature, but one can also fancy having much by nature. We often like a science merely on account of its exterior, without being familiar with what is inside. Fontanelle was one of the most universal minds. He could make everything agreeable and easy. An Italian asserted [that there was] a metempsychosis of talent and claimed to prove that on the day Michelangelo, a great man, died, Galileo Galilei was born, and when he died, Newton was born <only the first was a genius>.[155] But that is a mere play of the wit, for the soul was indeed with Newton already in the womb. The author[156] says the lack of talent could be replaced by practice. Whatever seems easy, was not always easy for the writer. Thus Rousseau says[157] that those of his plays that are especially beautiful also required of him an especially great deal of diligence. Leibniz is considered a universal mind. But actually Leonardo d'Avinci seems to have been such a person. He was the founder of a school of painting in Italy, was great in all the arts, had familiarity with every science, and was completely in control of himself. He was a painter, poet, sculptor, musician, handsomely built, candid, etc.

Indeed, when he was already near death and heard that the king was coming to visit him, he summoned up his courage so that he almost appeared to be not weak at all.[158] The historical talent requires memory. A critical talent requires knowledge of the rules of logic, aesthetics, and a good power of judgment. Hence he is no critic who has a sen-
25:1310   sation of beauty but cannot specify any ground other than his sensation. Habit replaces the lack of talent through practice, and consists in a *habitus*.[b] – But it is nonetheless immediately distinguished from natural talent.

The natural talent that cannot be acquired through any labor or through any practice is genius. It is distinguished from talent not so much in degree as in quality. It is the originality of talent.

[a] mind: *Geist*; universal mind: *allgemeiner Kopf.*
[b] Trans.: habit

ON GENIUS. 2 I

Genius derives from *genius*, peculiar spirit.[a] The ancients ascribed *ingenium* to everything and understood by it a natural constitution and predisposition of a thing. There are abilities that can be attained by diligence, but genius is what cannot be brought about that way, but rather derives merely from the peculiar natural predisposition. Thus there are geniuses of the power of imagination. For all the products of taste cannot be produced according to rules, but rather according to a predisposition of the mind peculiar to each person. In German works, there is often much diligence, but not much genius. – Hence one cannot learn this; rather, genius is required for it. Through diligence, it is true, one will make a poem error-free, but one will not actually be composing. – The ancients called that genius because they thought of it as insertion[b] and believed that it came from a peculiar spirit of someone else. The poets themselves often believed in inspiration[c] because at times something occurred to them that afterwards never came to mind again, even when they tried very hard at it. Genius is originality of talent.

Not everything that is original is for that reason worthy of imitation. There can be an original of foolishness, an originality of the incorrect use of the power. – Genius does not imitate rules, but rather brings forth products that themselves are in turn rules. It is through freedom from the constraint of rules that one produces new ones, which, however, must be worth imitating. When I extract other rules from rules that are known, it is talent, but not genius. For example, such are the inventions in mathematics and philosophy, etc. The rules of the genius must be fruitful. In language, one must follow the rules. Genius gives new rules. Thus Michelangelo was a genius, as he built St. Peter's Church in Rome according to a completely new invention, which later became a model for all times.[159] – Matters[d] of genius are those that cannot be learned in accordance with rules. Mathematics and philosophy are not matters of genius. Mathematics can be learned. Thus Newton was, it is true, a human being of great talent, but not of genius, as he himself said.[160] He had achieved his book *Principia philosophiae naturalis* through twenty years of diligence. But genius is not a very great talent, but rather an original talent. – One cannot learn genius, nor bring it about through one's own diligence; rather, it is based on the special natural predisposition. Matters of genius are those that aim at the power of imagination in relation to taste. Taste does not direct itself in accordance

25:1311

---

[a] peculiar spirit: *eigenthümlicher Geist*; *genius*: *Genius*; Genius: *Genie.*
[b] *Eingebung*   [d] *Sachen*
[c] *Begeisterung*

with rules *a priori*; I cannot at all justify my taste. Taste is thus the proportion of the mental powers. In the case of taste, it is not my taste, but my sensation, which judges. The learner must [have] natural aptitude, the teacher talent. The inventor with regard to taste must have genius. Now, from improper usage, people call all talents geniuses. – Genius is permitted a freedom from the constraint of rules. Poetry is a matter of genius, hence *licentia poetica*[a] – eloquence not so much so; but a genius cannot be unruled either. Geniuses free themselves from rules, since their products themselves become rules. He is, so to speak, a privileged mind. The mechanism of instruction through *imi-*

25:1312   *tationes Ciceronianas,*[161] regular preparation of letters, verses, etc., and through the mechanism of government, when limits are imposed on reason and the understanding, is repugnant to genius and its emergence. Genius must not be suppressed, but rather cultivated. – Through mechanism in schools, the pupil becomes so accustomed to it that he cannot proceed at all without rules. One should not therefore instruct the boys in eloquence; rather, one should have them read good poets and orators. The *Imitationes* are not imitations[b] – for it requires a great deal of spirit in order to be completely equal to a man and thus it actually [requires] precisely such genius; rather, it is an aping.[c] So mechanism in the civil condition, too, is very harmful because there the human beings are utter machines, and contingent errors cannot be remedied because there are no independent thinkers[d] there. Virtuosi are headstrong and have many passions, for example for drink, etc., etc.

Mechanism is very useful in soldiering; for here an entire army operates like a single great machine, and the strength of armies derives from this. The oriental peoples are brave enough, but they are not subordinate to a mechanism, and the latter depends on a discipline.

Geniuses are moody and dependent on their moods. They cannot compose all the time, just at certain times. However, geniuses are probably not as moody as virtuosi; the latter are artists in execution, the former are artists in invention. – Genius can be opposed to the mechanical mind. Genius creates epochs; however, the mechanical mind is still more useful, since it creates regular order. A mechanical mind is commonplace. Genius appears to be based on a kind of disproportion in the cognitive power. The geniuses of the power of imagination have for the most part a bizarre appearance, are crippled, etc. But geniuses are[e] always illustrious. Although geniuses have freedom from rules, one must

---

a   Trans.: poetic licence
b   *Nachahmungen*
c   *Nachäffung*

d   *SelbstDenker*
e   *ist*

not for that reason mock all rules. There are genius-apes^a who in the process thus began by transgressing the rules, who wanted to elicit in others the thought that they were geniuses, and so began at the end. Genius-apes seek originality without worthiness of imitation. He who has good inspirations is not yet a genius, for inspirations cannot be rules. Genius is for the most part coarse like Shakespeare – he lacks polish; Homer, too. The virtuoso polishes it away; Virgil is like this. To genius belong the power of imagination, power of judgment, spirit, and taste, just as to a painting belong expression, design (correctness), composition (fineness) and coloring (proper mixture of colors). – 25:1313

Lack of power of judgment is more offensive than lack of power of imagination. Prudence^b is punctiliousness, and thus seems not to belong to genius, but excessive daredevilishness does not belong to it either; thus the means^c [is] purposiveness. With spirit there must be unity of principle, so that the mental powers will be moved harmoniously. The creation of genius is to be attributed to the power of imagination. Spirit is power of imagination combined with understanding. But power of judgment combined with sensibility is taste. The word "spirit" is often used to indicate something enlivened.^{d} But what does something that is enlivened do? – Something enlivens when it sets the power of imagination into motion. This is the most active mental power, which also gives material for activity to the other powers. But with spirit there must also be a concept, for nothing can be pleasing when the understanding is not in play. The foundation of genius is having spirit. Taste involves choosing from what is given, not inventing something new. Hence a genius can have little taste, and someone with a great deal of taste can have little genius. A taste is probably required for genius; but it is nothing essential; rather, it belongs to [its] perfection. Ages of true taste are also ages of enlightenment and mature power of judgment. Taste comes primarily from long experience. It is cautiousness in the choice of that which pleases. It limits the daring of genius. Wherever therefore good taste dominates, there are also fewer geniuses; for instance, in England [there are] more geniuses than in France.

If the product of genius is not in keeping with taste, then it^e is despised and dismissed.^{162}

With genius, the power of imagination must not be fettered, and yet there must not be mere chimeras. There is a fine, small boundary here. Genius thus borders very closely on delirium. 25:1314

---

^{a} *GenieAffen*

^{b} *Klugheit*. Stark and Brandt note that this word might be corrupt.

^{c} *das Mittel* ^{d} *belebtes*

^{e} *er*. This pronoun may refer to taste (*der Geschmak*) rather than *das Product* or *das Genie*.

Genius either shoots into the root, i.e., power of judgment, which is found among the Germans; or into the crown, that is, power of imagination, which occurs with the Italians; or into the flower, i.e., taste, with the French; or into the fruit, spirit, with the English. The latter have a profound, very heavy*[a]* wit. Italians love splendor. – The French [are the] legislators of taste. – A great deal of understanding is always concealed in the English products of wit, as in all of their writings. Gerard[163] in particular has attempted to discover the authentic constitution of genius. – The question is whether nature also gave talent, to the person it gave a propensity.

One cannot infer this with certainty. To be sure, it is true that a genuine genius often displays itself early. He who through natural predisposition has more than others have through diligence, the French call *élève de la nature.*[b] A certain Brindley calculated all[c] the costs of the canals of Lord Bridgewater, the only ones in Europe.[164] *Ingenia praecocia*, children who are clever early, are not geniuses; they either die prematurely or later are ordinary human beings. – Such were Pascal, Heinecken, and Baratier. *Ingenia praecocia* are mere plays of nature that soon pass. They also do not live long, as Baratier became a doctor at the age of twelve and died at eighteen.[165] Great men did not show anything out of the ordinary in their youth, as Clavius, a great mathematician, was given to the blacksmith in his youth because of his lack of ability.[166] *Ingenia praecocia* are also often self-taught; they are naturalists in the sciences, and they are mostly in Switzerland because one is free there. But instruction is still better. For otherwise one never has a correct foundation. Such was Pascal, who invented various propositions of Euclid and gave his name to them.[167] Slowness does not indicate a lack of talent, but is instead a slow preparation.

Gigantic erudition is cyclopic, one-eyed, when it consists merely in historical knowledge and the other eye – reason, philosophy – is missing. A genius sometimes indicates vast erudition, but it must be regulated; otherwise it is mere chaos without life. Historical knowledge makes one haughty; philosophy humbles. –

Matters of genius can often be a disadvantage to the nation and produce contempt for diligence and laborious sciences. A great invention now draws towards itself a host of heads that imitate it, and a great genius strikes down a host of similar heads that do not dare step forward. The rarity of genius comes from this.

25:1315

---

[a] *Zentnerschweren*   *[b]* Trans.: pupil of nature
[c] Following Brandt and Stark's suggestion: *alle* (all). They also conjecture: *allein* (alone). Mro: *alles* (all).

SECOND SECTION OF THE PART[a]

ON THE FEELING OF PLEASURE OR DISPLEASURE

This will be more interesting than the preceding, since it concerns our delight.[b] But it is all the more difficult to provide distinct concepts of it. [A] feeling of pleasure or displeasure is either subjective, when we have a sensation of it in ourselves, or objective, when we have a sensation of it in an object. The delight in my condition itself is enjoyment, and what I enjoy is agreeable.[c] The delight in the object is either through the senses, i.e., the beautiful, or through the understanding, i.e., the good. The delight in the object is delight of judging;[d] that in the subject, delight of sensation. Thus delight is of three kinds: <u>agreeable</u>, <u>beautiful</u>, and <u>good</u>. The <u>agreeable</u> is that which pleases the private sense, the <u>beautiful</u> is that which pleases universally; both, however, please sensibly. – – The good, by contrast, is that which pleases in accordance with rules of the understanding. Hence I can only say: something is agreeable "to me." With the beautiful, we believe and demand that it is pleasing others as well. Hence we argue with each other over the beautiful. The agreeable is enjoyable;[e] the beautiful properly pleases; the good is approved.[f]

25:1316

1.[g] The agreeable: everyone strives after it, and the idea of [the] uninterrupted comfort[h] of life is called happiness. – Every discomfort or pain requires us to leave our present condition, and this is its definition. But comfort is the sensation that moves us always to prolong the condition we are in. Enjoyment: every moment we seek it and are driven to leave the condition we are in: hence it seems that we have pain incessantly. – One says if time passed really quickly, one was really enjoying oneself. Thus when we always alter our condition every moment, we are enjoying ourselves. Enjoyment therefore seems to consist in the cancellation of pain, and pain actually seems to predominate in us. The Italian Count Verri[168] <(Meiners translated his writing on the nature of enjoyment)> says, among other things, that the beautiful arts and sciences are means against the nameless pains of boredom. If we always had enjoyment, that would not benefit us at all, for we would not be conscious of our life. With pain we actually feel our existence. Boredom is incessant, nameless pain. Sensitive persons often have it. <u>Pleasures are physical and ideal.</u> The more the human being has the latter in his control, the more means

---

[a] Brandt and Stark indicate that "Section of the Part" was added to Mro at a later time, which is presumably why it was not underlined by the transcriber.
[b] *Wohlgefallen*
[c] agreeable: *angenehm*; enjoyment: *Vergnügen*.
[d] *Beurtheilung*   [f] gebilligt
[e] *vergnügt*
[g] There are apparently no subsequent subsections that correspond to this one.
[h] *Annehmlichkeit*

he has to eliminate pain, but the more he also needs that same thing. Pain is an ill,[a] but the remembrance of it is ridiculous or indifferent for us; one remembers a moral ill with ill yet again. We do not want to live again under the conditions that we already had during childhood, for we are never satisfied with our condition and always want to pass into another. The savages are not driven to activity by enjoyment, but by pain, that is to say, by hunger. – Work is pain which, however, when we succeed is eliminated by a new enjoyment. Entertainment is an agreeable occupation in idleness. Work is a wearisome occupation the purpose of which is agreeable. Why do we seek out company at the table? Not for the reason that through the various subject matters that are spoken about, we are always brought from one condition to another. If a time that we believed we really enjoyed were actually full of enjoyment, we would regret that it did not last longer. But, on the contrary, we are always glad that the time passed by so quickly. This shows that we always endeavor to rush through time instead. But this has the following uses.[b] With us, pain is now always the spur[c] of activity. If we were not driven by pain from one condition into another, we would always remain in one condition and do nothing. Admittedly, we could have also been moved to activity [in another way], such that we depart from our condition out of the prospect of a great enjoyment in the future. But Providence has determined pain to be the spur to our activity. Novels are thereby always more titillating for us, the more often strokes of fortune and misfortune alternate within them. They also therefore cannot describe married life, for the uniformity occurring in it would be displeasing to us. Hence no one has ever been able to depict marriage's good fortune, rather they have continued the story further; in this way they have interjected a marriage-devil.[d][169] In human beings, continuous enjoyment never occurs; rather, pain and enjoyment must always alternate. The human being therefore works, which in itself is pain, but which afterwards furnishes him the best and purest enjoyment. – If one does not work, one becomes bored. Pain makes time [feel] long, for we then feel our entire existence, for example, during a surgical operation. – Dissonances are pains, but they serve all the more to enhance[e] the enjoyment in the harmonic. Thus what is agreeable about tobacco consists in the fact that pain and enjoyment always alternate there and the previous pain is always eliminated by the enjoyment. What human beings love to the point of passion is a pain

25:1317

25:1318

---

[a] *Übel*

[b] Reading, as in Mar: *folgenden Nutzen* (the following uses). Mro: *immer den Nutzen* (always has uses).

[c] Reading, as in Mar: *der Stachel* (the spur). Mro: *die Seele* (the soul).

[d] *Eheteufel*, a person thought to cause disagreements between spouses.

[e] *heben*

that is always canceled by an enjoyment. Some have killed themselves out of boredom, for example Lord Mordaunt in Paris shot himself and left behind a note reading: "To eat, drink, go to balls and comedies, to caress mistresses, etc. – are these all the pleasures of this world? Then I want to seek new ones in another world."[170] Hence the French used to say: "The English shoot themselves in order to pass time." – In order to drive away boredom, one seeks out work. – Even games, for example, card games: why is it agreeable, why does it become the most violent passion that extirpates all other inclinations? – The interest here is due to the concern for losses and the alternation of losing and winning; thus the alternation of enjoyment and pain is the reason that it pleases. Games also cultivate, make us equanimous, accustom us to restrain our affects, and can thus have an influence on morality. When we are in pain, time becomes long, in enjoyment, [it is] short. We thus feel the duration of our life more in pain; enjoyment makes us forget the duration of our life. Enjoyment is the feeling of the promotion of life, pain is the feeling of the hindrance of life. (Enjoyment is no feeling of life, for I feel the latter just as well, and even much better, when in pain. It is also not mere promotion of life; there are medicines that, however, do not cause any enjoyment because they are not noticeable. Some have claimed that the degree of pain conforms to the degree of hindrance, but that is false, for example, in the case of toothaches. Enjoyment is not a positive savoring,[a] where something is added to the feeling of our condition, but rather merely negative and consists in the cancellation of pain. Life has a certain measure beyond which it does not go, that is, health. But now a continuous enjoyment would intensify life to infinity, and thus when it went beyond that measure it would again weaken [us]; hence pain, which cancels health, must always precede, and enjoyment then consists in the cancellation of this hindrance and the promotion of life towards health.) There can thus be a great hindrance to life that, however, we do not feel, and then there is no pain, for example a lung that is going bad. The feeling can be great, and the promotion or hindrance small. The magnitude of the enjoyment or pain is based on the magnitude of the feeling; life in itself cannot be felt, but only its promotion or hindrance. Thus the healthy person is he who feels nothing, and thus a human being will never find himself completely healthy. With regard to enjoyment, our life has little value, for the pain that one has a sensation of balances it out. – The value of our life consists merely in the good we have done. And despite all the innumerable pains, we nevertheless wish for life. Satisfaction from savoring[b] would be positive, from comfort[c] negative; we do not have the former in this world, but when we are satisfied with our

25:1319

---

[a] *Genuß*
[b] *Genuß*

[c] *Gemächlichkeit*

actions and with ourselves, and that arises out of the consciousness of good actions, then we are happy here.

All our happiness is comparative, according to which the things that cause us pain are different for each human being and for each people. – Voltaire says: "Hope and sleep are two things that aim at the promotion of our life."[171] We see from this that our greatest happiness here consists in work. It is peculiar that the time that seems short to us while it is happening appears long afterwards, and that the time that seemed long to us while it lasted appears short later. But that occurs because work fulfills time most soundly and at the same time thus shortens [it], and because work fills up time so much it afterwards appears long to us, for we can remember a great deal from it, whereas on the contrary a time in which we did nothing and therefore became long, later seems to us to have been short, as we represent it to ourselves as an empty time and we cannot remember anything from it. He who cannot be affected by anything is indifferent;[a] he who cannot be set into motion by anything is equanimous.[b] Our mind is moved if it is unable to value the entire worth of its condition. He who finds no enjoyment in anything, or whom nothing pains, is indifferent. But he who does not have a sensation of either joy or sadness is equanimous. – Joy and sadness consist not merely in sensations, but also in reflections; animals do not have the latter, although they have enjoyment and pain. Indifference comes from temperament. But equanimity [comes] from principles. The former should not be praised and is instead a [kind of] lifelessness; he who values his enjoyment so greatly that he believes that it alone makes him most fortunate or unfortunate, is not equanimous. It is thus said of such a person that he rejoices like a child and mourns like a woman. – Gamblers are often completely equanimous, but often that merely seems to be so, for sometimes things go for them just as they go for a person who said to another who was surprised by his apparent equanimity: "But the devil hasn't lost anything by this, for I have blasphemed on the inside all the more."[172] – In order to be equanimous, one needs only to consider that nothing in our life is as important as our good conduct alone. Equanimity is opposed to a moody character, which does not depend on principles but only on influences, partly from the body, partly from other circumstances. – The equanimous person always has a cheerful heart, and that is the pleasure[c] that Epicurus praises. – In order to obtain equanimity, one must not commit one's heart to things that are not in our control (and that is everything except our morality and learning to practice the *sustine* and *abstine*[d] of the Stoics).[173] Equanimity is the firmness of our mental

25:1320

---

[a] *Gleichgültig*
[b] *gleichmüthig*
[c] *Wollust*
[d] Trans.: endure and abstain (*sustine et abstine*)

disposition. A moody mental disposition has no firmness whatsoever, but is as unsteady as a reed; that is a miserable condition. (Mood[a] should be distinguished from humor,[b] which is the original jestfulness[c] that lies in a human being's disposition.) One can enjoy pleasures, but they all have to be such that we can dispense with them without having ill-humor; then we are masters of our feeling, and what is more excellent? We can acquire equanimity through culture. Through science we establish in ourselves an inner foundation with which we can completely enjoy and entertain ourselves without needing other things aside from ourselves. Sensitivity[d] is also suited to the equanimous, and is the faculty of being able to have a sensation of the agreeable and disagreeable. Touchiness[e] is the condition in which one is easily carried away by every sensation. This latter is [a] weakness, the former is [a] strength. For one needs the former in order to be able to choose for others what they will enjoy. – Such touchiness has now become very fashionable (with touchiness one creates sheer ideals rather than rational reflections. Sensitivity does not come from the senses, but from concepts. – In our actions we must not orient ourselves according to sensations, for these give no determinate rule and always mislead us. So, too, with moral feeling. Sentiment[f] could also be called sentimentality,[g] just like garrulity.[h] He who feels all impressions equally is pampered.[i]) To cry with someone who is poor and not help him is childishness. For, in the first place, instead of one unfortunate person, there will in that case be two, and in the second place, such people afterwards imagine that in so doing they have done a good deed.[j] First one must fulfill one's duties and pay one's indebtedness; afterwards one can think of magnanimity. Always being disposed to laughter and cheerfulness is [worth] nothing; always being sad even less. But a good, serene mood that takes important things to be important and trifles to be nothing: that is the right mental disposition that is fitting for the human heart. The good mood must express itself even when rebuking vice. This consists either in abhorrence or in ridicule; the former places us in an adverse mental disposition, but the latter preserves the good mood for us and is also more efficacious; for the thing, by being abhorred, is after all still represented as important, as I will not hate what is unimportant, and one is often thereby tempted to hate people, too. But by using ridicule I make the vice utterly unimportant. – Thus piety with a good mood is the best. Gravitas, so it seems, is not fitting for human nature and arises only by compulsion, for by inclination one merely plays. Others will be

25:1321

---

[a] *Laune*
[b] *vom launigten*
[c] *Scherzen*
[d] *Empfindsamkeit*
[e] *Empfindlichkeit*

[f] *Empfindelei*
[g] *Empfindseeligkeit*
[h] *Redseeligkeit*
[i] *Verzärtelt*
[j] *Handlungen*

satisfied with a man who is always satisfied with himself, for they have nothing to fear from him. But one should fear an unfortunate man on account of his envy. Letting something weigh on one's mind[a] is distinct from taking something to heart.[b] The former occurs when I view something as an essential diminution of my happiness, without making it an incentive to my actions. That is contrary to nature. For nature gave us pain so that it would be a spur to our activity. But taking something to heart is not improper. Here we must have a sensation of something insofar and as intensely as it is necessary for it to become an incentive to our actions. We should not let even our own needs weigh on our mind, but merely take them to heart. It is nothing, merely to do penitence for something but not improve anything. We cannot cancel the past, but surely [we can alter] the future (as far as our voluntary actions are concerned). Hence we must look merely towards the future. – It is believed that when one lets something weigh upon one's mind for a long time, the impression thereby becomes indelible and will thereby constantly become an incentive. But that is false, for rather, as Tetens says in his *Destiny of the Human Being*,[174] a thought that has for a long time become annoying becomes detestable to a person afterwards. – We must always try to increase our enjoyment. When it comes to our pleasures, we always have other ones in view. Hence in our youth we must not try to enjoy every possible pleasure, so that we have something left over in old age. For we judge everything according to the end. If we are doing well at the end, then it seems to us that our entire life is fortunate; and if we are not doing well, then it seems to us that our entire life was bad. Enjoyment in aftertaste is longer-lasting than in foretaste. Nature has wisely arranged it this way. Abstemiousness should therefore be praised not merely as virtue, but also as prudence. Pleasures are either of service for our culture or are not. The former are long-lasting pleasures. The more I enjoy them, the more I will be capable of them. The pleasures that are not of service for culture, but merely for enjoyment, make us even duller and less capable of them. To the cultivating pleasures belong in particular: 1. society with women, where wit is preeminently developed 2. furthermore, the sciences 3. luxury,[c] or a dispensable expenditure with taste. Luxury refers to the quality of things, *luxuries*;[d] debauchery[e] to the quantity of things; the Poles still have *luxuries*. – Luxury is part of a cultivated age. Home[175] says luxury is the comfort that makes one soft. Hence the English have no luxury, for they ride, drive, etc. But

25:1322

---

[a] *Etwas sich zu Gemüthe ziehen*, as in having an abiding grief about something.
[b] *etwas zu Herzen nehmen*
[c] *luxus*. In the Academy Edition, this sentence lacks the number "1."
[d] *luxuries*. Since Kant uses the English word, I have italicized it.
[e] *Schwelgerey*

luxury can make us soft, and hardened, too. It dominates in certain ages. In previous times there were *luxuries*. Thus in the year 1400, when the order of moderation was founded, where the law was that knights were not allowed to intoxicate themselves for two years, the knights were only permitted to drink seventeen goblets of wine. – Thus Charles IV[176] restricted the weddings to ten tables and ten persons at each table. An object can be agreeable to us and yet enjoyment in the object can displease us; for we judge (here sensibility and understanding create the contrast) our enjoyment through an even higher enjoyment. Thus there are bitter joys. On the contrary, something can be disagreeable to us that pleases us after all. Thus, for example, pain concerning a beloved person pleases us because love is something noble. Such distressed people who mourn out of magnanimity do not want to let themselves be consoled, for they think it is a duty to mourn. Those are sweet pains: these arise when the pain has something noble as its object. The word "penitence,"[a] which is a discharge of punishment for the crime, is also based on this. It is the inner torment of oneself. The understanding approves of this punishment and the human being thus practices it. However, it does not provide the least advantage. But the enjoyment can please the understanding, in addition to sensation. Thus a human being's taste creates much enjoyment for him, but he enjoys even more the fact that he has taste. The human being finds a delight [in the fact] that he shows beneficence to someone. But he also enjoys [the fact] that he can show beneficence and has the inclination to do so; the first arises from sympathy, the other from maxims. So, too, with pain there is something that also still pleases[b] us. Thus, with envy, we seem by nature to have a great predisposition to it. Thus LaRochefoucauld says: "There is something in the misfortune of our best friends that does not entirely displease us"[177] – for with the increase of others' perfection, our egoism suffers; hence we like to see that they are humbled. Envy is painful to us and we cannot approve of it. Envy, gloating, ingratitude are the three diabolical vices because they have no use whatsoever. – We enjoy an ability much more when we have acquired it ourselves: that is a new source of enjoyment for the understanding. When we have brought pain upon ourselves, we feel it all the more; for example, when playing a game, I am not as sensitive when I lose through fate as when I lose because of my own fault. The former was an individual incident, but the latter can be a general cause of future losses. When we have slipped up and the harmful consequence fails to materialize, we are certainly discontented over the mistake. It is like this with moral actions, too. – When we have escaped a great danger, nevertheless a shudder always comes over us. What is better, to suffer

25:1323

25:1324

---

[a] *Buße*
[b] Following Brandt and Stark's suggestion: *gefällt* (pleases). Mro: *mißfällt* (displeases).

when guilty or innocent? In the latter case, I still always give my actions approval, while on the other hand I become indignant and infuriated. But through consciousness of guilt I become dejected; the guilty person is shamed by his pain. Enjoyment is enlarged through comparison with other people's pain, and pain is enlarged through comparison with other people's enjoyment. (Hume[a] counts as poverty not poor eating and drinking, but being poorly dressed and not being able to appear in society.[178]) Thus one feels the comfort of a warm oven more when a storm is raging outside or when there is bad weather. Hence one must not come up to a distressed person with a serene mien, for he would prefer that all of heaven mourn for him, and that consoles him. Pain is alleviated when we know that we could have easily suffered an even greater loss. – Pain is mere sensation. Sadness [is] when I consider myself unfortunate. It is a judgment on the worth of my entire condition. But pain [is] merely a partial sensation. – A man of principles can never be unfortunate. He can surely feel pain, but not sadness. This latter is a new pain that arises from one's feeling that his pain outweighs his entire enjoyment.

25:1325

We feel mediately or immediately pleasure or displeasure;[b] the mediate one itself does not please me, but rather only the purpose [does]. We are thus considering the immediate enjoyment. This is either agreeable, beautiful, good, or disagreeable, ugly, evil. The agreeable pleases in the sensation, and distinguishing the agreeable requires merely senses or feeling; but distinguishing the beautiful requires the power of judgment, and power of judgment with regard to the beautiful is taste. Distinguishing the good requires reason <understanding, judgment>, sentiment. What is agreeable to me has charm for me. The agreeable pleases me alone; but the beautiful must be valid for everyone, for it is based on the object.[c] Hence Winckelmann[179] says: "Men have merely true beauty, but women do not." They have only a charm for the men. One woman will not think another one to be so beautiful. With beauty, all sensations must be in accordance with rules in proportion;[d] no disharmony must occur; that is why it is not tasteful when one adorns oneself with gold.

Taste has universal validity; hence there is only one. He who can choose for his private sense has appetite;[e] but he who chooses for the universal sense has taste. With taste, something pleases us because it cultivates. It increases our ability to feel such delight, but the pleasure of enjoyment[f] wears out the pleasure and its faculty more and more. All

---

[a] Reading, as in Mro: *Hume*. Brandt and Stark suggest: *Home*, i.e., Henry Home.
[b] *Lust oder Unlust*   [c] *beruht auf dem Obiect*
[d] Following Brandt and Stark's suggestion: *Regeln in Proportion* (rules in propotion). Mro: *Proportion in Regeln* (proportion in rules).
[e] *Appetit*
[f] enjoyment: *Genusses*; pleasure: *Vergnügen*; delight: *Wohlgefallen*.

objects of taste are sociable. They can be sensed by many people without any one person getting ahead. There are only two senses, hearing and sight, that allow for objects of taste. A very large number of human beings can view a painting without it losing anything. Music can likewise be heard by many people. These pleasures through these senses can be communicated to society; for that reason they are sociable. But their pleasures do not impose themselves on others. Smell can also be communicated, but it imposes itself; hence it is not sociable. – Taste is thus the ability to choose socially. One must confirm the rules of taste out of experience, otherwise one is uncertain [about] whether one can immediately know them already beforehand.[a] They also tolerate exceptions, for they are borrowed from experience. It is always possible to dispute taste; one cannot demonstrate[b] it. Taste becomes more universal the more cultivated the nation becomes. The writings of the ancients have taste, for they have retained their glory[c] already for so long. Taste is merely for society. A great means of social entertainment is the meal. Taste belongs to the sociable meal; hence this ability to choose socially has also been named taste. The beautiful conveys with it a comfort; but it is not for this reason beautiful, but rather because it pleases universally. A judgment of taste should be distinguished from an inclination of taste.[d] The latter is the interest that I take in taste. When I am on a deserted island, it is true that I will find this or that beautiful, but I will find no interest in it. The useful will outweigh the beautiful. The inclination of taste grows in accordance with the degree of the inclination to sociability. Hence the French have the great inclination to taste. Sociability is good, but social inclination[e] is not. One must always be able to do without society. Living well belongs to sense, and the propensity to it is called luxury.[f] Living well, with taste, belongs to the power of judgment, and the propensity to it is luxury. Living well is a multitude of agreeable sensations that exceeds the degree of our needs. Luxury is good in that the arts are thereby brought into bloom. In the case of luxuries, the multitude of means is not at all suited to the purpose. Everything is in excess. We thus ennoble our nature through luxury and are thereby brought closer to morality. One says that one has appetite, but not that one has taste, for the latter is based on the approval of others and is an honor. The noble class cannot be a model of taste, nor can fashion; rather, society is [a] model of taste. One must therefore enter into diverse societies. –

One can have a judgment of taste and not an inclination of taste; the latter is vanity. (It is based on the social inclination; hence unsociable

---

[a] *ob man sie gleich schon vorher wißen kann*

[b] *demonstriren*   [c] *Ruhm*

[d] inclination of taste: *GeschmaksNeigung*; judgment of taste: *GeschmaksUrtheil.*

[e] *gesellschaftliche Neigung*   [f] *luxus*

25:1327 people have no taste, and tasteless people are unsociable. Taste prefers the beautiful to the useful. But if one places importance on a different benefit, one has no inclination of taste. Here the inclination to the beautiful outweighs the inclination to the useful and good. The prevailing inclination of taste of a people is its luxury; that is the first step towards corruption, but is not yet corruption, for the beautiful can be reconciled with the useful and good. This is purified taste. However, human beings cannot observe the measure, but rather let the beautiful prevail; if it suppresses utility, it is harmful. The beautiful must not be a need, but [must be] dispensable. The merely useful is not beautiful, and what is chosen from taste is merely beautiful, not useful. Luxury promotes industry, for there are more needs there. It has vanity as an incentive, but one must not hold it as a model. Extravagance that makes one sick is contrary to taste. The enjoyment of life with taste is living well, and the due proportion^a of living well to sociability, good way of living. A feast^b is distinguished from a banquet.^{c} The former is a number of unfamiliar persons without social discussion. If there are too many of them, it is a <u>carousal</u>.^{d} At a banquet there is a number of familiar persons who constitute a society. Luxury is an enlargement of taste in quality. Thriftiness belongs to taste, and when it is perfect for the achievement of taste, it is exactly good taste. If luxury makes one soft, it is corrupting. If expenditure on the dispensable increases, individual persons grow poor, but not the state, for it gives work again to many hands. If our needs grow, then our enjoyment grows, but our discontent does as well. The happiness of our life thus does not depend on taste, but culture surely does. Taste brings forth arts and science because they belong to the dispensable and in part they themselves are an object of taste. In this way taste cultivates. But because the crude inclinations that are opposed to culture are also thereby moderated, we learn decorum,^{e} to make ourselves well-liked by others and hence become more suitable for society: taste cultivates in this way. We thereby become ever more capable of social intercourse and pleasures. Now the world is already beginning to become civilized. Drunkenness in society has already ceased; dueling will soon cease as well. It is true that taste does not make a person moralized,^{f} but it does prepare the

25:1328 way for it. The human being loses his coarseness, becomes more ideal [and] more capable of enjoying comfort, hence also more capable of idealized incentives to virtue. One often errs when one believes that vices cease on account of religion. That often occurs merely on account of

^{a} *Angemeßenheit*
^{b} *Schmaus*
^{c} *Gastmahl*

^{d} *Gelag*
^{e} *Wohlanstand*
^{f} *moralisirt*

taste. Purists[a] in morality rail against taste as [a kind of] pampering. But we can bring forth no virtue in a coarse human being; hence he must already be prepared and refined, otherwise he will not feel ideal reasons. Deficiencies in taste are also a cause of the absence of important virtues.)

We enjoy something twice as much when we see that others like it and that we are good company. Thus a garden is more [suited] for social gathering than a forest, for it has more order; that is why people prefer to bring social gatherings into the garden rather than the forest, because through its order the garden holds a social gathering together more. It is a meritorious talent and redounds to one's honor. Vanity therefore has a large share in it.

There are apers of taste.[b] – When approval is based not on the nature of the thing, but rather on a conventional approval. – A fashion is like that – this is aimed merely at the manner, not the purpose, of the thing. It is an object of imitation to the extent that it is first beginning. For an object of imitation that has already lasted a long time is custom. Fashions are trifles; for that reason one can take part in them in order not to appear to be an eccentric, and to give importance to trifles. Fashion gives us a uniform, so to speak, and thereby makes us sociable. But complete uniformity[c] in style of dressing, as in Sweden,[180] is again unbearable – fickleness in fashions, always being the first, is vanity. This is the value that one gives to things merely for the sake of general approval. – When it comes to fashions, to want to choose by employing one's understanding is also nothing. Understanding cannot be shown in such trifles. – It makes no difference whatsoever whether the dress is cut this way or that. It is peculiar that we become so accustomed by fashion that we find everything apart from it to be ridiculous, and when the ridiculous becomes fashionable, then we find it beautiful. Thus the Chinese find blue eyes ridiculous.[181] In Valais, where almost all of the people have goiters, when a foreigner without goiter entered a church, the people began to laugh, and indeed so much that the preacher had to remind them, namely, like this:[182] "You should not be surprised that nature has not lent this foreigner this ornament of goiter, and should recall *Sirach*, which says: 'Ridicule not the afflicted'."[183] (Thus writing style is also a fashion; this was especially so in the last century in France. When fashion is so inflated that it becomes ridiculous, one is appalled and goes to the other extreme.) Luxury populates. If it has risen to the highest degree, it depopulates and promotes the deterioration of the state. – At which time the great masterpieces of taste also appeared, which are genuine beauty.

25:1329

---

[a] Following Stark and Brandt's suggestion: *Puristen*. They also suggest *Rigoristen* (Rigorists). Mro has: *risten*, preceded by a small space.

[b] *GeschmaksAffen*

[c] uniformity: *Einformigkeit*; uniform: *Uniform*.

Fashions cannot occur in painting, sculpture. (Thus fifty years ago in the pulpits one still preached against wigs. Now no one may appear in the pulpit without a wig.) (The English *Spectator*[184] says one can predict fashions, especially for women, for they are supposed to be like trees. When the branches below are pruned, they sprout up into the crown, and vice versa. Thus when the hooped skirts become smaller, the head finery grows bigger and bigger, and vice versa.) Beauty has a charm to it.

25:1330

We also judge[a] in accordance with charm. In the case of human beings, we judge according to the sex. A woman whom we find very ugly as a female would still be found very attractive as a male. Accordingly Heidegger, a Swiss man who gave oratorios in London, that is, performed music in public, was a very ugly man, and in a social gathering he said in jest that surely no man could be found in London who was uglier than he was. Another man bet him on this and brought forward an old drunk woman, to everyone's immediate laughter. But Heidegger did not yet concede defeat, but rather said: "We want to switch. Let her take my wig and let me take her corset." – Heidegger looked like a witch. But she looked like a quite handsome male.[185]

Winckelmann[186] says: "Beauty, in the case of human beings and the judgment thereof, is sensual."[b] In the case of women we also require charm, but that is not true beauty – the true beauty is therefore masculine, as the ancients said. It is peculiar that, when judging beauty, we judge the height[c] of a human being in accordance with an ideal of the greatest beauty.

From where do we get this ideal? Since we have seen various human beings of different sizes, the impressions do indeed vanish, but they do so in such a way that they converge and there remains with us a certain average that we take to be the true proper size and in accordance with which we judge[d] all others.

25:1331

One can also quickly find the average size by calculating, namely if one adds the length of several thousand full-grown human beings and then divides that with their number. – In this way we also get such an average of the proportion of the head to the body, the nose to the head. Thus one could, from the calculations of all the limbs of many human beings, especially for example the nose, the head, etc., always find out the average, and thus the perfect proportion, too. As a consequence of this, every country has its own average size. In the Greek profiles, one finds the noses running on the same line as the forehead; that is noble. – Just as the beautiful is distinguished from the agreeable, so, too, must it be distinguished from the good. The beautiful is based on the concord of the understanding and sensibility insofar as it is promoted by the

---

[a] *urtheilen wir mit*
[b] *wohllustig*
[c] *länge Proportion*
[d] *beurtheilen*

concord. Hearing and sight are the beautiful senses. They not only provide nourishment to sensibility, but also provide the understanding with something to think. Painting [and] sculpture surely cultivate the beautiful; music does not do so that much. I have no concepts thereof other than merely [one] of harmony. It cultivates in that it spurs on the sensible power of judgment, draws [it] out from what is crude. It makes the heart soft and receptive to more delicate impressions, especially ideal charms and emotions.[a] Yet this cultivation is of a different kind than that of sight. For this latter gives concepts to the understanding. Music enlivens us, and promotes and makes it easier for us to dwell on our thoughts better, and is thereby a good motion. But we cannot recount anything about the music. Sherlock[187] says: "When travelers come to Italy they are entirely enchanted by a beautiful female opera singer; meanwhile the Italians play cards in the loges, and when a famous male singer takes the stage, they stand up a little." – That is the best. – Those who greatly abandon themselves to music are superficial minds for the most part. One must therefore not let children learn music intensely. Charm is distinguished from emotion;[b] the former is promotion, enlivening, of the vital force through a stimulus – hence piquant things have a charm. Emotion is inhibition of the vital force that is strengthened merely after that. Emotions penetrate more deeply. The dissonances of music likewise inhibit the animal spirits.[c] – Charm is loved. Emotion elicits admiration. Young people have a great deal of vital force; hence they prefer emotions; they therefore love tragedies. – Old people love charm more, not emotion, because the emotions remain longer with them, [but] vanish quickly with the young. We must not judge beauty according to charm, [and] especially not according to emotions. For they mislead very much. Poems that surely are emotional[d] do not have true beauty. Klopstock is like this.[188] His writings therefore cannot be translated into any other language. He has a kind of un-German that looks like something ancient, as if it were hewn out of rock. Beautiful and good come into affinity. The good pleases from objective grounds, the agreeable from subjective grounds, [and] the beautiful from objective and subjective grounds at the same time. – I can therefore paint the good beautifully, but not the agreeable, not the charming; otherwise virtue becomes a coquette – as the beautiful serves for the recommendation of the good. The human being becomes refined the more he finds taste in the beautiful. Distinguishing the agreeable requires sense. Distinguishing the beautiful requires sensibility and understanding. Animals therefore cannot have a sensation of beauty. Distinguishing the good requires reason. As an animal a person can have a sensation of the agreeable, as a human being a sensation of

25:1332

---

[a] *Rührungen*

[b] emotion: *Rührung*; Charm: *Reiz.*

[c] *LebensGeister*

[d] *die wol Rührungen sind*

the beautiful, and insofar as one raises himself above his humanity, a sensation of the good. – The good is either mediately or immediately good. The mediately good pleases us as a means to a good end, and that is the useful (nature has often hidden the useful behind the beautiful, for example in human beings the exterior is beautiful but the internal structure is useful; the skeleton is merely useful. If the beautiful is contrary to the useful, it is not even beautiful, for example when a column is thicker above than it is below.)

We are here speaking merely of the immediately good, and that is merely the morally good. The agreeable and beautiful please*a* immediately. So does the morally good. When we act in a morally evil way, it can be advantageous in particular cases; but we certainly dislike it as a universal rule. This liking and disliking*b* therefore arises from reason alone. For I like whatever can be valid as a universal law, thus that which agrees with my reason.

The good is considered in universality. The beautiful [is considered] in particularity. Virtue has inner worth and thus does not want to be recommended through advantages. That would be a market price. But it can have an affection price,*c* which is based on its beauty.[189] For there is no self-interest connected with it. – Having a sensation of the good requires sentiment, way of thinking – having contradictions in one's head is not sentiment. – Sentiment is very different. Everyone must surely recognize that it is either wrong or right; but the sensations accompanying this judgment are very diverse. Sentiment is actually the feeling of pleasure or displeasure at good and evil. Taste requires merely practice, culture. Cognition of good and evil requires instruction. Sentiment, and the formation thereof, requires that one can paint virtue more beautifully and vice in an uglier manner, can depict both with lively colors, and can make it more intuitable through [the use of] history. Some people can have a good sentiment, and nevertheless do not act well on account of this. Thus it is said of Queen Christina in Sweden that she always spoke and wrote cleverly, but acted imprudently.[190] Skill is [the] ability to apply one's talent to discretionary ends. – Good-naturedness tries to apply skill to merely great ends. A great and a good prince should therefore be distinguished. The former is he who possesses great natural predispositions to discretionary ends, be they good or evil. Good-naturedness, when it is based on temperament, is not moral. – Good-naturedness is negative; then it is called so much as harmlessness; this comes from stupidity, weakness. – Positive good-naturedness is based on maxims, principles that the human being follows in his actions. Maxims are not

25:1333

---

a gefällt   *b* Gefallen und Mißfallen
c Following Brand and Stark's suggestion: *Affektionspreis*. Mro reads, with *der* possibly corrupt: *affectiv der Preis*.

innate, but surely instinct is. Great[a] is he who has an ability to do much good [and] also evil. It arouses admiration. Probity earns inner approval from the human being, but attestations of honor do not. Through taste one becomes civilized; through formation of the way of thinking [one becomes] moral. Very often one takes civilization to be moralization. Honesty is now greatly honored, but that is not good, for then it must be very rare, but honesty must be ordinary, since it is the bare minimum, and whoever does not have it is a rogue. It is thought that it would be better if the good human beings were separated from the evil ones, but through such mixing the evil give up their maliciousness and the good ones are thereby even more tested in [their] goodness. The enjoyment that the agreeable provides, and the beautiful, comes from the outside. The good grants us an enjoyment from ourselves. The good and virtue are not merely natural gifts, but must also be learned. Rousseau believed the former,[191] Home the latter.[192] We must therefore learn maxims of the good early on. People who do not like to hear moral discussions usually have a great deal of self-seeking and self-interest. Many people do not have an interest in anything.

25:1334

ON THE FACULTY OF DESIRE SECOND CHAPTER[b]

The faculty of desire presupposes feeling of pleasure or displeasure, and this cognition.[c] Something can please us and yet we can be indifferent to its existence. It is like this with the beautiful. – Desire is the delight[d] in the existence of the object. It often produces an effort aimed at the existence of the thing and is thus the cause of an action insofar as the thing is in my control. – Therefore not every delight is desire. Desire is also called volition.[e] Either our reason, or our inclination, wills according to the diverse kinds of our delight. When reason does not will something that the inclination wills, reason is often used in the service of inclination, as reason must find out the means by which inclination can attain its end. Such is the case with most actions of human beings; inclination rules us through sensations that penetrate more strongly than the concepts of reason. This makes for the difference between 1. lower faculty of desire, where the inclination is incentive, and 2. upper faculty of desire, where reason is incentive. Reason is in play in both. Inclination presupposes that we are familiar with the object, but instinct is desire before cognition of the object. Sexual instinct, appetite, etc., are like this; an inclination can arise out of instinct. A habitual sensible desire is inclination, hence

---

[a] *Groß*
[b] Brandt and Stark indicate that "Second Chapter" was added to Mro at a later time.
[c] *und diese Erkenntniß.*
[d] *Wohlgefallen*   [e] *Wollen*

we must be on our guard. For otherwise we will become dependent on them. – They put us in the [position of] needing to do something without investigating why. Thus we must not learn to do anything out of habit, not even virtue. Otherwise it loses its worth. – All desires have a relation to activity. They are a basis of the effort of our power to make something actual; these are active desires. Often we do not exercise them because we see that the object is not in our control. Nature has given us merely active desires, but we also surely have idle desires, *pia desideria.*[a][193] Thus we often wish that something would not have happened which, however, now is impossible. And strangely our wish is more urgent, the more we see that the object is not in our control. It is necessary that we always first have idle desires, for we must will, then afterwards examine whether we can make the objects actual. Nature has given us idle desires in order thereby to move us to try our power. Rousseau[194] believes that one should lead a young human being to love for a woman because then, out of love for her, he will exert all his power to do anything and guard himself against all excesses. But he will be distracted by the love, then wish to exert his power, which, however, distraction will not let come to fruition. It is senseless and harmful to foster idle desires when we have recognized them as such. To this therefore belong the *pia desideria*, repentance,[b] which is good merely insofar as it impels us to cancel the consequences thereof and to act better in the sequel. – This occupation with time past makes us inactive in subsequent time. There are also vague and indeterminate desires that drive us to leave the present condition and go into an indeterminate future condition of which we know nothing. Of this kind is boredom, which actually consists in the fact that time lasts too long and bothers us. Boredom is not very prevalent among natural human beings, but rather where luxury prevails; with women it gives rise to vapors.[c] It is more prevalent among young, lively people than among the old. It arises from the habit of finding one's contentment in enjoyment.[d] Ultimately we grow weary of this and thus boredom arises. Enjoyment also uses up the vital force, whereas work strengthens it and provides an immediate satisfaction. – There is no boredom in the state of coarseness, for they[e] do not have that many concepts. Their imagination[f] does not represent to them that many kinds of possible pleasure, the non-possession of which they would be tormented by and which can arouse boredom in them. Thus the Caribbean sits for whole hours with his fishing rod by the river without becoming impatient, even when he does not catch the slightest thing.[195]

25:1335

25:1336

---

[a] Trans.: pious desires
[b] *Reue*
[c] *Vapeurs*
[d] *Genuße*
[e] *sie*, i.e., people in such a state
[f] *Imagination*

Boredom is the disgust that one has for a condition in which one finds oneself. – It is the great ill and the cause of much evil. One must already learn early in childhood how to keep oneself safe from it. One tries to pass the time by reading books. But if in doing so one does not aim to learn from it, one falls back into boredom immediately after reading. But when I read to learn something from it, I am working while learning and I then thereby pass the time while reading. But I also gather something [from it], the recollection of which can also drive away my boredom in the future. Using our mental and vital force for actual ends is the most respectable allocation of time and it also strengthens our vital force, for subsequent satisfaction can perhaps arise. The constant occupation with amusements eventually causes disgust at all amusements and thereby boredom and, in addition, disgust at work. It is a nameless pain. Some people also believe in passing the time[a] by smoking tobacco, but when at some point they have to stop on account of a malady or something, they feel unbearable boredom. One thus also flees to strong drink and games; games and tobacco consist in a change of sensations and in the variation of objects, where our power of imagination receives enough material and nourishment and thus drives away our boredom. Tobacco occupies our imagination[b] through the various shapes that the smoke takes on. Hence in the dark tobacco does not taste good in the same way or even at all; for we continually think that the pipe has gone out. An amusement of one sense must always be bound up with yet another one, if it is to have a great value for us. – Accordingly, if in the darkness we cannot distinguish veal and mutton meat, the sense of sight must enter in. Strong drinks drive away our boredom by robbing us of consciousness. Savage peoples get the greatest delight from this. To be sure, it does not taste good to them at first; but once they see that it intoxicates, then they burn for it. Displeasure in work is the next path to boredom. – Even repose must always be connected with an occupation, for a total repose exhausts our power just like the greatest work. – We must have work, i.e., occupation with constraint, for occupation during idleness, which is not connected with constraint, does not protect us from boredom and is good merely during repose. The propensity for work or industriousness is the best inclination, and one must try to acquire this. – Hence we must become accustomed to work from an early age on, and in this regard it is harmful to want always to instruct children while they are playing. It is peculiar that most human beings posit freedom in indolence and slavery in work. Hence the freest nations love indolence more, and indolent people imagine something respectable in it and believe that they are nobility. Work seems to convey something slavish with it, and

25:1337

[a] Reading, as in Mar: passing the time (*Zeit*). Mro: getting over boredom (*Langeweile*).
[b] *Imagination*

the human being is also not able to pass his time without putting certain fetters and bonds on himself. For the human being cannot properly use his freedom; he who does not shrink from the hindrances of working is brave, and he who happily goes immediately to work is vigorous. Nature entices us to work through the fact that the greater the hardship is, the more enjoyment we feel afterwards from it. Thus even children attempt all dangers and prefer to seek something in an arduous and dangerous way when they could attain it more easily. – Although desiring[a] seems to mean just as much as needing,[b] nevertheless we have a source of desires in us whose objects we do not need at all. Moral desires[c] are like this. Here we desire something on account of the representation that something might be good, and we desire what we do not need yet others do. Whatever we do not need is dispensable. When we can always imagine that something that we desire is dispensable, we have true satisfaction. For need bothers us. We commonly desire most strongly what is least in our control. Thus, for example, we strongly desire honor and it is after all least in our control, for it is based on the will of others to give us approval. It seems nature has given us such strong drives for what is difficult in order to exercise our power. – Falling in love is like this as well. Here, too, we indeed do not have whether a woman loves us or not in our control. – Independence from sensible stimuli[d] is moral freedom. One acquires this through the strength of virtue – that must occur during youth. But we attain it through the reduction of the strength of the drives in old age, yet there it is based on the reduction of passion and is not properly a growth in freedom. Old age becomes free of many enticements[e] though insensitivity. Moreover, mere reduction and insensitivity does not bring about moral freedom from enticements either, but rather morality itself must also be underlying it. <Freedom does not consist in the incapacity of desires.> The sermons of the old to the youth concerning abstemiousness therefore produce nothing because the youth see that the old can speak so well about it because they no longer get any enticements therefrom, are no longer suited for it. – One must say to the youth: "You could perhaps enjoy all pleasures,[f] but you must also save some for the future, for otherwise you might feel boredom in old age." (Freedom does not occur in the desires, but only in the will. Desires are not directly in our control, but perhaps [are so] indirectly in that we weaken them. Freedom is directed at the decision about which desires one wants to fulfill. It is what is characteristic of human beings, for animals have instincts that they must follow blindly. People who have more desires are also less free. Thus the rich man is less free than

25:1338

---

[a] *Begehren*
[b] *Bedürfen*
[c] *Die Moralische Begierden*

[d] *Anreitzen*
[e] *Reitzen*
[f] pleasures: *Vergnügen*; enjoy: *genießen*.

the poor man.) Through too much enjoyment of all possible pleasures they all become wearisome, and one becomes completely dull to all of them, [so] that afterwards one is no longer able to enjoy pleasures at all. Prudence therefore commands that one be frugal here. We must always leave many pleasures left over and unenjoyed so that afterwards we can always increase our pleasure. For if we cannot do so we become feeble and wearied, even if we also have enough other ones.

25:1339

The kinds of feeling of pleasure or displeasure[a] are sensitivity, feeling, and affect, and those of the faculty of desire are propensity, instinct, inclination, and passion.

1. Propensity (*propensio*). Possibility of the origin of desires; this can occur even if the desire is not actually there yet. Thus the Nordic peoples have a propensity for strong drinks. All women have a propensity for adornment; hence Amst.[196] defines a woman as an animal that likes to adorn herself.

2. Instinct is an actual desire, but without clear cognition of the object. One such desire is the one concerning the sexual inclination. [Another is] a child's desire to suck milk. It goes beyond the resources of philosophy to be able to explain instinct properly.

For example, if I were to adduce the reasons why the birds in Africa often build their nests in small branches that hang over the water, that is to say, whether or not they had considered that if they had not affixed their nests to small branches over the water, the apes would tear them down.[b]

3. Inclination is a habitual desire –.

Everyone thus has his permanent desires, for example, for playing, for drink. Having inclinations is no good fortune. But surely if on the other hand the human being had no inclinations, one would find no activity in him. If an inclination for a thing has become so strong and habitual that it suppresses all other inclinations, then it is called

4. Passion. With passion, one is not able to compare the inclination with the sum of all other ones. Passion is blind in that it does not want to adopt the judgment and conclusion of the understanding. –

25:1340

Affect and passion arise out of a disporportion when the sensation in the inclination grows so much that it becomes greater than the entirety of all inclinations. Passion and affect are distinct. Affect is the sensation that exceeds all other sensations and which impedes us from comparing it with the sum of all remaining sensations. Small objects commonly cause the strongest passions and affects. For the mind is not able to grasp large objects as readily as small ones. Hence it is also excited far more suddenly by the latter than by the former. Affect is [a] sensation and thus

---

[a] *Lust oder Unlust*
[b] This is a fragment in the Academy Edition.

must not be counted as belonging to the faculty of desire, but rather belongs to the feeling of pleasure or displeasure. But passion belongs to the faculty of desire. These are therefore the kinds or levels of the faculty of desire. Now we want to go over the kinds or degrees of the feeling of pleasure or displeasure. The feeling of pleasure or displeasure has three levels.

1.) Sensitivity is the capacity to receive pleasure or displeasure. Feeling is the state where one feels pleasure or displeasure. Mental movement[a] is a feeling of pleasure or displeasure that draws our entire attentiveness to it. If it makes us incapable of comparing this sensation with the sum of all sensations, it is affect.[b] It makes us lose our self-control, makes us incapable of voluntarily guiding our mental powers. It compels us to direct our attentiveness to it alone and to nothing else. With mental movement, it is after all still always in our control to direct our attentiveness to something else if we want to, but affect does not allow us to ponder[c] at all. With affect, we believe we are either completely fortunate or unfortunate. But here we act very irrationally, for we estimate our fortune or misfortune not in accordance with the whole sum of our sensations, but rather merely in accordance with one sensation, with a part of the sum; affect is thus blind. Affect is distinct from passion. – Affect is like a sudden storm that quickly ceases. But passion is like a continuous gush[d] that does not cease, but grows more and more with time. It can also never be properly extirpated. Affect disappears by itself. What affect does not do at once, it does not do ever. Passion is cautious, affect not at all. – Affect makes us imprudent, for in its throes we do not at all know what we should do. Passion makes us unwise, in that here we do not at all keep in mind the ultimate purpose. One can do as one pleases with a person who is in the throes of affect. One can transpose someone from one affect into another, but that in no way helps the power of self-control. Persons who have little affect do not for that reason have little passion, and vice versa. Many peoples have few affects yet passions that are all the stronger, e.g., the Indians have more vengefulness than anger – this comes from a [kind of] cowardice. Affect is like a drunkenness that one sleeps off – passion is like a long-lasting dementia. The French have much affect, but not that much passion.

Affectlessness is not insensibility. – One calls affectlessness "phlegm." And that is the temperament of a wise person. A human being without affect has a calm mind. –

25:1341

---

[a] *GemüthsBewegung*: since it includes laughter (Mro 25:1349), this seems better translated as "mental movement" than "emotion."
[b] *Affect*   [d] *Strom*
[c] *nachdenken*

There are affects of joy, of discontent, etc.; affects merely strike the senses in some people, in others the mind. To become irritated by something is to become indignant to the point of being bothered, and that relates to the mind. Becoming enraged relates to the external eruption of indignation; [it] relates to sense.[a] It is true that it strikes our sensation, but it does not penetrate the mind. The affects that penetrate the mind are the most harmful. Even joy must not penetrate to this degree. Human beings often die from such strong affects. Human beings thus die from both joy and sorrow, [and] even more from joy; that happens because in sorrow we gather together all of our powers in order to counter it.[197] But in joy we give ourselves up completely. The Stoics understood their *apateia*[b] as mere affectlessness. – One often wishes for affect, it is true, but not passion. One must distinguish vivacity from affect. The Italian has much affect, the Frenchman mere vivacity. They can represent all kinds of affects at will; for that reason they are very well suited to be actors. He who can vividly imagine an affect can do this better than he who himself has such an affect.

Great poets often were not full of affect, e.g., Young. It is very good 25:1342 to reproduce affects, to berate without actually being angry. For in the case of an actual affect we suffer more than the others. But we can never voluntarily transpose ourselves into an actual affect. Orators can stir [us] without being stirred. They also must not be stirred during their speech; otherwise they cannot speak in a manner befitting their subject matter. They must have sensations perhaps, but [they must] not be in the throes of affect. He who is in the throes of affect becomes speechless, and if one speaks with greater diction it is a sign that the affect is already cooling down. He can thus put the mind in motion without being in the throes of affect. The mind must be in repose when the soul is in motion. This is the state of true repose.

A human being can feel great pains without feeling grief over it. When I consider the ill by using my understanding, I weigh it over in my mind. Soul, heart, reveals the sensation. The soul can thus be in motion, but the mind must always be in repose. That is the consciousness of our condition insofar as the judgment about the worth of this condition is pronounced by the understanding. – We are blameworthy when we let ourselves come into the throes of affect; but when we are already in it, we are not capable of pulling ourselves out of it and then are not blameworthy. All affects surprise us, but some surprise us so suddenly that we cannot prepare ourselves for it in the slightest. Anger and fear are like this – the affect impedes us from attaining even the end on account

---

[a] *Sich erzürnen geht auf den äußerlichen Ausbruch des Unwillens geht auf den Sinn.* Cf. Mro 25:1347.
[b] Trans.: apathy.

of which it arises. Thus fear, when it is very great, makes us completely incapable of fleeing from [the object]. Why does nature do that? – In the case of animals, that happened so that, due to their incapacity to flee, they would be prey for the predators, which is their destiny after all. – In the case of human beings, these harms should produce the desire to get rid of the affects as much as possible. One considers some affects to be an honor, e.g., being angry and [a] hero is supposedly good. We sympathize with certain affects such as sadness, but not with affects such as anger, where instead we feel antipathy. – For we fear that the angry person will automatically attack us. – Anger is not merely a defensive affect, but also an offensive one. – If we are supposed to overcome affects, why did nature give them to us then? Nature did not give us affects, but only the predisposition to them, and she gave this to our animality. For in the state of animality, where after all the first human beings were, the affects served to double all of their powers and thus provided for their preservation. If the human being has emerged from animality, he does not need the affects anymore and must suppress them. Nature thus implanted the affects in us only provisionally and it gave them to us as a spur to activity, as it were, in order to develop our humanity. In opposition to affect is equanimity, the state of inner repose of the soul, not apathy but affectlessness.*a* – If it comes from temperament, it is phlegm.*b* – Furthermore, in opposition to affect is the capacity to control oneself with composure during a surging affect. – Socrates[198] possessed this, for when he was once in a dispute with a brutish man and the latter attacked him crudely, Socrates began to speak in a gentle tone only. After the dispute was over, one of his students said to him that he had noticed that Socrates had been in the throes of affect because he had forced himself to speak in a tone that was gentler than his usual one. Socrates agreed with him and said, "One cannot remove*c* the human being." – The capacity to govern oneself is in opposition to passion. – In that case one never loses his self-control. – The agreeable and disagreeable affects are alike in terms of their kind, but we can be transposed more easily into an agreeable affect than into a disagreeable one. The affect aims at the present, past, and future, especially at the latter. – Affect can be present, but its prospect is the future. If this latter is unforeseeable, the affect is unbounded.

25:1343

A sudden affect is alteration.*d* Affect stems from the joyful or sad prospect that we anticipate and that the imagination makes*e* even greater.

---

a affectlessness: *Affecktlosigkeit*; apathy: *Gefühllosigkeit*. In the Academy Edition this sentence lacks punctuation.
b *phlegma*, i.e., it derives from the phlegmatic disposition.
c *ausziehen*   *e* Mar: *macht*; Mro: *ausmacht*.
d *Alteration*

Thus sadness.[a] It arises out of the effects of the representation of a long future duration of pain, not out of the present pain itself. – Whoever is therefore not at all worried about the future can also be free of many affects. 1. Fear and 2.[b] hope belong to the disagreeable affects. Both are always found together, and depending on whichever is sizeable, the affect is called either fear or hope. With fear there is after all still always the possibility of the opposite [happening], for otherwise it would be certainty. – We do not fear whatever is certain. Hope and fear make one cowardly. Thus the delinquent is most despondent when his fate is uncertain, but he gets courage when his misfortune is inevitable. It is better to hope for nothing and prepare oneself for all ills, than to be constantly driven between fear and hope. Hope often makes one blind about the present. With hope I do not make any arrangements to prevent the opposite [from happening], and it is also like this with fear, and here I can be unfortunate. – Fear and hope are also often not affects at all. Fear without affect is concern. To be without fear and hope is virile and steadfast. There are people who always dine on sweet hopes. Sadness with hope can be hope in two ways: either in order to become free of the ill or to become accustomed to it; this latter is patience, a feminine virtue. – Sadness without hope is despair,[c] where the human being no longer feels any worth in his existence. Sorrow[d] is a sensation that relates to the present state. It becomes sadness when the reflection about our entire future state is added to this, when we then take our entire future lifetime to be unfortunate. – Sadness is not at all[e] pain, but a natural means of cautioning against future ill. – We are contemptuous of a person who is sad. – Depression[f] is sorrow that cannot be alleviated – the human being must never be sad, but one cannot avoid sorrow. Despair is either melancholic or savage; the former arises out of grief.[g] The latter [arises] out of indignation toward life and one's fate. Human beings often take their lives in both states. – The former is surely stoutheartedness, the latter timidity. One therefore cannot chastise every suicide for [involving] timidity. – Cato[199] also killed himself so that by his example the Romans would be encouraged not to surrender to Julius Caesar. He thought: if I give myself up to Caesar I will thereby tempt many others to do the same. – One must never consider life to be important and [must] view its joys and woes as child's play; hence Democritus did this better than Heraclitus.[200] – The best [thing] here in this world is therefore a constantly cheerful heart; in this way I

25:1344

25:1345

---

[a] *So die Traurigkeit.*
[b] The Academy Edition lacks this number "2."
[c] *Verzweifelung*
[d] *Betrübnis*
[e] *zu nichts*
[f] *Niedergeschlagenheit*
[g] grief: *Gram*; savage: *wild.*

am a friend to all human beings. By contrast, an unfortunate person is an enemy to human beings and one must fear him.

The degrees of fear are: angst, anxiety, terror, horror.[a] A sudden fear is a scare. –

Timidity is opposed to stouteheartedness. – A stouthearted person does not get scared. A courageous person may perhaps be scared, but does not yield. – The two are not found together. Montesquieu[201] says that stoutheartedness derives from the disposition of the body.

Stoutheartedness is opposed to fear; courage is opposed to fright. – The first is a matter of temperament – the second is based on deliberation. Stoutheartedness disappears as soon as one learns to have insight into the danger. One often encounters it in young people. In his travel writing, De Luc[202] recounts that he traveled with Fräulein von Schwellenberg, court lady to the Queen of England; she showed no fear on the roads over the highest mountains and was completely stouthearted when even a man would lose heart. But her courage went away as soon as she saw an animal, etc., for she thought it would feed on her. A human being with a stouter body, a hardened way of living, will not be scared so easily,[b] for he believes he will get through [the danger]. In the case of a great fear, nature produces evacuations [in us], but that does not yet count as despondency. Cowardice is despondency without honor. That is a contemptible fear. The French call such a dishonorable coward a *poltron*.[c] If one shirks one's duty when there is danger, one is a poltroon. This word derives from *pollex truncatus*. For the ancients who were cowardly cut off their thumbs so that they could not draw a bow and so did not have to fight in battle. The more someone has a valuable life, the sooner he puts it in danger, and the less valuable the life, the less this human being will put it in danger. The more significant a human being is in the state, the sooner he risks his life, and the more insignificant and worthless he is, the more he will want to preserve his life. This is based on a concept of honor, and this in turn on a sublimity of attitudes. One kind of stoutheartedness is recklessness. Charles XII had this kind of stoutheartedness.[203] The reckless man blindly rushes into all dangers and does not value his life at all; that does not bring any honor. One also calls that daredevilishness. Since stoutheartedness is based on temperament, it is quite possible that it can degenerate into a kind of rage. The Turks call those who venture into battle delirious, but after all they esteem them because they sacrifice themselves for the masses.[204]

Courage is preeminently worthy of esteem, because it arises out of maxims. Plutarch[205] says: "The Greeks had more courage in death than

25:1346

---

[a] *Angst, Bangigkeit, Grauen, Entsetzen*
[b] Reading, as in Mar: *leicht* (easily). Mro: *gleich* (immediately).
[c] Trans.: poltroon, coward

in battle,[a] but with the Germanic tribes it was the opposite: the former thus had genuine courage, the latter only stoutheartedness." – Among the savage peoples one finds only stoutheartedness, not courage, and for them this is considered to be the most excellent virtue and it alone determines the choice of the chief. – A stouthearted person possesses organs [such as] a strong breast, strong lungs that allow expansion. The Indians have no true courage.[206] For if they are surrounded they throw down their weapons and let themselves be hacked down. True courage is not an affect, but phlegm. –

There is a state in which the human being is not fearful, but becomes perplexed or bewildered. This is the first attack, which often eventually ends up in strong courage, if the blood that initially pressed on the heart too much gradually withdraws and the human being breathes more freely. Where there is true courage, the courage for dueling will be wholly absent. For the human being has the most courage whenever he has justice on his side. But with dueling the feeling of unjust dealings on the part of human beings is always present, so the conscientious and right-thinking man will never duel. Courage for a duel is always the result of stupidity and crude sentiment. Countries in which the princes allow duels still have exceedingly gothic taste and lack true enlightenment and formation. Where duels are even required, things look sadder still. For the savages the greatest merit is martial courage. It is very peculiar that war itself is a means to culture. For, because human beings transgressed the law and its boundaries, war was thereby indispensable in order to recover lost rights. Now through war human beings enter into association with each other more and the arts and sciences thereby become widespread, as one can see in the features of foreign peoples, for example, the Goths, Longobards. Through war, after the declaration of peace, a bond among peoples is forged that had never been there before. – And in this manner wars, with all of their inhumanity, have cultivated after all.

25:1347

Very much akin to fright is: 1.) Anger, which arises out of the surprise of outrage. Anger is sorrow that is manifested outwardly. Sorrow that is internal is vexation. If the internal trouble is continuous, it is resentment and becomes a passion. Anger is disagreeable. But if it is voluntary, its motion is not disagreeable, but agreeable. – But if one meets with resistance and it is involuntary, it is disagreeable. There are two kinds of anger. a.) When one becomes pale. One must fear him, for he sees the danger that he wants to rush into through the employment of his anger. b.) When one becomes red. One does not have to fear him, for he feels his timidity and does not know how to comport himself, but afterwards

[a] im Treffen

449

he retains a [feeling of] resentment within him, since he is aware of his blushing and it annoys him. –

2.) Admiration, which arises out of surprise, in that it is a sudden release of anticipation. – There are sensations that are not affects, yet nevertheless can become them. For instance, respect, elevated[a] admiration, and then the affect astonishment; in all of these the mind is put into the frame[b] of stretching beyond its limits. Gratitude, pity, can also become affects. – Sympathy with feeling is either physical, if distant objects have an effect on one another without having the slightest connection; this is ridiculous, but is still adopted by many. Nowadays one has invented physiological sympathy, which concerns joy and woe.[207] One is very unfortunate if this turns into an affect. Through sympathy one only becomes tender and does not help the other at all. Friendship, as an affect, is love. It quickly ceases.

3.) Shame, which arises out of the surprise[c] of coming into other people's contempt. –

Anger is a vigorous quality and is far preferable to hatred, which is a gloomy quality. Anger is not only dangerous for the person who is the target of a human being's outrage, but also for everyone else. Hence we do not sympathize with the angry person, but resist him, since we believe that in the midst of an angry person we ourselves are in danger, and when one is angry in our presence we see that as bad, too. The affect of anger subsides, extends the powers, and in such a manner even produces a level of activity, whereas hatred weakens us. Admiration arises out of a surprise, when the anticipation is extended by a sudden release.

Surprise must be distinguished from admiration. It[d] arises when one is astounded by something. It is an inhibition of the vital forces, which thereafter gush forth all the more rapidly. –

Shame is the feeling [we have] when we believe that we are contemptible in the eyes of others on account of a mischief. It therefore arises out of the sudden fear of disrespect. One here fears not only the disrespect, but also the fact that one will be ashamed. It is thus a twofold fear. A human being will not be ashamed in the dark, but only in the presence of others who can observe him in whatever light he should present himself. One therefore must not tell a child that he should be ashamed because: 1. a child cannot be ashamed, since he does not commit anything that is capable of shame. 2. In so doing the child receives a shock[e] that produces shyness and timorousness. Because one shames the human being in front of everyone else, often not only the guilty person

25:1348

---

[a] *hoher* 	[b] *Faßung*
[c] Reading, as in Mro: *Ueberraschung*. Brandt and Stark suggest *Erwartung* (anticipation, expectation).
[d] *Sie*, i.e., surprise. 	[e] *Reiz*

blushes, but the innocent do as well. Nature seems to have implanted in the human being this impulse to the sense of shame in order to betray 25:1349 him when he lies. One can say in general that the affects have something agreeable about them and have a degree of activity, but shame and disgust depress us. – But chiefly disgust depresses us very much, and it can never be aroused for fun, but appears just as if it were actual. One can therefore put every [kind of] affect into a poem with the exception of disgust. Disgust is either physical or ideal; the former is an inhibition of the appetite. Physical disgust is based on the senses and is rife with fancy.[a] Ideal disgust is the opposite of ideal enjoyment – ideal disgust arises when disrespect ascends into an affect, where one belittles a human being [as being] below the value of humanity. Disrespect is also [a kind of] rejection, not mere indifference. Some vices evoke aversion combined with disgust, others with dread; e.g., lechery belongs to the former. There are mental movements that, however, are in fact only predispositions toward such movements:

1.[b] Laughter. This arises out of the sudden but harmless reversal of expectation. For instance, Charles II of England once visited a very famous schoolteacher, Busby,[208] in London. Busby was very impolite towards the king and did not allow him to sit. As the king was leaving, the teacher said outside, "Your Majesty, pardon my rudeness. I cannot let the students notice that someone else is above me; otherwise, etc." 25:1350 Abbot Terrasson, translator of Homer and [author of] *Dissertation on the Merits of the Ancients and the Moderns*, went down the street fully dressed yet with his nightcap on.[209] Everybody laughed but he said, "I have amused everyone in Paris today without it costing me anything, or them either." Cheerful laughter is quite distinct from laughter at someone's expense, which always indicates a degree of malice. But the proud person is laughed at; malicious laughter can be used to mock a railleur, for, since such types really enjoy ridiculing others, people are glad when they can laugh at someone bent on ridiculing others. – Why is it that children love to play practical jokes? A practical joke is an action that may cause outrage in the other, yet afterwards soon leads to the eruption of laughter. Laughter can be elicited mechanically by tickling, but in that case there is nothing agreeable about it. In laughter the muscles are twitched and move to one side, then move just as much back to the other side, and swing until they are still at last. This occurs in precisely the same way with ideal laughter. For all of our actions are connected with bodily movements, even if we do not realize it. Ideas primarily extend the nerves here, but go toward the diaphragm. Through this extension the nerves oscillate and outwardly promote the peristaltic motion and

[a] *voller Einbildung*
[b] The Academy Edition lacks any numbers that would continue this series.

by this means promote the entire well-being of the body. Thus laughter is just as useful as it is healthy. Laughter occurs when all of a sudden one sees oneself faced with the opposite[a] [of what one expected]. We are here moved back, as it were. It is malevolent to laugh when the other cannot laugh with you. One must therefore not laugh when another falls – that is childish. Absurdities must not[b] underlie the laughter, but rather something reasonable. Witticisms[c] only arouse smiles. A practical joke or April Fool's jokes are not suited to make everyone laugh, for often they are harmful to the others. – Gloating is laughing about another person's troubles. When one person teases another person and he answers back with teasing, it is amusing. But one must be cautious and first see whether

he is in the right mood. If he does not answer back one must stop; otherwise one might insult him. The ancient satirists offer little material for laughter, whereas the moderns offer more. Laughing easily and about everything is vulgar, but men of spirit really like to laugh. One can remember a hearty laugh for a long time. It is an agreeable aftertaste. Laughter is a social mental movement, for when others laugh one laughs with them, often without knowing the reason. Laughing when alone is not allowed. Many maladies are relieved through laughter. Grinning is a [kind of] laughing in order to please others. Derisive laughter [is] when one smiles with a ridiculing mien.

Absurdity does not really produce any enjoyment; if one were to tell about some absurdity in a way that was not serious,[d] the absurdity would remain but the laughter would be missing. The mind must faithfully be led down a false path. Hence the person who wants to make others laugh must not let that be noticed. It is best if he can produce the absurdity in the last lines. Crying is opposed to laughter. It is connected with sighing; the latter is the sound of inhaling, the former of exhaling. During crying an excretion such as tears comes out. But during laughter one can sometimes shed tears. Crying has something agreeable [about it]. It is an outbreak of sweet sensation whereby the pain is resolved. We also fall into tears from magnanimity, gratitude. We turn our face away from a human being who expresses his pains a great deal. But we weep before a human being who devotes all of his effort in order to suppress the outbreak of pain so as not to disturb us, for he is so polite and magnanimous toward us. It is merely with noble things that we cry about others. For the most part we cry when the other does not cry, and laugh when the other does not laugh. Hence we laugh about a funny story that is told very seriously. We weep over features of magnanimity because we would like to find beneficence and love of humanity everywhere, and since we find the

---

[a] *ins Gegentheil versetzt*
[b] Brandt and Stark indicate that "not" was added to Mro at a later time.
[c] *Bons Mots*   [d] *nicht ernsthaft erzählen*

practice of these here, we sink into tenderness. Here we have good will and a longing to imitate that. But since we feel that we are unable to do it, we thus sink into woefulness; this produces crying; but this is not a sign of grief, but already a resolution of it. Crying is a respite for grief; the person who is crying thus no longer feels as much pain. When crying one makes similar facial features to those made when laughing, only the eyes move in a different way. Women cry straightaway about anything, particularly when they are angry. One also cries from malice when one feels one is powerless to avenge oneself. There are head-breaking texts of which one cannot make any sense, heart-breaking texts that stimulate [one] to affects, and neck-breaking texts, such as those of the new geniuses, that deviate from every rule. 25:1352

Timorousness is the concern over losing our worth in the judgment of others. In particular, it is the propensity toward this concern.

One does not have very much confidence in oneself to appear dignified in the eyes of others. This does not arise out of examination of oneself, but is already such a propensity [to do so], which either comes from education or from far too great an opinion and estimation of others and far too great a demand on oneself. It can be alleviated through society. Shame is a fear or embarrassment that arises out of the consciousness of one's timorousness. Humiliation thus makes one even more timorous. Hume[210] says that impudence is a good gift of nature. For the impudent human being places himself completely above the judgments of others and can thus display his talents in the most advantageous light and give them free play, but thereby one also elicits the arrogance[a] of others. – He says further: "One can never learn how to be impudent. For if one attempts it once and fails in that attempt, one will be even more unfit for future attempts." Opposed to timorousness is candor; this latter is the consciousness of one's worth without impinging on the worth of others.

The other extreme, and diametrically opposed, is presumptuousness, from "to threaten,"[b] because such people have such miens that always threaten a person with being crude. – Similarly, *lüderlich* does not derive from *Lieder*, but from *Luder*.[c][211] Impertinence wants to force others to give their approval. Modesty is either in attitudes, and that is moderation in claims; this is a virtue. But there is also a [kind of] modesty in manner; shame expresses itself only before the eyes of others, and thus not in front of the blind, nor in absence, nor in the dark. For shame arises out of the fear that another person would look at our timorousness. If he therefore cannot see us, the shame also ceases. – Hence writers are often very candid in writing and very timorous in social intercourse. 25:1353

[a] *Hochmuth*
[b] presumptuousness: *Dräustigkeit* (spelled *Dreistigkeit* today); to threaten: *Dräuen*.
[c] *lüderlich*: licentious, loose; *Lieder*: songs, airs; *Luder*: hussy.

Shame thus applies merely to decency. – Savages are not timorous – for they know nothing about the differences among human beings, that a person would be inferior. – And shame arises when I consider myself to be insignificant and others to be important. Timorousness arises out of servitude and subjugation. The reluctance to make others enraged is gentleness; the reluctance to give offense to others is sweetness; the indifference about whether one makes others enraged is crudity; the inclination to give offense to others is malice. – Whoever is inclined to make others enraged is mocking; whoever is inclined to vilify others and thereby give offense to them is slanderous.[a] – The cautiousness against not offending the slightest touchiness is masculine delicateness. Feeling the least [bit of] disagreeableness is feminine delicateness. The former is sensitive tenderness, *tendresse*;[b] the latter is susceptible tenderness.[c] The *ataraxia* of the Pyrrhonians[212] is liberation from affects; the apathy of the Stoics is liberation from passions. Whoever stifles affect can always be sensitive; he just does not allow his feeling to become an affect. This person is also of a stronger mind than the one who abandons himself to affects. The Stoics considered apathy to be the mark and requisite of a wise person – a constant peace[d] of mind that we do everything purposively and with deliberation. – In contrast, the heart can be moved since this is a spur to activity. The human being can be resolute, fervent, and eager, yet without having our self-control taken away.

ON THE PASSIONS CHAPTER 3[e]

Affects belong to feeling, passions to the faculty of desire. All passions are grounded on inclination insofar as they do not merely incite us, but dominate [us]. It is a dominating inclination that makes reason unable to compare it with the sum[f] of all inclinations. Passions are very harmful if we do not want to make an inclination into a passion; the satisfaction of the inclination must therefore always remain dispensable[g] for us. Then the enjoyment of the inclination is a pure addition to my happiness. – All inclinations are either formal or material. The former merely relate, without distinction of the objects, to how we partake of the object of our inclination. Material inclinations relate to determined objects. Formal inclinations relate to the state that contains the condition of satisfying all inclinations without distinction.

25:1354

---

[a] slanderous: *medisant*; mocking: *moquant*.
[b] *empfindsame Zärtlichkeit, tendresse*   [d] *Ruhe*
[c] *empfindliche Zartlichkeit*
[e] Brandt and Stark indicate that "Chapter 3" was added to Mro at a later time.
[f] Reading, as in Mar: *der Summe*. Mro: *den Sinen* (the senses).
[g] Reading, as in Mar: *entbehrlich* (dispensable). Mro: *unentbehrlich* (indispensable).

There are two formal inclinations: the inclination to freedom and to means.[a] – (Freedom is the negative condition – the human being can only satisfy his inclinations if nothing impedes him, and then he has freedom.) The former is the inclination to determine oneself according to one's own inclination and to be independent of the inclination of others. It is thus actually negative inclination; the satisfaction of my inclinations is not promoted through this, but rather the impediments to them are merely cleared out of the way. I acquire nothing through this, but only make myself independent of other inclinations. If one is not free, one is a slave and must direct oneself according to the inclinations of others, and then one is not happy. Even if one knows how to use his freedom a little, one surely will find his fortune in freedom. If freedom ceases, the personality of the human being also ceases. Most animals have an insurmountable propensity toward freedom. But they cannot reflect on it. Whoever has been a slave for a long time becomes base from it; but if one has been free, he will quickly help himself up.[b] The positive formal inclination is means,[c] or the possession of the ways of satisfying our inclinations, e.g., honor, etc. Freedom is the first thing that a human being demands; the human being does not sacrifice complete freedom to the highest good. I can merely hope to be fortunate and satisfied according to my conceptions,[d] but then I must have freedom. Freedom therefore underlies the hope for happiness. Freedom is twofold 1.) Freedom under laws is civil freedom. 2.) Freedom without laws is barbaric. One can also have a freedom under laws that, however, have no authority. This is Polish freedom. Savages have barbaric freedom. They also thus scoff at the Europeans who must obey. Barbaric freedom is a state of animality. Laws are limitations under the condition that our freedom exists with the freedom of others. – We very much want the freedom of others to be limited to the benefit of our own, but we do not want to have our own freedom limited. – But that is unreasonable. There is after all always an advantage to the laws. We believe we are free when we try to isolate ourselves; for that reason we really like to go to the countryside. – In cities one is more constrained. One is there limited by the laws of social intercourse, of fashion, and by judgments of others. The slave cannot act nobly because he does not act according to his own principles. The opinion[e] of freedom gives us the fancy that we are noble human beings, and then sometimes we actually become noble as well. The English are like this. Regents must thus see to it that their subjects have an opinion[f] of freedom; they achieve this by preventing one

25:1355

---

[a] *Vermögen*

[b] Reading, as in Mro: *heraufhelfen* (help himself up). Mar: *heraus helfen* (help himself out).

[c] *Vermögen*

[d] *Begriffen*

[e] *Meinung*

[f] *Opinion*

subject from oppressing and elevating himself above another. Barbaric freedom creates a great opinion of our worth and therefore arrogance and laziness. Thus savages also work little, for they think that freedom consists in laziness since work after all is coercion; lazy nations are also arrogant; the Spanish are like this. The Arabs in the desert consider themselves nobler than those in the cities. Nobility is also supposed to have derived from the Arabs,[213] for the oldest nobility does not extend to the year 1000.[a] Thus a husband, even if he rules the household, must rule it in such a way that the wife has an opinion of freedom. One says *mundus regitur opinionibus.*[b]

General remarks about the formal inclinations. They are the strongest of all, for they lie merely in the idea and do not relate to any determined object, but to infinity. They are the ground of all of the remaining inclinations; if they cannot be satisfied, all of our remaining inclinations cannot be satisfied either.

The inclination to means is based on the aim of having an influence on other human beings. (The more power I can use for my will, the more ends I achieve. But the number of powers I can use is based on the extent of the influence.) – This influence can be threefold: 1. through respect from others, through honor; 2. through fear others have of us, i.e., authority; 3. through one's own interest, i.e., through money. This last influence is the strongest. Money makes everyone compliant. Brahma, the Brahmin say, came into the world to pay a visit to a virtuous people. He appeared in the temple and set aside a day in which all the people could come together and each request something, but only one thing, from him. When the day came, they all shouted: money! It is no wonder, for by means of money one can procure everything else. Respect is based on the choice of others, on a kind of magnanimity. If I demand respect, I lose it for sure. We may well compel others through authority, but we will also experience all [kinds of] possible resistance in response. Some people perhaps let themselves profit more from inspired respect than from money or fear; but they are also the few exceptions. All people thus seek to accumulate money in order thereby to have influence on others, which they need more in old age than in youth. – They can perhaps expect respect on account of previous merits, but these can be forgotten and the respect itself is uncertain. Parents can also win over their children with money. But they are also suspicious of their children with regard to money, for if their children in turn have children, they will care more for them than for their parents; nature has so willed it in order to preserve progeny. From the three ways of having influence on human beings, three passions arise: vainglory, mania for dominance,

25:1356

[a] *bis auf 1000 Jahr reicht . . . nicht.*
[b] Trans.: the world is ruled by opinions.

and greed. These three passions each have their own particular age in human beings. Vainglory belongs to youth, the mania for dominance to manhood, and greed to old age; in particular, by means of honor we have influence on the opinions of human beings, by means of authority we have influence on their fear, and by means of money we have influence on their interest. The inclination to be loved so as to have an influence is not a passion. We do not make very much for ourselves this way. Love also does not tie other human beings to our interests as much as honor. Vainglory is not love of honor.[a] Love of honor is based on an immediate worth, but vainglory is based on a mediate one, namely, insofar as it is of service for having influence on others in other people's eyes. Love of honor arises out of modesty and is frank. Vainglory is violent, hypocritical. Arrogance is base, for it requires others to estimate their worth as less than our own, that is, requires them to be base. Whoever demands others to be base is base himself. Vainglory thus insults and is most hated and resisted. It only wants to get outward respect. One can thwart the aims of the vainglorious person most easily. One can slight him without even saying anything to him, merely through indifference. Mania for dominance appears to be for only a few, but everyone surely seeks it in small ways. In society, setting the tone is not exactly mania for dominance, but showing off is. Mania for dominance is even more detested than arrogance. Mania for dominance is unjust. If it is combined with authority, it is rather certain, as is the case, e.g., with monarchs. (Accordingly, in vainglory there is actually no true love of honor. An arrogant person is able to appear abject to those who are higher than him, just as he wants others to appear abject to him. The arrogant or vainglorious person wants to be judged by others outside the measure of equality. The lover of honor [wants to be judged] according to the measure of equality. – Meanwhile, even some vainglorious people are polite. Arrogance is hated, for it is a kind of injustice against the human race. Arrogance is stupid, for it is the stupidest means of acquiring respect, since with it one despises human beings and yet wants one person to respect another one. If a man of good standing preserves his dignity, it is good; but if he allows a pretension to honor to be displayed, he becomes ridiculous. For this reason, prudent nobles are always patronizing. Being jealous over social rank is generally greater among men than women. For virtue, beauty, etc., make women more similar to each other; [but] within the noble class, women are more jealous than men. For in the case of men, nobility is hereditary, but with women it is not very certain. But the less certain my preeminence is, the more I attempt to make whatever small preeminence I have perceptible to others. If we wish to be prudent, we must conceal[b] our vainglory. If

25:1357

[a] love of honor: *Ehrliebe*; vainglory: *Ehrsucht*.
[b] *verheelen*

457

one sees himself forced to show politeness to others, he resists the slight-est courteousness.[a] But if it is up to us, we lavish him with it. Pride[b] is the resistence to giving nourishment to arrogance. It should actually be called pride of self, natural pride. – If someone declares something in an arrogant tone, we immediately find contradictions in it that we would not find otherwise. The former pride is true love of honor. It is worse to be without love of honor than without conscience. For a human being who no longer has any love of honor is no longer capable of morals – but if a human being has no conscience and yet still has love of honor, surely he can still be led to have a conscience. *Point d'honneur*[c] is the foam of honor, [and it] did not exist in ancient times. It is a tender sen-sation, since one believes that his whole honor will be toppled over by a trifle. People with much *point d'honneur* are very quarrelsome and often do not have a correct concept of honor at all. They have it, as women do, merely in the ears. For not paying one's debts is no disgrace for them. –) The mania for dominance is found in everyone. The stronger person always oppresses the weaker if he can do so. We find that every-where in history. Even children possess it. For they dominate animals. It is much effort for the one who dominates, and where does this drive come from for the human being? From love of freedom. We are con-cerned that others might begin to dominate us and that we might lose our freedom; for that reason we make the surest move and we ourselves dominate. – It arises merely out of fear; hence it also happened that human beings spread themselves out over the entire earth. – Greed is inclination for acquisition. –

Inclinations that relate to means without making use of them are incli-nations of delusion. Delusion is the imagined value of a means, without making use of it. – Thus human beings find an immediate enjoyment in money. For after all it only has a value if it is used as a means. Money can only be used when it is spent. – But money grants us an ideal enjoy-ment when I imagine all the pleasures I can get from it. I procure true enjoyment when I select one of these ideal pleasures and actually try to attain it by using money. – Most human beings, especially in old age, choose ideal enjoyment and hold onto money. But this is an enjoyment of delusion, for it is based merely on the imagination.[d] The avaricious person is just as poor as [he would be] if he had no money. – An avaricious person is especially incurable in old age. Avarice exists in the fantasy; for that reason, just like the power of imagination, it has no boundaries.

25:1358

---

[a] Reading, as in Mar: *Artigkeit* (courteousness). Mro: *Höflichkeit* (politeness).
[b] *Stolz*
[c] Trans.: "point of honor," as in making a question of honor out of something, giving it a particular importance
[d] *Einbildung*

The avaricious person[a] is completely opposed to reason; hence one cannot argue him out of it through reason. He always understands rational grounds, but he finds more enjoyment in ideal than real enjoyment, and one cannot change his power of imagination. Money is a kind of power, and the surest kind. In their ways of speaking, nations directly reveal their avarice. Thus the Englishman says[214] of someone who has 100,000 pounds sterling: he is "worth" 100,000 pounds sterling, almost as if the human being in himself were of no worth. The Dutchman says he "commands" 1,000 pounds. The former is an expression that is arrogant, whereas the latter is an expression of mania for dominance. The material inclinations refer to benevolence[b] and comfort. The former is [an] inclination of enjoyment; the latter is [an] inclination for removing all impediments. In youth we have inclinations of living well in our view, and in old age, inclinations of comfort. There are occupations in play that are agreeable in themselves, and [occupations] in work, which is only immediately agreeable. Occupations of play belong to living well; occupations of work, which I can do when I want to, are comforts. But if I apply myself to work without coercion, it is not work but play. – Living well develops more talents because it produces more activity, but also more vices and inconvenience.[c] Comfort is innocence, but the life of the human being thereby withers away, as with the savages. It is uselessness.

25:1359

The human being's passion is again aimed at human beings and not at things. One can have great inclination for things, but not passion.

Inclination to society and to sex are the inclinations of living well that can become passions. He who has inclination for society in general is unfortunate – for society must never become a need. – The sexual inclination is greater than the inclination to society in general. The inclination for a long life can also often become almost a passion. (Life is empty for us when through too much luxury we have already made all kinds of enjoyment dull for ourselves, and then we are inclined to suicide. The love of life varies greatly according to the degree of amenity in life.) Nature has given us the inclination to life for our self-preservation and the sexual inclination for the preservation of the species. – As inclinations, they are both regarded as fair and becoming to the human being, but they are rebuked as passions. But, as a passion, love of life is even more despised than sexual love. Too great a love of life indicates a childish timidity. Considered through reason, life has no worth whatsoever, [but] merely insofar as its transformation[d] is worthy of it. If it is not, life

25:1360

---

[a] *Er*
[b] *Wohlwollen*. The transcriber may have intended *Wohlleben* (living well).
[c] Reading, as in Mro: *Unbequemlichkeit* (inconvenience). Mar: *Bequemlichkeit* (convenience).
[d] *Wandel*

has no worth whatsoever; hence there are cases where we must risk our life in order to act justly. But it is moral fantasy*a* to place no value in one's life and to consider the sexual inclination as improper; those are purists in morals who want us to be guided by grounds of the understanding alone and not by any animal drives whatsoever, which appertains only to pure spirits. Circumspection regarding the preservation of life is found among the aged; moreover, often more fear of death [is found with them] than with youth. –

(He whose life is worth the least respects it the most, and he whose life is worth the most respects it the least. The former esteems it so much because he is not acquainted with any goods nobler than this and therefore is not capable of any nobler actions; this latter [esteems it] because he is acquainted with higher duties and knows that life in itself is not a good,*b* but rather that, if we cannot use it, life is lost to us. Hence a man who demonstrates heroism in dying we lift up highly, even if he is a scoundrel, for we think that he must surely have had a predisposition to the good. We despise the man who is fainthearted in death. But this is always an ambiguous sign, for with certain maladies we appear fainthearted even if inwardly we are not so, and with certain maladies we can with all innate cowardice present ourselves as stouthearted, namely if the maladies are mild, e.g., consumption.) The human being must die at some point, and if important duties command him to put his life in danger, then he must do so. But it is no heroism to want to rid oneself completely of sexual inclination. It would seem that in both cases the human being is raising itself above animality, but with the latter I am raising myself above humanity, and that is not acceptable. – But in various peoples a high level of wisdom and overcoming has been posited in order to suppress the sexual inclination. The sexual inclination can be expressed toward the whole species in general, but its end and the particulars one shrouds in secret; this delicateness has cultivated us a great deal. Nature willed it in order to protect us from brutal animality.

25:1361 The sexual inclination is actually not a passion, but rather only a stronger instinct that is periodic, as one sees in the savages. It only becomes a passion through the power of imagination, and through the cultivation of the power of imagination this sexual inclination is called love. But as long as it is brutal and aims merely at enjoyment,*c* it is only animal instinct. – But as soon as it is connected to benevolence and aims at the happiness of the other, it becomes genuine love. It must not be like love of roast beef, which one carves up. A lord in parliament[215] once

---

a *Phantasterei*
b Reading, as in Mar: *kein Guth ist* (is not a good). Mro: *keine Glukseeligkeit sei* (is no happiness).
c *Genuß*

spoke like this of patriotic love. He said, namely: "England is like roast beef, and the love of country is like the love of roast beef. Everyone cuts off his piece and must take his piece, too." Sexual love brings the human being a certain measure of honor, whereas too much love of life is cowardice and brings disgrace. The latter is self-seeking in that it aims merely at self-preservation. But sexual love is already connected to a concern for others in that it has the propagation of the species as its basis. Sexual love is love that shares itself with others. But love of life [is] private love; hence sexual love is nobler. Nature implanted in human beings no passions, only inclinations, and it is only fantasy that turns these into passions. Hence nature also did not want us to observe the apathy of the Stoics with regard to passions and affects. Nature implanted in human beings only strong drives, which are raised even higher through the cultivation of the power of imagination. But for this reason it also demands that reason grow^a in exactly the same proportion as the inclinations do so that the understanding can maintain the mean among these inclinations. Happiness arises only out of the principle of reason. Hence only the human being, not the^b animal, can be happy or unhappy. But the human being is also never happy *in concreto* or fully satisfied with his existence. Nature willed this so that we would be merely in constant progress towards happiness here. Here nature treats us almost as it does the honeybadger following the honeyguide[216] at the Cape of Good Hope,^{c} in that it constantly shows us happiness always in prospect, but never lets us satisfy our appetite for it. Hence inclinations that constantly change are very suited to nature, but passions are not. Passions, when they become heightened, make it so that one always acts in opposition to one's own aims. Thus the ambitious person constantly acts contrary to his own aims, as he always wants to be honored and lets it be noticed, so the others erect the greatest obstacles in opposition to him.

    25:1362

There are inclinations that do not originally derive from nature, but that can be called acquired inclinations. The latter are acquired in society, namely, in domestic society. Social entertainment consists of:

    1.) Conversation; this in turn is three-fold: a. telling stories b. reasoning^d c. joking.

In the social gathering^e one usually begins the discussion with the weather. It is also the most natural [way], since it is of general interest. Thus with the following saying the Italians speak of a person who enters into the social gathering and becomes quite perplexed when glancing around it: "He lost the Tramontana." This is the northern wind which,

    25:1363

---

^{a} Reading, as in Mar: *wachsen* (grow). Mro: *wechseln* (change).
^{b} Reading, as in Mar: *das* (the). Mro: *als* (as an).
^{c} *Cap bonspei* ^{e} *Gesellschaft*
^{d} *Raisonniren*

just like the Sirocco (southern wind), troubles them a great deal. Hence in all social gatherings they also first speak of the wind.

At the table, one commonly begins with telling stories, for reasoning is always connected with quarreling, even if it is conducted in the gentlest manner. It would not be a good sign, then, if a social gathering were to begin with arguments. The end of the discussion is for joking, for, since the joke is a [kind of] play, it is agreeable and light and causes an agreeable reverberation, as the last thing that one hears leaves behind the strongest impression on human beings.

2.) Play. This is threefold: a. the play of sensation; b. the play of skills, e.g., dance; and c. the play of luck.

With conversation, one must keep in mind these general rules:

1. One must only speak about what interests everyone in general.

2. One must not want to show off.

3. One must not allow a deadly silence to break up [the discussion], for otherwise the discussion cannot pick up again quickly.

4. In such circumstances, one must then play something in the social gathering that re-animates the conversation.

5. Above all, cantankerousness must be kept at a distance, and this resignation is the gentle tone in society. –

6. In the case of disagreement, one has to be careful above all about the tone of voice one uses when one disagrees. – For this very often offends, even if the words are not otherwise offensive. It is otherwise the best opportunity for conversation and entertainment. As for gambling,[a] one cannot always speak ill of it because it concerns skill and luck. Yet when gambling becomes a passion, it becomes extremely dangerous. But gambling is nevertheless the passion[b] of a well-cultivated human being in that it amuses as well as provides for a recollection of the mind, since the mind,[c] and thereby passion itself,[d] is gradually weakened through the conversation. – But if gambling becomes the main attraction and not merely an episode in the entertainment, it is extremely harmful –.

25:1364 Social intercourse serves to moderate the egoism of human beings, and he who shies away from society is called a misanthrope.[e] – Rousseau was such an anthropophobe,[f] and everyone of whom it is said: "They would have many enemies." – Such a person is better called an anthropophobe, for he wishes human beings [to be] better than he is. He wishes them all the best, but he just wants to have nothing to do with them. Misanthropy derives from an erroneous concept of one's own importance and from a dark representation of the human being. When one is

[a] *Spiel*
[b] Following Brandt and Stark's suggestion (*Leidenschaft*). Mro: *Eigenschaft* (attribute).
[c] *er*
[d] *diese selbst*
[e] *Misanthrop*
[f] *Anthropophobus*

in society, one must always speak with other people; otherwise the society becomes timid and is wary of this person as if he were a spy. Hence the ancient Germans held wine to be so necessary in society, in order to forget one's attentiveness to oneself through drinking. True politeness is merely negative and consists in not saying rude things to people; positive politeness is when one always says a courtesy or small flattery to them. –

ON THE ASSOCIATION OF THE SOUL WITH THE BODY CHAPTER 4[a]

Here one can note the following:

1. We can arrive at our [own] mind and that of others through the body, and in turn we can arrive at the body through the mind, namely, its cultivation. The body in turn has an effect on and presses on the mind, and the mind likewise does so to the body. Accordingly, Brinckmann,[217] a doctor in the Palatinate, tells a story about a great general: he was a courageous man, but as soon as he had a bit of acid in the stomach and in the first canals of the digestive tract, he immediately became the most cowardly dastard.

2. If we want to take reciprocal influence into consideration, we must look at what:

a. voluntary influences the mind has on the body. We should not discuss this here. For these influences are sufficiently known, and the understanding must modulate them here.[b]

b. involuntary influences the mind has on the body. Sudden vibration, as in affects, belongs here; the affect creates this breach in that it overpowers the understanding. It is, as it were, the electrical shock that suddenly restrains the lifeblood in the ganglion and hinders its calm transition to vital sensation. (James Johnstone[218] says in the *English Transactions*: the ganglia are to be considered as little brains, which, however, all remain under the brain's control. There is a small accumulation point for the lifeblood within these, as in the brain, from which, as is well known, the lifeblood flows out and then further proceeds in the ducts. Now there are increasingly more nodes in the nerves, the closer they are to the bowels or diaphragm.) This restraint results in the accumulation of the nerve fluid, and its onward flow, at this point now doubled, creates this quick and sudden vibration. One finds examples of these influences of the mind on the body in Gaubius, a great physiologist,[c] *Dissertatio de regimine mentis quatenus medicorum est*,[219] and in Zimmermann's *Medical*

25:1365

---

[a] Brandt and Stark indicate that "Chapter 4" was added to Mro at a later time.

[b] Mro: *hier*. Brandt and Stark suggest *nur* (only).

[c] The Academy Edition has a period here. It was necessary to alter this sentence's punctuation.

Experiences,[220] [and] Krueger's *Experimental Theory of the Soul*.[221] The newest work is from Moritz.[222] In Gaubius there are remarks that are

25:1366 preeminently worth reading: e.g., one about a dog whom a boy dragged away while it was in the act of copulating, upon which the dog bit the boy, who then became delirious. The bite of a rooster also causes this during such a period [of mating]. Zimmermann tells of Boerhaave's cure that all the children in a school received after the sight of one of these episodes.[223]

Many people have died from the sudden vibration of the affects. However, more have died from joy. –

All of these influences are hard to explain.

C. involuntary influences the body has on the mind.

Thus a woman had a curious propensity to steal when she was pregnant.[224] From the time of conception up to the birth, it was completely impossible for her to refrain from stealing. But as soon as she had given birth, she sent back everything that she had stolen, which she had carefully hidden during that time. – Thus we also find similar examples in Moehsen's[225] (a doctor in Berlin)[a] *Pharmacology*, [and] Halle's

25:1367 *Natural Magic*,[226] in the preface – both of these adduce sure examples of witches, who as such were brought before the Inquisition. They themselves related that they were witches, and that they had danced with the devil on the Brocken during Walpurgis Night. The cause was probably this: they had smeared themselves with salve and narcotic things, e.g., henbane, and its application on the temples in particular had taken away their understanding and set their power of imagination into such an unruled and unreined fanaticism.

All of these examples are hard to explain. Indeed, Gaubius considers his own example to be impossible to explain, for, if one surely knows that women who are pregnant possess a very intense craving that the ancients called *pica* (the nose's longing for tobacco is also called *pica nasi*[b][227]) which is increased all the more by being partial [to the object], then in that case there is no example and no grounds of explaining it.

SECOND, OR PRACTICAL, PART OF ANTHROPOLOGY, WHICH CONCERNS THE CHARACTERISTIC[c] OF THE HUMAN BEING.

As the first part of anthropology contains the physiology of the human being and thus, as it were, the elements out of which the human being is

---

[a] Parentheses added.   [c] *Characteristic*
[b] Trans.: pica of the nose

composed, so the practical part of anthropology is the one that teaches us how human beings are constituted in their voluntary actions.

The characteristic of the human being consists:

1.) in what is characteristic of the human being and

2.) in the moral character*[a]* of the human being itself.

To what is characteristic of the human being, where I consider the human being as a product of nature and look at what distinguishes him from other products, that is, character more broadly,*[b]* belong. –

a.) the natural aptitude*[c]* or the natural predisposition

b.) the temperament or sensibility

c.) the natural character or the way of thinking of the human being in general. –

25:1368

To the moral character of the human being itself, where I consider him as a free being, belong. –

a.) the character of the sexes

b.) the character of the nations*[d]*

c.) and the character of the human species

When I sketch the character of a thing, in so doing I consider the natural difference it has with respect to other things (the natural character is easy to find, but the moral character is hard to find). But the character of the human being is very distinct from this. It is the character of a being that has something persistent. Consequently, the character of freedom.

FIRST SECTION

FIRST CHAPTER

ON NATURAL APTITUDE

Natural aptitude in general is that which in the human being is fit for a purpose. It is a human being's ability*[e]* to learn and nature's call to the uses of talents. – It is a property through which one is fit and usable for purposes. Therefore it is passive. By contrast, talent, when one is skillful, is using something for purposes. It is therefore active. –

Natural aptitude consists. –

1) in the capacity*[f]* to take on forms. –

2) in the capacity to invent.

Capacity is specifically attributed to the natural predisposition and is properly called natural aptitude; ability, by contrast, is also called talent,

---

[a] *Moralischen Character*
[b] *der Character latius*
[c] *Naturell*
[d] *Nationen*
[e] *Vermögen*
[f] *Fähigkeit*

even if it, too, is natural predisposition. Thus the natural aptitude properly means what is passive; but the natural aptitude is also the spirit. It is like this with animals; e.g., a dog [is] of a good natural aptitude if it is easy to train. An example of a natural aptitude among human beings, e.g., the Germans, is the willingness to adopt discipline. Other peoples have a good temperament but a poor natural aptitude. It is no eulogy when it is said of somebody: he has a good heart, he lets a person proceed with him as he wishes. For here one is not taking into consideration the ability to do good, but the capacity to endure anything. One must actually see the good heart as sensibility, as temperament comes into play with it. – One ascertains the natural aptitude of children and servants in order to discover in them the side that can best be steered and dominated. One ascertains the temperament of elders, teachers, and rulers, in order to comply with them. – It is said[228] that the Russians have much natural aptitude, but little genius. Hence they are good students but poor teachers, and experience shows that not even a single Russian has become a good teacher, as they bring all of their teachers in from foreign countries. <u>Spite</u> is contrariness towards one's commander that arises out of resentment, and <u>nodding</u>[a] is contrariness towards one's superiors out of a stupid pride, with the aim of playing a trick on him. The former is a quality of the Russians, the latter of the Poles. –

Good mind[b] and good heart are very different from each other. Natural aptitude is theoretical and practical. As the capacity to learn something, natural aptitude is theoretical; natural aptitude is good practically when one is able to be steered and compliant; that is the good mind. It is to be distinguished from the good heart and good character. The good mind aims at tolerance and is negative goodness.[c] It is thus pleasing to other people, for a good-minded person never gets in the way of others and one can proceed with him as one wishes. He is of little use to the world, for he is merely passive, but he is thus also not very harmful. The good heart belongs to temperament and is active. It is therefore also often betrayed by others, for it is blind just like other passions. Good character is positive goodness;[d] that is the best. A good mind is more fitting for a woman, a good heart more fitting for men. The Germans have good mind, can be steered well, and do not conceal themselves very much either, as do other nations, e.g., the Italians. –

Women conceal themselves far more and are also far more skilled than men in pulling out secrets from others, but they keep their own secrets

---

[a] *Niken*, today spelled *Nicken* (nodding). Here: giving apparent assent with the intention of not doing what one agrees to do. Cf. Mro 25:1413.
[b] *Gut Gemüth* [d] *positive Bonitaet*
[c] *negative Bonitaet*

safe. Such steadfastness and persistence are good qualities. A good mind, in contrast, is a weakness.

The expression about a woman, "she has a good mind," is very ambiguous. One thereby reveals her weakness and how easy it is to dispose and steer her toward anything.

25:1370

SECOND CHAPTER

ON TEMPERAMENT

One can actually call temperament that which is characteristic of the vital force. It is the sum total of incentives. It must be distinguished from the habitual mental disposition[a] of the human being. The latter is a person's mental state through which he is more disposed[b] to one way of doing and forbearing than other ones. One says of the disposition of the human being: he has [a] mood.

There is also, however, a habitual mental disposition, but one should not regard this as temperament. Some reasonable men[229] have remarked that one should expose a girl to many agreeable things when raising her. For just by laughing more frequently their facial features acquire an agreeable formation of cheerfulness and they [acquire] a habitual disposition to joviality which will be very useful to them in marriage. –

The habitual disposition can even improve the faulty temperament and remedy it.

Temperament is twofold:

1.) The temperament of the body, which indicates the mixture or composition of the constituent parts of the human being. – To this belong:

a. the constitution, the construction, the firmness of the body.

b. the complexion, or the mixing of the fluid with the solid parts. –

c. the temperament considered medically, and this is the mixture of the fluid parts with themselves.

2.) The temperament of minds

On a.) The constitution is based on the bones and other solid parts; these are the bases of life.

On b.) The complexion is based on the ducts and on the mixture of the fluids. They thus contain the basis of the inner vital motion.

On c.) The temperament is based on the nerve structure, thus on the sensation of the vital motion.

On 2.) With the temperament of the soul, it depends on two elements only: a. on the faculty of sensation[c] b. on the faculty of desire. Any

[a] *GemüthsDisposition*　　　　　　　　[c] *EmpfindungsVermögen*
[b] *aufgelegt*

25:1371 creature that can have a sensation and is active (or can desire, for thereby it surely expresses activity) lives. According to this division, we now have a fourfold sensibility of the soul:

1. The sensibility of sensation, to which belong:

a.) The Sanguine Sensibility[a] (light-bloodedness), where a preponderance of satisfaction with our condition dominates. With the sanguine person, sensations are easily aroused, but they do not last long either. He thus does not readily feel sensations for a long time afterwards.

b.) The Melancholic Sensibility (heavy-bloodedness), where a preponderance of displeasure with one's condition dominates. The sensations of melancholics are aroused with great difficulty, but they last a long time.

2. The sensibility of activity. Here belong:

a.) The Choleric Temperament (hot-bloodedness, fullness of affect) where the incentives take effect quickly and strongly, but do not last long. –

b.) The Phlegmatic Temperament (affectlessness, cold-bloodedness). With regard to activity, the temperament is not moved easily,[b] but it also continues a long time. – Accordingly:

1. The Sanguine Temperament: easy excitability and equally easy volatileness constitute the sanguine person. –

He is thoughtless, careless; hopes easily; promises quickly and sincerely, but rarely upholds it in that afterwards he cannot live up to it since he does not foresee the difficulties that are looming before him; for that reason he is a poor debtor. – He is merry and full of good things, for grief arises from reflecting on sensations. Carelessness makes him ever hopeful and cheerful, for nothing disturbs cheerfulness more than cares. Nothing penetrates his mind deeply; hence the most important things are only important to him for a moment, and he considers everything only superficially. He is amicable, but does not share grief with others, for he can console himself very easily. Therefore one has made constant cheerfulness into what is essential about the sanguine person. But it is a mere consequence of the great excitability, and equally easy volatileness, of his sensations. (Likewise, in the case of the melancholic person, the constant sadness is a mere consequence of his deeply penetrating and long-lasting sensitivity.) The sanguine person loves fashion, as this

25:1372 consists in the variability in the selection of objects of taste. Hence the French are sanguine, too. They are also therefore the merriest nation.

[a] *die Sanguinische Sinnes Art*. Each of the four headings has been capitalized, whereas the Academy Edition capitalizes two of them. This also applies below, where Kant discusses each temperament.
[b] Reading, as in Mar: *leicht* (easily). Mro: *lange* (for a long time).

He is always merry, and however one is disposed, that is how one looks at things. Thus everything is an object of joy to him. – He is variable and does not give real importance to any matter, but quickly makes it into a matter of ridicule. He thus often gives a comical importance to unimportant things. He has an *esprit des bagatelles*,[a] which is very welcome in social gatherings. He is thus good company and even loves it very much, for there he is in his element, but he is not a good friend, for he does not bother himself with the affairs of others, nor even with his own. He is not a human being who has evil intentions, but rather a hard-to-convert sinner, for his repentance never lasts long. He is good-minded, but not good-hearted. He is a friend of pity, for it affects[b] him quickly, and whatever he can do at that moment, he also does. But pondering over it is boring for him. He is full of good precepts and resolutions, but is variable. His disposition[c] is a happy one,[d] but not for that reason also a good temperament.

2. The Melancholic Temperament. Here a discontent with life dominates. This is not a basic feature of the melancholic's temperament; rather, the heavy and long-lasting impression of sensation is. Melancholy[e] must stem from this displeasure with life, which in turn must be derived from the deep penetration of the sensations on the mind. For that reason he is also called pensive,[f] for he feels everything deeply. He attaches great importance to all things; that is why he broods over an object for a long time. The mind becomes disturbed in the sensation of life through this assiduity, and melancholy thus arises. (The melancholic has in general a habitual attachment to all representations.) Even enjoyment upsets the melancholic more than it pleases him; for once he becomes merry, he is totally giddy because everything makes an impression on him so deeply. The cause of his sadness is that everything appears to him to be so important, for he fears losing the agreeable, and then he views the agreeable as a great ill. The sanguine's temperament is thus more in keeping with nature, as he[g] will surely attach importance to a thing; for the thing is not in our control for long in that our life is short and, after all, the importance of the thing ceases when our life ends. A propensity for suspiciousness that is difficult to remedy arises in him from this apprehension of everything, just as the sanguine[h] in turn trusts everyone. The melancholic finds difficulties in every matter, where

25:1373

---

[a] Trans.: spirit for trifles   [c] *Gemüths-Art*
[b] *afficirt*
[d] This clause and "but is variable" are both found in Mar, but are absent in Mro.
[e] *Schwermuth*
[f] pensive: *tiefsinnig*; deep penetration: *tiefen Eindringen*.
[g] *er*   [h] *Sanguinicus*

everything seems easy to the sanguine person; the cautiousness of the melancholic arises from that, and he is excellently fit for practical matters that require cautiousness. He does not readily make promises, but he does keep them. He does not feel that he himself is adequate, for since he finds difficulties everywhere and places importance in everything, according to him not enough is ever done. The melancholic is grateful, the sanguine is not. But he is also just as revengeful as he is grateful, and he holds a grudge in his heart. The fact that he is grateful derives from the importance he places on everything. He is enthusiastic in religion and easily [becomes] fanatical;[a] the sanguine is nothing less than that, for he does not bother himself over it and never investigates. He is just as enthusiastic in friendship and patriotic love. The melancholic can be very virtuous, [but] also very vicious. The sanguine, by contrast, has no particular virtues and vices and is more indifferentist.[b] If the melancholic has a great deal of understanding, he becomes an enthusiast; if he has little understanding, he becomes a fantast or fanatic;[c] with the enthusiast, the power of imagination is unreined; with the fantast, it is unruled.[d] I can still tame the former, for it is mere exaggeration of the rules, but not the latter, for it is without all rules.

3. The Choleric Temperament. It is very active, but not industrious. He is exceedingly full of affect; this arises out of the great activity of quickly removing every obstacle that opposes his activity and undertaking. Anger arises from this, but this anger should be viewed not as a basic feature of the choleric temperament, but as a consequence of his quick and intense incentive to activity. He likes to command, but he is not disposed[e] to do something himself, for he is too hasty. – He is therefore most unbearable when he has to obey, but he is good when he can command. He can be an honest man and a just judge, if he alone dominates. But if he is contradicted, he often acts unjustly because he really wants to assert his right. As for his decorum, he has no taste but is stiff instead, for he wants to appear respected before human beings. For this reason, he adopts another course, always watches himself, and is thus constrained. On account of his mania for dominance, he loves monarchy. He is not stingy,[f] but instead has an avarice of the greedy kind, for it is true that he gives, but he does so only to be connected

25:1374

[a] fanatical: *schwärmerisch*; enthusiastic: *enthusiastisch*.
[b] *indifferentistisch*, as in indifferentism in morality or religion.
[c] fanatic: *Schwärmer*; fantast: *Phantast*.
[d] unruled: *regellos*; unreined: *zügellos*.
[e] Reading, as in Mar: *aufgelegt* (disposed). Mro: *auferlegt* (enjoined, imposed).
[f] *filzig*

to others. He is vehement but not assiduous. One counts anger as chief among his affects, and among his passions, ambition. The choleric is easily drawn into quarrels on account of his quick excitability to action. If he is a cleric, he meddles in everything and is a busybody.[a] He is orthodox or professes the prevailing religion, where one can enforce opinions with the club of Hercules. – He is orderly with regard to work. He has a great opinion of his cleverness and also appears to be cleverer than he is. Order, which pageantry always evokes, contributes a lot to this, as it always provides a kind of importance to things. – In general, he appears more than is, and he will create pageantry more for the display than for the enjoyment.[b] In religion he is hypocritical. He is polite in ceremonies, as well as stiff. He is offensive in his tone and hardly gets along with his equals, but among persons where he has the reputation of a protector, he is excellent. Rarely is much genius found among such people, but talent perhaps. Two cholerics do not at all get along well with each other in society. He is a better relative than a friend, for with a friend there must be equality, but as a relative he can add to his reputation as a protector. –

4. The Phlegmatic Temperament can be considered in two ways.

a.) As weakness, and then it is insensibility, sluggishness in resolutions and actions; this is ignoble, for the incentives consist merely in animal enjoyment. It is base, since it acquiesces to everything.

b.) As strength, when activity is aroused slowly; but [it is] all the more enduring when desires are aroused. Phlegm considered as strength is the most excellent temperament, for his activity is in keeping with his principles. Before he acts, he thinks over everything precisely first. – He does not easily become heated, let alone carried away. He is completely in control of himself and his affects and has true strength of soul. But there are few people like this. This phlegm seems to be the maturation of the judgment of the soul. [Prince] Eugene was a phlegmatic; Schwerin, a choleric.[230] Fabius Cunctator,[231] as well as a Hungarian general Corvinus,[232] who also always retreated and thereby won in the end. His symbol was: *Vir fugiens iterum pugnat.*[c][233] Such a phlegmatic is called a philosopher, for one requires the latter to bear everything with equanimity. Phlegm gives us advantage over others. For the vehemence with which the choleric is placed into affect makes him blind. The phlegmatic is patient, the choleric impatient. He is also industrious. In religion he will be enduring, not just go for prayers. – The latter is very frugal, for nature loves diversity; if there were many such phlegmatics, things would all be brought into order. – He is completely impartial, merely

---

[a] *die Polypragmosyne*
[b] *Genuß*

[c] Trans.: The man who flees will fight again.

a spectator, and he will therefore write[a] comically or satirically. The phlegmatic is not vehement and rash; he does not let difficulty bother him. The choleric bounces off the phlegmatic person like [the projectiles of] ballistas and catapults bounce off a woolsack, for the choleric there runs into a cold-blooded man. He has firm resolve and gets a genuine advantage over others without seeking it. This temperament acts in the place of wisdom, for [although] these persons often do not have true wisdom, they nevertheless have what one demands of a practical philosopher. That is why one is wont to call them philosophers, too. The phlegmatic is not vain, for trifles do not affect[b] and excite him. The phlegmatic does not glisten and thus does not arouse jealousy either; by contrast, the choleric glistens a great deal and for just that reason he also arouses envy.[c] However, for this reason the worth of the phlegmatic is not very easily recognized either, for he handles everything slowly. The phlegmatic is the best husband, since he never starts bickering. In the good sense, it is the happiest temperament.

25:1376

The habitual inclination to temperament depends on education, social intercourse, way of living, and on acquired principles. Women must be brought up free so that a sanguine temperament is prevalent in them. Merchants get their phlegmatic temperament primarily from their way of living, and the phlegmatic temperament of the Dutch perhaps stems more from their way of living than from their mental disposition. With regard to religion:

1. the sanguine is easily a ridiculer; 2. the melancholic is fanatical; 3. the choleric hypocritical and orthodox; 4. the phlegmatic indifferentist.

In office, 1. the sanguine is distracted and disorderly 2. the melancholic is punctilious and scrupulous 3. the choleric has mania for novelty and mania for fame 4. the phlegmatic is mechanical and likes to leave everything as it as was.

In the sciences, 1. the sanguine is popular 2. the melancholic is deep or obscure and for the most part original 3. the choleric is incorrect but methodical 4. the phlegmatic is very sweeping yet without much content and laborious in the process.

In social intercourse, 1. the sanguine entertains with jokes 2. the melancholic with reasoning[d] 3. the choleric with stories 4. the phlegmatic with teasing.[e] The following verse expresses his temperament:

And with this I do something, too –
In an armchair I watch you.[234]

---

[a] Reading, as in Mro: *schreiben* (write). Mar: *speilen* (play).
[b] *afficiren*
[c] envy: *Neid*; jealousy: *Jalousie*.
[d] *Vernünfteln*
[e] *Zwiken*, from "to pinch, tweak"

THIRD CHAPTER

ON PHYSIOGNOMY

Physiognomy should be an art from which to deduce and guess the interior from the exterior. It is a science of the external marks of the temperament, talent, and character of human beings. External marks can be found in the human being either as peculiar [to it], or as merely accessory or contingently. Formation[a] belongs to the former; costume, gait, eating, etc., belong to the latter; the former ones properly belong to physiognomy; however, Lavater[235] also purports to recognize the temperament from the latter [kinds]: for instance, from the various ways in which each person writes. But this derives from the diversity of the muscles, just as every wagon rattles differently indeed. One cannot give any universal concept of physiognomy, for it is based merely on sensations. It thus also cannot be communicated to others or serve any use because it does not have a secure foundation. After Baptista Porta,[236] who compared human beings to animal forms, Lavater brought it back again. But he is a man who is more accustomed to sensation than to distinct concepts and who speaks about sensations[b] when he is filled with them.[c] In physiognomy it is difficult to speak without pictures, but we should nevertheless speak of whatever is necessary here. – It is generally agreed that the soul has such an influence on the body that it reveals itself even in the body's structure. But who can acquaint us with these characters so well that one could form an infallible science out of it? True, it is generally accepted that we can grasp some features of the human being with the power of imagination, but we cannot easily render these features of a human being as comprehensible as a mathematical figure, for we cannot communicate them to another person. This impression of the imagination[d] remains locked inside us as it were; hence this cannot be brought to firm concepts, and thus a science will never emerge from it. It is most certain that we can recognize something about the temperament and character of the mind from the external formation of the body, and this even occurs with animals, too. For the body must be in keeping with the quality of the soul. To physiognomy belong:

1. The construction[e] or the body. The perfect, proportioned, beautiful structure is the median of the structure belonging to several things of one kind. The perfect, beautiful structure is thus the principle for the judging[f] of the beautiful. Beauty lies in the concepts that we get from experience. True beauty is natural beauty and not the artist's imaginary

25:1377

25:1378

---

[a] *Bildung*
[b] *Empfindungen*
[c] *empfindungsvoll*
[d] *Imagination*
[e] *Bauwerk*
[f] *Beurtheilung*

ideal, whose harmony[a] exists only in the imagination. – It is noted[237] that a bodily structure that is entirely regular always designates a very ordinary, average human being who has few capacities. (Nature seems to have a certain proportion. If it[b] has turned about more in the body, the soul has become worse, and vice versa.) Genius is infirm as it were, and some singularities of the temperament are always noticeable; e.g., the virtuoso is often stubborn, sullen. In the case of genius, by bringing perfection to a locality, nature has produced an infirmity. From the concept of original beauty the concept of median size emerges, and thus also the concept of the median size of the powers and capacities of the human being. In geniuses of the power of imagination, one chiefly finds that a certain disproportion is prevalent in their body, e.g., Socrates, Pope.[238] – True ugliness emerges out of the features of the face that betray malice.

Can an ugly thing[c] perhaps be brought forth in nature as a natural product? No, for if we had broad cognition of its purposes, if we knew the use of all of its limbs, then nothing produced from the rules of nature would appear to us as ugly, but rather as truly beautiful, for in the course of nature everything is beautiful. Ugliness is merely relative in comparison with others. If we keep regularity in mind, then the ugly, too, is regular. Nothing can be altered about it, otherwise one appears ten times worse. A general once lost his nose in combat; since it was very large and had made him look disfigured, he wanted a really attractive one – and thus had the best waxen nose sent from Paris. But when he had the new nose put on, he looked ten times uglier. He therefore had to have his old one put on again.[239] All frailties belong to an abnormal condition.[d] We therefore call a face ugly-grotesque[e] because we are not able to see the proportion that was necessary for every face. For, it was necessary to have diversity in the facial predispositions, and this predisposition was already made from nature at the time when it created the first human being and planted in him the semen to many thousands of others. No human being, with all of the art in fantasy, is able to trace these features. One can easily distinguish, in a series of paintings, the painter's ideal from the live original to be encountered. It follows from this that there is no ugly face from nature; the ugliness is mere variation.[f] Maliciousness[g] of temperament and character is true ugliness. It is designated by a derisive mien and a spiteful face. If an evil[h] temperament turns into an evil character, the ugly facial features express themselves

25:1379

---

[a] *Ebenmaaß*
[b] *sie*
[c] *eine Häßlichkeit*, also "a deformity"
[d] *Statu praeternaturali*
[e] *häßlich grotesk*
[f] *bloß Varietaet*
[g] *Bösartigkeit*
[h] *böses*

even more distinctly. We detest such a thing. We could even grow fond of the grotesque face, but we could not grow fond of evil miens.

2. Facial structure.[a] Here we should note:

a). The profile or the cross section of the face. We cannot properly present our face to ourselves because we do not see our face in the mirror as we do in profile, for the eye depicts us on a plane and does not show us the elevations; hence we cannot immediately recognize ourselves in pictures. The forehead of the Americans is very overgrown with hair. Among the Greeks, the nose runs parallel to the forehead; this is a perpendicular profile; that is allowed for the men,[b] but not the women. The eyes then lie deep in the head. The ancients viewed whoever had a hump on the nose as a satirist.[240] Crimped noses are remnants from the Huns. The Chinese have their upper jaws and upper teeth out front; we have the opposite.[241] –

In [the work of] an old physiologist[c] Baptista Porta, one finds many animal heads, just as in Lavater there are human heads. Female foreheads are much more rounded than male ones, which are flatter. The profiles of each nation are also different.

25:1380

Lavater believes that angular heads house a great deal of talent, and that is also why he depicts the head of Erasmus of Rotterdam.[242] –

3. Facial features are predispositions to miens, and these are facial features that are put into play. Miens are gestures through which one expresses his present thoughts. Engel's *Mimic* discusses this.[243] Facial features are arranged according to the temperaments. –

Lichtenberg[244] believes that the facial features derive from the miens, as the facial features are first established through education and habit. Lavater claims that facial features are derived from nature and are not habitual miens. – He is right. The miens one has when thinking are completely different from those during speaking, for in the latter the human being adopts the mien that most behooves him given his aim. But if the human being is in repose, the miens are very different from these. Lavater[245] says that the miens of a human being after his death still reveal good-naturedness even if he lived with a great deal of maliciousness. (He thus believes that such [a person] must have therefore had a good predisposition after all.) But[d] this would prove Lichtenberg's thesis. The cause is perhaps this: the miens of the dead have lost their demeanor through the mind's influence, which now is absent, and the miens of maliciousness are molded like this only through the mind's influence. Miens are also taken for facial features.

---

[a] *GesichtsBildung*   [b] *den Männern laßt das*

[c] Reading, as in Mro: *Physiologen* (physiologist). Brandt and Stark suggest "physiognomist" (*Physiognomen*).

[d] *Allein*

Quite surprisingly, education [and] way of living also accustom miens to a position [on the face]. (A famous thief[246] in court had a restless, savage face like a savage predator, for he had been engaged in his trade for a long time. A prince, whom no one has to command, thereby acquires an appearance of greatness and self-confidence; this is a kingly face. One dif-

25:1381 ferentiates between a distinguished[a] and a common face. A distinguished face is one that always expresses fine sensation. One acquires it through a great deal of social intercourse with human beings and cultivation. A common face is one that is clumsy and thus not at all pliant.[b] As Baptist Porta[247] remarked, there is a certain similarity between human beings and animals, e.g., between a donkey and a lazy human being. If a human being is lost in thought, he appears different from the way he usually is, [and] sometimes as scowling, as Hume was when he was at the fireplace, leading Rousseau[248] to infer something evil [about Hume]. On the basis of miens, one infers [what a person is] thinking. In *Tristram Shandy*, a person says: "Aristotle says that when one thinks about the future, one looks up at the heavens. When one thinks about the past, one looks down at the earth. My father is looking straight ahead, so he is not thinking anything at all."[249] Some people appear as if they are completely dead and yet have an agreeable mien when speaking. Innate defects include, among others, having crossed eyes, when one eye is stronger than the other. One cannot infer anything from this. But if a person is not otherwise cross-eyed and just crosses his eyes toward the tip of his nose when speaking, he is lying whenever he is doing that. Just as he is taking an artificial path in thought, his eyes take one as well. The presumptuous glance and the derisive bent[c] are adverse to us. The presumptuous man is not candid. He could not care less about things, and we must always fear encountering rudeness in him. The derisive bent displays a scornful laughter. – The bent toward cheerful laughter must not be continuous. For being friendly all the time reveals a common education. Lavater[250] says: "If one's physiognomy changes, one's way of thinking changes as well, and vice versa." But a human being can become thicker, fatter, fuller in the face, and that may change his mien a great deal – but not his way of thinking. The disposition of the mind can change as a result of particular circumstances, way of living, freedom, constraint, etc., but not

25:1382 the way of the mind.[d] –) Thus one can immediately see in his miens that a human being who has lived in the countryside into his fortieth year lacks fineness and polish. Thus there are miens that often are unique to an entire people. (In order to bring about a cheerful social gathering for women, one must have them laugh often.) Indeed, even dissimilarity in

---

[a] *vornehmes*
[b] *und so gar nicht biegsam*
[c] *Zug* (usually translated as "feature").
[d] way of the mind: *GemüthsArt*; disposition of the mind: *GemüthsDisposition*.

religions yields dissimilarity in miens, and change in the religious ceremonies and its concepts changes these miens, too. Thus Herodotus[251]
laments that human beings with very awful gestures went to the gods'
altars, just as their ancestors did. – People who are enthusiastic[a] in religion also have a grotesque look. – The Tahitians and the Italians have
a great deal of expression in their faces.[252] On the basis of miens one
can make inferences about temperament, but one can make inferences
about character only to an extent, for most people adopt the character to
which they are predisposed by their temperament. But we cannot infer
anything at all about talent, and what is found in Lavater is ridiculous,
for this surely does not put facial features into play at all. One would,
otherwise, have to deduce it from the profile. –

Great rogues do not have any miens at all, but instead are dreamy.
The Bashkirs knew immediately whether a German, Russian, or Frenchman came to them. Lavater[253] says: "The English have smoother skin
than the Germans, and therefore in old age the Germans become more   25:1383
wrinkled than the English." The Greeks' profile comes from the average
of inwardly-turned and prominent noses.

Painters distinguish character and caricature; this latter is exaggeration of a character. In his caricature paintings Hogarth[254] distinguished
himself most exquisitely; an actor can do this as well if he exaggerates his
role's character. It is generally agreed that there are national faces; one
sees this in the different paintings of the various nations. In the pictures
of Italians one almost always finds eyes looking up, and in their paintings
one finds faces that are always full. The faces of base scoundrels say nothing, and when they are asked something they answer quite distracted, as
if they were absent. But the faces of sly scoundrels always express this
slyness; this is confirmed by the observations of people who often inter-
acted with criminal felons and have had a great deal to do with them.
Female faces are often beautiful yet with evil character, as with the Marquise de Brinvilliers[255] at the end of the previous century. A first-rate
mixer of poisons, she killed her father, uncle, and siblings with poison,
etc., and in order to test the poison's power she even administered it with
the soups she sent to the hospital. When it became known, she fled, but
was captured and burned.

Pernety[256] tells of a man from Brandenburg who came to Paris to
meet a parliamentary councilor and saw this painting [of her]. He did
not know the person; the parliamentary councilor left him and came
back soon after and found him still there before the painting. He asked
him what he found in it. "Beauty," he said, "one cannot deny her, but if
it is like the original, then a devil surely inhabited this person." During   25:1384
his trip, Grimm[257] visited the Bastille, Newgate, and other prisons, and

[a] *Enthusiastisch*

found that all scoundrels show a certain strength of nerves and thereby a certain superiority, which they also actually use, even if poorly. It is generally agreed that people always have a certain strength of spirit and talent that could make them into great human beings, had they not gotten into the position where they misused them. The question is: Does physiognomy change? Not very likely; it is merely formed. But one can certainly fit one's miens to another demeanor through one's way of living, just as these are formed in the same way through an earlier way of living. Hence a father said to his son as he sent him off to the Academy: "My boy, come back to me with the same face."[258] There is much that is agreed to in physiognomy so that to some extent one could indeed be acquainted with the temperament and the character of the human being, but to want to judge the entire soul and the entire character of the human being from the face [and] facial features would be impudence and uncharitableness. For we would likely be inclined to make a scoundrel out of the human being who had a vile formation[a] because one could already read this from his features. Every human being has a kind of physiognomy, and often one does not hire a servant, does not become somebody's friend, because there is something off-putting about his facial structure. On the whole, then, it is good to engage in[b] the observation of human faces.

FOURTH CHAPTER

ON THE PROPER CHARACTER OF HUMAN BEINGS, OR ON THE CHARACTER OF FREEDOM

Proper character is character of freedom. Everything else that nature gave to the human being as predisposition, his natural aptitude, temperament, physiognomy, does not constitute his proper character. Character is the will of the human being in accordance with principles. But what is characteristic of the free will constitutes the proper character of the human being, and this is the character of the human being in the strictest sense, and one calls it way of thinking.[c] Practical character is independent of one's temperament. Talent is called proficient, temperament fortunate, and character good or the opposite. The character of each human being is based on the dominion of maxims. Character could thus also be defined as the determination of the human being's power of choice through lasting and established maxims. The human being has three powers.

25:1385

[a] *Bildung*
[b] *sich mit . . . abzugeben*

[c] *DenkungsArt*

1. Talent; this determines the human being's market price and relates to the use[a] of the human being.[259]

2. Temperament determines the affection price[b] of the human being and relates to the human being's feeling.

3. Character determines the inner worth of the human being and determines its merit.[c]

Talent is valued through itself; if one is equipped for all kinds of purposes, talent is <u>cultivated</u>. Temperament is favored through itself; if one is destined for happiness or is neglected in a stepmotherly way, temperament is <u>disciplined</u>. Character is respected or feared. By means of character, one[d] is destined to general well-being. Character is <u>moralized</u>. With talent, the purpose is aimed at other ones; with temperament, the purpose of the human being is aimed at itself; and with character, the purpose is aimed at the entire creation. – Temperament must be tamed, suppressed, or nurtured. Character is a certain characteristic of the will to use all natural gifts. It is not innate, which is why we can blame it. But not temperament and talent. A human being has a way of thinking if he has certain practical principles.[e] He has a way of thought,[f] however, if he has logico-theoretical principles.[g] Character secures freedom. He who sets no rules of conduct has no character. A man has a character if others know what they have to do to abide by him. I cannot rely on temperament, for the human being can still act otherwise, but I can rely on character. Character only appears in the mature years. During youth one does not yet have it. Often one attains it only very late in life and many do not attain it at all.

25:1386

Talent and temperament can be replaced by something else that is equivalent to it, if one of them is missing. But a lack of character or way of thinking cannot be replaced by anything. For we attribute character to the human being as a merit; the other natural predispositions are only fortunate merits[h] and cannot be imputed to it as something meritorious at all. To character belong: 1. the fact that the human being has a will at all.

2. The fact that the human being has his own will. This is not to be confused with stubbornness,[i] for stubbornness belongs to temperament and indicates an ungovernableness with respect to inclinations; but it is very bad to be stubborn; that is why it is indeed necessary to have a will

---

[a] Following Brandt and Stark's suggestion: *Gebrauch* (use). Mro: *Werth* (worth).
[b] *AffektionsPreis*
[c] Following Brandt and Stark's suggestion: *sein Verdienst* (its merit). Mro: *ihren Gebrauch* (their use).
[d] *er*
[e] *Prinzipien*
[f] *DenkArt*
[g] *Grundsätze*
[h] *merita fortunae*
[i] *Eigensinn*

of one's own, for this consists of established, lasting maxims. Whoever does not have a will of his own cannot turn down anything and whoever lacks even an evil character [is, e.g.,] a dawdler, drunkard, gambler, and someone whom everyone uses as an object of his eccentricities and follies. But whoever wants to have a will of his own must also deliberate for himself and must not pay attention to how others judge him. Thus, in order to have his own will, he must not follow and consult his own instincts and moods, but his unyielding and determinate principles, and he must not follow these out of habit, but carefully deliberate on them each time.

3. That the human being has a steadfast will and acts according to it: this is the main work of character. It must not accrue from moods. There must not be any exceptions at all; otherwise the exceptions will bring the rules to naught. Whoever acts only according to moods is capricious.[a] I cannot deduce anything about good or evil character on the basis of actions, for they can arise from temperament; the human being must have good maxims, that is, practical principles. When it comes to indifferent things, one must prepare youth for character early. One must teach them not to promise lightly, but to deliberate on every resolution. If they resolve to do something by themselves, one must thereby teach them to persist. In short, when it comes to trifles, one habituates them to act according to rules first; in particular one must prevent them from imitation. Whoever affectedly feigns[b] a character and always does the opposite of what is in fashion is an eccentic and ridiculous. Friendliness is a very good virtue in society, but it must not become childish. Stubbornness is from temperament if it comes from a lack of sympathetic inclination; it is from talent if it comes from a lack of conviction; and it is from character if its principles are stronger rather than the opposite. The latter is good. There are three kinds of maxims. 1. Maxims of dietetics: when one eats, sleeps, walks, wakes up, etc. 2. Maxims of social intercourse and 3. Maxims of morals. One can make exceptions to maxims that are not sufficiently determined, but only for the improvement of other maxims. A friend who has character is an unwavering friend. If he gets angry, he will not hate someone and speak badly of him. A man of character is a great man, but not yet good on account of that. The maliciousness of temperament can be raised through good character. We respect character. This is love for what outweighs our self-love. We do not like to interact with whomever we respect, for that always impairs our self-love. We certainly like to love, but we like being respected even more. Rousseau[260] says, "You all want to hate me, but I want to make you respect me." (The evil character elicits

25:1387

---

[a] *wetterwendisch*   [b] *affektirt*

respect as well, as with Sulla in Rome. The rigid disposition[a] arouses admiration in the beginning but afterwards becomes indifferent, as with Charles XII.[261])

What ways of practicing character are there? One must 1. keep his word to himself and also 2. keep his word to others. The human being must only legislate to himself. He must keep his word to himself; otherwise he loses all respect for his reason and for his own character. For if one does not keep his word to himself the first time, nothing is achieved. For instance, if he has resolved to get up early always and this resolution is always neglected while carrying it out, nothing is achieved. The human being who cannot believe in himself with respect to his own resolutions feels the hopelessness of not being able to procure all the good that he could have procured. But he must also keep his word to others; which includes: 1. that one not lie 2. that one keep one's word. Whoever lies has no real character and he is always something contemptible, but I must also keep my word; this presupposes that, before I promise, I first deliberate about everything. – Many persons who have a character of their own often become heretics of taste, or eccentrics.[b] An eccentic is one who apes originalities, but in fact this does not indicate any character. A character actually consists in the unyielding adherence to principles; already in youth one can contribute something to attaining it. Not every temperament is equally inclined to adopt a character; for instance, the melancholic first adopts a character, [but] the sanguine does not do so very easily. However, it is actually not based on temperament, but on the human being's freedom. In order to create a character, these are very useful:

1. Unwavering observation of principles and the attempt to make them consistent and ready at any occasion.

2. The representation of the contemptibility of a human being without character.

It is hard to distinguish between good-naturedness[c] of temperament and goodness[d] of character. A physiognomist,[262] looking at the facial features of Socrates, discerned a corrupt mind (temperament); the latter even admitted it to him, and merely said that through persistent practice he had shaped this mental predisposition into a good character. – Goodnaturedness is well-meaning temperament. It is hard to recognize one's own character. Good character is negative, also positive. The negative is the lack of an evil character, which includes three parts: a. lying b. falsity and affectation c. abjection and flattery. For here one sacrifices one's worth, and a human being with true character must know how to value the latter. Flattering and pretending to be friendly in front of someone

25:1388

25:1389

---

[a] *steife Sinn*
[b] *Sonderlinge*

[c] *Gutartigkeit*
[d] *bonitaet*

while being false behind one's back indicates a man without character. One can call someone a good man without presupposing anything, but if one calls him an upright man, one always presupposes character. – Chattiness, meeting in a society with others and speaking badly of a human being who was once my friend but broke with me due to certain circumstances, always indicates a human being with no character at all. Friendship preeminently has something so noble about it that one must avoid a break, inasmuch as one can do this; and if it ever occurs, one should preserve all of the friend's secrets that he holds in his soul, and must use nothing to his disadvantage. Otherwise the Italian proverb would become true: "Treat your friend as if one day he might be your enemy."[263] But that is an abhorrent proverb, for, put another way, it amounts to: "Only pretend to be someone's friend, but deep down do not be one."

The positive side [of good character] includes: 1. its being constant and good in general, not good out of mere interest 2. in society not abusing other people's trust. Even if one can speak completely freely and without reservation in public societies, one still must not divulge what is said. For, as it were, a pact is made there. A human being who recounts everything without distinguishing between what can be recounted and what cannot be, is indiscreet and incapable of any character; when he can make this distinction and nevertheless does not act according to it, he is malicious (it is even contemptible for us to speak badly of someone whose friendship one previously cherished).

25:1390

3. One must not only abhor evil, but, when something evil is said in a society, also oppose oneself to it, not keep silent.

4. One must have genuine love of honor, not ambition[a] and vanity. One must not go about with the unworthy,[b] for that means *noscitur ex socio qui non, etc.*[c]

It is not shameful when a noble goes about with an inferior person who has good character, but when an inferior person who has good character interacts with a noble who has an evil character, it is vanity, if not sheer vainglory.[d] Vanity is: whatever in itself has no value is nonetheless valued merely on account of fashion. Maxims must not be fashionable. Good-naturedness of temperament must be distinguished from that of character. The former wants the good from inclination, the latter from duty. The doctrine[e] of tenderheartedness, mere pity that is not built

---

[a] *EhrGeitz*   [b] *nichtswürdigen*

[c] Kant is referring to the proverb, *Noscitur ex socio, qui non conoscitur ex se.* (One who is not recognized from himself can be known from his company.)

[d] Reading, as in Mar: *gar Ehrsucht* (sheer vainglory). Mro: *wahre Ehrliebe* (true love of honor).

[e] *Lehre*

on principles, is very contrary to character. In this Gellert[264] held that his moral philosophy aims more at inclination than at duty; in the end, all good character is eradicated by aroused sensations. Inclination can change if its cause disappears. Hutcheson,[265] who is also like this, says: "Duty is whatever one feels to be good." Now whoever does not have a sensitive soul is therefore also unable to recognize duty. Likewise all religious observation that comes from fear and punishment rather than from principles is contrary to moral character, just as is all performance of the good carried out with advantage in mind. –

Certain occupations offer more opportunity to build character than other ones. Because poets have a great flexibility in representing and taking on all sorts of characters, they cannot have an unyielding character. One sees this also from their biographies. Young [was] like this.[266] Actors of passion,[a] musicians, dancers, etc., also rarely have character, for they love what is changeable, and this does not agree with character. That is why only people with little disposition to character become musicians and poets. Speculative scholars are generally free from all other passions; only science interests them; hence they lack the incentive to other passions and thus have a good character. David Hume[267] notices this, for he says that it is not easy to find a professional man of learning who is not an honest man. This same Hume[268] also says that clergymen, if they do not have a good sensibility,[b] easily fall into hypocrisy and dissimulation [concerning the level of their devotion]; they do this in order to avoid shocking the masses and they refrain from doing a great deal of what they could do. This derives from the delusion of human beings, from the fact that they demand so much from them. Soldiers and citizens are more disposed to good character, for they are not forced in this way. *Rustica gens, etc.*[c] is a principle of brutal financial advice, as Sulzer[269] says. Likewise, it is also bad to presuppose malice in everyone, for then I see myself as evil. Deficiency in character is thoughtlessness. The corruption of character is falseness. Deficiency of character can be brought about in several ways. Thus the proverbs *rustica gens, optima flens pessima ridens,*[d] "Everyone for himself, God for us all," etc., make a human being thoughtless, as it teaches him false maxims and thereby hardens his heart. Furthermore, [the notion] that God hates unbelievers,[270] if understood improperly and wrongly used, can turn the human being into a hater of a great number of human beings. In short, whoever lets himself be ruled by example has no predisposition to character, for the good character does not originate from nature, but must be acquired. The acquisition

25:1391

25:1392

---

[a] *Spieler von Passion*   [b] *SinnesArt*
[c] Kant is referring to: *Rustica gens est optima flens et pessima ridens.* (A rustic people is good when crying and bad when laughing.)
[d] See previous note.

of character includes: 1. education – for males it must rest on principles, for females, on honor. –

2. Having the predisposition to character through reflection and conversation with friends about moral things. –

3. Through sincere adoption of unyielding principles. – One can call this the philosophical rebirth, if, that is to say, one turns from rule by instincts to rule by principles.

4. Circumspection regarding the inviolableness of principles. One must be an object of respect even in one's own eyes. –

SECOND SECTION

ON THE ACTUAL CHARACTER OF THE HUMAN BEING.
FIRST CHAPTER

ON THE CHARACTER OF THE SEXES

25:1393

In all products of art where just as much should be organized by a small power as by a great one, art is required. Nature wanted the happiness of both sexes. Nature did not give women[a] as much strength of body and soul as it gave men; it still wanted them to be as happy as men; thus it had to give them more art in the application of power and had to give man a simple application of his power. Man is made for nature, and woman[b] for man. In the end, through man, woman also rules nature. In the civilized condition, woman[c] and her character perhaps have to be observed in the finest Parisian ladies. In the refined condition, the germ of nature develops in the female sex more than in the male one. Female[d] weakness is the weakness of nature, but actual strength for the male nature. For the fact that men can provide assistance makes them loved by women. If their strength were equal, a rivalry would arise. If a union should arise, it cannot come about through equality, but through a mutual need. One calls the weakness of the female sex femininity.[e] Nature wanted the part of the human race that is responsible for reproduction not to be daring. On the other hand, through this femininity woman even rules man. For uniformity is opposed to the exact union of two persons. Thus, for example, two scholars from the same specialty will never become friends. Woman is weak by nature; man is weak through his wife. David Hume[271] made the remark that a woman[f] does not become angry[g] if one ridicules her sex, but that she becomes terribly enraged if one ridicules marriage. (Otherwise, one can also reproach woman for

---

[a] *Weibern.* Kant appears to use *Weib* and *Frau* interchangeably throughout this section.
[b] *Frau*
[c] *Weib*
[d] *Weibliche*

[e] *Weiblichkeit*
[f] *Frauenzimmer*
[g] *böse*

anything, just not her age.) The cause of that lies in this. Women[a] know quite well that the male sex will never lose respect for their sex, but they seem to be concerned that at some point marriage could be seen with disdain. This enrages them, for if that were the case they would lose their influence on men, and their worth would be placed far below that of men. One must never ridicule femininity. For if one ridicules it, one ridicules oneself. For the other sex still dominates the male sex through this femininity. It had earned the greatest domination during the period of chivalry, of which some traces are found, even if only from fashion, in Spanish animal fights. Moreoever, women could, if they wanted, acquire a great domination over the male sex through their charm. Women must be brought up through delicateness[b] when it comes to honor, through candor, not compulsion. Vice must be represented to them from its indecent and detestable side. Thus, when in company women with such an education are full of confidence and not bashful at all. By contrast, young boys made of the best material, that is, of mind, understanding, and heart, are very bashful if they enter into company with well-educated women. Women[c] do not have respect for men who are dolls and who want to play narcissus. By contrast, men are often enchanted by doll-like women. Women have a solid judgment in this. The female sex is for the cultivation of the male sex, for with them it attains 1. the cultivation of the useful 2. the cultivation of the beautiful. Women do not have as fine a taste as men. For, because they themselves are a fine object of taste, they certainly cultivate the taste of the male sex, but do not cultivate it themselves. There is a specific difference between the corresponding properties that we attribute to the male and female sexes. Thus, for instance, completely different standards are to be assumed for the male and female understanding. Man thinks according to principles; woman thinks that how others think is likewise true for her. Women agree with the common opinion because they go for common approval, and they cannot attain this if they oppose the common opinion. Man has honor in himself, woman in what is outside her. With respect to religion, woman must not speculate, but should accept what the church says. With respect to their honor, with women it depends on what people say about them; but with men on how they must judge themselves. Women see only what others say about them, but men what others think about them if they judge impartially. With respect to sentiment, the incentive for the male sex must be honor, but for the female sex, virtue. With respect to domestic income, the attribute of men is to earn and that of woman to save. Thus women also accept gifts before men do, as the latter believe that in so doing they are indebting themselves. It is also good that women

25:1394

---

[a] *Frauenzimmer*   [c] *FrauensPersonen*
[b] *Delicatesse*

are not generous, for they do not know how much it has cost to earn
something. – Man also has an interest in what is public, in addition to
his private interest; but woman has an interest only in her domestic concerns. It would also be very peculiar if woman were to be concerned
about war and peace and wanted to take part in some state; hence in
Poland there is no just form of government, for only the women rule
there, and the latter love peace and only care for the private interest.
Perhaps no women have had as much done to them as the wives of Job
and Socrates. Job's wife had been concerned about his generosity and
later cut him off for that reason, for she took it to be the cause of his
misfortune.[272] Socrates's wife asked him if he would like to give up his
mission of improving the world, and, when she saw that he did not care
about the domestic interest very much and that this was his reason for not
accepting any gifts, she also let him be. – By the way, Socrates was very
content with her. Thus Richardson,[273] the author of *Pamela*, *Clarissa*,
Grandison, has a bookseller in London, a woman, repeat something out
of Cicero [and] Seneca, but with the addendum "as my brother said to
me,"[274] as if she were afraid of having read Cicero himself. – This is on
the mark. Woman is intransigent, but always seeks to put her husband at
peace. – Women are not likely to be as friendly with each another as men
are. This comes from the fact that men only have an inclination to please
a single person, but women to please the entire male sex. With them, this
inclination cannot fall on a single person, otherwise it would be coquetry
or calculated play of charm. Women want to be sought after, but men
seek themselves; hence there is a determinate rivalry among women; this
even expresses itself in fashion, if they alike know that dress makes them
really attractive in men's eyes. In their court cases, women thus prefer
to have male judges rather than female ones, and if a woman judges she
will always first find the woman in the wrong. Women do not preen
themselves for the sake of men, but to outdo their peers. In front of a
husband, they prefer to appear in a negligee. Women refuse; men accept.
The women have to be like this; otherwise they would depend too much
on the man. The man must make an effort, and the woman does not
have the option of proposing; she would look down on this. In choosing,
man is more delicate than woman as well as more delicate with regard
to looks. For she has nothing but acceptance and rejection and cannot
take the initiative, which she would really like to do. She looks more at
wealth and station than at outer figure and reputation. With her all charitable acts are to be regarded as grace, but with man as duty. Through
refusal the woman draws the man to her, and she can continue this in
marriage; in this way she dominates the man. The man, if he already
has a wife, no longer seeks to be found pleasing by women; but the wife
seeks to please other men even when she is married. For she can indeed
become a widow and then not have the choice again. The woman puts

up with intolerant jealousy of men, but not suspicious jealousy. Tolerant jealousy is extremely ridiculous, for surely the husband did not have to marry at all and limit himself to his wife; through marriage he has a totally exclusive privilege with regard to his wife. One who is a tolerant thinker concerning his wife is a cuckold.[a] This comes from the word *Rehhahn*, which means a capon that has a horn on its head. Emperor Charles could not put up with jealousy in his realm, since he introduced a society that was called the cuckold's[b] society, which was very tolerant with regard to the women in it.[275] In botany, it is called *cucurbitare*, from *Kürbiß*. In Arabic one has a word for it that also derives from the word 'cock'. Woman is affectionate in sensations, but not in the way of thinking; that is the man. She lays all her troubles on man because she cannot bear any of them.   25:1397

The question is often raised: who should rule[c] in marriage? In marriage the wife should dominate[d] through inclination. The husband should rule over inclination through understanding. – For example, if a prince wanted to make plans for some festivity, he could certainly do it. However, if the minister presented to him the miserable state of the exchequer that would therefore have unaccounted charges, this would motivate the prince to forgo his plans, and thus the minister would rule and the prince would still dominate. In this way, the husband must also be the advisor and leader of the wife's will. A young wife dominates an older husband, and an older wife will be dominated by a younger husband. Matrimonial love is intolerant in itself.[e] Matrimonial love and tolerance are *contradictio in adjecto.*[f] This tolerance makes the husband contemptible and detestable in his wife's eyes, for she believes that he scarcely values his treasure since he hardly watches over her. Debaucheries[g] committed by the male sex before marriage are not taken as much into account as those done by the female sex. – A man's freedom is narrowed by marriage, and a woman's freedom is extended. The wife thinks that a man who is married does not have to look for another woman, for she could stand in for the entire sex; he will thus not have to be unfaithful in marriage. But a man thinks that a woman[h] will not be faithful in marriage if, when she was unmarried, she risked a great deal and still went down forbidden paths; for now that she is married she risks less [and] can use the husband as a cover.   25:1398

With respect to family, it is usually the mothers who raise sons, and those sons who demonstrate much vivacity are usually called momma's boys. Women in general really love the vivacity of males; by contrast,

---

[a] *Hahnrey*
[b] *Rehhans*
[c] *regieren*
[d] *herrschen*

[e] *an sich*
[f] Trans.: contradiction in terms
[g] *Die Ausschweifung*
[h] *Frauenzimmer*

daughters are usually raised by their fathers. Sons who possess a good way of thinking thus always prefer their mothers and obey them, indeed they get a lasting enjoyment from this, and a kind of magnanimity is revealed by the fact that they let themselves be controlled[a] by their mothers and obey her until her death. Hence it is not good if sons take their mothers in after marriage. For the wife is then a nobody in the house. However, this is not the case with daughters and their mothers. Daughters have more devotion to their fathers and preside over the household, for they do not allow themselves to be controlled by their mothers.

SECOND CHAPTER

ON THE CHARACTER OF NATIONS

If many characters are found within a people,[b] the entire people has no character. This is a remark that Hume[276] makes about the English. – It is completely correct because if the individuals each have a distinct character, they do not constitute a whole. The people is thus without character because it lacks uniformity.

One can count four learned nations[c] in Europe, namely: 1. the French 2. the Italians 3. the English 4. and the Germans, to which the Swiss, the Dutch, the Danish, and the Swedish also belong. All of these peoples are mixed with German peoples and tribes. According to Denina,[277] the Italians [are mixed] with Ostrogoths in particular and have also gained a great deal in the process. The feudal government originates from the German peoples; the current system of states is grounded on it and is better than the previous one.

25:1399

1. The French. They have a mature national character, for the individuals have so much uniformity with one another that nobody has much character of his own. They make changes often; they turn the great into the small and the small into the great and important. With them, everything becomes old. Inoculation[d] had become fashionable for not long; thus one again began to get rid of it merely because it had already become old. It is the land of taste. They are originators of taste and its master at the same time. With respect to conduct,[e] they are civilized without being virtuous, sociable without the objective of bringing about their well-being, and in their societies and theaters they do not put up with the slightest equivocal expression; [they are] astonishing patriots without taking the slightest part therein. They are patriots from vanity,

[a] beherrschen
[b] Volk
[c] Nationen
[d] Inoculation
[e] Conduite

not from devotion to their home country. The French possess anything that can give them a polished outward appearance without too much effort. – As authors they are popular, the cause of which are the societies, as there is more bonding within the social ranks and not as vast a distance between the social ranks as with the Germans. With them popularity is the *summum bonum*; it constitutes what is characteristic of the French and brings the same conduct[a] to all the social ranks. Thus one can say that one finds great conduct there, while in England one finds great erudition. The French language has words that cannot be expressed in German at all; this is because they express attributes of their character, for example, *frivolité*[b] (a scholar's inclination to represent the small as great and the great as small, and thus [to make] a satire, if one cannot manage to poke fun at it). In similar fashion, the word *conduite*, a good way of living.

Gallantry[c] is an obliging courtesy that flatters the inclination and vanity of another person. It can also be directed at men. – It was something unfamiliar to the Greeks and Romans; one can see that in the odes of Horace, for when he presents eulogies to Maecenas, in the end he surely offers the greatest ones.[278]   25:1400

Point d'honneur[d] can be compared to the *puncto iuris*, or a matter where justice or injustice is in dispute. The *point d'honneur* is a [kind of] scrupulosity[e] in honor that is not based on any concepts or maxims. One indeed commonly imagines that the French lack genuine honor: one errs in doing so, however. Only among the French does one find people who, out of honor in battle, do more than they should.

The *point d'honneur* is like a case of conscience in casuistry;[f] jousts among knights, and duels after that, originated from it. According to the original arrangement, someone who was attacked could not engage in a duel, only someone who was insulted with the accusation that he had committed some wrong could do so. In France there is a court of *point d'honneur* made up of upright marshals: nobles who, due to their honorable position, collect money, are sued if they do not pay back their debts, and then are claimed to be without honor. –

Petit maitre means, approximately, a minor ruler who nonetheless at the same time acts like he has a reputation of great importance.[279] The name originated with Marshal de Condé. One calls a person who has   25:1401 the utmost cultivation of morals and manners a *petit maître*. One cannot translate it with fop,[g] because that is a well-groomed ape. A *petit maître* is a person who shows off the tone of the court in society and therefore

---

[a] *gleiche Conduite*
[b] *Frivolite*
[c] *Galanterie*
[d] Trans.: point of honor
[e] *scrupulositaet*
[f] *Casus conscientiae in der Casuistic*
[g] *Stuzer*

acts as if he were very familiar with the court. A German who imitates the court but does not quite reach it[a] is a *macaque*.

Flippancy[b] is the manner of saying something to someone with a certain freedom.

Coquetry[c] is the calculated play with one's charm; it is to please a person to visible desire. One must not translate it with *Buhlschwesteren*.[d]

All of these aforementioned faults of the French are forms of politeness taken to the extreme.

France is also the land of fashion. – Fashion is the need to have a style[e] that begins first; if the need becomes general, it is a need plain and simple. It is not Versailles that sets fashion, but the common people in Paris, and the court must adjust itself accordingly. The Orientals all have the same habit in clothing and spelling and have no fashion; perhaps fashions usually come from the theater. In France the women set the tone, and the woman who usually sets the tone is called the woman of good tone.[f] (Tone, i.e., the worth according to which one values the thing.) The ladies' offices of spirit[g] also originate in the same way. – An affected[h] way of [being a] chaste and peculiar lady is called a prude. One calls *précieuse* a lady who demands an affected kind of respect. –

The French are interested in whatever their king undertakes. They are very willing to bear all burdens, so long as they receive some enjoyment. Thus the court also always arranges for festivities. Every scholar makes the effort to present a book at court. Every one speaks of the king with warmth. However, this is not devotion to the king but vanity, as they honor themselves through the honor of an illustrious king, and so believe that they are profiting from their own luster. If he is well past the years of flippancy, the Frenchman is liked. But if he must display his character, he is disliked, for he thinks that only his nation is clever and satirizes all the other ones. Thus he also thinks that his language is the best and believes that everyone has to learn it. Therefore, if a German makes mistakes while speaking French, they correct him without laughing, as if he were their pupil. If they learn to speak German, one must laugh because they have fun with whatever is fitting for their character. They therefore also rarely learn to speak German properly; they also do not care if they pronounce a name in this way or that. One sees this also in their writings. The Frenchman is not clean, but dainty. The English are the cleanest; they don fresh clothes every day. Grimm[280] says: "One

25:1402

---

[a] *Der ihn nachahmende aber nicht nachkommende Deutsche*
[b] *Etourderie*   [c] *Coquetterie*
[d] *Buhlschwesteren*, a woman who engages in an illicit love affair
[e] *Manier*   [g] *bureaux d'Esprit*
[f] *de bon ton*   [h] *affektirte*

need only seek the French cuisine in order to receive something disgusting on the table." For the meats there are quite inferior, and when they
snort or puff out tobacco, it all falls on the meat; and the French are quite
opposed to foreigners, polite but not hospitable. The women are very
understanding; they are not beautiful, but are very likable, very entertaining but not homemakers, and Rousseau[281] claims that the women
are far more loyal friends than the men. The French very much love
witticisms[a] and cannot live without them; they are *suaviter in arte sed non
fortiter in re.*[b] They love bold judgment and judge themselves to be bold
in philosophy; thus their writings always only glisten for a while. If he
cannot make a joke, the Frenchman is profound, but if he can manage
to do it, he prefers to put aside the profundity just to be able to make
the joke. In what concerns the laws, they are very rigid and the proceedings tumultuous. The police tyrannize, and a *lettre de cachet* can come
like a bolt from the air. The criminal laws are outwardly rigid and one
proceeds according to them without any form at all. One finds the greatest intolerance next to the greatest freespiritedness, but the government   25:1403
believes that, because the French are inconstant, the Protestants would
quickly run riot if there were tolerance. The history of the Protestants[282]
and Jean Calas is an example of this.[283] But the French rehabilitate him
afterwards, that is, if they break an innocent person on the wheel or hang
him and then declare him to be innocent after more precise investigation, they solemnly reestablish his honor. – Calas was rehabilitated in
this way, too.

   2. The Spanish: although their king was a prince from the Bourbon
house,[284] he was unable to change their customs after all. Perhaps the old
Moorish blood is responsible for this. They are the exact antipodes of the
French; they hold strong and fast to their old customs, and, like Oriental
peoples, are set apart without observing many sciences. They do not
have any desire to travel; they also do not learn any French. The word
grandezza[c] thus rightly designates a reputation that even every peasant
gives himself and arises out of the feeling of his imagined worth. The
merchants have preeminently something noble about them and are the
most honorable in the world. For if a war between Spain and England
breaks out, an edict is immediately issued that says they should not pay
their debts to the English merchants, but they pay it anyway, even at the
risk of their own lives.[285] Their table is poorly furnished. They eat little
in terms of quantity and quality. A German traveler with his entourage
thus made a great deal of commotion because he consumed so much,
and the Spanish ran together to see the Germans eat. The city Saragossa

---

[a] *bon Mots*
[b] Trans.: gentle in art but not resolute in execution
[c] *Grandezza*, "magnificence, grandeur"

25:1404   thus forbade him to enter the city in response, for they feared not having enough food.[286] –

The nation has few pleasures. Only a dance called the fandango has such a charm for the people that, if someone does such a dance, the people dance in the street. The nation is somewhat cruel; this is shown by the bullfights and their *auto da fé*[287] where the [people wearing a] *sanbenito*[a] are burned if their paper caps are painted with devils and upright torches; but the ones with the torches facing downward are only expelled from the country. They have a propensity toward the romantic.[b] In Spain every reform falls hard because the Spaniards hold rigidly and firmly to their old customs, for when the king[288] merely wanted to abolish the cape

25:1405   and broad-brimmed hats in order to reduce the number of scoundrels, a revolt rose up against him.

3. Italians. In this country, as in France, the taste for art is the taste for conversation. The gondoliers sing such beautiful duets that many singers do not sing them more beautifully than they do. The Italians are very sociable, but also very clever. They are full of much affect and are earnest. Do murders arise as a result of their affect? The Frenchman is vivacious without affect; he loves everything that creates pageantry. They[c] are jocular, but they cannot tolerate teasing.[d] They prefer public festivities, e.g., *Carnevale*, to private ones. They have rooms that are more splendid than comfortable. Rousseau says: "They have splendid rooms and sleep in rats' nests."[289] The *cicesbei*[e] were originally guards and have now become suitors.[290] – *Cicesbei* or attending knights[f] are actually people who attend to ladies, but a man of reputation and honor can appear with his wife, without a *cicisbeo*. They have splendid churches with mosaics and frescos. – They understand masterfully how to get money out of the bag, but also how to circulate it; they invented all of that, e.g., the banks, the collateral loans, and lotteries such as the one in Venice. There are artists who engage with a great deal. Inequality of fortunes is very large with the Italians. It has not been like that in England for a long time. – The *polenta*, a porridge made from Turkish wheat, and chestnuts constitute their typical sustenance. – Their spirit is planted very deeply, but their politics rests on very slippery cornerstones. The Roman court is a model in politics. The Italians have many bandits, whom one calls

25:1406   *bravos*, and many preparers of poison.

It properly arose here. A certain Lady Toffana[291] under Charles VI invented a poison that killed slowly and was made up of arsenic and the

---

[a] With Brandt and Stark, reading Mro's *Santonito* as *sambenito* (sanbenito). Mar: *Subjecte* (subjects).
[b] *zum Romantischen*
[c] *Sie*, i.e., the Italians
[d] *Neken*

[e] *Cicesbei*
[f] *Cavalieri serventes*

convallaria lily; after she had killed 30 men, she was discovered, fled to a cloister and found protection there, and there she also died. The Italians have the greatest aversion to the court [and] civil police,[a] and the latter are half dishonorable in their eyes. They have the vivacity of the French, but are focused through the understanding. In France, the commonest man has more sociable taste than in other countries, whereas in Italy he has more taste for art. The promotion of taste is part of the Frenchman, the promotion of pomp part of the Italian.

The social gatherings of the Italians do not aim at culture as much as the French ones do. The Italian social gatherings are comparable to the stock exchanges, where one comes and goes. But one gets to know many human beings there; otherwise these gatherings have no use. – By contrast, in France they cultivate very exquisitely, and whoever has been in France for a year and learned nothing, either could not learn anything or did not want to. –

4. The English. David Hume[292] makes the remark that every individual in the entire nation has his own character. One actually cannot find as many eccentrics in any other country as in England. – Indeed, one finds that there it is a proper honor to be unique. They appear to hate all imitation and nevertheless love fashion. – Stubbornness is often a sign of a stupid mind, but also of a firm character. In France, everyone up to the commonest man has more good spirit[b] than anywhere else, but here [in England] they have more good sense,[c] more teaching. The English newspapers probably contribute very much to this, for they are so full of diversity of every kind, and one always finds in them something for clever people and fools; they are read all over and in noble houses they are even regarded as servants. When they read the newspapers, the nobles only hear a pronouncement of their dominance. The Englishman works hard and briskly until the very end, but only until it is dinnertime. Afterwards he goes to the taverns and then argues about politics and religion. Many wondrous conceptions emerge from tarrying there, but it surely cultivates the spirit of the nation. They therefore have wonderful clubs. Prosperity goes farthest in England. England is the true land of machines. They shorten and lighten their labor very much with these machines; hence their labors are paid the best there; thus if the French want to possess correct and precise astronomical instruments, they import them from England. Simplicity and uniformity are conspicuous in their labors, and they exquisitely demonstrate their utility and usability. One can always learn something from the English writings. They are well worked out, and when one has read it one must not ask,

25:1407

---

[a] *Diener Sbirri*, armed police soldiers in Italy
[b] *bon Esprit*   [c] *bon sens*

"Why might the author have written that?" This is not the case with the writings of the French.

Montesquieu, one of the greatest minds[a] of the French, put in his work on the spirit of the laws nothing but merely incipient ideas that lack reality. No state will be improved by this book. There is also much playful wit in it, e.g., he writes a chapter on the despotic government, where he merely says: "If the savage from Java wants to get the fruit of a tree, he skins it and eats the fruit."[293] This is an image of the despotic government. Perhaps this is warranted, admittedly, but it is a peculiar chapter on account of this image. The English are polite without ceremonies, their mood and their wit are original, and the Frenchman surely loses when it comes to ridicule. The genuine opposition[b] between English and French and the national hatred between them is based on the different forms of government. Out of vanity the Frenchman always praises the

25:1408 king.[c] The Englishman does not easily put up with the reputation of the king and loves freedom. The Frenchman seeks by contrast to promote the reputation of his king as much as possible. There is thus a contrast here. – The former is the attribute of the slave, the latter of the savage. If the Englishman sees us as apes, then one can see them as bears. He is polite, but not flattering. He finds pleasure in stubbornness and lets himself be coerced by others the least. Sharp[294] says in his travels: "In France everyone is polite except for the innkeepers, and in England everyone is impolite except for the innkeepers." For in France one is simply polite when it comes to compliments, but they are not at home[d] with real services. But it is the reverse with the English. The Englishman is hospitable; he invites people, but does not like doing so. In their social gatherings they are without any ceremonies; they thus even meet foreigners with indifference. His foods are excellent, but they do not create such garnishing[e] for it as the Germans. The Germans are the most hospitable nation, namely, they entertain a person with formality. This is what Paoli's colonel tells Boswell, as they had both been in Germany.[295] –

Like the French, the English travel around in order to be contemptuous of everything. If they travel, they always attend clubs with travelers from their nation and get to know just the taverns there; in his travels the German tries to become acquainted with the nation. One must therefore be astounded at what miserable conceptions of other countries the greatest English geographers have, e.g., those of Guthrie, who edited *General History of the World* with Gray, of the Prussians.[296]

---

[a] *Geister*

[b] Reading, as in Mro: *antipodische* (opposition). Mar: *Antipathie* (antipathy).

[c] In Mar, this sentence reads: "The Frenchman loves his king due to boasting."

[d] *zu Hause*   [e] *apparatus*

England is the paradise of women.[a] Despite all of the gallantry of the men in France, the woman dominates more in England than France. They are very popular with the innkeepers when they travel, for they consume a large amount; that is why they are the most popular foreigners in Rome.

25:1409

5. Germans. The phlegmatic temperament prevails here. They are a mixed people at the very least. Mechanism is here the greatest incentive that puts everything in motion. With them order is in all things. Thus one finds mechanism in the government and preeminently in the army; hence their army is the best, and the French, with all of their patriotism, and the English, with all of their daredevilishness, cannot do what the Germans with their mechanism can do. They are inventors in everything that can be brought out by observation and experience. Thus they are chiefly strong in chemistry. They are better discoverers than inventors. When it comes to politeness, they are punctilious or forced. They cannot at all assume the easy manner[b] of the French. They are always somewhat wooden, and one never finds a good actor among the Germans. The Germans translate everything, and one could advise other nations to learn German, for they could then dispense with all the other languages. The Germans have no national pride. Some writers[297] now want to encourage national pride, but that [lack] is a good quality that one should not get rid of. The cause perhaps lies in the fact that they are divided into many small states and do not constitute a whole nation. The Germans are good colonists and do not depend much on their homeland. Thus Cook[298] met a German in Kamchatka [and] on the Island Savu,[299] positioned laterally with respect to Java; one can indeed meet them anywhere the force of religion does not dominate. They are more cultivated than the Polish, Russians, etc.; their punctiliousness runs contrary to genius; with regard to genius they are ranked below the French, English, and Italians. They work on a thing only so long as it has to do with their diligence. As soon as it becomes a thing of genius they hand it over to the French. Thus Kepler in fact discovered the trajectories of the planets, but Newton explained this far better and exactly through his discovery of the weights of the bodies. It is this way in chemistry, too. Black in Edinburgh invented the analysis of the air.[300] The German has talent for scholarship and composure, but more judgment than spirit. He distinguishes profoundly and exactly, and has a great mania for titles. He speaks of a person in the singular and plural.[c] The German language is very rich in synonyms; it is therefore more suited for philosophy than French, for the latter has many words with multiple meanings. It is very pure and every mixing from foreign languages is

25:1410

25:1411

[a] *Frauenzimmer*
[b] *das air degagée*

[c] *im Singulari und Plurali*

immediately noticeable, e.g., *Genie*, from *ingenium* or *genius*. It is not like this in other languages. The French take, e.g., a Latin word, add a French ending, and immediately it sounds completely French; in particular, in a solemn speech, a foreign word in the German language sounds most ridiculous. A priest once said[301] at the conclusion of his sermon: "If you do this you will become like this, you will promote your own well-being, and I will be much *obliged*."[a] Germans love pleasures that can be enjoyed at a phlegmatic pace,[b] and these are meal and drink. The Germans are hospitable not so much out of friendship as to be able to invite himself as a guest, as it were. They are very disciplined and gladly accept discipline. This constitutes what is mechanical and punctilious in school education. Dispositions toward being very long-winded, a designed letter, *Imitationes Ciceronianae*,[302] etc., suppress all genius and inventiveness, due to the punctiliousness they have already been accustomed to in their youth. They are patient in work, but they do not work with as much purposiveness as the English. They have much erudition; the many citations in their writings come from this, but often these already seem to be on the decline. They leave many marks in the area of invention, e.g., Otto Guericke,[303] the vacuum pump, etc., but they do not know how to use this invention. He must leave further execution and improvement to others. He is very systematic, so that he gave many sciences a systematic dressing, e.g., *iure publico*.[c] He accepts a reform willingly. And Rousseau is perhaps right in saying that Abbé de St. Pierre's[304] recommendation of a league of nations, where disputes among nations would be decided through proceedings[d] rather than war, could come into existence. Germany would like to be the midpoint here. This is also proved by many examples of peacefully settled disputes at the Diet at Regensburg.

25:1412

We now pass over the Danish, Swedish, Dutch, and Swiss, for these are Germanic nations. We therefore turn:

6.[e] To the <u>Poles</u>. In what concerns the political constitution they have a brutal freedom from the laws. One can attribute the repressions of the Poles, which are comparable to the feuds of the ancient Germans, primarily to this. They are vivacious, but without much wit and inventiveness. We find no good, original authors among them. The Poles are frivolous and therefore like to choose the French as models. They are not good hosts and are slow to pay, even if they always want to borrow because they never have money. They love splendor, but without any purity. Their dance depicts their character well. It begins with a

---

[a] *obligiren*. Kant's point is that the Latinate sounds strange in German.
[b] *mit dem Phlegma*
[c] Trans.: public law.
[d] Mar: *Prozesse*. Mro: *Processionen*.
[e] The number "1" in the Academy Edition has been changed to "6" to continue Kant's series.

Spanish *grandezza* and ends with a *mazurka*. The Pole is easily led,[a] but not civilized. There is no middle class in Poland; rather, everyone is either nobility or a peasant (the middle noble is only a titular noble). The noble man calls the peasant a *chlopiec*.[305] There the women are in the middle of the great world and the most distinguished state matters are handled in their rooms. – The Poles love their personal freedom, but they would sell their home country if they had to. They are very ceremonious and always address each other with "My sir." They are soft and certainly not as tough as the Russians. –

7. Russians have a stern attitude. They are actually an Asian[b] nation. They hate every other nation and hide their hatred only as long as they fear violence. Russian servants are loyal to their masters only as long as their fortune lasts, and later perhaps even help increase their misfortune. That is why Russian nobles prefer German servants. Spite[c] is secret enmity under the appearance of submissiveness; one attributes this to the Russians. Nodding[d] is hidden contumacy under the appearance of obedience, and one imputes this to the Poles – and one sees this also in Polish domestics. It generally consists in doing the opposite of what was instructed. It is a misconceived pride, and one plays a trick on his master because of it. One also finds this among children. The Russian is easily disciplined but hard to lead, and if Poles and Russians are led, they surprisingly become a diminished version of the French. The Russians really love commerce, and this perhaps comes from the fact that many crafts and artisans are not as common there as in other countries. The Russian peasant must be self-taught, one who himself makes his wheel, wagon, and sleigh. The Russian peasants travel around a great deal, and as a result of this and because they must purchase what they need, they are much more cultivated than the Prussian and Swabian peasants. – Therefore, whenever in a given nation the peasant is very refined, the nation as a whole is quite stupid. This seems to be a paradox, but it is nevertheless confirmed by experience and it can also be explained by this: namely, when a nation is more cultivated, it increases the number of people who practice the specialized arts that one learns mechanically. The peasant can then meet his needs at little cost and stay with his agricultural business. The Russians, etc., do not insist on anything in the spirit of the sciences and cannot understand and teach anything out of principles. Among their painters they have good copyists, but they have not had a single original painter. They are very inclined to remain under despotism. [They are] like the Oriental peoples who cannot create any concept of freedom for themselves and thus do not love freedom as much as the Poles do. The Orientals imagine all forms of government

25:1413

[a] *conduisert*
[b] *asiatische*
[c] *Tüke*
[d] *Niken*

25:1414 to be monarchical. They therefore always call the Prince of Orange the "King of Holland." They personify the East Indian Company by calling it John Company. Hence Sparrman, whom the Company sent on a trip to the Kaffirs,[a] called himself a "son of John Company."[306] They have a great respect for him, and they would quickly lose it if they knew that John Company was a society of merchants.

The Turks are honest, brave, sober, earnest, and proud. Among the ordinary people there is much common sense, and notwithstanding despotism, much pride and confidence in oneself. There is no slavery among them, for they have Christian slaves. The government is barbarian. They do not want to adopt any culture, or least of all discipline. If a Turk traveled through Europe, which he calls Frankestan just as he calls all of the European nations Franconia,[b] due to the thought of the Franks' invasion of the Ottoman empire, he would name: 1. France the land of fashion 2. Spain the land of ancestry (for one cares a great deal about ancestors there, so that often a duke marries the daughter of a peasant just because she comes from ancient, unmixed Spanish blood) 3. Italy the land of splendor 4. England the land of moods 5. Germany the land of titles 6. a land, the land of spite, once the land of boasting.[c][307] –

We have now sketched the character of the nations. Anyone is free to take away or add to these descriptions if he has profound reflections and data for it. It cannot be denied that a characterization is often accompanied by a caricature, but often the character of a nation is also a true caricature.

Now the political constitution of the form of government, education, in short, everything that pertains to anthropology, is grounded on the depiction of this national character. –
25:1415

THIRD CHAPTER

ON THE CHARACTER OF THE HUMAN SPECIES

One sees what is characteristic of the human species if one places the human being next to the animal and compares the two. In the system of nature, the human being belongs to the animal kingdom. However, if I see the human being as part of the world system, he belongs to the rational beings. Thus,

1. One can ask about the human being seen as an animal species, that is, in his physical character: a. Is the human being determined by nature to walk on two feet or four? Rousseau[308] contends the latter.

---

[a] *an die Caffern*   [b] *Franken*
[c] *6. Ein Land, das Land der Tüke eins das Prahlerland*, perhaps a reference to Russia, although it could refer to Poland or even Turkey.

A great Italian anatomist Moscati[309] joins him. He proves this from: 1. pregnancy, as the child in the fifth month of the pregnancy turns over in the uterus and comes down with his head. This would create much discomfort for the child and mother. If, however, the mother went on all fours, the child would lie horizontally. 2. the circulation of the blood, which would course much more easily through the body if it proceeded in the horizontal position and could not ascend; but this paradox was also sufficiently resolved by others from the corporeal structure of the human being.

Linneaus[310] also categorizes human beings in a different way, into *homines diurnos* and *nocturnos.*[a] The *cockroach albinos*[b] or Dondos, [a] people from western, central Africa, can only see in the dark; he calls them *nocturnos*. The human being is able to live in any climate, but an animal cannot do this. This ability derives from the human being's reason, for in order to nourish himself he can make use of any product, products from both land and sea.

The Negroes in Senegal eat plants that have not yet completely decomposed [and] soil that the Senegal River tosses up on the banks as sludge, which contains some fat.[311]

b. Is the human being a herbivorous or a carnivorous animal? On account of the structure of the stomach he is better classified as the latter, since herbivorous animals have a thick stomach. The vegetable foods bring acidic and alkaline moisture[312] into the human body; experience shows that. Milk from wet nurses that are fed with plain meat [is] not acidic when one cooks it and even adds drops of lemon juice. Wet nurse's milk that has been made after eating plain vegetables is similar to cow's milk; hence it is better for the infants if the wet nurses eat meat frequently.   25:1416

c. Is the human being a predator or not? The human being does not have a set of jaws or claws as predators do, yet compared to the animals he is much more fearsome than the strongest predator on account of his might with regard to deliberation.

d. Is the human being created for society or not? The human being is not created for the hive like the bees, but he is also not placed in the world as a solitary animal; rather, on the one hand, he has a propensity toward society due to his needs, which are far greater for him than for the animals. On the other hand, the human being also has a principle toward unsociability, for a society that is too large limits and discomforts him, and forces him to be on his guard. It can be supposed that human beings must have to a great extent displaced each other from their dwellings because one finds them in the most barren regions, where they certainly

---

[a] Trans.: diurnal and nocturnal humans
[b] *Die Kakerlaks Albinos*, presumably from near Dondo, Angola

would not have gone without force; but [without this displacement] the earth would also surely not be completely populated.

2. Considered as an intelligence for the world system, the human being is of a completely special kind.

A. Compared to the animal. Every animal already knows through instinct what it has to do, with the exception of birds; the latter learn their song from older birds. Experience teaches this, for some birds, if they have not yet heard their parents sing much, can produce the song of other species of birds. The main difference with human beings is that they must be taught. One who gives the instruction is an instructor,[a] but one who disciplines is a tutor.[b] The first lesson is instruction in language, for it is hard to believe that it is innate for the human being, for if it were there would have to be only one language now. The second difference consists in:

B. [The fact that] the human being has himself to thank for everything. On the one hand this is a great honor that nature has bestowed on us; but on the other hand it is a great burden since in the process it becomes very difficult to become happy and promote and maintain one's prosperity.

C. With the animal, every individual reaches the destiny[c] of its being in this life already. With the human being, the species first reaches the destiny of humanity from generation to generation, since a generation always adds something to the enlightenment of the previous one, and thus it makes the [next] generation more perfectly endowed than it was. The human being has himself to thank for enlightenment not only in arts and sciences, but also in morals.

D. Which is best, the rough state of nature or the civilized one where the human being is cultivated? The latter state, which, however, we do not yet know and where all the germs of the human being will have been developed for the best constitution[d] of the civil society, will be the best. There are two endpoints of the enlightenment and of the progress of human destiny – namely:

1.) the crude state of the human being (state of nature)

2.) the cultivated state (civilized state)

The intermediate state between these two is the worst. In the first one, the human being was happy negatively; in the other one, he will be happy positively. The intermediate state between these two is the time of luxury, refinement, taste, sociability, etc. Now to that extent Rousseau is certainly right to prefer the state of nature to this state. But this does not apply to the civilized state; but that the human being should arrive at this civilized state through much discomfort, war, and its vile consequences, this occurred because, at least on our globe, pain for the human being

[a] *informator*
[b] *Hofmeister*
[c] *Bestimmung*
[d] *Constitution*

is a spur of activity. Every creature surely reaches his destiny in the end, i.e., reaches the time in which all of its natural predispositions are developed and come to maturity. The main difference from the animals, for the human being, is that with him the entire species first reaches its destiny through several generations. – It is admittedly hard that others should first reap the fruits of our brooding efforts, but experience and the annals of human history show us this without the possibility of making any objection to the contrary. The crude state of nature was good in some respects, since human beings inclined toward noble simplicity and did not know any needs or desires (though only out of ignorance). But, if poets and philosophers call this age the golden and fortunate one, this occurs out of a propensity toward laziness. This age was the time of the crudest ignorance, for human beings nourished themselves from trees like apes and did not need to work due to a lack of needs. One could call the age of the developed culture of humanity the true golden age; the former age was the infancy of human beings, and only one who wishes to be a child could desire it. 25:1418

E. But how does it come about that human beings have brought so much evil upon themselves through culture? –

α. The natural stages do not coincide with the civil ones; from this an antimony of good and ill*a* arises. In the state of nature, the human being is much better able to propagate his kind as well as to support it immediately. – In the state of nature, the human being is able to generate his species as early as the age of sixteen, and in the state of nature he would thereupon also already be able to maintain his species. In the intermediate state, it is true that the human being is perhaps able to propagate his species, but he is not able to maintain it. He is first able to do this around the thirtieth year. If, namely, he is sixteen years old, in the former state he is thus already a man, but in the latter state he is a youth. Now here a contradiction arises. But if the natural stages ran parallel to the civil ones, many vices would go away, e.g., if the human being were first able to propagate in his thirtieth year.

The human being was determined by nature to maintain himself and his species, but nature also wanted him to come out of the state of nature. From the perspective of the first aim, nature had to give him the drive to propagate early, but on the other hand he had to deviate from nature, and from that a conflict arose which, with regard to the good that the latter aim produced, surely itself was the root of some ill with regard to the former aim. 25:1419

2. The drive toward culture has no relationship to the length of the lifespan, for if the human being reaches his sixtieth year, when he could make use of the attained culture the most, he becomes obtuse, slows

---

a Uebels

down,[a] and must vacate his place to another person. However, this also was necessary, for if no human being stood down, human beings would crowd each other out. In this way the wisdom of Providence had to institute this disproportion. But this culture itself makes the human being abandon the state of nature. It is bound up with many hardships and, due to the disproportion between a lifetime and intellectual curiosity, the human being must hurry and even incur hardship by himself. –

3. The human being is free by nature, and all human beings are by nature equal.[b] – In this the human being also differs from animal nature – for the human being is an animal that needs a master and cannot exist without a head.[c] And here again a hardship arose from culture, as one sees the inequality among human beings arise through it, which in turn results in the oppression of the less cultivated. Rousseau's three paradoxes[313] are based on this.

1. Of the harm to human beings done by culture or the sciences

2. Of the harm to human beings done by civilization[d] or by inequality in the civil constitution; but one cannot think of a civil constitution without inequality; accordingly, of the harm to human beings done by the civil constitution. –

25:1420

3. Of the harm done by the artificial method in moralizing

On 2. We can maintain culture and civilization only in the inequality of the civil constitution, although this inequality is very disagreeable. Indeed even war, the greatest ill,[e] is even a means of attaining culture and of reaching the final destiny of human beings. –

Here we have only spoken of the animal determination of the human being. But now we must speak also of the spiritual determination of the human being. If this is done, the animal determination of the human being will no longer stand in opposition to its spiritual determination. – In short, Rousseau examined only the one side of the matter in his paradoxes. He attended only to the harms that the departure from the state of nature seems to have caused, but did not attend to the advantages arising through the culture of the human being; this opposition between the animal and spiritual nature of the human being itself ultimately contributes to the production of the final destiny of the human being. –

For if, e.g., the human being is at the age when he can propagate but not yet maintain his species,[f] then he is required to leave behind

---

[a] *vegetirt*
[b] Following Brandt and Stark's suggestion: *gleich* (equal). Mro: *einander gleich* (equal to one another).
[c] *Oberhaupt*   [e] *Uebel*
[d] *Civilisirung*   [f] *Art*

animality and make it possible to maintain his species through industry and the application of his powers. And thus in part arose the sciences and the arts. – Evil[a] originates out of the opposition between humanity and animality, or between the physical, natural predispositions and the moral ones; the inevitable evil in the determination of the human being is the spur toward the good that the human being must perform. – There are three natural predispositions in the human being: 1. laziness 2. cowardice and 3. falsity.

On 1. Laziness itself ultimately becomes an incentive for industry and thus is even useful, without taking into consideration that scoundrels, as well as every human being, would commit much more evil if they did not have this propensity. For all labors are driven by the prospect of laziness, which puts them into motion. Our natural powers would also in the end be overextended and severed if nature had not placed a counterweight in the human being, that is, such a propensity to repose and inactivity. –

On 2. If all human beings had as much stoutheartedness as some exceptional individuals have, if no fear of death controlled them, then every human being who got in a fight would perish. Hence nature thus gave the human being cowardice in order to protect him from the various dangers into which by his own volition he could throw himself. – Moreover, this predisposition was necessary in order to maintain the species. –

25:1421

On 3. The human being is secretive and at most is frank only when he supposes he has encountered a genuinely good moral character. He would also be contemptible, if he were too frank. From this [kind of] reservation[b] arise dissimulation (reserve[c]) and simulation (hypocrisy[d]), which together constitute the character of falsity. The human being wants to give himself priority over others; one wants to dominate others, and this brings about hypocrisy and falsity. Hence, when civil society is more developed, the human being becomes more and more false. De Luc says:[314] "Human beings are not as cruel as one represents them. If only they did not have a certain secret falsity, they [would] assist each other gladly." – It has already been adduced that if one takes a human face and changes only a part of it without changing the other parts, a disproportion and true caricature arises. It is also like this with the moral qualities of the human being. If one changes one quality but not all of them, all proportion is immediately ruined. It is thus a good thing that as long as human beings are not yet completely civilized, they are not frank. For if they were that way, endless harm would arise through the improper use of this frankness by the ill-disposed. If the natural predispositions

---

[a] *Böse*
[b] *Zurükhalten*

[c] *Zurükhaltung*
[d] *Verstellung*

are developed only half way, they simply bring about evil, yet all of the good pertaining to the final destiny is nevertheless ultimately produced through this evil. The human being is unsociable and in the state of nature every foreigner is an enemy; as Cicero[315] also remarks, *hostis* used to mean nothing other than foreigner. – This unsociability arouses fear, drives human beings from one pole to the other, and in the process populates the earth. Thus the savages view every foreigner as an enemy, and they also eat anything that falls into their hands. Thus the knight Marion du Fresne[316] reports that during his travels savages once captured and ate fifteen of his sailors, and adds that the human being is a fearsome animal if he is not in civil society. It is hard to prove to savages that one is their friend. Among the New Hollanders,[a] one does this through nose contact. Only then can one actually enter into their dwellings, *hippahs*, which are inaccessible sites on steep cliffs by the sea and places that are fortified by palisades.[317] But the tight civil association is further brought about by this unsociability; this produces more culture and refinement of taste. Without this unsociability there would never have arisen a firm civil association, but at most only the arcadian life of a shepherd, i.e., a life full of laziness with the best attitudes, whereby the human being would never be perfected or cultivated and would not be more esteemed than any other animal species. One still finds such a life in Tahiti,[318] where laziness dominates all the inhabitants, as the sea offers them fish and fruits give them their bread. Even their fishing is also an idleness that only appears to be busy. However, unsociability drove human beings into the state where one strove for the belongings of others and thereby came into collision with others, and because of this they were required to elect to adopt a commanding head and in this way to bring the systematic into the civil condition.[b] Through culture the needs of the human being became great, and this was also a tie that linked human beings more firmly to one another. Thus laziness was fought against and the human being was required to be industrious and hard working. The civil state is therefore the only condition in which all the natural predispositions of the human being can be developed. The civil condition is now again either a state[c] or a power,[d] the first according to its internal condition, the second according to its external condition. But the latter do not make up a universal association, for they do not recognize any laws above them. War then also arises from this because a state fears the power of another; this is barbarism. – It is not clear from this if it will cease. One can call "barbaric freedom" every freedom of the human being that is not restricted through laws, but instead is without ties and is connected with the oppression of others. – The princes, the rulers of the state, are to be

25:1422

25:1423

[a] *Neuhollaendern*, i.e., the Māori
[b] *Zustand*
[c] *Staat*
[d] *Macht*

viewed as individual human beings in the condition of savagery, for they recognize no laws other than those that they make themselves and they carry out everything with other states by using force. It is true that they derive everything through dispossessions*a* while the opposing member does just the same, but by doing this just as little is determined about who has right as is determined through war; rather, who has greater force determines what right is. – Thus even Rousseau³¹⁹ says: "It is better to be their enemy than their citizen." For through these wars the states become barbaric even on the inside. In order to avoid this barbaric state, there must be:

1. A rule of law. 2. A judge who administers justice.*b* 3. A power that holds strong oversight over these judicial sentences. In this way the Amphictyonic League³²⁰ of the Greeks and the plan³²¹ of St. Pierre and Rousseau would be satisfied, although the princes still ridicule it as they do other chimeras. Now is such a condition likely to ever arrive? One must at least hope for it, and in fact a similar kind of institution has actually already been created for that purpose. For we already no longer deal so directly with war, but rather there are mediators who seek to prevent wars and who also perhaps need threats against the assailants, if from the reason, *tum tua res agitur paries dum proximus ardet,*c or from what La Fontaine*d* mentions in his fable of the frogs.³²² One frog told another one that the bulls and steers were at war with each other, and the other replied, "What is that to you?" and the first frog replied, "The bulls that were defeated retired to the marsh and could crush us all." – But it is not clear if this condition will appear. For there will first have to be a long-lasting government. –

25:1424

The civil constitution includes:

1. Freedom. This includes: 2. the law, or the restriction of the freedom of an individual in order not to disturb the freedom of another; besides this, there must also 3. be an authority that applies the laws. Freedom without laws and force is the freedom of the savages and nomads. With this [kind of] freedom, I am always in danger of losing my freedom. Freedom with law and force creates equality among human beings. But freedom with laws and without force is the most absurd thinkable, and it is the true Polish freedom. Freedom with force and without law is a *contradictio in adjecto,*e for that is unthinkable. Force and law without freedom is despotism, and it is the Turkish government. There is

---

a *Deductionen*   *b* *der Recht spräche*

c Kant loosely quotes from Horace, *Epistles* 1.18.84–85: *Nam tua res agitur, paries cum proximus ardet, et neglecta solent incendia sumere uires.* (When your neighbor's wall is on fire, it is your own concern: and neglected flames are likely to gain in strength.)

d Following Stark and Brandt's suggestion: *La Fontaine.* Mro: *La Motte.*

e Trans.: contradiction in terms

little difference between a Polish government and a despotic government with regard to the evil that arises therefrom; the former state can never constitute a harmonious whole. Hatred of the law is a true mark of a barbarian condition. – They prefer to tolerate the greatest drudgery rather than remove something according to the laws. – The Turks and Russians belong to this kind, and their true antipodes are the English, who recognize nothing as right that does not happen in accordance with the laws. This again reveals a high degree of civilization. For human beings, the state of nature is to be viewed as most perfect in the beginning. This first state is therefore the state of innocence. Evil, as well as the good that lies within human beings, has not yet germinated. – Now the first attempt that the human being makes of his freedom is always faulty.

25:1425

All the evil and all the ill that the human being commits arises from the crudity of nature with respect to the use of our freedom. All kinds of ills arose because human beings crowded each other out, for they had not yet thought of the rule through which freedom was restricted, or through which the public will would be restricted to a final purpose without restricting the private will. The wisdom of Providence availed itself of war and discord in order to produce culture.

The *status civilis* is a particular state[a] to which human beings in the crude condition do not submit and that has a commanding head over it who: 1. can legislate laws and 2. has the authority[b] to require adherence to these laws. Seeing how the civil condition distinguishes itself from the other one already belongs to the cultivation[c] of the civil condition. Now civil society is the means whereby the cultivation of the human being is produced and in which he gets closer and closer to his final destiny. A tree that grows in the open field grows crooked and bent, but in the forest it grows straight, as its branches cannot expand very much because other trees rob it of sun and space. This is the true image of the savage and civilized conditions. In the civilized condition one resists the arbitrary expansion of another person. He cannot thoughtlessly enjoy his freedom because law and authority restrict him. In the civil condition the human being must act according to competition among wills and he cannot do what he wants. Only here will his talents and capacities be able to be developed. But this civil condition arose only through a series of ills, since, namely, the freedom of one person hindered the freedom of another. The perfection of the civil condition is based on the development of the natural predispositions for the final[d] destiny of the human being. Humanity is now on the outermost boundaries of civilization, but

---

[a] *Staat.* The term *status civilis* means "civil condition."
[b] *Gewalt*   [d] *endlichen*
[c] *Cultur*

not of morality.[a] The great masterpiece that nature has striven to bring forth through the perfect development of the natural predispositions is the perfect, civil constitution or its agreement with the ends of humanity. Now why have all the ancient civil constitutions been overturned? The cause of this is the lack of such constitutions, since they were perhaps of service for the flourishing of the arts and sciences but not for maintaining the state, when through luxury it had arrived at a high level of needs per individual. Accordingly, all of the laws of the Greeks lacked force,[b] and the force of the Oriental peoples lacked laws. Virtue and vice, religion, and arts and sciences are products of the political constitution. For when a state has ascended to a high degree of culture, the multiplicity of needs grows through luxuries and this leads to the stifling of freedom. Now, however, people who are used to freedom do not want to let their freedom be limited, and the destruction of the state arises in this way. It was like this in the case of the Greeks. All that was great and sublime in the sciences comes from them, and the rest is not worth our attention. But they could not maintain themselves because there was no force that limited them. – Now if human beings come (not through concoctions to improve the civil condition; no human being can have insight into this because he who has force in hand will not abdicate from the throne) to have insight into the best civil constitution, then what should we think of international law? International law will not, then, become any better through war, but rather through a judicial sentence. The kings will themselves no longer administer justice, but will submit themselves to a universal amphictyonic league. Then a universal peace will reign over our globe. The natural predispositions aim at the development of our talents through 1. the highest cultivation 2. civilization 3. moralization. To date we are still without a plan in culture, and luxury only enlivens it. The majority of human beings are still crude and the basic development of our talents is still missing. Even the sciences merely satisfy the taste of the time and do not aim at universal benefits. As for civilization, with us it is simply more an effect of taste and fashion, whereas it should be grounded on maxims toward what is best in general. To date we are only refined and polished, but we lack what constitutes a good citizen. As for morality, we can say that we have not yet gotten very far. If we praise virtue, we do so only because we cannot deny its worth and we want people to see that we have it. Customs without virtue, sociability without righteousness and friendship, and vanity without true love of honor, indicate well enough that morality does not yet have right standing with us.

Now what are the means of improving the civil society and constitution? 1. education 2. legislation 3. religion.

25:1426

25:1427

---

[a] *Moralitaet*   [b] *Gewalt*

<However, all three must be public and in conformity with nature; through religion the inviolable seal must be imprinted on morals.>

On 1. Education must be negative. It must omit everything that is contrary to nature. The child should already be good as a child. All harsh coercion in the cultivation of talents must be omitted so that afterwards, when they come into freedom, they do not become lazy. The children's freedom should thus remain with them, and yet they must be required to act from duty.

On 2. Legislation must also be negative. It must not limit the freedom of the citizen, but rather each citizen must, so to speak, have his voice and yet at the same time be held to act according to the laws.

On 3. Religion must also be negative. – All learned definitions must be omitted from the discourse, even if erudition itself has to be found in religion.

We are in a threefold immaturity, so to speak.

1. As children in the household setting, where one must always act according to the standards^a of others.

2. In the civil condition. We are oriented by laws that we did not legislate and that we often do not even know, for in the case of laws as well, science swells to a puff of erudition that we ourselves cannot know. He who has no property, but must act according to what he has and be content with it, is called a child. – But now one finds that in every state that is despotic, monarchic, aristocratic, etc., human beings are always immature. Why is that the case? The human being is constituted in such a way that he can never exist without a master,^{b} for if he did not have one he would restrict the freedom of the other. For this reason, therefore, human beings are required to elect a head.^{c} Now one cannot, however, get this head from a higher class of creatures. The head is a human being, and he therefore needs other people above him; but this does not go on and on, and in this manner justice and freedom are found in the authority of a human being. Now suppose also that this human being were perfectly just. Could there ever be such a person?

3. We are in a pious immaturity. – One still prescribes to human beings religious concepts that they either must not examine or are not able to, even if we otherwise have enough skill. There is something convenient about this immaturity, for as it were one keeps for himself a curator who cares about his practical affairs. A king^{323} once had his confessor tell him what he had to do to become blessed – the confessor prescribed a spate of ceremonious actions, fasting, deprivation, etc. But the king, who was very punctilious, told his confessor that the latter had to sign that note

25:1428

---

^{a} Urbildern ^{c} Oberhaupt
^{b} Herrn

so that, if something were forgotten, it would not change his (the king's) reckoning. He wanted to comply with what was written down.

We see that anyone can modify religion as he pleases because one accepts everything without examining it. An eloquent example of this is perhaps Mohammed, whose wisdom was probably not very extensive. – We cannot blame the clerics for everything that is deficient in religion, either, for it certainly requires an astonishingly great deal to cleanse and purify the concepts of an entire public. In the end we will perhaps see that, concerning the well-being of the world, everything depends on education, and here the government should think more about religion and morality[a] in order to make human beings better. – But they do not focus on that very much because they have the power in their hands and can use force to compel immoral people to act in accordance with the laws. In schools they thus concentrate more on writing, arithmetic, reading, etc., than on basic education in religion as the foundation of morality and its seal. From all of this, we see that the final destiny of   25:1429 humanity will then be reached, if we have a perfect civil constitution, i.e., if we find ourselves in the highest degree of cultivation, civilization, and moralization so that we reach such a condition, a condition where the general well-being of the whole of humanity is no longer interrupted by wars and various ills, where the highest culture, civilization, and moralization is reached, where a general peace on earth will reign, and where conflict among princes will be resolved through judicial sentences; in short, where the state of nature will no longer stand in opposition to the civilized one. That we can one day attain this condition can certainly be hoped for. But what Providence will use as a means thereto remains inscrutable and completely impossible for us to discover because our reason here approaches the boundaries of perpetual reason, which alone is in a position to foresee and to order future things, means, and ends. Finis. 31 October.

Finis

---

[a] *Moralitaet*

Anthropology Busolt, 1788–1789

Translator's introduction

This is both the latest and the briefest of the lecture transcriptions published in Volume 25 of the Akademie Ausgabe, comprising about 100 printed pages in that edition. It was apparently the work of a single transcriber. This text is fragmentary, and omits the organizing divisions found in *Friedländer*, *Menschenkunde* and *Mrongovius*. But it seems to follow the same general pattern as the other lecture transcriptions, both early and late, covering first the theoretical faculty, then the faculty of taste, and finally the faculty of desire.

The selections here are from the introductory remarks about methodology, self-consciousness and obscure (or unconscious) representations, and also from Kant's first mention of the three maxims of thinking, presented in several of his later published works: the *Critique of the Power of Judgment*, *Anthropology from a Pragmatic Point of View*, and the *Jäsche Logic*.

Lecture of the Winter Semester 1788-1789 [?] Based on the transcription Busolt

[Excerpts]

TRANSLATED BY ALLEN W. WOOD 25:1435

PROLEGOMENA

One makes a distinction among scholastic cognition and worldly cognition.

One has scholastic cognition if one can communicate one's information according to a certain system. One possesses worldly cognition, however, when one can teach another this information in conversations or in society in such a way that one leaves out what has little interest and yet is intelligible enough, and it is consequently agreeable. Whoever cannot do this is called a 'pedant'. A pedant, apart from this, can be a skilled man, but is only lacking in the respect just mentioned --. What concerns us in the world for the most part, what sets in motion our inclinations, our desires, and our will, is the human being. Worldly cognition is thus just the same as cognition of the human being. When this observation of human beings (*anthropography*) is brought to a science, it is called 'anthropology', and one attains to this science:

1) through long and manifold experiences and through travels.

Remarks: If one wants to collect anthropological information through travels, then one must previously have a sufficiently connected knowledge of human beings and with it a certain plan, so that one can arrange the observations of the differences among human beings that one sees in travels.

2) If one makes attentive observations of oneself and with other human beings.

Such a knowledge of human beings is possible because we have daily opportunity in our business affairs and in society to acquire anthropognosis. If through experiences without any aim and through observations we get knowledge of human beings for ourselves and present them in a connection, according to a certain method, or in a word, systematically, then they are a science, which one calls 'anthropology'.

515

There are three species of doctrines:

25:1436 1) We must seek to acquire skill; through theoretical sciences that can be used for all sorts of discretionary works.

2) We must make an effort to form ourselves according to the manner of thought and the capacities of the human beings with whom we have to do, so that we do not become too difficult or too much of an obstacle to them. Anthropology teaches us this, by showing how we can use human beings to our end. The rules of prudence are taught not in the schools but in worldly cognition.

3. The doctrine of wisdom. This leads us not merely to advantages but [teaches us] how through powers of the soul we can do without things that are not necessary, and how we can find the best choice in our action. One can express these three species of doctrine in another way and more briefly:

1. through the scholastic science in which we are *cultivated*.

2. through the doctrine of prudence in which we are *civilized*.

3. through the doctrine of wisdom, in which we learn to treasure ourselves or in which we become *moralized*.

Furthering doctrines of skill are practical

------ morals ---- moral

------ prudence --- pragmatic

Thus a history is of great utility and a source of anthropology, if it is treated pragmatically, so that, namely, I can draw a doctrine of prudence from history, which makes me prudent and careful in respect of the choice of my actions, because I become ever more acquainted with the constitution of human beings. Such a pragmatic anthropology is now our end. It should not be a theoretical anthropology, which merely poses questions and contains in itself only psychological investigations; on the contrary, we want to give instruction as to how through observation one might come to be acquainted with the constitution of human beings so as to be able to use them here to our end. One might pose a question here: whether it is possible to get a complete anthropology. That does not matter, because the human being's mind can deceive itself very much. Anthropology rests on empirical data, given through experience. The 25:1437 latter one has either

a) through art, and specifically

aa) through observation when observe the object as long as we want

Remark: The human being, however, does not want to be observed. For as soon as one notices and sees it, he will either dissemble or deceive himself. In both cases the human being is not the one he was at first. If one wants to observe, then he must not be noticed at all doing it.

bb) Through experiments. Through them the human being can also not be observed. One can indeed make experiments with animals and things, but not with human beings, because as soon as he notices it, he will do precisely the opposite of what one wants him to do. So if I want to annoy him, he will straightway be certain to complain.[a]

b) Through general experience of others.

Although in this way anthropology will be imperfect, it is still indispensable and of great utility.

1. In the art of education.[b]

2. In respect of the influence we have on others. Especially those in command, who by a suitable knowledge of human beings can go to work in an entirely different way, since without it not everything can be accomplished by force.

3. In respect of the influence on morality and religion, since one can give these duties the power of incentives through this knowledge.

This chararacteristic (for anthropology is properly a *characteristic*) is divided into doctrines in regard to their methods:

1. Of the character of the person
2. ------ of sexes
3. ------ of nations
4. ------ of the species

It is difficult to know humanity according to all its principles, because we cannot make a comparison between human beings and other rational beings. Hence it is a great matter to determine the character of humanity in anthropology.

25: 1438

ON CONSCIOUSNESS OF ONESELF

'I' is that on which the human being places the greatest attention. In all thoughts and actions, he places a worth on his person. The interest of the human being accumulates to the concept 'I'. If, however, in a society someone constantly intrudes the I, then one calls him an 'egoist', and calls the thing 'egoism'. This is a great error, and advertises the fact that he has little prudence and especially little manners. For one always gains more if one brings other human beings to speak of himself. This way of bringing others along, so that he shows his own skill and his worth over against me, is the best way of gaining the other's inclination and respect.

Montaigne, although his way of writing was rude, has gained enduring approval. He speaks always of himself, but because he is presenting a knowledge of humanity, he cannot properly do otherwise and tests himself and his inclinations in order from it to draw conclusions about others.

---

[a] *lermen*. The text here seems to be corrupt.
[b] *Erziehungskunst*

The moral egoist is the one who blinds himself so that he places little value on what is outside himself. One must keep a tight rein on this emotion of self-love.

The aesthetic egoist is the same one just talked about. Except that he says something about himself by not begrudging the privilege to others.

The physical egoist who always puts himself in the position of an object. – Thus, for example, people who are hypochondriacs constantly pay attention to themselves, and since they always have themselves as an object, they often utter something absurd in society. All this feeling of oneself is actually counterproductive. For what I feel is of no use. The more information one has about objects, however, the more useful one is. With an ever-present feeling of oneself, one loses one's entire activity and liveliness, the human being becomes a true dreamer, because his imagination, which is not led by his understanding, produces all sorts of chimaeras and the worst moods and follies. With-

25:1439 drawal from this self-feeling is an elevation of the mind which is effected if I let my mind roam into different representations through a voluntary distraction in society. By which ceases the attention to oneself. A healthy soul is always concerned with something outside itself. A sick soul is always concerned ever and again with itself, and thus arises fantastic beings and enthusiasm. – Through great attention one is either awkward[a] or affected. One is awkward when in social relations one observes too great a punctiliousness and thus in the end excites mistrust against oneself. One does not know how to show oneself to advantage. But all this comes from paying too much attention to oneself. From this discomfiture it arises that the human being makes things worse than he would have otherwise. Not to be awkward is therefore a great advantage.

One is affected when in social relations one strives that another should have a favorable opinion of one's person. But this affectation actually excites laughter or sympathy in other people. Human beings can also easily conclude that apart from the affectation he is nothing at all. At best, such a human being can be humiliated by indifference and mockery.

Naïveté is a natural way of behaving, without art, where truthfulness and freedom are combined. If one is not awkward or affected, then one can have this naïveté. It is a nature that looks like art. – The attention to external propriety does not reveal itself, but there is nonetheless a modesty, which, however, is without premeditation. – But one does not always use the word with this significance: on the contrary, usually those one calls 'naïve' are children, young ladies and peasants. One also calls this an *air dégagé*.

[a] *genirt*

ON OBSCURE REPRESENTATIONS

Obscure representations are those of which we are conscious not immediately, but rather through their effects. Everything contained in our
memory lies in the field of obscure representations. Many dispute the 25:1440
existence of obscure representations and say: How can one be convinced
of the existence of obscure representations if we are not conscious of
them? To this one can answer: It is not necessary to be conscious through
sensation, if one can come to consciousness by inferences. Thus the
ancients, for example, explained the shimmer of the Milky Way as a
light of many stars, even though they did not know the stars in this Way
due to their lack of telescopes.

These obscure representations actually exist and play a great role in
human beings. If the human being became conscious all at once of all
these representations, then he would be astonished by the great store
of them. Yet the faculty for deriving these representations is so limited in us that they come to light only individually and on occasion. –
One can represent the human soul as a map, whose illuminated parts
are the clear ones, especially bright, the distinct ones, and the unilluminated parts signify the obscure representations. Obscure [ones] occupy
the biggest place, and are the ground of the clear ones. Human beings
are often become a play of obscure representations. If a human being has
doubts about a thing, and in this thing the representations are obscure,
that is a scruple. If they become clear, then they are objections. These
obscure representations are an agreeable arrangement for those human
beings, because the alteration of light and shadow is much loved, e.g. a
witty notion. The sudden displacement of thoughts in us and the sudden
livening of our power of thought is agreeable, because in the case of an
apparently initial obscurity, a host of thoughts is discovered to us all at
once. By means of obscure representations we seek either to strengthen
or weaken the strength of an impression, e.g. by means of the word 'com- 25:1441
modity'[a] the strength of the impression is very much weakened, because
I come to this one through a host of other representations and in time
the representation loses its impression. Through artificially obscurings,
by which the imagination is made to create more, it happens that the
impression of a representation becomes so much the stronger, e.g. in all
the expressions of gallantry belonging to both sexes. As soon as obscurity
betrays the slightest traces of light, our attention strains itself.

Our sense is often somewhat clear, but we are not conscious of it and
we can first become conscious of it through inferences. Thus, e.g., when
someone is walking into the distance, one believes one sees him, but not
his eyes, his nose, and the like. But if I do not see his eyes, I also do not

[a] *Commotitaet*

see a spot as large as his eyes, and so it comes that in the end we do not see him at all. But we do see him, so we must also see the parts of him. Here is another example. Suppose the moon is a body like the earth, as it actually is; then it must have animals and other things like our earth. If there is a horse on the moon, then I must see it, for if I do not see it, then I also do not see the spot that is as big as a horse on the moon; and hence all spots too that are not as big as a horse, I do not see all of them; consequently I also do not see the entire moon. But I do see the moon, and also its parts, consequently also this horse, but I am not conscious

25:1480 of it...

OF THE PRINCIPLES OF THINKING

1. Thinking for oneself
2. Thinking in the place of another
3. Always thinking in agreement with oneself.[1]
Thinking for oneself helps one to:
a) make his reason the highest touchstone of truth.

b) have better grounded insight into what one generates from thinking for oneself, so that it never will or can escape from one. But one must also be able to put oneself in the place of another, in order to think the matter over from another point of view. One must also be able to think consistently,[a] so that one principle can subsist along with another. Yet someone who has actually false principles can also think consistently. – Enthusiasm judges inconsistently. The lack of ability to think in the place of another is not good. One must be able completely to put oneself in the position of another, because then one can protect oneself well against false judgments. Consistent thinking is also very good, especially when 25:1481 the principles are good, for then all the consequences must also be good. It is very advantageous to be consistent in the maxims for one's actions, as long as the maxims are good. This usage is twofold: theoretical, which has to do with consistent judgments, and practical, which has to do with consistent conduct, acting according to good principles, and determining one's will according to them. One could call the use of reason that does not permit disputation[b] 'mechanism' or 'despotism'. Every mechanical power of thought is false, for one that is accustomed to it will never achieve anything good, because one can never be compelled to that of which one ought to be convinced at the same time through principles.

The use of reason is very necessary. For in order to learn, one needs memory and understanding, to apply what one has learned one needs judgment; in order to examine it by turning back to the principles of the rules, and extending one's judgment, to this belongs reason. For

[a] *Consequent*   [b] *Räsoniren*

the first skill is required which consists in knowing and being able, and rests on understanding. To the second belongs prudence, to bring your knowledge to the man, to use and be able to apply his skill toward his ends. For the third, wisdom to judge about the true worth of things. This is a need of reason.

The judging of true worth proceeds according to principles and not according to particular taste and examples. 'Rationalizing'[a] ought to mean 'using reason', but properly it is only an empty use of reason which contains nothing in regard to the true ends. Wisdom is a practical use of reason. Thinking for oneself is enlightenment or thinking according to a commonly ruling maxim. Extensive information does not belong to this: instead, it is only using your own reason as the supreme touchstone of truth. To think in the place of another is the concept of broad mind-edness[b]. – A narrow-minded person[c] is not one who has learned little, but who has no broad-minded concepts. His mode of thought is limited, he cannot put himself in the place of another, but judges merely from his own standpoint in his own way, and never sees a matter from another point of view. Such a human being one calls 'narrow-minded' because he has limited and not broad-minded concepts. – To think consistently is also called 'well-grounded thinking',[d] so that one always remains in connection and is in agreement with another. This mode of thought is the finest. Extraordinary attentiveness is required for it. Hence very few human beings think this way, which is also actually good, for the greatest ills arise when one thinks consistently with false principles. They nonetheless remain of great importance. But much, and especially much experience, pertains to refraining from erring principles, so as to discover all other errors and to judge the connection precisely.

25:1482

Philosophy is the legislator of reason in every species of human knowing. We have need of it everywhere, because it teaches us how we may make use of the supreme touchstone of truth. Principles or fundamental concepts and fundamental rules require attentiveness to one kind of object. This is very necessary and also very difficult, because there should be only one kind of object of thoughts and not of the senses. Mathematics can be of much aid for attentiveness through intuition. But if one wants to direct one's attention to concern with one kind of object immediately through concepts of reason, this is very difficult. The distraction of thought, where one can attend to nothing more, applies to speculative minds. Distraction is voluntary and involuntary; it is voluntary when one lets one's thoughts roam voluntarily to all kinds of objects, and chiefly in society where there is speaking. In society one can best distract oneself

---

[a] *Vernünfttteln*, which could also be translated 'ratiocinating', 'quibbling', or 'arguing'.
[b] *Ein erweiternder Begriff*   [d] *Gründlich denken*
[c] *Ein Bornierter*

25:1483 and give his thoughts free rein. Only society must (as Lord Chesterfield expresses it), like the number of the muses, not be more than nine, and like the graces, it must be not be less than three.[2] For otherwise society divides itself into smaller parts and comes to ruin through this. The genuinely agreeable that is to be communicated by the society is lacking, and so the proper delight ceases. In a small society there is still talking, but it is done in secret. In general here there is lacking the right style for intimacy and the proper spirit of communication. In such societies the expression of laughter also has its place in talking, i.e. if someone in such a society wants to make it smaller and for this reason begins to talk to the whole society; then no one hears him, but he will be teased on this side and that. Shortly he jumps into the laughter but no one respects him, whether he started it or not. But in a society that is not divided up (which can take place only when the society is not too large), it goes otherwise; there the communication is general, intimacy has its place, the mind is voluntarily brought to distraction by all kinds of objects and one is at the same time strengthened by this movement of the mind, because the mind is led to different objects.

Distraction is [also] *involuntary*. If in this state one is drawn to something to which one does not want to turn his attention. If servants, who otherwise have nothing to think about, are distracted, then they have in their heads either an intrigue or something to worry about or a love story. The first is probably the case. If ladies, who always roam about with their thoughts and therefore rightly belong in society – when they are distracted,[a] then either they are in love or something else of the sort is ruling them. This involuntary distraction is a sickness in which attention is always directed to oneself, and are indulging the thought that awakens displeasure. Human beings who have this sort of subtle distraction and always build castles in the air, are of no use in society and are harmful and a burden on society. Such people are commonly considered the fools of society. For if a distracted person is in society then there is
25:1530 always something to laugh at....

DOCTRINE OF METHOD

The character: is twofold, either the character of a thing or that of a human being. The character of a human being is the mark distinguishing one human being from another, or the human being from another being. This is the character of the person, that of the sex, that of a nation, and finally the character of the species. One can consider the human being

[a] *Distrahiret*

as a nature and as a free being. As a natural being one considers him according to the predispositions encountered in him, and that is the character of the human being as an animal. With this consideration we have made a beginning. The character of a human being as a free being is posited in his will.

OF THE CHARACTERISTIC OF THE PERSON

Talent or natural aptitude[a] shows the temperament. Further the character or mode of thought is added to it. These elements constitute the character of the human being *in sensu latiore*. Natural aptitude signifies the natural predispositions in regard to receptivity. Every human being has a certain ground from this natural aptitude. This natural aptitude is the receptivity of a disposition or a teaching or discipline, under 'discipline' one understands the limitation of inclination through a certain rule. – Discipline is properly negative. The human being assumes discipline when he himself denies it so far that he accommodates himself to others. A pliant natural aptitude is always good for those who educate it, otherwise it is no great praise. For such a human being can also easily assume bad forms. One understands under natural aptitude also the natural predisposition, and that is called 'talent', and if this talent has originality,[b] then it is called 'genius'. We soon count as temperament that which we reckon to the natural aptitude. The good mind signifies harmlessness in a human being, especially it means that such a human being easily accommodates others, lets himself be turned away to where others will have him. We therefore see that it too is no praise for a human being. There are very good people who nonetheless assume vices merely from a desire to please. Mere wishes do not attest straightway to a good heart. Good heartedness can be judged only from the deed. The English call themselves a good hearted nation. But others will not always concede that to them. Good naturedness signifies, so to speak, an instinctiveness and not doing good according to principles. 25:1531

The temperament is properly what is characteristic of the life-force, insofar as it does not belong to the rationality of the human being. The temperament is corporeal and psychological, of the body and the soul. It was customary with the ancients to seek the cause of temperament in the constitution of the body; but that is not comprehensible. The temperament of the soul is the proportion of the incentives. Talent contains the proportion of cognition, one can call the temperament the "mode of

[a] *Naturell*   [b] *Originalitaet*

sense". Life consists in the feeling of pleasure and displeasure and consists in activity. If the feeling is determined, then that is the incentives, but we can look to the activity for the determining ground and then it is the temperament of activity.

In regard to the feeling, the temperaments are [The text breaks off at this point].

Editorial notes

General introduction

1 See Holly L. Wilson, *Kant's Pragmatic Anthropology* (Albany: State University of New York Press, 2006), p. 7. Chapter 1 of this book provides an excellent brief and lucid discussion of the history of Kant's interest in anthropology, and of the scholarly controversies over it.

2 See *ibid.*, p. 123.

3 One account of the origins of anthropology, albeit one that sees Kant and Herder as rivals and takes Herder's side, is John Zammito, *Kant, Herder and the Birth of Anthropology* (University of Chicago Press, 2002). Herder's organicist approach involved a rejection of the Enlightenment idea of an underlying and unifying "human nature" and especially of the idea of seeking for general laws of human behavior. Kant accepts the Enlightenment goal of discovering a basic human nature that is common to all peoples and all times, and at least pays lip service to the idea of general laws. But he acknowledges the wide variation in the manifestation of human nature among human beings, which makes it all the harder to discover. Kant's "pragmatic" approach to anthropology, and also the natural (biological) teleology that he employs regulatively in his philosophy of history, took a big step in the direction that Herder was to pursue.

4 For a good review of this controversy, beginning with its nineteenth-century roots, and an interesting suggestion about how it might be resolved, see Wilson, *Kant's Pragmatic Anthropology*, Chapter 1, especially pp. 15–26.

5 As identified by the editors, Werner Stark and Reinhard Brandt, VA 25:1565–1658. See Brian Jacobs and Patrick Kain, Introduction to Jacobs and Kain (eds.), *Essays on Kant's Anthropology* (Cambridge, Eng,: Cambridge University Press, 2003), p. 7.

6 See the introduction by Werner Stark and Reinhard Brandt to the *Vorlesungen über Anthropologie, Kants Schriften* 25:VII-CLI, and also Werner Stark, "Historical Notes and Interpretive Questions," in Jacobs and Kain (eds.), *Essays on Kant's Anthropology*, pp. 15–37.

7 Paul Guyer, "Beauty, Freedom and Morality," in Jacobs and Kain (eds.), *Essays on Kant's Anthropology*, pp. 135–163.

8 These passages are discussed by Werner Stark, "Historical Notes and Interpretive Questions," in Jacobs and Kain (eds.), *Essays on Kant's Anthropology*, pp. 23–25.

9 For a fuller discussion of these two functions of practical anthropology, see Robert B. Louden, "The Second Part of Morals," in Jacobs and Kain (eds.), *Essays on Kant's Anthropology*, pp. 60–84.

Anthropology Collins 1772–1773

1 "The most useful and least advanced of all human knowledge seems to me that of man" (Jean-Jacques Rousseau, *Discourse on the Origin of Inequality*, Preface (Paris: Gallimard, 1969), 3:122.

2 Kant seems to be borrowing this phrase from his friend J. G. Hamann, *Abälardi virbii Chimärische Einfälle über den Briefe die neueste Literatur betreffend*, J. Nadler (ed.), *Sämmtliche Werke* (Vienna: Herder, 1949–1957), 10:164: "This descent into the Hell of self-knowledge paves the way for deification" (cf. *Conflict of the Faculties*, Ak 7:55).

3 Kant is doubtless alluding to the views of Wolff and Baumgarten, who treated empirical psychology as a part of metaphysics. Cf. *Metaphysics L1* Ak 28:221–224, *Critique of Pure Reason* A848–849/B876–877.

4 Johann Joachim Spalding (1714–1804); cf. *Moral Philosophy Collins*, Ak 27:244.

5 Charles Bonnet (1720–1793), Swiss physiologist. Kant is no doubt also referring here to Ernst Platner, the German physiologist whose *Anthropologie für Ärtzte und Weltweisen* (1767, 2nd edn. Leipzig: Dukische Buchhandlung, 1772) was the avowed occasion for Kant to begin lecturing on anthropology. The book was reviewed by Kant's friend Marcus Herz in the *Allgemeine deutsche Bibliothek* 20 (1773); in reference to this review, Kant wrote to Herz about Platner's "futile inquiries as to the manner in which bodily organs are connected with thought" (Ak 10:146).

6 Kant knew the self-examinations of Michel Eyquem de Montaigne (1533–1592) in the edition of Johann Daniel Tietze (Titius), *Versuche nebst des Verfassers Leben, nach der neuesten Ausgabe des Herrn Peter Coste ins Deutsche übersetzt*, 3 vols. (Leipzig, 1753, 1754, 1755). The criticisms by Pascal and Malebranche were included in Volume 3 as an appendix (3:639–640 and 3:642–643).

7 Cf. *Moral Philosophy Collins*, Ak 27:459 and Ak 23:411; Kant's source for this story seems to be Karl Günther Ludovici [Ludewig], *Ausführlicher Entwurff einer vollständigen Historie der Leibnizischen Philosophie. Zum Gebrauch seiner Zuhörer*, 2 vols. (Leipzig, 1737), 2:230.

8 Cf. Plato, *Phaedrus* 250c.

9 Cf. Diogenes Laertius, *Lives of the Greek and Roman Philosophers* 10:39, and Lucretius, *On the Nature of Things* 1:265–364.

10 Cf. Descartes, *Meditations, Oeuvres* (ed. Charles Adam and Paul Tannery) (Paris: Vrin, 1964), 7:27.

11 For the distinction between *anima* and *animus*, see Lucretius, *De rerum natura* 3:136–140 and *Anthropology Parow* 25:247.

12 Cf. Cicero, *De fato* 5 § 10 and *Tusculan Disputations* 4:80. Also Joseph Addison and Richard Steele, *Spectator* (ed. Gregory Smith) (London, 1963–1964), No. 86, which Kant would have known in the following edition: *Der Zuschauer* (trans. Louise Adelgunde Victoria Gottschedin) 9 vols. (Leipzig, 1749–51), 2:71–72. Many authorities think Cicero's source for this was a no longer extant dialogue entitled *Zopyrus* written by Phaedo (of the Platonic dialogue by the same name; see Diogenes Laertius, *Lives of the Philosophers* 3:105). Cf. also Plato, *Charmides* 155d, which involves a pun on the name 'Zopyrus' while alluding to Socrates' being "inflamed" by looking inside a youth's cloak.

Anthropology Parow 1772–1773

1 See *Anthropology Collins*, Note 3.
2 Kant may be thinking of Cicero, *De legibus I*, 22 § 58, in which "the knowledge of how we know" is identified with both "wisdom" and "philosophy," and is said to be "the mother of all good things."
3 See *Anthropology Collins*, Note 6.
4 "If the King of Spain signs a document, then this does not occur through the signing of his name, but rather by means of the words "YO EL REY," i.e. 'I the King', but in letters to foreign princes he writes his name." Eobald Toze, *Der gegenwärtige Zustand von Europa, worin die natürliche und politische Beschaffenheit der Europäische Reiche und Staaten aus bewährten Nachrichten beeschrieben* (The present condition of Europe, in which the natural and political properties of European empires and states are described from confirmed reports), 2 vols. (Bützow/Wismar, 1767).
5 See *Anthropology Collins*, Note 8.
6 Perhaps a reference to the Stoic philosopher Epictetus, author of the *Enchiridion*, who was a slave. Cf. also Seneca, *Epistulae morales* 5:17.
7 See *Anthropology Collins*, Note 9.
8 Regarding the claim about Locke, see Rousseau, *Discourse on the Origin of Inequality*, Note XII, *Oeuvres Complètes* 3:214-215, cf. Locke, *Second Treatise on Government*, VII §§ 79–80. The 'Italian physician' is Pietro Moscati, *Von dem körperlichen wesentlichen Unterschiede zwischen der Struktur der Thiere und der Menschen* (trans. Johann Beckmann) (Göttingen, 1771), pp. 23–44.
9 Cf. Aristotle, *History of animals* 5551a.
10 "Strike, you are striking not Anaxarchus but only his vessel." Montaigne, *Essay on Gluttony*, which Kant knew in this edition: *Versuche nebst des Verfassers Leben, nach der neuesten Ausgabe des Herrn Peter Coste ins Deutsche übersetzt*, tr. and ed. Johann Daniel Tietze (Titius), 3 vols. (Leipzig, 1753, 1754, 1755), 1:681, cf. Diogenes Laertius, *Lives of the Philosophers* 9:59.
11 Lucretius, *De rerum natura* 3:136–140; cf. *Anthropology Collins* 25:16.
12 Cf. *Anthropology Collins* 25:18.
13 See *Anthropology Collins*, Note 12.
14 Cf. Romans 7:23.
15 Kant's source for this story is not known. In *Anthropology Collins* 25:19, the man is described as the inhabitant of one of the "aracadian islands."

Anthropology Friedländer 1775–1776

1 David Hume was a great historian, as well as a great philosopher. His History of England in six volumes (1754–62) went through over fifty editions between his death in 1776 and the beginning of the nineteenth century. Kant would have known it in the translation by Johann Jacob Dusch: Hume, *Geschichte von Großbritannien*, 2 vols. London and Edinburgh, 1762–1763.
2 Ernst Platner, *Anthropologie für Ärtzte und Weltweise* (Leipzig, 1772).
3 *The Spectator* was a daily publication of 1711–12, running to seven volumes in length, founded by Joseph Addison and Richard Steele in England after they met at Charterhouse School. In its aim to "enliven morality with wit, and to temper

wit with morality," *The Spectator* adopted a fictional method of presentation through a "Spectator Club," whose imaginary members extolled the authors' own ideas about society. Whiggish in tone, *The Spectator* generally avoided party-political controversy. The paper was revived without the involvement of Steele in 1714, appearing three times weekly for six months, and these papers when collected formed the eighth volume. Eustace Budgell, a cousin of Addison's, also contributed to the publication, as did Alexander Pope, Thomas Tickell, and Ambrose Phillips. Kant probably knew it through the following German edition: *Der Zuschauer* (trans. Louise Adelgunde Victoria Gottschedin), 9 vols. (Leipzig, 1749–1751).

4 Kant knew the self-examinations of Michel Eyquem de Montaigne (1533–1592) in the edition of Johann Daniel Tietze (Titius), *Versuche nebst des Verfassers Leben, nach der neuesten Ausgabe des Herrn Peter Coste ins Deutsche übersetzt*, 3 vols. (Leipzig, 1753, 1754, 1755).

5 In the translation by Tietze (see previous note) the criticisms of Montaigne by Pascal and Malebranche were included in Volume 3 as an appendix (3:639–640 and 3:642–643).

6 Plato, *Theaetetus* 149a.

7 Kant is probably referring to the optical projection instruments using lenses and mirrors, the forerunners of today's slide and overhead projectors, first invented in the seventeenth century and more commonly called "magic lanterns," although a print reproduced in *Instruments and the Imagination* (by Thomas L. Hankins and Robert S. Silverman [Princeton University Press, 1995], 67) also uses the term "Optical Box." (I am indebted to Phillip R. Sloan, *University of Notre Dame* for this reference.) As Hankins and Silverman report, first used for entertainment, in the eighteenth century magic lanterns also began to receive the attention of natural philosophers and were introduced in instruction to illustrate the laws of optics. The Swiss mathematician, Leonhard Euler, who joined the Berlin Academy of Sciences at the urging of Frederick the Great in 1741 and became an important member of the Berlin Enlightenment, himself designed such a projecting instrument in 1750 and described these inventions in his *Letters to a German Princess* (43–58). Kant repeatedly mentions Euler by name in his published writings from 1755 through 1802. In his Inaugural Dissertation of 1770, he explicitly refers to Euler's *Letters to a German Princess* (Ak 2:414, 419). Thus we can assume he was familiar with Euler's discussion of these magic lanterns.

8 "It belongs to no understanding to follow the opinion that is presently the most general. But it takes understanding to adhere to an opinion in this day to which all human beings will adhere only in thirty years. The opposite of this, or complete idiocy, is this: that in an enlightened age one still cleaves to the old errors... Respect for the world does not consist in following common errors but rather in laying before it well proven paradoxes. One must take note of future opinions." Jean Abbé Terrasson, *La philosophie applicable à tous les objets de l'esprit et de la raison* (Paris, 1754), translated by J. C. Gottsched (Leipzig, 1756), pp. 110, 112.

9 Aristotle, *De Mundo* 395a; cf. *Meteorology* 341b.

10 George Lyttleton, *Dialogues of the Dead* (London, 1760), translated as *Gespräche der Verstorbenen*, by J. G. H. Oelrichs (Berlin, 1762), p. 22.

11 Kant's reference here is to the theory of a music of color in the writings of Louis Bertrand Castel (1688–1757); see also the footnote in Kant's *Reflexionen on Anthropology* (Ak 15: 694–695). Johann Gottlob Krüger (1715–1759) improved on Castel's notion of a melody of color.

12 Cervantes, *Don Quixote*, Book 5, Chapter 13, which Kant would have known in the two-volume German edition of Leipzig, 1734: "I need only hold [my wine] before my nose to know immediately what fruit it is … The one took only a few drops on his tongue, and the other merely smelled it: the former said it tasted of iron, and the latter that it smelled of leather." German edition 2:138.

13 Aristotle: "My dear friends, there are no friends." (Diogenes Laertius *Lives of the Ancient Greek and Roman Philosophers* 5.1.21.) This was a favorite saying of Kant's: see *Metaphysics of Morals* 6: 470; *Anthropology* 7:152; *Moral Philosophy Collins* 27:424, cf. *Groundwork* 4:408. But the quotation by Diogenes Laertius, supposedly from Aristotle, may be based merely on a textual corruption: Compare *Eudemian Ethics* 1245b20: "He who has [many] friends has no friend." (The only difference is a misplaced hard breathing mark.)

14 The German editors indicate a corruption of the text here which cannot be clarified. They suggest a comparison with Ak 29: 20–22, 32, Kant's lectures on philosophical encyclopedia. In a sub-section entitled "History of Logic," having commented on the multiple meanings of the verses of the Scholastics, Kant notes that someone else faults Virgil's poetry for its lack of rhyme and concludes that everything which is repugnant to taste is barbaric.

15 Apparently a reference to Johann August Eberhard, *Neue Apologie des Sokrates, oder Untersuchung der Lehre von der Seligkeit der Heiden* (Berlin, 1772).

16 These lectures were given in the winter and spring of 1775–1776, just as the American Revolutionary War was in the process of breaking out. The battle of Lexington had been fought on April 19, 1775, but American independence (July 4, 1776) had not yet been declared.

17 Edward Young (1683–1765), English poet and dramatist. His satires appeared 1725–1728 under the title *The Universal Passion*.

18 *Hudibras* is a mock-heroic poem written by the English poet, Samuel Butler (1612–1680). It is a satire on Puritanism inspired by the seventeenth-century Spanish novel *Don Quixote*. The first part of *Hudibras* was published in 1663, the second part in 1664, and the third part in 1678.

19 Oliver Goldsmith (1728–1774), an Anglo-Irish writer of histories, biographies, plays, and poetry, whose one novel *The Vicar of Wakefield* appeared in 1766. For a later reference by Kant to Swift's satires, see *Perpetual Peace*, Ak 8:353n.

20 La Fontaine's "The Limbs and the Stomach" included in Book III of his *Fables*. It is perhaps better known through Shakespeare's use of it in *Coriolanus*, Act 1, Scene 1. But its original source was Aesop's *Fables*.

21 A reference to Herder's *Essay on the Origin of Language* (1772), Part 1, Third Section: "As so many ancients say, and as so many moderns have repeated without sense after them, comes from the sensible life: that, namely, poetry is older than prose!"

22 Alexander Pope, *Essay on Man* (1740).

23 Region of Swiss Alps bordering northern Italy, where endemic cretinism associated with goiter was found. In his *Anthropology from a Pragmatic Point of View*,

Kant refers to the "cretins of *Walliserland*" in the course of his discussion there of the weaknesses of the mind with regard to the faculty of cognition. Reinhard Brandt notes in his commentary on this passage that in the Dohna lectures, the reference is to a kind of people inhabiting the Pyrenees, with a marginalia referring to a travelogue by a Baron Carbonnipres (*Kommentar zu Kants Anthropologie* [Hamburg: Felix Meiner, 1999] 211–212).

24 Apparently a reference to Anthony Ashley Cooper, Third Earl of Shaftesbury, "A Letter Concerning Enthusiasm," *Characteristics of Men, Manners, Opinions, Times* (ed. John Robertson) (Indianapolis: Bobbs-Merrill, 1964), pp. 5–42. Locke had condemned "enthusiasm" in *Essay Concerning Human Understanding*, Book 4, Ch. 19, and it was Locke's opinion that prevailed in most Enlightenment thought, including Kant's disparaging use of the German term *Schwärmerei* (e.g. *Critique of Practical Reason* 5:84–86; Metaphysics of Morals 6:409). But see also his praise for the "wishful participation that borders closely on enthusiasm [*Enthusiasm*]" that is felt by spectators of the French Revolution (*Conflict of the Faculties*, Ak 7: 85).

25 Cf. John 2:10.

26 Leibniz, *Monadology* § 22.

27 Nader Shah or King Nader (1688–1747), the founder of Afsharid Dynasty, ruled Persia from 1736–1747. He was a harsh ruler, given to paranoia, who had his own son blinded. His commanders eventually assassinated him, but he killed two of the assassins before he succumbed. It is not clear how he is supposed to illustrate the oriental disposition to pictorial thinking, but Kant's reference is apparently to Mirsa Mahadi Khan Msanderani Mohammed, *Geschichte des Nadir Schah Kaysers von Persien*, trans. Th. G. Gadebusch (Greifswald, 1773).

28 Christina Augusta, also known as Christina Alexandra (1626–1689) was the only surviving child of Gustavus II Adolphus, King of Sweden at the beginning of the Thirty Years' War. Christina was Queen Regent of Sweden from 1632 until 1654. After converting to Catholicism and abdicating her throne, she lived in France and in Rome (where she is buried in St. Peter's Basilica). Descartes accepted an invitation to her court in 1649, where he died of pneumonia in February, 1650. Kant's unfavorable opinion of Queen Christina was apparently derived from Johann Arkenholz (translated into German by Johann Friedrich Reifstein), *Historische Merkwürdigkeiten die Königinn Christina von Schweden betreffend...* 4 vols. (Leipzig & Amsterdam, 1751–1760).

29 Baumgarten, *Metaphysica* § 638.

30 This anecdote was published in the *Monthly Review* of 1772. See David Brewster, *The Life of Sir Isaac Newton* (London, 1831), p. 341.

31 This story is from Abbé Terrasson, *La philosophie*, pp. 35–56, cf. *Anthropology from a Pragmatic Point of View* 7:264.

32 Cf. *Anthropology from a Pragmatic Point of View*, Ak 7:210.

33 The notion dates back to the sixteenth century and the popular belief that such blemishes were the result of cravings which the pregnant woman could not satisfy. The form the blemish took was connected by some with the kind of craving in the particular case.

34 Christian Rickmann, *Von der Unwahrheit des Versehens und der Hervorbringung der Muttermahle durch die Einbildungskraft* (Jena, 1770).

35 Plato, *Republic* 534b–d.

36 Compare Kant's discussion of misology in his *Groundwork of the Metaphysics of Morals* (Ak 4:395–396). There the hatred for reason arises from the recognition that its efforts, both in the invention of all the arts of common luxury and in the sciences, result in more trouble than in happiness.

37 Henry Fielding, *The History of Tom Jones, a Foundling* (1749), which was translated into German by Horst Höckendorff (Hamburg, 1750).

38 The suicide of Philip Mordaunt was well known in the eighteenth century through its description by Voltaire in his *Philosophical Dictionary*: "Philip Mordaunt, German-cousin of the famous count of Peterborough, was known in all the courts of Europe and advertised himself as a man of the world who had known many kings; this Philip Mordaunt, I say, was a man of twenty-seven years, handsome, well-favored, rich, born of illustrious blood, who could pretend to anything, and what was worth even more, passionately beloved by his mistress. This Mordaunt was taken by a disgust with life; he paid his debts, wrote to his friends to bid them goodbye, and even wrote some verses whose last lines may be translated into French as follows:

L'opium peut aider le sage;	Opium may help the sage,
Mais selon mon opinion,	But in my opinion,
Il lui faut au lieu d'opium	What he needs in place of opium
Un pistolet et du courage.	Is a pistol and some courage.

He conducted himself according to his principles and dispatched himself with a pistol shot, without having any other reason than that when the soul is discontented with its body as one is discontented with one's house, it is necessary to leave it. It seems that he died because he was disgusted by his happiness." (*Œuvres complètes de Voltaire* [Paris: Antoine Augustine Renouard, 1819], v. 34, p. 313.)

39 The English poet Edward Young (1683–1765), served from 1730 until his death as rector at Welwyn (see note to 25:517).

40 A similar passage is found in the Prieger lectures (1777/78) (per editors' note): "But that is hard (*Schlim*) to have a will, since one always thereby thinks that it depends on the will to do it every time, and this is however the reason why people postpone their conversion."

41 Drawing on Kant's discussions elsewhere, this sentence might be understood as follows. The mere proximity to one another is the occasion for the eruption of all the misanthropic vices (and hence barbarity), but this stage is also part of the process in which nature brings about the cultivation and culture of human beings.

42 Henry Home, Lord Kames (1696–1782), *Sketches of the History of Man* (London, 1774–1775), German translation by Anton Ernst Klausing: *Versuche über die Geschichte des Menschen* (Leipzig, 1774), Book 1, Essay 8, "Growth and Effects of Luxury," 1:391–392. Home is the source for Kant's use of the word 'Kritik'; he is cited by Kant also in his lectures and reflections on logic, as well as his correspondence. Home's main work, *Elements of Criticism* first appeared in German in 1763–1766 in three volumes under the title *Grundsätze der Critik*.

531

43 Christian Fürchtegott Gellert (1715–1769) was a German writer who was named professor at Leipzig in 1742 and enjoyed the reputation of being the arbiter of good taste in Germany, even being called 'the most reasonable of all German savants' by Frederick the Great.

44 Francis Hutcheson (1694–1746), an Irish-born Scottish philosopher, was one of the most powerful influences on Kant, especially in the areas of moral philosophy, aesthetics and anthropology. His *Essay on the Nature and Conduct of the Passions and Affections with Illustrations on the Moral Sense* (London, 1728) was translated into German by Johann Gottfried Gellius: *Abhandlung über die Natur und Beherrschung der Leidenschaften und Neigungen . . .* (Leipzig, 1760). Kant appears to have got his distinction between *Leidenschaft* and *Affekt* from Hutcheson, though it is questionable whether they are the same distinction in the two philosophers.

45 Baumgarten, *Ethica philosophica* (Halle, 1763) § 287.

46 Compare the discussion on 25:568.

47 Compare Kant's discussion on 25:574.

48 See discussion on 25:564–565.

49 Seneca, *Epistulae morales* 1 Ep. 9, "Epistle IX, On Philosophy and Friendship," *Epistles*, trans. Richard M. Gummere, Loeb Classical Library (Cambridge, MA: Harvard University Press, 1917), 43–67. cf. *Metaphysics of Morals* 6:457.

50 Johann Peter Brinckmann (1746–1785), *Brief über die Würkung des Blattereiters bey der Inoculation* (Düsseldorf: Neue Buchhandlung, 1774).

51 Virgil, *Aeneid* 4:791–792: "Woman's a thing / Forever fitful and forever changing."

52 See *Reflexionen zur Anthropologie* Ak 15:497. Here Kant speaks of the strength and weakness of either the nerves or fibres which must be taken into account with temperament. As effects of the constitution of the body, how and the extent to which they are moved depends on temperature.

53 However, it is worth bearing in mind, especially given Kant's immediate connection with the practical, that in other texts (for example, the *Religion within the Boundaries of Mere Reason*), he also explicitly identifies *Herz* with power of choice (*Willkür*).

54 See note to 25:583. Christian Fürchtegott Gellert, *Moralische Vorlesungen* (Leipzig, 1770), 1:224.

55 Cf. Hume, "Of National Characters," *Essays Moral, Political, Literary* (1742) 1, Essay XXI.

56 Compare the discussion on shame on 25:599–600.

57 See 25:560.

58 Mazurian = natives of Mazovia, a Polish territory.

59 Genesis 1:27.

60 Cf. Kant, *On the Different Races of Human Beings* (1775), Ak 2:439.

61 Johann Joachim Winckelmann (1717–1788), *Abhandlung von der Fähigkeit der Empfindung des Schönen in der Kunst* (Dresden, 1763).

62 Rousseau, *Émile*, *Œuvres complètes* (Paris: Garnier-Flammarion, 1966), 4:411.

63 This propensity on Kant's part to "etymologize" (as has been in evidence repeatedly in these lectures) was noted by his contemporaries, visitors, and earliest biographers, with the general observation that these efforts were sometimes

pertinent, but also often unsuccessful. See Brandt's Introduction to his *Kommentar zu Kants Anthropologie* (Hamburg: Meiner, 1999), pp. 42–43.

64 Johann Jacob Heidegger: Kant repeats this story in even more explicit detail in a footnote in his *Anthropology from a Pragmatic Point of View* (7:300) referring there to Heidegger as a "German musician in London."

65 Johann Friedrich Karl Grimm, *Bemerkungen eines Reisenden durch Deutschland, Frankreich, England und Holland in Briefen an Seine Freunde* (Altenburg, 1775), 3:334–335.

66 Johann Kaspar Lavater, 1741–1801, Swiss philosopher and theologian. Kant's reference is to his widely read and translated *Physiognomische Fragmente* (1775–1778), which founded the study of physiognomy.

67 George Louis le Clerc Comte de Buffon, *Allgemeine Historie der Natur* (Hamburg, 1750–1782), 2:250, which, however, does not say what Kant here reports.

68 The similarity of human to animal features was a recurrent theme in the physiognomy of Lavater. See note to 25:668.

69 Lavater, *Physiognomische Fragmente* 1:79–83.

70 *Ibid.*, 1:183.

71 William Hogarth (1697–1764), English painter and engraver, known for his depiction of moral themes.

72 Carl von Linné (Carolus Linnaeus), 1707–1778, Swedish botanist.

73 Kant alludes to the same example in his *Reflexionen zur Anthropologie* (*Reflections on Anthropology*). In the footnote (R 1498, Ak 15:776); Kant took the anecdote about the Marquise Brinvilliers (1630–1676) from Antoine-Joseph Pernety's *La connaissance de l'homme moral par celle de l'homme physique* (1776), with the German translation prepared under the title, *Des Abbts. Ant. Jos. Pernety Versuch einer Physiognomik, oder Erklärung des moralischen Menschen durch die Kenntniss des physischen* (1784) (Pernety's Attempt at a Physiognomy, or the Explanation of the Moral Human Being through Knowledge of the Physical). Other manuscripts give alternate spellings for Pernety – Pernelle, or even Bernetti – and provide more details of Brinvilliers's atrocities, poisoning her father, uncle, and siblings, as well as poisoning the soup sent to patients in hospitals; she was caught and apparently burned at the stake.

74 William D. Dampier (1652–1715): an English captain who published an account of his travels in 1690 as *New Voyage Around the World by Captain William Dampier* (a French translation appeared in 1701).

75 Kant reviewed Moscati's treatise (a talk by Peter Moscati in Pavia, where he was professor of anatomy) in 1771: *Von dem körperlichen wesentlichen Unterschiede zwischen der Structur der Thiere und Menschen* (*On the Essential Corporeal Difference between the Structure of Animals and Human Beings*) (Ak II, 421–425). Kant notes that Moscati shows that going on all fours is the natural posture suited to our physical anatomy, that while we obviously can go upright, habitually doing so in fact leads to discomforts and illnesses attributable to our erect posture (harm to both mother and child in pregnancy, heart disease, problems with the circulatory system and gastronomical tract), which further is taken to prove that it was through reason that we were induced to deviate from our initial constitution natural to us as animals. The cultivation of the germ of reason (*Keim der Vernunft*) laid in our nature, on the other hand, destines us for society (at the cost of these

physical ills). It is clear in his review, that Kant finds Moscati's account very persuasive.

76 Daniel Defoe, *The Life and Surprising Adventures of Robinson Crusoe...* (1719) (Oxford, 1927), 1:177.

77 *Mit dem Bösen aus Freiheit*, echoing the statement on 25:691 that "it pleased providence to draw good out of the root of evil," as well as being reminiscent of the opening lines of Rousseau's *Émile* and agreeing also with Kant's account in *Conjectural Beginning of Human History*. See also 25:682 for the first expression of this question in this discussion.

78 Depending on context, *Weib* expresses such nuances as "skirt," "doll," "bitch," etc., while *Frauenzimmer* likewise bears such nuances as "broad," "hussy," or "skirt." Notably too, both terms, *Weib* and *Frauenzimmer*, have the neuter gender in German which means that the corresponding pronoun is "it" (and not "she"); it carries the implication, in other words, that the woman is thus viewed wholly as an object. When Kant refers to women in general, i.e. for the plural form, he uses *das Frauenzimmer*. Up to this point in the lectures, Kant's only usage of *Frau* has been in the explicit context of a reference to "wife" (*Mann und Frau* being the usual way of expressing "husband and wife"). Kant's admission here of the offensiveness of his choices of terminology in ordinary life is rather telling; by his own admission then, it cannot be said that the terms connoted something less offensive in the eighteenth century than they do today. Indeed, as Reinhard Brandt too notes in his *Kommentar*, Kant's misogyny can only be described as relentless or "uncontrollable" (*unbezähmbar*, 261). As Brandt accurately sums it up: "Kant denies the woman an independent reason (as Aristotle denies it to the slave by nature), she is [held] neither capable of science in cognition, nor of the feeling of the sublime in aesthetics, nor of the formation of character in ethics, nor can she become an active citizen, nor even enter into and conclude independent business contracts" (*Einleitung*, 19). It should also not go unremarked that Kant presented this viewpoint to his students every year for at least a quarter of a century (in its most concentrated form in these anthropology lectures, but also elsewhere) with all the authority he carried as teacher, professor, philosopher, and civil servant of the state.

79 This distinction of *herrschen* and *regieren* as Kant uses it here does have an ety-mological basis. *Herrschen* comes from *Herr sein*, being the lord, or the elder, and hence the power here derives from one's position and can simply be a matter of asserting will or inclination in order to prevail over another. *Regieren* comes from the Latin for "leading, guiding, steering," and hence here the principle is fundamental as the source of the order. Reinhard Brandt's commentary on this is also very helpful (*Kommentar*, 440–441).

80 Kant is referring to an institution of education based on Lockean, Rousseauian, and Enlightenment principles first founded in 1774 in Dessau by Johann Bern-hard Basedow. The school (the Philanthropin) and the program of educa-tion it initiated had the support of the authorities at all levels. It was estab-lished under the auspices of the local sovereign in Dessau (Leopold Friedrich Franz). The Prussian Minister in charge of education as of 1771, Karl Abra-ham von Zedlitz, was sympathetic to the *Philanthropinismus* movement (whose proponents' writings outlived the actual Institute). In addition to Basedow,

the proponents included Christian Heinrich Wolke, D. Karl Friedrich Bahrdt, Christian Gotthilf Salzmann, Joachim Heinrich Campe, Ernst Christian Trapp, and Piere Villaume. For his first set of lectures on pedagogy (1776/77), Kant used Basedow's *Methodenbuch* as the basis for his course, only changing at the behest of his superiors to Bock's *Lehrbuch der Erziehungskunst für christliche Eltern und künftige Jugendlehrer* in the summer of 1780.

81 In his writings, Basedow referred to his conception of public schools as "nurseries" (*Pflanzgärten*) in which "virtue, patriotism, and the public happiness" were to be cultivated. The use of "*Pflantzschule*" here is likely a variation of Basedow's term. Kant himself frequently makes use of horticultural imagery, including the sense of cultivation closely connected with the original Latin root of *cultura*.

82 Cf. Kant's *Lectures on Ethics*, Ak 27:102, 248, 484, 29:603.

83 Locke, *Some Thoughts Concerning Education* (London, 1693), §§ 7–8. Cf. Rousseau, *Émile, Oeuvres complètes*, 4:162.

84 Rousseau, *Émile, Oeuvres complètes*, 4:208; cf. 4:59–60.

85 Compare Kant's discussion on 25:599–600.

Anthropology Pillau 1777–1778

1 See *Anthropology Collins*, Note 6.

2 Benjamin Franklin, *Briefe von der Elektrizität* (1758), trans. Johann Carl Wilke (Wiesbaden: Heilbronn, 1783), p. 28.

3 Samuel Butler (1612–1680). Kant's likely source for this was Samuel Johnson, quoted in *Merkwürdigkeiten zur Geschichte der Gelehrten, und besonders der Streitigkeiten derselben, aus dem französischen übersetzt* (Leipzig, 1763–1764), 7:210.

4 Baumgarten, *Metaphysica* § 655 deals with the faculty of pleasure and displeasure.

5 Pietro Verri, *Idee sull'indole del piacere* (Livorno, 1777); translated by Christoph Meiners as *Gedanken über die Natur des Vergnügens* (Leipzig, 1777).

6 Cf. Sextus Empiricus, *Against the Mathematicians*, 1.196–197.

7 "Pleasure is intuition, or intuitive cognition of whatever perfection, whether true or apparent." Wolff, *Psychologia empirica* (1738), *Gesammelte Werke* II, 5, § 511 (Hildesheim: Olms, 1968), p. 389.

8 Verri, trans. Meiners, op. cit. in note 5, pp. 4–5.

9 Jean Sylvain Bailly, *Histoire de l'astronomie ancienne* (1775), trans. Christian Ernst Wünsch, *Geschichte der Sternkunde des Alterthums bis auf die Errichtung der Schule zu Alexandrien*, 2 vols. (Leipzig, 1777), 1:70.

10 The Zend-Avesta is the holy scripture of Zoroastrianism, the religion of ancient Persia. Bailly found in it apparent references to cities as far north as the 49th parallel, from which astronomical measurements were supposedly taken.

11 Compare *Religion within the Boundaries of Mere Reason*, Ak 6:139–141 and notes; *Lectures on the Philosophical Doctrine of Religion*, Ak 28:1073–1076. Kant's source is apparently Pierre Sonnerat, *Reise nach Ostindien un China auf Befehl des Königs vom Jahr 1774 bis 1781* (Zürich, 1783), 1:166. Cf. *The End of All Things*, Ak 8:329 and note.

12 See *Anthropology Parow*, Note 8.

13 See Genesis 3:19.

14 Rousseau, *Discourse on the Origin of Inequality Among Men* (1755).

15 Presumably, a reference to *Of the Social Contract* (1762).

16 Presumably, a reference to *Émile, or on Education* (1762).

17 Presumably, a reference to *Extract from the project for perpetual peace* (1764), based on the *Project to Render Peace Perpetual in Europe* (1713), by Charles Irenée Castel, Abbé de Saint-Pierre.

Menschenkunde *1781–1782?*

1 Ernst Platner, *Anthropologie für Ärzte und Weltweise* (Leipzig, 1772). See also Kant's letter to Marcus Herz, written toward the end of 1773, where Kant draws further contrasts between his own approach to anthropology and that of Platner.

2 Samuel Sharp, *Letters from Italy, describing the customs and manners of that country, in the years 1765, and 1766. To which is annexed, an Admonition to gentlemen who pass the Alps, in their tour through Italy* (London, 1766), pp. 258–259. (The exact source of Kant's remark is not certain.)

3 Alexander Gottlieb Baumgarten, *Metaphysica*, 4th edn. (Halle, 1757). Kant frequently used this work as a text for his lectures. The paragraphs from the *Metaphysica* dealing with empirical psychology form the official text for the anthropology lectures, though Kant does not stick closely to them.

4 Kant repeats this famous trifold distinction later in the *Groundwork of the Metaphysics of Morals* (4:434–435) and in *Anthropology from a Pragmatic Point of View* (7:292). See also *Mrongovius* 25:1333, 1385.

5 See also *Collins* 25:221–222, *Parow* 25:429.

6 David Hume, in his essay "The Sceptic," writes: "It is certain, that a serious attention to the sciences and liberal arts softens and humanizes the temper, and cherishes those fine emotions, in which true virtue and honour consists. It rarely, very rarely happens, that a man of taste and learning is not, at least, an honest man, whatever frailties may attend him" (*Essays, Moral, Political, and Literary*, ed. Eugene F. Miller [Indianapolis: Liberty Press, 1987], p. 170). See also 15:872 and *Mrongovius* 25:1391.

7 Here Kant foreshadows his famous claim in the *Groundwork of the Metaphysics of Morals* that "a good will seems to constitute the indispensable condition even of worthiness to be happy" (4:393). Cf. *Mrongovius* 25:1333, 1385.

8 See also Kant's later discussion of price versus dignity in the *Groundwork* 4:434–435.

9 Cf. Cicero, *Philippics* VI 3 § 7: "In the circumstances, the Senate's decree is not altogether remiss; the embassy has some element of severity; would that it involved no delay! For as in the conduct of most things slowness and procrastination are hateful, so this war especially asks for speed" (trans. Walter C. A. Ker, *The Loeb Classical Library* [Cambridge: Harvard University Press, 1926]). See also *Anthropology from a Pragmatic Point of View* 7:186 and *The Conflict of the Faculties* 7:97, 99.

10 Charles XII (1682–1718), King of Sweden. The classic biography is Voltaire's *Histoire de Charles XII*. See also *Anthropology from a Pragmatic Point of View* 7:293 and *Mrongovius* 25:1346, 1387.

11   Anthony Ashley Cooper, Third Earl of Shaftesbury (1671–1713), in his essay, "*Sensus Communis*: An Essay on the Freedom of Wit and Humour" (1709), writes: "Now the variety of Nature is such, as to distinguish everything she forms, by a peculiar original character, which, if strictly observed, will make the subject appear unlike to anything extant in the world besides" (Part IV, Section III; in Shaftesbury, *Characteristics of Men, Manners, Opinions, Times*, ed. John M. Robertson [London: Grant Richards, 1900]). See also *On the Use of Teleological Principles in Philosophy* 8:166.

12   Georg Christoph Lichtenberg (1742–1799), German physical scientist, mathematician, essayist, and philosopher. The Academy editors, while unable to locate the exact source of Lichtenberg's remark, draw readers' attention to his work *Über Physiognomik; wider die Physiognomen. Zur Beförderung der Menschenliebe und Menschenkenntniß* (1778), reprinted in Lichtenberg, *Schriften und Briefe*, 3rd edn., ed. Wolfgang Promies (Frankfurt am Main, 1994), vol. III. See also *Mrongovius* 25:1380.

13   Johann Caspar Lavater (1741–1801), Swiss theologian, mystic, and physiognomist; author of *Physiognomische Fragmente zur Beförderung der Menschenkenntnis und Menschenliebe* (1775–1778), 4 vols. Lavater and his theory of physiognomy are satirized by Lichtenberg in the latter's *Über Physiognomik* (see n. 12). See also Lavater's letter to Kant of April 8, 1774 and Kant's two replies (10:165–166, 175–180).

14   Alexander Pope (1688–1744), English poet, author of *An Essay on Man* (1732–1734). Cf. *Mrongovius* 25:1378.

15   William Hay, *Deformity. An Essay* (London, 1754). See also *Parow* 25:289, *Pillau* 25:789.

16   William Hogarth (1697–1764), English painter, engraver, and author. See also *Collins* 25:233, *Friedländer* 25:671.

17   Cf. Martial, *Epigrams* 1.3, 5–6: "Young men, old men, boys – they all have noses like a rhino" (ed. and trans. D. R. Shackleton Bailey, Loeb Classical Library [Cambridge: Harvard University Press, 1993]). See also *Anthropology from a Pragmatic Point of View* 7:299, *Mrongovius* 25:1379.

18   In his *Über Physiognomik* (1778).

19   See also *Pillau* 25:828 and *Mrongovius* 25:1307. The exact title of the book in question is *Bemerkungen eines Reisenden durch Deutschland, Frankreich, England und Holland in Briefen an seine Freunde* (Altenburg, 1775). Published anonymously, the author was later revealed to be Johann Friedrich Karl Grimm.

20   The Academy editors here cite a long passage from Johann Jacob Volkmann, *Neueste Reisen durch Spanien vorzuglich in Ansehung der Künste, Handlung, Oekonomie und Manufakturen aus den besten Nachrichten und neueren Schriften zusammengetragen* (Leipzig, 1785), 2 vols., 1:114, where the author elaborates on the same topic. See also Mrongovius 25:1404 and *Anthropology from a Pragmatic Point of View* 7:316.

21   Here the Academy editors cite from Volkmann, *Neuste Reisen durch Spanien*, 1:51–52. See also *Mrongoivus* 25:1404 and *Anthropology from a Pragmatic Point of View* 7:316.

22   The Academy editors here refer readers to Erich Adickes, *Untersuchungen zu Kants physischer Geographie* (Tübingen, 1911), p. 303.

23 This statement prefigures Kant's famous opening proclamation in his essay, *An Answer to the Question: What is Enlightenment?* (1784): "*Sapere aude* [trans.: dare to be wise]! Have courage to make use of your *own* understanding! is thus the motto of enlightenment" (8:35).

24 Alexander Pope (1688–1744), English poet. In his *Moral Essays* (1731–35), he writes:

> In Men, we various Ruling Passions find;
> In Women, two almost divide the kind;
> Those, only fix'd, they first or last obey,
> The Love of Pleasure, and the Love of Sway.
> (Epistle II. *Of the Charakters of Women*, 207–210)

Kant refers to the same passage in *Anthropology from a Pragmatic Point of View* 7:305.

25 See Job 2: 9–10. See also *Anthropology from a Pragmatic Point of View* 7:308 and *Mrongovius* 25:1395. The Academy editors also draw attention here to an anonymously published essay entitled "Ehren-Rettung Der Xanthippe" ("Saving the Honor of Xanthippe"), *Acta Philosophorum* 1 (1715): 103–125; as well as to a passage from Moses Mendelssohn's 1767 work *Phädon, oder über die Unsterblichkeit der Seele* (*Phaedo, or On the Immortality of the Soul*), where Mendelssohn argues that Xanthippe was "not of such an evil temperament as is normally believed" (*Moses Mendelssohn: Gesammelte Schriften*, ed. Alexander Altmann, Jubiläums Ausgabe [Stuttgart: Frommann, 1971], 3.1:20).

26 See *Menschenkunde* 25:1084–1085.

27 See also *Anthropology from a Pragmatic Point of View* 7:308.

28 Hume, at the beginning of his essay "Of Love and Marriage," writes: "I know not whence it proceeds, that women are so apt to take amiss everything which is said in disparagement of the married state; and always consider a satyr upon matrimony as a satyr upon themselves" (*Essays*, ed. Miller, p. 557). This essay appeared in the first edition of Hume's *Essays* (1741), but was withdrawn after 1760. See also *Anthropology from a Pragmatic Point of View* 7:309, *Parow* 25:458, and *Mrongovius* 25:1393.

29 The Academy editors refer readers here to Hermann Samuel Reimarus, *Allgemeine Betrachtungen über die Triebe der Tiere, hauptsächlich über ihre Kunsttriebe: Zum Erkenntnis des Zusammenhanges der Welt, des Schöpfers und unserer selbst,* [...], [*General Considerations Concerning the Instincts of Animals, primarily their Mechanical Instincts: Toward Cognition of the Interconnection of the World, the Creator, and Ourselves, ...*], 2nd edn. (Hamburg, 1762), § 153, pp. 385–386. At the beginning of this passage, Reimarus states: "We crawl at the beginning on all fours, however this nevertheless indicates, even in the construction of our body, a distant natural vocation to walking upright."

30 Here the Academy editors refer readers to Peter Camper, "Etwas vernünftiges vom Orang Utang" ["Something Reasonable on the Orangutan"], *Goettinger Taschen Calender vom Jahr 1781*: 40–64, esp. pp. 62–63; Erich Adickes *Untersuchungen zu Kants physischer Geographie* [*Inquiries in Kants Physical Geography*] (Tübingen, 1911), pp. 115–116; and also to Eberhard August Wilhelm Zimmermann, *Geographische Geschichte des Menschen, und der allgemeinen verbreiteten*

vierfüßigen Thiere, [. . .] [*Geographical History of the Human Being, and of the universally dispersed four-footed Animals, . . .*], 3 vols. (Leipzig, 1778–1783), 1:117–124. See also *Anthropology from a Pragmatic Point of View* 7:322.

31 The Academy editors refer readers here to John Hunter, *The Natural History of the Human Teeth: Explaining their Structure* [. . .] (London, 1780), esp. p. 128.

32 See in particular the section entitled "Concerning Human Beings" in Kant's *Lectures on Physical Geography* (9:311–320).

33 See also Kant's famous opening to his essay, *An Answer to the Question: What is Enlightenment?*: "Enlightenment is the human being's emergence from his self-incurred immaturity" (*selbst-verschuldete Unmündigkeit*) (8:35). Mary Gregor renders *Unmündigkeit* as "minority"; *Mündigkeit* as "majority."

34 Kant also discusses these famous three questions in the *Critique of Pure Reason* (A 805/B 833). A fourth question (What is the human being?), to which the first three all relate, appears later in his letter to Stäudlin of May 4, 1793 (11:429), the *Jäsche Logic* lectures (9:25), and the *Metaphysik Pölitz* lectures (28:533–534).

35 See also *Idea for a Universal History with a Cosmopolitan Aim* 8:23, Review of Herder's *Ideas for a Philosophy of the History of Humanity* 8:64, and *Parow* 25:425.

36 Miltiades was an Athenian general who commanded at Marathon in 490 BC, during the Persian Wars.

Anthropology Mrongovius 1784–1785

1 For an etymology of *pedante* that conflicts with Kant's own, see Manlio Cortelazzo and Paolo Zolli, *Dizionario etimologico della lingua italiana* (Bologna, 1987), vol. 4, p. 879. Cf. 24:626ff.

2 Ernst Platner (1744–1818), German physician and philosophy professor in Leipzig. *Anthropologie für Aertzte und Weltweise* (Leipzig: Dyck, 1772). See also the translation of Collins, n. 5, in the present volume.

3 Johann Jakob Engel, *Ueber Handlung, Gespräch und Erzehlung* (1774). Cf. Johann Christoph Gatterer's essay, "*Vom historischen Plan, und der darauf sich gründenden Zusammenfügung der Erzählungen,*" in: *Allgemeine historische Bibliothek von Mitgliedern des königlichen Instituts der historischen Wissenschaften zu Göttingen*, ed. Gatterer (Halle, 1767–1771), vol. 1, pp. 15–89.

4 Terence, or Publius Terentius Afer (*c.*195/185–159 BCE), Roman dramatist. Chremes is the character in Terence's play *Heauton Timorumenos* (The Self-Tormentor) who says, "*Homo sum: humani nil a me alienum puto*" (I am a human being: therefore I consider nothing that is human to be foreign to me). Cf. Kant's reference in *Parow* 25:414.

5 Alexander Gottlieb Baumgarten (1714–1762), *Metaphysica*, 4th edition (Halle, 1757), reprinted at 15:3–54. See "Empirical Psychology" (§§ 504–699), Section 1, "Existence of the Soul," § 504.

6 Claude Adrien Helvétius (1715–1771), French philosopher and author of *De l'esprit* (On the Mind) (Paris, 1758). The source of Kant's reference, however, cannot be found in *De l'esprit*.

7 Michel Eyquem de Montaigne (1533–1592), French philosopher and author of the introspective *Essais* (Essays) (Bordeaux, 1580).

8 Kant has Pascal and Malebranche in mind; see Collins, n. 6, in the present volume. Their criticisms were found in the third volume of the German translation of Montaigne's *Essays*: Michel de Montaigne, *Versuche, nebst des Verfassers Leben, nach der neuesten Ausgabe des Herrn Peter Coste ins Deutsche übersetzt* (Leipzig, 1753–1754), 3 vols., trans. Johann Daniel Titius (Tietze), ed. Pierre Coste.

9 Adam Bernd, *Eigene Lebens-Beschreibung, Samt einer Aufrichtigen Entdeckung, und deutlichen Beschreibung einer der grösten, obwol großen Theils noch unbekannten Leibes- und Gemüths-Plage* [...] (Leipzig, 1738).

10 Johann Caspar Lavater (1741–1801), Swiss physiognomist. See his (anonymous), *Geheimes Tagebuch. Von einem Beobachter Seiner Selbst* (Leipzig, 1771). See also Johann Caspar Lavater (published anonymously), *Unveränderte Fragmente aus dem Tagebuch eines Beobachters seiner Selbst; oder des Tagebuches Zweyter Theil, nebst einem Schreiben an den Herausgeber desselben* (Leipzig, 1773).

11 See Plato, *Thaetetus* 149a.

12 The source of this passage in Buffon's writings is unknown, but cf. *Observations* 2:237 and 28:853. Descartes also describes how he was affected in this way at a young age; see Descartes, Letter to Chanut, The Hague, June 6, 1647, *Oeuvres de Descartes* (Paris, 1897–1913), ed. Charles Adam and Paul Tannery, *Correspondance*, vol. 5, p. 57.

13 Cf. *Logik-Philippi* (*c.*1772) 24:360–363; and 24:517.

14 For instance, Sextus Empiricus (*c.* second century CE), a Pyrrhonian skeptic or follower of Pyrrho of Elis (*c.*360 BCE to *c.*270 BCE), argued that we should always suspend our judgments so as not to commit any errors, thereby attaining peace of mind. See Sextus Empiricus, *The Skeptic Way: Sextus Empiricus's Outlines of Pyrrhonism*, trans. Benson Mates (Oxford University Press, 1996).

15 The *Preisfrage* (prize question) raised by the Berlin Academy of Sciences in early 1780 was a version of this question. See also Menschenkunde 25:882.

16 Kant is referring to a middle and late seventeenth-century debate about philosophical sin (*philosophische Sünde*). On *peccati philosophici*, see also Baumgarten, *Initia* § 117 (= AK 19:57). Cf. Kant's notes for his anthropology course, 15:672.

17 Kant presumably has Hamann and Herder in mind. Cf. Adickes in AK 15:336–337; 344–345.

18 Cf. Jean Terrasson, *Philosophie, nach ihrem allgemeinen Einflusse auf alle Gegenstände des Geistes und der Sitten* (Leipzig, 1756), p. 110. Originally published as *La philosophie applicable à tous le objects de l'esprit et de la raison* (Paris, 1754).

19 This phrase was used by Claudio Aquaviva (1543–1615), a general of the Society of Jesus and author of *Industriae ad curandos animae morbos* (Efforts to Cure the Diseases of the Soul) (Venice, 1606).

20 Cf. Friedländer 25:485. For this distinction, see Aristotle, *De mundo* (On the Universe), 395a 29–30. "To sum up, some of the phenomena which occur in the air are merely appearances [*kat' emphasin*], while others have actual substance [*kath' hypostasin*]." *The Complete Works of Aristotle* (Princeton University Press, 1984), ed. Jonathan Barnes, "On the Universe," pp. 626–640, trans. E. S. Forster, on p. 631.

21 Cf. Francis Bacon (1561–1626), "Distributio operis" (Distribution of the Work), in *Novum organum* (The New Organon) (1620), in *The Works of Francis Bacon*, 14 vols. (London, 1857–1874), in vol. 1, p. 138.

22 This passage may be compared to *Critique of Pure Reason*, A 51/ B 75.

23 See Plato, *Phaedo* 82d–83b. See also Democritus, Fragment B 159, in Hermann Diels and Walther Kranz, *Die Fragmente der Vorsokratiker* (Berlin, 1956, eighth edition), vol. 2, pp. 175f.

24 Alexander Pope (1688–1744), *Essay on Man* (London, 1732–1734), 2.107–108: "On life's vast ocean diversely we sail, / Reason the card, but passion is the gale." German translation: "*Ist die Vernunft nun der Magnet; / so sind die Leidenschaften Winde*"; in: *Versuch vom Menschen, [...] nebst verschiedenen andern Uebersetzungen und einigen eigenen Gedichten. Nebst einer Vorrede und einem Anhange von Briefen*, trans. Barthold Heinrich Brockes and J. B. Zinck (Hamburg, 1740), on vol. 2, p. 98. Cf. Kant 15:677 and ApH 7:267.

25 Christoph Meiners (1747–1810), philosopher and historian, professor in Göttingen. See his *Historia doctrinae de vero deo omnium rerum auctore atque rectore. / Pars prima qua veterum gentium eorumque sacerdotum de divina natura opiniones explicantur. / Pars altera, qua Graecorum philosophorum de rerum ortu et divina natura opiniones illustrantur* (Lemgo, 1780).

26 Christoph Meiners, *ibid.*, pp. 187ff., discusses Orpheus but does not claim that he taught philosophy in verses. See also ApH 7:191.

27 Kant presumably has Hamann and Herder in mind. See also Mro 25:1227 above.

28 The King James Version (1611) reads: "For this is the love of God, that we keep his commandments: and his commandments are not grievous." Martin Luther's translation is: "*Denn das ist die Liebe zu Gott, daß wir seine Gebote halten; und seine Gebote sind nicht schwer.*" Cf. Kant 15:679; 6:179; and ApH 7:147.

29 See also Rel 6:193–194 and ApH 7:148.

30 See Johann Gotthelf Lindner, *Lehrbuch der schönen Wissenschaften, insonderheit der Prose und Poesie*, 2 vols. (Königsberg/Leipzig, 1767, 1768), vol. 2, p. 75: "*hänseln* [banter, tease], to admit into the league, hence Hanseatic League, and because there were all sorts of customs there, it thereafter meant to mock, hence the hare [*Hase*] is called *Hänselchen* [little Hansel] in fables because of the little man he makes."

31 Cf. François Marie Arouet de Voltaire, *Die Metaphysik des Neuton, oder Vergliechung der Meinungen des Herrn von Leibnitz und des Neuton*, trans. Gottlieb Christian Mosheim (Heimstädt, 1741). Originally published as *Elémens de la philosophie du Neuton* (Amsterdam: Etienne Ledet, 1738).

32 On the accusation of "charlatanry" aimed at Voltaire, the editors refer to H. A. Korff, *Voltaire im literarischen Deutschland des XVIII. Jahrhunderts. Ein Beitrage zur Geschichte des deutschen Geistes von Gottsched bis Goethe*, 2 vols. (Heidelberg, 1917), vol. 2, p. 505.

33 Conte Francesco Algarotti (1712–1764), an Italian who spent some years at the court of Frederick the Great, wrote *Newtonianismo per le Dame* (1736), which was translated into all the major European languages, including English (in 1737), French (*Le Neutonianisme pour les dames* [Amsterdam, 1741]), and (from the French) German: *Jo. Newtons Welt-Wissenschaft für das Frauenzimmer. Oder Unterredungen über das Licht, die Farben, und die Anziehende Kraft. Aus dem*

Italiänischen des Herrn Algarotti, durch Herrn Du Perron de Castera ins Französische und aus diesem ins Teutsche übersetzet (Braunschweig, 1745). Cf. Kant's reference to Algarotti at *Observations on the Feeling of the Beautiful and Sublime* 2:230.

34 Voltaire, *Abhandlung über die Religionsduldung* (Leipzig, 1764), originally published as *Traité sur la tolérance, à l'occasion de la mort de Jean Calas* (Geneva, 1763). Voltaire's treatise led to the reversal, in 1765, of a death sentence that had been enforced on Jean Calas on March 9, 1762. Cf. below Mro 25:1403.

35 Bernard Le Bovier de Fontanelle (1657–1757), French writer. See his *Dialogen über die Mehrheit der Welten. Mit Anmerkungen und Kupfertafeln*, ed. Johann Ehlert Bode and trans. Wilhelm Christhelf Sigmund Mylius (Berlin, 1780). Originally published as *Entretiens sur la pluralité des mondes* (Paris, 1686), and translated into English: *Conversations on the Plurality of Worlds*, trans. H. A. Hargreaves (Berkeley: University of California Press, 1990).

36 See Karl Friedrich Wilhelm Wander, *Deutsches Sprichwörter-Lexikon. Ein Hausschatz für das deutsche Volk*, 5 vols. (Leipzig, 1867–1880), vol. 1, column 942: "The lazy man drags himself to death, the industrious man runs himself to death. The lazy man prefers to drag a great deal only one time, just to avoid going twice alongside the activity of the industrious man. The industrious man carries little, but goes often."

37 On the basis of the so-called certificate of invitation (*Einladungspatent*) of February 2, 1732 issued by the Prussian King, Friedrich Wilhelm I, numerous Protestants from the diocese of Salzburg moved to East Prussia. On May 27, 1732, they reached Pillau, then moved to Königsberg, settling mainly in the region of Gumbinnen. Despite initial difficulties, the settlements prospered.

38 Cf. Friedländer 25:539; and 15:227. A similar anecdote was published in "Monthly Review for October 1772"; see *British Biography; or an Accurate and impartial account of the lives and writings of eminent persons* [. . .], 10 vols. (London, 1773–1780); see British Biographical Archive, microfiche 814, n.110. See also David Brewster, *The Life of Sir Isaac Newton* (London, 1831), p. 341.

39 Albrecht von Haller, *Grundriß der Physiologie für Vorlesungen*, trans. Konrad Friedrich Uden, 2 parts (Berlin, 1781). See part 1, ch. 12, § 431. Cf. Denis Diderot, "Additions à la lettre sur les aveugles" (*c.*1782) in: *Oeuvres philosophiques*, ed. P. Vernière (Paris, 1956), on p. 152: "I have heard of a blind person who recognized the color of cloths by touching them." See also Edmund Burke, *A Philosophical Enquiry into the Origin of Our Idea of the Sublime and Beautiful* (London, 1757). The latter was translated (based on the fifth edition) by Christian Garve, as *Philosophische Untersuchungen über den Ursprung unsrer Begriffe vom Erhabnen und Schönen* (Riga, 1773); see Garve, pp. 201–202.

40 Georges-Louis Le Clerc, Comte de Buffon, "Dissertation sur les couleurs accidentelles," in *Memoires de l'Académie Royale des Sciences, Année 1743* (Paris, 1746), pp. 147–158, on pp. 151–153.

41 Joseph Huddart, "Von einigen Personen, welche keine Farben unterscheiden konnten, an D. Priestley," in J. S. T. Gehler (ed.), *Sammlungen zur Physik und Naturgeschichte von einigen Liebhabern dieser Wissenschaften*, vol. 1.5 (Leipzig, 1779), pp. 637–640.

42 That is, we are not always thankful or grateful for them.

43 Kant's source is unknown.

44 See François Xavier de Charlevoix, *Histoire et description generale de la Nouvelle France, avec le Journal historique d'un voyage fait par ordre du Roi dans l'Amérique Septentrionnale*. 3 vols. (Paris, 1744). See the 22nd letter, dated August 1721; vol. 3, p. 322.

45 The source of Kant's example is unknown.

46 Presumably a reference to François Rabelais (*c.*1494–*c.*1553), French Renaissance writer, but the source of Kant's claim could not be determined.

47 Kant's source is unknown.

48 On the Koryak people in Siberia, see Johann Gottlieb Georgi, *Beschreibung aller Nationen des Rußischen Reiches, ihrer Lebensart, Religion, Gebräuche, Wohnungen, Kleidungen und übrigen Merkwürdigkeiten*, 4 vols. (St. Petersburg, 1776–1780). On the Koryaks, see p. 348; on this kind of intoxication among Siberian peoples, see pp. 77f.

49 Wild rosemary is known as *ledum palustre* or Marsh Labrador tea, a herb once used as a gruit in brewing beer.

50 See Pierre Bayle, *Historisches und Critisches Wörterbuch, nach der neuesten Auflage von 1740 ins Deutsche übersetzt*, ed. Johann Christoph Gottsched, 4 vols. (Leipzig, 1741–1744); for the entry on Augustine, see vol. 1, p. 401. Originally published as *Dictionnaire historique et critique* (fifth edition, Amsterdam, 1740). On *crapula* as "surfeiting," see Augustine, *Confessions*, x.31.45.

51 See Herodotus, *Histories*, book 1; Tacitus, *De origine et situ germanorum*, ed. Alf Önnerfors (Stuttgart, 1983), on p. 22; and Laurence Sterne, *The life and opinions of Tristram Shandy, gentleman*, 9 vols. (London, 1760–1767). German translation: Johann Joachim Christoph Bode (trans.), *Das Leben und die Meynungen des Tristram Shandy* (Berlin, 1763–1767).

52 On Cato the Elder, see Horace (65–8 BCE), *Carmina* (Odes) III.21.11–12: "even the virtue of venerable Cato is said to have grown warm with wine." On Cato the Younger, see Seneca, *De tranquillate animi* (On Tranquility of Mind), IX.17.4. Cf. 6:428 and ApH 7:171.

53 Jonathan Swift (1667–1745), English writer. The Academy editors cite this German translation: Jonathan Swift, ed. Johann Breitenfels, *Satyrische und ernsthafte Schriften*, 8 vols. (Hamburg/Leipzig, 1756–1766). Swift's famous maxim was the matter of some eighteenth-century controversy; e.g., Patrick Delaney calls it "detestable," in Delaney, *Observations upon Lord Orrery's Remarks on the Life and Writings of Dr. Jonathan Swift* (London, 1754), p. 142.

54 See Joseph Addison and Richard Steele, *Spectator* (London, 1711–1714). The passage reads, in Gregory Smith (ed.), *Addison & Steele and others, The Spectator*, 4 vols. (London, 1963–1964), no. 509, vol. 3, p. 108: "I say, Mr. Hobson kept a Stable of forty good Cattle always ready and fit for Travelling; but, when a Man came for an Horse, he was led into the Stable, where there was a great Choice; but he obliged him to take the Horse which stood next to the Stable-Door; so that every Customer was alike well served according to his Chance, and every Horse ridden with the same Justice: From whence it became a Proverb, when what ought to be your Election was forced upon you, to say 'Hobson's Choice'." German translation: Richard Steele and Joseph Addison (eds.), *Der Zuschauer* (The Spectator), Louise Gottschedin and Victoria Adelgunde (trans.), 9 vols. (Leipzig, 1749–1751). Cf. Adickes's note in AK 15:736–737.

55 Pseudo-Longinus, *De sublimate* (On the sublime), trans. Herbert Lord Havell (London: Macmillan, 1890), xii.4–5, p. 27: "The sublimity of Demosthenes is generally sudden and abrupt: that of Cicero is equally diffused. Demosthenes is vehement, rapid, vigorous, terrible; he burns and sweeps away all before him; and hence we may liken him to a whirlwind or a thunderbolt: Cicero is like a widespread conflagration, which rolls over and feeds on all around it, whose fire is extensive and burns long, breaking out successively in different places, and finding its fuel now here, now there."

56 Kant's source is George Lyttleton and Elizabeth Montagu, *Dialogues of the Dead* (first edition, London, 1760), dialogue xxii, where François Rabelais says to Lucian (on p. 238, second edition, London, 1760): "Good Sense is, like a Dish of plain Beef or Mutton, proper only for Peasants; but *a Ragout of Folly*, well dressed with *a sharp Sauce of Wit*, is fit to be served at an Emperor's Table." Cf. Friedländer 25:491.

57 Jakob Böhme (1575–1624), German philosophical mystic and founder of modern theosophy. Originally a cobbler, Böhme is the author of *Aurora* (1612) and other theological writings.

58 Francis Hutcheson (1694–1746), *An Essay on the Nature and Conduct of the Passions and Affections, with Illustrations on the Moral Sense* (London, 1728). The editors cite these pages in the German translation: *Abhandlung über die Natur und Beherrschung der Leidenschaften und Neigungen und über das moralische Gefühl insonderheit* (Leipzig, 1760), Johann Gottfried Gellius (trans.), pp. 33, 66, 68, 81, 94, 235, 351.

59 A reference would be expected in: Nicolas Fuß, *Lobrede auf Herrn Leonhard Euler, in der Versammlung der Kayserlichen Akademie der Wissenschaften zu St. Petersburg den 23. Octob. 1783 vorgelesen [...]* (Basel, 1786), but Fuß mentions no anecdotes to which the text could be referring. Dieudonné Thiébault, *Mes souvenirs de vingt ans de séjour à Berlin [...]*, 5 vols. (Paris, 1804), contains an anecdote to which Kant could be referring; see (in the fourth edition of 1826), vol. 5, p. 13. But it remains unclear how in the mid-1780s Kant could have learned of Thiébault's anecdote.

60 See Jacob Hofer, *Dissertatio curiosa-medica De Nostalgia, vulgo Heimwehe oder Heimwehsucht* (Basel, 1678).

61 Apparently a reference to subsequently well-known "errors of judgment" [*Fehlurteile*] in Johann Caspar Lavater, *Physiognomische Fragmente, zur Beförderung der Menschenkenntniß und Menschenliebe*, 4 vols. (Leipzig/Winterthur, 1775–1778).

62 Philipp Dormer Stanhope, 4th Earl of Chesterfield (1694–1773), British diplomat and man of letters. He alludes to the French adage in: *Letters [...] to His Son [...]* (London, 1774). The editors cite this German translation: *Briefe an seinen Sohn [...]*, 6 vols., trans. Johann Gottfried Gellius (Leipzig, 1774, 1775, 1776, 1777); see vol. 4 (1776), p. 183.

63 Johann Heinrich Zedler's lexicon contains an extensive article on rhubarb (*Rhabarber*); see Johann Heinrich Zedler (ed.), *Grosses vollständiges Universal-Lexikon aller Wissenschaften und Künste, welche bishero durch menschlichen Verstand und Witz erfunden und verbessert worden*, 64 vols. (Leipzig/Halle, 1732–1750), in vol. 31, columns 1028–1055.

64 In other writings, Kant speaks of a kind of enthusiasm that is an affect (ApH 7:254, 269; KU 5:272). In the third *Critique*, Kant defines enthusiasm as "the idea of good with affect" and connects it to the sublime (KU 5:272ff.), and he associates red with the idea of sublimity (KU 5:302).

65 The claims in this passage can be compared to those at KU 5:275.

66 For this reference to "discretion" and Swift, see David Hume, "Of Qualities Useful to Ourselves," in *An Enquiry Concerning the Principles of Morals*, part 2. Brandt and Stark cite this German translation: David Hume, *Vermischte Schriften*, 4 vols., ed. Johann Georg Sulzer et al. (Hamburg/Leipzig, 1754–1756), on vol. III (*Sittenlehre der Gesellschaft*), p. 136.

67 See the work of German poet and mathematician Abraham Gotthelf Kästner (1719–1800), *Einige Vorlesungen. In der Königlichen deutschen Gesellschaft zu Göttingen gehalten*, 2 vols. (Alternburg, 1768, 1773), on vol. 1, p. 102. The observation about *sot* and *fat* is mentioned in the review of the *Deutsche Bibliothek der schönen Wissenschaften*, vol. 2 (1768), pp. 716–720.

68 See *Angenehme Beschäftigungen in der Einsamkeit, oder tausend Stück auserlesener Anecdoten*, 2 vols. (Leipzig, 1775, 1777), on vol. 2, pp. 117f.; and Karl Friedrich Müchler, *Anekdotenlexikon für Leser von Geschmack*, 2 vols. (Berlin, 1784), on vol. 2, pp. 36f.

69 *Bull* derives from Middle English *bull* ("falsehood, trivial statements, fraud"). The verb *to bull*, dating from the 1530s, means "to mock, cheat." Cf. Friedländer 25:506.

70 Jean-Baptiste Colbert (1619–1683), French statesman, founder of the French Academy of Sciences. It appears that the mention of Colbert is based on an undetermined publication that followed the prize question of the Parisian Academy of Sciences. E.g., see Jacques Necker, *Lobrede auf Johann Baptist Colbert, die den Preis der Königlichen Akademie der Wissenschaften zu Paris erhalten hat* (Dresden, 1781), p. 48: "Colbert was tirelessly occupied with the expansion of the sciences; he expanded the royal library and the botanical garden; he had the observatory built; he hired Huygens and Cassini to France; finally under his aegis the Academy of Sciences arose." However, sayings such as the one Kant mentions cannot be identified in Necker's work.

71 Ehrenfried Walther von Tschirnhaus (1651–1708), German mathematician and scientist. See Tschirnhaus, *Die Curiöse Medicin, darinnen die Gesundheit des Leibes in sehr wahrscheinlichen Gedancken in XII. Reguln vorgestellet / Und wie solche durch gar leichte Mittel zu unterhalten gezeiget wird* (Frankfurt/Leipzig, 1688), rule 11, pp. 162f. This work was originally published as *Medicina Corporis* (Amsterdam, 1686).

72 See the work of Athenaeus of Naucratis (*c.*170–*c.*230 CE), *Deipnosophistae*, in *The Deipnosophists in Seven Volumes*, trans. Charles Burton Gulick (Cambridge, MA and London: Harvard University Press, 1957), vol. X, 419 c–d. Cf. ApH 7:278.

73 Kant's source is unknown.

74 See the play by Jean Jacques Rutledge (1742–1794), written anonymously: *Le Bureau d'Esprit, Comédie en cinq Actes et en prose* (Liège, 1776). The satirical play, which appeared in the fall of 1777, characterizes Marie Thérèse Rodet Geoffrin (1699–1777) and is directed at the *philosophes*. The literary source for Geoffrin's saying remains unknown.

75 Kant's source is unknown.

76 Jonathan Swift (1667–1745), *A Tale of a Tub* (London: John Nutt, 1704). German translation: *Mährgen von der Tonne. Nebst übrigen dazugehörigen Schriften*, trans. Johann von Breitenfels, pseudonym of Johann Heinrich Waser (Hamburg, 1758).

77 Jonathan Swift, *Martinus Scriblerus, Peri Bathous: or, of the Art of Sinking in Poetry* (London: Benjamin Motte, 1727). German translation: *Anti-Longin, Oder die Kunst in der Poesie zu kriechen*, ed. Johann Christoph Gottsched, trans. Johann Joachim Schwabe (Leipzig, 1734).

78 See David Hume, *The History of Great Britain*, 2 vols. (Philadelphia: M'Carty and Davis, 1836), vol. 2, p. 654: "Hudibras is perhaps one of the most learned compositions that is to be found in any language." (First published in London/Edinburgh: Gavin Hamilton et al., 1754–1762.) Kant mentions Samuel Butler (1612–1680), English author of *Hudibras* (1663–1678), at Friedländer 25:518.

79 Samuel Butler, *Hudibras*, part 2, canto 3, lines 1023ff.: "Upon the bench I will so handle 'em / That the vibration of this Pendulum / Shall make all Taylors' yards, of one / Unanimous Opinion."

80 Samuel Butler, *Hudibras*, part 2, canto 2, lines 317–320: "Why should not conscience have vacation / As well as other courts o' th' nation / Have equal power to adjourn, / Appoint appearance and return [?]"

81 Samuel Butler, *Hudibras*, part 3, canto 3, lines 261–264: "If th' ancients crown'd their bravest men / That only sav'd a citizen, / What victory could e'er be won, / If ev'ry one would save but one [?]"

82 Samuel Butler, *Hudibras*, part 1, canto 3, lines 607–610: "In all the trade of war, no feat / Is nobler than a brave retreat: / For those that run away, and fly, / Take place at least of th' enemy."

83 Samuel Butler, *Hudibras*, part 3, canto 1, lines 277–280: "What makes all doctrines plain and clear? – / About two hundred pounds a year. / And that which was prov'd true before, / Prove false again? – Two hundred more."

84 See Guillaume Raynal, *Anecdoten zur Lebensgeschichte berühmter französischer, deutscher, italienischer, holländischer und anderer Gelehrten*, 2 vols., trans. Johann Adam Hiller (Leipzig, 1762–1764). Originally published as *Anecdotes littéraires, ou Histoire de ce qui est arrivé de plus singulier et de plus intéressant aux écrivains françois* [...] (Paris: Chez Durand, 1752).

85 The sources of Kant's remarks about Swift and Sterne remain unknown.

86 Kant's source is unknown.

87 Jean-Baptiste Colbert, founder of the French Academy of Sciences.

88 Tungus: now called Evenks, a northern Asia people. See Johann Gottlieb Georgi, *Bemerkungen einer Reise in Rußischen Reich im Jahre 1772*, 2 vols. (St. Petersburg, 1775), vol. 1, p. 248.

89 Peter Abelard (1079–1142), French theologian and philosopher.

90 See (anonymous) *Angenehme Beschäftigungen in der Einsamkeit, oder tausend Stück auserlesener Anecdoten*, 2 vols. (Leipzig, 1775, 1777), vol. 1, pp. 169f. See also Friedrich Nicolai, *Vade Mecum für lustige Leute enthaltend eine Sammlung angenehmer Scherze witziger Einfälle und spaßhafter kurzer Historien aus den besten Schriftstellern zusammengetragen*, 7 vols. (Berlin, 1764–1777), vol. 3, pp. 160–161.

91 Johann Buno (1617–1697), German theologian and pedagogue. See Johann Buno, *Tabularum mnemonicarum, quibus historia universalis, cum sacra tum profana, a condito mundo, per aeras nobiliores & quatuor monarchias ad nostrum usque aetatem deducta, simulacris et hieroglyphicis figuris delineata exhibetur clavis* [. . .] (Lüneburg, 1664). For the quote, "Erasmus quasi, er aß eine Muß: oder eras mus, in deme er Satyrice vieler böse mores rodirte," see this German translation of the work: *Historische Bilder / Darinnen idea historiae universalis, eine kurtze summarische Abbildung der fürnehmsten Geist- und Weltlichen Geschichte* (Lüneburg, 1672), p. 199.

92 On Caesar, see *ibid.*, Johann Buno (Lüneburg, 1672), p. 205.

93 See Johann Buno, *Memoriale juris civilis Romani, quo tituli omnes et praecipuae leges* [. . .], 2 vols. (Hamburg, 1673,1674); for the illustration, see Digest, bk. 38, ch. 16, p. 70.

94 For the saying, "*Tantum scimus, quantum memoria teneamus,*" see Hans Walter, *Lateinische Sprichwörter und Sentenzen des Mittelalters in alphabetischer Anordnung*, 6 vols. (Göttingen, 1963–1967), on vol. 5, p. 262, no. 31057c. Kant quotes this maxim in *Lectures on Pedagogy* 9:472.

95 Plato, *Phaedrus* 274e–275b.

96 John Wallis (1616–1703), English mathematician. See John Wallis, *Opera mathematica*, 3 vols. (Oxford: 1693, 1695, 1699), vol. 2 (1693), ch. 103, p. 450. Wallis is mentioned in Christian Wolff, *Psychologia empirica* (Frankfurt/Leipzig, 1738), § 197.

97 Kraken is a mythical sea-monster that was said to appear off the coast of Norway.

98 Erik Pontoppidan (1698–1764), Danish bishop and historian. See Erik Pontoppidan, *Versuch einer natürlichen Historie von Norwegen [. . .] Aus dem Dänischen übersetzt [. . .]*, 2 vols., trans. by Johann Adolph Scheiben (Copenhagen, 1753, 1754), on vol. 2, pp. 345ff.

99 Giovanni Pico della Mirandola (1463–1494), Italian philosopher and scholar. See under "Pico (Johann) Herr von Mirandola und Concordia," in Johann Heinrich Zedler's *Universal-Lexikon, Grosses vollständiges Universal-Lexikon aller Wissenschaften und Künste, welche bishero durch menschlichen Verstand und Witz erfunden und verbessert worden*, 64 vols., ed. Johann Heinrich Zedler (Leipzig/Halle, 1732–1750), on vol. 28, column 59.

100 Julius Caesar Scaliger (1484–1558), Italian humanist known for his wide learning.

101 Politian, or Poliziano (1454–1494), Italian humanist and philologist.

102 Antonio Magliabecchi (1633–1714), Italian bibliophile, scholar, and librarian to Cosmo III, Grand Duke of Tuscany. Kant's source is Joseph Spence (1699–1768). See Joseph Spence, *A Parallel; In the manner of Plutarch: between a most celebrated Man of Florence; and One scarce heard of, in England*, in: "*Fugitive Pieces on various subjects, by several authors.*" (London: 1757); see edition of 1761, vol. 2, pp. 321–357, on pp. 323–335.

103 Baumgarten, *Metaphysica*, fourth edition (Halle, 1757), "§ 589–§ 594, Sectio VII: Facultas fingendi."

104 Kant's source is unknown.

105 See Johann Gramm, *Abhandlung vom Schießpulver; Wenn es in Europa erfun-den worden, und wie lange es unter den Dänen üblich sey?* (Leipzig, 1755), in Johann Daniel Tietze et al. (eds.), *Allgemeines Magazin der Natur, Kunst und Wissenschaften* (Leipzig, 1753–1767), vol. 5, pp. 137–263; see pp. 229–230.

106 Jean Jacques Barthélemy (1716–1795), French writer. See his "Réflexions sur quelques monumens Phéniciens, et sur les Alphabets, qui en résultent," in: *Histoire de l'académie royale des inscriptions et belles-lettres avec les mémoires de littérature, tirés des registres de cette académie depuis l'année MDCCLVIII, jusques et compris l'année MDCCLX* (Paris, 1764), vol. 30, pp. 405–426.

107 Kant's source is unknown. Thomas Savery (*c.*1650–1715), an English inventor, was granted a patent for his pump in 1698. By the mid-1760s, James Watt (1736–1819) had developed a working model of the modern steam engine.

108 That is, Francis Bacon (1561–1626), English philosopher.

109 Marcus Fabius Quintilian (*c.*35–*c.*86 CE), Roman rhetorician. See his *Institutio oratoria*, II.15.

110 Kant's reference is unknown, but he may be referring to Achille III de Har-lay, Count of Beaumont (1639–1712), who was chosen first president of the Parliament of Paris in 1689 and was known for his caustic wit.

111 Cf. Quintilian, *Institutio oratoria*, XII.10.16–17; and Mro 25:1226–1227 above.

112 Kant's source is unknown.

113 See Alexandre Jérôme Loiseau de Mauléon, *Berühmte Rechts-Händel bey ver-schiedenen Parlamentern in Frankreich. Aus dem Französischen, mit Anmerkun-gen* (Berlin, 1777). Cf. François Gayot de Pitaval, *Erzählung sonderbarer Rechtshändel, sammt deren gerichtlichen Entscheidung. Aus dem französischen übersetzt*, 3 vols. (Leipzig, 1747), originally published as: *Causes célèbres et inter-essantes, avec des judgements qui les ont décidées* (Paris, 1734–1743).

114 Edmund Waller (1606–1687), English poet. Waller's poem to Cromwell is "A Panegyric to my Lord Protector," and that to Charles II, "To the King, upon His Majesty's Happy Return." See Simon Ratzeberger (probable author), *Vade Mecum für lustige Leute enthaltend eine Sammlung angenehmer Scherze witziger Einfälle und spaßhafter kurzer Historien aus den besten Schriftstellern zusammenge-tragen*, ed. Friedrich Nicolai, 7 vols. (Berlin, 1764–1777), vol. 2, pp. 183–184 (no. 264). Cf. (anonymous) *Angenehme Beschäftigungen in der Einsamkeit, oder tausen Stück auserlesener Anecdoten*, 2 vols. (Leipzig, 1775, 1777); vol. 1, p. 136. Cf. also Samuel Johnson, *Biographische und critische Nachrichten von einigen englischen Dichtern. Aus dem Englischen übersetz und mit Anmerkungen vermehrt*, trans. Christian Friedrich von Blankenburg, 2 vols. (Altenburg, 1781–1783), vol. 2, p. 276.

115 Waller is said to have replied: "Sir, we poets never succeed so well in writing truth as in fiction."

116 Barthold Heinrich Brockes (1680–1747), German poet. See Brockes, *Irdisches Vergnügen in Gott* [...], 2 vols. (Hamburg, 1724, 1725).

117 Albrecht von Haller (1708–1777), "Die Alpen" (1729).

118 John Milton, *Paradise Lost* (London: Samuel Simmons, 1667). German transla-tion: *Episches Gedichte von dem Verlohrnen Paradiese. Uebersetzet und durchgehends mit Anmerckungen über die Kunst des Poeten begleitet*, trans. Johann Jacob Bodmer (Zürich/Leipzig, 1742).

119 Virgil's *Eclogues* depict the lives of Arcadian shepherds.

120 Friedrich Gottlieb Klopstock (1724–1803), German poet. Cf. Mro 25:1332 below and Collins 25:97.

121 Plutarch, *On Superstition*, 166c: "Heraclitus says that people awake enjoy one world in common, but of those who are fallen asleep each roams about in a world of his own." In: *Moralia*, trans. Frank Cole Babbitt, vol. 2 (Loeb Classical Library, 1928).

122 Santorio Santorio (1561–1636), Italian physiologist, author of *De statica medicina* (Concerning Static Medicine) (1614). By weighing the intake and excretion of solids and liquids, Santorio there proposed that the majority of consumed food was lost from the body via "imperceptible perspiration" (*perspiratio insensibili*). See Santorio Santorio, *Aphorismi de Medicina Statica cum Scholiis* [...], ed. Andreas Rüdiger (Leipzig, 1762), Section VII ("De Animi Affectionibus"), pp. 111–122, and aphorism XXXXV of Section VII.

123 See Johann Kaspar Lavater, *Physiognomische Fragmente, zur Beförderung der Menschenkenntniß und Menschenliebe*, 4 vols. (Leipzig/Winterthur, 1775–1778), vol. 2, pp. 194–196.

124 Kant's source is: *British Biography; or an Accurate and impartial account of the lives and writings of eminent persons* [...], 10 vols. (London, 1773–1780); see British Biographical Archive, microfiche 814, no. 109.

125 Francesco Petrarch (1304–1374), Italian poet, whose *Il Canzoniere* (Songbook) is presumably devoted to Laura de Noves (1310–1348). For the story of Petrarch's response, see Antonio da Tempo, "Francesco Petrarca," in *Le vite di Dante, Petrarca et Boccaccio scritte fino al secolo decimosesto*, ed. Angelo Solerti (Milan, 1904), p. 333.

126 Kant's source is unknown.

127 Kant is referring to Section X "Praesagitio" (§§ 610–618) of Pars III of Baumgarten's *Metaphysics*.

128 See, e.g., 1 John 5:3.

129 If the parallel between the two mystics is not an error of the transcriber, it is likely that "Molignon" refers to Jeanne Marie Bouvier de la Mothe Guyon (1648–1717). Cf. the contrast between her and Antoinette de Bourignon (1616–1680), a Flemish mystic, in Johann Caspar Lavater, *Physiognomische Fragmente*, vol. 3, p. 227. Cf. also Kant's remark on Bourignon at ApH 7:133.

130 See the (anonymous) book by Louis-Claude de Saint-Martin (1743–1803), French mystical philosopher: *Irrthümer und Wahrheit, oder Rückweiß für die Menschen auf das allgemeine Principium aller Erkenntniß*, trans. Matthias Claudius (Breslau, 1782). Original title: *Des Erreurs et de la Vérité* (Of Errors and Truth) (Lyon, 1775).

131 Artemidorus Daldianus (*c.* second–third century CE), soothsayer from Ephesus (in what is now Turkey), author of *Oneirocritica* (The Interpretation of Dreams). See Artemidorus, *The Interpretation of Dreams*, second edition, trans. R. J. White (Torrance, CA: Original Books, 1990), bk. 1, preface.

132 Kant's source is unknown.

133 See Jean-Jacques Rousseau, *Second Discourse* (1756). Cf. ApH 7:186.

134 On Friedrich Balthasar Schönberg von Brenkenhof (1723–1780), see August Gottlieb Meissner (anonymous), *Leben Franz Balthasar Schönberg von*

Brenkenhof, Königl. Preuß. geheim. Ober- Finanz- Kriegs- und Domänenrath (Leipzig, 1782), pp. 191–192. The source for the anecdote about Prussian Minister Heinrich Rüdiger von Ilgen (*c.*1650–*c.*1728) is unknown.

135   Cf. ApH 7:191, where Kant claims that with discursive cognition, the sign "accompanies" the concept as a guardian in order to reproduce the concept.

136   Philo of Alexandria (*c.*20 BCE–C.50 CE), Hellenistic Jewish philosopher. On the number seven, see Philo, *De opificio mundi* (On the Creation of the Cosmos), §§ 89–128. Marquis d'Argentean has not been identified.

137   See Albrecht von Haller, *Onomatologia medica completa* [. . .], ed. Johann Peter Eberhard (Ulm/Frankfurt/Leipzig, 1772), columns 96–97. This critical year was said to arrive every seven years and presumed to mark a person's passage into the next life stage. Cf. ApH 7:194. Romulus and Numa Pompilius, respectively, were the first two legendary Roman kings.

138   Cf. *Critique of Pure Reason* A134/B173. *Casus in terminis* refers to a case that is to be determined by a simple subsumption under the law as it is written, whereas *casus discretivi* requires the critical power of judgment.

139   This passage can be compared to the opening of Kant's essay (1784), "An Answer to the Question: What is Enlightenment?" at 8:35.

140   Philipp Dormer Stanhope, 4th Earl of Chesterfield (1694–1773), British diplomat. See Chesterfield, *Briefe an seinen Sohn* [. . .], trans. Johann Gottfried Gellius, 6 vols. (Leipzig, 1774, 1775, 1776, 1777), vol. 3 (1775), p. 130 and vol. 4 (1776), p. 96.

141   Although the source of this claim has not been ascertained, in a similar passage at ApH 7:209 Kant refers to Adam Smith, *An Inquiry into the Nature and Causes of the Wealth of Nations* (London, 1776), II.iii.36.

142   Cornelius de Pauw (1739–1799), Dutch historian and geographer who served as a diplomat at Frederick the Great's court. Apparently either Kant or the transcriber confused the book's title ("Americans"). See Cornelius de Pauw, *Philosophische Untersuchungen über die Aegypter und Chineser* [. . .], trans. Johann Georg Krünitz, 2 vols. (Berlin, 1774), vol. 2, pp. 339–340. Originally published as *Recherches philosophiques sur les Égyptiens et Chinois*, 2 vols. (Berlin, 1773).

143   See William Dampier (1651–1715), *Reise nach den Südländern. Neu-Holland u.a. Welcher beygefüget* [. . .]. *4. Theil. Aus dem Engellischen ins Französische und aus diesem ins Teutsche übersetzt* (Frankfurt/Leipzig, 1714), p. 162. Originally published as *A New Voyage Round the World* (London, 1697). Cf. ApH 7:304.

144   The source is unknown.

145   Gotthold Lessing (1729–1781), German dramatist, philosopher, and author of *Nathan the Wise* (1779), to which Kant refers in a similar comment at Menschenkunde 25:886.

146   The story, which comes in numerous versions, derives from French Humanist scholar Guillaume Budé (1467–1540). See Claude Adrien Helvétius, *Discurs über den Geist des Menschen* [. . .], ed. Johann Christoph Gottsched, trans. Johann Gabriel Forkert (Leipzig/Liegnitz, 1760), vol. 4, 1, p. 483. See also Friedrich Nicolai (ed.), Simon Ratzeberger (probable author), *Vade Mecum für lustige Leute* [. . .], 7 vols. (Berlin, 1764–1777), vol. 2, p. 123, no. 188. Cf. Friedländer 25:541; and ApH 7:210.

147 Christoph Girtanner, "Fragmente über J. J. Rousseau's Leben, Charakter und Schriften," in: *Göttingisches Magazin der Wissenschaften und Literatur*, ed. Georg Christoph Lichtenberg and Georg Forster (Gottingen, 1781), p. 283.

148 See Siegmund Jacob Baumgarten and Johann Salomo Semler (eds.), *Sammlung merkwürdiger Lebensbeschreibungen grösten Theils aus der britanischen Biographie*, 10 vols. (Halle, 1754–1770), vol. 8, p. 318.

149 The inhabitants of the Valais canton in Switzerland were subject to goiters. Cf. Mro 25:1328–1329 below.

150 See Louis-Claude de Saint-Martin (anonymous), *Irrthümer und Wahrheit* [. . .], trans. Matthias Claudius (Breslau, 1782). Original title: *Des Erreurs et de la Vérité* (Of Errors and Truth) (Lyon, 1775).

151 See Louis-Claude de Saint-Martin (anonymous), *Tableau Naturel des Rapports qui existent entre Dieu, l'Homme et l'Univers* (Natural Table of Relations that Exist among God, Man, and the Universe), 2 parts (Edinburgh, 1782).

152 The sources of the three stories in this paragraph are unknown.

153 Johann Friedrich Karl Grimm (1737–1821), German physician. See his (anonymous), *Bemerkungen eines Reisenden durch Deutschland, Frankreich, England und Holland in Briefen an seine Freunde*, 3 vols. (Altenburg, 1775).

154 Jean-Jacques Rousseau, *Selbstgespräche auf einsamen Spaziergängen. Ein Anhang zu den Bekenntnissen*, trans. Karl Gottfried Schreiter (Berlin, 1782). Originally published as *Les Rêveries du promeneur solitaire* (Reveries of the Solitary Walker) (Geneva, 1782). Kant himself also displayed the tendencies of a hypochondriac.

155 Christian Joseph Jagemann, "Leben und Schriften des Galileo Galilei," in: *Magazin der Italienischen Litteratur und Künste*, ed. Christoph Jagemann, 8 vols., vol. 7 (Dessau/Leipzig, 1783), pp. 1–235; see esp. pp. 162–163 and 174. Jagemann refers to Giovanni Batista Clemente de' Nelli, *Vita e commercio letterario di Galileo Galilei*, 2 vols. (Lausanne, 1793). But Nelli (vol. 1, pp. 20–21) criticizes the supposed metempsychosis and shows that Galileo's death and Newton's birth did not coincide temporally.

156 Apparently a reference to § 639, the last paragraph in Sectio XII of Pars III in Baumgarten's handbook.

157 The source has not been ascertained.

158 The (disputed) claim that da Vinci died in the arms of the French king Francis I is found in Christian Joseph Jagemann, *Geschichte der freyen Künste und Wissenschaften in Italien*, Vol. 3, 3 (Leipzig, 1781), p. 671. See also Giorgio Vasari, *Le vite de piú eccelenti architetti, pittori, et scultori italiani, da Cimabue a tempi nostri* (Florence, 1550). At vol. 1, p. 42, in their translation of Vasari, *Leben der ausgezeichnetsten Maler, Bildhauer und Baumeister von Cimabue bis zum Jahr 1567*, 6 vols., trans. Ludwig Schorn and Ernst Förster (Worms, 1983), Schorn/Förster write: "Vasari's story of the king's presence at Leonardo's death is factually without basis."

159 Kant's claim could be based on this piece of travel writing: Johann Jacob Volkmann, *Historisch-kritische Nachrichten von Italien, welche eine Beschreibung dieses Landes, der Sitten, Regierungsform, Handlung, des Zustandes der Wissenschaften und insonderheit der Werke der Kunst enthalten*, 3 vols. (Leipzig, 1777), vol. 2, pp. 47f.

160   On Newton's self-assessment, see *British Biography* [...], 10 vols. (London, 1773–1780); British Biographical Archive, microfiche 814, no. 109: "In one of his letters to Dr. Bentley, speaking of his discoveries, he says, 'If I have done the public any service this way, it was due to nothing but industry and patient thought.'" Cf. Isaac Newton, *Philosophiae naturalis principia mathematica* (London, 1687).

161   Dolet defended the imitation of Ciceronian Latin in this work. See Stephani Doleti (Étienne Dolet), *Dialogus de imitatione Ciceroniana, adversus Desiderium Erasmum Roterodamum, pro Christophoro Longolio* (Leiden, 1535). Cf. Mro 25:1411 below.

162   On the "dismissal" of taste in cases of conflict with genius, cf. *Critique of the Power of Judgment* 5:319.

163   Alexander Gerard (1728–1795), Scottish writer and philosopher. See his *An Essay on Genius* (London, 1774), translated into German by Christian Garve as *Versuch über das Genie* (Leipzig, 1776).

164   See Johann Ludewig Hogrewe, *Beschreibung der in England seit 1759 angelegten, und jetzt gröstentheils vollendeten schiffbaren Kanäle, zur innern Gemeinschaft der vornehmsten Handelsstädte* [...] (Hannover, 1780), pp. 90 and 124.

165   Jean Henry Samuel Formey, *La vie de Mr. Jean Philippe Baratier, Maître ès Art, & Membre de la Société Royale des Sciences de Berlin* (Franfurt/Leipzig, 1755). Cf., in the unpaginated foreword, the reprint of a letter from Formey of March 24, 1755. Baratier was born on January 19, 1721, near Nuremberg, the son of a French pastor. He learned to read at the age of three. His first publication was a Hebrew dictionary (1730). In March 1735 he earned his doctorate in Halle under Lange; in the same year be became a member of the Berlin Academy of Sciences. He died on October 5, 1740. His father anonymously published *Merckwürdige Nachricht von einem frühzeitig gelehrten Kinde* (Stettin/Leipzig, 1728). See also ApH 7:227.

166   On Christoph Clavius (*c.*1537–1612), German astronomer and mathematician, see Joseph Addison and Richard Steele, *Addison & Steele and others, The Spectator*, 4 vols., ed. Gregory Smith (London, 1963–1964), no. 307, vol. 4, p. 422: "The Story of Clavius is very well known; he was entered in a College of Jesuits, and after having been tryed at several Parts of Learning, was upon the Point of being dismissed as an hopeless Blockhead, till one of the Fathers took it into his Head to make an Assay of his Parts in Geometry, which it seems hit his Genius so luckily, that he afterwards became one of the greatest Mathematicians of the Age." Cf. Maladies 2:260; ApH 7:204.

167   Blaise Pascal, *Pensées sur la religion et sur quelques autres sujets* (Amsterdam, 1688). German translation: *Gedanken* [...] *mit Anmerkungen und Gedanken*, ed. Johann Friedrich Kleuker (Bremen, 1777); on his discoveries see its foreword, pp. xxxv f., an excerpt from a biography written by Pascal's sister.

168   Count Pietro Verri (1728–1797), Italian philosopher and political economist. See Pietro Verri (anonymous), *Gedanken über die Natur des Vergnügens*, trans. Christoph Meiners (Leipzig, 1777), pp. 14, 16, and 64. Originally published as *Idee sull' indole del piacere* (Ideas on the Nature of Pleasure) (Livorno, 1773). Cf. ApH 7:232.

169 Kant is referring to the novel by the English writer Henry Fielding (1707–1754), *The History of Tom Jones, a Foundling* (London, 1749). Cf. ApH 7:164.

170 Although the exact source for Kant's anecdote has not been ascertained, see the anonymous work, *Supplemente zum Anekdotenlexikon für Leser von Geschmack* (Berlin, 1785), p. 91, about the suicide of a certain Philipp Merdant.

171 François Marie Arouet de Voltaire, *Der Heldengesang auf Heinrich den Vierdten, König von Frankreich*, trans. Friedrich Heinrich von Schönberg (Dresden, 1751), pp. 107–108. Originally published as *La Ligue, ou Henri le Grand, poëme épique* (Geneva, 1723).

172 Kant's source is unknown.

173 See Aulus Gellius (Latin compiler, *c.* mid-second century CE), *Noctes atticae* (The Attic Nights), 2 vols., ed. P. K. Marshall (Oxford: Clarendon Press, 1968), 17.19.6.

174 Kant or the transcriber may have mistakenly conjoined the name of the German philosopher Johann Nicolas Tetens (1736–1807) with a book by Johann Joachim Spalding (1714–1804), *Die Bestimmung des Menschen* (The Destiny of the Human Being) (1748). However, Kant's claim is found neither in Tetens's *Philosophische Versuche über die menschliche Natur und ihre Entwicklung* (Philosophical Essays on Human Nature and its Development), 2 vols. (Leipzig, 1777) nor in Spalding's book.

175 Henry Home, Lord Kames (1696–1782), *Sketches of the History of Man* (London, 1774); see Sketch 7, "Progress and Effects of Luxury." German translation: *Versuche über die Geschichte des Menschen*, 2 vols., trans. Anton Ernst Klausing (Leipzig, 1774–1775).

176 Apparently this is a reference to the Holy Roman Emperor Charles IV (1316–1378), but no source has been identified.

177 François Duc de LaRochefoucauld (1613–1680), *Refléxions, ou Sentences et maximes morals* (Paris, 1665). The quote is found in LaRochefoucauld, *Oeuvres complètes* (Paris, 1825), Supplément no. xv, p. 402. Cf. Philipp Dormer Stanhope, 4th Earl of Chesterfield, *Briefe an seinen Sohn* [. . .], trans. Johann Gottfried Gellius, 6 vols. (Leipzig, 1774–1777), in vol. 2 (1775), p. 148.

178 No relevant passage in David Hume's works has been found. The editors Brandt and Stark suggest that Henry Home may have been intended, as in Menschenkunde 25:1103. Adam Smith, however, connects poverty to the want of a linen shirt and leather shoes to wear in public. See Adam Smith, *An Inquiry into the Nature and Causes of the Wealth of Nations* (London, 1776), book 5, chapter 2, article 4, "Taxes upon consumable Commodities," in Adam Smith, *An Inquiry into the Nature and Causes of the Wealth of Nations*, 2 vols., ed. R. H. Campbell et al. (Oxford: Clarendon Press, 1976), vol. 2, pp. 869–870.

179 Johann Joachim Winckelmann (1717–1768), German art historian. See his *Abhandlung von der Fähigkeit der Empfindung des Schönen in der Kunst, und dem Unterrichte in derselben* (Dresden, 1763); and *Briefe an seine Freunde in der Schweiz* (Zürich, 1778).

180 See Mro 25:1299 above, where Kant repudiates the laws governing dress in Denmark. Cf. ApH 7:209, 250.

181 Kant's source is unknown. Cf. ApH 7:299.

182 See Friedrich Nicolai (ed.), *Vade Mecum für lustige Leute* [...], 7 vols. (Berlin, 1764–1777), vol. 1, p. 90, no. 107. Cf. Mro 25:1303 above.

183 Sirach 4:4 (King James Version): "Reject not the supplication of the afflicted; neither turn away thy face from a poor man."

184 The *Spectator*, an English daily literary publication (founded in 1711) edited by Joseph Addison and Richard Steele. *Spectator* No. 98, Addison's entry of June 22, 1711, begins: "There is not so variable a thing in Nature as a Lady's Head-dress: Within my own Memory I have known it rise and fall above thirty Degrees...I find most are of [the] Opinion, they are at present like Trees new lopped and pruned, that will certainly sprout up and flourish with greater Heads than before." Cf. No. 127, Addison's entry of July 26, 1711.

185 On the Swiss musician Johann Jakob Heidegger (1666–1749), see Jacob Friedrich von Bielfeld, *Des Freyherrn von Bielfeld freundschaftliche Briefe nebst einigen andern*, 2 vols. (Danzig/Leipzig, 1770), on vol. 1, pp. 348–349. Originally published as *Lettres familieres et autres* (La Hague, 1763). Cf. ApH 7:300n.

186 Johann Winckelmann, *Abhandlung von der Fähigkeit der Empfindung des Schönen in der Kunst* [...] (Dresden, 1763); and *Briefe an seine Freunde in der Schweiz* (Zürich, 1778). Cf. Mro 25:1325 above.

187 See the work of British travel writer Martin Sherlock (1750–1797), *Neue Briefe eines Engländers auf seiner Reise nach Italien, Genf, Lausanne, Strasburg, Berlin, Deutschland, Senlis und Paris* (Leipzig, 1782); see p. 178 (32nd Letter) and p. 183 (34th Letter). Originally published as *[Nouvelles] Lettres d'un voyageur Anglois*, 2 vols. (London, 1780).

188 On Klopstock, cf. Mro 25:1282 above and Collins 25:97.

189 Cf. Mro 25:1385 below and 15:775, 865, 868. On *Affektionspreis*, see also *Groundwork* 4:434–435.

190 See Johann Arckenholz, *Historische Merkwürdigkeiten die Königinn, Christina von Schweden betreffend* [...], trans. Johann Friedrich Reifstein, 4 parts (Leipzig/Amsterdam, 1751, 1752, 1760).

191 Jean-Jacques Rousseau, *Émile ou de l'Éducation* (The Hague, 1762), which was translated into German in 1762 by Johann Joachim Schwabe.

192 Henry Home, Lord Kames, *Elements of Criticism*, 3 vols. (Edinburgh, 1762). German translation: *Grundsätze der Critik*, 3 vols., trans. Johann Nicolaus Meinhard (Leipzig, 1763–1766).

193 *Fromme Wünsche* (Pious Desires) (Antwerp, 1624) is the title of a text by the Belgian Jesuit Hermann Hugo (1588–1629). Philipp Jakob Spener (1635–1705) chose the same title for his book (1675) *Pia desideria oder herzliches Verlangen nach gottgefälliger Verbesserung der wahren evangel. Kirche* (Pious Desires, or Heartfelt Desire for God-pleasing Reform of the True Evangelical Church), in which he demanded an internalization of faith and provided the program for Pietism, which was the faith of Kant's parents. See the entry, "Pia desideria," in Georg Büchmann, *Geflügelte Wörte* (Munich, 1959).

194 See Jean-Jacques Rousseau, *Émile ou de l'Éducation* (The Hague, 1762), Book 5.

195 Kant's source is unknown. Cf. ApH 7:233.

196 This (apparently abbreviated) name "Amst." is difficult to decipher. The reference could not be identified.

197 Kant's source is unknown. Cf. ApH 7:254–255 and *Menschenkunde* 25:1154.

198 See Seneca, *De ira* (On Anger) III.13.3.

199 Cato the Younger, or Marcus Porcius Cato Uticensis (95–46 BCE), Roman statesman. Kant's source is unknown.

200 On child's play, see Heraclitus, Fragment B 52. Heraclitus was known in antiquity for his melancholy and weeping, Democritus for being the "laughing philosopher." See, e.g., Seneca, *De ira* II.10.5.

201 Charles-Louis de Secondat, Baron Montesquieu (1689–1755), author of *De l'esprit des lois* (The Spirit of the Laws) (Geneva, 1748). However, it is possible that this reference to Montesquieu is due to a transcriber's error. Cf. ApH 7:256.

202 Jean André de Luc (1727–1817), French geologist. See his *Lettres physiques et morales sur les montagnes et sur l'histoire de la terre et de l'homme* (The Hague, 1778), 5th letter.

203 In 1713 Charles XII (1682–1718), King of Sweden, fought in the *kalabalik* at Bender (present-day Moldova), where Ottoman soldiers eventually captured him. On Charles XII, cf. Pillau 25:804–805, *Menschenkunde* 25:1129, and ApH 7:256.

204 Kant's source is unknown. On this passage, cf. ApH 7:256.

205 This reference could not be found in Plutarch's works.

206 Kant's source is unknown.

207 The source of Kant's reference to "physiological sympathy" cannot be found.

208 Richard Busby (1606–1695), British teacher. See Friedrich Nicolai (ed.), Simon Ratzeberger (probable author), *Vade Mecum für lustige Leute* [. . .], 7 vols. (Berlin, 1764–1777), vol. 4, pp. 196–197, no. 298. See also (anonymous) *Angenehme Beschäftigungen in der Einsamkeit* [. . .], 2 vols. (Leipzig, 1775, 1777), vol. 1, pp. 140f. It is unclear how Kant knew the name of the teacher.

209 Jean Terrasson (1670–1750), French author and philosopher. In the literary debates of the time he favored the Moderns. Kant is presumably referring to Terrasson's *Dissertation critique sur L'Iliade d'Homère, où, à l'occasion de ce poème, on cherche les règles d'une poétique fondée sur la raison et sur les exemples des anciens et des modernes* (Paris, 1715). Whether Terrasson provided a translation of Homer is unknown. Brandt and Stark locate the source of Kant's story in Johann Christoph Gottsched (ed.), *Philosophie, nach ihrem allgemeinen Einflusse, auf alle Gegenstände des Geistes und der Sitten* (Leipzig, 1756), pp. 46f. (First French edition: *La philosophie applicable à tous les objects de l'esprit et de la raison* [. . .] [Paris, 1754].) For the anecdote, see also Friedländer 25:540 and ApH 7:264.

210 Hume writes: "Nothing carries a man through the world like a true genuine natural impudence." David Hume, "Of Impudence and Modesty," in *Essays: Moral, Political, and Literary*, ed. Eugene F. Miller (Indianapolis: Liberty Fund, 1985, 1987), p. 553. Hume's essay appeared in the first edition of *Essays, Moral, Political, and Literary* (Edinburgh: A. Kincaid, 1741).

211 Kant's etymologies here and in the previous sentence, on *Dräustigkeit*, are not generally accepted today. On both, cf. ApH 7:258.

212 See Sextus Empiricus, *Hypotyposes* (Outlines of Pyrrhonism) I.10.

213 Kant's source is unknown.

214 Kant's source is unknown. Cf. ApH 7:312.
215 Kant's source is unknown. Cf. 15:483, 859.
216 Honeyguide birds were said to lead both humans and honeybadgers, or ratels, to bee hives. See Georg Forster (ed.), Anders Sparrmann and Christian Heinrich Groskurd (trans.), *Reise nach dem Vorgebirge der guten Hoffnung, den südlichen Polarländern und um die Welt, hauptsächlich aber in den Ländern der Hottentotten und Kaffern in den Jahren 1772 bis 1776* (Berlin, 1784), pp. 480–495, esp. p. 487.
217 Johann Peter Brinckmann (1746–1785), German physician. See his *Beyträge zu einer neuen Theorie der Gährungen* (Düsseldorf/Cleve/Leipzig, 1774), pp. 74–75. Cf. ApH 7:256 and Friedländer 25:619–620.
218 James Johnstone (1730–1802), Scottish physician. See James Johnstone, *Essay on the Use of the Ganglions of the Nerves* [. . .], in *Philosophical Transactions*, ed. Royal Society of London (London, 1764; reprint 1774), vol. 54, pp. 177–184, on pp. 87–88: "Ganglions besides, instead of being instruments subservient to the will, are almost peculiar to nerves, distributed to parts, the motions of which are totally involuntary. [. . .] and granting Ganglions to be, as is ingeniously conjectured by Lancisi and Winslow, subsidiary brains, or analogous to the brain in their office [. . .]." Cf. James Johnstone, *History of a Foetus born [. . .] to which is subjoinded a Supplement of the Essay on the Use of the Ganglions, published in Philosophical Transactions for 1764* [. . .], in *Philosophical Transactions*, ed. Royal Society of London (London, 1767; reprint 1774), vol. 57, pp. 118–131, on pp. 64–66: "To conclude, the ganglia, respecting their structure, may justly be considered as little brains, or germs of those nerves detached from them, consisting, according to Winslow, of a mixture of cortical and nervous medullary substance [. . .]."
219 See Hieronymus David Gaub, *Sermones academici de regimine mentis, quod medicorum est* (Leiden, 1776). Gaub or Gaubius (1705–1780), a German physician and student of Hermann Boerhaave (1668–1738) at the University of Leiden, is also author of *Institutiones Pathologiae Medicinalis* (Leiden, 1758).
220 See the work of the German physician Johann Georg Zimmermann (1728–1795), *Von der Erfahrung in der Arzneykunst* (Zürich, 1763–1764; 1777).
221 See the book by German physican Johann Gottlob Krüger (1715–1759), *Versuch einer Experimental-Seelenlehre* (Halle/Helmstedt, 1756).
222 See the work of German psychologist Karl Philipp Moritz (1757–1793), *Aussichten zu einer Experimentalseelenlehre an Herrn Direktor Gedike* (Berlin, 1782).
223 For the story about children whose epileptic episodes were transmitted to other children through a kind of imaginative sympathy, and on Boerhaave's threatening to brand them with hot metal, see Johann Zimmermann, *Von der Erfahrung in der Arzneykunst* (Zurich, 1777), book 4, chapter 11, pp. 646–648. It is unclear where Boerhaave discusses this in his work. Cf. Menschenkunde 25:953–954.
224 Kant's three anecdotes about the dog, the rooster (cf. Menschenkunde 25:1154–1155), and the pregnant woman (cf. Pillau 25:814) all derive from Gaub's *Sermones academici de regimine mentis* (1776).
225 Johann Carl Wilhelm Moehsen [Möhsen] (1722–1795), physician in Berlin. See his *Geschichte der Wissenschaften in der Mark Brandenburg, besonders der Arzneiwissenschaft* [. . .] (Berlin/Leipzig, 1781). Although there appears to be

no text by Moehsen that is called *Pharmacology*, paragraphs §§ 42–45 (especially pp. 439f.) of the *Geschichte* are pertinent to Kant's remarks.

226 Johann Samuel Halle (1727–1810), German writer. See his *Magie, oder, die Zauberkräfte der Natur, so auf den Nutzen, und die Belustigung angewendet werden*, 4 vols. (Berlin, 1783, 1784, 1785, 1786), vol. 1 (1784 edition), "Introduction to Magic," p. XXIII.

227 Johann Heinrich Cohausen, *Satyrische Gedanken von der Pica Nasi* [...] (Leipzig, 1720).

228 Kant's source is unknown. Cf. Friedländer 25:542.

229 Kant's source is unknown.

230 The transcript's "Eugen" refers to Prince Eugene of Savoy (1663–1736), Austrian commander and statesman. The reference to "Schwerin" may be to Kurt Christoph Count of Schwerin (1684–1757), a Prussian field marshal; or to Otto Magnus of Schwerin (1701–1777), a Prussian general. On Kurt Christoph of Schwerin, see also the contemporary biography in Karl Friedrich Pauli, *Leben grosser Helden des gegenwärtigen Krieges*, 9 parts (Halle, 1758–1764), part 1, pp. 59–126.

231 Quintus Fabius Maximus Verrucosus (280–203 BCE), Roman general and consul five times betwen 233 and 209 BCE. He was called "Cunctator" (the Delayer) because he carried out a war of attrition against the more powerful Carthaginian general Hannibal, who was attacking the Romans in Italy.

232 "Corvinus" perhaps refers to Hungarian general and ruler János Hunyadi (Johannes Corvinus) (*c.*1407–1456).

233 From Tertullian, *De fuga in persecutione* (On Fleeing from Persecution), ch. 10, 1: "*Qui fugiebat, rursus sibi proeliabitur*" (He who flees will fight again). See also Hans Walter, *Lateinische Sprichwörter und Sentenzen des Mittelalters in alphabetischer Anordnung*, 6 vols. (Göttingen, 1963–1967), on vol. 5, p. 758, no. 33531g: "*Vir fugiens denuo pugnabit*" (The man who flees will fight again).

234 The lines read: "*Und damit ich auch was thu / Seh ich euch im Lehnstuhl zu.*" The author and title of the poem are unknown.

235 Lavater cites French naturalist Georges Buffon (1707–1788), *Histoire naturelle générale et particulière* (Paris, 1749), while mentioning voice, gait, posture, gesture, and costume; see Johann Caspar Lavater, *Physiognomische Fragmente*, vol. 4, p. 417. On handwriting, see Lavater, *Physiognomische Fragmente*, vol. 3, pp. 110–114, 4th section, 4th fragment, "On the Character of Handwritings."

236 Giambattista della Porta, or (Giovanni) Battista Porta (*c.*1540–1615), Italian physiognomist and author. See his *Della fisonomia dell'huomo* [...] *Tradetti de Latino in Volgare* [...] (On the Physiognomy of Man, translated from Latin into Italian) (Padua, 1607), bk. 4, ch. 2, pp. 173–174. The work is a translation of della Porta's *De humana physiognomonia* (Sorrento, 1586).

237 Kant's source is unknown.

238 The English poet Alexander Pope (1688–1744) had many health problems. On Socrate's ugliness, see Plato's *Symposium*; cf. Cicero's *De fato*, 5 § 10 and *Tusculan Disputations* IV, 37, §§ 80–81. Cf. Mro 25:1388.

239 That is, he replaced the smaller nose with a model of his real nose. Kant's source and the general to whom he refers are unknown. Cf. Friedländer 25:555, 666.

240 See Martial (Marcus Valerius Martialis), *Epigrams* 1.3,6. Cf. ApH 7:299.

241 See Johann Joachim Schwabe (ed.), *Allgemeine Historie der Reisen zu Wasser und zu Lande* [...], 21 vols. (Leipzig, 1747–1774), on vol. 6 (1750) p. 343. Cf. ApH 7:299.

242 Desiderius Erasmus Roterodamus (1466–1536), Dutch humanist. Cf. Johann Caspar Lavater, *Physiognomische Fragmente*, vol. 2, pp. 267–268, although Lavater does not mention angular heads.

243 That is, the work by German philosopher and writer Johann Jacob Engel (1741–1802), *Ideen zu einer Mimik*, 2 parts (Berlin, 1785/1786). A review of the first part appeared in February 1785 in *Göttingische Zeitungen von gelehrten Sachen* (Göttingen, 1753–1801). Engel was a member of the Enlightenment movement in Berlin and taught philosophy at a secondary school. Kant published a revised and enlarged version of his essay "Of the Different Races of Human Beings" in Part Two of Engel's *Der Philosoph für die Welt* (The Worldly Philosopher) (Leipzig, 1777).

244 Georg Christoph Lichtenberg (1744–1799), German physicist and writer. Cf. Lichtenberg, *Über Physionomik; wider die Physiognomen. Zur Beförderung der Menschenliebe und Menschenkenntniß. Zweyte vermehrte Auflage* (Goettingen, 1778), vol. 3, p. 282.

245 Johann Lavater, *Physiognomische Fragmente*, vol. 2, pp. 33–35. Cf. ApH 7:301.

246 The source of Kant's reference is unknown.

247 Cf. Giambattista della Porta, *Della fisonomia dell'huomo* [...] (Padua, 1607), bk. 2, ch. 6, p. 51.

248 See Jean-Jacques Rousseau's letter to David Hume of July 10, 1766.

249 Laurence Sterne (1713–1768), *The life and opinions of Tristram Shandy, gentleman*, 9 vols. (London, 1760–1767), bk. 2, ch. 7: "It is said in Aristotle's Master Piece, 'That when a man doth think of any thing which is past, – he looketh down upon the ground; – but that when he thinketh of something that is to come, he looketh up towards the heavens.' My uncle Toby, I suppose, thought of neither, for he look'd horizontally."

250 Although this claim agrees with the gist of Lavater's *Physiognomische Fragmente*, a textual passage that precisely corresponds with the claim has not been located.

251 Kant seems to have confused Herodotus with Thucydides. See Thucydides, *The Peloponnesian War*, bk. 2, 52.4.

252 Johann Hawkesworth, *An Account of the Voyages undertaken [...] in the Southern Hemisphere* [...] (London, 1773). See the German translation by Johann Friedrich Schiller, *Geschichte der See-Reisen und Entdeckungen im Süd-Meer* [...], 3 vols. (Berlin, 1774), vol. 2, p. 185. On Italian facial expressions, cf. Pillau 25:830.

253 Johann Lavater, *Physiognomische Fragmente*, vol. 3, p. 178 and p. 191; and vol. 4, p. 269.

254 William Hogarth (1697–1764), English engraver and author of *Analysis of Beauty* (London, 1753).

255 For this story about Marie Madeleine Marguerite d'Aubray, Marquise de Brinvilliers (1630–1676), see François Gayot de Pitaval, *Causes célèbres et interessantes, avec des jugements qui les ont décidées* (Paris, 1734–1743). Cf. the German translation, *Erzählung sonderbarer Rechtshändel* [...], 3 vols. (Leipzig, 1747),

vol. 1, pp. 331–390, esp. p. 334. On Brinvilliers, cf. Friedländer 25:672 as well as the next note below.

256 See the work of the French Benedictine and mystic Antoine-Joseph Pernety (1716–1801), *Discours sur la physionomie et les avantages des connoissances phy-sionomiques* (Berlin, 1771), p. 470. Cf. the German translation, *Versuch einer Physiognomik, oder Erklärung des moralischen Menschen durch die Kenntniß des physischen*, 3 vols. (Dresden, 1784–1785), vol. 1, pp. 59–60. Lavater cites Per-nety's passage in French in: Johann Lavater, *Physiognomische Fragmente*, vol. 1, pp. 180–181. At Friedländer 25:672–673, Kant tells a similar story, drawn from Pernety, about the supposedly diabolical character of Brinvilliers; cf. 15:776.

257 Johann Friedrich Karl Grimm (anonymous), *Bemerkungen eines Reisenden* [...], 3 vols. (Altenburg, 1775), vol. 3, pp. 334–335. Cf. ApH 7:302 and Friedländer 25:668.

258 See Johann Lavater, *Physiognomische Fragmente*, vol. 4, p. 99.

259 On this passage, cf. Mro 25:1333, ApH 7:292, and *Groundwork* 4:434–435.

260 See Jean-Jacques Rousseau, *Narcisse ou l'amant de lui-même* [...] (Geneva, 1781).

261 On Charles XII of Sweden, cf. Mro 25:1346 above. On Roman politician Lucius Cornelius Sulla (*c*.138–78 BCE) and Charles XII, cf. ApH 7:293.

262 See Joseph Addison, *Spectator* No. 86, entry of June 8, 1711. See also Cicero, *De fato*, 5 § 10, which mentions the physiognomist "Zopyrus," and Cicero, *Tusculan Disputations* bk. IV, 37, §§ 80–81. Cf. Friedländer 25:634.

263 See Joseph Addison, *Spectator* No. 225, entry of November 17, 1711: "*Tully* [Cicero] has therefore very justly exposed a Precept delivered by some Ancient Writers, That a Man should live with his Enemy in such a manner, as might leave him room to become his Friend; and with his Friend in such a manner, that if he became his Enemy, it should not be in his Power to hurt him."

264 See the posthumous work by German poet and professor Christian Fürchtegott Gellert (1715–1769), *Moralische Vorlesungen* [...] (Moral Lectures), ed. Gott-lieb Leberecht Heyer et al., 2 vols. (Leipzig, 1770), vol. 1, p. 224 and vol. 2, p. 394. Cf. Friedländer 25:629–630.

265 Francis Hutcheson, *An Inquiry into the Original of our Ideas of Beauty and Virtue; in Two Treatises* (London, 1725), 2nd Treatise, sect. 7, para. V.

266 Edward Young (1683–1765), poet and author of *The Complaint: or, Night-Thoughts on Life, Death, and Immortality* (London, 1742). Cf. Menschenkunde 25:1117 and Friedländer 25:575.

267 David Hume, "The Skeptic," in *Essays, Moral, Political, and Literary*, p. 170: "It rarely, very rarely happens, that a man of taste and learning is not, at least, an honest man, whatever frailties may attend him."

268 On dissimulation among clergymen, see David Hume, "Of National Charac-ters," in *Essays: Moral, Political, and Literary*, pp. 199–200.

269 Johann Georg Sulzer (1720–1779), Swiss philosopher. The exact source is unknown. Cf. ApH 7:332 and *Groundwork* 4:410n.

270 Kant's source is unknown; cf. 15:872.

271 David Hume, "Of Love and Marriage" (1741), in *Essays, Moral, Political, and Literary*, p. 557. Cf. Friedländer 25:715.

272 See Job 2:9 (New American Standard Bible): "Then his wife said to him, 'Do you still hold fast your integrity? Curse God and die!'" On the wives of Job and Socrates, cf. ApH 7:308.

273 Samuel Richardson (1689–1761), English novelist. Kant is referring to Richardson's *Pamela: or, Virtue Rewarded*, 2 vols. (London, 1740–1741); *Clarissa: or, the History of a Young Lady* (London, 1748); and *The History of Sir Charles Grandison* (London, 1753–1754). On Richardson, cf. Observations 2:224 and ApH 7:121, 163.

274 Samuel Richardson, *Pamela* (London, 1740–1741). In German translation Richardson's heroines introduce their pithy reflections with this set phrase (*wie mein Bruder mir gesagt hat*).

275 Neither the emperor nor society could be identified, but Kant may be referring to Charles VII (1697–1745) or Charles VI (1685–1740).

276 David Hume, "Of National Characters," in *Essays: Moral, Political, and Literary*, p. 207. Cf. ApH 7:311 and Friedländer 25:630.

277 Carlo Giovanni Maria Denina (1731–1813), Italian historian. See his *Staatsveränderungen von Italien in vier und zwanzig Büchern entworfen*, trans. Johann Jacob Volkmann, 3 vols. (Leipzig, 1771–1773), vol. 1, pp. 374–375.

278 See Horace, *Carmina* (Odes) I.1 and III.30. Caius Cilnius Maecenas (*c.*100 BCE–8 CE) was a Roman author, diplomat, and patron to Virgil and Horace.

279 See (anonymous) *Angenehme Beschäftigungen in der Einsamkeit, oder tausend Stück auserlesener Anecdoten, gesammelt von* *, 2 vols. (Leipzig, 1775, 1777), vol. 2, pp. 163f.

280 Johann Friedrich Karl Grimm (anonymous), *Bemerkungen eines Reisenden* [. . .], 3 vols. (Altenburg, 1775), vol. 1, p. 269.

281 It is unclear which passage in Rousseau's work Kant has in mind.

282 The Tolerance Edict of Nantes, issued on April 13, 1598 by Henry IV of France, was replaced by the Edict of Fontainebleau, which Louis XIV issued in October 1685.

283 Voltaire's *Traité sur la tolérance* (1763) argued that the death penalty enforced on Jean Calas on March 9, 1762, should be revoked in a retrial that took place in 1765. Calas's conviction was ultimately overturned. Cf. Mro 25:1236.

284 Philippe V, Duke of Anjou and Louis XIV's grandson, assumed Spanish rule as the first Bourbon on November 1, 1700, and thereafter the War of Spanish Succession ensued. Philippe V ruled, with a brief interruption in 1724, until 1746.

285 See Montesquieu, *De l'esprit des lois* (The Spirit of the Laws) (Geneva, 1748), bk. 19, ch. 10, and bk. 20, ch. 14.

286 The source of this story is unknown.

287 Kant's claim may have been influenced by the anonymous piece, "Historische Nachricht vom Ursprung, Stiftung, von den Fortschritten, Grundsätzen und vom gerichtlichen Verfahren der Inquisition" (Historical News of the Origin, Foundation, Progress, Principles, and Legal Proceedings of the Inquisition), published in the first year of "Litteratur und Völkerkunde" (Dessau, 1782/1783) pp. 44–72, pp. 118–147, and pp. 230–254; see esp. pp. 237 and pp. 239f. On the *auto da fé* and *sanbenito*, cf. *Observations* 2:245.

288 Kant is referring to the Spanish revolts, the Esquilache Riots, against Charles III in March 1766.

289 In *The Social Contract* (1762), bk. 3, ch. 8, Rousseau claims that in Madrid there are superb reception rooms yet bedrooms like rat holes. It remains unclear why Kant applied Rousseau's remark about the Spaniards to the Italians. Cf. ApH 7:317.

290 A *cicisbeo* was the professional gallant of a married woman in eighteenth- and nineteenth-century Italy. He attended her at all public entertainments since it was considered unfashionable for the husband to be her escort.

291 Lady Giulia Toffana (Tofana/Tofania) was a Sicilian woman who mixed and sold poisons in early seventeenth-century Rome. See Johann Georg Keyßler, *Neueste Reise durch Teutschland, Böhmen, Ungarn, die Schweitz, Italien, und Lothringen* [...], 2 vols. (Hannover, 1741–1742), vol. 2, 57th letter, pp. 234–235.

292 Cf. Mro 25:1398 and the corresponding endnote.

293 See Montesquieu, *The Spirit of the Laws* (Geneva, 1748), bk. 5, ch. 13.

294 Samuel Sharp (*c.*1700–1778), English physician and author of travelogues. See his *Letters from Italy, describing the customs and manners of that country* [...] (London, 1766). Cf. ApH 7:315.

295 James Boswell (1740–1795), Scottish writer. See his *An Account of Corsica, the Journal of a Tour to that Island; and Memoirs of Pascal Paoli* (Glasgow/London, 1768). Pascal Paoli (1725–1807) was a Corsican patriot and general. Boswell tells of a conversation he had about Germany with one of Paoli's officers, Suzzoni, who had served in Germany; both Suzzoni and Boswell thought very highly of German hospitality. Cf. Parow 25:431.

296 William Guthrie (1708–1770), English writer and John Gray (dates unknown), British writer. Guthrie and Gray's *General History of the World* (London, 1767) was translated by Carl Renatus Hausen as *Die Geschichte der Deutschen* (Leipzig, 1767). Volume 9 of *Allgemeinen Weltgeschichte* (1767) contains Hausen's revised portrayal of the Germans, "Die Geschichte von Deutschland" (The History of Germany), but Kant does not seem to be referring to this here.

297 Kant is perhaps referring to the work of the Swiss doctor Johann Georg Zimmermann, *Vom Nationalstolze* (On National Pride) (Zurich, 1768), ch. 17, pp. 387ff. Cf. ApH 7:318. At Menschenkunde 25:1040f., Kant says that cosmopolitan interest should be preferred to the national interest and that, moreover, the former helps secure the latter.

298 James Cook (1728–1779), British explorer, did not himself reach Kamchatka, but died in February 1779 in an encounter with indigenous peoples in the South Sea. His expedition reached Kamchatka in April 1779. See also Georg Forster, *Fragmente über Kapitän Cooks letzte Reise* (Fragments on Captain Cook's Last Voyage) (1780).

299 Savu: the Indonesian island also known as Sawu, Sabu, Sawoe, or Hawu. See Johann Hawkesworth, *Geschichte der See-Reisen und Entdeckungen im Süd-Meer* [...], trans. Johann Friedrich Schiller, 3 vols. (Berlin, 1774), vol. 3, pp. 306–307.

300 Contrary to Kant's remark, Scottish chemist Joseph Black (1728–1799) is not generally credited with the discovery of the chemical analysis of atmospheric air, but rather Joseph Priestley, Antoine Lavoisier, or Carl Wilhelm Scheele.

301 The origin of the anecdote is unknown. Cf. Johann Gotthelf Lindner, *Lehrbuch der schönen Wissenschaften, insonderheit der Prose und Poesie*, 2 vols. (Königsberg/Leipzig, 1767, 1768), vol. 2, p. 84.

302 See Stephani Doleti, *Dialogus de imitatione Ciceroniana* [...] (Leiden, 1535). Cf. Mro 25:1311 above.

303 German scientist Otto von Guericke (1602–1686) invented the vacuum pump in 1650, and its first public demonstration took place in 1654 at the Reichstag in Regensburg.

304 Charles-Irénée Castel de Saint-Pierre (1658–1743), French cleric and writer. Abbé St. Pierre, a secretary at the congress preceding the Treaty of Utrecht, proposed a project for perpetual peace, publishing the first two volumes of his *Projet pour rendre la paix perpetuelle en Europe* in 1713. See Rousseau, *Extrait du projet de paix perpétuelle de Monsieur l'Abbé de Saint-Pierre* (1761). See also Kant's essay *Toward Perpetual Peace* (1795). Kant had been aware of St. Pierre's project for several decades, as a reflection dated around 1755 reveals (6:241).

305 *Chlopiec* is related to the Polish word *chlop*, meaning *fellow* or *guy* as well as *peasant*. The Latin *iuvenis* (youth) corresponds to *chlopiec*. The latter may have either a neutral or a derogatory connation, depending on the context.

306 See Georg Forster (ed.), Anders Sparrmann and Christian Heinrich Groskurd (trans.), *Reise nach dem Vorgebirge der guten Hoffnung* [...] (Berlin, 1784), pp. 347f.

307 The transcriber may have meant to write *der Türken* (of the Turks), for Kant associates the Turks with pride and self-confidence, but that reading would conflict with the fact that it is a Turk who is traveling through Europe. Given the reference to *Tüke* (spite) and the Russians above at 25:1413, the clause, as written, probably refers to Russia. At ApH 7:312, however, Kant mentions Poland ("the land of lords") at this very point in a similar list and, moreover, claims that Russia and European Turkey lie outside Frankestan. Cf. Friedländer 25:657 and, on the Turks and Russians, Mro 25:1424.

308 Rousseau, *Discours sur l'origine et les fondements de l'inégalité parmi les hommes* (Second Discourse) (Amsterdam, 1755). Cf. Remark III, where on the contrary Rousseau asserts that there are better reasons for claiming that the human being is a biped.

309 Pietro Moscati (1739–1824), Italian physician and natural scientist. Cf. Friedländer 25:676–677 and Kant's *Review of Moscati's Work* (1771) 2:421–425.

310 Carl von Linné (1707–1778), Swedish natural scientist; cf. his *Systema naturae per regna tria naturae, secundum classes, ordines, genera, species* [...], 3 vols. (Holm, 1766–1768), vol. 1, pp. 28–33. See also Georges Buffon, *Histoire naturelle générale et particulière*, 3 vols. (Paris, 1749), vol. 3, p. 399. Cf. ApH 7:322f.

311 Kant's source is unknown.

312 For a contrary view, see Rousseau, *Émile* (1762). The source of Kant's claim is unknown.

313 See Rousseau's *First Discourse* (1750), *Second Discourse* (1754), *Émile* (1762), and *The Social Contract* (1762). Cf. Kant's *Conjectural Beginning of Human History* (esp. 8:116–118), which appeared in the January 1786 issue of the *Berlinische Monatsschrift*.

314 Perhaps a reference to the work of French geologist Jean André de Luc, *Lettres physiques et morales sur les montagnes et sur l'histoire de la terre et de l'homme* (The Hague, 1778).

315 See Cicero, *De officiis*, bk. 1, section 37.12, which reads, in the translation of Walter Miller (Cambridge, MA and London: Harvard University Press, 1913): "This also I observe – that he who would properly have been called 'a fighting enemy' (*perduellis*) was called 'a guest' (*hostis*), thus relieving the ugliness of the face by a softened expression; for 'enemy' (*hostis*) meant to our ancestors what we now call 'stranger' (*peregrinus*)."

316 Marc-Joseph Marion Du Fresne (*c.*1729–1772), French voyager, was among the crew killed and eaten in New Zealand by Māori. Kant's description derives from a report written by Du Fresne's second-in-command, Julien Crozet. With the assistance of Alexis-Marie Rochon, Crozet's journal was published as *Nouveau voyage à la mer du sud, commencé sous les ordres de Marion* [...] (Paris: Barrois, 1783), and a German edition appeared in Leipzig later in 1783.

317 On the fortified dwellings, see Johann Hawkesworth, *Geschichte der See-Reisen und Entdeckungen im Süd-Meer* [...], trans. Johann Friedrich Schiller, 3 vols. (Berlin, 1774), vol. 2, pp. 337–339 and p. 324.

318 See Johann Hawkesworth, *ibid.*, vol. 2, pp. 194–195.

319 Cf. Rousseau, *Jugement sur la paix perpétuelle* (Geneva, 1782). Whether Kant had read this text as early as the mid-1780s remains questionable, however.

320 Such leagues or councils helped the independent Greek states maintain peaceful relations with one another. The congresses or assemblies, made up of deputies from the confederated states of ancient Greece, engaged in political and religious matters such as protecting the Delphic oracle.

321 Cf. Rousseau, *Extrait du projet de paix perpétuelle de Monsieur l'Abbé de Saint-Pierre* (1761).

322 See Jean de La Fontaine (1621–1695), *Fables*, "The Two Bulls and the Frog," bk. 2, fable 4.

323 The source of Kant's story is unknown. According to Brandt and Stark, Kant appears to have had in mind King Philip IV of Spain (1605–1665).

Anthropology Busolt 1788–1789

1 This is the first known statement by Kant of these three rules, which first appeared in a published work in the *Critique of the Power of Judgment* (KU 5:294–295). But cf. *Reflexion* 1486, Ak 15:715, Jäsche Logik 9:57, and *Anthropology from a Pragmatic Point of View* 7: 220, 228.

2 Philip Dormer Stanhope, 4th Earl of Chesterfield (1694–1773). Cf. *Anthropology from a Pragmatic Point of View* 7:278, *Metaphysics of Morals* 6: 428, *Pillau* 25:776, *Menschenkunde* 25:1088, *Zusätze* 25:1540, 1543, 1551.

Glossary

Abbildung	formation of an image; direct image formation
Abbruch tun	break off, impair; infringe upon
Aberglaube	superstition
Aberwitz (vesania)	delusional reason, lunacy; (insanity for *Wahnwitz*)
Abfolge	succession (cf. *Folge, Sukzession, Nacheinander, Reihenfolge*)
(sich) abgeben	occupy oneself, concern oneself, spend time with
Abgemessenheit	exactness
abgeschmackt	vapid, tasteless, in poor taste
Abgunst	spite; aversion, loathing, antipathy
Abhandlung	treatise
Ablauf	lapse
ablegen	lay aside, get rid of, renounce, etc. [see *entsagen*]
ableiten	derive; deduce, infer, divert [derive = *herleiten*]
Abscheu	disgust, aversion
Abscheulichkeit	odiousness
Absicht	intention; aim
absondern	separate, abstract, set aside
Absprung	leap
abstammen	descend
Abstammung	ancestry; derivation
Abstechung	contrast
abteilen	partition, divide up
abwechselnd	intermittent, alternating
Abwechselung	variety
abweichen	deviate
abweisen	dismiss; refuse, decline
Abwesenheit (absentia)	absent-mindedness
Achtsamkeit	circumspection

Glossary

Achtung	respect
Affect/Affekt	affect
Ähnlichkeit	similarity
All	(the) all
allenthalben	everywhere
allgemein	general; universal
Allheit	totality (cf. *Totalität*)
Andacht	devotion
Anfangsgründe	first principles
Anfechtung	impugnment
angeboren	innate
angemessen	suited to, in keeping with, etc.
angenehm	agreeable
angewöhnen	accustom
Angewohnheit	habituated way [to distinguish from *Gewohnheit*]
angreifen	strains
(darauf) ankommen	depends
Anlage	predisposition
Anleitung	guidance
Anmaßung	arrogance; arrogation
annehmen	assume; *Annehmung* = assumption, adoption; accept, take on, admit of
Annehmlichkeit	agreeableness; convenience, amenity, comfort; *Unannehmlichkeit* = drawback
Anordnungen	orders, directives, rulings, making arrangements
Anschaffung	acquisition
anschauen	intuit
anschaulich gemacht	made intuitable (made concrete, given concrete shape)
Anschauung	intuition
Ansehen	reputation, repute, standing
ansehnlich	respectable
Ansehung	regard
Anspruch	claim
Anstand	decency
Anständigkeit	decency, propriety, respectability
anstellen	institute; carry out (pursue, conduct – e.g. research)
Anstrengung	exertion
antreffen	encounter, find
antreiben	urge, impel, goad
Antrieb	impulse
anweisen	assign
Anwendung	application

arglistig	guileful
Art	way, species, kind, manner
Aufbewahrung	keeping; safekeeping, custody
aufbieten	summon (up), muster
aufbringen	anger
auffassen	grasp [*fassen*], take it to mean
Aufforderung	requirement, demand
Aufgabe	problem; task
Aufgang	sunrise, rising on the part of anything, a way or path up, staircase
aufhalten	check
aufklären	clarify, enlighten
Auflösung	solution, resolution, dissolution
Aufmerksamkeit	attentiveness; attention for *Attention* and *attendiren*
Aufmunterung	enlivening
aufnehmen	adopt, receive, take in/up
Aufrichtigkeit	sincerity; uprightness
Aufschluß	elucidation
Aufsprung	saltation
aufwallend	surging
aufwecken	awaken, wake
(in die) Augen fallen (zu machen)	(make) evident
Ausbildung	completing formation; schooling, training
Ausdehnung	extension
ausdenken	excogitate
Ausdeutung	explanation [to distinguish from *Auslegung* = interpretation]
Ausdruck	expression
ausfindig machen	discover, bring to light
ausführlich	exhaustive
Ausführung	execution
ausgeben	pass off as/for
Auslachen	derision
auslöschen	erase, extinguish
ausmachen	constitute, settle; +make out; find out
ausrotten	extirpate
Äußeres	external (thing)
äußern	express, manifest, show
aussetzen	expose
aussinnen	devise
austeilen	dispense

ausüben	exercise, perform, practice, exert [save "carry out" for *ausführen*]
Auswickelung	uncovering
ausziehen/Auszug	excerpt
Bau	structure
beben	quake, tremble [see *zittern*]
bedenken	bear in mind [consider for *betrachten*]
bedeuten	signify; mean
Bedeutung	significance, meaning
bedienen (sich zu)	to avail/help oneself to ["make use of" for *Gebrauch machen*]
bedingt	conditioned; contingent
Bedürfnis	need
Beförderung	promotion
befremden	appear strange, strike as odd
befriedigen	satisfy, appease [the desires]
Befriedigung	satisfaction (use for *Wohlgefallen*); fulfillment, appeasement
Befugnis	authorization, warrant
begatten	breed
(sich) begeben	resort
Begebenheit	event; occurrence (use "event" for *Ereignis*)
Begehrungsvermögen	capacity of desire; faculty of desire
Begierde	desire; *Begierden* = desires/appetites
begnügen	be content with
begreifen	comprehend
begrenzen	bound (cf. *einschränken*)
Begriff	concept
beharren	persist; insist on
beharrlich	persevering, unwavering; persistent, abiding
Beharrlichkeit	perseverance; persistence
behaupten	assert; contend
behend	adroit
behutsam	cautious
beibringen	convey, impart, teach
Beifall	approval
beilegen	ascribe
Beispiel	example
bejahen	affirm
bekennen	acknowledge; admit, confess
beklagen	deplore
belebt	animated, enlivened, stimulated; see *beseelen*

Glossary

Belebung	animation
Belehrung	teaching
Beleidigung	offense, affront
Belieben	likings, as you like, suit yourself; [*nach Belieben* = at one's discretion]
beliebig	discretionary; this or that, arbitrary, optional
belustigen	entertain
Bemerkung	observation; observation, remark
bemühen	endeavor
benebeln	befuddle
benehmen	deprive
Benennung	term; designation, nomination
Beobachtung	observation
bequem	convenient
(sich) bequemen	conform
Beredsamkeit	eloquence
berichtigen	correct
beruhen	based on, due to
Beschaffenheit	property, constitution; characteristic(s)
beschäftigen (sich)	be concerned; occupy
Beschäftigung	occupation
Beschauung	contemplation (*contemplatio*)
Bescheidenheit	modesty, unassumingness, unpretentiousness
beschuldigen	charge, accuse
beschwerlich	arduous (wearisome, troublesome)
beseelen	animate
besinnen	call to mind, recollect
besonder	particular; particular, special
besorgen	provide, attend; *besorgt* = concerned
beständig	constant, steadfast; constant
bestätigen	confirm
bestehen	subsist, exist, consist; *bestehend* = persist(ing)
bestimmt	destined, determined, determinate
Bestimmung	vocation, destiny; determination, vocation
betrachten	consider, examine [save for *erwegen*], regard, inspect
Betrachtung	consideration
Betragen	behavior, bearing, deportment
betreffen	concern, regard, refer to, relate to
Betrübnis	depression; distress
Betrug	fraud, deception
beurteilen	assess, judge
Beurteilung	estimation, judgment, appraisal

bewegende Kraft	motive force
Bewegung	motion; agitation
Bewegungsgrund	motive (cf. *Triebfeder*)
Beweis	proof
Beweisgrund	ground of proof; argument
bewundern	admire
Bewußtsein	consciousness
bezeichnen	denote, signify, mark, stand for
Bezeichnung	designation (see *Bennenung, nennen*)
Beziehung	relation, reference (cf. *Verhältnis*, Relation)
Bild	image
bilden	to form; educate, school
Bildung	education; formation
Bildungsziel	pedagogical goal
billig	equitable, fair; acceptable
Billigung	assent, approval; *Beifall* = synonym
bleibend	abiding, lasting
Blendwerk	semblance, mirage (cf. *Schein, Illusion*)
Blödigkeit	timorousness: see *Schüchternheit*
blödsinnig	idiotic
bloß	mere, merely
Boden	terrain, land
bösartig	malicious [*Bösartigkeit*: maliciousness]
Bösewicht	scoundrel
boshaft	malevolent
Bosheit	malice
bündig	binding, valid, conclusive, to the point
bürgerlich	civil
Classe	species
consequent	resolute; consistent [*Folgerichtig* = consistent]
Cultur	cultivation; culture, cultivation
dahero	hence
darstellen	exhibit, present
Darstellung	exhibition, presentation; display
dartun	demonstrate, establish
Dasein	existence
Dauer	duration
dauerend	continual (lasting, in context); *fortdauerend* = lasting
Demut	humility
Demütigung	humiliation

denken	think, conceive
Denkungsart	conduct of thought; way of thinking
Denkungskraft	power of thought
Deutlichkeit	distinctness, clarity
Dichten	poesis (n.), engage in poesis (v); compose, composition
Dichter	poet
Dichtung	fiction, literature (of a people, of an epoch), literary/poetic works
Dichtungsvermögen	fictive prowess (in context)
Ding	thing (cf. *Sache*)
Ding oder Unding	something real or an absurdity; *Ding* = actual matter
doch	surely, after all, but, however, yet
dreihärig/dreihaarig	crafty
Dreistigkeit	presumptuousness
dulden	tolerate
Dummdreistigkeit	impertinence
Dummheit (stupiditas)	stupidity
Dummkopf	stupid
dunkel	obscure
durch	through, by
durchgängig	thorough(going); *allgemein geltend* = generally, universally, as a rule
durchtrieben	sly; wily [save cunning for *List*]
dürftig	meager, poor, shabby, needy, straitened
eher	more likely
Ehrbarkeit	integrity
Ehrbegierde	ambition; desire for honor
Ehre	honor
Ehrfurcht	reverence
Ehrlichkeit	honesty, frankness
Ehrliebe	love of honor
Ehrsucht	ambition; obsessive ambition, vainglory [i.e. need "ambition" for *Ehrbegierde/geiz*]
ehrwürdig	respectable; honorable (*ehrenwert*); see *ansehnlich*
Eifersucht	jealousy
eigen	proper, peculiar; proper
Eigendünkel	self-conceit
Eigenliebe	egoism, narcissism (to distinguish from *Selbstliebe* = self-love)

Glossary

Eigenschaft	quality; attribute; property
eigensüchtig	egotistical; keep "selfish" for *selbstsüchtig* (also for *Eigennutz*)
eigentlich	real; actual (*wirklich*), true (*wahre*), proper (*eigen*)
eigentümlich	peculiar
(das) eigentümliche	peculiarity
einbilden	convince, believe, imagine, fancy, etc. (context dep.)
Einbildung	imagination; imaginative formation; fancy, conceit
Einbildungskraft	power of imagination
Eindruck	impression
Einerleiheit	identity; makes no difference, uniformity, monotony
Einfall	inspiration
einfallen	come to mind
Einfalt	simplemindedness; artlessness (simplicity)
Einfältig	simple
Einheit	unity; homogeneity; see *gleichartig*
einhellig	(with) unanimity
einige	some, few, several
einräumen	admit, concede, grant, acknowledge, etc.
einschieben	insert
einschläfern	lull to sleep
einschlagen	pertains, relative to, bearing on, dealing with
einschränken	limit
Einschränkung	qualification, limitation
einsehen	have (gain) insight into, see; +understand; realize, appreciate
Einsicht	insight
einstimmen	harmonize
einstimmig	being of one voice, in unanimity; to be in accord with oneself
Einstimmung	agreement
Einteilung	division [see *Abstechung*]; classification
Eintracht	unity and concord
Einwilligung	consent
(ein) Einziger	singular
Ekel	loathing
Elend	misery
Empfänglichkeit	responsiveness; receptivity
empfinden	feel, be sensible of, have a sensation of

empfindlich	sensitive, acute, etc. (context dep.); susceptible (where contrast is made with *empfindsam* = sensitive)
Empfindlichkeit	touchiness (in context)
Empfindsamkeit	sensitivity
Empfindung(en)	sensation; feeling; sensations (leave feeling for *Gefühl*)
Emsigkeit	industriousness
endlich	finite
Endzweck	final purpose
entbehren	dispense with
Entfaltung	unfolding
entdecken	discover
Entgegensetzung	opposition
enthalten	contain
Enthaltung	abstention
entlehnen	borrow (fm; *herleiten* = derive; *annehmen* = adopt; assume)
entsagen	renounce, etc. [see *ablegen*]
Entschließung	decision
entspringen	arise
entstehen	arise; originate, emerge
entwerfen	designs, devise, draw up; see *aussinnen, ersinnen*
Entwickelung	development
Entzückung	transport into raptures, to be carried away
erbarmen	pity
Erbauung	edification
erdenken	think up
erdichten	poetically invent; invent
erdichtet	fictional
(Bild der) Erdichtung	poetically invented image; poetic invention
erdulden	endure [see *dulden, geduldig*]
Ereignis	event (cf. *Begebenheit*)
Erfahrungs-	experiential
erfinden	invent; see *Erdichtung*
Erfindung	invention
Erfolg	results, success
erfordern	require, demand, need
erfreuen	take pleasure (delight) in
ergötzen	take delight in
Ergötzlichkeit	amusement
erhaben	sublime
erhalten	maintain, preserve, obtain, keep
erheben	elevate, heighten

Erhebung	elevation
erheitern	amuse
erinnern	remind [*sich erinnern* = remember]
erkennen	cognize, recognize
Erkenntnis	cognition
Erklärung	declaration (*declaratio*); explanation, definition, declaration
erlangen	attain
Erläuterung	clarification, elucidation
erlöschen	lapse
Ermahnung	admonition
Erörterung	exposition
ersinnen	contrive
Erste	first member (of a series)
ertragen	bear, endure
erwägen/erwegen	consider; weigh/examine (*erwägen* = *in Betracht ziehen, prüfen*
erwecken	arouse [awake = *erwachen*]
erweisen	prove, demonstrate; establish
erweitert	enlarged, extended
Erweiterung	amplification, expansion; save enlargement for *Vergrößerung*
erworben	acquired (by own efforts/work)
erzeugen	produce, generate
Erziehung	upbringing; rearing, education
ewig	eternal; perpetual
excoliren	tend (to); cultivate
Exempel	exemplary instance
Fähigkeit	capacity
(Urteil) fällen	pass (a judgment)
Falschheit	duplicity
faselnd	babbling
fassen	grasp; *Mut fassen* = pluck up/muster courage
Faßung	composure, self-control
Faulheit	indolence, laziness
Fehler	failing, fault, defect, mistake
fein	fine
Feld	sphere, domain
Fertigkeit	facility; skill; accomplished observance (*habitus*)
Festigkeit	firmness
festsetzen	establish
figürlich	figurative (*speciosum*)
fingieren	fabricate

fixirt	defines, sets
Fleiß	industry; diligence
fließen aus	follow, proceed, results
Folge	consequence; sequel, sequence, result
Folge leisten	comply
folgen	follow
folgerichtig	consistent
folgern	conclude (cf. *schließen*)
Folgerung	consequence
folglich	consequently
fordern	require, demand, ask,
fördern	promote, advance, further
Fortgang	advance (*Progressus*); progression, progress
Fortschreiten	progress; *Fortschritt* = progress, advance
Fortsetzung	continuation
Freimütigkeit	candor
Freude	joy
(sich) freuen	glad (happy, pleased, delighted) about
Fröhlichkeit	cheerfulness
fromm	pious
fruchtbar	prolific
Fruchtbarkeit	fecundity
Fürst	prince
Fürwahrhalten	take to be true; regard as true
Ganze	whole, entirety
gänzlich	entirely
Gattung	species, genus; race [*Classe* = species]
Geberde/Geberdung	= *Gebärde* = gesture [save mien for *Mien*, expression for *Ausdruck*, posture for *Stellung*]
Gebot	command
Gebrauch	use, employment
Gebrechen	infirmity
Gedankending	thought-entity (*ens rationis*)
geduldig	patient
gefallen	please
Gefallen	liking; favor, kindness
Gefräßigkeit	voraciousness
Gefühl	feeling
Gefühllosigkeit	apathy
Gegenbild	counterimage
Gegenbildung	analogue or symbolic formation
Gegenhaß	reactive hatred

(auf etwas) gehen	aim (in the sense of "directing one's/its efforts); (refer: in context)
gehören	appertain, belong
gehörig	relevant, appropriate, essential
Geist	spirit; mind, spirit
Geistestalente	intellectual talents
Geistlichen	clerics, clergymen
Geiz	avarice; stinginess
gekünstelt	factitious, artificial
Gelassenheit	composure
Gelegenheit	occasion
gelehrig	quick to learn, teachable
Gelehrigkeit	aptness, etc.
Gelehrte	scholar
gelten lassen	accept as valid, etc.
Gemächlichkeit	comfortableness; *Ungemächlichkeit* = discomfort
gemäß	in keeping with
gemein	common
gemeine Menschenverstand/ vernunft	common (human) understanding (*gesund* = sound)
Gemeinnützigkeit	common good
Gemeinschaft	community, association (in context)
gemeinschaftlich	mutual
Gemeinsinn	common sense (*sensus communis*)
Gemeinwesen	commonwealth, community
Gemüt	mind, heart
Gemütsstimmung	attunement of mind; mental attunement
Gemütskräfte	powers of mind; mental powers
Gemütsverfassung	frame of mind
genießen	enjoy, relish, savor
Genuß	enjoyment
Gerechtigkeit	justice, righteousness
Gerichtshof	court, tribunal
gering/Geringe (Person)	slight, negligible, insignificant, humble person
Geschäft	concern, business, practical affairs
geschäftig	busy, active (*tätig*)
geschehen	happen
geschicht(s)	obsolete sp. of *geschieht*
Geschicklichkeit	skill; skillfulness
geschickt	skillful, adroit, suited for, dexterous
Geschmack	taste
Geschöpf	living being, creature

geschwind	swift
gesellig	sociable
gesellschaftlich	social
Gesetzgeber	legislator, lawgiver
Gesetzgebung	legislation, lawgiving
Gesetzmäßigkeit	lawfulness, conformity with law
gesetzt	sober
Gesinnung	disposition; attitude; comportment of mind
gesittet	well-mannered, civilized, well-bred
Gestalt	form, figure; shape
gewähren	offer, grant, allow, accord
Gewalt	force, authority; control
Gewissen	conscience
Gewissenhaftigkeit	conscientiousness
gewöhnen	become accustomed
Gewohnheit	habit; habit, custom [see *Angewohnheit*]
Glaube	belief, faith
gleichartig	homogeneous; similar, uniform; see *Einheit*
Gleichgewicht	equilibrium
Gleichgültigkeit	indifference
Gleichheit	equality
Gleichmütigkeit	equanimity
Glied	member
Glück	good fortune; luck
Glückseligkeit	happiness
(nicht) gönnen	begrudge; *gönnen* = not to begrudge
grämen	fret, worry, grieve
Grausamkeit	cruelty
Grenze	bound(ary)
Grille	whim
grob	crude, rude
Groll	resentment
Größe	magnitude
grüblerisch	pondering; *grüblend* = brooding (in context)
Grund	ground, basis, reason; *zum Grunde liegen* = underlies
Grundkraft	fundamental power
Grundlage(n)	foundation; fundamentals, fundamental principles
Grundsatz	principle
grundsatztreu	true to (fundamental) principle(s)
gültig	valid
gutartig	good-natured
Gutartigkeit	good-naturedness, friendliness

gutherzig	kind-hearted
Gütigkeit	charity, kindness
habitus	proficiency [*Fertigkeit* = proficiency]
Habsucht	greed
(an die) Hand (geben)	furnish, make available
Handlung	activity (for *innere Handlung*, e.g. in general of reason) act (*Handlung* or *Tat* as *factum noumenon*, inner moral judgments) action (*Tat* = *factum phenomenon*, concrete outer actions) act(ion)
Hang	propensity
Haß	hatred
heften	rivet; shackle
heftig	violent; *Heftigkeit* = violence, vehemence
Heil	well-being
Heimlichkeit	confidentiality (*Geheimniß*, secret); secretiveness
Heiterkeit	mirth (distinguish from *Fröhlichkeit*, cheerfulness)
hemmen	inhibit
heraufsteigen	mount
herausbekommen	make out
herausbringen	generate
(auf eins) herauskommen	come (amount) to the same thing
herbeirufen	summon
herbeischaffen	procure
herkommen	derive (fig. sense); (see *herleiten*)
herleiten	derive
Herrschaft	domination; dominion
herrschen	prevail (over), dominate (*beherrschen*, also "govern," "control")
Herrschsucht	tyranny; craving for dominance
hervorbringen	produce, bring forth
Herzhaftigkeit	heartiness
Heuchelei	hypocrisy
hinabgehen	descend
hinlänglich	sufficient [see *zulänglich*]
hintergehen	trick, get the better of (deceive for *betrügen*)
Hinterlist	insidiousness, craftiness, etc. (*Betrug* = deceit; *List* = cunning, ruse)
hinzufügen/setzen	add
Hirngespinst	figment of the mind; chimera, pipe dream
Hochschätzung	esteem

Inbegriff	sum total
irre	deranged, confused
Irrtum	error
karg	frugal
Kausalität	causality
Keim	germ; rudiment
Keim des Guten	rudiment of good, germ of good
Kenntnis	knowledge; acquaintance, information, knowledge
Klarheit	clarity
Kleinigkeit	trifle
(der) Kleinste	humblest man
Klugheit	cleverness, prudence
Klügling	sophistical reasoner; smart aleck
kommen (in)	enter into (i.e. *in Verhältnisse kommen*, enter into relations)
kommen (darauf)	to think of
Kopf	brain, mind, very smart person; head
Kraft	power; power, strength(s), force; force, power
Kühnheit	daring; also for the French *hardiesse*
Kummer	grief; troubles, worries, heartache
Kunststück	feat, trick
Kürze	brevity
lächerlich	foolish, ridiculous
Lage	position
läppisch	foolish, silly
das läßt nich	that is not seemly
Laster	vice
Lauf	course
Laune	mood, temper
launig	humorous
Läuterung	purification
lebendig	lively, spirited
Lebensgeister	animal spirits
Lebenswandel	conduct of life
Lebensweise	way of life
Lebhaftigkeit	liveliness, vivacity
lediglich	solely, strictly
Lehre	doctrine, teaching; see *Belehrung*
Lehrgedicht	didactic poem
Lehrling	apprentice
Lehrsatz/spruch	theorem

Leichtigkeit	facility, agility, ease
leichtsinnig	thoughtless, careless
leidend	passive, suffering
Leidenschaft	passion
Leistung	performance
Leit-	guiding
Leitfaden	guide; guiding thread, guide, clue
lenken	steer [save "direct" for *richten/orientieren*]; see *regieren*
lenksam	tractable
letzter Zweck	ultimate purpose
Leutescheuen	timidity, anthropophobia
List	ruse, cunning
locken	tempt (save entice for *reizen*)
Lust	pleasure
Macht	power, might
Mannigfaltige	manifold; multiplicity
Mannigfaltigkeit	manifold; variousness, diversity
Maschinenwerk	mechanical means
Maß und Ziel	moderation
Mäßigkeit	moderation
Mäßigung	self-control
Materie	subject (matter)
mehrere	several, various, sundry
meinen	hold an opinion; opine
Meinung	opinion; estimation
Menge	multitude, multiplicity, amount
Mensch	human being
Menschenfreund	humanitarian
Menschenliebe	love of human beings, philanthropy; love of humanity
Menschheit	humanity
Menschlichkeit	humanity
merklich	considerable, noticeable, distinct, marked
Merkmal	mark
mißbilligen	disapprove
Mißfallen	dissatisfaction; dislike
Mißgunst	grudgingness
Mißtrauen	mistrust
Misvergnügen	discontentment
mit sich selbst einstimmig	(think) in one voice; to be in accord with oneself
Mitfreude	sympathetic joy; sharing/partaking in another's joy

Mitgefühl	compassion
Mitleid	compassion; pity (*Mitgefühl* = compassion; *Mitleidenschaft* = commiseration); (sympathetic) sadness, pity
Mitleidenschaft	compassion; commiseration
Mitteilung	communication
mitwirkenden	cooperative
Moral	morals, moral philosophy
Moralität	morality
mühsam	laborious
Mündigkeit	majority; maturity [majority = *Majorennitaet*]
mürrisch	sullen
müßig	idle
Mut	spirit, courage, courageous spirit; *Unmut* = ill humor
mutig	spirited, courageous
Mutlosigkeit	discouragement
nach	in accordance (with), according to, after
Nachahmung	imitation, emulation
Nachbildung	reproductive image formation; imaging the past
Nacheinandersein	succession
Nachfolgen	following after, following in the same steps, being a successor to; succeed
nachgehen	pursue
nachhängen	indulge, give way to
Nachläßigkeit	carelessness, negligence, neglect
nähern	approximate
Naturanlage	natural aptitude; natural predisposition
Naturell	natural aptitude; Kant identifies *Naturell* with *Naturanlage* (ApH 285); natural temper
Naturlehre	doctrine of nature
Naturrecht	natural right
Naturtriebe	natural drives
Neid	envy [jealousy, used for *Eifersucht*]
Neigung	inclination
nennen	designate
Nennung	mention
nichtig	nugatory
Niederschlag	suppression (in context)
Niederträchtigkeit	meanness
niedrig	base
nötig	needed (necessary)

Nötigung	constraint; necessitation
Notwendigkeit	necessity
Oberhaupt	head
Obersatz	major premise
oberst	supreme
Obliegenheit	(something) incumbent upon (one)
Obrigkeit	authority
öffentlich	public
ohngefehr	= *ungefähr* = approximation; chance
Ort	locality, place
Peinlichkeit	awkwardness [embarrassment: *Verlegenheit*]; punctilious
Perzeption	perception (cf. *Wahrnehmung*)
Pflanzgärten	nurseries
pflegt	wont to, etc.
Pflicht	duty (fm, *officium*); *-mäßig* = in conformity with; = *-widrig* = contrary to
Pfropfen	graft(ing)
Phantast/phantastisch	eccentric (both as n & adj) / fancied
preisgeben (sich)	abandon, surrender, yield, give oneself up; = *aussetzen* = expose; sacrifice; divulge, reveal, disclose
Probierstein	touchstone
Progressus	advance
Pünktlichkeit	accuracy
quälen	plague, torment
Rache	vengeance; revenge, retribution
rauschend	heady
Recht	right
Rechtens	laid down as right
rechtlich	rightful, honorable, having to do with rights, by right
rechtmäßig	in conformity/accord with right, legitimate
Rechtsanspruch	verdict, sentence
rechtsschaffenen	upright, righteous
Rechtschaffenheit	uprightness
Rede	speech, oration
Redlichkeit	probity
Redner	orator
rege machen	animate, rouse

Regung(en)	impulse, stirrings, caprice
regieren	manage, rule, govern [etymologically, related to *führen/leiten*]
Reich	kingdom
reif	mature
Reihe	series
Reihenfolge	succession (cf. *Folge, Nacheinander, Abfolge, Suksession*)
rein	pure (cf. *lauter*)
reiz	(v) enticed; charming
Reizbarkeit	irritability, sensitiveness; excitability (*Erregbarkeit*)
reizend	charming
richten	direct, orient
Richtigkeit	correctness or rightness, truth, advisability, appropriateness, regularity, soundness
Richtmaß	standard
Richtschnur	guideline
Richtung	direction, orientation
roh	crude (*grob*), unrefined, callous, rough, rude, brutal
Ruhe	repose
in Ruhe	calm (in reference to mind; *Gemütsruhe* = calmness, composure)
rühmen	praise
rührend	touching; *rühren* = stir
rüstig	energetic, vigorous
Sache	thing; subject
sagen wollen	mean
sapientiae	wisdom
sapor	taste
Satz	proposition, sentence, principle
Schadenfreude	gloating; malice; malicious delight in other's misfortunes
schädlich	harmful
schaffen	create
schal	insipid
scharf	keen
Scharfsinn	acuity; *scharfsinnig* = acute; keen-witted
Schatz	store
Schätzung	appraisal; *schätzen* = value, estimate
Schaudern	shudder

Schauer	shiver
Schauplatz	stage
Schein	semblance; illusion; also "look(s)"
Schelm	rogue
scherzhaft	jestingly
schickanieren	quibble
schildern	describe, depict, portray
Schläfrigkeit	drowsiness
schlau	shrewd
schlechthin	absolutely
schließen	infer
Schluß	inference, conclusion
schmälern	diminish, detract from
Schmerz	pain
schön	beautiful
schöne Kunst	fine art
Schranke	limit(ation)
Schüchternheit	timidity; shyness; see *zaghaft*
schulgerecht	systematic, methodical, according to rule
Schulwissenschaft	theoretical learning
Schwärmerei	enthusiasm; fanaticism; raptures
Schwere	gravity
Schwermut	depression; melancholy [see *Tiefsinnigkeit*]
Schwermütig	melancholy [see *Tiefsinnigkeit*]
Seelengröße	magnanimity (greatness of soul)
Seelengüte	kindheartedness (goodness of soul)
Seelenstärke	strength of mind/soul
(auf etwas) sehen	set great store by, be particular about, be careful with/about
seicht	banal
Selbsterhaltung	self-preservation
Selbstgefühl	self-awareness
Selbstschätzung	self-esteem
Selbstsüchtig	self-seeking; selfish
Selbsttätigkeit	spontaneity
Selbstzufriedenheit	self-contentment
Seligkeit	blessedness
Seltenheit	rarity
setzen	posit, place, put
sichern	secure, assure, guarantee
Sinn	sense, meaning
Sinnengenusse	sensual enjoyments
Sinnenwelt	world of sense

Sinnesart	[conduct of] sensibilities, sensibility (fm; Kant uses as synonym for temperament, *Gefühls- und Begehrungsvermögen*)
sinnlich	sensible
Sinnlichkeit	sensibility
sinnreich (perspicax)	perceptive; perspicacious, ingenious
Sitten	morals, customs; manners
sittlich	moral
Sittlichkeit	lived morality, moral life; morals; ethical life
sittsam	demure
Sittsamkeit	propriety; modesty (but see *Bescheidenheit*); [*Anständigkeit* = propriety]
sogleich (sofort)	instantly
Sollen	ought
sowohl . . . als	both . . . and, as well as
Spott	ridicule
spüren	perceive, sense, feel, get a taste of
Standhaftigkeit	steadfastness
Stärke	intensity; force, power, might, strength, vividness
Stillstand	cessation
Streit	dispute (to distinguish from *Widerstreit*, conflict)
Stück	element, item
stumpf	dull [senses]; *stumpfe Kopf (obtusum caput)*: obtuse
subaltern	subordinate
Sucht	mania, addiction; obsession
Tadel	blame; rebuke
tadeln	reproves (to distinguish from *vorwerfen*)
tapfer	brave
Tapferkeit	fortitude
Tat	deed
tätige Wesen	actors
Tätigkeit(en)	activity, actions, works; activity
Tatlosigkeit	lack/absence of activity
taugen	fit for
Tauglichkeit	fitness
Teil	part
teilbar	divisible
teilnehmend	sympathetic
Teilnehmung	participation; sympathy; *Anteil nehmen/Anteilnahme* = sympathy
Thor	fool
Thorheit	folly, foolishness

Tiefsinnigkeit (melancholia)	melancholy
Tierheit	animality
tierisch	brutish (to distinguish from *animalisch*); use "bestial" for *viehisch*
tilgen	eradicate
toll	delirious
Tollheit	delirium
Tollheit, allgemeine (delirium generale)	general delirium
Tollheit, bestimmt (delirium circa objectum)	monomaniacal delirium
Traurigkeit	sadness; sorrowfulness
treiben	incite
Treuherzigkeit	candor; artlessness, guilelessnes, etc.
Trieb	instinct; drive, impulse [*Antrieb* = impulse]
Triebfeder	incentive (*Bewegungsgrund* = motive); motivation, motive spring
Trockenheit	dryness
Tugend	virtue
Tun und Lassen	what is done and left undone; doing and forbearing, actions, acting and refraining from acting
Übel	ill; ills; vile (when synonymous with *böse*)
Übelbefinden	affliction
Überdruß	weariness, surfeit
übereinkommen	coincide
Übereinkommen	accord (noun)
übereinstimmen	agree; use harmonize for *zusammenstimmen*
überfallen	overcome
überfliegend	extravagant
Überfluß	affluence (in context)
Übergang	transition
übergehen	pass (into)
überhaupt	indeed, in general, in fact, at all
überlegte	deliberate
Überlegung	reflection; deliberation
Übermut	arrogance, haughtiness
Überredung	persuasion
Übertretung	transgression
überwiegen	predominate, outweigh
Überzeugung	conviction
Umfang	domain

Umgang	(social) intercourse, association, dealings, relations
Umschweif	detour
Umstand	circumstance
Umwandlung	conversion, transformation
unablässig	persistent
unbestechlich	inexorable
unbrauchbar	inept
Undankbarkeit	ingratitude
Undurchdringlichkeit	impenetrability
Unempfindlichkeit	insensitivity
Unendliche	infinity; *unendlich* = infinite
unerforschlich	inscrutable
unerweislich	indemonstrable
ungereimt	absurd; inconsistent, incongruous [*Ungereimtheit*: incongruity]
Unglück	misfortune
Unlauterkeit	disingenuousness; impurity
Unlust	displeasure
unmäßig	excessive, immoderate
unmittelbar	directly; immediate, immediately
unrecht	wrong
Unredlichkeit	insincerity; dishonesty
unrichtig	false
Unschuld	innocence
unsinnig	foolish
Unsinnigkeit (amentia)	senselessness, mindlessness, psychosis
unterdrücken	suppress
Unterhalt	maintenance, support, upkeep
(sich) unterhalten	entertain, converse
Unterhaltung	entertainment
unterlassen	refrain from, desist, forbear, stop, leave off, discontinue
Unterlassung	default (juridical sense of term), omission; omission, neglect
Unternehmung	initiative, transaction, enterprise
Untersatz	minor premise
unterscheiden (sich)	differs from; non-refl: distingish
Untersuchung	investigation
Unterweisung	instruction [*Unterricht* = synonym]
unterwerfen	subject to [save for *stehen unter*], subjugate, v/r: yield
Untugend	vice; lack of virtue
unveränderlich	constant

Unvernunft	irrationality, unreasonableness; *vernünftig =* rational/reasonable
Unverschämtheit	impudence
unwandelbar	unwavering
Unwille	indignation
Unwissenheit	ignorance
Unzufriedenheit	dissatisfaction
Urbild	archetype
Urbildung	archetypal formation
Urheber	author, agent; author
Ursache	cause, causal agency, causal agent
Ursprung	source
ursprünglich	original
Urteil	judgment
Urteilskraft	power of judgment
Urwesen	original being
verabscheuen	abhor
verachten	be contemptuous of; despise
veränderlich	variable
verändern	change, alter, transform
Veränderung	alteration; variation, change
veranlassen	occasion
Veranstaltung	organization
verbergen	conceal (to distinguish from *verhehlen*)
verbieten	prohibit
verbinden	bind, obligate
Verbindung	combination
Verbot	prohibition
verdächtig	suspect; questionable, dubious, suspicious
verdienstlich	meritorious; *Verdienst =* merit
Veredelung	refinement (things), ennoblement (humans), grafting
vereinigen	unite, unify
verfahren	proceed
Verfeinerung	refinement
verfließen	elapse; blend, mingle
verfügen	dispose
Vergehen	transgression
Vergesellschaftung	association
Vergleichung	comparison
Vergnügen	enjoyment; as v. = enjoy [see *genießen*]
Vergnügungen	delights, pleasures, [save entertainment for *Unterhaltung*]

vergnügt	merry, gay, cheerful
Vergrößerung	enlargement
Verhalten	conduct
Verhältnis	relation(ship)
verhehlen	hide, disguises; see *verbergen*
Verheißung	promise
verhindern	impede, prevent
Verhöhnung	ridicule
verkehrt	errant; topsy-turvy, wrong, upside down, reverse
Verkehrtheit	folly (see *Torheit*); state of being upside down
Verknüpfung	connection
Verlegenheit	embarrassment
Verleihen	lending
Verletzung	violation
Verleumdung	slander
vermindern	diminish, reduce, lessen, minimize [see *verringern*]
vermittelst	by means of
Vermögen	faculty; power, ability; faculty, capacity, power, wealth, means, resource; capacity
vermuten	assume, surmise, anticipate, suspect
verneinen	deny, negate
Vernunftanlage	rational aptitude
Vernünftelei	sophistical reasoning
vernünfteln	ratiocinate, rationalize
vernünftelnd	sophistical
Vernunftglaube	rational faith
Vernunftkünstler	artificer of reason
Vernunftschluß	syllogism, inference of reason
vernunftwidrig	contrary to reason
Verpflichtung	obligation (*obligatio*)
verraten	disclose, divulge, betray, reveal
verringern	diminish [see *vermindern*]
verrückt	insane
verschafft	procured; *verschaffen* = furnish
Verschiedenheit	dissimilarity
Verschuldung	fault, culpability
versetzen	transpose
(sich) versprechen	to expect, etc. [idiomatic use in context]
Verstellung	dissimulation; misrepresentation, hypocrisy
Versuch	attempt, try, experiment

verteilen	divide; distribute, allocate, etc. (*zerteilen* = disperse, break up)
Vertrauen	trust
Vertraulichkeit	confidence, intimacy
verwandeln	transform; change, alter
Verwandtschaft	affinity; kinship, relationship
verweisen	refer; expel
Verwirrung	confusion
Verzückung	rapture
Vielheit	plurality
Volk	nation, people
vollkommen	perfect
vollständig	complete
Vorbild/ung	anticipatory image formation; imagining the future
vorbringen	put forward, present, bring forward, produce, etc.
vorhersagen	= *vorraussagen:* predict
vorläufig	preliminary, provisional
vornehm	noble; distinguished, refined, genteel
Vorrat	supply
Vorsatz	resolve
Vorschrift	precept
Vorsehung	providence
vorsetzlich	intentional
vorstellen (sich)	represent, imagine
Vorstellung	conception, representation; representation; presentation
Vorstellungskraft	power of [conception] representation
vortrefflich	excellent
vorwerfen	reproach
vorziehen	prefer
wacker	valiant; plucky (when used to describe passions), brave (see *tapfer*)
wagen	risk, venture, take a chance
Waghals	daredevil
Wahn	delusion
Wahnsinn (dementia)	delusional sensation; dementia, insanity; madness
Wahnsinnige	mental patient
Wahnwitz (insania)	delusional understanding/wit; insanity
wahr	true, veritable, real, right, proper, correct

wahrnehmen	perceive, discern
Wahrnehmung	perception
Wahrsagung	fortune-telling
wandelbar	changeable
Wechsel	change
wechselseitig	reciprocal
wechselsweise	reciprocally
Wechselwirkung	interaction
wegfallen	cancel(ed) (also omitted, abolished, cease); disappear
Wegweiser	guides, signposts
Weißagung	prophecy
Weltall	world-whole
Weltbegriff	cosmological [or] cosmopolitan concept
Weltbürger	cosmopolitan citizens
weltbürgerlich	cosmopolitan
Weltganze	world-whole
Weltkenntnis	knowledge of the world [*der Welt, des Weltgetriebes, anderer Länder*]
Weltklugheit	prudence
Weltkörper	heavenly body
Weltreihe	world-series
Weltweisheit	philosophy
Weltwissenschaft	cosmology
Wesen	being, essence
Widerlegung	refutation
widersetzen	resist (distinct from *entgegensetzen, widerstreiten*)
widersinnig	absurd, preposterous, nonsensical
Widerspruch	contradiction
Widerstand	resistance
Widerstreit	conflict, opposition
Wiedergeburt	rebirth
Wiederholung	repetition
Wiederkehr	recurrence
Wildheit	unruliness
Wille	practical desire; will
Willensbestimmung	determination of volition
Willkür	power of choice; (power of) choice
willkürlich	arbitrary, voluntary, chosen
wirken	effect, produce
wirkende Ursache	efficacious cause, efficient cause

wirklich	actual, real
Wirklichkeit	actuality
wirksam	efficacious; operative, forcible
Wirkung	effect; operation
Wirkungen	operations
wirkt zurück	impacts
Wissen	knowledge
Wissenschaft	science
Witz (ingenium)	wit; ingenuity
vergleichende Witz	comparative ingenuity
(ingenium comparans)	
vernünftelnde Witz	sophistical ingenuity
(ingenium argutans)	
witzig	ingenious; witty
Witzling	joker
Wohl und Heil	prospering and well-being
Wohlbefinden	well-being
Wohlfahrt	welfare
Wohlgefallen	satisfaction; being pleased
Wohl(sein)	well-being
Wohltätigkeit	beneficence
Wohltun	beneficence
Wohlverhalten	good conduct
Wohlwollen	benevolence
wollen	will; want
Wollen	volition
Würde	dignity
Würdigkeit	worthiness
Wut	fury
zaghaft	timid
Zank	quarrel
zart	delicate
Zeichenlehre	semiotics
Zeitfolge	temporal sequence
Zergliederung	analysis
Zerstreuung (distractio)	distraction
Zerteilung	disintegration
zielbewußt	goal-directed, conscious of one's goal
zittern	tremble, shiver, quiver
Zorn	anger, resentment
Zucht	discipline; correction
zuerst	first, at first, initially, in the beginning

zufällig	contingent; fortuitous; *zufälliger Weise* = accidentally
Zufriedenheit	satisfaction, contentment
Zugänglichkeit	affability; accessible, approachable, amenable
zugleich	simultaneous, at the same time
Zugleichsein	simultaneity
zukommen	befits
Zulänglichkeit	adequacy [see *Hinlänglich*]
Zurechnung	reckoning; imputation; *zurechnen* = impute
zurechnungsfähig	responsible, accountable; as juridical term, soundness of mind thus to be accountable
zurecht kommen	get along
zureichenden Grund	sufficient reason; *zureichend* = sufficient
zürnen	bear a grudge, harbor a resentment
zurückhalten	restrain, check
Zurückhaltung	reserve
zurückrufen	recall
zurückrufend	recollective
Zusammengesetztes	composite
Zusammenhang	connection, interconnection, nexus
Zusammensetzung	composition; *zusammensetzen:* assemble, compose, put together
Zusammenstellung	juxtaposition; compilation
zusammenstimmen	harmonize; see *übereinstimmen*
Zustand	state, condition; state of affairs
zuwider	repugnant, against, contrary to, opposed to, abhorrent to
Zwang	coercion, compulsion; constraint, duress
zwar	it is true . . . but, may be . . . but
Zweck	end; purpose
zweckmäßig	purposive, appropriate, suitable
Zweckmäßigkeit	purposiveness
zweideutig	equivocal
Zwietracht	disunion and discord

Bibliography

Original edition

Kant's Vorlesungen über Anthropologie, bearbeitet von Reinhard Brandt und Werner Stark. *Kants Schriften*. Ausgabe der Akademie der Wissenschaften zu Göttingen. Berlin: Walter de Gruyter, 1997.

Works on Kant's Anthropology

Brandt, Reinhard. *Kritischer Kommentar zu Kants Anthropologie in pragmatischer Hinsicht*. Hamburg, 1999.

Cohen, A., *Kant and the Human Sciences: Biology, Anthropology and History*. London, 2009.

　(ed.) *Kant's Lectures on Anthropology: A Critical Guide*. Cambridge, forthcoming.

　(ed.) special issue of *Studies in History and Philosophy of Science* on "Kantian Philosophy and the Human Sciences," 39(4) 2008.

Failla, Mariannina. *Verità e saggezza in Kant. Un contributo all'analisi della logica e dell'antropologia*. Milan, 2000.

Ferrari, Jean (ed.). *L'Année 1798: Kant et la naissance de l'anthropologie au siècle des Lumières: actes du colloque de Dijon, May 9–11, 1996*. Paris, 1997.

　(ed.) *L'année 1798. Kant. Sur l'anthropologie*. Paris, 1997.

Firla, Monika. *Untersuchungen zu Verhältnis von Anthropologie und Moralphilosophie bein Kant*. Frankfurt a. M., 1981.

Foucault, Michel. *Introduction to Kant's Anthropology*, ed. Roberto Negro, trans. Roberto Negro and Kate Briggs. Cambridge, MA, 2008.

Frierson, Patrick R. *Freedom and Anthropology in Kant's Moral Philosophy*. Cambridge, 2003.

Goldmann, Lucien. *Mensch Gemeinschaft und Welt in der Philosophie Immanuel Kants*. Dissertation, Zürich, 1945. Reprint: Frankfurt am Main, 1989.

Gregor, Mary J. "Introduction," *Anthropology from a Pragmatic Point of View*. Hague, 1974.

Heidenmann, D. H. (ed.) *Kant Yearbook Anthropology*: 3/2011. Berlin, 2011.

Jacobs, Brian and Kain, Patrick (eds.). *Essays on Kant's Anthropology*. Cambridge, 2003.

Kim, Soo Bae. *Die Entstehung der Kantischen Anthropologie und ihre Beziehung zur empirischen Psychologie der Wolffschen Schule*. Frankfurt am Main, 1992.

Lestition, Steven O. "Kant's Philosophical Anthropology: Texts and Historical Contexts, Continuity and Change," PhD Dissertation, University of Chicago, 1985.

Louden, Robert B. *Kant's Human Being: Essays on His Theory of Human Nature*. Oxford, 2011.

   Kant's Impure Ethics. Oxford, 2000.

Manganaro, Paolo. *L'antropologia de Kant*. Naples, 1983.

Munzel, G. Felicitas., *Kant's Conception of Moral Character: The 'Critical' Link of Morality, Anthropology and Reflective Judgment*. Chicago, 1999.

Nobbe, Frank. *Kants Frage nach dem Menschen: die Kritik der ästhetischen Urteilskraft als transzendentale Anthropologie*. Frankfurt am Main, 1995.

Otte, Rainer. "Die Ordnungen des Leibes in der Aufklärung: Kants Anthropologik under ihre historischen Voraussetzungen." Dissertation. Tübingen, 1986.

Potestà, Andrea. *La pragmatica di Kant. Saperi al confine tra antropologia e criticismo*. Milan, 2004.

Schmidt, Claudia. "Kant's Transcendental and Empirical Anthropology of Cognition." Dissertation, University of Iowa, 1999.

Sturm, Thomas. *Kant und die Wissenschaften vom Menschen*. Paderborn, 2009.

Sussman, David G. *The Idea of Humanity. Anthropology and Anthroponomy in Kant's Ethics*. New York, 2001.

Svare, Helge. *Body and Practice in Kant*. Dordrecht, Holland, 2006.

Van de Pitte, Frederick. *Kant as Philosophical Anthropologist*. The Hague, 1971.

Wenzel, Uwe. *Anthroponomie: Kants Archäologie der Autonomie*. Berlin, 1992.

Wilson, Holly L. *Kant's Pragmatic Anthropology*. Albany, NY, 2006.

Wood, Allen W. *Kant's Ethical Thought*. New York, 1999.

Zammito, John. *Kant, Herder and the Birth of Anthropology*. Chicago, 2002.

Index

animality (*cont.*)
  in conflict with humanity 217–230
  in desires 133
  and difference between the sexes 233
  and freedom 330
  and *intelligens* 263
  mistrust in society 330
  and rationality 33, 52
  and sexual inclination 460
  as source of development of good in
    human beings 217
  as source of ill 20
  the Stoics on 19
  and sympathy 157
  temperament and 52
animals
  compared with human beings 19, 33,
    50, 51, 141, 233, 239, 274, 294,
    326, 348, 361, 437, 442, 498–502
  and natural laws 277
  our duties towards 157
  profile compared with human 208
  propensity toward freedom 455
  self-preservation instinct 138
animus 20, 34, 40, 51
anthropognosis 515
anthropography 515
"Anthropological Characteristic" 8,
  10
"Anthropological Didactic" 8, 10
anthropology 1, 16
  as a characteristic 517
  Introduction to 343–509
  Kant on 1, 41–42, 48
  Kant's lectures 2–5
  major parts of 7, 8
  methododology in 8, 15–20
  and moral philosophy 9
  nature and need for 41–42
  Part II 171–181
  and physiology 15–20
  the purpose of 49
  relationship with metaphysics 2, 4,
    15, 31, 50
  rules of prudence 48
  as a science 515
  sources of 292, 346–347, 516
  The Utility of 262
  use of term 292, 344
  uses 343, 344, 346, 517
  see also moral anthropology; physical
    anthropology; practical

anthropology; pragmatic
  anthropology; scholastic approach
Anthropology Busolt *see Busolt*
Anthropology Collins *see Collins*
Anthropology Friedländer *see*
  Friedländer
Anthropology from a Pragmatic Point of
  View (Kant) 2, 5, 7
  and development in lectures 10
Anthropology Mrongovius *see*
  Mrongovius
Anthropology Parow *see Parow*
Anthropology Pillau *see Pillau*
apathy 118, 445, 454, 461
apes 212, 213
  genius-apes 423
  orangutan 326
aphorisms 267, 389, 395
appearances 31, 74
  the assessment of 106
  compared with feeling 23
  deceptive 53
  differences in the sexes 249
  and impression 54
  mere 19
appetite 432, 433
Arabs 456
architecture 111, 266, 269
Aristippus 270
aristocracy 156
Aristotle 60, 75, 104, 476
armies
  mechanism in 422
  standing 278, 357
arrogance 416, 417, 418, 456, 457
art 219–225, 516
  appears as nature 173, 266
  of obscuring 355
  in women 230, 240, 321, 484
artificiality 16, 32, 54, 352
arts 216, 225, 265, 433, 503
  development of the species of the
    277–279
  fine and useful 266
  formative 268, 269
  of industry and of genius 268
  taste and feeling 24, 198
  that produce an object that can charm
    us 269
  with or without spirit (mechanical)
    269
  see also fine arts

Index

prudence 98, 167, 168, 291, 292, 344,
    410, 443
  the doctrine of 345, 516, 521
  as punctiliousness 423
  ways to arrive at 344, 430
Prussians 366, 408, 494
psychology 2, 31, 50, 264, 292
  metaphysical 294
  on the Peculiar Characteristic of
    Every 113–120
  see also empirical psychology
public life, character in private and 309
public office
  difference in sexes 412, 485
  and temperament 305, 472
punctiliousness 365, 423
pyrotechnics 269
Pyrrhonians, *ataraxia* 454
Pythagoras 363
  Theorem 264

Quintilian, Marcus Fabius 399

Rabelais, François 5, 64, 77, 376, 382
races
  character of 10, 320–321
  difference of 327
  different phyla 320–321
  four 320
  white 321
ratiocination 107, 411
rationality, and animality 33, 348,
    498–502
rationalizing 521
reason 1, 17, 22, 31, 34, 101, 410
  animated through poetry 93
  architectonic use of 111
  combined with passions 168, 461
  cultivation of 39, 295, 331, 411, 414
  and deliberation 164
  determines the particular from the
    universal 143
  development in children 251, 252
  as a faculty of cognition from
    concepts 111–112, 410
  as a faculty of cognition of principles
    411
  and freedom 330
  hatred of *see* misology
  as human 19
  as legislator 411
  liking and disliking 438, 439

limits of its use 111
maxims of sound 109–110
misuse of 276
On the Use with Regard to the
  Practical 106–113, 520
perpetual 509
in pursuit of happiness 4, 461
and the senses 21
sickness of 112
and soul 32
speculative rules of 110, 414
and speech 213
technical use of 111
teleological inner order of 41
and thinking for oneself 520
universal bases and principles of 107
and universal judgment 56
versus nature in the affects and
  passions 164–169
and well-being 127–131
reflection 55, 57, 68, 291, 379, 484
  animals incapable of 51, 428
  and judgment 52
  love due to 161
  on pain 34
  on representations 101–103
  sadness from 300
  on sources of human action 262
  utility and insight is 23
  versus sensitivity 146–150
religion 279, 329, 507
  belief that vices cease on account of
    434
  and character 309, 483
  in child's education 254
  facial features and 314
  fasting in 365
  and fear of punishment 308
  immaturity in 508
  and insight 254
  and knowledge of human beings 49
  and mien 477
  and morality 79, 228
  negative 329, 508
  and passion 144
  subjective principles in 262
  and temperament 305, 472
  use of anthropology to 345, 517
  women and 249, 485
religions
  threefold concepts in 275
  tolerance of other 411